Lecture Notes in Computer Science 1521

Edited by G. Goos, J. Hartmanis and J. van Leeuwen

Springer

Berlin
Heidelberg
New York
Barcelona
Hong Kong
London
Milan
Paris
Singapore
Tokyo

Branislav Rovan (Ed.)

SOFSEM'98:
Theory and Practice
of Informatics

25th Conference on Current Trends
in Theory and Practice of Informatics
Jasná, Slovakia, November 21-27, 1998
Proceedings

 Springer

Series Editors

Gerhard Goos, Karlsruhe University, Germany
Juris Hartmanis, Cornell University, NY, USA
Jan van Leeuwen, Utrecht University, The Netherlands

Volume Editor

Branislav Rovan
Comenius University, Department of Computer Science
SK-84215 Bratislava, Slovakia
E-mail: rovan@fmph.uniba.sk

Cataloging-in-Publication data applied for

Die Deutsche Bibliothek - CIP-Einheitsaufnahme

Theory and practice of informatics : proceedings / SOFSEM '98,
25th Seminar on Current Trends in Theory and Practice of
Informatics, Jasná, Slovakia, November 21 - 27, 1998 / Branislav
Rovan (ed.). - Berlin ; Heidelberg ; New York ; Barcelona ; Hong
Kong ; London ; Milan ; Paris ; Singapore ; Tokyo : Springer, 1998
    (Lecture notes in computer science ; Vol. 1521)
    ISBN 3-540-65260-4

CR Subject Classification (1998): C.2, D, F, H

ISSN 0302-9743
ISBN 3-540-65260-4 Springer-Verlag Berlin Heidelberg New York

© Springer-Verlag Berlin Heidelberg 1998
Printed in Germany

Typesetting: Camera-ready by author
SPIN 10692809   06/3142 – 5 4 3 2 1 0   Printed on acid-free paper

Preface

This volume contains the invited papers and papers selected for presentation at the 25th conference on Theory and Practice of Informatics — SOFSEM '98, held in Jasná, Slovakia, November 21–27, 1998.

The SOFSEM conference series started in 1974 as a local event in Czechoslovakia and from the very beginning became the top domestic event in software theory and practice. It has been unique in several respects, being a mix of winter school, conference, and advanced workshop. It brought together professionals from academia and industry and provided an opportunity for both theoreticians and practitioners to learn about the new developments in a broad range of computer science subjects via a series of invited talks. The conference gradually evolved into an international event, keeping most of its original characteristics. It features a relatively large number of invited talks, refereed papers (contributed papers), and refereed poster contributions. In addition, time and space for flash communications, industrial presentations, and exhibitions are provided.

SOFSEM is every year the result of a considerable effort by a number of people. Its Advisory Board (Dines Bjørner, Manfred Broy, Michal Chytil, Peter van Emde Boas, Georg Gottlob, Keith G. Jeffrey, Maria Zemankova) and Endowment Board (Keith G. Jeffrey, Jan Pavelka, František Plášil, Igor Prívara, Branislav Rovan, *vice-chair*, Jan Staudek, Jiří Wiedermann, *chair*) is in process of being transformed into a Steering Committee. All members of these committees have devoted special attention to the silver jubilee SOFSEM and I am glad to acknowledge this. As usual, the core of the work has been done by the Program Committee and the Organizing Committee listed below. Special thanks go also to the referees who helped to evaluate the 48 submissions, from which 18 papers have been selected by the Program Committee for presentation at the conference and for publication in the Proceedings.

The invited talks are traditionally grouped into a number of tracks chosen by the Endowment Board for that particular year. SOFSEM '98 has a special silver jubilee track featuring five talks with a historic aspect in the area of models of computation (R. Freivalds), algorithms (G. Ausiello), formal (M. Broy) and practical (D. Rombach) aspects of software, and database systems (G. van Emde Boas-Lubsen an P. van Emde Boas). In addition, four more tracks of invited talks are featured: Parallel and Distributed Computing (M. Boasson, U. Kastens, and P. Ružička), Electronic Commerce (P. Hanáček, W. Lamersdorf, B. Preneel, L.A.M. Strous, and Ch. Vanoirbeek), Electronic Documents and Digital Libraries (R. Lüling, Ch. Nikolaou, C. Roisin), and Trends in Algorithms (B. Chor, A. Marchetti-Spaccamela, R. Niedermeier, J. Rolim). All but one of these talks are documented in this volume (two of them as abstracts only).

The decision of Springer-Verlag to make available in parallel the electronic versions of the volumes published in the LNCS series adds extra duties to the volume editors. Perhaps this is the necessary price for the convenience the computer science community is enjoying. I would like to thank all the authors who did their best to follow the guidelines. It would be very difficult (if at all possible) to produce the volume in time without the technical assistance of Miroslav Chladný (Comenius University, Bratislava), who also designed and operated the electronic support for the work of the Program Committee. Last but not least, I would like to thank Springer-Verlag for the traditionally excellent and smooth co-operation in producing this volume.

September 1998   Branislav Rovan
                                    SOFSEM '98 Program Committee Chair

SOFSEM '98

Organized by

Slovak Society for Computer Science
Czech Society for Computer Science
Slovak Research Consortium for Informatics and Mathematics

In co-operation with

Faculty of Mathematics and Physics, Comenius University, Bratislava
Institute of Informatics and Statistics, Bratislava
Faculty of Natural Sciences, Šafárik University, Košice
SOFTEC, Ltd., Bratislava
Faculty of Electrical Engineering and Information Technology, Slovak University
    of Technology, Bratislava
Institute of Informatics, Slovak Academy of Sciences, Bratislava
Faculty of Informatics, Masaryk University, Brno

Sponsors

The principal sponsors of SOFSEM '98 are:

Andersen Consulting   *IBM*
Digital Slovakia   *SAP Slovensko*

We also appreciate the sponsorship of the following companies:

ERCIM   *ORACLE Slovensko*
Microsoft Slovakia   *VSŽ Informatika*

Telenor Slovakia provided the Internet connection to the conference site and a
mirror site for the SOFSEM '98 Web page.

Program Committee

Kurt Bauknecht	University of Zürich, CH
Dines Bjørner, *vice-chair*	Technical University of Denmark, Lyngby, DK
Janos Demetrovics	Hungarian Academy of Sciences, Budapest, H
Viliam Geffert	Šafárik University, Košice, SK
Georg Gottlob	Vienna University of Technology, Vienna, A
Nicolas Hermann	LORIA, Nancy, F
Vašek Hlaváč	Czech Technical University, Prague, CZ
Mojmír Křetínský	Masaryk University, Brno, CZ
Klaus-Jörn Lange	Tübingen University, DE
Ľudovít Molnár	Slovak Technical University, Bratislava, SK
Pekka Orponen	University of Jyväskylä, FI
Jan Pavelka	DCIT, Prague, CZ
František Plášil	Charles University, Prague, CZ
Veith Risak	Techno-Z FH TKS, Salzburg, A
Branislav Rovan, *chair*	Comenius University, Bratislava, SK
Wilhelm Schäfer	University of Paderborn, DE
Anton Scheber	SOFTEC, Bratislava, SK
Witold Staniszkis	Rodan System, Warsaw, PO
Gerard Tel	Utrecht University, NL
Imrich Vrťo	Slovak Academy of Sciences, Bratislava, SK
Judith Wusteman	University College Dublin, IRL

Referees

M. de Berg, H.L. Bodlaender, G. Castagna, W. Castelnovo, C. Castro, I. Černá,
V. Chevrier, F. Damiani, L. Dreschler-Fischer, T. Eiter, F. Fages, H. Fernau,
V. Geffert, G. Gottlob, P. de Groote, T. Hagerup, M. Hermann, V. Hlaváč,
T. Hrúz, I. Kalaš, U. Kastens, M. Kaufmann, S.T. Klein, M. Křetínský, M. van
Kreveld, A. Kučera, K.-J. Lange, P. Mederly, F. Meyer auf der Heide, M. Mid-
dendorf, P. O'hIceadha, P. Orponen, J. Pavelka, T. Plachetka, F. Plášil, K. Rein-
hardt, Ch. Ringeissen, V. Risak, L. Ronyai, R. Rosati, B. Rovan, P. Ružička,
P. Sanders, W. Schäfer, A. Scheber, L. Škarvada, L. Stacho, W. Staniszkis,
W. Strasser, M. Stumptner, S.D. Swierstra, O. Sýkora, G. Tel, H.S. Thomp-
son, H. Tompits, B. Uhrin, M. Veldhorst, I. Vrťo, F. Wotawa, J. Wusteman

Organizing Committee

Gabriela Andrejková, Martin Bečka, Radovan Červenka, Ivona Dostálová, Mar-
cela Gschillová, Vanda Hambálková, Jozef Jirásek, Rastislav Kráľovič, Zuzana
Kubincová, Dana Pardubská, *vice-chair*, Igor Prívara, *chair*, Martin Stanek,
Marek Tamajka

Table of Contents

Invited Talks

Contributed Papers

Software Architecture for Distributed Reactive Systems

Maarten Boasson

Universiteit van Amsterdam, Department of Computer Science
Kruislaan 403, 1098 SJ Amsterdam, the Netherlands
boasson@wins.uva.nl

Hollandse Signaalapparatern B.V.
P.O. Box 42, 7550 GD Hengelo, the Netherlands
boasson@signaal.nl

Abstract. Due to the many possible interactions with an ever changing environment, combined with stringent requirements regarding temporal behaviour, robustness, availability, and maintainability, large-scale embedded systems are very complex in their design. Coordination models offer the potential of separating functional requirements from other aspects of system design. In this paper we present a software architecture for large-scale embedded systems that incorporates an explicit coordination model. Conceptually the coordination model consists of application processes that interact through a shared data space - no direct interaction between processes is possible. Starting from this relatively simple model we derive successive refinements of the model to meet the requirements that are typical for large-scale embedded systems. The software architecture has been applied in the development of commercially available command-and-control, and traffic management systems. Experience confirms that due to the resulting very high degree of modularity and maximal independence between modules, these systems are relatively easy to develop and integrate in an incremental way. Moreover, distribution of processes and data, fault-tolerant behaviour, graceful degradation, and dynamic reconfiguration are directly supported by the architecture.

1. Introduction

Due to the many possible interactions with an ever changing environment, combined with stringent requirements regarding temporal behaviour, robustness, availability, and maintainability, large-scale embedded systems, like traffic management, process control, and command-and-control systems, are very complex in their design. The tasks performed by these systems typically include: (1) processing of measurements obtained from the environment through sensing devices, (2) determination of model parameters describing the environment, (3) tracking discrepancies between desired state and perceived state, (4) taking corrective action, and (5) informing the operator, or team of operators, about the current and predicted state of affairs. All tasks are very closely related and intertwined, and particularly in large-scale systems, there is a huge number of model parameters, which are often intricately linked through numerous dependencies. It is therefore a very natural approach to design the software for such systems as a monolithic entity, in which all relevant information (deductive knowledge and actual data) is readily accessible for all the above mentioned parts.

There is, however, a strong and well-known reason to proceed differently: a software system thus conceived is very difficult to implement, and even more difficult to modify should the purpose of the system be changed, or the description of the environment be refined. Adopting a *modular* approach to design, the various functions implemented in software are separated into different modules that have some independence from each other. Such an approach - well established today as standard software engineering practice - leads to better designs, and reduces development time and the likelihood of errors.

Unfortunately, with today's highly sophisticated systems, this is still not good enough. In addition to the functional requirements of these systems, many non-functional requirements, such as a high degree of availability and robustness, distribution of the processing over a possibly wide variety of different host processors, and (online) adaptability and extendibility, place constraints on the design freedom that can hardly be met with current design approaches. A methodology for the design of large-scale distributed embedded systems should provide (a basis for) an integral solution for the various types of requirements. Traditional design methods based on functional decomposition are not adequate. The sound principle of modularity needs therefore to be further exploited to cover non-functional requirements as well.

Recently, coordination models and languages have become an active area of research [10]. In [11] it was argued that a complete programming model consists of two separate components: the computation model and the coordination model. The computation model is used to express the basic tasks to be performed by a system, i.e. the system's functionality. The coordination model is applied to organize the functions into a coherent ensemble; it provides the means to create processes, and facilitates communication. One of the greater merits of separating computation from coordination is the considerably improved modularity of a system. The computation model facilitates a traditional functional decomposition of the system, while the coordination model accomplishes a further decoupling between the functional modules in both space and time. This is exemplified by the relative success of coordination languages in the field of distributed and parallel systems.

Since the early 80's we have developed and refined a software architecture for large-scale distributed embedded systems [3], that is based on a separation between computation and coordination. Below, we first present the basic software architecture, after which we shall focus on the underlying coordination model. We demonstrate how the basic coordination model can be gradually refined to include non-functional aspects, such as distributed processing and fault-tolerance, in a modular fashion. Next we indicate how formal techniques can be introduced for reasoning about systems built according to this architecture. A short example illustrates various aspects of system design. We conclude with a discussion of our experiences in the design of commercially available command-and-control, and traffic management systems.

2. Software Architecture

A software architecture defines the organisational principle of a system in terms of types of components and possible interconnections between these components. In addition, an architecture prescribes a set of design rules and constraints governing the behaviour of components and their interaction [5]. Traditionally, software architectures have been primarily concerned with structural organisation and static interfaces. With the growing interest in coordination models, however, more emphasis is placed on the organizational aspects of behaviour and interaction.

In practice, many different software architectures are in use. Some well-known examples are the Client/Server and Blackboard architectures. Clearly, these architectures are based on different types of components - clients and servers versus knowledge sources and blackboards - and use different styles of interaction - requests from clients to servers versus writing and reading on a common blackboard.

The software architecture, named SPLICE, that we developed for distributed embedded systems basically consists of two types of components: *applications* and a *shared data space*. Applications are active, concurrently executing processes that each implement part of the system's overall functionality. Besides process creation, there is no direct interaction between applications; all communication takes place through a logically shared data space simply by reading and writing data elements. In this sense SPLICE bears strong resemblance to coordination languages and models like Linda [7], Gamma [1], and Swarm [18], where active entities are coordinated by means of a shared data space.

2.1. The Shared Data Space

The shared data space in SPLICE is organized after the well-known relational data model. Each data element in the shared data space is associated with a unique *sort*, that defines its structure. A sort definition declares the *name* of the sort and the *record fields* the sort consists of. Each record field has a type, such as integer, real, or string; various type constructors, such as enumerated types, arrays, and nested records, are provided to build more complex types.

Sorts enable applications to distinguish between different kinds of information. A further differentiation between data elements of the same sort is made by introducing identities. As is standard in the relational data model, one or more record fields can be declared as *key* fields. Each data element in the shared data space is uniquely determined by its sort and the value of its key fields. In this way applications can unambiguously refer to specific data elements, and relationships between data elements can be explicitly represented by referring from one data element to the key fields of another.

To illustrate, we consider a simplified example taken from the domain of air traffic control. Typically a system in this domain would be concerned with various aspects about flights, such as flight plans and the progress of flights as tracked from the reports that are received from the system's surveillance radar. Hence, we define sorts *flightplan*, *report*, and *track* as indicated in figure 1.

Sort *flightplan* declares four fields: a flight number, e.g. KL332 or AF1257, the scheduled time for departure and arrival, and the type of aircraft that carries out the flight, e.g. a Boeing 737 or an Airbus A320. By declaring the flight number as a key field, it is assumed that each flight plan is uniquely determined by its flight number.

Sort *report* contains the measurement vector of an object as returned at a specific time by the system's surveillance radar. The measurement vector typically contains

sort *flightplan*
    key *flightnumber* : string
    departure : time
    arrival : time
    aircraft : string

sort *report*
    key *index* : integer
    measurement : vector
    timestamp : time

sort *track*
    key *flightnumber* : string
    timestamp : time
    state : vector

Figure 1: Sort definitions - an example

position information. A unique index is attached to be able to distinguish between different reports.

Through a correlation and identification process, the progress of individual flights is recorded in sort *track*. The state vector typically contains position and velocity information on the associated flight number, that is computed from consecutive measurements. The timestamp identifies the time at which the state vector has been last updated.

2.2. Applications

Basically, applications interact with the shared data space by writing and reading data elements. SPLICE does not provide an operation for globally deleting elements from the shared data space. Instead, data can be removed implicitly using an overwriting mechanism. This mechanism is typically used to update old data with more recent values as the system's environment evolves over time. Additionally, applications can hide data, once read, from their view. This operation enables applications to progressively traverse the shared dataspace by successive read operations. By the absence of a global delete operation, the shared dataspace in SPLICE models a dynamically changing information store, where data can only be read or written. This contrasts the view where data elements represent shared resources, that can be physically consumed by applications.

SPLICE extends an existing (sequential) programming language with coordination primitives for creating processes and for interacting with the shared dataspace. More formally, the primitives are defined as follows.

- **create**(*f*): creates a new application process from the executable file named *f*, and run it in parallel to the existing applications.

- **write**(α, *x*): inserts an element *x* of sort α into the shared data space. If an element of sort α with the same key value as *x* already exists in the shared dataspace, then the existing element is replaced by *x*.

- **read**(α, q, t): reads an element of sort α from the shared dataspace, satisfying query q. The query is formulated as a predicate over the record fields of sort α. In case a matching element does not exist, the operation blocks until either one becomes available or until the timeout t has expired. If the latter occurs, a timeout error is returned by the operation. The timeout is an optional argument: if absent the read operation simply blocks until a matching element becomes available. In case more than one matching element can be found, one is selected non-determinstically.

- **get**(α, q, t): operates identically to the read operation, except that the element returned from the shared dataspace becomes hidden from the application's view, that is, the same element cannot be read a second time by the application.

The overwriting mechanism that is used when inserting data elements into the shared dataspace potentially gives rise to conflicts. If at the same time two different applications each write a data element of the same sort and with the same key value, one element will overwrite the other in a nondeterministic order. Consequently one of the two updates will be lost. In SPLICE this type of nondeterministic behaviour is considered undesirable. The architecture therefore imposes the design constraint that for each sort at most one application shall write data elements with the same key value.

As an illustration we return to the air traffic control example from the previous section. Consider an application process that tracks the progress of flight number n. This application continuously reads new reports from the surveillance radar and updates the track data of flight number n accordingly. The application process can be defined as indicated by the code fragment in figure 2.

```
t := get(track, flightnumber = n);
repeat
    r := get(report, true);
    if correlates(r, t) then
        update(t, r);
        write(track, t);
    end if
until terminated(t);
```

Figure 2: Coordination primitives - an example.

The application first reads the initial track data for flight number n from the shared dataspace. The initial data is produced by a separate application that is responsible for track initiation. The application then enters a loop where it first reads a new report r from the shared dataspace. If the report correlates with the current track t, as expressed by the condition $correlates(r, t)$, then track t is updated by the newly received report, using the procedure $update(t, r)$. The updated track is inserted into the shared dataspace, replacing the previous track data of flight number n. This process is repeated until track t is terminated. Termination can be decided, for instance, if a track did not receive an update over a certain period of time.

3.   Refinements of the Architecture

The shared dataspace architecture is based on an ideal situation where many non-functional requirements, such as distribution of data and processing across a computer network, fault-tolerance, and system response times, need not be taken into account. We next discuss how, through a successive series of modular refinements, a software architecture can be derived that fully supports the development of large-scale, distributed embedded systems.

3.1. A Distributed Software Architecture

The first aspect that we consider here is distribution of the shared data space over a network of computer systems. The basic architecture is refined by introducing two additional components. As illustrated in figure 3, the additional components consist of *agents* and a *communication network*.

Each application process interacts with exactly one agent. An agent embodies a local database for storing data elements, and processing facilities for handling all communication needs of the application processes. All agents are identical and need no prior information about either the application processes or their communication requirements. Communication between agents is established by a message passing mechanism. Messages between agents are handled by the communication network that interconnects them. The network must support broadcasting, but should preferably also support direct addressing of agents, and multicasting. An application process interacts with its assigned agent by means of the interaction primitives from section 2.2. The interaction with agents is transparent with respect to the shared dataspace model: application processes continue to operate on a logically shared dataspace.

The agents are passive servers of the application processes, but are actively involved in establishing and maintaining the required inter-agent communication. The communication needs are derived dynamically by the collection of agents from the read and write operations that are issued by the application processes. The protocol that is used by the agents to manage communication is based on a *subscription* paradigm that can be briefly outlined as follows.

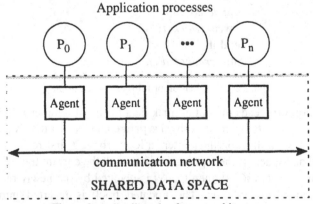

Figure 3: A distributed software architecture

First consider an application that performs a write operation. The data element is transferred to the application's agent, which initially stores the element into its local database, overwriting any existing element of the same sort and with the same key value.

Next consider an application that issues a read request for a given sort. Upon receipt of this request, the application's agent first checks whether this is the first request for that particular sort. If it is, the agent broadcasts the name of the sort on the network.

All other agents, after receiving this message, register the agent that performed the broadcast as a *subscriber* to the sort carried by the message. Next, each agent verifies if its local database contains any data elements of the requested sort, previously written by its application process, in which case copies of these elements are transferred to the newly subscribed agent. After this initial transfer, any subsequently written data of the requested sort will be immediately forwarded to all subscribed agents.

Each subscribed agent stores both the initially and all subsequently transferred copies into its local database, overwriting any existing data of the same sort and with the same key value. During all transfers a protocol is used that preserves the order in which data elements of the same sort have been written by an application. This mechanism in combination with the architecture's design constraint that for each sort at most one application writes data elements with the same key value, guarantees that overwrites occur in the same order with all agents. Otherwise, communication by the agents is performed asynchronously.

The search for data elements matching the query of a read request is performed locally by each agent. If no matching element can be found, the operation is suspended either until new data of the requested sort arrives or until the specified timeout has expired.

Execution of a get operation is handled by the agents similarly to the read operation, except that the returned data element is removed from the agent's local database.

As a result of this protocol, the shared dataspace is selectively replicated across the agents in the network. The local database of each agent contains data of only those sorts that are actually read or written by the application it serves. In practice the approach is viable, particularly for large-scale distributed systems, since the applications are generally interested in only a fraction of all sorts. Moreover, the communication pattern in which agents exchange data is relatively static: it may change when the operational mode of a system changes, or in a number of circumstances in which the configuration of the system changes (such as extensions or failure recovery). Such changes to the pattern are rare with respect to the number of actual communications using an established pattern. It is therefore beneficial from a performance point of view to maintain a subscription registration. After an initial short phase each time a new sort has been introduced, the agents will have adapted to the new communication requirement. This knowledge is subsequently used by the agents to distribute newly produced data to all the agents that hold a subscription. Since subscription registration is maintained dynamically by the agents, all changes to the system configuration will automatically lead to adaptation of the communication patterns.

Note that there is no need to group the distribution of a data element to the collection of subscribed agents into an atomic transaction. This enables a very efficient implementation in which the produced data is distributed asynchronously and the latency between actual production and use of the data depends largely on the consuming application processes. This results in upper bounds that are acceptable for distributed embedded systems where timing requirements are of the order of milliseconds.

3.2. Temporal Aspects

The shared dataspace as introduced in section 2.1, models a persistent store: data once written remains available to all applications until it is either overwritten by a new instance or hidden from an application's view by execution of a get operation. The persistence of data decouples applications in time. Data can be read, for instance, by an application that did not exist the moment the data was written, and conversely, the application that originally wrote the data might no longer be present when the data is actually read.

Applications in the embedded systems domain deal mostly with data instances that represent continuous quantities: data is either an observation sampled from the system's environment, or derived from such samples through a process of data association and correlation. The data itself is relatively simple in structure; there are only a few data types, and given the volatile nature of the samples, only recent values are of interest. However, samples may enter the system at very short intervals, so sufficient throughput and low latency are crucial properties. In addition, but to a lesser extent, embedded systems maintain discrete information, which is either directly related to external events or derived through qualitative reasoning from the sampled input.

This observation leads us to refine the shared dataspace to support volatile as well as persistent data. The sort definition, whose basic format was introduced in section 2.1, is extended with an additional attribute that indicates whether the instances of a sort are volatile or persistent. For persistent data the semantics of the read and write operations remain unchanged. Volatile data, on the other hand, will only be visible to the collection of applications that is present at the moment the data is written. Any application that is created afterwards, will not be able to read this data.

Returning to the air traffic control example from figure 1, the sort *report* can be classified as volatile, whereas the sorts *track* and *flightplan* are persistent. Consequently, the tracking process, as specified in figure 2, does not receive any reports from the surveillance radar that were generated prior to its creation. After the tracking process has been created, it first gets the initial track data and then waits until the next report becomes available.

Since the initial track data is produced exactly once, the tracking process must be guaranteed to have access to it, otherwise the process might block indefinitely. This implies that the sort *track* must be persistent.

The subscription-based protocol, that manages the distribution of data in a network of computer systems, can be refined to exploit the distinction between volatile and persistent data. Since volatile data is only available to the applications that are present at the moment the data is written, no history needs to be kept. Consequently, if an application writes a data element, it is immediately forwarded to the subscribed agents, without storing a copy in the application's local database. This optimization reduces the amount of storage that is required. Moreover, it eliminates the initial transfer of any previously written data elements, when an application performs the first read operation on a sort. This enables a newly created application to integrate into the communication pattern without initial delay, which better suits the timing characteristics that are typically associated with the processing of volatile data.

3.3. Fault-tolerance

Due to the stringent requirements on availability and safety that are typical of large-scale embedded systems, there is the need for redundancy in order to mask hardware failures during operation. Fault-tolerance in general is a very complex requirement to meet and can, of course, only be partially solved in software. In SPLICE, the agents can be refined to provide a mechanism for fault-tolerant behaviour. The mechanism is based on both data and process replication. By making fault-tolerance a property of the software architecture, the design complexity of applications can be significantly reduced.

In this paper we only consider failing processing units, and we assume that if a processor fails, it stops executing. In particular, we assume that communication never fails indefinitely and that data does not get corrupted.

If a processing unit in the network fails, the data that is stored in this unit, will be permanently lost. The solution is to store copies of each data element across different units of failure. The subscription-based protocol described in section 3.1 already implements a replicated storage scheme, where copies of each data element are stored with the producer and each of the consumers. The basic protocol, however, is not suffi-cient to implement fault-tolerant data storage in general. For instance, if data elements of a specific sort have been written but not (yet) read, the elements are stored with the producer only. A similar problem occurs if the producers and consumers of a sort hap-pen to be located on the same processing unit.

The solution is to store a copy of each data element in at least one other unit of fail-ure. The architecture as depicted in figure 3 is extended with an additional type of component: a persistent database. This component executes a specialized version of the subscription protocol. On start-up a persistent database broadcasts the name of each persistent sort on the network. As a result of the subscription protocol that is exe-cuted by the collection of agents, any data element of a persistent sort that is written by an application, will be automatically forwarded to the persistent database. There can be one or more instances of the persistent database executing on different processing units, dependent on the required level of system availability. Moreover, it is possible to load two or more persistent databases with disjoint sets of sort names, leading to a dis-tributed storage of persistent data.

When a processing unit fails, also the applications that are executed by this unit will be lost. The architecture can be refined to support both passive and active replication of applications across different processing units in the network.

Using passive replication, only one process is actually executing, while one or more back-ups are kept off-line, either in main memory or on secondary storage. When the processing unit executing the active process fails, one of the back-ups is activated. In order to be able to restore the internal state of the failed process, it is required that each passively replicated application writes a copy of its state to the shared dataspace each time the state is updated. The internal state can be represented by one or more persist-ent sorts. When a back-up is activated, it will first restore the current state from the shared dataspace and then continue execution.

When timing is critical, active replication of processes is often a more viable solu-tion. In that case, multiple instances of the same application are executing in parallel, hosted by different processing units; all instances read and write data. Typically, active replication is used when interruption of services cannot be tolerated.

The subscription-based protocol can be refined to support active replication transparently. If a particular instance of a replicated application performs a write operation, its agent attaches a unique replication index as a key field to the data element. The index allows the subscribed agents to distinguish between the various copies that they receive from a replicated application. Upon a read request, an agent first attempts to return a matching element having a fixed default index. When, after some appropriate time-out has expired, the requested element is still not available, a matching element with an index other than the default is returned. From that moment on it is assumed that the application corresponding to the default index has failed, and the subscription registration is updated accordingly. The index of the actually returned data element now becomes the new default.

A general overview of the distributed software architecture supporting fault-tolerance based on the various data and process replication techniques is given in figure 4.

3.4. System Modifications and Extensions

In the embedded systems domain requirements on availability often make it necessary to support modifications and extensions while the current system remains on-line. There are two distinct cases to be considered.

- The upgrade is an extension to the system, introducing new applications and sorts but without further modifications to the existing system.

- The upgrade includes modification of existing applications.

Since the subscription registration is maintained dynamically by the agents, it is obvious that the current protocol can deal with the first case without further refinements. After installing and starting a new application, it will automatically integrate.

The second case, clearly, is more difficult. One special, but important, category of modifications can be handled by a simple refinement of the agents. Consider the problem of upgrading a system by replacing an existing application process with one that implements the same function, but using a better algorithm, leading to higher quality

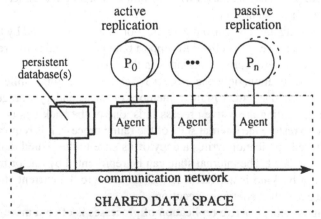

Figure 4: Supporting fault-tolerance.

results. In many systems it is not possible to physically replace the current application with the new one, since this would require the system to be taken off-line.

By a refinement of the agents it is possible to support on-line replacement of applications. If an application performs a write operation, its agent attaches an additional key field to the data element representing the application's version number. Upon a read request, an agent now first checks whether multiple versions of the requested instance are available in the local database. If this is the case, the instance having the highest version number is delivered to the application - assuming that higher numbers correspond to later releases. From that moment on, all data elements with lower version numbers, received from the same agent, are discarded. In this way an application can be dynamically upgraded, simply by starting the new version of the application, after which it will automatically integrate and replace the current version.

4. Formalisation

In this section we will briefly sketch ongoing work in developing a theoretical framework for SPLICE and SPLICE-based systems.

Process algebras provide a well-known formal method for reasoning about distributed systems [17][12]. Processes in SPLICE are sequential processes, that interact with each other by means of read and write actions on the shared dataspace. It therefore seems natural to study SPLICE in the context of *Communicating Sequential Processes* (CSP [12][13]). In CSP-like algebras, the semantics of processes is given in terms of traces: the behaviour of a process is represented by sequences of its communication actions. Unlike CSP, communication actions in SPLICE are not synchronized. Therefore, we use a process algebra for *Data-Flow Networks* (DFN), an asynchronous variant of CSP, as basis for a SPLICE Process Algebra (SPA). In DFN, output is never blocked: the environment is always ready to accept data. DFN is subsumed in *Receptive Process Theory*, RPT [15]. A general explanation of DFN in the context of CSP can be found in [13]. The development of SPA is inspired by [16] where another sub-theory of RPT is presented which is based on delay-insensitive communications.

In SPA we model SPLICE processes at a certain level of abstraction, where we focus on the communication behaviour of processes. Processes in SPA are typically denoted by P, Q and R; different sorts are typically denoted by a, b, and c. Processes have an input and an output alphabet, denoted with $i(P)$ and $o(P)$ respectively. These alphabets define the sorts that can be read or written by P according to the subscription paradigm of SPLICE. We abstract from the agents; their role as manager of communication is integrated in the semantics of the operators in SPA. The local data space is modelled with an *after* operator. Communication between different processes is expressed by *parallel composition*. The idea is that data $a.v$ (of sort a and value v) written by P is read by Q (given that $a \in o(P)$ and $a \in i(Q)$; i.e. P is a publisher of a and Q is subscribed to a). We do not make assumptions about Q actually reading $a.v$, we only assume that Q eventually will have $a.v$ in its local data space. In general, there may be multiple subscribers of sort a, but only one publisher.

In SPA, the coordination primitives of SPLICE are written as:

- $a!v$: Write an element of sort a and value v. We demand that $a \in o(P)$ if P is the process publishing $a.v$. Writing is never blocked by the environment.

- $a?x$: Read an element x of sort a (nondestructive read). We demand that $a \in i(P)$ if P is the process that reads an element of sort a. The read operation is blocking when no x is available.
- $a?\bar{x}$: Get (read and remove) an element x of sort a (destructive read). We demand that $a \in i(P)$, with P the process performing this operation. The get operation is blocking when no element of sort a is available.
- $P/a.v$: P after reception of data $a.v$ ($a \in i(P)$). In terms of SPLICE, $a.v$ has been stored in the local data space of P.
- $P \parallel Q$: Parallel composition of P and Q.

Just as in DFN, we have to impose some syntactic restrictions on processes in SPA. It is required that $i(P)$ and $o(P)$ are finite, that the output alphabet is non-empty, and that the input and output alphabets are disjoint:

$$o(P) \neq \varnothing \qquad i(P) \cap o(P) = \varnothing$$

The host language is replaced by an abstract programming language based on guarded commands [9]. This language has operators for nondeterministic choice, prefixing, guarded-choice, and recursion.

Using the SPA operators presented above we can express several coordination primitives, such as asynchronously writing, (non)destructively reading, dynamic process creation, process replication, et cetera. Via SPA we can use DFN to represent the SPLICE primitives. The laws of the algebra define valid program transformations for SPLICE processes. Details are beyond the scope of this paper, however, and the reader is referred to [8].

The goal of the formalization is to support the design of SPLICE-based systems within a process algebra. Design rules and guidelines can be formally derived and used to improve the development process. Design rules put (extra) constraints on the composition of program constructs; guidelines streamline the task of developing programs that conform to the design rules. The benefit of restricting the design freedom through design rules, is the guarantee of certain emergent system properties. Therefore, the next step is to focus on the definition of design rules and related guidelines.

Another step is to extend the read and get operations with the query mechanism of SPLICE; that is, an element is read when it is available *and* when the given query yields for this element; otherwise, the operation blocks. With such a mechanism we can distinguish the order in which data is read. Because reordering read operations in the presence of queries might introduce deadlock, we will need to impose restrictions on the use of the query mechanism. Complete understanding of these restrictions is only possible through the use of mathematical techniques.

Besides the coordination primitives, there are other important features of SPLICE to be expressed. We mention real-time and fault-tolerant behaviour. Currently, we can express data and process replication in SPA; future work will focus on design rules for fault-tolerant behaviour and on the introduction of temporal properties in our formal framework.

5. Example

To demonstrate the benefits of SPLICE in designing complex systems, a full-scale example should be presented. This is clearly beyond the scope of this paper, and we therefore restrict ourselves to an academic problem, with nevertheless interesting properties.

Imagine a rectangular grid of railway tracks, intersecting at regular intervals, such that trains cannot change from one track to another. Now suppose there is exactly one train on each of the n east-west tracks, and on each of the n north-south tracks. Each train has a given amount of time it should spend going from one end of its track to the other. Trains only move either from west to east, or from north to south. When reaching the end of a track, a train jumps back to the beginning and repeats its journey with a new deadline for reaching the other end. The journey times are random perturbations over a preset time given for each train separately. Trains are required to:
* travel safely,
* meet their deadlines, to the extent possible, and
* as much as possible, provide passengers with a comfortable journey,
with decreasing relative importance in the order given.

Now suppose that a train cannot be trusted to carrying out a given schedule; it will therefore be impossible to compute for each train what the best schedule for a given journey would be. (Note that the random variations on the travel times from start to finish already make computing a globally optimal schedule for all trains impractical.) It will thus be necessary to control the trains dynamically: depending on the actual situation, trains need to adjust their speeds to fulfil the requirements.

There are several possible solutions to this problem. At a high level of abstraction, there is the distinction between central and distributed control. Central control, although intuitively attractive for its (perceived) conceptual simplicity has the drawback of poor scalability [6]. In the case of distributed control, there are different ways of organizing the control function: it may either be associated with the railway tracks, or with the trains themselves.

The solution presented here is based on the following principle:

Every train periodically makes available its status. The status contains the following information:

```
time,               -- time at which status was produced
position,           -- position of head of train at "time"
nextX,              -- next crossing
onX,                -- either 0 when not on a crossing,
                    -- or crossing number of occupied crossing
length,             -- length of the train
speed,              -- speed at time "time"
acc,                -- acceleration at time "time"
delay,              -- delay w.r.t. schedule at time "time"
action taken,       -- action relating to collision avoidance
maximum speed,
maximum acceleration,
maximum deceleration
```

Each train in addition obtains status information for those trains that it might conceivably collide with. All trains then independently, and without further communication, determine what their course of action must be for satisfying the requirements. In order to do so, all trains obey the same set of traffic rules. Evaluating the rules every time new information is obtained then allows the trains to autonomously (i.e. without interaction with other trains) decide what action is appropriate.

The following set of rules has been implemented (the rules marked * are necessary for safety and cannot be removed; the others are optional):

	condition	action
*	conflicting decisions	east-west train has priority
*	train already on Xing	keep going
*	other train on Xing	wait for Xing to be clear again
*	other train has taken action	take complementary action
	different delays	most delayed has priority
	different speeds	faster train has right of way
	different lengths	shortest train goes first
*	otherwise	east-west has priority

5.1. Discussion

There are two aspects that merit discussion. One is the validity of this solution, the other is its implementation.

The argument that trains will meet the requirements consists of several parts. One approach would be to first show that the set of behavioural rules is sufficient to prevent accidents, under the assumption that trains detect an imminent collision in time to brake. Second, conditions would then have be specified that guarantee the validity of that assumption. And finally it must be shown that if there is no collision danger (any more), a train will focus on meeting its deadline

This paper's topic being distributed reactive systems, we will limit the discussion to the implementation of the solution using SPLICE.

5.1.1. Structure of the solution

The essence of the solution is that each train has information about the behaviour of all other trains, or at least the relevant subset of them (trains on parallel tracks will never collide, and thus there is no need for information about such trains). SPLICE provides an ideal mechanism for organizing this information exchange. As explained above, the model underlying SPLICE is a shared dataspace, upon which individual application programs may perform actions, like reading and writing of data elements.

The obvious approach, is therefore to model each of the trains as a separate program, where programs only differ in their parametrization to indicate track and static train properties. Each program consists of an endless cycle, in which it repeatedly requests data from SPLICE, then determines whether action is necessary, and subsequently writes its current state to SPLICE. This cycle is repeated at the required sample rate, which in the case of our experiments was 5 times per second. Note that in general there is a relationship between sample rate, maximum allowable speed, and network geometry.

5.1.2. Scalability issues

For scalability, and in order to improve efficiency, it is desirable to limit the amount of data to be communicated to a minimum. Clearly, with a track-grid of size n, there are n^2 communications necessary for all the trains to obtain information about all the others travelling in a different direction. Thus, minimizing the amount of information to be exchanged can make a huge difference in network load.

In addition, since a train cannot collide with another train on a track that has been crossed already, it is not necessary for a train to obtain status data from trains on those tracks. So, as a train moves from the beginning of its track to the end, the number of potentially dangerous trains reduces monotonously, and consequently, the train program's processing requirements should diminish accordingly. Since in our simulation, trains are randomly distributed over the network as a result of the random perturbations in their schedules, the average processing load should benefit from exploiting this observation. Note that in a real setting the expected processing load for a train would probably be very low, and the only necessary optimization would be in reducing communication requirements.

5.1.3. Implementation

Forgetting about a possible optimization in which the sample rate for a particular train is made dependent on its speed, both optimizations can be very easily expressed using SPLICE. To achieve a minimal communication load, the first improvement is to split the state data into two separate structures: one that describes (pseudo-) static properties of a train and therefore only changes rarely, if ever, and another that describes the actual position, speed and other variable attributes of a train. Simple as this may appear, this approach introduces the difficulty of ensuring that the properties and dynamic data for a particular train are always processed together. Clearly, if the properties data never change, it suffices to read them once only, during a program initialization phase. If however, due to unforeseen circumstances a train's abilities may suddenly change, this data will have to be read at unpredictable moments. The shared dataspace provides a solution that is both elegant and effective. SPLICE supports subscriptions to so-called multi-sorts: collections of individual sorts that must be processed together, and that are related through a common key (as illustrated in figure 1). Depending on the needs of the application program, data can be retrieved from SPLICE in different ways; one of them will return fresh data for all those sorts that have received an update since the last read operation, and stale (previously read) data when no new data has been received. SPLICE ensures that in either case the data of the different sorts making up the multi-sort, form a coherent set, as expressed through the common key. Thus, rather than producing information in complete records, the data is assembled at the consuming side, for which the application only needs to provide a specification. This mechanism rather strongly contrasts with traditional message-passing and client-server systems, such as e.g. object oriented designs, where the burden is upon the producer of information.

Preventing state data from trains on parallel tracks to be needlessly communicated is slightly more difficult. The first step is for a train program to express interest in orthogonal trains only. This is easily accomplished in SPLICE through the built-in fil-ter-mechanism, which permits a content-dependent refinement of the subscription to be specified. Thus, provided the track-direction of a particular train is encoded in the state data, it is possible to express that only data is required where the direction is dif-ferent from one's own. SPLICE will evaluate this filter expression for all incoming data elements (of the relevant sort), and will discard those that fail the test. Depending on the structure of the application, SPLICE may decide to evaluate the filter expression at the producer's site, rather than at the consumer's, for better utilizing the available communication bandwidth. Note that this involves migrating the filter from the con-sumer location (where it is defined), to the producer's site.

Both techniques can be illustrated with the following example, taken verbatim from the *trains* program:

```
char dir_filter[64];
char *df = dir_filter;
```

A filter expression is a string expressing a condition, that is compiled into byte (or machine) code by SPLICE upon its definition.

```
struct sp_consumer_part train_state[]={
    {sp_use_sort(train_descr),"@id","",0,NULL,1,&df},
    {sp_use_sort(state_descr),"@id","",0,NULL,1,&df}};
```

This declaration describes a multi-sort, consisting of two constituent sorts: "train_descr" and "state_descr", as adumbrated above.

```
sprintf(dir_filter, ".id %c 0",
                myself.track_dir == dir_hor ? '<' : '>');
```

This statement generates the actual filter expression: "id" is the common key in both sorts, and encodes the track the train is using. Negative track numbers are N-S tracks, positive track numbers are W-E tracks. Since there is only one train per track, this pro-vides unique identification of a train. For ease of programming, the static data "myself" in addition contains an enumeration type giving the track direction: "track_dir". Thus, depending on the train's direction, SPLICE will check for positive or negative "id" values in received data, and discard the unwanted instances of parallel trains.

```
ts_cons=sp_start_consuming_multi(app,2,train_state,
                1,&w,NULL,
                "splice","","",NULL,SP_SYNC_DEFAULT);
```

This statement, finally, starts the multi-sort subscription.

In order to prevent processing of data on tracks already behind a given train, another mechanism is used. Rather than refining interest in subscribed data through filter expressions, we use the query facility to exclude this data from being returned to the application.

```
q=sp_define_query(ts_cons,"@track==%p matching @tail<=%f",
                &p_track,Xings[myself.track]);
```

This way, the data will always be available in the local instance of the shared dataspace, which in a subsequent cycle of the train over its track will be needed for processing anyway.

The choice between the filter and the query mechanism is partly a matter of taste, and partly one of efficiency. Filter expressions cannot contain references to program variables and it is relatively expensive to install a filter, whereas query expressions may link data fields to actual program states. Since a new filter would have to be installed after every intersection, it was decided to use the query mechanism, even though communication overhead cannot be reduced in this way.

5.1.4. Simulation results

The program has been implemented in C and was executed on UltraSparc machines, running at 300 MHz, among others. The largest size gird that has been experimented with, was 100x100 tracks, resulting in 200 train processes running concurrently. It was found that a single machine could not fulfil the processing requirements and consequently executed the train programs at a lower periodicity. Instead of the requested 5 Hz, programs cycled at approximately 3 Hz. This still presents an average number of SPLICE dataspace updates of 30000 per second, in addition to an equal number of read operations and 600 executions per second of the Finite State Automaton that implements the decision procedure for a train. This resilience against overload is typical of systems designed for a shared-data architecture, and strongly contrasts with other design approaches.

Running the same experiment on two machines, connected by standard (10 Mbit/sec) Ethernet, proved near the limit of the communication channel, but easy on the processors, that achieved 50000 dataspace updates per second. The limitation caused by the channel is largely due to the fact that all write operations on the shared dataspace result in separate packets; since there is little data in a packet, this is far from optimal. Since the program requires all communication to be reliable, frequent collisions can have a snowballing effect: SPLICE guarantees the order of messages in reliable communication, and missing messages will therefore be retransmitted. Once the effective capacity of the network is reached, this can easily lead to an explosion of collisions. An improvement can be obtained by collecting a number of data elements in a single packet: this will reduce the number of Ethernet packets, at the cost of somewhat greater latency. SPLICE provides mechanisms that allow this packaging to occur automatically, without having to compromise the solution (thus, maintaining the independence between individual train programs in particular).

6. Conclusion

Due to the inherent complexity of the environment in which large-scale embedded systems operate, combined with the stringent requirements regarding temporal behaviour, availability, robustness, and maintainability, the design of these systems is an intricate task. Coordination models offer the potential of separating functional requirements from other aspects of system design. We have presented a software architecture for large-scale embedded systems that incorporates a separate coordination model. We have demonstrated how, starting from a relatively simple model based on a shared data space, the model can be successively refined to meet the requirements that are typical for this class of systems. Finally, We have indicated how formal techniques can be used to support development of SPLICE-based systems.

Over the past years SPLICE has been applied in the development of commercially available command-and-control, and traffic management systems. These systems typically consist of some 1000 applications running on close to 100 processors interconnected by a hybrid communication network. Experience with the development of these systems confirms that the software architecture, including all of the refinements discussed, significantly reduces the complexity of the design process [4]. (In [2] the authors argue that SPLICE lacks global control mechanisms, and that consequently understanding and debugging systems tend to be difficult. Unfortunately, the arguments given are either inapplicable or wrong; in addition, our experience does strongly contradict their statement.) Due to the high level of decoupling between processes, these systems are relatively easy to develop and integrate in an incremental way. Moreover, distribution of processes and data, fault-tolerant behaviour, graceful degradation, and dynamic reconfiguration are directly supported by the architecture.

Acknowledgements

The contributions by Edwin de Jong, Paul Dechering, and Erik Boasson, without whom little would have been achieved, are gratefully acknowledged.

References

[1]   Banatre, J.-P., Le Metayer, D.: Programming by Multiset transformation. Communications of the ACM, Vol. 36 (1993) 98-111

[2]   Bergstra, J., Klint, P.: The discrete time TOOLBUS - A software coordination architecture. Science of Computer Programming, Vol 31 (1998) 205-229

[3]   Boasson, M.: Control Systems Software, IEEE Transactions on Automatic Control. Vol. 38 (1993) 1094-1107

[4]   Boasson, M.: Complexity may be our own fault. IEEE Software (1993)

[5]   Boasson, M.: Software Architecture special issue (guest editor). IEEE Software 1(995)

[6]   Boasson, M., Mouaddib, A.: Comparison of two solutions to a reactive planning problem. Proc. of Avignon (1994)

[7]   Carriero, N., Gelernter, D.: Linda in Context. Communications of the ACM, Vol. 32 (1989) 444-458

[8]   Dechering, P. et al: Formalization of a Software Architecture for Embedded Systems: a Process Algebra for SPLICE. To appear

[9]   Dijkstra, E.W.: A Discipline of Programming. Prentice Hall (1976)

[10]   Garlan, D., Le Metayer, D. (Eds.): Coordination Languages and Models. Lecture Notes in Computer Science Vol. 1282 (1997)

[11]   Gelernter, D., Carriero, N.: Coordination Languages and their Significance. Communications of the ACM, Vol. 35 (1992) 97-107

[12]   Hoare, C.A.R.: Communicating Sequential Processes, Prentice Hall (1985)

[13]   Hoare, C.A.R., Jifeng, H.: Unifying Theories of Programming. Prentice Hall (1998)

[14]   Jackson, K., Boasson, M.: The importance of good architectural style. Proc. of the workshop of the IEEE TF on Engineering of Computer Based Systems, Tucson (1995)

[15]   Josephs, M.B.: Receptive Process Theory. Acta Informatica 29(1992) 17-31

[16]   Josephs, M.B., Udding, J.T.: An Overview of DI Algebra. In Proc. of the 26th Annual Hawaii Int. Conf. on System Sciences. IEEE CS Press (1993) 329-338

[17]   Milner, R.: Communication and Concurrency. Prentice Hall (1989)

[18]   Roman, G.-C., Cunningham, H.C.: Mixed Programming Metaphors in a Shared Dataspace Model of Concurrency. IEEE Trans. of Software Engineering, Vol. 16 (1990) 1361-1373

A Logical Basis for Modular Software and Systems Engineering[*]

Manfred Broy

Institut für Informatik, Technische Universität München, D-80290 München, Germany

Abstract. We introduce a logical and mathematical theory for the specification of system components and the typical steps of the development process. In particular, we identify three patterns of development
- refinement within one level of abstraction,
- transition from one level of abstraction to the other,
- implementation by glass box refinement.

We introduce refinement relations to capture these three dimensions of the development space. We give verification conditions for these refinement steps. In this way, a logical basis for the development of systems is described.

1   Introduction

For a discipline of modular system development firmly based on a scientific theory we need a clear notion of components and ways to manipulate and to compose them. In this paper, we introduce a mathematical model of a component with the following characteristics:

- A component is *interactive*.

- It is connected with its environments by named and typed *channels*.

- It receives *input messages* from its environment on its *input* channels and generates *output messages* to its environment on its *output* channels.

- A component can be *nondeterministic*. This means that for a given input history there may exist several output histories that the component may produce.

- The interaction between the component and its environment takes place in a *global time* frame.

Throughout this paper we work exclusively with discrete time. Discrete time is a sufficient model for most of the typical applications for information processing systems. For an extension of our model to continuous time see [16].

Based on the ideas of an interactive component we can define forms of composition. We basically introduce only one form of composition, *namely parallel composition with feedback*. This form of composition allows us to model *concurrent execution* and *interaction* of components within a network. We briefly show that other forms of composition can be introduced as special cases of parallel composition with feedback.

For the systematic stepwise development of components we introduce the concept

---

[*] This work was carried out within the Forschungsverbund ForSoft, sponsored by the Bayerische Forschungsstiftung and the project SysLab sponsored by Siemens-Nixdorf and partially supported by the Deutsche Forschungsgemeinschaft under the Leibniz program.

of *refinement*. We study three refinement relations namely *property refinement*, *glass box refinement*, and *interaction refinement*. We claim that these notions of refinement are all what we need for a systematic top down system development.

Finally, we outline that our approach is *compositional*. This means that a refinement step for a composed system is obtained by refinement steps for its components. As a consequence, global reasoning about the system can be structured into local reasoning about the components. Compositionality relates to *modularity* in systems engineering. The contribution of this paper is the relational version of the stream processing approach as developed at the Technische Universität München (under the keyword FOCUS, see [11], [12]). Moreover, the paper aims at a brief survey on this approach.

We begin with the informal introduction of the concept of interactive components. This concept is based on communication histories called streams that are introduced in section 3. Then a mathematical notion of a component is introduced in section 4 and illustrated by a number of simple examples. Section 5 treats operators for composing components into distributed systems. In section 6 we introduce three notions of refinements to develop systems and show the compositionality of these notions. Again all described concepts are illustrated by simple examples.

2 Central Notion: Component

We introduce the mathematical notion of a component and on this basis a concept of component specification. A component specification is given by a description of the syntactic interface and a logical formula that relates input and output histories.

The notion of component is essential in systems engineering and software engineering. Especially in software engineering a lot of work is devoted to the concept of *software architecture* and to the idea of *componentware*. Componentware is a catchword in software engineering (see [15]) for a development method where software systems are composed from given components such that main parts of the systems do not have to be reimplemented every time again but can be obtained by new configurations of existing software solutions. A key issue for such an approach are well designed *interfaces* and *software architectures*. Software architectures mainly can be described as distributed systems, composed of components. For this, a clean and clear concept of a component is needed.

In software engineering literature the following informal definition of a component is found:

> A *component* is a physical encapsulation of related services according to a published specification.

According to this definition we work with the idea of a component which encapsulates a local state or a distributed architecture. We provide a logical way to write a specification of component services. We will relate these notions to glass box views, to the derived black box views, and to component specifications.

3 Streams

A *stream* is a finite or infinite sequence of messages or of actions. Streams are used to represent communication histories for channels or histories of activities. Let M be a given set of messages. A stream over the set M is a finite or an infinite sequence of elements from M. We use the following notation:

M^* denotes the finite sequences over M with the *empty* sequence ⟨⟩,

M^∞ denotes the infinite sequences over M (that can be represented by mappings $\mathbb{N} \setminus \{0\} \to M$).

A stream is an element of the set M^ω which is defined by

$$M^\omega = M^* \cup M^\infty$$

On streams we specify the prefix ordering for x, y ∈ M^ω by the formula

$$x \sqsubseteq y \equiv \exists z \in M^\omega: x\hat{\ }z = y$$

Here x^z denotes the concatenation of the stream x to the stream z. If x is infinite then x^z = x.

Throughout this paper we do not work with the simple concept of a stream as introduced so far but find it more appropriate to work with so called *timed streams*. A timed stream represents an infinite history of communications over a channel or an infinite history of activities that are carried out in a discrete time frame. The discrete time frame represents time as an infinite chain of time intervals of equal length. In each time interval a finite number of messages can be communicated or a finite number of actions can be executed. Therefore we represent a communication history of a system model with such a discrete time frame by an infinite sequence of finite sequences of messages or actions. By

$$(M^*)^\infty$$

we denote the set of timed streams. The k-th sequence s.k in a timed stream s ∈ $(M^*)^\infty$ represents the sequence of messages exchanged on the channel in the k-th time interval or the sequence of actions executed in the k-th time interval.

In the following, we use streams exclusively to model the communication histories of sequential communication media called channels. In general, in a system several communication streams occur. Therefore we work with *channels* to identify the individual communication streams. Hence, in our approach, a channel is just an identifier in a system that is related to a stream in every execution of the system.

Throughout this paper we work with some simple notation for streams that are listed in the following. We use the following notation for a timed stream x:

z^x   concatenation of a sequence z to a stream x,

x↓i   sequence of the first i sequences in the stream x,

S©x   stream obtained from x by deleting all messages that are not elements of the set S,

$\overline{x}$ finite or infinite stream that is the result of concatenating all sequences in x.

We may also consider timed streams of states to model the traces of state-based system models. In the following, we restrict ourselves to message passing systems, however.

4   Syntactic and Semantic Interfaces

In this section we introduce a mathematical notion of components. We work with typed channels.

4.1 I/O-Functions

Let a set S of *sorts* or *types* be given. By C we denote a set of typed channels. We assume that we are given a type assignment for the channels in the set C:

$$\text{type: } C \rightarrow S$$

Given a set C of typed channels a *channel valuation* (let M be the set of all messages, by [T] we denote for a type T its set of elements) is an element of the set defined as follows:

$$\vec{C} = \{x: C \rightarrow (M^*)^\infty: \forall\, c \in C: x.c \in ([\text{type}(c)]^*)^\infty\}$$

A channel valuation $x \in \vec{C}$ associates a stream of elements of type type(c) with each channel $c \in C$. The operators on streams induce operators on valuations by pointwise application.

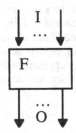

Fig. 1. Graphical Representation of a Component F with Input Channels I and Output Channels O

Given a set of typed input channels I and a set of typed output channels O we introduce the notion of a *syntactic interface* of a component:

        (I, O)   syntactic interface,

        I   set of typed input channels and,

        O   set of typed output channels.

In addition to the syntactic interface we need a concept for describing the *behavior* of a component. A behavior is a *relation between the input histories and the output histories.*

Input histories are represented by valuations of the input channels and output histories are represented by the valuations of output channels. We represent the black box behavior of a component, by a set valued function the semantic interface:

$$F: \vec{I} \rightarrow \wp(\vec{O})$$

Given $x \in \vec{I}$, by F.x we denote the set of all output histories which a component with behavior F may produce on the input x.

Of course, a set valued function, as well known, is isomorphic to a relation. We prefer set-valued functions to emphasize the roles of input and output. We call the function F an *I/O-function.*

4.2 Specification of I/O-Functions

Using logical means, an I/O-function F can be described by a logical formula relating the streams on the input channels to the streams on the output channels. Syntactically therefore such a formula uses typed channels as identifiers for streams.
A specification of a component provides the following information:

- its syntactic interface, describing how the component is connected to its environment,

- its behavior by a specifying formula Φ relating input and output channel valuations.

This way we obtain a specification technique that gives us a very powerful method to describe components.

Example. As simple but very fundamental examples of components we specify a merge component MRG, a transmission component TMC, and a fork component FRK as follows:

MRG

in x: T1, y: T2	
out z: T3	
$\bar{x} = T1 \copyright \bar{z}$	
$\bar{y} = T2 \copyright \bar{z}$	

Here let T1, T2, T3 be types (in our case we can see types simply as sets) where T1 and T2 are assumed to be disjoint and T3 is the union of the sets of elements of type T1 and T2. We specify the proposition x ~ y for timed streams x and y of arbitrary type T by the logical equivalence:

$$x \sim y \equiv (\forall\, m \in T: \{m\}\copyright \bar{x} = \{m\}\copyright \bar{y})$$

Based on this definition we specify the component TMC.

TMC

in z: T3	
out z: T3	
z ~ z'	

Here we use the convention for channel identifiers z that occur both as input and as output channels: in the specifying formula we write z' to denote the output channel z. The simple specification TMC states that every input message occurs also as output message by the component, and vice versa. However, messages may be arbitrarily delayed and overtake each other.

FRK

in z: T3	
out x: T1, y: T2	
$\bar{x} = T1 \copyright \bar{z}$	
$\bar{y} = T2 \copyright \bar{z}$	

Note that the merge component as well as the TMC component as they are specified here are fair. Every input is finally processed and reproduced as output. ☐

We use the following notation for a component F to refer to the constituents of its syntactic interface:

In(F)   the set of input channels I,

Out(F)   the set of output channels O.

By the specifying formula of a specification of an I/O-function F we may prove properties about the function F.

4.3 Properties of I/O-Functions

In the following we introduce some basic properties for I/O-functions. An I/O-function

$$F: \vec{I} \to \wp(\vec{O})$$

is called

- *properly timed*, if for all times $i \in \mathbb{N}$ we have

$$x{\downarrow}i = z{\downarrow}i \Rightarrow F(x){\downarrow}i = F(z){\downarrow}i$$

- *time guarded* (or *causal*), if for all times $i \in \mathbb{N}$ we have

$$x{\downarrow}i = z{\downarrow}i \Rightarrow F(x){\downarrow}i+1 = F(z){\downarrow}i+1$$

- *partial*, if $F(x) = \varnothing$ for some $x \in \vec{I}$ and *total* otherwise.

- *realizable*, if there exists a time guarded function $f: \vec{I} \to \vec{O}$ such that

$$\forall x \in \vec{I} : f.x \in F.x.$$

- *fully realizable*, if for all $x \in \vec{I}$: $F.x = \{f.x: f \in [\![F]\!]\}$

  Here $[\![F]\!]$ denotes the set of time guarded functions $f: \vec{I} \to O$, where $f.x \in F.x$ for all x.

- *time independent* (see [9]), if $\overline{x} = \overline{z} \Rightarrow \overline{F.x} = \overline{F.z}$

A specifying formula Φ for a component with the set of input channels I and the set of output channels O represents a predicate

$$p: \vec{I} \times \vec{O} \to \mathbb{B}$$

This predicate defines an I/O-function

$$F: \vec{I} \to \wp(\vec{O})$$

by the equation (for $x \in \vec{I}$)

$$F.x = \{y \in \vec{O}: p(x, y)\}$$

Given a specification with a specifying formula, we either may prove that the specified I/O-function fulfills certain of the properties introduced above. Another option is to add certain of these properties as schematic requirements to specifications.

Adding time-guardedness as a requirement on top of the predicate p leads to the inclusion greatest function F' such that $y \in F'.x$ implies $p(x, y)$ and F' is time guarded. This way we obtain the following definition for the function F'. Let F' by the inclusion largest function such that:

$$F'.x = \{y \in \bar{O}: p(x, y) \wedge \forall\, x' \in \bar{I}, k \in \mathbb{N}:$$

$$x{\downarrow}k = x'{\downarrow}k \Rightarrow \exists\, y' \in \bar{O}: y{\downarrow}k{+}1 = y'{\downarrow}k{+}1 \wedge x' \in F'(y')\}$$

Time guardedness adds the principle of causality between input and output to a specification.

Example: Transmission Component

Consider the transmission component TMC of the example above. In this case we have $p(x, y) = x \sim y$. Assuming time guardedness we get the function

$$F'.x = \{y: x \sim y \wedge \forall\, x', k \in \mathbb{N}: x{\downarrow}k = x'{\downarrow}k \Rightarrow \exists\, y': y{\downarrow}k{+}1 = y'{\downarrow}k{+}1 \wedge x' \sim y'\}$$

From this we easily prove

$$y \in F'.x \Rightarrow \forall\, m \in T3, k \in \mathbb{N}: \#\{m\}{\copyright}\,x{\downarrow}k \geq \#\{m\}{\copyright}\,y{\downarrow}k{+}1$$

This formula is a simple consequence of the fact that for each input history x we can find an input history x' such that $x{\downarrow}k = x'{\downarrow}k$ and

$$\overline{x'{\downarrow}k} = \overline{x'} \qquad\qquad \square$$

Time-guardedness is a very basic notion. It models the asymmetry between input and output. For time independent deterministic I/O-functions time guardedness has a strong relationship to *prefix monotonicity*.

As pointed out above, notions like time independence or time guardedness are logical properties that can be either added as properties to specifications explicitly or proved for certain specifications. It is easy to show for instance that MRG, TMC, and FRK are time independent. If we add time guardedness as a requirement then all three specified I/O-functions are fully realizable.

4.4   State Transition Specifications

Often it is more appropriate to describe a component by a state transition system with input and output. In such a case we have to describe the data state, the initial state, and the state transition relation.

We describe the data state of a transition system by a set of typed state attributes V that can be seen as programming variables. Mathematically, then a data state

$$\eta: V \to \bigcup_{v \in V} [\text{type}(v)]$$

is a valuation of the attributes by values of the corresponding type. In addition we use a finite set W of control states. A state of the component is a pair (w, η) consisting of a control and a data state. By Σ we denote the set of all states.

A state transition machine is given by an initial state σ_0 and a state transition function

$$\Delta: (\Sigma \times (I \to M^*)) \to \wp(\Sigma \times (O \to M^*))$$

Often it is helpful to describe a state transition machine by a state transition diagram in a graphical way. A state machine diagram consists of a number of nodes representing control states and a number of transition rules represented by labeled arcs between the control states. This is in particular an alternative to our logical characterization of I/O-functions. A state transition machine describes also an I/O-function. We show in the following how to associate an I/O-function to a state transition machine.

The state transition function Δ as introduced above describes a function

$$B_\Delta: \Sigma \to (\vec{I} \to \wp(\vec{O}))$$

that associates with every state $\sigma \in \Sigma$ an I/O-function $B_\Delta(\sigma)$ that describes the behavior of the system in this state. B_Δ provides the black box view onto Δ.

For each state $\sigma \in \Sigma$, each input pattern $z \in (I \to M^*)$, and each input channel valuation $x \in \vec{I}$, we specify the black box function B_Δ for the given state σ by the equation

$$B_\Delta(\sigma).(\langle z \rangle^\frown x) = \{\langle t \rangle^\frown y: \exists \sigma' \in \Sigma: (\sigma', t) \in \Delta(\sigma, z) \wedge y \in B_\Delta(\sigma').x\}$$

This is a recursive definition of B_Δ. In particular, B_Δ is not uniquely determined by the equation, in general. We choose the inclusion greatest solution of the equation for B_Δ.

State transition machines can als be used as implementation of I/O-functions. In particular, we may generate program code for certain classes of state transition machines. We come back to this issue under the heading glass box refinement.

5 Composition Operators

In this section we introduce a notion of *composition* for components. We prefer to introduce only one very general form of composition and later define a number of other composing forms as special cases.

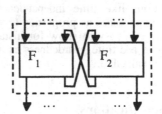

Fig. 2. Parallel Composition with Feedback

Given I/O-functions with disjoint sets of input channels (where $O_1 \cap O_2 = \emptyset$)

$$F_1 : \vec{I}_1 \to \wp(\vec{O}_1), \qquad F_2 : \vec{I}_2 \to \wp(\vec{O}_2)$$

we define the parallel composition with feedback by the I/O-function

$$F_1 \otimes F_2: \vec{I} \to \wp(\vec{O})$$

where the syntactic interface is specified by

$$I = (I_1 \cup I_2) \backslash (O_1 \cup O_2), \ O = (O_1 \cup O_2) \backslash (I_1 \cup I_2).$$

The resulting function is specified by the following equation (here $y \in C$ where $C = I_1 \cup I_2 \cup O_1 \cup O_2$):

$$(F_1 \otimes F_2).x = \{y|O: y|I = x|I \wedge y|O_1 \in F_1(y|I_1) \wedge y|O_2 \in F_2(y|I_2) \}$$

Here y denotes a valuation of all the channels of F_1 and F_2. By y|C we denote the restriction of the valuation y to the channels in C.

Let Φ_1 and Φ_2 be the specifying formulas for the functions F_1 and F_2 respectively; we obtain the specifying formula of $F_1 \otimes F_2$ simply by

$$\exists\, z_1, ..., z_k\colon \Phi_1 \wedge \Phi_2$$

where $\{z_1, ..., z_k\} = (I_1 \cap O_2) \cup (I_2 \cap O_1)$ are the internal channels of the system.

For this form of composition we can prove the following facts by rather straightforward proofs:

(1)   if the F_i are *time guarded* for i = 1, 2, so is $F_1 \otimes F_2$,

(2)   if the F_i are *realizable* for i = 1, 2, so is $F_1 \otimes F_2$,

(3)   if the F_i are *fully realizable* for i = 1, 2, so is $F_1 \otimes F_2$,

(4)   if the F_i are *time independent* for i = 1, 2, so is $F_1 \otimes F_2$.

If the F_i are total and properly timed for i = 1, 2, we cannot conclude, however, that the function $F_1 \otimes F_2$ is total. This shows that the composition works only in a modular way for well-chosen subclasses of specifications.

Some further forms of composition that can be defined by $\otimes$ are listed in the following (we do not give formal definitions for them, since these are quite straightforward):

- renaming of channels: $F[c/c']$

- feedback without hiding: $\mu\, F$

  let $F\colon \vec{I} \to \wp(\vec{O})$, then we define: $\mu\, F\colon \vec{J} \to \wp(\vec{O})$ where $J = I\backslash O$ by the equation (here we assume $y \in \vec{C}$ where $C = I \cup O$):

$$(\mu\, F).x = \{y|O\colon y|I = x|I \wedge y|O \in F(y|I)\}$$

- sequential composition $F_1 ; F_2$

  Sequential composition of the components F_1 and F_2 requires $O_1 = Out(F_1) = In(F_2) = I_2$.

In the special case where $O_1 = I_2 = (O_1 \cup O_2) \cap (I_1 \cup I_2)$ we can reduce sequential composition to parallel composition with feedback as follows:

$$F_1 ; F_2 = F_1 \otimes F_2$$

A simple example of sequential composition (where $O_1 = I_2$) is the composed component MRG;FRK as well as FRK;MRG.

Example: Feedback for the Component TMC

In this example we study the result of a composing form like feedback in its dependency on the additional requirement of time guardedness. If we do not require time guardedness then the specification μ TMC boils down to the specifying formula

$$z \sim z$$

which is equivalent to true. Assuming time guardedness we get in addition the requirement

$$\forall\, k \in \mathbb{N}\colon \overline{z{\downarrow}k} \sim \overline{z{\downarrow}k+1}$$

from which we can conclude by the fact that $z{\downarrow}0 = \diamond$ by induction that $\bar{z} = \diamond$.   □

This example demonstrates that time guardedness is an essential assumption to make feedback into an operator that mirrors the causality of the operational data flow principle.

6   Refinement for System Development

Refinement relations (see [13]) are the key to formalize development steps (see [8]) and the development process as it is advocated in software engineering process models. We work with the following basic ideas of refinement relations:

- *property refinement* - enhancing requirements - allows us to add properties to a specification,

- *glass box refinement* - designing implementations - allows us to decompose a component into a distributed system or to give a state transition description for a component specification,

- *interaction refinement* - relating levels of abstraction - allows us to change the granularity of the interaction, the number and types of the channels of a component (see [10]).

We claim that these notions of refinement are sufficient to describe all the steps needed in the idealistic view of a strict hierarchical top down system development. The three refinement concepts mentioned above are explained in detail in the following.

6.1   Property Refinement

Property refinement allows us to replace an I/O-function by one with additional properties. A behavior

$$F: \vec{I} \rightarrow \wp(\vec{O})$$

is refined by a behavior

$$\hat{F}: \vec{I} \rightarrow \wp(\vec{O})$$

if

$$\hat{F} \subseteq F$$

This relation stands for the proposition

$$\forall \, x \in \vec{I}: \hat{F}(x) \subseteq F(x).$$

Obviously, property refinement is a partial order. In particular, the refinement relation of property refinement is transitive, which garantees that iterated steps of property refinement can be composed into one step of property refinement.

A property refinement is a basic refinement step as it is needed in requirements engineering. In the process of requirement engineering, typically the overall services of a system are specified. This, in general, is done by requiring more and more sophisticated properties for components until a desired behavior is specified.

Example. A specification of a component that transmits its input on its two input channels to its two output channels (but does not necessarily observe the order) is specified as follows.

TM2

in x: T1, y: T2
out x: T1, y: T2
$\forall\ m \in T1: \{m\} © \bar{x}' = \{m\} © \bar{x}$ $\forall\ m \in T2: \{m\} © \bar{y}' = \{m\} © \bar{y}$

We want to relate this specification to the simple specification of the time independent identity TII that reads as follows:

TII

in x: T1, y: T2
out x: T1, y: T2
$\bar{x}' = \bar{x} \wedge \bar{y}' = \bar{y}$

Given these two specifications we immediately obtain that TII is a property refinement of TM2.

$$\text{TII} \subseteq \text{TM2}$$

A proof of this relation is straightforward (see below).   ☐

The verification conditions for property refinement are easily obtained as follows. For given specifications S_1 and S_2 with specifying formulas Φ_1 and Φ_2, the specifications S_2 is a property refinement of S_1 if the syntactic interfaces of S_1 and S_2 coincide and if for the specifying formulas Φ_1 and Φ_2 we have

$$\Phi_1 \Leftarrow \Phi_2$$

In our example the verification condition is easily obtained and reads as follows:

$$(\forall\ m \in T1: \{m\} © \bar{x}' = \{m\} © \bar{x}) \Leftarrow \bar{x}' = \bar{x}$$
$$\wedge \quad (\forall\ m \in T2: \{m\} © \bar{y}' = \{m\} © \bar{y}) \Leftarrow \bar{y}' = \bar{y}$$

The proof of this condition is obvious.

Property refinement can also be used to relate composed components to given components (see also glass box refinement in section 6.3). For instance, we obtain the following refinement relation

$$(\text{MRG}\ ;\ \text{FRK}) \subseteq \text{TII}$$

Again the proof is quite straightforward.

As we have shown the additional assumption of schematic properties to specifications such as time guardedness, time independence or realizability is a strengthening of the specifying predicate. Therefore it is a step in the property refinement relation.

Property refinement is characteristic for the development steps in requirements engineering. It is also used in the design process where decisions are taken that introduce further properties for the components.

6.2 Compositionality of Property Refinement

In our case, the proof of the compositionality of property refinement is simple. This is a straightforward consequence of the simple definition of composition. The rule of compositional property refinement reads as follows:

$$\frac{\hat{F}_1 \subseteq F_1 \qquad \hat{F}_2 \subseteq F_2}{\hat{F}_1 \otimes \hat{F}_2 \subseteq F_1 \otimes F_2}$$

The proof of the soundness of this rule is straightforward by the monotonicity of the operator $\otimes$ with respect to set inclusion.

Example. For our example the application of the rule of compositionality reads as follows. Suppose we use a specific component MRG1 for merging two streams. It is defined by

MRG1
in x: T1, y: T2
out z: T3
$z = \langle\rangle\char94 f(x, y)$
where
$f(\langle s\rangle\char94 x, \langle b\rangle\char94 y) = \langle s\char94 b\char94 f(x, y)$

Note that this merge component MRG1 is both deterministic and time dependent. According to our rule of compositionality and transitivity of refinement, it is sufficient to prove

$$\text{MRG1} \subseteq \text{MRG}$$

to conclude

$$\text{MRG1;FRK} \subseteq \text{MRG;FRK}$$

and by the transitivity of the refinement relation

$$\text{MRG1;FRK} \subseteq \text{TII}$$

This shows how local refinement steps and their proofs are schematically extended to global proofs. $\quad\Box$

The usage of the composition operator and the relation of property refinement leads to a design calculus for requirements engineering. It includes steps of decomposition and implementation that are treated more systematically in the following section on glass box refinement.

6.3 Glass Box Refinement

Glass Box Refinement is the classical concept of refinement that we need and use in the design phase. In glass box refinement we replace a system description by a more detailed one adding implementation information.

In the design phase we typically decompose a system with a specified black box behavior into a distributed system architecture or we represent (implement) its behavior by a state transition machine. In other words, a glass box refinement of a component F is a special case of a property refinement where the reined system descriptions are of the form

$$F_1 \otimes F_2 \otimes ... \otimes F_n \subseteq F \qquad\qquad \textit{design of an architecture}$$

or of the form

$$B_\Delta(\sigma_0) \subseteq F \qquad\qquad \textit{implementation by a state machine}$$

where the I/O-function $B_\Delta(\sigma_0)$ is defined by a state machine Δ (see [19] and section 4.4) and σ_0 is its initial state.

Accordingly, a glass box refinement is a special case of property refinement where the refining component has a special syntactic form. In the case of a glass box refinement that transforms a component into a network, this form is a term composed of a number of components.

Example. A very simple instance of such a glass box refinement is already shown by the proposition

$$MRG\ ;\ FRK \subseteq TII$$

It allows us to replace the component TII by two components. $\qquad\qquad\square$

Hence, a glass box refinement works with the relation of property refinement and special terms representing the refining component. Thus the construction of implementations and their correctness proof can be carried out fully within the framework of refinement. The compositionality of glass box refinement is a straightforward consequence of the compositionality of property refinement.

6.4   Interaction Refinement

Interaction refinement is the refinement notion that we need for modeling development steps between levels of abstraction. Interaction refinement allows us to change

- the number and names of input and output channels,
- the granularity of the messages on the channels

of a component.

An *interaction refinement* requires two functions

$$A:\ \vec{C}' \to \wp(\vec{C}) \qquad R:\ \vec{C} \to \wp(\vec{C}')$$

that relate the abstract with the concrete level of a development step leading from one level of abstraction to the other.

Given an abstract history $x \in C$ each history $y \in R(x)$ denotes a concrete history representing x om the concrete level. Calculating a representation for a given abstract history and then its abstraction yields the old abstract history again. This is expressed by the following requirement:

$$R\ ;\ A = Id$$

Let Id denote the identity relation. A is called the *abstraction* and R is called the *representation*. R and A are called a *refinement pair*.

For nontimed components it is sufficient to require for the time independent identity TII (as a generalization of the specification TII given in section 6.1 to arbitrary channel sets)

$$R\ ;\ A \subseteq TII$$

Choosing the component MRG for R and FRK for A immediately gives a refinement pair for nontimed components. Fig. 3 illustrates how the refinement pair relates the abstract and the concrete levels.

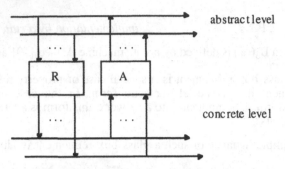

Fig. 3. Communication History Refinement

Interaction refinement allows us to refine components, given appropriate refinement pairs for the input and output channels. The idea of an interaction refinement is visualized in Fig. 4.

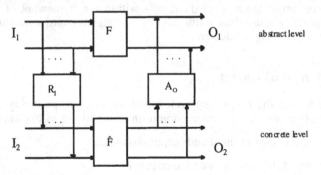

Fig. 4. Interface Interaction Refinement (*U-simulation*)

Given interaction refinements

$$A_I: \vec{I}_2 \to \wp(\vec{I}_1) \qquad\qquad R_I: \vec{I}_1 \to \wp(\vec{I}_2)$$
$$A_O: \vec{O}_2 \to \wp(\vec{O}_1) \qquad\qquad R_O: \vec{O}_1 \to \wp(\vec{O}_2)$$

for the input and output channels we call the I/O-function

$$\hat{F}: \vec{I}_2 \to \wp(\vec{O}_2)$$

an *interaction refinement* of

$$F: \vec{I}_1 \to \wp(\vec{O}_1)$$

if one of the following propositions holds:

$$\hat{F} \subseteq A_I ; F ; R_O \qquad\qquad\qquad U^{-1}\text{-simulation}$$

These are different versions of useful relations between levels of abstractions. A more detailed discussion is found in [13].

Example. We obtain

$$TMC \subseteq FRK; TII ; MRG$$

as a simple example of interaction refinement by U^{-1}-simulation. The proof is again straightforward.   ☐

Interaction refinement is used heavily in many practical system developments, although not introduced formally, there. It supports the definition of a formal relation between layers of abstraction. This way it can be used to relate the layers of protocol hierarchies, the change of data representations for the messages or the states or the introduction of time into system developments. Interaction refinement is a Galois connection.

In our model, in particular, input and output histories are represented explicitly. This allows us to apply classical ideas (see [17], [18]) of data refinement to communication histories. Roughly speaking: communication histories are nothing than data structures that can be manipulated and refined like other data structures.

7. Conclusions

What we have presented in the previous chapters is a comprehensive method for a system and software development which supports all the steps of a hierarchical stepwise refinement development method. It is compositional and therefore supports all the modularity requirements that are generally needed.

The presented method provides, in particular, the following ingredients:

- a mathematical notion of a syntactic and semantic interface of a component,

- a formal specification notation and method,

- a precise notion of composition,

- a mathematical notion of refinement and development,

- a compositional development method,

- a flexible concept of software architecture,

- concepts of time and the refinement of time (see [16]).

What we did not mention throughout the paper are concepts that are also available and helpful from a more practical point of view including

- systematic combination with tables and diagrams,

- tool support in the form of AutoFocus (see [4]).

The simplicity of our results is a direct consequence of the specific choice of our semantic model. The introduction of time makes the model robust and expressive. The fact that communication histories are explicitly included allows us to avoid all kinds of complications like prophecies or stuttering and leads to an abstract relational view of systems.

Of course, what we have presented is just the scientific kernel of the method. More pragmatic ways to describe specifications are needed. These more pragmatic specifications can be found in the work done in the SysLab-Project (see [7]) at the Technical University of Munich. For extensive explanations of the use of state transition diagrams, data flow diagrams and message sequence charts as well as several versions of data structure diagrams we refer to this work.

Acknowledgment

It is a pleasure to thank Ketil Stølen, Max Breitling, and Jan Philipps for a number of comments and helpful suggestions for improvement.

References

1. M. Abadi, L. Lamport: The Existence of Refinement Mappings. Digital Systems Research Center, SRC Report 29, August 1988
2. M. Abadi, L. Lamport: Composing Specifications. Digital Systems Research Center, SRC Report 66, October 1990
3. L. Aceto, M. Hennessy: Adding Action Refinement to a Finite Process Algebra. Proc. ICALP 91, Lecture Notes in Computer Science 510, (1991), 506-519
4. F. Huber, B. Schätz, G. Einert: Consistent Graphical Specification of Distributed Systems. In: J. Fitzgerald, C. B. Jones, P. Lucas (ed.): FME '97: 4th International Symposium of Formal Methods Europe, Lecture Notes in Computer Science 1313, 1997, 122-141
5. R.J.R. Back: Refinement Calculus, Part I: Sequential Nondeterministic Programs. REX Workshop. In: J. W. deBakker, W.-P. deRoever, G. Rozenberg (eds): Stepwise Refinement of Distributed Systems. Lecture Notes in Computer Science 430, 42-66
6. R.J.R. Back: Refinement Calculus, Part II: Parallel and Reactive Programs. REX Workshop. In: J. W. de Bakker, W.-P. de Roever, G. Rozenberg (eds): Stepwise Refinement of Distributed Systems. Lecture Notes in Computer Science 430, 67-93
7. R. Breu, R. Grosu, Franz Huber, B. Rumpe, W. Schwerin: Towards a Precise Semantics for Object-Oriented Modeling Techniques. In: H. Kilov, B. Rumpe (eds.): Proceedings ECOOP'97 Workshop on Precise Semantics for Object-Oriented Modeling Techniques, 1997, Also: Technische Universität München, Institut für Informatik, TUM-I9725, 1997
8. M. Broy, B. Möller, P. Pepper, M. Wirsing: Algebraic Implementations Preserve Program Correctness. Science of Computer Programming 8 (1986), 1-19
9. M. Broy: Functional Specification of Time Sensitive Communicating Systems. REX Workshop. In: J. W. de Bakker, W.-P. de Roever, G. Rozenberg (eds): Stepwise Refinement of Distributed Systems. Lecture Notes in Computer Science 430, 153-179
10. M. Broy: Compositional Refinement of Interactive Systems. Digital Systems Research Center, SRC Report 89, July 1992, To appear in JACM
11. M. Broy, F. Dederichs, C. Dendorfer, M. Fuchs, T. F. Gritzner, R. Weber: The Design of Distributed Systems - An Introduction to Focus. Technische Universität München, Institut für Informatik, Sonderforschungsbereich 342: Methoden und Werkzeuge für die Nutzung paralleler Architekturen TUM-I9202, January 1992
12. M. Broy, F. Dederichs, C. Dendorfer, M. Fuchs, T. F. Gritzner, R. Weber: Summary of Case Studies in FOCUS - a Design Method for Distributed Systems. Technische Universität München, Institut für Informatik, Sonderforschungsbereich 342: Methoden und Werkzeuge für die Nutzung paralleler Architekturen TUM-I9203, January 1992
13. M. Broy: Interaction Refinement – The Easy Way. In: M. Broy (ed.): Program Design Calculi. Springer NATO ASI Series, Series F: Computer and System Sciences, Vol. 118, 1993
14. M. Broy: Algebraic Specification of Reactive Systems. M. Nivat, M. Wirsing (eds): Algebraic Methodology and Software Technology. 5th International

Conference, AMAST '96, Lecture Notes of Computer Science 1101, Heidelberg: Springer 1996, 487-503

15. M. Broy: Towards a Mathematical Concept of a Component and its Use. First Components' User Conference, Munich 1996. Revised version in: Software-Concepts and Tools 18, 1997, 137-148

16. M. Broy: Refinement of Time. M. Bertran, Th. Rus (eds.): Transformation-Based Reactive System Development. ARTS'97, Mallorca 1997. Lecture Notes in Computer Science 1231, 1997, 44-63, To appear in TCS

17. J. Coenen, W.P. deRoever, J. Zwiers: Assertional Data Reification Proofs: Survey and Perspective. Christian-Albrechts-Universität Kiel, Institut für Informatik und praktische Mathematik, Bericht Nr. 9106, Februar 1991.

18. C.A.R. Hoare: Proofs of Correctness of Data Representations. Acta Informatica 1, 1972, 271-281

19. N. Lynch, E. Stark: A Proof of the Kahn Principle for Input/Output Automata. Information and Computation 82, 1989, 81-92

20. M. Broy: Mathematical System Models as a Basis of Software Engineering. J. van Leeuwen (ed.): Computer Science Today. Lecture Notes of Computer Science 1000, 1995, 292-306

21. M. Broy: A Functional Rephrasing of the Assumption/Commitment Specification Style. Technische Universität München, Institut für Informatik, TUM-I9417, June 1994, Revised and Extended Version to appear in: Formal Methods in System Design

22. C. Klein: Anforderungsspezifikation durch Transitionssysteme und Szenarien. Promotion, Fakultät für Informatik, Technische Universität München, Dezember 1997

23. M. Broy, K. Stølen: FOCUS on System Development. Springer 1999 (to appear)

24. B.Möller: Algebraic Structures for Program Calculation. Marktoberdorf Summer School 1998

From Quartets to Phylogenetic Trees

Benny Chor*

Dept. of Computer Science, Technion
Haifa 32000, Israel.

Abstract. Constructing phylogenetic (or evolutionary) trees from biological data is a classical problem in biology, and it still is a major challenge today. Most realistic formulations of the problem, which take errors into account, give rise to hard computational problems. In this survey paper we concentrate on *quartet based* tree reconstruction methods. We briefly describe the general tree reconstruction problem, and discuss the motivation for using quartet based reconstruction. We then turn to the computational complexity of this reconstruction task. Finally, we give a high level description of some algorithms and heuristics for constructing trees from quartets.

1 Introduction

Given a set of taxa (a group of related biological species), the goal of phylogeny reconstruction is to build a tree which best represents the course of evolution for this set over time. The leaves of the tree are labeled with the given, extant taxa. Internal nodes correspond to hypothesized, extinct taxa. Because events of taxon divergence are assumed to be rare, the sought after tree is bifurcating (or binary), with internal nodes of degree 3. (In case of ambiguous data one might have to resort to multifurcating trees, which are less informative.) In early days, morphologic features were mostly used to study evolution. Today, molecular data are the primary basis for phylogenetic analysis of evolution, but other sources of information (for example paleontology, anatomy, and morphology) are also in use. For simplicity, most of our exposition will concentrate on molecular sequence data.

The first step in constructing a tree is to collect from an updated database either DNA (typically genes), RNA, or amino acid sequences for all taxa under study. (For the sake of simplicity, we will restrict ourselves to proteins.) Homologous sequences (detected by similarities, or low edit distances) from different taxa are then grouped together. Homologous sequences for different taxa often have the same functionality (*e.g.* insulin, hemoglobin, etc.) and are assumed to be descendents of a common ancestral sequence. Their degree of similarity gives an indication of the time when two taxa diverged. Since the mutational process is assumed to be probabilistic in nature and to operate locally, we expect

---

* Partially supported by the Fund for Promotion of Research at the Technion. benny@cs.technion.ac.il.

that longer periods of time since divergence imply more accumulated mutations. However, different proteins may evolve at different rates. Combining this with the stochastic nature of the process, it is clear that single proteins, viewed separately, may give conflicting indications as to the history of evolution. To overcome this "noise effect" it is thus advisable to employ longer sequences, obtained by concatenating many homologous sequences together.

In general, phylogeny reconstruction methods are divided into *character-based* and *distance-based* methods. Character based methods work directly on character data that represent various biological features. These methods try to produce a tree which minimizes the total number of changes along tree edges. Distance based methods start by computing "evolutionary distances" between pairs of taxa. Then a tree with weighted edges whose pairwise tree distances approximate the evolutionary distances is sought.

1.1 Organization

In Section 2 we briefly describe character based and distance based reconstruction methods. With long enough input sequences, these methods will succeed in correctly reconstruction the tree, with high probability. But "long enough" might be way longer than currently available sequences. What compounds this problem is the fact that molecular data are not available evenly for all taxa of interest. In Section 3 we explain this data disparity problem, and its implications on the above mentioned reconstruction methods. This motivates the introduction of quartet based phylogenetic reconstruction . In Section 4 we specify the quartet reconstruction problem, and quote known results on the its computational complexity. In Section 5 we describe some algorithmic approaches and heuristics to solving the problem. Finally, Section 6 describes some computational results and presents a few open problems.

2 Character and Distance Based Reconstruction

2.1 Character-Based Methods

A character-based method considers qualitative characters of the input taxa. Any such character is a partition of the input set according to the value each taxon takes. Each equivalence class defined thus is called a *character state*. For example, a DNA sequence is composed of the 4 nucleotides characters A, C, T, G. An RNA sequence is composed of the 4 nucleotides characters A, C, U, G. Finally, a protein sequence is composed of the 20 amino acid characters A, C, D, E, F, G, H, I, K, L, M, N, P, Q, R, S, T, V, W and Y. Sequences originating from different species are aligned via a *multiple sequence alignment* process. Where needed, gaps are inserted into the sequences so as to maximize the resemblance of the sequences to each other when laid out one on top of the other. Thus, each position of an aligned amino acid sequence (called *site*) is a character with twenty one states (20 amino acids and the gap symbol –). Table 1 exhibits

Table 1. Multiple sequence alignment of the sequences for the protein *insulin-like growth factor II*, corresponding to four species: (1) Human (PRI), (2) Mouse (MUR), (3) Sheep (RUM), and (4) Chicken (OUT). An asterisk indicates complete agreement at a given site, while a dot indicates significant biochemical similarity. Three letter initials stand for the taxon to which each specie belongs

```
(1)    MGIPMGKSMLVLLTFLAFASCCIAAYRPSETLCGGELVDTLQFVCGDRGFYFSRPASRVS
(2)    MGIPVGKSMLVLLISLAFALCCIAAYGPGETLCGGELVDTLQFVCSDRGFYFSRPSSRAN
(3)    MGITAGKSMLALLAFLAFASCCYAAYRPSETLCGGELVDTLQFVCGDRGFYFSRPSSRIN
(4)    MC-AARQILLLLLAFLAYALDSAAAYGTAETLCGGELVDTLQFVCGDRGFYFSRPVGRNN
       *     . ..* ** **.*  .  ***  ****************  *********  *


(1)    RRS-RGIVEECCFRSCDLALLETYCATPAKSERDVSTP-----PTVLPDNFPRYPVGKFF
(2)    RRS-RGIVEECCFRSCDLALLETYCATPAKSERDVSTS-----QAVLPDDFPRYPVGKFF
(3)    RRS-RGIVEECCFRSCDLALLETYCAAPAKSERDVSAS-----TTVLPDDFTAYPVGKFF
(4)    RRINRGIVEECCFRSCDLALLETYCAKSVKSERDLSATSLAGLPALNKESFQKPSHAKYS
       **  ********************  *****.*.      ... . *       *.


(1)    QYDTWK-QSTQRLRRGLPALLRARRGHVLAKELEAFREA-KRHRPLIALPTQDPA-HGGA
(2)    QYDTWR-QSAGRLRRGLPALLRARRGRMLAKELKEFREA-KRHRPLIVLPPKDPA-HGGA
(3)    QSDTWK-QSTQRLRRGLPAFLRARRGRTLAKELEALREA-KSHRPLIALPTQDPATHGGA
(4)    KYNVWQKKSSQRLQREVPGILRARRYRWQAEGLQAAEEARAMHRPLISLPSQRPP-APRA
       .  *. .*. **.* .* *****  .  *  *   **  ***** ** . *      *


(1)    PPEMASNRK
(2)    SSEMSSNHQ
(3)    SSEASSD--
(4)    SPEATGPQE
        * .
```

the result of running the multiple sequence alignment program CLUSTAL W on four amino acid sequences. The output of the multiple sequence alignment is an $|S| \times |C|$ matrix, where S is the taxa set and C is the character set. (In the example of Table 1, $|S| = 4$ and $|C| = 189$.) Each entry denotes a state which a particular taxon exhibits for a given character. Such matrix serves as the input for a character based method. Given the aligned sequences (with inserted gaps) for each taxon, a natural approach is to build a tree with the internal nodes, as well as the external ones, labeled by sequences. The labels at the leaves are given as input, while the tree topology and the internal labels are computed by the algorithm. The goal is to minimize the number of "mutations" along adjacent tree edges that are required in order to explain the data at the leaves. This leads to a minimization problem, where the objective function is the sum of Hamming distances between neighboring sequences along tree edges. More refined approaches give different prices to different changes. This "price" measures the log likelihood of a local change, as not all point mutations are equally likely [12]. The sum of costs of aligned locations determines a cost function for any pair of sequences. The global optimization criterion for *maximum parsimony* is *minimizing* the sum of costs between neighboring sequences. The general maximum parsimony problem is NP-hard [10, 20, 29], but finding the internal labeling for a given topology can be done efficiently [18, 30]. This leads to algorithms which scan many different topologies and output the most parsimonious one.

Another approach tries to construct a tree such that for each character, the node-sets that correspond to any character state form a connected subgraph. Maximizing the number of characters for which this is true is called the *maximum compatibility* problem. This problem, too, is NP-hard [11, 36]. A phylogeny satisfying both maximum parsimony and maximum compatibility is called *perfect phylogeny*. Deciding if the data supports a perfect phylogeny was shown to be NP-hard (by an equivalence to the *triangulating colored graphs* problem [7], and by a reduction from the *betweenness* problem [40]). Although hard in the general case, polynomial-time algorithms for perfect phylogeny exist in cases where some of the input parameters (the number of states or the number of characters) are fixed [34, 3, 2, 31].

2.2 Distance-Based Methods

A distance based phylogeny method would typically start by performing all *pairwise alignments* of the input sequences. For each alignment the *edit distance* between the two sequences is computed. This gives rise to a symmetric zero-diagonal $|S| \times |S|$ *distance* matrix. The goal is to produce a phylogeny whose induced metric represents the input data in the best way possible. If the input distance matrix M is realizable by a tree and its induced path lengths, then M is said to be *additive*. The special case where all leaves have the same distance from the root is called an *ultrametric*. Ultrametric trees correspond to the biological theory that substitutional events in different species occur at the same rate (this is the "molecular clock" assumption, nowadays popularly discredited).

Given an additive metric, constructing the tree is easy [43]. The problem is that real-life input is erroneous. Some of the errors are inherent in the assumed model of evolution. Therefore, we seek phylogenies with induced metric which approximates the "best possible" tree metric under some criterion. Again, most of the problems in this domain are NP-hard.

One popular heuristic approach is *agglomerative clustering*. It works iteratively, and at each iteration two nodes are joined into one parent node. Examples include the popular *Neighbor Joining* method [19], the *Fitch-Margoliash* method [19], and BIONJ [21].

As it turns out, approximating ultrametrics under the L_∞ criterion is doable in polynomial time [23, 39, 15, 42]. Consequently, there are algorithms that use an approximated ultrametric to produce an approximation of the additive metric [1, 9].

Table 2. An illustration of the data disparity problem

	PRI	MUR	RUM	LAG	INS	OUT
insulin-like growth factor II	+	+	+	−	−	+
insulin	+	+	+	+	−	+
angiotensin-converting enzyme	+	+	−	+	−	+
HCG beta	+	+	+	+	−	+
acetylcholine receptor	+	+	+	−	+	+
GABA-A receptor alpha-1 subunit	+	+	+	−	−	+
guanine nucleotide-binding protein	+	+	+	−	−	+
growth hormone	+	+	+	+	−	+
prolactin	+	−	+	+	−	+
endothelin 2	+	+	+	+	−	−
TGF-beta2	+	+	−	−	−	+
histamine H2 receptor	+	+	−	−	−	−
serotonin receptor	+	+	−	+	−	−
PAI-1	+	+	+	−	−	−
alpha globin	+	+	+	+	+	+

3 Motivation for Quartet Based Reconstruction

We demonstrate the data disparity problem by considering the example of mammals. The specie most extensively studied is humans. Next in popularity come model species like rats and mice, and certain species of economic/agriculture importance, like cows and sheep. On the other hand, neither government nor industry is going to finance an armadillo genome project in the foreseeable future. Thus we are doomed to stay with significant disparities in available sequence data between different taxa for many years to come.

To illustrate the situation, Table 2 depicts a portion of the available data matrix for 6 taxa (5 mammalian taxa and one non-mammalian "outgroup") vs. 15 protein sequences. The rows correspond to specific proteins, while the columns correspond to specific taxa. A "+" in the (i, j) entry indicates that i-th protein sequence is known for the j-th taxon, while a "−" indicates that it is unknown. The three letter initials stand for the following taxa: PRI = Primates (humans, apes and monkeys), MUR = Muridae (rats, mice, hamsters, voles), RUM = Ruminantia (cows and sheep, but not pigs or horses), LAG = Lagomorpha (rabbits and hares), INS = Insectivora (hedgehogs and shrews), OUT = Outgroup[2] (chicken). In this small table, all 15 protein sequences are known for PRI, 10 are known for LAG, and just 2 are known for INS. In actuality, there are even more "−" entries than what is implied by Table 2. Looking at

---

[2] The outgroup is an auxiliary input which assists in determining the root of the phylogenetic tree. See Section 4 for more details.

actual numbers [37] as recently extracted from the HOVERGEN database [13] with respect to 23 mammalian taxa and one outgroup taxon, the number of sequenced proteins vary from 621 for Primates down to 3 for Chrysochloridae (golden moles). This gives a mean of 135 and a median of 19 proteins with known sequence per taxa. The number of taxa for which a specific protein was sequenced varies in a similar fashion. Most proteins, totaling 363, are sequenced for only 4 taxa, while only 3 are sequenced for as many as 20 taxa (out of 24 taxa).

Given the data disparity problem, molecular phylogeneticists must frequently decide on a trade off between the number of taxa and the amount of molecular data used in a study. If we restrict ourselves only to sequences that are common to all the taxa under study, we may end up ignoring the vast majority of data. The tree constructed this way will be strongly biased towards the evolution of the few over represented proteins. If, on the other hand, we insist on taxa for which a large number of protein sequences are known, we end up with a small number of taxa (this is referred to as "taxonomic sampling"). Both character based methods and distance based methods have as their starting point a list of sequences that are known for all taxa under study. Therefore, both methods are effected by the data disparity problem. This implies that in order to utilize all available data, a different approach is called for.

One way to try and circumvent the data disparity problem is to make, for each taxa, a long sequence which is the concatenation of individual sequences. Where sequence information is not known, we concatenate the appropriate number of "missing data" symbols. These long sequences could then serve as a basis for either character based or distance based methods. The problem with this approach is that most of these long concatenated sequences will consist mainly of "missing data" symbols. As a result, the quality of the resulting trees tends to be poor.

An approach that tries to utilize all available data while avoiding the problem of taxonomic sampling is the *four taxon approach* suggested in [24] and used in [26, 26]. The key idea is to consider small subsets of taxa (say of size ℓ), one at a time. For each such subset, take all proteins that are known for all taxa in the subset. Using this collection of common sequences, apply either maximum parsimony or distance based methods to infer the phylogeny of each subset. Since small phylogenies are easier to infer than large ones, this step is computationally feasible. The advantage of this approach is that each protein that is common to at least ℓ taxa will influence the tree construction. Such protein need not be common to all n taxa. This means that many more sequences will be utilized, and fewer will be "wasted".

What kind of information can one expect to get? Different subsets will usually share different proteins. The rates of evolution for different proteins might differ substantially. So we cannot use any metric (or distance) information across different subsets in a uniform way. What we get is just topologic information – *unrooted* trees with ℓ leaves each. It is clear that smaller ℓ leads to better utilization of sequence information. But how small can ℓ be? Trees on $\ell = 2$ leaves are

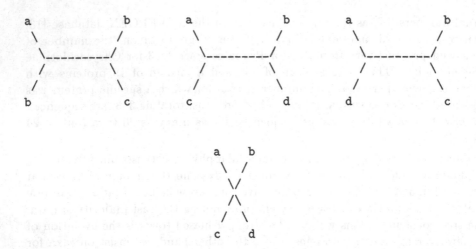

Fig. 1. The possible unrooted trees for the taxa set $\{a, b, c, d\}$. Three bifurcating quartets (top), and the multifurcating star (bottom)

simply one edge connecting the two leaves. For $\ell = 3$, there is only one unrooted tree on three leaves – the star. So neither $\ell = 2$ nor $\ell = 3$ yield informative data. The minimal value of ℓ which can give rise to an informative, input dependent tree topology is $\ell = 4$. For each subset of 4 taxa, there are three possible unrooted bifurcating phylogenetic trees. Such quadruple of taxa with an associated bifurcating topology is called a *quartet*. There is one more topology – the star, which is multifurcating. Figure 1 depicts these possibilities. A quartet can be viewed a partition of the four taxa into two pairs of taxa (*e.g.* $\{a, b\}$ and $\{c, d\}$). This subdivision expresses the most supported topology, given the sequence data common to all four taxa. Such a quartet is denoted $ab|cd$.

After the list of quartets has been determined, the goal of quartet based reconstruction is to find a phylogenetic tree which maximizes the number of "satisfied quartets". Combinatorially, the justification for the quartet based approach is that if all $\binom{n}{4}$ quartets are given with the right topology, then the underlying tree is uniquely determined, and can be efficiently constructed. Of course, in reality there are errors, so a tree consistent with all given quartets may not exist. In the next section we define the problem exactly, and discuss its computational complexity.

4 Problem Description and Complexity

The problem is defined over a set of n taxa, numbered $1, \ldots, n$. The input consists of a set of k such quartets. We denote the associated taxa and partition for the j-th quartet by $a_j b_j | c_j d_j$. No two quartets share the same set of four taxa. Each input quartet is accompanied by a positive weight, denoted by C_j, which represents the confidence in the quartet topology. We will first describe how these confidence values are computed.

After each four-taxon phylogenetic tree is inferred, a measure of reliability or confidence for this topology is assessed. The confidence value is a real number in the range $[0, 1]$. It should reflect two factors: how solid is the plurality of sequences supporting the quartet topology (i.e., the strength of the phylogenetic signal), and what is the size of the sequence population used to build the tree. *Bootstrap* [17] is a common method of computing the confidence values. Random positions of the original sequences are chosen independently (with repetition) to generate sequences whose length equal the original length. For each such re-sampling, a phylogenetic tree is computed. The bootstrap value equals the fraction of these reconstructions that yield the original quartet topology (notice that this value can be lower than $1/3$).

4.1 Specifications

The output in the quartet based reconstruction problem is an unrooted tree with n leaves, which are labeled by the input taxa. Given a tree T and a quadruple $\{a, b, c, d\}$, we can compute the quartet topology induced by T, using the following procedure. First, all leaves but a, b, c and d are deleted from the tree. Edges adjacent to these deleted leaves are also removed. Next, internal nodes with degree two are contracted and deleted, so their two adjacent nodes become connected. This process is repeated until no internal nodes of degree two are left. As we observed earlier, there are four possible induced topologies for the quadruple — the three quartets and the star topology (which can be induced only by a multifurcating tree). Given a specific quartet and the induced four taxa subtree, we say that the quartet is *unresolved* if the tree induces the star topology on the four taxa. Otherwise, the quartet is either *satisfied* (if the topology induced by the tree equals the quartet's topology), or *violated*.

Given a tree T and a set of quarters Q, we would like to know how well does T represent Q. To do this, we find the subset of quartets $S \subset Q$ that are satisfied by T, and the subset of quartets $U \subset Q$ that are unresolved by T. We now define the *score* of the tree as follows:

$$\mathtt{score}_Q(T) = \sum_{s \in S} C_s + \frac{1}{3} \sum_{u \in U} C_u .$$

That is, we add the confidence weights of the satisfied quartets, plus one third of the weights of the unresolved quartets. This latter term was chosen because there are three possible pairings for every quadruple. Therefore this term equals the expected increase to the tree score that will result from a random bifurcation of the tree (performed at nodes with more than two descendents). Even though we prefer to construct bifurcating trees, we introduce a measure which is "fair" with respect to multifurcating trees as well. We are now ready to formulate the problem precisely.

Definition 1. The *quartet based reconstruction* problem is defined as follows: Given a set of quartets Q, together with associated confidence scores, find a tree T which maximizes $\texttt{score}_Q(T)$.

4.2 Complexity

Suppose we are given a full list of $\binom{n}{4}$ quartets over n taxa (one quartet topology for each quadruple). Then it is easy to check if there is a bifurcating tree which satisfies all quartets, and to construct this (unique) tree if it exists. We first identify a pair of "sibling taxa", contract them, update their associated quartets, and continue iteratively. If we get stuck, the data is inconsistent. However, given $k \leq \binom{n}{4}$ quartets, the decision problem "is there a tree which satisfies all quartets" is NP-complete [7, 40]. Given a list of weighted quartets Q, an upper bound on the score of any tree is $\sum_{q \in Q} C_q$. This upper bound can be achieved only if there exists a tree that satisfies all quartets. Given $k \leq \binom{n}{4}$ quartets, we assign weight 1 to each quartet in the list, and 0 to all remaining quartets. The existence of a tree which satisfies all k quartets is therefore equivalent to the existence of a tree whose score equals k. This immediately implies that maximizing the score of a tree with respect to a partial (or weighted) list of quartets is NP-hard. A careful look at Steel's reduction from the betweenness problem reveals that maximizing the score of a tree is even MAX SNP complete. This means that there is an absolute constant $\varepsilon > 0$ such that finding a tree whose score is at least $1 - \varepsilon$ of the maximum score is NP-hard (even if there is a tree satisfying all the quartets).

NP-completeness and hardness results imply that there is little hope to find polynomial time algorithms. But such results are asymptotic, applicable to "worst case" input instances. In particular, when trying to reconstruct phylogenetic trees, it is worthwhile to consider what is a "typical" problem size and what is the nature of "typical" input instances. While one may consider trees with hundreds or thousands taxa, it turns out that much smaller values of n are still of biologic interest. For example, investigations of mammalian evolution often involve instances where n, the number of taxa, is between 15 to 24. With such values, "mild" exponential time algorithms may be of practical interest. In addition, while available sequence data contain lots of errors, it is reasonable to expect that these errors are not designed by an adversary, but are rather of some stochastic nature. One may therefore hope that efficient heuristics can be effective in approaching optimal solutions on such data.

Before proceeding to more advanced methods, we point out that the simple, exhaustive search methods seem infeasible even for modest values of n (say $n = 15$). The number of unrooted bifurcating trees [16] with n leaves is $(2n - 5)! / \left(2^{n-3}(n - 3)! \right)$. For $n = 15$ the number of such trees is just below 8×10^{12}. For a full list, the number of quartets is $\binom{15}{4} \approx 1,300$. So an algorithm which goes over all quartets for every tree would take more than 10^{16} steps. Performing that many steps is not a feasible task on "reasonable" contemporary machines.

4.3 Rooting the Tree

Recall that the goal of phylogeny reconstruction is to build a tree which best represents the course of evolution. In particular, to understand which events occured earlier and which ones took place later, the tree should be *rooted*. But the input to quartet based reconstruction is a list of quartets, which are inherently *unrooted*. How can one hope to construct a rooted tree given unrooted information?

Indeed, to root the tree we need some auxiliary information, not included in the quartets. This information is the identity of *outgroup* among the n taxa. This outgroup is an external taxon, which does not belong to the same family as the other taxa. (In our example the outgroup is chicken, while all others are mammalian.) If indeed the identification of the outgroup is correct, then this taxa was the earliest to diverge from the remaining taxa. We first produce an *unrooted* tree according to the optimization criteria. Then we root the tree by forcing the outgroup to be an immediate descendent of the root.

We note that the problem of generating rooted tree is considered hard for all tree reconstruction methods. The use of an outgroup is a standard trick in the other methods as well.

5 Algorithms

Published quartet methods include the Buneman tree [8, 6], the short quartet method [14], neighbor-joining variants [25, 26, 27], and quartet puzzling [41]. See also [42] for a comprehensive survey, and [4] for a different formulation of the problem, termed split decomposition. Most of these heuristics deal with unweighted quartets (i.e., each quartet has the same significance). Some also require as input the full set of $\binom{n}{4}$ quartets. The general maximization problem with weighted quartets is MAX SNP complete. However Li *et. al.* have recently obtained a polynomial time approximation scheme for the "dense" version of the problem: Unweighted case with a full list of $\binom{n}{4}$ quartets [32].

A "geometric" heuristic, based on semi definite programming, and an "exact" algorithm, based on dynamic programming, are described in [5]. These two approaches are global, and can handle weighted quartets. Due to space limitations, we describe in detail only three approaches: Quartet puzzling, the geometric heuristic, and the exact algorithm.

5.1 Quartet Puzzling

Quartet puzzling applies a simple greedy procedure (called "puzzling step") for combining quartets into bifurcating trees. To avoid local traps, this puzzling step is repeated many times, and the order of the taxa is permuted at random in each repetition. Finally, the many resulting trees are combined to one tree (which could be multifurcating) by "majority consensus" [33].

Consider a run of the greedy procedure, and for simplicity assume the (random) order of the taxa is $a, b, c, d, e, f, \ldots$. The quartet topology for a, b, c, d

serves as an "anchor" for the tree. A counter is associated with each of the five edges in this anchor, and all counters are initialized to 0. Then the next taxa e is examined. The taxa e should be added to the current tree by branching off one of the existing edges. Suppose $ij|ke$ is a quartet from the input, and i, j and k preceded e in the random order, so that these three taxa already appear as leaves in the current tree. Consider the internal node O in the tree where the three paths $i - j$, $i - k$ and $j - k$ intersect. Deleting O splits the tree into three disjoint subtrees. In order not to violate the $ij|ke$ quartet, e should branch off some edge in the subtree containing k. Branching off an edge from either the "i subtree" or the "j subtree" would violate $ij|ke$. To indicate this violation, the counter of every edge in these two subtrees is incremented by 1. The process repeats for other such quartets involving e. At the end of the current step the counter of every edge in the current tree contains a non-negative integer, indicating how many quartets involving e will be violated if e is to branch off this edge. The edge with minimum count is chosen (if there are two or more such edges, one is chosen at random). After e is added to the tree, e does not change its place with respect to previous taxa. Then, all counters are zeroed, and the next taxa f is examined. This greedy process is repeated until all n taxa are examined and placed.

Both the puzzling step and majority consensus are extremely efficient, so quartet puzzling is a fast heuristic with good reported results. As presented in [41], the quartet puzzling algorithm requires non weighted input of all $\binom{n}{4}$ quartets. However, if we update the counter of violating edges by the weight of the violated quartet (rather than by 1), weighted input can be handled. Thus, it seems that quartet puzzling is applicable to the general, weighted case as well. However, to our knowledge no experiments in this direction were done.

5.2 The Geometric Heuristic

The geometric heuristic [5, 35] is a "global" method, which assigns to each taxa a point on the boundary of the unit sphere in $\mathcal{R}^n$. The embedding is built using "hints" from the input set. For example, if the quartet $ab|cd$ is in the list, we try to place a and b close to each other, but a and d far apart. Once the points are embedded in $\mathcal{R}^n$, a clustering heuristic converts the embedding into a tree.

Semidefinite Programming: The paradigm of SDP — semidefinite programming plays an important role in combinatorial optimization and in many approximation algorithms (see [28]). Let $\langle v_i, v_i \rangle$, denote the inner product of two points v_i and v_j in $\mathcal{R}^n$. We can use SDP to efficiently solve (with any desirable precision) any optimization problem of the form (the $c_{ij}, a_{ij}^{(k)}, b^{(k)}$ are reals):

Find n vectors $v_1, \ldots, v_n \in \mathcal{R}^n$ so as to maximize the quantity

$$\sum_{i,j} c_{ij} \langle v_i, v_j \rangle,$$

subject to the constraints

$$\sum_{i,j} a_{ij}^{(k)} \langle v_i, v_j \rangle \leq b^{(k)}$$

We will use this formulation of SDP to find an embedding of n points which represent the n taxa.

Geometric embedding of taxa: We will generally denote the embedding of taxon i by the point v_i in $\mathcal{R}^n$. Given a list of k quartets $a_j b_j | c_j d_j$ and confidence values C_j $(j = 1, \ldots, k)$, we solve the following semidefinite program:

maximize:
$$\sum_{1 \leq j \leq k} C_j(\langle a_j, b_j \rangle + \langle c_j, d_j \rangle)$$
$$-0.5 \sum_{1 \leq j \leq k} C_j(\langle a_j, c_j \rangle + \langle a_j, d_j \rangle + \langle b_j, c_j \rangle + \langle b_j, d_j \rangle)$$

subject to
$$\langle v_i, v_i \rangle = 1 \quad (1 \leq i \leq n)$$

The n constraints force the points v_i to the boundary of the unit sphere. The quartets' input is incorporated into the objective function, which embodies many local requirements into a single expression. (This approach was motivated by the approximation MAX CUT algorithm in [22].) Consider the quartet $ab|cd$ with confidence level C. Its maximum contribution to the objective function occurs when a and b are placed at the same point, while both c and d are placed at the antipodean point on the unit sphere. In this case $\langle a, b \rangle = \langle c, d \rangle = 1$, while $\langle a, c \rangle = \langle a, d \rangle = \langle b, c \rangle = \langle b, d \rangle = -1$. The overall contribution of the quartet will be $4C$ with this embedding. The worst embedding places a and c together, and b and d at the antipodean point. This will contribute $-4C$ to the objective function. The semidefinite program will therefore look for a global embedding which maximizes "good" quartet placements and tries to avoid "bad" ones.

By experimenting with this approach, it turned out that small variants of it are helpful in improving the final result (the produced tree). One such variant is ignoring quartets with low confidence in the objective function. Only quartets with confidence level above a certain threshold (90% for example) are included. One possible explanation why this may prove helpful is that low confidence quartets probably carry most of the inconsistencies, and their inclusion may lower the value of the objective function. It was also discovered that by imposing additional constraints, one gets (small) improvements in the score of the tree. For example, forcing the points to maintain some small pairwise distance by adding the $\binom{n}{2}$ constraints

$$\langle v_i, v_j \rangle \leq 1 - \varepsilon \quad (1 \leq i < j \leq n)$$

for some positive ε (say $\varepsilon = 0.25$). This "represses" the SDP's tendency to find embeddings where points are very close to each other. This tendency has a negative effect on the tree building method, which we describe next.

Geometrical Clustering: Having solved the SDP problem, one seeks a tree that reflects the geometric data. For instance, if two points reside in the same geometric vicinity, they should have a common ancestor which is not too much high up the resulting tree. To this end, we employ a simple clustering heuristic. The program is initialized with n clusters, each containing a single point. An invariant kept by the algorithm is that each cluster has a point in $\mathcal{R}^n$ associated with it. This is the case at initialization, and remains true as new clusters are formed. At each step of the algorithm the number of clusters is decreased by one, by removing two "old" clusters and adding a new one. This defines a tree, as the newly-added node represents the father of the two deleted nodes in the output tree. The selection of the clusters to be removed is done by calculating the pairwise distances between points associated with clusters, and selecting the pair having the shortest Euclidean distance. The point associated with the new cluster is the center of mass of the points of the removed clusters (the "mass" of a point being the number of taxa it represents). When the number of clusters reaches one, the tree is completed. The resulting tree is rooted, but we disregard the rooting, since the input is inherently unrooted. To root the tree we use the identity of the outgroup taxon. We remark that this clustering heuristic is a special case of the general neighbor joining approach [38].

5.3 The "Exact" Algorithm

Since the underlying problem is NP-hard we can not hope to give a polynomial time algorithm to solve it optimally. However, in this subsection we show how an optimal phylogenetic tree can be found, using a dynamic programming algorithm, with a "mild" exponential running time [5, 35]. The method is applicable to instances with modest size (say $n \leq 21$).

The following discussion deals with *rooted* bifurcating trees. For a node v, its left and right children will be denoted by v_ℓ and v_r, respectively. Given a rooted tree T and a node v in it we denote by $T(v)$ the subtree of T rooted at v. We denote by $L(T)$ the set of leaves (*i.e.*, taxa) of the tree T. For a pair of nodes u, v the *least common ancestor* of u and v, $\mathrm{lca}(u, v)$ is defined as an ancestor p of both u and v such that no node in $T(p)$ other than p is an ancestor of both u and v. (This definition is extendible to a larger number of nodes.)

Definition 2. Given a quartet $q = ab|cd$ and a tree T, the *quartet* least common ancestor of q, $\mathrm{qlca}(q)$ is defined as a node p that is the lca of two or more pairs of elements from $\{a, b, c, d\}$, and no node in $T(p)$ except p is the lca of two or more pairs of elements from $\{a, b, c, d\}$.

The following equivalent definition is helpful for implementing the algorithm.

Definition 3. Given a quartet $q = ab|cd$ and a tree T, the qlca of q is a node p such that

1. $|L(T(p)) \cap \{a, b, c, d\}| \geq 3$.
2. For any child s of p, $|L(T(s)) \cap \{a, b, c, d\}| \leq 2$.

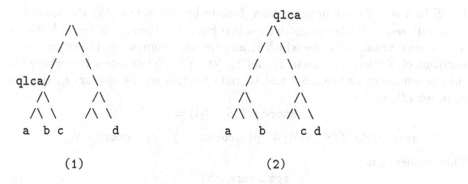

Fig. 2. Two possible arrangements of a qlca for quartets over $\{a, b, c, d\}$

It is not hard to see that every quartet q has a unique qlca(q). Figure 2 illustrates two qlca arrangements. The first arrangement demonstrates a case where the qlca is different from the least common ancestor of the four leaves.

Lemma 4. *Given a tree T and a quartet q, the subtree rooted at qlca(q) determines whether q is satisfied in the tree T.*

Corollary 5. *Given a quartet $q = ab|cd$ and a tree T, let $v = $ qlca(q). Then T satisfies q if and only if at least one of the following holds:*

1. $\{a, b\} \subseteq L(T(s))$.
2. $\{c, d\} \subseteq L(T(s))$.

Where s is either v's left child ($s = v_\ell$) or v's right child ($s = v_r$).

The Algorithm: Let Q be a fixed set of input quartets. Let T be a rooted tree, and v a node in T. We denote by SAT$_Q(T(v))$ the set of quartets $q \in Q$ such that q is satisfied by T, and qlca(q) is a node in $T(v)$. Let TOP$_Q(T(v)) \subset$ SAT$_Q(T(v))$ be the set of quartets in Q that have v as their qlca and are satisfied by T. The following equality describes a partition of SAT$_Q(T)$ to three disjoint subsets

$$\text{SAT}_Q(T(v)) = \text{TOP}_Q(T(v)) \cup \text{SAT}_Q(T(v_\ell)) \cup \text{SAT}_Q(T(v_r)) \ . \qquad (1)$$

(The equality follows from Lemma 4.) For a set $A \subseteq Q$ of quartets, let $\text{sum}(A) \stackrel{\text{def}}{=} \sum_{q \in A} C_q$ denote the sum of their weights. The *score* of the subtree $T(v)$ (with respect to Q) is defined as

$$\text{score}_Q(T(v)) \stackrel{\text{def}}{=} \text{sum}(\text{SAT}_Q(T(v))) \ .$$

By Equation (1)

$$\text{score}_Q(T(v)) = \text{sum}(\text{TOP}_Q(T(v))) + \text{score}_Q(T(v_\ell)) + \text{score}_Q(T(v_r)) \ . \qquad (2)$$

Let S be a set of three or more taxa. Denote by $\textsf{opt\_score}_Q(S)$ the maximum score with respect to Q among all trees that have S as their set of leaves [3]. We denote by $\textsf{opt\_tree}_Q(S)$ a tree which attains the maximum score. For every proper partition of S into two subsets S_1 and S_2, let $T(S_1, S_2)$ denote a tree whose left subtree equals $\textsf{opt\_tree}_Q(S_1)$ and its right subtree equals $\textsf{opt\_tree}_Q(S_2)$. By equation (2), we have

$$\textsf{score}_Q(T(S_1, S_2)) =$$

$$\textsf{sum}(\text{TOP}_Q(T(S_1, S_2))) + \textsf{opt\_score}_Q(S_1) + \textsf{opt\_score}_Q(S_2) \ .$$

This implies that

$$\textsf{opt\_score}_Q(S) = \qquad\qquad\qquad\qquad\qquad\qquad (3)$$

$$\max_{S_1 \cup S_2 = S} \left(\textsf{sum}(\text{TOP}_Q(T(S_1, S_2))) + \textsf{opt\_score}_Q(S_1) + \textsf{opt\_score}_Q(S_2) \right) \ .$$

Let $\langle S_1, S_2 \rangle$ be a partition of S which attains the maximum, then $\textsf{opt\_tree}_Q(S)$ is defined as $T(S_1, S_2)$.

Equation (3) yields a recursive algorithm to compute the optimal tree (with respect to the given list of weighted quartets, Q): Given Q and S, go over all partitions $\{S_1, S_2\}$ of S, and choose a partition which maximizes

$$\textsf{sum}(\text{TOP}_Q(T(S_1, S_2))) + \textsf{opt\_score}_Q(S_1) + \textsf{opt\_score}_Q(S_2) \ .$$

This partition defines which taxa belong to the left subtree, and which to the right one. Apply the procedure recursively until each subtree has size smaller than 3. An optimal tree may be constructed by means of backtracking the partitioning steps.

The drawback of this recursive algorithm is that the score of each set S is recomputed whenever S is encountered as a subset in a partition. (Thus if S is of size i, its score will be computed 2^{n-i} times.) In order to avoid this wasteful repetition, employ the dynamic programming paradigm. We make a record of computed $\textsf{opt\_score}_Q(S)$ values, so that we will not have to recompute them. To do this, we scan the subsets $S \subseteq \{1, 2, \ldots, n\}$ by increasing size of S. This guarantees that in the computation for a set S, all subsets of S are already scanned over. It can be shown that by employing dynamic programming, the running time of the exact algorithm for an input of k quartets over n taxa is $k3^n$, and that $\Theta(2^n)$ memory is required.

6   Concluding Remarks

The geometric algorithm and the dynamic programming algorithm were implemented in [35]. Together with the quartet puzzling algorithm, they were tested on real data, corresponding to $\binom{15}{4}$ weighted quartets over 15 taxa – 14 mammalian orders and an outgroup taxon. (For quartet puzzling, the weights were ignored.) These quartets were derived from the HOVERGEN database [13]. The

---

[3] By the definition, trees with one or two leaves do not contain any qlca, so for sets S of size 1 or 2 we define $\textsf{opt\_score}_Q(S) = 0$.

Table 3. Results of running the three algorithms on real sequence data

Method	Score (% upper bound)	% Satisfied Quartets	Running Time
Puzzling	71.6%	68.1%	10 seconds
Geometric	72.1%	68.7%	5 seconds
Exact	73.4%	70.2%	7 minutes

results are described in Table 3. Running times are measured on a $30K machine, in 1997 prices (Sun Ultra-4 at 300 MHz). The fact that the score of the optimal tree is only 73.4% indicates that the input is not very reliable. We note that despite this fact, the resulting trees seem to make biological sense.

From the algorithmic point of view, there are a number of interesting open problems related to quartet base reconstruction. For realistic datasets, any decrease of the exponent's base for an "exact" algorithm will be significant. (Currently the dynamic programming algorithm takes about 5 days for datasets with $n = 20$ on the same hardware.) A different direction is to prove any performance guarantees for either the quartet puzzling or the geometric reconstruction methods. A tree chosen at random is expected to satisfy one third of the quartets. However, we are not aware of any efficient algorithm for reconstructing trees from weighted quartets whose output is guaranteed to be above one third of the maximum.

Acknowledgments

Thanks to Marc Robinson for supplying updated information and answering my endless questions, and to Marc, Metsada Pasmanik, and Ron Shamir for comments on earlier drafts. Parts of this survey are based on [5, 35]. I am grateful to Amir Ben-Dor, Dan Graur, Giddy Landan, Ron Ophir, and Dan Pelleg for the many things I've learnt from them while working on the quartets project.

References

1. R. Agarwala, V. Bafna, M. Farach, B. Narayanan, M. Paterson, and M. Thorup. On the approximability of numerical taxonomy (fitting distances by tree metrics). In *Proceedings of the Seventh Annual ACM-SIAM Symposium on Discrete Algorithms*, pages 365–372, New York/Philadelphia, 28–30 January 1996. ACM/SIAM.
2. R. Agrawala and D. Fernandez-Baca. A polynomial time algorithm for the perfect phylogeny problem when the number of character states is fixed. *SIAM Journal on Computing*, 23(6):1216–1224, 1993.
3. R. Agrawala and D. Fernandez-Baca. Simple algorithms for perfect phylogeny and triangulating colored graphs. *International Journal of Foundations of Computer Science*, 7(1):11–21, 1996.

4. H.-J. Bandelt and A. Dress. Reconstructing the shape of a tree from observed dissimilarity data. *Advances in Applied Mathematics*, 7:309–343, 1986.

5. A. Ben-Dor, B. Chor, D. Graur, R. Ophir, and D. Pelleg. From four-taxon trees to phylogenies: The case of mammalian evolution. In Sorin Istrail, Pavel Pevzner, and Michael Waterman, editors, *Proceeding of the Second Annual International Conference on Computational Molecular Biology*, pages 9–15, 22-25 March 1998. To appear in JCB. http://www.cs.technion.ac.il/Labs/cbl/download/bcgop97.ps.gz.

6. V. Berry and O. Gascuel. Inferring evolutionary trees with strong combinatorial evidence. Research Report CS-RR-341, Department of Computer Science, University of Warwick, Coventry, UK, March 1998. http://www.dcs.warwick.ac.uk/pub/reports/rr/341.html.

7. H.L. Bodlaender, M.R. Fellows, and T. Warnow. Two strikes against perfect phylogeny. In W. Kuich, editor, *Automata, Languages and Programming, 19th International Colloquium*, volume 623 of *Lecture Notes in Computer Science*, pages 273–283, Vienna, Austria, 13–17 July 1992. Springer-Verlag.

8. P. Buneman. The recovery of trees from measures of dissimilarity. In F.R. Hodson, D.G. Kendall, and P. Tautu, editors, *Anglo-Romanian Conference on Mathematics in the Archaeological and Historical Sciences*, pages 387–395, Mamaia, Romania, 1971. Edinburgh University Press.

9. J. Cohen and M. Farach. Numerical taxonomy on data: Experimental results. In *Proceedings of the Eighth Annual ACM-SIAM Symposium on Discrete Algorithms*, pages 410–417, New Orleans, Louisiana, 5–7 January 1997.

10. W.H.E Day. Computationally difficult parsimony problems in phylogenetic systematics. *Journal of Theoretical Biology*, 103:429–438, 1983.

11. W.H.E Day and D. Sankoff. Computational complexity of inferring phylogenies by compatibility. *Systematic Zoology*, 35:224–229, 1986.

12. M.O. Dayhoff, R.M. Schwartz, and B.C. Orcutt. A model of evolutionary change in proteins. *Atlas of Protein Sequence and Structure*, 5:345–352, 1978.

13. L. Duret, D. Mouchiroud, and M. Gouy. Hovergen: a database of homologous vertebrate genes. *Nucleic Acids Research*, 22(1):2360, 1994.

14. P. Erdös, M. Steel, L.A. Székely, and T. Warnow. Constructing big trees from short sequences. In P. Degano, R. Gorrieri, and A. Marchetti-Spaccamela, editors, *Automata, Languages and Programming, 24th International Colloquium*, volume 1256 of *Lecture Notes in Computer Science*, pages 827–837, Bologna, Italy, 7–11 July 1997. Springer-Verlag.

15. M. Farach, S. Kannan, and T. Warnow. A robust model for finding optimal evolutionary trees. *Algorithmica*, 13(1/2):155–179, January 1995.

16. J. Felsenstein. The number of evolutionary trees. *Systematic Zoology*, 27:27–33, 1978.

17. J. Felsenstein. Confidence limits on phylogenies: An approach using the bootstrap. *Evolution*, 39:783–791, 1985.

18. W.M. Fitch. Towards defining the course of evolution: minimum change for a specified tree topology. *Systematic Zoology*, 20:406–416, 1978.

19. W.M. Fitch and E. Margolaish. Construction of phylogenetic trees. *Science*, 155:279–284, 1967.

20. L.R. Foulds and R.L Graham. The steiner problem in phylogeny is NP-complete. *Advances in Applied Mathematics*, 3:43–49, 1982.

21. O. Gascuel. BIONJ: An improved version of the NJ algorithm based on a simple model of sequence data. *Molecular Biology and Evolution*, 14(7):685, 1997.

22. M.X. Goemans and D.P. Williamson. Improved approximation algorithms for maximum cut and satisfiability problems using semidefinite programming. *Journal of the Association for Computing Machinery*, 42(6):1115–1145, November 1995.

23. J. Gower and G. Ross. minimum spanning tress and single linkage cluster analysis. *Applied Statistics*, 18:54–64, 1969.

24. D. Graur. Towards a molecular resolution of the ordinal phylogeny of the eutherian mammals. *FEBS letters*, 325(1/2):152, 28 June 1993.

25. D. Graur. Mammalian phylogeny: using every available molecule. In *Proceedings of the Training Course in Molecular Evolution*, pages 6–8, Bari, Italy, 1996. CIHEAM.

26. D. Graur, L. Duret, and M. Gouy. Phylogenetic position of the order lagomorpha (rabbits, hares and allies). *Nature*, 379(6563):333, 1996.

27. D. Graur, M. Gouy, and L. Duret. Evolutionary affinities of the order perissodactyla and the phylogenetic status of the superordinal taxa ungulata and altungulata. *Molecular Phylogenetics and Evolution*, 7(2):195, April 1997.

28. M. Grötschel, L. Lovász, and A. Schrijver. *Geometric Algorithms and Combinatorial Optimization*. Springer-Verlag, Berlin, 1987.

29. D. Gusfield. The steiner tree problem in phylogeny. Technical Report 332TH, Yale university, New Haven, September 1984.

30. J.A Hartigan. Minimum mutation fits to a given tree. *Biometrics*, 29:53–65, 1973.

31. S. Kannan and T. Warnow. A fast algorithm for the computation and enumeration of perfect phylogenies when the number of character states is fixed. In *Proceedings of the Sixth Annual ACM-SIAM Symposium on Discrete Algorithms*, 1995.

32. Ming Li, 1998. Personal communication.

33. T. Margush and F.R. McMorris. Consensus n-trees. *Bull. of Math. Biology*, 43(2):239–244, 1981.

34. F.R. McMorris, T. Warnow, and S. Kanan. Triangulating vertex colored graphs. *SIAM Journal on Discrete Math.*, 7(2):296–306, 1993.

35. D. Pelleg. *Algorithms for Constructing Phylogenies from Quartets. M.Sc. Thesis and Software*. Computer Science department, Technion, June 1998. http://www.cs.technion.ac.il/Labs/cbl/publications.html.

36. C. Phillips and T.J. Warnow. The asymmetric median tree — a new model for building consensus trees. *Discrete Applied Mathematics*, 71(1–3):311, 1996.

37. Marc Robinson, 1998. Personal communication.

38. N. Saitou and M. Nei. The neighbor-joining method: A new method for reconstructing phylogenetic trees. *Molecular Biology and Evolution*, 4, 1987.

39. R.R. Sokal and P.H.A. Sneath. *Principles of numerical taxonomy*. A Series of books in biology. W.H. Freeman, San Francisco, 1963.

40. M. Steel. The complexity of reconstructing trees from qualitative characters and subtress. *Journal of Classification*, 9(1):91–116, 1992.

41. K. Strimmer and A. von Haeseler. Quartet puzzling: A quartet maximum-likelihood method for reconstructing tree topologies. *Molecular Biology and Evolution*, 13(7):964–969, 1996. Software available at ftp://ftp.ebi.ac.uk/pub/software/unix/puzzle/.

42. T. Warnow. Some combinatorial optimization problems in phylogenetics. Unpublished manuscript, 1998.

43. M.S. Waterman, T.F. Smith, M. Singh, and W.A. Beyer. Additive evolutionary trees. *Journal of Theoretical Biology*, 64:199–213, 1977.

Reuse Methods for Construction of Parallel Software

Christoph Eilinghoff, Uwe Kastens

University of Paderborn

Abstract. The development of efficient parallel programs requires expertise in the application domain as well as deep knowledge of parallel algorithms, languages and tools for the construction and execution of parallel programs. We present a method to make such expertise available in an domain specific tool set. Its construction is based on extensive use of a variety of powerful reuse methods. It automates a large amount of the software construction process, such that users need not know about parallelism.

1 Introduction

The development of an efficient parallel program needs expert knowledge of the architecture of the parallel machine and its development tools. The fundamental differences of machines with respect to concepts as shared or distributed memory, synchronous or asynchronous communication, tightly or loosely coupled processors are visible in the programming language, in different abstract programming models, and give even rise to different algorithms. Hence, reuse of precoined solutions is much more difficult than in the case of sequential programs, where software reuse can be based on one programming model and highly portable languages. [1]

In our approach a tool set makes the expert knowledge of a specific domain available, such that users can characterize their problem instance on a high level of abstraction without knowledge of parallelism. The tool set creates efficient parallel software using development tools, dedicated libraries and components. The tool set is constructed by experts in the particular domain of parallel programming. A variety of reuse methods is extensively used, e. g. libraries of generic components, software architectures, generators, manufacturing procedures.

We understand this approach mainly as a demonstration of an engineering strategy, rather than as the development of particular production tools.

The main aspects of our approach are

- We aim at automated software construction, rather than at the support of interactive development steps.

---

[1] This work was supported by DFG Sonderforschungsbereich 376: "Massive Parallelität: Algorithmen, Entwurfsmethoden, Anwendungen".

– The reuse covers the construction process, and hence, reaches beyond passive, composable program structures.
– We aim at restricted problem domains, rather than at a wide range of parallel programs.

The approach has been applied in the construction of two tool sets, one for parallel branch-and-bound programs and one for parallel sorting. A complete description of the project and its results can be found in [8]. The general engineering strategy and many ideas and techniques have been carried over from our construction of a successful tool set for a completely different domain: the Eli system for automated language implementation.

The paper is structured as follows. In section 2 we describe a scenario of parallel branch-and-bound implementation in order to show what kind of expertise needs to be made reusable. An overview on reuse methods is given in section 3. Section 4 introduces the concepts of the tool set. The remaining sections emphasize the most effective reuse methods within the tool set.

2 Development of Parallel Programs

The development of programs for parallel machines requires knowledge of a variety of specific topics: the application area, algorithmic methods for a parallel programming model that fits to the particular machine, parallel programming languages, and machine specific tools for program implementation and execution. High quality and efficient software requires expertise in all these areas. Hence, it is very desirable to make some knowledge of experts in parallel programming available to those who are experts in an application area. In the following we consider a more concrete scenario in order to elaborate what kind of expertise is needed to develop efficient parallel programs.

Assume software is to be constructed for an application in the area of planning of machine usage: A set of jobs has to pass a linear sequence of production stages. Each job needs a specific amount of time in each stage. Each stage is equipped with a certain number of equal machines. A schedule is to be computed such that the time until the last job is finished is minimized. This problem is called a flow shop problem with multiple processors (FSMP) [1]. It belongs to the class of NP-hard combinatorial optimization problems [13]. However, in practice upto medium size problem instances are solvable on massively parallel machines using branch-and-bound algorithms.

A branch-and-bound algorithm explores a tree structured solution space [11]. The nodes represent partial solutions where some of the decisions are made, e. g. some jobs are allocated in the schedule. There is a branch function which creates successors of a given node by enumerating all possibilities of one more decision being bound. Some leafs of the tree represent legal solutions. They have costs associated which are to be minimized. The cost function is defined for the inner nodes, too, such that it estimates a lower bound of any solution created from that node. It is used to refine the most promising nodes first, and not to explore subtrees which can't have a better solution than the best one found so far.

At this point we can characterize what the minimal problem specific part of the program is: the functions for branching, bounding, and cost computation, the data type that implements solution tree nodes, and the application program which provides the problem data and uses the result. Note that these program parts are not influenced by parallelism. The main part of the branch-and-bound implementation does not directly depend on the specific problem. It could be subject to reuse.

The above description sufficiently characterizes a sequential branch-and-bound algorithm. However, parallel ones need a much deeper algorithmic consideration: Distributed worker processes explore sets of subtrees, which are to be stored in distributed data structures (priority queues). The efficiency heavily depends on suitable load balancing strategies to keep the workers busy without disturbing them by unnecessary communication.

Additional tasks have to be solved for the parallel solution: initialization and termination of the worker processes, distribution of the problem data and output of the results. Hence, the modular decomposition of the parallel solution significantly differs from a sequential one.

Even on this abstract level algorithms can not easily be reused for any parallel machine. They must fit with respect to different parallel programming models: shared or distributed memory, synchronous or asynchronous message passing, or data parallel concepts. The same holds even more on the level of implementation: There are either programming languages specific for a certain programming model, e. g. Occam-2 [2] for distributed memory and synchronous communication via channels, or otherwise general programming languages like C are extended by constructs for a specific programming model. Hence, even if there are libraries that support certain tasks, their portability is rather restricted. Interface specifications like PVM [10] and MPI [14, 7] provide some standardization at least for the message passing model.

Finally, on the technical level of program installation, execution and debugging tools are used which are specific for the particular parallel machine. Even accessing a parallel machine often requires a significant amount of specific technical knowledge.

The above analysis demonstrates that all aspects considered below the level of characterizing the problem specific part of the branch-and-bound method belong to the expertise needed for the development of this kind of parallel program. Furthermore, one easily recognizes that such expertise can not be made simply available by some library of functions. More sophisticated reuse methodes are needed.

3 Software Reuse

Our approach for construction of domain specific tool sets is based on systematic application of the most powerful reuse methods in order to make expert knowledge available to non-experts. This section gives a brief overview on those aspect of software reuse. A comprehensive survey and taxonomy can be found in [17] and a status report in [20].

Software reuse is the construction of software systems from existing components in contrast to their development from scratch. It is not only code that can be reused, but any kind of intermediate product of the development process, e. g. specifications and system structures. Even manufacturing procedures or decision rules may be subject to reuse.

Reuse of components does not only decrease time and costs of software development. Even more important, reuse may increase software qualities of the products, e. g. reliability, adaptability, and efficiency. That effect can be achieved if experts for a particular task develop reusable components of high quality by applying state-of-the-art design and techniques. Although reusers do not have those knowledge and skills, they can reproduce such quality. Reuse may even enable users to solve an implementation task. Take for example a parser generator. It encapsulates sophisticated expert knowledge for the construction of powerful and efficient parsers. Most of its users would not be able to develop such products, even if they could spend plenty of time.

In our approach a tool set is built by experts for a certain domain of parallel programming, and is used by non-experts to create software from high level descriptions. In terms of reuse methods such a tool set is considered as an application generator [3]. It reuses complete system designs and creates implementations from specifications. In terms of our scenario in section 2, a branch-and-bound problem is specified, and a parallel implementation is created from it.

Application generators have a high potential payoff, with respect to the conceptual distance spanned from the specification to the implementation, as well as in terms of the code expansion (ratio of specification size to program size) [17]. However, such great leverage is only possible if the application domain is sufficiently narrow to allow the automation, and if many different variants of software in that domain need to be constructed.

For building such tool sets several powerful reuse methods have to be applied in order to encapsulate a variety of expertise as discussed in the scenario of section 2. The **software architecture** [21] of systems in the application domain is fixed upto a certain degree and reused for each of the created variants. In a known modular decomposition of a system the interfaces between components can also be fixed. Hence, variants of components can be created independently, and a combinatorial explosion of the number of variants can be avoided. Krueger characterizes software architecture reuse in [17] as large-scale system design reuse and also points out the relation to application generators.

The components of a tool set have to cooperate in a certain preplanned way in order to create a complex software system. Such software **manufacturing processes** can be modeled, programmed and executed by tool control systems like Make [9] or Odin [5, 4]. Here the knowledge of construction steps, their dependencies, input/output relations and parametrization, as well as intermediate results are reused. The power of this reuse method lies in its programmable activities, which even allows to reuse rule based decisions in the construction process. The method belongs to the category of more general software development processes where both persons and tools are involved [18].

Generic instantiation of software components mainly supports reuse of program structures, data structures, or algorithms. Abstract schemas are reused on instantiation where the generic parameters are substituted by concrete types, functions, statements, or other program constructs. The concept is closely integrated in several programming languages, e. g. in Ada, C++, Eiffel. The technique of macro substitution can yield similar effects, however without any checks for consistency. The skeletons of [6] are based on comparable concepts: They describe parallel algorithmic schemas in the notation of higher order functions.

Finally it should be mentioned that a system of actively cooperating tools can itself contain generators which contribute components to the whole product.

The Eli system [23, 12, 15] is an example for a tool set that is constructed on the base of reuse methods as described above. Its domain is the construction of software systems for language processing. It can be considered as an application generator that consists of many cooperating tools.

The software architecture of the generated products is a widely accepted decomposition model for language processors. Its fixed interfaces guarantee that the components created by different tools fit together. Several generators are integrated in the Eli system, e. g. generators for scanners, parsers, attribute evaluators, and definition tables. There is even a generator which completes the concrete and the abstract grammar and creates the parser grammar as input for the parser generator. It is clear that such activities form a complex manufacturing process. It is described for and controlled by the Odin system.

A library of reusable generic modules is embedded in the system. A module implements the solution of a common subtask of language implementation, e. g. basic concepts for name analysis according to scope rules as in C. Several instantiations allow to have different scope rules for different kinds of identifiers, e. g. variables and labels. Such a module consists of specifications for generators and program components written in several different languages. Hence, the generic parameter substitution has to be done by language independent text replacement.

By this means the Eli system embodies expert knowledge in the domain of language implementation, and provides state-of-the-art implementation techniques for non-experts. Its principles have provided ideas, methods, and techniques for the construction of the tool sets for parallel program domains.

4 Tool Set Structure

This section describes the overall structure of tool sets for the development of domain specific parallel programs according to our approach. We illustrate the description using components and properties of BBSYS, the system for construction of programs that use branch-and-bound algorithms. However, the concepts apply to other application topics as well.

BBSYS incorporates expert knowledge for the implementation of parallel branch-and-bound programs. The support reaches from mechanisms of accessing the parallel machine to load balancing strategies for distributed worker algorithms. The knowledge is encapsulated such that users need not be concerned with aspects of parallel solutions. They just contribute information that characterizes their problem instance, e. g. data types representing branch-and-bound solutions.

From the user's view the system is organized in four levels (Fig. 1). They represent increasing levels of abstraction of support for parallel program development from access to the parallel machine upto software creation in the specific application domain.

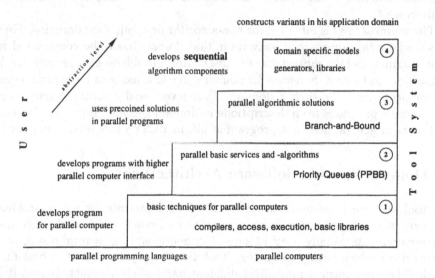

Fig. 1. Conceptual levels of the tool set

The lowest level (1) abstracts from techniques that are specific for the particular parallel machine, e. g. compilation, configuration, and execution of programs, and allocation of processors. The tools on this level are scripts that call compilers and other components of machine specific platforms. Standard libraries for message passing, are also allocated on this level. At present several different platforms are supported, e. g. workstation clusters, Transputer systems, and the SIMD computer MasPar MP1. On this level mainly manufacturing procedures are reused.

Level 2 contributes utilities, parallel algorithms, and data structures which are typical for the particular application domain. In case of BBSYS those are load balancing libraries and parallel implementations of priority queues, like the PPBB library [22]. Hence, we have reuse of precoined domain specific standard components.

Level 3 is the algorithmic level. Here the modular decomposed components of the algorithmic solutions are allocated - in our case for branch-and-bound algorithms. Variants for different problem characteristics and different programming paradigms are organzid in a library. The library modules have generic parameters which are substituted on instantiation by problem specific data types and operations. The structure of the resulting program is determined by a domain specific software architecture for branch-and-bound programs. Hence, on this level users select module variants from the library to be used for certain components in the software architecture and supply generic parameters for the particular program instance. This level hides the parallel solution from the user. His contributions can be made in terms of sequential branch-and-bound concepts, i. e. branching, bounding, and cost functions, and a data type for solutions. We here have reuse of generic schemes of algorithms and data structures within a fixed software architecture.

The topmost level is intended for non-algorithmic application domains. They are suited for this approach if software in that domain has to be constructed in many variants, and if a subtask has to solve complex problems that require parallel machines to be used. Software for planning machine usage in large production environments could be such a domain. That level usually contains generators which create programs from descriptions in domain specific languages. On this level users in general need not program at all. In BBSYS this level is not used.

5   Domain Specific Software Architecture

The tool sets are constructed to produce software variants for many problem instances in their application domain, in this case branch-and-bound programs. The requirements usually vary in several dimensions, e. g. a minimizing or a maximizing problem, compute one or all solutions, apply depth-first or best-first search. The consequences may affect different parts of the product. Hence, it is extremely important to have a suitable modular decomposition that is applicable for all variants. Then consequences of a requirement can be localized. For example, the software architecture holds for all target machines. For a particular one specific modules are selected for certain components in the software architecture. Thus, the construction of variants is kept manageable.

Fig. 2 shows the software architecture for BBSYS. The boxes represent modules, the arcs show the use relation. The central concept of a parallel branch-and-bound implementation is realized in the worker module together with the data module for distributed work load. Variants are created for example by selection of alternative modules for load balancing depending on the network topology of the target machine.

The modules above the shaded part represent the part of the application program which supplies the problem data and uses the solution from the branch-and-bound algorithm, as well as the problem specific data types and functions required by the generic instantiations. They consist of sequential code and are provided by the user.

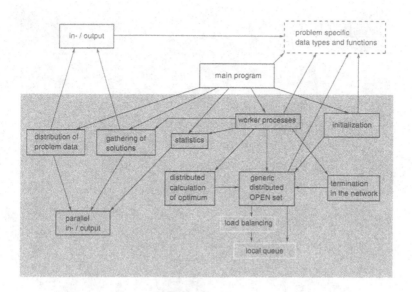

Fig. 2. Software architecture for parallel branch-and-bound

Of course, most of the modules are generic. They are instantiated with generic parameters, like data types for problem instances and solution representation, with functions for branching, bounding, cost computation, etc. We use a very general language independent mechanism for generic instantiation. It replaces generic parameters just textually. It allows any kind of program construct to be substituted on instantion, e. g. types, statements, expressions, or complete functions. The module designer has to use this technique carefully, because there are no checks for consistency of parameter substitution as in more restricted genericity of programming languages.

6   Software Manufacturing

Our tool sets build software for parallel machines. The manufacturing process itself is rather complex, involves several different tools, and many intermediate products. It incorporates expert knowledge which is reused in order to automate the construction. It may be considered as a work-flow model for specific software development which in our special case is executed without human interaction.

A typical example for a rather sophisticated process is contained in the lowest level of our tool sets. It comprises the steps necessary to install and execute a program on a SC-320 Transputer system using the INMOS-C-Toolset. Fig. 3 illustrates the process for a sorting program that consists of two C modules and a description of the process topology (in the top row). The latter is processed by a generator, which creates configuration information to be added to the compiled and linked C-modules, and to be used to allocate processors on the machine.

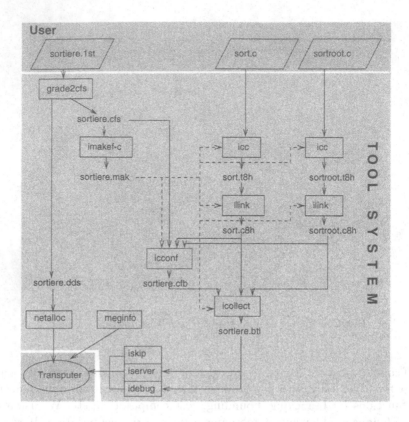

Fig. 3. Reuse of a manufacturing procedure (INMOS-C-Toolset)

Another situation where active manufacturing steps are needed in our tool set is the selection of one of several algorithmic variants, e. g. of a load balancing module, on the base of problem characteristics and machine properties.

The complete manufacturing process throughout all levels of our tool set is modeled for the tool control system Odin. A so-called derivation graph is formulated in Odin's specification language. It describes the inputs and outputs of each tool call and the data flow through the system. Odin's interpreter uses that graph to determine which steps, with which arguments are to be executed in which order for a given request. The intermediate products are kept in a cache. They are reused for a subsequent request, if the products they depend have not changed. This is one of Odin's advantages compared with the Unix tool Make, which serves similar purposes.

The reuse of manufacturing processes as described in this section is typical for our approach. Its effects can not be achieved by other powerful reuse methods which are based on passive program structures, e. g. skeletons, object-oriented hierarchies, or frameworks.

7 Program Generators

Program generators are one of the most powerful reuse methods. They incorporate the knowledge of how to create a solution from a declarative description of a problem instance.

As an example we consider a tool that creates configuration files for parallel programs. The network structure of machines like the SC-320-Transputer systems can be adapted to fit well to the process structure of the program, in order to save time for routing steps. In order to do this the INMOS-C-Toolset requires to supply three configuration files, the desired processor net, the process net from the view of the program, and a mapping between both. As the file contents are closely related and the notation is rather clumsy for being written manually, a generator is well suited for that task. It creates the three files from a single annotated graph, which is drawn using a general purpose graph editor.

This generator raises the level of abstraction significantly from the low level operational notation of configuration files upto a graph notation that also has a visual representation. Furthermore, the generator checks for structural consistency. This generator supports the design of almost arbitrary process nets. That facility is not used in BBSYS. The generator is integrated into an earlier tool set of ours which supports program development for communication structures, that can be specified explicitly.

8 User Interface for Software Configuration

Using a tool set like BBSYS can be considered as a software configuration task: The user provides several items of information, which describe properties of the particular problem instance, state requirements on the results, and contribute program fragments for specific data types and functions. The items are related to each other, and they have to be consistent and complete with respect to a set of rules that drive the software construction process. Those rules and the design of the input information structure encode expert knowledge of correct and effective usage of the system. It is embedded in a configuration program and its graphical user interface.

The configuration program is generated by the tool LaCon from a description of the structure and the kind of information, and from rules for consistency and completeness. According to the description it creates a window hierarchy with suitable input components and an implementation of the rules and of a help mechanism. Initially LaCon has been developed as a tool for specifying variants of domain specific languages [19, 16]. However, it is sufficiently general to be used as a generator for configuration programs in any domain.

The input items are organized in a hierarchy of windows. Each window comprises information of a certain topic. Fig. 4 shows the root window and two windows from levels below it. The hierarchy expresses the level of abstraction of the information: Upper levels are expressed in terms of branch-and-bound concepts, whereas lower levels allow to influence the created software more directly. Information on those detailed levels can be omitted, defaults are then used

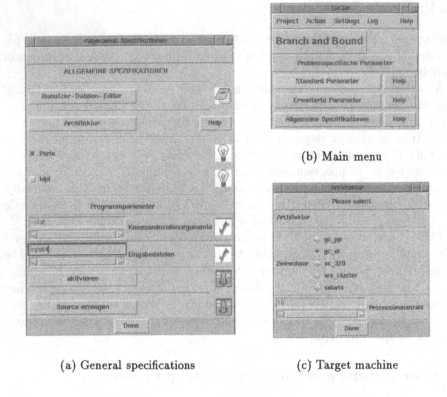

(a) General specifications   (c) Target machine

Fig. 4. Configuration with graphical user interface

instead. Users may completely abstract from the parallel branch-and-bound implementation.

The input components are generated from a small but sufficient number of graphical widgets for different kinds of information: e. g. a binary decision whether a minimizing or maximizing problem is stated, a number for the branch degree if it is fixed, a selection out of several target machines. Program fragments like a type or a function are contributed using dedicated editors. They present frames to be filled in for the particular item.

Fig. 5 shows an example for the violation of a consistency check. It is taken from a detailed specification level. The selected local heap strategy does not fit to the request for backtracking mode. The error description is automatically generated from the violated rule.

9 Conclusion

We presented a method for construction of tool sets which support the development of parallel programs in specific domains. Expert knowledge of efficient use of parallel machines, languages, programming models, algorithmic methods,

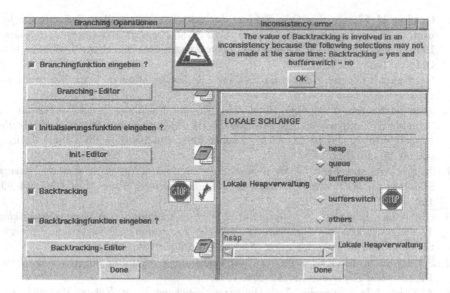

Fig. 5. Consistency violation

and on the software manufacturing process is made available for non-experts in parallel programming.

Our approach is based on powerful methods of reuse to automate software construction: A domain specific software architecture is the basis of compositional reuse. Variants are created by selecting and instantiating generic modules from a library. The manufacturing process is modeled for and executed by a tool control system. A generated configuration program with a graphical user interface guides users towards consistent and complete specifications on a high level of abstraction.

The approach has been demonstrated by a tool set for parallel branch-and-bound programs. It has been successfully used for the construction of flow shop scheduling software. The tool construction process has been repeated for another algorithmic domain, parallel sorting. It is left for future work to apply the approach to further domains, and to get even closer to applications by domain specific generators on the topmost tool level as described in section 4.

References

1. Klaus Brockmann and Wilhelm Dangelmaier. Ein paralleler Branch-&-Bound-Algorithmus zur Minimierung der Zykluszeit in Fließlinien mit parallelen Maschinen. Technical report tr-rsfb-97-044, reihe sfb, Universität-GH Paderborn, Fachbereich Mathematik-Informatik, June 1997.
2. Alan Burns. *Programming in Occam 2*. Addison-Wesley Publishing Company, 1988.
3. J. Craig Cleaveland. Building Application Generators. *IEEE Software*, 5(7):25–33, July 1988.

4. Geoffrey M. Clemm. The Odin System. In Jacky Estublier, editor, *Software Config-uration Management: selected papers ICSE SCM-4 and SCM-5 workshops*, volume 1005 of *Lecture Notes in Computer Science*, pages 241–262, Seattle, Washington, October 1995. Springer.

5. Geoffrey M. Clemm. The Odin System - Reference Manual, Odin Version 1.15, 1995.

6. John Darlington, Yi-ke Guo, Hing Wing To, and Jin Yang. Parallel Skeletons for Structured Composition. In *Proceedings 5th Principles and Practice of Parallel Programming*, pages 19–28. ACM, August 1995. Published as SIGPLAN Notices, volume 30, number 8.

7. Jack J. Dongarra, Steve W. Otto, Marc Snir, and David Walker. A Message Passing Standard for MPP and Workstations. *Communications of the ACM*, 39(7):84–90, July 1996.

8. Christoph Eilinghoff. *Systematische Konstruktion anwendungsspezifischer Werkzeugsysteme zur Entwicklung paralleler Programme*. Dissertation, Universi-tät-GH Paderborn, Fachbereich Mathematik-Informatik, 1998.

9. S.I. Feldman. MAKE - a program for maintaining computer programs. *Software Practice and Experience*, 9:255–265, 1979.

10. Al Geist, Adam Beguelin, Jack Dongarra, Weicheng Jiang, Robert Manchek, and Vaidy Sunderam. *PVM 3 User's Guide and Reference Manual*. Oak Ridge National Laboratory, May 1993.

11. Bernard Gendron and Teodor Gabriel Crainic. Parallel branch-and-bound algo-rithms: survey and synthesis. *Operations Research*, 42(6):1042–1066, November 1994.

12. R.W. Gray, V.P. Heuring, S.P. Levi, A.M. Sloane, and W.M. Waite. Eli: A Com-plete, Flexible Compiler Construction System. *Communications of the ACM*, 35(2):121–131, February 1992.

13. J.N.D. Gupta. Two-stage hybrid flowshop scheduling problems. *Journal of the Operational Research Society*, 34:359–364, 1988.

14. Rolf Hempel. The MPI Standard for Message Passing. In Gentzsch and Harms, editors, *High-Performance Computing and Networking '94*, volume 797 of *Lecture Notes in Computer Science*, pages 247–. Springer Verlag, April 1994.

15. Uwe Kastens. Executable Specifications for Language Implementation. In *Proceed-ings 5th Symposium on Programming Language Implementation and Logic Pro-gramming*, volume 714 of *Lecture Notes in Computer Science*. Springer Verlag, August 1993.

16. Uwe Kastens and Peter Pfahler. Compositional design and implementation of domain-specific languages. In R.N. Horspool, editor, *In Proc. Systems Implemen-tation 2000 Conference*, pages 152–165. Chapman and Hall, 1998.

17. Charles W. Krueger. Software Reuse. *ACM Computing Surveys*, 24(2):131–183, June 1992.

18. L. J. Osterweil. Software Processes are Software Too. In *Proceedings 9th Inter-national Conference on Software Engineering*, pages 2–13, Monterey, CA, March 1987. IEEE.

19. Peter Pfahler and Uwe Kastens. Language Design and Implementation by Selec-tion. In *Proceedings 1st ACM-SIGPLAN Workshop on Domain-Specific-Languages, DSL '97, Paris, France*, pages 97–108. Technical Report University of Illinois at Urbana-Champaign, January 1997.

20. Rubén Prieto-Díaz. Status Report: Software Reusability. *IEEE Software*, 10(5):61–66, May 1993.

21. Mary Shaw and David Garlan. *Software Architecture*. Prentice-Hall, 1996.
22. Stefan Tschöke and Thomas Polzer. Portable Parallel Branch-and-Bound Library, PPBB-Lib, User Manual, Library Version 2.0. Technical report, University of Paderborn, November 1996.
23. William M. Waite, V. P. Heuring, and U. Kastens. Configuration Control in Compiler Construction. In *International Workshop on Software Version and Configuration Control '88*, Stuttgart, 1988. Teubner Verlag.

Compiling Horn-Clause Rules in IBM's Business System 12 an Early Experiment in Declarativeness

Ghica van Emde Boas - Lubsen[1] and Peter van Emde Boas[2]

[1] IBM, the Netherlands, PO Box 24, 1420 AA Uithoorn; emdeboas@nl.ibm.com
[2] ILLC - WINS, University of Amsterdam,
Plantage Muidergracht 24, 1018 TV Amsterdam; peter@wins.uva.nl

Abstract. The tight connection which exists between the fragment of Prolog now known by the name Datalog [27] and the various calculi and algebras for Relational Database Systems was observed at several places in the late 70-ies and early 80-ies. The problem was to make this idea operational and to build a system which implemented it. Such systems today are known as *Deductive Databases*.

We describe the history of a hardly known project from the mid 80-ies where a prototype realizing this goal was produced. We explain why the Relational Database system called *Business System 12*, developed by IBM in the Netherlands, and which became operational in 1983, turned out to provide the right functionality. We also indicate how this project influenced subsequent projects aimed at enhancing the degree of declarativeness in interfaces with database systems.[1]

What we understand we can formalize; what is formalizable can be automated, and you will discover that someone has built it.

1 The Great Idea

Deductive Databases arose in the 1980-ies out of the confluence of three technologies which came to age by the end of the 1970-ies. First, by 1980 the *Relational Database* had become the preferred model of database technology. Secondly, due to the initial success of *Expert Systems*, Artificial Intelligence was returned to grace. Finally, with the proliferation of the language Prolog the concept of *Logic Programming* became a prominent activity in Artificial intelligence, if not in computer science in general.

People observed that, notwithstanding the substantial differences in conceptual frameworks, these three approaches to conceptual information processing

---

[1] Evidently the actual developments in the fields of Databases, Logic Programming and Artificial Intelligence go far beyond the small part which the authors observed and participated in. The observations and opinions expressed in this paper therefore don't pretend to present a complete view on history, but rather to reflect the insights and positions held by the authors during these developments

were storing and combining information in similar ways. Thus the idea arose to substitute the computational strategies from one field for the slower methods used in another. For example one might use the database engine from a Relational Database system in order to compute the results which would be produced by backtracking in Prolog.

Such a cross fertilization of technologies held great promises for all fields involved. Databases were much more powerful when crunching raw data than interpretation based Prolog systems. Secondary benefits from Database technology, like security, sharing and persistence, would become available to AI almost free. On the other hand database technology would benefit from the *declarativeness* of Prolog, where one can introduce new concepts and use them in the same way as concepts stored in the system directly. It would also provide a monolingual alternative for the rather heterogeneous ad hoc formalisms used for providing structural information about data and constraints to the database. That at the *procedural level* the match would be less than perfect (e.g., the order in which answers would be produced would be different in the two worlds), was something one could live with.

In this section we give our perspective on the state of the art in Databases, Ai and Logc programming around 1982. With a familiar example we show how relations are expressed in the three formalisms. Finally we explain our *compilation based* approach to building a Deductive Database. In section 2 we describe our project from 1984, where a fragment of Prolog indeed was compiled onto an existing database system. How the functionality of our prototype can be extended is discussed in the third and final section.

The reader should note that a number of terms naming and identifying concepts relevant to our project (terms like *Deductive Databases* and *Datalog*) still had to be invented in 1984. Using these phrases in our paper therefore is in fact an anachronism.

1.1 The Theater

On the left side of the scene a team of engineers is programming a huge mainframe machine; on the other side a group of logicians is writing strange looking formulas on a blackboard....

Relational Databases The main cause for the success of the Relational Database model as proposed by Codd [5] is its clean and conceptual semantics over a well understood mathematical model: relations are subsets of Cartesian products of Domains. Relations can be used both for describing *entities (objects)* by listing their characteristic properties as a tuple of values, and conceptual *relationships* between such entities. The conceptual world from the system designer (as represented in an entity-relationship scheme [4]) can be mapped to a Relational Database scheme, consisting of domains, attributes, tables and various constraints. This mapping is well understood and forms a basic ingredient of elementary database courses.

Relations in mathematics are used to represent the meaning of *predicates* in *first order predicate logic* (standard Tarskian semantics), so it is natural to use first order logic as a language for talking about the contents of databases. By 1980 the appropriate fragment of first order predicate logic had been described. This fragment today is known in various syntactic dialects by the names *domain calculus* or *tuple calculus*. The core of the prominent language SQL is a dialect of tuple calculus.

These calculi can be used to give a *declarative* description of *derived relations* in terms of *primitive relations* stored in the database[2]. Derived relations are evaluated by subjecting the primitive relations to suitable *algebraic operations* which live in the mathematical structure known by the name *relational algebra*. Well known relational operations are, *select, project, union, product, (natural) join* and *difference*. However, a single description may correspond to a large variety of equivalent expressions in the relational algebra, all yielding the same result, but with possibly different processing costs. It is the task of a *query optimizer* to produce, for a given logical or algebraic expression, an equivalent one with optimal processing costs.

An important shortcoming of the Relational Database model is the lack of abstraction mechanisms at the level of domains: what for one observer is a primitive value may turn out to be a composed structured object for another. In the relational model attribute values are selected from domains consisting of atomic values only. The need for *composite structured values* has resulted in the *nested* relational model. Computer Industry however has moved in a different direction: in the world of *Object Orientation* composite structured objects are the norm, and by making them persistent the *Object Oriented Database* is obtained. However, by taking this road all the secondary functionality of databases had to be recreated, and along the way the nice features of the relational model, particularly those related to its clean mathematical semantics and *declarativeness*, where lost. *Object-Relational Databases* [26] represent an attempt to preserve the best of both worlds.

These semantic issues on how to represent information and how to express queries, should not make us forget the prime purpose of a database system: *providing a secure, stable and persistent environment where a community of users may concurrently access, query and update large volumes of shared data*. Database technology primarily is concerned with the technological problems of realizing these "secondary" features.

Artificial Intelligence and Logic Programming In this paper an *Artificial Intelligence* project is a project involving some form of logical inference by symbolic means. Other important activities in AI like natural language processing, image processing, robotics, knowledge representation and extraction or computational research on models of the human mind will be disregarded.

---

[2] today, in Deductive Databases the terms *intensional* and *extensional* are used for expressing this distinction

Researchers in symbolic inferencing and theorem proving in the early development of AI, used first order predicate logic as a universal representation language. *Resolution* based theorem provers were used and obtained sometimes reasonable results. Resolution is a strategy for theorem proving which hardly resembles the strategies used by humans. For a full treatment of the strategy I refer to standard textbooks like [3, 14]. The strategy requires several steps. The logical expression of assumptions and the (negated) conclusion are transformed into a collection of *clauses* build from *literals* having *terms* as arguments. The resulting list of terms is subjected to an iteration of *unifications, substitutions* and *resolution* steps, aiming for a derivation of the *empty clause*. If this succeeds one obtains a *refutation proof* showing that the negated conclusion is inconsistent with the assumptions thus proving the required result. If the resolution proof *fails* the substitutions computed can be used for constructing a *countermodel* for the conclusion.

The bad news is that the resolution strategy is highly nondeterministic: *indefinite clauses* lead to a branching structure of cases which all should be explored. Moreover, iterated substitutions on terms occurring in the clauses may lead to a combinatorial explosion. Worst of all, the method is incomplete, as some satisfiable formulas turn out to posses only infinite models, which will never be searched out to completion in a resolution proof.

In many practical situations this combinatorial explosion doesn't occur, which makes actual work in AI feasible. People saw a reason why this happened. Frequently the formulas used belong to the fragment known by the name *Horn clauses*, clauses with at most one *positive* literal. This property reduces the number of available literals on which a clause may be resolved to at most one, and thus one of the important sources of the combinatorial explosion is removed. The nondeterminism of the resolution method can be replaced by the deterministic depth first search backtracking strategy known today by the name *SLD resolution*. The language *Prolog*, which originated out of a natural language processing project but which to a large extent was founded on Kowalski's work on resolution theorem proving, actually has SLD resolution for the Horn Clause fragment as its computational model. [6]

Using SLD resolution the combinatorial explosion due to the growth of terms remains. However if we remove from Prolog the function symbols in terms (together with many features residing outside the computational core like build-in predicates having side effects) we obtain the "pure" core language known today by the name *Datalog*.

One of the claimed advantages of the language is its *declarativeness*: a Prolog program is a list of first order formulas which express the structure of the model to be constructed, just written in a rather unconventional dialect of predicate logic. On the other hand there exists a Prolog interpretator which actually builds the model described by the rules, and the user doesn't have to be bothered about the details on how the interpreter obtains its results. Note however that there is a major semantic difference with the interpretation of logic used by ordinary mathematicians: in predicate logic a set of formulas describes a family of models, whereas the Prolog interpreter produces a preferred *minimal* model. For people working in AI this difference was no problem at all, since they were looking for minimal models as interpretations anyhow. Curiously enough such a minimal model is also taken to be the natural interpretation for the contents of a (relational) database.

A major contribution to the popularity of Prolog was the selection around 1982 by the Japanese of this language as vehicle for their Fifth Generation Project, and the impact this choice had on research in computer science around the world.

Logic programming is the Computer Science research area where the above intuitive notions are investigated and formalized. Notwithstanding the fact that the field dates from the 1970-ies it lasted until the early 1990-ies before a complete satisfactory mathematical correct formalization of the theory of logic programming which was free from the errors caused by the interaction between syntax and semantics, appeared in the literature.

1.2 The Players

In the centre of the scene a group of people is having a picnick. They are discussing how they are related to each other...

We stick to the traditional example of family relations among humans to illustrate the similarities and differences between the various Computer Science fields mentioned above.

Consider the statement that Dorothy is an aunt of Jessica. This can describe two different relations: it may be the case that Dorothy is a sister of one of Jessica's parents, or it can mean that Dorothy has a husband Fred which is a brother of one of these parents, thus becoming Jessica's uncle. It can even mean both relations at the same time. Sisterhood is a defined relation as well. Dorothy is a sister of Thomas, since they share parents and are not the same person; moreover Dorothy is a female person. Parenthood and marriage are relations which are not defined in terms of other relations, and the same holds for the gender, date of birth and name of people. Existence of a set of entities called people is assumed, together with the possibility of identifying people by name. These notions are considered to be basic notions when talking about family relations. A further distinction is that gender, date of birth and name are *unary* properties of people, whereas parenthood and marriage are *binary relations*. In fact marriage has a hybrid nature: as a relation it connects two people, and at the same time it is an *entity* in itself having properties like a date of marriage (and possibly a date of termination).

First order logic is a convenient language to express such relations. In this particular case we might write something like:

$$parent(Gerti, Jessica) \land sister(Gerti, Dorothy) \Rightarrow aunt(Dorothy, Jessica)$$

or preferably, since it is a general rule, using logical variables

$$\forall G, J, D[parent(G, J) \land sister(G, D) \Rightarrow aunt(D, J)]$$

a similar rule for sisterhood reads:

$$\forall X, Y, Z[parent(Z, X) \land parent(Z, Y) \land X \neq Y \land female(X) \Rightarrow sister(X, Y)]$$

Information about the primitive relations in logic is expressed by atomic assertions like: $female(Gerti)$ or $parent(Gerti, Jessica)$.

The corresponding rules written in a Prolog become:
```
aunt(D,J) :- parent(G,J), sister(G,D)
sister(X,Y) :- parent(Z,X),parent(Z,Y),X ≠ Y, female(X)
female(X):- person(X,'F',Any) .
```
showing that the order of the implication is reversed, and that the quantifiers are omitted (by convention free variables are understood to be universally quantified). The basic information is presented by means of *facts* which are stored in the Prolog *database* which in fact is just a collection of lines in the program:
```
person(Gerti,'F',19240713).,
marriage(Fred,Dorothy,19411013).
```
which illustrates that the unary properties of entities are written in a format resembling database tuples, rather than using a collection of unary predicates.

In a Relational Database model people will be represented by a (stored) database table whose structure can be expressed by a structure declaration like:
```
PERSON(NAME:STRING(20),GENDER:{'M','F'},BIRTH:NUM(8) # KEY(NAME) )
```
Gerti now can be represented by a tuple like (Gerti,F,19240713) in the PERSON table. Other base relations describing parenthood and marriage. are represented by relations as well:
```
PARENT(PAR:STRING(20),CHILD:STRING(20) # KEY(PAR,CHILD) )
MARRIAGE(HUSB:STRING(20),WIFE:STRING(20),DATE:NUM(8)
# KEY(HUS,DATE), KEY(WIFE,DATE) )
```
and by inserting the appropriate tuples the basic family relations are described.

Having provided the required facts and rules we hope that our computer system indeed will be capable to derive the fact that Gerti is an aunt of Jessica.

In Prolog one may submit a query like: ?- aunt(Dorothy,Jessica) hoping that the system will return the answer 'YES'. The Prolog interpreter, using its SLD resolution, will first discover that Gerti is a parent of Jessica, and subsequently attempt to solve the subgoal of establishing that Dorothy and Gerti are sisters, which eventually will succeed by invoking the rule for sisterhood, but not before having inferred along the way that Dorothy is female.

Extracting the same information from the relational database would require to invent an algebraic or logical relational expression representing the aunt relation. We might describe the sister relation by:
```
SISTER(A,B) =
SEL( PROJ(( PARENT(X,A) JN PARENT(X,B) ,(A,B) ) , A ≠ B )
JN PROJ( SEL(PERSON(A,G,Arb), G = 'F', (A) )
```

and this complicated expression must be joined with the parent relation to obtain one of the two contributing relations for aunthood. Once the view definition for aunthood is constructed one can evaluate it on the database hoping that in the resulting table the tuple (Dorothy,Jessica) will show up. If the database contains a large number of people it might even be advantageous to submit a query selecting the tuple (Dorothy,Jessica) from the view describing aunthood: the database optimizer may push the selection down in the algebraic expressions thus reducing the size of the intermediate results and the processing time for the query.

Observe the distinction between the definition of this derived sister relation (called a *view definition*) and the table produced by evaluating it in the database (the *view instantiation*).

This example illustrates what declarativeness is all about: in Prolog we have specified the rules and the system navigates towards a solution. In a Relational database we have to do a lot of thinking before we can submit the right query to the database.

1.3   The Play

Disturbed by the fierce debate the engineers and logicians drop their activities and join the family, in an attempt to solve the dispute...

In the above example the Prolog approach offers a reasonable degree of declarativeness. However, inspection of how the Prolog inference process will proceed if run against a substantial fact database, will show that the computational process can be quite inefficient. Moreover, there is no actual database system against which the Prolog system operates; the Prolog system contains a fact database stored explicitly in the program. Consequently none of the secondary benefits of database technology like persistence, security and sharing will be available.

Declarativeness is also a property ascribed to the Database Interface language SQL. Since SQL is claimed to be *relationally complete* it should be possible to formulate an equivalent of the definitions given in Prolog. However, the resulting expressions will become far more complex than the ones given in the previous section. Worse, in the version of SQL available around 1982, due to the lack of a Union operator, it would have been impossible to express the aunt relation by means of an expression, and one would need a process for evaluating this relation.

Even if the database interface language is truly relationally complete the problem remains how to *obtain* the required relational expressions. In Prolog, as in mathematics and logic, a complex definition is expanded into a chain of more simple definitions, terminating at basic notions. The corresponding feature in relational databases would be a *view definition* being expanded into a chain of other view definitions, ultimately arriving at the tables stored directly in the databases. This requires view definitions to be invokable as easily as stored relations. Yet another feature which the database systems around 1982 didn't offer [29].

Finally the translation itself. Life will remain hard if every Prolog defini-tion must be translated by hand into a corresponding relational expression. The translation, however, is not hard to automate. The strategy how to perform it can be found in textbooks like [27]. Yet there remains the difference between knowing how to do it in principle and actually building a system doing it. Such automated systems are now known by the name *Deductive Databases*.

The ideal of Deductive Databases is to combine the user friendly declara-tive world of Prolog with the information crunching power of existing relational database systems. Isolate a fragment of Prolog which can be evaluated by means of relational algebra on a database system, automate the translation, and build a system which uses as much computational power from the database engine as feasible. Next enjoy using for free the secondary benefits of the database sys-tem which you no longer have to reinvent for your AI system: sharing data, concurrency, transaction management, security and so on...

The core fragment of Prolog for which this translation exists is known by the name *Recursion-free Safe Datalog*. This fragment consists of rules describing predicates in Prolog defined by a non-recursive[3] system of Horn clauses, starting from a finite collection of basic relations. Terms do not contain function symbols. The rules moreover satisfy a *safety condition* preventing the occurrence of free variables in the answer as given by the Prolog interpreter. This condition is required in order to keep the derived relations bounded. For such rules the defined predicates have an extent which can also be described by algebraic relational expressions having base tables corresponding to the basic relations as atoms. The translation process moreover can be mechanized.

As illustrated by the extensive literature on the topic *Logic and Databases* around 1980 this semantic relation itself was reasonably understood. Yet most projects in this area worked on the basis of the so-called *tuple at a time* approach. The AI system no longer needs to store its fact database inside the program, if the resulting facts can be represented by tuples in a relational database. But the combinatorial processing of this information is still performed at the side of the AI inference engine and therefore the power of the database system itself is severely under-utilized. None of the secondary benefits of database technology becomes available to the AI system.

One may wonder why so few projects in the early 1980-ies went beyond this tuple at a time approach. As we conjecture, the lack of an appropriate relational database system may have been an important cause....

2 The Prolog - BS12 Interface Project

Inspired by the hype provoked by the Japanese Fifth Generation project and its challenge to the rest of the world [22] the first author, using her experience as a participant for several years in the development of IBM's product Business

---

[3] The full language Datalog allows for recursive definitions also; in the last section of this paper we explain how such recursive rules can be treated in a compilation based deductive database.

System 12, noted the correspondence between backtracking in Prolog and evaluating expressions in a relational database. Initial ideas on this approach were presented at a workshop at the Free University in Amsterdam, early 1984 [17]. This workshop was dominated by proponents of the tuple at a time approach resulting is disbelief among the audience. Still convinced of the suitability of BS12 as a vehicle for realizing this idea, she arranged a student internship at IBM for C.J.F. Doedens, who developed a working prototype within 9 months. His report [12] constitutes the master thesis on which he graduated in Computer Science at the University of Amsterdam. See also [13]. The best accessible document describing the project is [20].

Since this paper focuses on the general ideas and historical backgrounds of the project we will not present a complete technical description of the translation process. The theory needed for constructing such a translator can be found in textbooks like Ullman [27]. Instead we discuss the requirements on an RDMS in order to be a suitable platform for realizing a compilation based deductive database system. BS12 indeed satisfies these requirements.

2.1 Business System 12

Business System 12 is the name of a Relational database system developed by IBM, the Netherlands in the early 1980-ies, building on the work of a group at Peterlee, UK. During the early stages of development there was little interaction with database development projects going on in the USA like system R. Blauw and Duyvesteijn from the University at Twente served as advisors. A first version of BS12 became operational in 1983. The system was offered as a service from the International Network in Zoetermeer in the Netherlands. There was never an installation delivered to clients; users accessed the system in a time shared environment. IBM management at some point in the 1980-ies decided no longer to support the product, after which the system gradually disappeared. However, a major application running on the system was a financial project build around the XSHARE database storing stock exchange rates of some 100000 companies over a period of five years, resulting in the (for this era tremendous) volume of 5GB! The fact that it turned out to be impossible to migrate this application to DB2 without loss of performance and functionality was the main reason why BS12 actually survived until approx. 1996.

It is difficult to find in the literature information about BS12; the reference manual [2] contains a full description but was made available primarily to users. A more superficial description of the functionality in the style as advocated in [25] constitutes the unpublished document [16]. A paper on concurrency issues appears in the proceedings of a Dutch national conference [7]. Andrew Warden, in reality Hugh Darwen, one of the designers of BS12 mentions the system with hindsight in [29].

In BS12 tables are relations, subsets of Cartesian products of domains, where columns are identified by named attributes; the rows correspond to the tuples in the relation. Domains are finite sets relating to one of the five basic types:

Character, Numeric, Name, Bit, Timestamp. The basic type **Name** represents a sort of strings with a normalization convention. It is the datatype used for table and attribute names. To every domain a default value can be assigned. Duplicate rows in a table are disallowed. Tables are homogeneous: all rows have the same attributes and domains. The ordering of rows in a table is insignificant.

The environment where the system had to operate: a time sharing environment where several customers are using the database system simultaneously, had severe consequences for the system architecture. Since competitors might share the use of the system they had to be protected against each other, both with respect to accessing information and the denial of service. Consequently, having a global catalogue of tables and/or views was unthinkable. Every user had access to his/her private dictionaries with the possibility of opening items for shared use.

A second important feature is the *monolingual* structure of the system interface. BS12 focusses on tables, being relations interpreted as sets. But processes, functions etc. are represented by objects which are also tables (*language tables*) which makes these objects accessible to relational operators. System information like the catalogues of tables, columns, or views are also stored in tables.[4]

A third important feature is the fully algebraic character of the system. The number 12 in the name BS12 refers to the presence of 12 relational operators:

- SELECT set comprehension on a table based on a selection criterion (subset of rows)
- PRESENT a hybrid combining projection and renaming (subset of columns)
- CALCULATE extends a table by a new attribute which functionally depends on the others where the dependency is given by an explicit formula
- GENERATE production of a single row relation computed from constant values
- SUMMARY a aggregate construct used for grouping, summation etc.
- JOIN the natural join
- MERGE a version of the outer join where nonmatching row are extended by default values rather than nils
- QUAD Cartesian product of relations
- DIFFERENCE relative set difference
- EXCLUSION symmetric difference of two tables
- INTERSECTION
- UNION

The Boolean operations (the last four in the list) do not require that the two argument relations are union compatible; if they are not the resulting table is projected on the attributes shared by both operands.

BS12 is algebraically complete: wherever a base relation can serve as an operand in an expression its role may be performed by a relational expression as well. Note that the result of evaluating an expression in this context always represents a relation considered as a set. Every relational expression in the algebra

---

[4] This makes it possible to construct the "paradoxical" Russell view consisting of those views which don't contain themselves as a row.

represents a *view* on the database. This view can not only be evaluated but the expression defining the view can be stored in a language table, which itself can be added to a user owned catalogue called the Table of Views. Moreover these definitions can be stored and modified during a session.

As we will indicate in the sequence both the algebraic completeness and the monolinguality are instrumental in making BS12 a suitable platform for the construction of a deductive database system.

2.2 The translation of safe non-recursive Horn-clauses into view definitions

Given a system of Horn-clause rules for a family of predicates, and given a collection of basic predicates used in these rules we want to interpret this systems as a definition of a collection of predicates in terms of the given basic ones. Assuming that the basic predicates correspond to stored tables in a relational database we want to obtain for the derived relations relational expressions in terms of the basic tables with the intended meaning.

In a preprocessing stage the clauses are ordered such that clauses sharing a predicate in the head are grouped together. The group defining a predicate which occurs in a subgoal in the body of some clause should precede the group containing this clause. Consequently clauses all whose subgoals invoke predicates corresponding to base tables or build-in predicates appear at the beginning of the list. If the system of Horn clauses is not recursive such an ordering can be obtained by topological sorting. For recursive families of Horn clauses such an ordering doesn't exist.

One additional complication may lead to meaningless expressions. The complication involves the occurrence of variables in the head which don't appear in the body, or only appear in build-in predicates. Semantically this means that the values assigned to the corresponding attributes in the relational tabel for this predicate have no designated domain and thus give rise to potentially unbounded relations. The problem is illustrated by rules like: `mortal(Everybody).` or `larger(X,Y) :- (X > Y)`.

The easy way out is to prohibit such unbounded relations by enforcing a so-called *safety condition* on Prolog programs.[5] The condition stipulates that in each rule all variables occurring in the head occur *bounded* in the body: Constants and variables occurring in a basic predicate or a predicate earlier in the order of definitions in the body occur bounded in the body. The same holds for variables occurring in a build-in predicate whose semantics enforces this variable to be functionally dependent on other bounded variables. All other variables are unbounded.

The translation of Horn-clauses into view definitions as described by Ullman [27] consists of three stages.

---

[5] Our safety condition follows [20]; it is slightly more general than the one given by Ullman [27], who requires equality in stead of functional dependence.

In the first stage a relational expression is constructed for every subgoal based on a relational predicate; the build-in subgoals are treated separately during the second stage. These relational expressions basically consist of the relation or view representing the predicate in the subgoal. However, due to the occurrence of constant arguments or multiple occurrences of a single variable the SELECT operator has to be invoked.

In the second stage the various expressions corresponding to the subgoals are joined together to yield an expression corresponding to the extent of the body of the rule. Build-in predicates (in this context primarily (in)equalities on numeric arguments) are translated to another select. Moreover, in order to accommodate for the positionally specified arguments in the subgoals in a relational algebra based on named attributes, frequently the expression corresponding to a subgoal frequently will have to be *renamed*. RENAME is also essential in order to arranged that shared variables between subgoals will correspond to common columns in a JOIN expression.

In the third and last stage the contributions of the various rules for a predicate must be put together to provide an expression which defines this predicate. A UNION of the subgoal expressions, after a PROJECT on the variable occurring in the head of the rule will suffice in case these subgoal expressions are union-compatible and have the same signature as the head predicate. However, due to the occurrence of repeated variables and constants in the head of individual rules the subgoal expressions in general are not union compatible. However, the semantic impact of such occurrence patterns in the head of a rule can also be expressed by extending the body with a few additional build-in subgoals. Ullman uses a preprocessing stage called *rectification of rules* which solves this problem. The impact is that the expressions for the body will include some more select conditions.

From the above description we can infer the requirements on the functionality to be satisfied by the RDMS in order to support a Datalog compiler as intended.

1. The translation requires that the relational operators SELECT, PROJECT, JOIN, RENAME and UNION can be used in expressions in an arbitrary nested way. Consequently, with a system like the earlier version of SQL which requires to form a Union by means of a process rather than an expression life will be quite unpleasant...
2. If systems of rules, rather than rules for a single predicate have to be translated conveniently, one needs to be able to invoke defined views on the same positions as basic tables. Views must be first class citizens.
3. In order to be able to add, remove and modify rules during a session the corresponding views must be inserted, deleted and modified in the database, without having to restructure the entire database after every change. This requires that the catalogue storing views and their definitions should be readily accessible and updatable during runtime.

As indicated before BS12 fully satisfied these three requirements. The PRESENT operator combines the functionality of a project and a renaming operator and the other three required operators: SELECT, JOIN and UNION are available. In the real world, the SQL based systems available in 1984 violated them all (a situation which, in the more recent SQL2 standard, is hardly improved since). This illustrates both why BS12 was the ideal RDMS for building our prototype and also explains why other groups never opted for a fully compilation based approach to deductive databases.

3 The Aftermath; Extensions of the Functionality of the Compilation Based Approach

Full Datalog includes a feature not covered by the translation process as described in the previous section: *Recursive definition of predicates*. Since Deductive Databases were rather popular in an academic environment where recursion is a well understood mechanism it was the first feature one wanted to add to the interface.

Full Prolog uses function symbols for building complex terms which are used for representing complex entities. These structures show a similarity with the structures in the nested relational model. A second extension involves the migration of our compiled based approach to a nested relational model.

Prolog itself supports the use of negated subgoals, by means of the *negation by failure* strategy. A much milder form of negation is offered in the relational database model by the DIFFERENCE operator. Therefore one wants to investigate whether some "tame" use of the negation operator can be added to the interface.

Finally, having numerical values in a Database is hardly useful if you can't compute on these values, preferably by invocation of symbolic expressions. One would like to see the functionality offered by spreadsheet programs to appear in a database system where the numeric constraints are described symbolically in the database scheme. This extension of functionality is investigated in the field called *Constraint Logic Programming* today.

Between 1984 and 1997 we have been involved with research projects aimed at the above extensions. Recursion and (nonrecursive) terms has been processed on our prototype system. For the negation the solution which is described in theory [27] evidently could have been implemented on our prototype, but we never did so. Finally, the extension with constraints became the focal point of the *RL-project*, which was initiated at the IBM San Jose Research Center[6] in 1985 and which was continued at the University of Amsterdam.

In this section we will discuss the first two extensions, since they were investigated in our project. For the negation problem we refer to the presentation of the problem and its solution for the class of *Stratified Programs* in Ullman [27]. With respect to the constraints we emphasize the tight connection between our project and the subsequent RL-project; for more technical details on **RL** and its prototype implementation see [9, 11].

---

[6] now known as the IBM Almaden research center

3.1 Beyond Relational Algebra: Recursion

Recursive definitions of predicates in Prolog are as little a part of logic as recursive definitions are allowed in the branch of mathematics called Algebra. They violate the basic principle in mathematics that defining an object in terms of itself is disallowed. Yet logicians, computer scientists and Mathematicians have learned to understand and operate on the notions defined using recursion. These "definitions" better be understood as equations, and equations may have a solution. In fact, in order to be meaningful these equations better have a unique, or at least a *preferred* solution. As it turns out this frequently happens to be the case (at least in those situations where indeed recursive definitions nowadays are commonly used, since otherwise...).

The existence of a preferred solution in computer science often can be based on the semantic principle attributed to Knaster and Tarski, known as the *least fixed point principle*. If interpreted over some abstract mathematical structure Ω a recursive definition can be interpreted by means of an equation of the form

$$X = \Phi(X)$$

where Φ denotes some *functional* over Ω, a mapping from Ω into itself. Assume that Ω is a structure on which some partial order $\sqsubseteq$ is defined, such that there exists a unique minimal element $\bot \in \Omega$, and such that least upper bounds for countable increasing chains are defined: if $X_0 \sqsubseteq X_1 \sqsubseteq X_2 \ldots$ is a countable increasing chain then $\bigsqcup_{n=0}^{\infty} X_n$ denotes this least upper bound.

The functional Φ is called *monotonous* if $X \sqsubseteq Y$ implies that $\Phi(X) \sqsubseteq \Phi(Y)$. The functional Φ is called *continuous* if it satisfies $\Phi(\bigsqcup_{n=0}^{\infty} X_n) = \bigsqcup_{n=0}^{\infty} \Phi(X_n)$.

The Knaster Tarski principle states that for a monotonous continuous functional Φ the equation $X = \Phi(X)$ has a minimal fixed point, which moreover can be computed by $\bigsqcup_{n=0}^{\infty} \Phi^{(n)}(\bot)$, where $\Phi^{(n)}(\bot)$ denotes n-fold iteration of Φ on $\bot$.

This principle has been used to assign meaning to recursive procedures in programming theory with great success [1], where it forms the theoretical foundation of the *Scott induction rule*.

For the semantics of Prolog rules, and its interpretation in the relational database model, we take for Ω the family of relations within a (fixed) Cartesian product of domains, where $\sqsubseteq$ denotes set-inclusion and $\bot$ denotes the empty relation. It is easy to see that the five relational operators invoked in our translation process: SELECT, PROJECT, JOIN, RENAME and UNION, all are monotonous and continuous, and so are the complex expressions produced by our translator.

In applying this principle one has to be aware that in general the use of recursion in Prolog invokes a set of predicate symbols rather than a single recursive predicate. After translation this would define a collection of relations in terms of themselves. However, by forming the Cartesian product of these relations, the system can be replaced by a single relation having a recursive definition, after which the Tarski Knaster principle can be applied.

Hence we know what the meaning of a recursively defined relation should be. Moreover, the Knaster Tarski principle tells us how to compute this meaning.

Starting with the empty relation we repeatedly submit the result obtained so far to the functional until no new tuples appear in the result. Where in the theoretical model this might require an infinite number of steps, in the database the process is guaranteed to terminate after finitely many steps, due to the fact that after all the domain Ω is finite. Thus increasing chains must become stable at some point, and it is easy to see that the first chain element X_i satisfying $X_i = \Phi(X_i)$ indeed equals the minimal fixed point.

From a practical perspective this evaluation method (the so called *naive evaluation scheme*) is highly inefficient since it will recompute the same tuples over and over again. The *semi-naive evaluation scheme* is an attempt to prevent some of these recalculations by rewriting the functional in such a way that only the "incremental part" is computed.

Much effort has been invested in building interfaces on databases capable of dealing with recursive definitions. In our project [20] we have performed some experiments with recursive rules using a compilation based approach. Rather than resubmitting the intermediate results as a table to the functional we compile a series of increasingly complex expressions representing the result of k-fold application of the rule and compiling it in relational algebra. This approach was enabled due to the architecture of BS12 where the user has access to his view definitions in the form of language tables. Furthermore the optimizer in BS12, which operated on some tree representation of the algebraic expressions, worked in such a dynamic fashion that the recursive expansion of the expressions and the optimization worked together in an incremental fashion. This made it possible to optimize these expressions at construction time. Once more the architecture of BS12 enabled us to investigate an approach followed by few others...

3.2 Beyond Datalog: Terms

Where Datalog supports as arguments in predicates only constants and variables, full Prolog allows terms build by application of functions to a number of terms also. Semantically a term violates the first normal form condition in databases where all attribute values have to be atomic values.

A typical example of a pair of Prolog facts illustrating terms is given by: owns(Lucy,Mug). in combination with owns(Lucy,book(Homer,Ilias)).

These two facts show that Lucy owns a mug for which no structure information is available, and a book with given author and title. In a Database property of the first sort is easy to represent; just store a tuple (Lucy,Mug) in the OWNS table. Property of the second type requires that one introduces another table BOOK for storing information about books, and subsequently storing in the OWNS table a tuple (Lucy,X), where X is something like a *foreign key* value referring to the BOOK table. At a slightly higher level of abstraction one would consider this value X to be an *object identifier*. But then we are leaving the relational model proceeding towards something like a nested relational or fully object oriented model.

This example illustrates a rather evident strategy for bringing Prolog terms within the scope of our compiled approach. However, several problems remains to be solved:

- Storing a foreign key or an object identifier requires some mechanism for generating these values, and since in the Prolog world these values are not required it becomes the task of the database system to do so. It is questionable whether the database will be able to figure out whether it is attempting to create a new object identifier for a tuple which it has seen already before: duplicate removal becomes a far more serious issue, like it is in the world of Object Orientation.
- Inventing a domain containing the entities which can become property is nontrivial since property can both be unstructured and structured. In Prolog this is no problem since Prolog is an untyped language.

In 1986 S.J.C. Elbers, a student in Mathematics at the University of Amsterdam, was given the assignment for his master thesis to construct at IBM Uithoorn an extension of the prototype of our Prolog-BS12 interface which would incorporate terms [15]. We knew that the first problem would be easy to solve given the fact that BS12 in its internal structure generates object identifiers (called *pseudokeys*) for all tuples anyhow. It was just a matter of making these pseudokeys available to the user of the system. The developers at IBM at that time turned out to be willing to design the required patch on its system for the purpose of our project (keeping in mind that it might be of use for themselves as well....)

The second problem was solved by systematically replacing columns by a collection of three columns, thus supporting the choice between an atomic value or an object identifier for all attributes. For atomic values the first column stores the value and the remaining two obtain a default value. For object identifiers the first column is a default value and the second and third column contain a table reference and a pseudokey value for that table respectively.

With this expansion of tables it turned out to be possible to extend our compiler in such a way that nonrecursive terms could be dealt with resulting in queries which provided the right answer. However we stumbled on yet another problem, this time having to do with Prolog itself.

Prolog, in its syntax hardly discriminates between functions and predicates. In the above example we might add a fact expressed by book(Vergil,Aeneas). This would be stored as an entry in the BOOK table as well. But a subsequent query for the existing books: ?-book(X,Y) would now return the result consisting of the Aeneas only. Due to the fact that the Ilias is mentioned only as a term unification with the predicate would fail for the Ilias. Evidently in our database table storing books this distinction would be lost.

In order to preserve this (counterintuitive?) behavior of the Prolog system Elbers had to divide each relation in the database into two sections, one corresponding to the predicate information and another representing the so-called *argument information*.

The resulting system became rather complicated, but it worked. Proving its correctness became however hard. Elbers has argued for its correctness by modeling his database design into Prolog yielding a *Flat Prolog* version of a given program. Next one could show that the Flat Prolog version of the program returns always the same answers as the original one. Subsequently, showing that the compiler preserves the meaning of the flat prolog program was not hard.

In this extension recursive terms were disallowed; they could give rise to cyclic structures which would force the database system into an infinite loop if traversed.

3.3 Constraints and Elimination: the RL-Project

Having numerical attributes in a database creates the wish to compute on such numerical values. Standard databases provide a restricted support for doing so.

On the one hand there are simple *calculate* operations where a new numeric attribute value is added to each tuple in a relation according to an explicitly specified formula (as implemented by the CALCULATE operator in BS12). The calculate operator doesn't belong to the core of relational algebra as required for relational completeness. It is unclear whether relations extended by a calculate can be subjected to further algebraic operations. For example: is it permitted for a user to perform a select on a attribute value which is computed to be the sum of two others?

On the other hand one has so-called *aggregate operators* where a table is grouped on the base of one attribute values and for each resulting group some other attribute is summed up to a total. The collection of aggregation operators which may be invoked is fixed and depends on the database system selected: *summation, maximum, minimum, counting* and sometimes logic operations like *exists* and *forall*. These operators don't belong to relational algebra and are in general not expressible in first order logic. The main reason for aggregates to exist in systems is that they are needed in practical applications like generating reports for companies. Needless to state that in most systems the user is not able to define his own aggregate operators (Stonebraker's Illustra being a notable exception).

As far as support for computations is offered it lacks one feature which is essential for databases: *reversibility*. When designing a database scheme one doesn't yet know what sort of queries will be submitted to the database. The selection which attributes will be submitted as input values in a query and which attributes will be asked for output is made when the query is submitted, and at that time the system will have to invent a navigation strategy through the available tables in order to generate the answers.

However, a calculate instruction is always understood to be evaluated in the direction given by the definition. Most systems lack the intelligence needed to infer that given attributes A,B,C, where C is calculated by C = A + B, the output value of B can be obtained from the input values of A,C by rewriting the calculate into B = C - A.

A more complicated situation involves systems: given the calculate instructions C = A + B and D = A - B, our knowledge on elementary mathematics learns us that we can compute the values of A,B from those of C,D, but we need a symbolic equation solver in order that some system can discover this fact.

In Prolog the situation is about as bad. The build-in predicate sum(A,B,C) only can be invoked to obtain a binding for C once bindings for A and B have been given. Symbolic equation solving is out of question.

Nowadays there exist extensions of logic programming which provide this additional functionality (the field of *Constraint Logic Programming*), but around 1986 not much work had been done. Moreover, the research done aimed at extending Logic Programming with constraint capabilities, and not to bring constraints within the scope of database technology. Yet such systems would be of great value for applications describing a physical system like an electronic circuit, a business application computing the impacts of various tax regulations, or a physiological model describing the blood circulation in a human body. In such models there are far more quantities in the model than actually will be stored in a table of data. Some quantities are fixed *constants* which preferably are written symbolically, some indeed are *observable* and *known*, some are *unknown* but *wanted*, and there are values which are unobservable, unknown and unwanted which simply arise as *intermediate* values in the equational model.

Full declarative reversibility means in this context that one describes the model by giving the system of equations, and submitting the information about the partition in known, wanted and intermediate variables at a later stage. The system must invent an evaluation strategy to compute the wanted variables from the known ones, eliminating the intermediate ones during the process.

In 1985 the second author held a visiting scientist position for eight months at IBM San Jose, as a member of a research group on Office Automation chaired by Peter Lucas. The aim was to establish a repository for business rules, to be accessed by multiple application programs, similar to the way a Database stores raw data. Business rules were to be understood to involve primarily algebraic numeric constraints (Austrian Social Security regulations being a prototype example). It became the author's task to invent a language for expressing contents of the repository. The resulting proposal for a language called **RL** appeared in [18]. This report presents a syntax for rules, and a semantic model for their meaning. The model was highly influenced by our experience from the Prolog/BS12 interface.

Rules could be given in three formats: *Tabular rules* correspond to relational database expressions (view definitions); *Clauses* correspond to Horn-clauses in Datalog and *Constraints* represent the algebraic constraints on symbolic attributes. Both Syntax and Semantics are based on the principle *Everything is a relation but not all relations are equal*. For example both tabulars and clauses describe named relations whereas the constraints describe an unnamed "world" relation. Tabulars are given as a program-wide global definition, whereas new clauses for an existing predicate can be given. Adding a clause behaves semantically as a union, whereas adding a constraint behaves as an intersection.

Reception of the proposed language was negative. Implementation of the ideas was expected to require at least three years. No activities in that direction took place at IBM. In fact the Office Automation project was killed several months after we left IBM. Still the RL project was revived at the University of Amsterdam. For his master thesis in Computer Science S.J. van Denneheuvel had written a symbolic equation solver in Prolog, to be used in some entirely unrelated project. Learning about **RL** he became interested in actually implementing it, and his equation solver turned out to be exactly the ingredient needed to do so. Construction of a small prototype with the intended functionality required only a few months. A more extended implementation and the related theory became the topic of van Denneheuvels ph.d. thesis. Papers describing the language, its implementation and an example of its use in a medical model are [10, 11, 23].

It is relevant to observe that this system once more is *compilation based*. A query in **RL** is analyzed by the symbolic equation solver, and subsequently translated into a select-join-calculate-project expression which can be submitted to a database system. BS12 would have been an ideal system to serve as a database back-end, but by the time the project arrived at this point, IBM in the Netherlands had lost all interest in experimenting with BS12 (the official policy at this time was to retire BS12 as soon as possible...)

After completing his thesis van Denneheuvel build a front-end to his system which compiled **RL/1** to SQL. This tool turned out to be useful even in the case no constraints were used, since the **RL/1** code for a database application is far more compact than its SQL equivalent. The language was used as a rapid prototyping tool in the early stage of a major development project of Syllogic, a high tech software corporation in the Netherlands[7]. Its awesome performance made the system useless for real applications in practice.

The last **RL** related project involves an Object Oriented extension called **OORL** which has been investigated in the years 1994–1997 by dr. E. Rotterdam as a postdoc at the University of Amsterdam. The report [24] describing this language which offers a declarative window on the inherently imperative world of Objects has not yet been finalized.

Conclusion

The projects we were involved with in the period 1983 until 1997 have proven that a compilation based approach to deductive databases is, in theory, possible. We never got to the point to determine whether the approach would yield acceptable performance for real life applications; this would require far more investments than we were able and motivated to spend. We also discovered that, starting from the clean mathematical model for the intended semantics, functionality from areas beyond datalog could be added, preserving a reasonable amount of transparency of the languages used.

These projects were made possible by circumstances which allowed to disregard the pressure to follow the main stream approaches investigated elsewhere.

---

[7] now a wholly owned subsidiary of Perot Systems

Moreover we found in BS12, a system which had been developed under a similar climate of independence, an ideal tool to perform experiments with our ideas.

References

1. de Bakker, J.W., *Mathematical theory of program correctness*, Prentice Hall, 1980.
2. Business System 12 Reference Manual, pre-release copy, IBM DCS-SC, Uithoorn, June 1983.
3. Chang, C-L., Lee, R. C-T., *Symbolic logic and mechanical theorem proving*, Academic Press, 1973.
4. Chen, P.P., *The entity-relationship model: toward a unified view of data*, ACM Trans. on Database Systems, 1(1), 1976, 9–36.
5. Codd, E.F., *Extending the data base relational model to capture more meaning*, ACM Trans. on Database Systems, 4(4), 1979, 397–434.
6. Colmerauer, A., Roussel, P., *The birth of Prolog*, in Bergin, T.J. jr., Gibson, R.G. jr., eds., History of Programming Languages - II, ACM Press, 1996,pp. 331–367.
7. du Croix, A.J., *Concurrency Considerations of Business System 12*, proc NGI-SION 1985 Informatica Symposium, NGI, Amsterdam, April 1985, pp. 501–509.
8. Date, C.J., *An introduction to Database Systems*, sixth edition, Addison Wesley, 1995.
9. van Denneheuvel, S., *Constraint solving on database systems; Design and implementation of the rule language RL/1*, ph.d. thesis, univ. of Amsterdam, Oct 29 1991.
10. van Denneheuvel, S., van Emde Boas, P., *The rule language RL/1*, in Tjoa, A.M., Wagner, R., eds., Database and Expert system applications, Proc. DEXA 1, Vienna, Aug, 1990, Springer Wien, 1990, 381–387.
11. van Denneheuvel, S., Kwast, K.L., van Emde Boas, P., de Geus, F, Rotterdam, E., *Symbolic computation in RL/1*, proc. DEXA'91, Berlin Aug. 1991, Springer Wien,1991, 559–564.
12. Doedens, C.F.J., *Logic Programming and Business System 12*, rep. TR 13.198 IBM INS-DC Uithoorn, Dec 1984; this document constitutes also the author's Master thesis in Computer Science at the Univ. of Amsterdam.
13. Doedens, C.F.J., *Logic Programming with a relational data base management system*, proc NGI-SION 1985 Informatica Symposium, NGI, Amsterdam, April 1985, pp. 485–500.
14. Doets, K., *From Logic to Logic Programming*, Foundations of Computing Series, the MIT press, 1994.
15. Elbers, S.J.C., *De compilatie van willekeurige Prolog structuren in een relationele database*, rep. IBM INS-DC TR 13.206, Jun 1986; (in Dutch); this document constitutes also the author's Master thesis in Mathematics at the Univ. of Amsterdam (rep. FVI-UvA-86-14)
16. van Emde Boas, H. , *Feature Analysis of Business System 12*, INS-DC IBM Uithoorn; unpublished internal memorandum, Oct 04 1984. (Facsimile edition: rep. ILLC-X-1998-01).
17. H. van Emde Boas-Lubsen, P. van Emde Boas *Logic programming in a relational database query language (working document)* in M.L. Kersten ed., Proc. Workshop Coupling PROLOG with Database management systems, VUA Jan 1984 Amsterdam, pp. 11–17

18. van Emde Boas, P. *RL, a language for enhanced rule bases database processing*, working document, rep. IBM research, RJ 4869 (51299), 1986

19. van Emde Boas, P., *A semantical model for the integration and modularization of rules*, proc. MFCS 12, Bratislava, Springer LNCS 233, 1986, 78–92.

20. van Emde Boas, H. , van Emde Boas, P., *Storing and evaluating Horn-clause rules in a relational database*, IBM J. of Research and Development, 30(1), 1986, 80–92

21. van Emde Boas, H. , van Emde Boas, P., Doedens, C.F.J., *Extending a relational database with logic programming facilities*, Rep. IBM, INS-DC Tr 13.195, Oct 1984

22. Feigenbaum, E.A., McCorduck, P., , *The Fifth Generation; artificial Intelligence and Japan's Computer Challenge to the World*, Addison Wesley, 1983.

23. de Geus, F., Rotterdam, E., *Decision Support in Anaesthesia*, ph.d. thesis Univ. of Groningen, Dec 02 1992.

24. Rotterdam, E., *OORL, a relational and Object Oriented Database Language*, in preparation

25. Schmidt, J.W. , Brodie, M.L., eds., *Relational Database Systems; analysis and comparison*, Springer 1983

26. Stonebraker, M., *Object-Relational DBMSs; the next great wave*, Morgan Kaufmann, 1996.

27. Ullman, J.D., *Principles of Database and Knowledge-base systems*, vol 1, Computer Science Press, 1988.

28. Ullman, J.D., *Principles of Database and Knowledge-base systems*, vol 2, Computer Science Press, 1989.

29. Warden A., *Adventures in Relationland*, in Date C.J., Relational database writings 1985-1989, Addison Wesley 1990, pp. 453–521.

Models of Computation, Riemann Hypothesis, and Classical Mathematics*

Rūsiņš Freivalds **

Abstract. Classical mathematics is a source of ideas used by Computer Science since the very first days. Surprisingly, there is still much to be found. Computer scientists, especially, those in Theoretical Computer Science find inspiring ideas both in old notions and results, and in the 20th century mathematics. The latest decades have brought us evidence that computer people will soon study quantum physics and modern biology just to understand what computers are doing.

1 Introduction

Twenty years ago graduates of my University used to say: "Why we were taught calculus and algebra? They are not at all needed in programmer's work." Of course, this saying characterized their jobplaces more than the profession. The main goal of my today's talk is to show that contemporary Computer Science needs very much of knowledge which is not considered as Computer Science. I might mention Quantum Physics, Biology but I will concentrate mainly on Classical Mathematics. I will try to show that Classical Mathematics has much to say to Computer Scientists. I even risk to predict that the next generation of Computer Science students will learn much more Classical Mathematics rather that the students now in the University.

My talk consists of several stories connected only in one way. All these stories show that Classical Mathematics has much to offer to us. Mostly, this is a survey of known results. However Theorem 32 seems to be new.

2 Models of Computation

Can we presume that human brain is purely deterministic? Perhaps, not. Indeed, assume from the contrary that it is. In this case the following paradox of responsibility arises. If I do something wrong, what can I be responsible for? All my reactions have been genetically preprogrammed in my organism, and nothing depends on me. However, if somebody believes I am still responsible for something, then this person assumes there is more in my brain but simple deterministic reactions to the environment.

* Research supported by Grant No.96.0282 from the Latvian Council of Science
** Department of Computer Science, University of Latvia, Raiņa bulv. 29, Riga, Latvia

Theoretical Computer Science has long ago developed a system of notions generalizing determinism. *Nondeterministic* and *probabilistic* algorithms were the first generalizations.

Nondeterministic machines constitute an important part of the Theory of Computation. However nondeterminism does not give and it is not able to give any mechanism of how to perform choices.

Probabilistic algorithms were first used during WWII for simulation and numerical analysis. Probabilistic Turing machines were introduced by de Leeuw et al. in [28]. The main result in this paper shows that every function computed by a probabilistic machine can be computed by a deterministic machine as well. This result seems to have a devastating effect on our discussion about the nature of human brain. If human brain can be considered as a computing device with unresricted computational resources, then by [28] a probabilistic brain can compute no more functions than a deterministic one, and our consideration of the brain as a probabilistic device does not help us to solve the responsibility problem. The probabilistic brain also cannot be responsible for anything because the reactions however probabilistic are nonetheless genetically preprogrammed.

M. Rabin [34] introduced probabilistic 1-way finite automata. They can be described by *stochastic matrices* $A(i)$ of size $n \times n$ corresponding to every letter in the input alphabet(where n is the number of the states of the finite automaton), a *stochastic column-vector* ξ (being the probability distribution among the states in the starting moment) and a 0-1 row-vector χ (being the description which states are accepting and which states are rejecting). By $A(x)$ we denote the product of the matrices $A(i_s)\ldots A(i_2)A(i_1)$ where $i_1, i_2, \ldots i_s$ are the symbols in the word x. The input word x is accepted if and only if

$$\chi A \xi > \frac{1}{2}.$$

M. Rabin [34] considered seperately the case of *bounded away probabilities* (he called this case *isolated cut-point*) when there is a positive number δ such that for arbitrary input word x either

$$\chi A \xi > \frac{1}{2} + \delta$$

or

$$\chi A \xi < \frac{1}{2} - \delta$$

and proved that 1-pfa with a probability bounded away from $\frac{1}{2}$ can recognize only regular languages, i.e. the same languages recognized by 1-way deterministic finite automata. If human brain can be considered as a computing device with maximally restricted computational resources (a 1-way finite automaton), then the same conclusion is obtained by M. Rabin's result [34].

There has been much work done to find where the advantages of probabilistic algorithms over deterministic ones lie. R. Freivalds [14] proved that palindromes can be recognized by a single-tape probabilistic Turing machine in time $n \log n$ while every deterministic machine of this type needs $\Omega(n)$ time to recognize palindromes. After the famous probabilistic algorithms for primality testing by R. Solovay and V. Strassen [38] the topic of probabilistic algorithms became increasingly popular. This caused increasing interest in comparison of capabilities of probabilistic, deterministic, nondeterministic machines as well. R. Freivalds [15] proved that probabilistic 1-way multitape and multihead finite automata can recognize languages non-recognizable by deterministic or nondeterministic automata of these types. Similar advantages of probabilistic automata and machines over their deterministic counterparts were proved in [15–18] for 2-way finite automata, 1-way counter, pushdown automata, and 1-way Turing machines with limitations on running time, space, reversals, etc. However the comparison of capabilities of probabilistic versus other types of machines is strongly limited by the well-known difficulty to prove good lower bounds for complexity of concrete (non-diagonal) languages. For instance, we know that probabilistic multitape Turing machines with arbitrary number of work-tapes can recognize in time $2n$ languages not recognizable in time n [20] but, on the other hand, we are not able to separate any running time less than $n^{\log n}$ from time $2n$ for the same class of machines in spite of highly sophisticated techniques used [26].

Recently a new type of algorithms has appeared, namely, *quantum* algorithms. Nobel prize winner physicist Richard Feynman asked in [12] what effects can have the principles of quantum mechanics, especially, the *principle of superposition* on computation. He gave arguments showing that it might be computationally expensive to simulate quantum mechanics on classical computers. This observation immediately leads to a conjecture predicting enormous advatages to quantum computers versus classical ones. R. Feynman left open even the crucial question whether or not quantum computers can compute any functions non-computable by classical (deterministic) computers. P. Benioff [6] gave early arguments on Feynman's problem, and later D. Deutsch [11] introduced the commonly used notion of the quantum Turing machine and proved that quantum Turing machines compute exactly the same recursive functions as ordinary deterministic Turing machines do.

Quantization has been introduced by Max Planck in 1900 [33]. Planck assumed a *discretization* of energy. That was a bold step in a time of the predominant continuum models of classical mechanics.

Mathematicaly all quantum mechanical entities are represented by objects of Hilbert spaces. A *Hilbert space* is a linear vector space over the field of complex numbers (with vector addition and scalar multiplication), together with a complex function for the scalar product. It seems that there have never been satisfactory explanations why complex numbers are used (but not, say, quaterions or more exotic number fields). The simplest explanation might be that physicists have developed such a theory, and it works, while theories based on real numbers only do not explain all the experiments.

Quantum mechanics differs from the classical physics very much. It suffices to mention *Heisenberg's uncertainty principle* asserting that one cannot measure both the position and the impulse of a particle simultaneously precisely. There is a certain trade-off between the accuracy of the two measurements. Another well-known distinction of quantum mechanics from the classical physics is the impossibility to measure any object without changing the object.

The fundamental atom of information is the quantum bit, henceforth abbreviated by the term 'qbit'.

Classical information theory is based on the classical bit as fundamental atom. This classical bit, henceforth called *cbit*, is in one of two classical states t (often interpreted as "true") and f (often interpreted as "false"). In quantum information theory the most elementary unit of information is the *quantum bit*, henceforth called *qbit*. To explain it, we first discuss a *probabilistic* counterpart of the classical bit, which we call here *pbit*. It can be t with a probability α and f with probability β, where $\alpha + \beta = 1$. A *qbit* is very much like to *pbit* with the following distinction. For a *qbit* α and β are not real but complex numbers with the property $\|\alpha\|^2 + \|\beta\|^2 = 1$.

Every computation done on qbits is performed by means of unitary operators. One of the simplest properties of these operators shows that such a computation is reversible. The result always determines the input uniquely. It may seem to be a very strong limitation for such computations. Luckily this is not so. It is possible to embed any irreversible computation in an appropriate environment which makes it reversible. For instance, the computing agent could keep the inputs of previous calculations in successive order.

The following features of quantum computers are important (but far from the only characteristic features of them).

- Input, output, program and memory are represented by qbits.
- Any computation (step) can be represented by a unitary transformation of the computer as a whole.
- Any computation is reversible. Because of the unitarity of the quantum evolution operator, a deterministic computation can be performed by a quantum computer if and only if it is reversible.
- No qbit can be copied. After the qbit is processed, the original form of it is no more available.
- Measurements may be carried out on any qbit at any stage of the computation. However any measurement destroys the information. More precisely, the measurement turns a qbit into a classical bit with probabilities dependent on the qbit.
- Quantum parallelism: during a computation (step), a quantum computer proceeds down all coherent paths at once. If managed properly, this may give rise to speedups.

Quantum finite automata were introduced twice. First this was done by C. Moore and J.P.Crutchfield [32]. Later in a different and non-equivalent way these automata were introduced by A. Kondacs and J. Watrous [27].

The first definition just mimics the definition of 1-way finite probabilistic only substituting *stochastic* matrices by *unitary* ones. Since now complex numbers are involved, multiplication to the row matrix χ is substituted by a non-linear operation "squaring modulos of the amplitudes corresponding to the accepting states and totaling these real numbers" denoted below by $B_\chi()$. The definition is as follows. 1-way quantum finite automata can be described by a *unitary matrix* A of size $n \times n$ (in the case of automata with n states) and a *complex column-vector* ξ (being the amplitude distribution among the states in the starting moment) and a 0-1 row-vector χ (being the description which states are accepting and which states are rejecting). The input word x is accepted if and only if

$$B_\chi(A\xi) > \frac{1}{2}.$$

The second definition is a bit more complicated. The states of the automaton are divided into *halting* and *non-halting* ones. The transition to a new state is made exactly as prescribed by the first definition but if the automaton reaches a halting state, the final measurement is made immediately.

The relation between capabilities of quantum and other finite automata is not yet completely described. 1-way quantum finite automata recognize only regular languages (hence they cannot do more than deterministic automata) but the quantum automata cannot recognize all the regular languages. For instance, the language $\{0,1\}^*1$ is not recognizable by any 1-way quantum finite automaton [27]. On the other hand, for some languages quantum automata can have much less complexity. It is proved by A. Ambainis and R. Freivalds [2] that, for arbitrary prime number p, there is a quantum 1-way finite automaton with $O(\log p)$ states recognizing the language "the length of the input word is a multiple of p " with a bounded probability of success while every deterministic and even probabilistic 1-way finite automaton needs p states.

It is well-known that if a language can be recognized by a probabilistic finite automaton with a probability $\frac{2}{3}$ (or any other number strictly exceeding $\frac{1}{2}$), then for arbitrary $\epsilon > 0$ the same language can be recognized with a probability $1 - \epsilon$. For quantum finite automata it is not so. A. Ambainis and R. Freivalds [2] show an example of a language which can be recognized by a QFA with a probability 0.65 but which cannot be recognized with a probability exceeding 0.9. The key-word used in these proofs most often is *Fourier transform*.

Quantum automata might remain a lesser known unusual modification of the standard definitions but two events caused a drastical change. First, P. Shor invented surprising polynomial-time quantum algorithms for computation of discrete logarithms and for factorization of integers [37]. Second, joint research of physicists and computer people have led to a dramatic breakthrough: all the unusual quantum circuits having no classical counterparts (such as *quantum bit teleportation*) have been physically implemented. Hence universal quantum computers are to come soon. Moreover, since the modern public-key cryptography is based on intractability of discrete logarithms and factorization of integers, building a quantum computer implies building a code-breaking machine.

The above-mentioned features of quantum computers seem unusual and hence one may think that their advent is highly unlikely. On the other hand, in the recent years physicists have performed series of crucial experiments showing that that all the basical elements needed for quantum computers can be indeed implemented. A quantum computer with 1 qbit memory has been built in IBM

Almaden Research center and a quantum computer with 4 qbits memory has been built in Los Alamos National Laboratory.

Another most unusual computation device has emerged quite recently. L. Adleman [1] succeeded in solving of the directed Hamiltonian path problem solely by manipulating DNA strings. DNA (deoxyribonucleic acid) is perhaps the most popular of the molecules in organic chemistry. DNA is responsible for keeping and transmitting the genetic information. Adleman's algorithm solves an NP-complete problem. Later papers on molecular computing mostly consider the possibility to build universal computers for NP-hard problems. Unfortunately (for our purposes) little is done to introduce notions for molecular computation on a lower level (finite automata, pushdown machines, etc.)

Any way, the recent decade has been rich in proposing mathematical notions for generalizations of deterministic computation devices. All these devices rely on unusually rich "built-in" parallelism. On the other hand, we still do not see a complete answer on what might be the adequate matematical model to describe behavior of human brain. This is a problem not only for physiologists, and first of all, this problem is not so much for them. Computer scientists can say rather much *what type of mechanism could possibly be in our brain to make the choices.* The models of computation existing now, most probably, are not the adequate ones. But which ones are?

3   Riemann Hypothesis and Complexity of Computation

Generating functions is an invention puzzling beginners very much. The unusuality of this notion is based mainly on the feeling that you "multiply miles by miles and get kilograms".

We consider an example showing the main idea of generating functions as they were introduced by Abraham de Moivre (1667 - 1754).

Definition 31 *Suppose that a random variable takes values*

$$
\begin{cases}
X_1, prob = p_1 \\
X_2, prob = p_2 \\
\quad \ldots \\
X_s, prob = p_s
\end{cases}
$$

The function

$$
\sum_{i=1}^{s} p_i t^{X_i}
$$

is called the **generating function** *of this random variable.*

Example. A dice can produce values 1,2,3,4,5,6 with probability $\frac{1}{6}$, respectively. Calculate the probability of the event "the total of results of two dices equals a."

In our example the generating function is

$$\frac{1}{6}(t^1 + t^2 + t^3 + t^4 + t^5 + t^6).$$

Squaring this, we obtain

$$\frac{1}{36}t^2 + \frac{2}{36}t^3 + \frac{3}{36}t^4 + \frac{4}{36}t^5 + \frac{5}{36}t^6 + \frac{6}{36}t^7 +$$

$$+\frac{5}{36}t^8 + \frac{4}{36}t^9 + \frac{3}{36}t^{10} + \frac{2}{36}t^{11} + \frac{1}{36}t^{12}.$$

It remains to find the coefficient of t^a. For instance, if $a = 5$, then the result is $\frac{4}{36}$.

The reader can check that the result is indeed correct. On the other hand, there is no sense to ask whether the variable t is real, complex or some other. This is a *formal variable* denoting merely the places where the corresponding numbers (the coefficients) can be found.

Generating functions used by de Moivre contained only a finite number of terms in these polynomials. Leonhard Euler (1707 - 1783) made the technique of generating functions to be a powerful tool to obtain complicated combinatorial results. In de Moivre's example we used multiplication of the generating functions. Euler's functions were represented by infinite power series (not merely by polynomials) and the operations used included even taking a derivative.

Next step in development of the generating functions was made by Johann Peter Gustav Lejeune Dirichlet (1805 - 1859). He used more complicated infinite series as the "place-holders" for the coefficients, namely *Dirichlet series*.

A Dirichlet series is

$$F(s) = \sum_{n=1}^{\infty} \frac{\alpha_n}{n^s},$$

where s can be a real or complex number. Following Euler, we consider the case of real values for s. $F(s)$ can be considered the generating function for the sequence $\{\alpha_n\}$.

However this is a more complicated object rather than the power series, the properties of Dirichlet series are rather similar.

(1) If $\sum \alpha_n n^{-s}$ a converges absolutely for an s, then it converges absolutely for every $s > s_0$.

(2) If $\sum \alpha_n n^{-s}$ converges absolutely for a $s > s_0$, then the derivative of

$$F(s) = \sum_{n=1}^{\infty} \frac{\alpha_n}{n^s},$$

can be calculated term-wise

$$F'(s) = \sum_{n=1}^{\infty} \frac{\alpha_n \log n}{n^s},$$

(3) If $F(s) = \sum \alpha_n n^{-s} = 0$ for $s > s_0$, then $\alpha_n = 0$ for all n.

(4) Absolutely converging Dirichlet series can be multiplied term-wise. The simplest Dirichlet series is the one defining Riemann zeta-function

$$\zeta(s) = \sum_{n=1}^{\infty} \frac{1}{n^s}.$$

corresponding to the sequence $\alpha_n = 1$. It converges for $s > 1$.

$$\zeta(2) = \sum_{n=1}^{\infty} \frac{1}{n^2} = \frac{\pi^2}{6}$$

$$\zeta(4) = \sum_{n=1}^{\infty} \frac{1}{n^4} = \frac{\pi^4}{90}$$

$$\zeta(2n) = \frac{2^{2n-1}B_n}{(2n)!}\pi^{2n},$$

where B_n is the Bernoulli number (L.Euler).

$$\frac{x}{e^x - 1} = \sum_{n=0}^{\infty} \frac{B_n x^n}{n!}.$$

The first Bernoulli numbers are

$B_0 = 1,$ $B_1 = -\frac{1}{2},$
$B_2 = \frac{1}{6},$ $B_3 = 0,$
$B_4 = -\frac{1}{30},$ $B_5 = 0,$
$B_6 = \frac{1}{42},$ $B_7 = 0,$
$B_8 = -\frac{1}{30},$ $B_9 = 0.$

Since the odd Bernoulli numbers equal 0, the corresponding values of the ζ-function also equal 0. These are called the *trivial roots* of the ζ-function. Below we will see other roots called *nontrivial roots* discussed.

Theorem 31 (L. Euler) *If $s > 1$, then*

$$\zeta(s) = \prod_{p} \frac{1}{1 - p^{-s}}.$$

Dirichlet used this technique to prove that arbitrary non-degenerated arithmetical progression contains infinetely many prime numbers.

Georg Friedrich Bernhard Riemann (1826 - 1866) was a mathematician who influenced the 19th century mathematics no less than any other his contemporary.

Riemann's doctoral dissertation was on the functions of a complex variable. This is why he along Augustin-Louis Cauchy (1789 - 1857) is considered as the father of the modern theory of the functions of a complex variable.

On June 10, 1854 B. Riemann delivered his academic lecture "**On hypotheses underlying geometry**" to get employment at Götingen University. This is the talk and this is the paper where Riemann geometry is described for the first time. The position he seeked for was not that of a full professor. It was a position of a "Dozent" corresponding to the position of an Associated Professor nowadays.

In 1859 B. Riemann was elected to become a member of the Berlin Academy of Science. According the Rules, the newly elected member was to present a short report on his scientific activities. B. Riemann presented a 8 page report "**On the number of primes less than a given magnitude**". Here he considered the function ζ introduced by L. Euler (above) as a function of a complex variable. Unfortunately, the function

$$\zeta(s) = \sum_{n=1}^{\infty} \frac{1}{n^s}$$

is defined not on all the complex plane but for $Res > 1$ only.

The complex variable allows new operations over the generating functions, among them being *Analitical Continuation* (allowing every analitical function defined on a non-trivial domain to be continued in a unique way to the whole complex plane), *Fourier transform* and its inverse:

If $f \in L_1$ and

$$g(\omega) = \int_{-\infty}^{\infty} f(t)e^{i\omega t}\, dt,$$

then the function $g(\omega)$ is uniformly continuous and bounded for $-\infty < \omega < \infty$ with $g(\omega) \to 0$ at $|\omega| \to \infty$.

If $g \in L_1$, then almost everywhere

$$f(t) = \frac{1}{2\pi} \int_{-\infty}^{\infty} g(\omega)e^{-i\omega t}\, d\omega.$$

The ζ function is the generating function for a rather simple sequence $1, 1, 1, \ldots$ However it can be used to construct generating functions for much more complicated sequences related to well-known notions in Number Theory.

$$\zeta^2(s) = \sum_{n=1}^{\infty} \frac{d(n)}{n^s}(s > 1)$$

where $d(n)$ is the number of divisors of the number n, including 1 and n.

$$\zeta(s)\zeta(s-1) = \sum_{n=1}^{\infty} \frac{\sigma(n)}{n^s}(s > 1)$$

where $\sigma(n)$ is the sum of all the divisors of the number n, including 1 un n.

$$\frac{1}{\zeta(s)} = \sum_{n=1}^{\infty} \frac{\mu(n)}{n^s} (s > 1)$$

where $\mu(n)$ is the Möbius function

$$\mu(n) = \begin{cases} 1 & \text{, if } n = 1; \\ (-1)^k & \text{, if } n = p_1 p_2 \ldots p_k \\ & \text{, where } p_1, p_2, \ldots, p_k \text{ are pairwise} \\ & \text{distinct prime numbers;} \\ 0 & \text{, if } n \text{ is divided by a perfect square.} \end{cases} \Big\}$$

$$\zeta(s)\zeta(s - k) = \sum_{n=1}^{\infty} \frac{\sigma_k(n)}{n^s} (s > 1).$$

Here $\sigma_k(n)$ is the sum of all the k-th degrees of the divisors of n.

$$-\frac{\zeta'(s)}{\zeta(s)} = \sum_{n=1}^{\infty} \frac{\Lambda(n)}{n^s} (s > 1)$$

where $\Lambda(n)$ is the von Mangoldt function.

$$\Lambda(n) = \begin{cases} \log n & \text{, if } n = p^m; \\ 0 & \text{, if } n \text{ is not a number } p^m. \end{cases} \Big\}$$

Euler had noticed that

$$n! = \int_0^{\infty} e^{-x} x^n dx (n = 1, 2, 3, \ldots).$$

This allowed to introduce the Γ-function

$$\Gamma(s + 1) = \int_0^{\infty} e^{-x} x^n dx (s > -1).$$

Riemann analytically continues the ζ-function

$$\zeta(s) = \frac{\Gamma(-s + 1)}{2\pi i} \oint_{+\infty}^{+\infty} \frac{(-x)^s}{e^x - 1} \frac{dx}{x}$$

where the integration contour is the positive real semi-axis. Now the function is analytical everywhere but a simple pole at $s = 1$.

The reader should notice the *genre* of Riemann's paper. This is not a journal paper. Rather this is a bureaucratic report to the chiefs. No wonder that it is not easy to distinguish between correctly proved statements and plausible conjectures.

Riemann **proves** that

$$\zeta(s) = \Gamma(-s+1)(2\pi)^{s-1}2\sin(\frac{s\pi}{2})\zeta(1-s).$$

By a substitution of the variable and multiplication to $\frac{s(s-1)}{2}$ Riemann obtains an **entire** function, i.e. a function without singular points

$$\xi(s) = \Gamma(\frac{s}{2}+1)(s-1)\pi^{-\frac{1}{2}}\zeta(s)$$

and proves that

$$\xi(s) = \xi(1-s).$$

Riemann **proves** that all the roots ρ of ξ are on the strip $0 \le Re\rho \le 1$ and **asserts** that the number of roots ρ with $0 \le Im\rho \le T$ is about

$$\frac{T}{2\pi}\log\frac{T}{2\pi} - \frac{T}{2\pi}$$

and the relative error is of the magnitude $\frac{1}{T}$.

This was proved by von Mangoldt only in 1905.

Next Riemann **asserts** that the number of roots with the real part $\frac{1}{2}$ and the imaginary part between 0 and T is about

$$\frac{T}{2\pi}\log\frac{T}{2\pi} - \frac{T}{2\pi}.$$

This is not proven even today.

Riemann **proves** that

$$\frac{\log\zeta(s)}{s} = \int_0^\infty J(x)x^{-s-1}dx(Res > 1)$$

where $J(x)$ starts at) for $x = 0$ and grows in jumps 1 for prime numbers, in jumps $\frac{1}{2}$ for squares of primes, etc.

By inverse Fourier transform Riemann obtains

$$J(x) = \frac{1}{2\pi i}\int_{a-i\infty}^{a+i\infty} \log\zeta(s)x^s\frac{ds}{s}(a > 1).$$

Since

$$J(x) = \pi(x) + \frac{1}{2}\pi(x^{\frac{1}{2}}) + \frac{1}{3}\pi(x^{\frac{1}{3}}) + \dots,$$

Riemann finally concludes that

$$J(x) = Li(x) - \sum_\rho Li(x^\rho) - \log 2 + \int_x^\infty \frac{dt}{t(t^2-1)\log t}, (x > 1)$$

where the sum $\sum\limits_{\rho}$ is taken over **all the non-trivial roots ρ of ζ.**

These formulas link explicitly properties of the ζ-function (being a continuous object) with the properties of distribution of primes among natural numbers (being discrete objects). This was a most unusual discovery because before that every mathematician considered continuous and discrete objects being two worlds apart.

Riemann's intension was to prove a famous conjecture proposed independently by Carl Friedrich Gauss (1777 - 1855) and Adrien Marie Le Gendre (1752 - 1833) in the years 1792 or 1793 asserting that the number of primes among the first x natural numbers was

$$\pi(x) \approx \int\limits_{2}^{x} \frac{dx}{\ln x}.$$

Since B. Riemann died early (at the age of 40), not much progress (and even interest) was shown during nearly 30 years. Finally, the Paris Academy of Science announced a competition (1890-1892) on filling the gaps in Riemann's proof. The prize was given to Jacques Salomon Hadamard (1865 - 1963) but he did not solve the problem yet. He did so but that was later. In 1896 both he and Charles Jean de la Vallee-Poussin (1866 -1962) independently proved the Gauss-Legendre hypothesis on the number of primes in 1896. The crucial point was to prove that there are no roots of ζ on the line $1 + it$.

The prime number theorem is important for Number Theory and sometimes is cited in papers on Complexity Theory (for instance, in [16]). However for our story the most important is the following paragraph in B. Riemann's paper having no formal connection with his topic.

B. Riemann finds number of the roots of his auxiliary function $\xi(t)$ in a certain domain is indeed as large as needed for his proof and adds: "One finds in fact this many real roots within these bounds **and it is very likely that all of the roots are real**. One would of course like to have a rigorous proof of this, but I have put aside the search for such a proof after some fleeting vain attempts because it is not necessary for the immediate objective of my investigation."

This is the famous Riemann Hypothesis. Nowadays it is usually formulated as an assertion about the ζ-function itself. It is asserted that all the nontrivial roots of the ζ-function have the imaginary part $\frac{1}{2}$.

As it was described above, the ζ-function was introduced by L. Euler. However impact of B. Riemann on the study of this fuction was so profound that nowadays the function's "official" name is Riemann ζ-function. The function was generalized in various ways (Dirichlet L-functions (1837), Hecke L-functions (1917, 1918, 1920), E. Artin L-functions (1931), etc.) Counterparts to the Riemann Hypothesis also were constructed. Since they are generalizations of Riemann ζ-function, no wonder that the counterparts the Riemann Hypothesis are also not yet proved or disproved.

Riemann Hypothesis have turned out to be not merely a difficult open problem but also a deep assertion on fundamental properties of mathematical objects.

Computer scientists know that NP-complete problems can be found in all areas of mathematics. Some of them seem to be algebraic problems, some other problems seem to belong to differential equations. However we know that all they are reducible one to another. Hence essentially this is the same problem under different disguises. The same situation is with the Riemann Hypothesis. Equivalent formulations of this conjecture are found in very many areas of the classical mathematics. For instance, F. Roesler [36] has published a paper with the title "Riemann hypothesis as an eigenvalue problem" (followed by a series of similar nature papers by the same author). The author studies eigenvalues $\lambda_n (1 \leq n \leq N - 1)$ of the matrix $A_N = (a_{m,n})_{2 \leq m,n \leq N}$, where $a_{m,n} = m - 1$, if $m|n$ and -1 otherwise. It turns out that Riemann hypothesis is equivalent to $det A_N = O(N!N^{-\frac{1}{2}+\epsilon})$

Roesler's paper is only one of very many possible examples of this kind. Riemann Hypothesis has become a kind of a new axiom. A new area of mathematics has been started containing results based on the assumption that Riemann Hypothesis is true. Who knows, this new area can later be proved independent of the other axioms (like Continuum Hypothesis or Axiom of Choice have been proved independent).

However Roesler's example (and so many other examples not mentioned here) shows that Theoretical Computer Science can also be a possible area for such results dependent on Riemann Hypothesis.. At this moment so-called Extended Riemann Hypothesis (the counterpart of the Riemann Hypothesis for Dirichlet L-functions) has had much deeper influence on Theoretical Computer Science. Nobody knows whether this is just a temporary effect or something more deep.

Gary Miller [30] constructed a deterministic algorithm to recognize primality of natural numbers which runs in polynomial time and is correct if the Extended Riemann Hypothesis is. The algorithm is short and clear.

Given an odd N. Let $N - 1 = 2^s \times m$. We choose a base b and compute the following sequence:

$$\{b^m, b^{2m}, b^{4m}, \ldots, b^{N-1}\}.$$

If either all entries are $+1$ or some entry before the last is -1, then we say that the sequence is **of type 1**. otherwise the sequence is **of type 2.**

b^m	b^{2m}	b^{4m}						b^{N-1}	
+1	+1	+1	+1	+1	+1	+1	...	+1	$type1$
x	x	x	...	x	-1	+1	...	+1	$type1$
x	x	x	...	x	+1	+1	...	+1	$type2$
x	x	x	x	x	x	x	...	x	$type2$
x	x	x	x	x	x	x	...	-1	$type2$

Algorithm.
(1) For each b less than $2(\ln N)^2$:
(2) **IF** the b-sequence of the number N is of type 2,
PRINT "COMPOSITE"
(3) **ELSE PRINT "PRIME"**.

Extended Riemann Hypothesis is used for very many algorithms produced for needs of Computer Science [4, 8, 21–23].

Now we consider the most popular computation model in the Theory of Computation, namely, multi-tape Turing machines. We will show that complexity of language recognition by these machines is closely related to Number Theory and, specifically, to the Extended Riemann Hypothesis.

A Turing machine is said to be *strongly* $L(n)$ space-bounded if no computation on any input of length n , uses more than $L(n)$ space. It is said to be *weakly* $L(n)$ space-bounded if for every accepted input of length n, at least one accepting computation uses no more than $L(n)$ space. DSPACE (L) or NSPACE (L) denotes the class of languages accepted by deterministic or nondeterministic $L(n)$ space-bounded Turing machines, respectively.

Turing machines with sublogarithmic space differ sharply from those which have logarithmic or greater space. If the function $L(n)$ is not fully space constructible, it is possible that a language A is weakly $L(n)$ space recognizable while $\bar{A}$ is not. We concentrate on languages A such that A is weakly *loglog*-space recognizable and $\bar{A}$ is weakly *log*-space recognizable. We denote this complexity class by DSPACE (log log, log).

Specifically, we consider the language

$$\text{NONSQUARES} = \{1^n \mid (\neg \exists k)(n = k^2)\}.$$

The complement of this language PERFECT-SQUARES needs deterministic space $\Omega(\log n)$ but the problem whether or not the language NONSQUARES is weakly *loglog*-space recognizable turns out to be related to open problems in Number Theory.

By standard methods one can prove that

1) the two languages are in DSPACE(log),
2) NONSQUARES have weak space complexity $\Omega(\log \log n)$,
3) PERFECT-SQUARES have weak space complexity $\Omega(\log n)$.

Conjecture 1. The language NONSQUARES is weakly recognized by a deterministic Turing machine in space $\log \log n$.

Hence under this conjecture NONSQUARES is in DSPACE(log log, log). The second conjecture seems to be weaker.

Conjecture 2. The language NONSQUARES is weakly recognized by a nondeterministic Turing machine in space $\log \log n$.

However we see below that Conjectures 1 and 2 are equivalent.

Legendre symbol $\left(\frac{n}{p}\right)$ is defined for integers n, p such that p is an odd prime, and n is not a multiple of p.

$$\left(\frac{n}{p}\right) = \begin{cases} +1, & \text{if there is } x \text{ such that } x^2 \equiv n \pmod{p}, \\ -1, & \text{if there is no } x \text{ such that } x^2 \equiv n \pmod{p}. \end{cases}$$

Jacobi symbol $\left(\frac{n}{m}\right)$ is defined as a generalization of Legendre symbol for $m = p_1 \cdot p_2 \cdot \ldots \cdot p_s$ where $p_1, \ldots, p_s$ are primes (some of them can be equal):

$$\left(\frac{n}{m}\right) = \begin{cases} 0, & \text{if } (m,n) \neq 1, \\ \left(\frac{n}{p_1}\right) \cdot \left(\frac{n}{p_2}\right) \cdot \ldots \cdot \left(\frac{n}{p_s}\right), & \text{if } (m,n) = 1. \end{cases}$$

Let $N^*(n)$ be

$$\begin{cases} \text{minimal } m \text{ such that } \left(\frac{n}{m}\right) = -1, & \text{if such an } m \text{ exists}, \\ 0, & \text{otherwise}. \end{cases}$$

By Theorem 3 in §2, Chapter 5 of [24] $N^*(n) = 0$ iff n is a perfect square. Otherwise $N^*(n)$ is an odd prime.

Conjecture 3. $N^*(n) = O(\text{poly } \log n)$.

Theorem 32 *Conjectures 1, 2 and 3 are equivalent.*

Proof. $(3) \to (1)$. The deterministic Turing machine considers all odd integers m in the order of their growth and tests whether or not the remainder modulo m of the length of the input word can be a remainder modulo n of a perfect square. If $N^*(n)$ never exceeds poly $\log n$, the space complexity never exceeds $\log \log n$.

$(1) \to (2)$. Obvious.

$(2) \to (3)$. Assume that NONSQUARES is recognized by a nondeterministic Turing machine in space $s(n) = O(\log \log n)$. Only $const^{s(n)}$ configurations of the work tapes are possible which is less than the length of the input word. Hence the machine inevitably repeats the configurations. Let $K(n)$ denote the l.c.m. of all the positive integers not exceeding $const^{s(n)}$. If a word w is accepted by the nondeterministic machine, and we consider a word w' such that $|w'| = |w| + K(n)$, then there is a computation accepting w' as well. Hence acceptance is determined only by the remainder of the length of the input word modulo $K(n)$. Hence $K(n) \geq N^*(n)$. If Conjecture (3) fails, then $N^*(n) \geq O(\text{poly} \log n)$. Then $K(n) \geq O(\text{poly} \log n)$ and

$$const^{(s(n))^2} \geq O(\text{poly} \log n)$$

$$(s(n))^2 \geq r \log n$$

$$s(n) \geq \sqrt{r \log n}$$

contradicting Conjecture (2). $\boxtimes$

Please notice that Conjectures (1) and (2) belong to the Complexity Theory while Conjecture (3) belongs to Number Theory.

Many persons consider Number Theory as a highly abstract area removed from anything practical. Equivalence between a problem in Complexity Theory and a problem in Number Theory not only certifies the real difficulties underlying the open problems in Complexity Theory but also shows that Number Theory is no more an area remote from Computer Science.

A. Cobham [9] proved (using the proof of M. Ankeny [3]) that Conjecture (1) is implied by the Extended Riemann Hypothesis. Hence all our Conjectures (1)-(3) are true in the mathematics where the Extended Riemann Hypothesis holds.

David Hilbert (1862-1943) placed Riemann Hypothesis in his famous list of the Hilbert Problems, i.e. the mathematical problems for whom he predicted to have the greatest impact on the development of mathematics. It seems that the mathematicians have agreed that Hilbert has been right in his choice. Any way, even without being solved this problem has created a fantastic impact. One can only wonder whether or not B. Riemann himself recognized the importance of his hypothesis.

I would like to add one more result on Riemann Hypothesis creating much impact. Arnaud Denjoy (1884-1974) equivalently interpreted Riemann Hypothesis in statistical terms. If the values of Möbius function were **random**, then they would be distributed statistically independent. With probability 1 then

$$\frac{M(x)}{\sqrt{x}} < (\ln x)^{\frac{1}{2}},$$

would be true. where

$$M(x) = \sum_{n \leq x} \mu(n).$$

Riemann Hypothesis is equivalent to

$$|M(x)| = O(x^{\frac{1}{2}+\epsilon}).$$

Whatever the results being obtained in this direction and whatever the perspectives of this direction. please remember that *randomness* is a notion deeply connected to *Kolmogorov complexity*.

The year 1941 brought a most unexpected continuation in these efforts of many mathematicians. André Weil (b. 1906) [39]proved Riemann Hypothesis for congruence ζ-functions in elliptic functions over finite fields. This line of research was continued by many persons but the strongest results were obtained by P. Deligne [10]. The results by Weil and Deligne unfortunately do not say anything about the original problem. These ζ-functions are no more generalizations of Riemann ζ-function.

It might be expected that these results duly respected as classics of the 20th century mathematics are surely very far from Computer Science. No, in our time the time distance between the highest and most abstract achievements of the classical mathematics and the applications of results in Theoretical Computer Science is brought to a minimum. Michael Ben-Or [7] and Eric Bach [5] have used Weil's theorem for their results. Ben-Or's result was in an area somewhat related to elliptic functions, but Bach used this theorem in a situation where the formulation of the problem had nothing in common with Riemann and Weil. He was interested in the reason why some random polynomial-time algorithms work so well in practice.

References

1. Leonard Adleman. Molecular computation of solutions to combinatorial problems. *Science*, 1994, vol. 266, p. 1021–1024.
2. Andris Ambainis and Rūsiņš Freivalds. 1-way quantum finite automata: strengths, weaknesses and generalizations. *Proc. 39th FOCS*, 1998
   http : //xxx.lanl.gov/abs/quant − ph/9802062
3. N. C. Ankeny. The least quadratic non residue. *Annals of Mathematics*, 1952, vol. 55, p. 65–72.
4. Eric Bach. Fast algorithms under the Extended Riemann Hypothesis: a concrete estimate. *Proc. 14th STOC*, 1982, p. 290–295.
5. Eric Bach. Realistic analysis of some randomized algorithms. *Journal of Computer and System Sciences*, 1991, vol. 42, No. 1, p. 30–53.
6. Paul Benioff. Quantum mechanical Hamiltonian models of Turing machines. *J. Statistical Physics*, 1982, vol. 29, p. 515–546.
7. Michael Ben-Or. Probabilistic algorithms in finite fields. *Proc. 22nd FOCS*, 1981, p. 394–398.
8. Johannes Buchmann and Victor Shoup. Constructing nonresidues in finite fields and the Extended Riemann Hypothesis. *Proc. 23rd STOC*, 1991, p. 72–79.
9. Alan Cobham. The Recognition Problem for the Set of Perfect Squares. *Proc. FOCS*, 1966, p. 78–87.
10. Pierre Deligne. La conjeture de Weil. *Publ. Math. Inst. HES*, v. 43, 1974, p. 273–307.
11. David Deutsch. Quantum theory, the Church-Turing principle and the universal quantum computer. *Proc. Royal Society London, A400*, 1989. p. 96–117.
12. Richard Feynman. Simulating physics with computers. *International Journal of Theoretical Physics*, 1982, vol. 21, No. 6/7, p. 467-488.
13. Ernests Fogels. On the zeros of L-functions. *Acta Arithmetica*, 1965, vol. 11, p. 67–96.
14. Rūsiņš Freivalds. Fast computations by probabilistic Turing machines. In *Theory of Algorithms and Programs*, J. Bārzdiņš, Ed., University of Latvia, Riga, 1975, p. 3–34 (in Russian).
15. Rūsiņš Freivalds. Recognition of languages with high probability by various types of automata. *Dokladi AN SSSR*, 1978, vol. 239, No. 1, p. 60–62 (in Russian).
16. Rūsiņš Freivalds. Fast probabilistic algorithms. *Lecture Notes in Computer Science*, 1979, vol. 74, p. 57–69.
17. Rūsiņš Freivalds. Probabilistic two-way machines. *Lecture Notes in Computer Science*, 1981, vol. 118, p. 33–45.
18. Rūsiņš Freivalds. Space and reversal complexity of probabilistic one-way Turing machines. *Annals of Discrete Mathematics*, 1985, vol. 24, p. 39–50.

19. Rūsiņš Freivalds and Marek Karpinski. Lower space bounds for randomized computation. *Lecture Notes in Computer Science,* 1994, vol. 820, p. 580–592.

20. Rūsiņš Freivalds and Marek Karpinski. Lower time bounds for randomized computation. *Lecture Notes in Computer Science,* 1995, vol. 944, p. 154–168.

21. Dima Grigoriev, Marek Karpinski and Andrew M. Odlyzko. Existence of short proofs for nondivisibility of sparse polynomials under the Extended Riemann Hypothesis. *Proc. Int. Symp. on Symbolic and Algebraic Computation,* 1992, p. 117–122.

22. Ming-Deh A. Huang. Riemann Hypothesis and finding roots over finite fields. *Proc. 17th STOC,* 1985, p. 121–130.

23. Ming-Deh A. Huang. Generalized Riemann Hypothesis and factoring polynomials over finite fields. *Journal of Algorithms,* 1991,vol. 12, No. 3, p. 464–481.

24. Kenneth Ireland and Michael Rosen. *A Classical Introduction to Modern Number Theory. Graduate Texts in Mathematics,* vol. 87, Springer-Verlag, New York-Heidelberg-Berlin, 1972.

25. Lila Kari. DNA computers, tomorrow's reality. *Bulletin of the EATCS,* vol. 59, p. 256–266.

26. Marek Karpinski and Rutger Verbeek. On randomized versus deterministic computation. *Lecture Notes in Computer Science,* 1993, vol. 700, p. 227–240.

27. Attila Kondacs and John Watrous. On the power of quantum finite state automata. In *Proc. 38th FOCS,* 1997, p. 66–75.

28. K. de Leeuw, E.F. Moore, C.E. Shannon and N. Shapiro. Computability by probabilistic machines. In *Automata Studies,* C.E. Shannon and J. McCarthy, Eds., Princeton University Press, Princeton, NJ, 1955, p. 183–212.

29. R.F. Lukes, C.D. Paterson, and H.C. Williams. Some Results on Pseudosquares. *Mathematics of Computation,* 1996, v. 65, No. 213, p. 361–372.

30. Gary L. Miller. Riemann's hypothesis and tests for primality. *Journal of Computer and System Sciences,* 1976, vol. 13, No. 3, p. 300–317.

31. Hugh L. Montgomery. *Topics in Multiplicative Number Theory. Lecture Notes in Mathematics,* 1971. vol. 227.

32. Cristopher Moore, James P. Crutchfield Quantum automata and quantum grammars. Manuscript available at
$http://xxx.lanl.gov/abs/quant-ph/9707031$

33. Max Planck. Über eine Verbesserung der Wien'schen Spectralgleichung. *Verhandlungen der deutschen physikalischen Gesellschaft 2* 1900, S. 202.

34. Michael Rabin. Probabilistic automata. *Information and Control,* 1963, vol. 6, p. 230–245.

35. Michael Rabin. Probabilistic algorithms. In *Algorithms and Complexity, Recent Results and New Directions,* J.F.Traub, Ed., Academic Press, NY, 1976, p. 21–39.

36. Friedrich Roesler. Riemann hypothesis as an eigenvalue problem. *Linear Algebra Appl.* 1986, vol. 81, p. 153–198.

37. Peter Shor. Algorithms for quantum computation: discrete logarithms and factoring. In *Proc. 35th FOCS,* 1994, p. 124–134.

38. R. Solovay and V. Strassen. A fast Monte-Carlo test for primality. *SIAM J. Comput.* vol. 6, No. 1 (March), 1977, p. 84–85. See also *SIAM J. Comput.,* vol. 7, No. 1 (Feb.), 1978, p. 118.

39. André Weil. Number theory and algebraic geometry. *Proc. Intern. Congr. Math.,* 1950, Cambridge, vol. 2, p. 90–100.

Security of Electronic Money

Petr Hanáček

Technical University of Brno,
Božetěchova 2, 612 66 Brno, Czech Republic
E-mail: hanacek@dcse.fee.vutbr.cz

Abstract. The realisation of electronic commerce process is very difficult without appropriate system for electronic payment. Of course it is possible to use some of the conventional payment instruments (e.g. payment cards, bills, payment orders), but these instruments do not fit with requirements for improving the commerce process. The resulting electronic commerce system would have disadvantages inherited from these conventional payment instruments. New electronic payment systems should be developed to satisfy all requirements of electronic commerce. The main idea of most of these systems is to convert conventional money to its electronic equivalent - electronic money.

1 Introduction

According to most definitions the electronic commerce system is a system, that performs electronically all (or almost all) activities, connected with conventional commerce process. The purpose of converting these activities into electronic form is to improve the commerce process, especially:

- to speed up the commerce process and the turnover of money (using faster medium for commerce process activities)
- to create new types of goods (especially electronic goods or "soft goods", e.g. electronic publications, electronic services, multimedia products)
- to make the commerce process more convenient for the customer
- to find new types of commerce activities (e.g. information retrieval services)
- to find new types of customers and to globalise the customer area

The growth of electronic commerce systems causes that requirements for suitable payment systems are quite urgent and important. A number of payment systems is proposed and some of them are implemented. But we are still not satisfied with the quality of existent payment systems and the evolution of these systems is still far from required status.

The problematics of electronic money is tightly coupled with the problematics of information system security and mainly with the problematics of cryptography. The design of functional electronic payment system is not so difficult. The design of functional and secure payment system is quite difficult and security mechanisms are usually the most important part of the payment system.

2 Electronic Commerce and Electronic Money

The term "electronic money" (according to [15]) has been used in different settings to describe a wide variety of payment systems and technologies. "Stored-value" products are generally prepaid payment instruments in which a record of funds owned by or available to the consumer is stored on an electronic device in the consumer's possession, and the amount of stored "value" is increased or decreased, as appropriate, whenever the consumer uses the device to make a purchase or other transaction. By contrast, "access" products are those typically involving a standard personal computer, together with appropriate software, that allow a consumer to access conventional payment and banking products and services, such as credit cards or electronic funds transfers, through computer networks such as the Internet or through other telecommunications links.

3 Basic Principles of Electronic Money

3.1 Properties of Electronic Money

When implementing an electronic money a big effort has been made to make an electronic money as close as possible to real, physical money. Okamoto and Ohta present in [13] following six properties of an ideal electronic payment system:

1. Independence. The security of electronic money does not depend on a special physical conditions. No special hardware is necessary and money can be sent over the network.
2. Security. Electronic money cannot be copied, modified, or double-spent.
3. Privacy, anonymity and non-traceability. Privacy of user is protected. Nobody can deduce the link between user and his payment. The customer may perform operations anonymously.
4. Off-line payment. The protocol for electronic payment between customer and merchant can be performed off-line. No direct link to third party (e.g. bank) is necessary.
5. Transitivity. The electronic money can be transferred to any other user.
6. Divisibility. The electronic coin C can be divided to any number of other coins. Any of these coins can have any value, smaller than C, and the sum of values of these coins is equal to the C.

Note, that these properties are properties of an *ideal* electronic payment system. No currently working electronic payment system meets all these properties together.

3.2 Implementation of Electronic Money

This section provides a general overview of the electronic payment systems products which we are interested in. Figure 1 illustrates the general structural model common to most electronic money systems, including participants and their interactions.

Electronic payment system contains following parties:

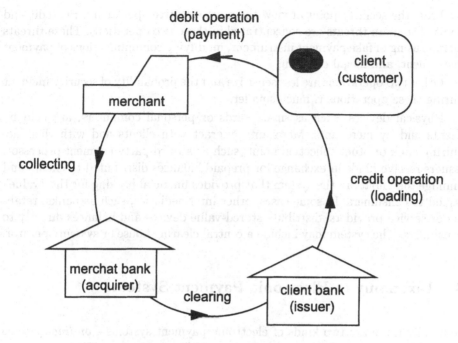

Fig. 1. General structure of electronic payment system

- Client (customer) - party that gets electronic money from client bank (issuer) and pays to the merchant.
- Merchant - party that gets electronic money from client and send these money (in the form of payment transactions) to the merchant bank (acquirer).
- Acquirer (usually the bank of merchant) - party that gets the transactions (i.e. electronic money) from its merchants and clears these payment transactions with appropriate issuer (client bank).
- Issuer (usually the client bank) - party that gives the electronic money to its clients and later receives these money from the acquirer.

The actions in this model are:

- Credit (loading) means transferring the monetary value from the issuer to the payment instrument (e.g. electronic purse) of client.
- Debit (purchase, payment) means transferring the monetary value from payment instrument of client to the payment instrument of merchant (that is usually payment terminal). In the terminal is then created payment transaction, that contains the electronic money and other payment details.
- Transaction collecting means transferring the payment transactions from the merchant to the acquirer.
- Payment clearing means clearing of payment request between acquirer and issuer.

From the security point of view the most sensitive operations are credit and debit. The main threats are concentrated in these two operations. These threats include using of fake payment instrument, modifying communications of payment instrument, and illegal crediting.

Other two operations are less sensitive and the probability of security incident during these operations is much smaller.

Physical devices, such as smart cards or personal computers, are held by clients and by merchants. Merchants interact with clients and with their acquiring bank or other collection point, such as a third-party payment processor. Issuers receive funds in exchange for prepaid balances distributed to clients and manage the "float" in the system that provides financial backing for the "value" issued to consumers. In some cases, other intermediaries, such as banks, retailers or service providers, distribute stored-value devices and balances directly to consumers. The system may include a central clearing house or system operator.

4 Taxonomy of Electronic Payment Systems

Generally there are two kinds of electronic payment systems - *on-line* systems and *off-line* systems. On-line systems require direct communication connection with the electronic money issuer (usually the bank) during every transaction (credit or debit). Off-line systems allow to perform payment transaction without such on-line connection with the issuer.

From privacy point of view the payment systems are divided to *identifiable* and *anonymous*. Identifiable payment system allows the issuer of electronic money to identify the participants of every transaction and gives him the possibility to trace the path of electronic money. Anonymous payment system preserves one of the property of real metal coins - the anonymity and untraceability. The issuer has no possibility to follow the path of electronic money. The anonymity of the payment system is quite desirable property of the payment system.

We also distinguish whether the payment system uses the intelligent token - *smart card* (sometimes called also *electronic purse* or *electronic wallet*) or it uses only non-intelligent payment instrument.

Next criterion is whether the payment instrument (magnetic card, smart card, personal digital assistant, personal computer) carries in itself an electronic monetary value (systems *with electronic money*) or it does not carries any value (systems *without electronic money*).

If the system uses the electronic money, we consider the implementation of value in the payment instrument. The value can be implemented using a *counter* (counter based systems) or using *electronic coins*.

According to the cryptographic mechanisms that are used, the electronic payment systems are based on *secret-key cryptography* or on *public-key cryptography*.

The taxonomy of electronic payment systems is shown at the following figure:

Electronic payment systems (EPS)

- EPS without electronic money
  - electronic banking (e.g. any home banking)
  - magnetic payment card (e.g. credit card)
  - payment smartcard (e.g. VISA Easy Entry)
  - network system without electronic money (e.g. SET)
- EPS with counters
  - prepaid smartcard card (e.g. telephone card)
  - electronic purse with electronic cheques
- EPS with electronic coins
  - electronic purse with electronic coins
  - network payment system with electronic coins

Fig. 2. Taxonomy of electronic payment systems

4.1 Electronic Payment Systems without Electronic Money

The most characteristic property of electronic payment systems without electronic money is that the payment instrument (e.g. magnetic payment card, smart card, or personal computer) does not contain any electronic money. The payment instrument performs only identification and authentication of the client and sometimes is used for cryptographic securing of the messages or for non-repudiation of the client. The messages, exchanged between the client and other party also do not contain any electronic money – they contain *orders to transfer money from account to account*. Payment systems without electronic money are typically *identifiable* and *on-line* payment systems. Typical examples of payment systems without electronic money are electronic banking systems, magnetic payment cards, payment smartcards, and computer network payment systems.

Electronic Banking System. Electronic banking systems can have many different names – home-banking, internet banking, Telebanking, etc. Electronic banking system performs exchange of banking information between bank and client using a personal computer, modem, and telephone line. System usually allows common passive operations with client accounts (e.g. examine account balance and history of account) and also some active operations (e.g. sending payment orders). It is clear from the nature of the electronic banking system that this system does not contain any electronic money.

Magnetic Payment Card. Magnetic payment card is used for withdrawal of the cash from ATM (Automatic Teller Machines) or for performing cashless payments. The card itself does not contain any electronic money. All relevant information are located in bank central computer and payment card (together with PIN) is used only for identification and authentication of client.

Payment Smartcard. Payment smartcard is used instead of magnetic payment card. The smartcard itself does not contain any electronic money and all information are stored in bank computer. Payment smartcard is direct replacement of magnetic payment card and has the same functionality as magnetic card. Its advantage is higher level of security – it is harder to copy it, it can locally verify the PIN code and it can effectively limit the number of unsuccessful PIN attempts.

Payment Systems for Computer Networks. Payment systems for computer networks are both without electronic money and with electronic money. Because of implementation complexity of electronic money the most of these systems are without electronic money. The main characteristics of these systems are that the payment instrument is personal computer and the communication is performed over the internet. It is desirable that no additional hardware is required on the client side. Because of relatively big computational power on the client side the cryptographic mechanisms are usually based on public key cryptography.

One of the most known payment system for computer networks is SET ([14]). In the second half of 1995 two separate draft specifications for making secure payments over insecure networks such as the Internet were published: the Secure Transaction Technology (STT) sponsored by Visa International and Microsoft, and the Secure Electronic Payment Protocol (SEPP) sponsored by MasterCard International. However, in early 1996 Visa International and MasterCard International published for comment a joint draft specification called Secure Electronic Transactions (SET). SET is aimed at transactions made using existing payment products, such as credit and debit cards, rather than electronic money products. The specification identifies five parties to any transaction: the cardholder, issuer, merchant, acquirer and payment gateway. The cardholder initiates the purchase across the network from his personal computer. Use is made of "trusted software" and authentication information on the PC.

SET specifies the use of message encryption, digital signatures and cryptographic certificates to provide confidentiality of information, integrity of payment data and authentication of cardholders and merchants. SET specifies RSA-based cryptography using 768, 1,024 or 2,048 bit keys and a hierarchy of certification authorities.

4.2 Electronic Payment Systems with Counters

The simplest implementation of electronic payment system with electronic money is to represent the money amount, carried by the client, as a value of *counter*, stored in the secure hardware token that is used as a payment instrument. When the payment instrument is credited, the counter is incremented by credited value. When the debit operation is performed, the counter is decreased by value paid. The system is rather simple and also the messages exchanged between parties are simple and independent on the exchanged monetary value. The security of such system relies on the security of payment instrument and on its resistance against unauthorised tampering. When the payment instrument is "broken" then the attacker can create an arbitrary amount of fictive money. The most common variants of counter-based payment system are prepaid card and electronic purse.

Prepaid Card. Prepaid cards (according to [16]) have developed first as a single-purpose payment instrument for which the card issuer and the merchant have been one and the same party (e.g. telephone cards or parking cards). Such cards have not raised central bank concerns because the value embedded in them (i.e. the value of counter) did not have a wide range of uses and, therefore, did not have the characteristics of money. Prepaid card is usually implemented by smart card, but in case of small amounts the magnetic card can be also used. The prepaid card is a typical *anonymous off-line* payment system.

Electronic Purse with Electronic Cheques. Drawing on the experience of prepaid cards a new payment instrument is under development in many countries: the multi-purpose prepaid card, also known as the "electronic purse". Electronic purses differ from other cashless payment instruments in that they are supplied in advance with generally accepted purchasing power. They can be loaded at bank counters, through Automated Teller Machines or through specifically equipped telephones, against a debit entry in a bank account, or against banknotes and coins. The embedded purchasing power is drawn down at the point of sale by an electronic device that can suitably adjust the information on the card.

Inside of electronic purse is again a *counter*, that directly represents monetary value. When the purse is debited, the counter decreases its value and purse issues an electronic message (electronic cheque) with debited value. The electronic cheque is cryptographically secured. The merchant stores received electronic cheques in its payment instrument (usually called *point of sale* or *payment terminal*) in the form of payment transactions. The transactions are then submitted by merchant to bank and consequentially the merchant's account is credited. The electronic purse is a typical *identifiable off-line* payment system.

4.3 Electronic Payment Systems with Electronic Coins

The main characteristics of electronic payment systems with electronic coins is that the payment instrument contains a number of digitally signed pieces of data – electronic coins. The value stored in the payment instrument is equal to the sum of values of individual electronic coins.

When the payment instrument is credited, the issuer creates the number of required electronic coins and sends it to the client payment instrument. The payment instrument only stores the electronic coins – it is used as storage media for electronic coins and also as a "guard" against double spending of the same electronic coin. In the moment of payment (i.e. debit operation) the payment instrument sends to the receiving party (usually to the merchant) an appropriate number of electronic coins. The electronic coins retain the most properties of real coins and payment system with electronic coins is usually an *anonymous off-line* system with *transitivity*.

From the security point of view the coin-based systems are better that counter-based systems. When the electronic purse with counter is "broken" (i.e. attacker knows the secrets stored in the purse), the attacker is able to create a big amount of fake electronic money, and the probability of identifying the attacker is usually small. When the electronic purse with coins is "broken", the attacker is still not able to generate any new electronic coin – he is able only to spend existing electronic coins twice or more times.

From the technical point of view the implementation of coin-based payment system is quite difficult and we are still not satisfied with current implementations. The main problem is already mentioned double-spending. The problem of double-spending is natural problem of electronic signature based electronic coins. The electronic coin has a lot of properties equivalent to real coins. But there is one property, that is inherently different – the ability to distinguish between an original and a copy. When the real coin is copied, it is usually easy to distinguish between original and fake copy. When the electronic coin is copied, the original and the copy are exactly the same. So the electronic coin could be spent many times, that is highly undesirable. There is no common and simple solution to this problem. One possible solution is before accepting of the electronic coin check in central database, whether this coin was already spent – this solution enforces on-line connection. Next possible solution is to use an "electronic guard" that is represented usually by the smartcard, that ensures that the coin is spent exactly once. This solution does not allow software-only implementation of payment instrument. There are also some other possibilities, but these have also disadvantages. The next problem of electronic coins is divisibility. Simple implementations do not solve divisibility and it could be sometimes difficult to combine available coins into desired amount. There are also some cryptographically-based solutions, but these solutions are usually difficult to implement and expensive.

The result is that in present the majority of payment systems with electronic money are counter-based payment systems and only few really working systems are coin-based. But coin-based systems have many advantages and in future we can expect that implementations of coin-based systems will be quite common.

5 The Role of Cryptography

The role of cryptography is very important in the design of electronic payment systems. The application of cryptographic mechanisms can help achieve objectives such as confidentiality, data integrity, authentication, and non-repudiation (see [15]).

The cryptographic mechanisms used in electronic payment systems include secret key encryption/decryption, one-way hash functions, challenge-response cryptographic protocols, digital signatures and key management protocols.

The cryptographic principles and building blocks described above are used to achieve security functions such as confidentiality, data integrity, authentication, and non-repudiation. Confidentiality is typically achieved by using triple-DES as the encryption method. Although it can also be done by applying asymmetric algorithms, owing to performance and price considerations the symmetric algorithms are generally preferred.

DES is also referred to as single-DES, to distinguish it from triple-DES. Triple-DES encryption consists of three consecutive operations (encryption; decryption; encryption) in which two DES keys are used (or a double-length DES key). Triple-DES has been developed in response to the increasing processing capabilities of computers and ensures that an exhaustive key search would still demand a considerable amount of resources.

Data integrity and authentication (including non-repudiation) are achieved by using DES, triple-DES and public key algorithms such as RSA, and by applying well-known hashing and MAC algorithms, such as MD-5, SHA-1 and RSA.

6 The Role of Tamper Resistant Hardware

The concept of tamper resistant hardware is tightly coupled with the concept of reference monitor. The reference monitor was defined in [1] and was standardised in [8]. The reference monitor concept was found to be an essential element of any system that would provide multilevel secure computing facilities and controls. Reference monitor is also a heart of the most of cryptographic modules using secret-key cryptography. An usual implementation of reference monitor is a reference validation mechanism, so we will define the reference monitor in this implementation (see [8]). Reference validation mechanism is defined as "an implementation of the reference monitor concept that validates each reference to data or programs by any user (program) against a list of authorised types of reference for that user." Three design requirements that must be met by a reference validation mechanism are:

1. The reference validation mechanism must be tamper proof.
2. The reference validation mechanism must always be invoked.
3. The reference validation mechanism must be small enough to be subject to analysis and tests, the completeness of which can be assured.

The most common implementation of this concept in electronic payment protocols is done by using the smart card as a payment instrument. The smartcard has such physical and logical properties that it complies to the three above conditions. The conditions are then met in following ways:

1. The reference validation mechanism is tamper proof because of physical properties of the used smartcard, that is designed as secure hardware, that is resistant against physical, electrical, electro-magnetic, and chemical tampering.

2. The reference validation mechanism is always invoked because of communication protocol, that is the only way to communicate with the smartcard.
3. The reference validation mechanism is small enough to be subject to analysis and tests, because of simplicity and standardisation of the communication protocol that is used.

For the long time the tamper resistance of smartcards and security processors was accepted without discussion. It was known, that large companies, like Intel or IBM, can successfully reverse-engineer complex chips, but everybody thought that this kind of attack is far beyond abilities of general attackers. The problem of evaluating the level of tamper resistance offered by a given product has been neglected by the security research community. It was discovered in the past that attacks on tamper resistance are possible also by small companies and even by individuals (see [4], [5]). The tamper resistance of smartcards and security processors has to be now closely examined product by product to discover possible vulnerabilities.

7 Example System of Smart Card Based Electronic Purse

Recently a new payment instrument has emerged: the multipurpose prepaid card or "electronic purse". It is a plastic card which contains real purchasing power, for which the customer has paid in advance. Although developments in the field of electronic purses are only at an early stage, the possibility of proliferation of such cards is a real one. In the future, if electronic purses were used in a great number of retail outlets, they would become a direct competitor not only to cashless payment instruments already in existence, but also to notes and coins issued by central banks and national authorities.

In following sections we will describe the proposed payment system, that is developed on the Department of Computer Science and Engineering, TU Brno. This payment system is developed in the framework of development the student smart card, that except other functions should have a property of electronic purse for closed payment system. The proposed system according the previously defined taxonomy is an electronic purse with electronic cheques, i.e. the system with counters.

The payment instrument contains inside a counter. The value of the counter is equivalent to the monetary value, that is stored in the payment instrument. The value of the counter can be changed using two operations - debit and credit. These two operations are equivalent to the two commands of payment instrument and have following semantics:

- Operation **CREDIT (VALUE)** increments the COUNTER by value VALUE. Input parameter of this operation is a credit value VALUE. The operation has no output parameters - returned is only the status that indicates successful performing the operation.
- Operation **DEBIT (VALUE)** checks whether value of the COUNTER is greater or equal than VALUE. If this is not the case, operation immediately

quits with status that indicates not successful performing of operation. Otherwise the operation decrements the COUNTER by value VALUE. Input parameter of this operation is a credit value VALUE. The operation has no output parameters - returned is only the status that indicates successful or unsuccessful performing the operation.

7.1 Security Requirements

From the functionality point of view the operations CREDIT and DEBIT are correct. From the security point of view are operations with such semantics not suitable, because they do not prevent against following attacks:

1. Tampering with the payment instrument. The value of counter can be modified (of course, increased) not only by performing the credit operation, but also using direct logical or physical manipulation with the payment instrument. These manipulations include patching in the case of software payment instrument or electrical tampering (e.g. using a microprobes injecting electrical signals) in the case of hardware payment instrument.
2. Using of fake payment instrument. This instrument emulates the behaviour of debit operation and gives to the client infinite amount of money without any crediting.
3. Modifying the communication between payment instrument and payment terminal. The communication could be modified in such way, that negative status code from unsuccessful debit operation is changed to positive status, although the payment instrument does not contain enough money to perform payment.
4. Illegal crediting of genuine payment instrument. This attack can be done simply by performing the credit command on the payment instrument.

In the following text we would like to describe the security concept of these two most sensitive operations - debit and credit - that prevents above attacks. The first attack is prevented by using the tamper resistant hardware and next three attacks are prevented by using cryptographic protocols.

7.2 Smart Card Used

The used smartcard is AT card. AT card is an authentication smartcard, adapted to cryptographic and prepaid card applications. It incorporates the ISO 7816-4 standard commands and return codes. AT card operating system must fulfil two main functions:

1. Be a general purpose operating system for smart card applications.
2. Provide security processing for authentication and prepaid applications

For the card user, the applications of AT card are many. Personal data such as medical history could be stored. It is possible to support financial applications such as EFTPOS, or to implement electronic wallet/cheque book functions all easily and securely from within the AT card system. In fact any application requiring the storage and retrieval of small to medium volumes of data with restricted or general access is possible from within the AT card structure. Use of recognised international standards where applicable makes the system acceptable across national boundaries making both the cards and the application developed for them internationally acceptable.

The communications protocol conforms to ISO/IEC 7816-3 in order to make the card readable from general purpose reading equipment. To achieve reliable and secure data transfer data encryption is based on the ANSI DES (X3.92-1981) algorithms and ANSI 3-DES algorithm. Message authentication is based upon ANSI X9.9-1982. The Table 1 summarises the AT card commands.

Table 1. AT card commands

VERIFY	Compares a card holder verification value (PIN) against a reference value.
SETPIN	Changes the card holder verification value (PIN).
READ BINARY	Reads data from a data file.
UPDATE BINARY	Updates data in a data file.
GET CHALLENGE	Generates an eight byte challenge and provides it to the external world.
PUT RANDOM	Initiates the computation of the session key, based on supplied random number sent from the reader.
INTERNAL AUTHENTICATE	Allows an external application to verify whether the card or an application on the card is authentic.
EXTERNAL AUTHENTICATE	Authentication of the external world based on a previously generated random number and a secret key.
DECREASE (DEBIT)	Decreases the value in a purse file by a specified amount and returns the new value.
INCREASE (CREDIT)	Increases the value in a purse file by a specified amount and returns the new value.

7.3   Cryptographic Protocol for Credit and Debit Operations

Operations credit and debit are cryptographically secured using so called MAC (Message Authentication Code). MAC is a way how to ensure authentication (i.e. proof of origin) of the secured message and the integrity (i.e. prevention against modification) of the message.

$MAC_K(M)$ is a fixed length value, usually 32 or 64 bit long, that is the function of message M and secret cryptographic key K (see Fig. 3). This value is computed by the creator (sender) of the message and is appended to the message. The recipient of the message which knows the same secret key K as creator can compute independently the MAC value according to received message M and

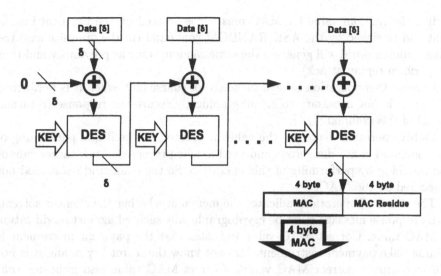

Fig. 3. Cryptographic mechanism MAC

his key K and then compare the value of received MAC and computed MAC. If both values are equal, the recipient can be sure, that:

1. The message was created by the creator that knows the secret key K, and
2. The message was not changed during the transmission.

Unfortunately MAC is not enough to protect the messages that contain the credit and debit commands because of replay attack. Replay attack allows attacker to capture a legal message with its MAC and send it later to the recipient. It is clear that e.g. replay of message with credit command means illegally increasing the value of payment instrument which is highly undesirable.

The solution to replay attack is to make every MAC unique by parametrizing it by the random value. The MAC value is computed over the message M and the random value Rnd that is unique for every command. Thus we need two new operations of payment instrument:

ASK RANDOM – (in AT card called GET CHALLENGE) that asks the payment instrument for random value that will be used by subsequent command
PUT RANDOM – that gives to the payment instrument the random value, created by the outside world that will be used by subsequent command

Now we can define the cryptographic requirements for the credit and debit operations:
Credit operation increases the value of counter, so the illegal performing of this command is highly undesirable and is against security policy. The command itself must be secured by the MAC to prevent illegal credits of payment instrument. Because payment instrument must prevent the outside world against fake

credits, the random value for MAC must be generated by the payment instrument and retrieved by the ASK RANDOM command (in the opposite case the "fake" outside world will generate the same random value as previously and thus can perform replay attack).

Because this operation always succeeds (of course only when it is performed legally), it is not necessary to cryptographically secure the response (returned status) of this command.

Debit operation decreases the value of counter, so the illegal performing of this command is not dangerous and need not be prevented. An attacker cannot gain anything by performing of this operation. So the command itself need not be secured by the MAC.

The status of operation indicates the merchant whether the client is solvent, so the response message must be cryptographically secured against modification by MAC value. Correct MAC value indicates that the payment instrument is genuine (fake payment instrument does not know the secret key K and it is not able to compute correct MAC value). Correct MAC value also indicates that the response message was not modified, i.e. that the client had on its payment instrument enough money to pay and that his counter value was decreased. Because the outside world (in this case the merchant) must be assured that the message is authentic, the random value for MAC must be generated by the outside world and entered by the PUT RANDOM command.

The resulting protocol for the credit and debit operations is shown on the Figure 4.

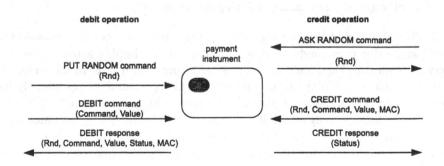

Fig. 4. Credit and debit commands

8 Conclusion

Electronic money products have the potential to provide important benefits to payment systems if implemented with appropriate security. These systems can not be made fully secure against all types of attack. Determining the appropriate level of security for a particular system should involve consideration of the magnitude of potential risks, the cost of implementing varying levels of security, the impact on the functionality of the product and the implications for privacy.

References

1. Anderson, J. P.: Computer Security Technology Planning Study, ESD-TR-73-51, vol. I, ESD/AFSC, Hanscom AFB, Bedford, Mass., October 1972 (NTIS AD-758 206).
2. Anderson, R..J.: Why Cryptosystems Fail, in Proceedings of the 1st ACM Conference on Computer and Communications Security (November 1993) pp 215-227
3. Anderson, R.J., Bezuidenhoudt, S.: On the Reliability of Electronic Payment Systems', in IEEE Transactions on Software Engineering v 22 no 5 (May 96) pp 294-301
4. Anderson, R.J., Kuhn, M.: Tamper Resistance - a Cautionary Note, in The Second USENIX Workshop on Electronic Commerce Proceedings, Oakland, California, November 18-21, 1996, pp 1-11
5. Anderson, R.J., Kuhn, M.: Low Cost Attacks on Tamper Resistant Devices appeared in M Lomas et al. (ed.), Security Protocols, 5th International Workshop, Paris, France, April 7-9, 1997, Proceedings, Springer LNCS 1361, pp 125-136, ISBN 3-540-64040-1.
6. Chaum, D. Fiat, A. Naor, M.: Untraceable electronic cash. (Springer-Verlag, Berlin, West Germany, p. 319-27, 1990)(Conference: Advances in Cryptology - CRYPTO '88. Proceedings, Santa Barbara, CA, USA, 21-25 Aug. 1988)
7. Biham, E., Shamir, A.: Differential Fault Analysis: Identifying the Structure of Unknown Ciphers Sealed in Tamper-Proof Devices, preprint, 10/11/96
8. Department of Defense Trusted Computer System Evaluation Criteria, DoD 5200.28-STDm December 1985, US Department of Defense, December 26, 1985
9. Even, S.: Secure off-line electronic fund transfer between nontrusting parties. (North-Holland, Amsterdam, Netherlands, p. 57-66, 1989) (Conference: Smart Card 2000: The Future of IC Cards. Proceedings of the IFIP WG 11.6 International Conference, Laxenburg, Austria, 19-20 Oct. 1987)
10. Security Requirements for Cryptographic Modules, FIPS PUB 140-1, Federal Information Processing Standards Publication, National Institute of Standards and Technology, U.S. Department of Commerce, January 11, 1994
11. Joye, M., Koeune, F., Quisquater, J.J.: Further results on Chinese remainder- ing, Universite Catholique de Louvain Technical Report CG-1997-1
12. Kocar, O.: Hardwaresicherheit von Mikrochips in Chipkarten, in Datenschutz und Datensicherheit v 20 no 7 (July 96) pp 421-424
13. Okamoto, T., Ohta, K.: Universal Electronic Cash, Proceedings of Crypto 91, p. 324-337, 1992, Springer
14. Secure Electronic Transaction Technical Specification, VISA, MasterCard, 1996
15. Security of Electronic Money, Report by the Committee on Payment and Settlement Systems and the Group of Computer Experts of the central banks of the Group of Ten countries, Basle, August 1996
16. Report to the Council of The European Monetary Institute on PREPAID CARDS by the Working Group on EU Payment Systems, May 1994.
17. Tunstall, J.S.: Electronic currency. (North-Holland, Amsterdam, Netherlands, p. 47-8, 1989) (Conference: Smart Card 2000: The Future of IC Cards. Proceedings of the IFIP WG 11.6 International Conference, Laxenburg, Austria, 19-20 Oct. 1987)
18. Integrated Circuit Card Specifications for Payment Systems, VISA, MasterCard, Europay, 1995

Algorithms Based on Randomization and Linear and Semidefinite Programming

Klaus Jansen[1], Jose Rolim[2]

[1] IDSIA Lugano, Corso Elvezia 36, 6900 Lugano, Switzerland,
email: klaus@idsia.ch
[2] University of Geneva, Computer Science Center, 23, Rue General Dufour, 1211 Geneva 4, Switzerland,
email jose.rolim@cui.unige.ch

Abstract. We study three methods based on linear programming and generalizations that are often applied to approximate combinatorial optimization problems. We start by describing an approximate method based on linear programming; as an example we consider scheduling of jobs on unrelated machines with costs. The second method presented is based on semidefinite programming; we show how to obtain a reasonable solution for the maximum cut problem. Finally, we analyze the conditional probabilities method in connection with randomized rounding for routing, packing and covering integer linear programming problems.

1 Introduction

Several approximation algorithms for combinatorial problems are somewhat related to linear programming or generalizations of linear programming. Once an optimization problem is formulated as an integer mathematical programming problem, the relaxation over the reals can be used to develop approximation algorithms in one of the following way:

1. Primal/dual algorithms: the algorithm finds a feasible solution for the problem of interest and a feasible solution for the dual of its relaxation; the ratio between the costs of the two solutions is at most some constant r. Then the solution is r-approximate.
2. Rounding: an optimum (or near-optimum) solution is found for the relaxation, and it is rounded to yield an integer solution. The ratio between the cost of the rounded solution and the fractional one is at most r. Then the rounded solution is r-approximate.

In the first case, the linear programming formulation is used just as a conceptual tool to prove the approximation bound. In the second case, the relaxation is actually solved. Rounding a fractional solution is, in general, a difficult task. Randomization is a primary tool. The algorithms we shall consider in this paper use linear programming, semidefinite programming and/or randomized rounding to find a solution.

This paper is organized as follows. In the next section, we study linear programming by showing how to derive an approximation algorithm for the particular case of scheduling jobs on unrelated machines with costs. We continue by describing a method based on semidefinite programming. As an example we show a randomized approximation algorithm for the maximum cut problems that randomly rounds the solution of a nonlinear programming relaxation. In the last section, we study more deeply the randomized rounding presented in the previous sections. Random rounding has been used to develop approximation algorithms for the maximum satisfiability problem and the constraint satisfaction problem among others. By the use of pessimistic estimators a de-randomized solution can be found.

2 Linear Programming

In this section we describe an approximation method based on linear programming. As an example we consider scheduling of jobs on unrelated machines with costs. This scheduling problem can be described as an integer program. We describe an approximation algorithm given by Shmoys and Tardos [25]. The algorithm consists of a linear programming LP relaxation followed by rounding the fractional solution. The rounding step is based on a minimum cost matching algorithm in a bipartite graph. Several approximation algorithms are based on linear programming; for a survey we refer to the book edited by Hochbaum [13].

A *linear program* LP has the following form:

$$
\begin{aligned}
& max \ \textstyle\sum_{j=1}^{n} c_j x_j \\
& \textstyle\sum_{j=1}^{n} a_{ij} x_j = b_i \quad i = 1, \ldots, m \\
& x_j \geq 0 \quad\quad\quad\quad j = 1, \ldots, n
\end{aligned}
$$

and can be solved in time polynomial in the size of the input [16, 11].

In the following, we describe the scheduling problem with *unrelated machines*. There are n independent jobs and m parallel machines where each job has to be processed by exactly one machine. Job j takes p_{ij} time units and produces cost c_{ij} when job j is executed on machine i, for $i = 1, \ldots, m$ and $j = 1, \ldots, n$. A *schedule* can be described by a mapping f that assigns a machine $f(j) \in \{1, \ldots, m\}$ to each job j. The *cost* of a schedule f is given by $\sum_{j=1}^{n} c_{f(j)j}$ and the *makespan* of a schedule is the maximum finishing time:

$$
max_{1 \leq i \leq m} \sum_{j|f(j)=i} p_{ij}.
$$

The approximation algorithm solves a bicriteria problem: optimizing the makespan and the cost of a schedule together. Lenstra, Shmoys and Tardos [17] have given a 2-approximation algorithm for the single criterion problem of minimizing the makespan. Furthermore, they have proved an in-approximability result for the single criterion problem: for any $\epsilon < \frac{1}{2}$ there exists no polynomial time $(1 + \epsilon)$ approximation, unless $P = NP$. Suppose that there is a schedule with total cost C and makespan T. The goal is an approximation algorithm that generates a schedule with makespan at most $2T$ and cost at most C. To do this we describe the scheduling problem as a integer linear program:

$$
\begin{aligned}
&min \ \sum_{i,j} c_{ij} x_{ij} \\
&\sum_{i=1}^{m} x_{ij} = 1 && j = 1, \ldots, n \\
&\sum_{j=1}^{n} p_{ij} x_{ij} \leq T && i = 1, \ldots, m \\
&x_{ij} \in \{0, 1\} && i = 1, \ldots, m; j = 1, \ldots, n \\
&x_{ij} = 0 && \text{if } p_{ij} > T
\end{aligned}
$$

Solving the integer linear program is a NP-complete problem. Therefore, we use a relaxation of the integer linear program. If we relax the binary constraints $x_{ij} \in \{0, 1\}$ and require only that $x_{ij} \geq 0$ for all i, j, we get a linear program called the *LP relaxation* of the integer linear program. We notice that the cost value of an optimum LP solution is a lower bound on the integral optimum cost value. Given an optimum solution $\bar{x} = (\bar{x}_{ij})$ of the linear program, we construct an integral assignment with total cost at most C and makespan at most $2T$. Clearly, the cost of any optimum fractional solution is bounded by C. To get an integral solution we build a *bipartite graph* $B(\bar{x}) = (V, W, E)$ with weights $x'(v, w)$ on the edges $(v, w) \in E$.

The bipartite graph consists of job nodes $W = \{w_j | j = 1, \ldots, n\}$ and of machine nodes $V = \{v_{is} | i = 1, \ldots, m, s = 1, \ldots, k_i\}$ where $k_i = \lceil \sum_{j=1}^{n} \bar{x}_{ij} \rceil$. The nodes $v_{i1}, v_{i2}, \ldots, v_{ik_i}$ correspond to machine i. In what follows, we construct the edges incident to nodes corresponding to machine i. We may assume that the jobs (for machine i) are sorted in non-increasing processing time order:

$$
p_{i1} \geq p_{i2} \geq \ldots \geq p_{in}.
$$

If $\sum_{j=1}^{n} \bar{x}_{ij} \leq 1$ then we have only one node v_{i1} for machine i. In this case we use an edge $(v_{i1}, w_j) \in E$ with weight $x'(v_{i1}, w_j) = \bar{x}_{ij}$ for each job j with $\bar{x}_{ij} > 0$. Otherwise, let j_1 be the minimum index with $\sum_{j=1}^{j_1} \bar{x}_{ij} \geq 1$. Then E contains the edges (v_{i1}, w_j) for $j = 1, \ldots, j_1 - 1$ for which $\bar{x}_{ij} > 0$ with weights $x'(v_{i1}, w_j) = \bar{x}_{ij}$ and one additional edge (v_{i1}, w_{j_1}) with weight $x'(v_{i1}, w_{j_1}) = 1 - \sum_{j=1}^{j_1 - 1} x'(v_{i1}, w_j)$. Using this definition, the sum of the weights among edges incident to v_{i1} is exactly 1. If $\sum_{j=1}^{j_1} \bar{x}_{ij} > 1$ then a fraction of the value $\bar{x}_{ij_1}$ is unassigned. We set $\bar{x}'_{ij_1} = \bar{x}_{ij_1} - x'(v_{i1}, w_{j_1})$; this is the remaining fraction of job j_1 for machine i. If $\sum_{j=1}^{j_1} \bar{x}_{ij} = 1$ then we have $\bar{x}'_{ij_1} = 0$.

Then, we proceed with the jobs $j \geq j_1$ and values $\bar{x}'_{ij_1}, \bar{x}_{ij_1+1}, \ldots, \bar{x}_{in}$, and construct edges incident to node v_{i2} in the same way as above. This procedure is iterated k_i times for the nodes $v_{i1}, v_{i2}, \ldots, v_{ik_i}$. The sum of the weights of edges incident to v_{is} ($s < k_i$) is exactly 1 and the sum of the weights of edges incident to v_{ik_i} is at most 1. We give an example of this construction with $n = 8$ jobs. We suppose that the jobs are sorted according to non-increasing processing times on machine 1, and suppose that $\bar{x}_{11} = \frac{2}{3}$, $\bar{x}_{13} = \bar{x}_{15} = \bar{x}_{16} = \frac{1}{2}$, $\bar{x}_{18} = 1$ and that $\bar{x}_{12} = \bar{x}_{14} = \bar{x}_{17} = 0$. The number of nodes for machine 1 is $\lceil \frac{2}{3} + \frac{3}{2} + 1 \rceil = 4$. The constructed edges with corresponding weights for the first machine are given in Table 1.

Table 1. The constructed edges with weights for machine 1

	w_1	w_3	w_5	w_6	w_8
v_{11}	$\frac{2}{3}$	$\frac{1}{3}$			
v_{12}			$\frac{1}{6}$	$\frac{1}{2}$	$\frac{1}{3}$
v_{13}				$\frac{1}{6}$	$\frac{5}{6}$
v_{14}					$\frac{1}{6}$

For each machine node v_{is} we define two values

$$p_{is}^{max} = max\{p_{ij}|(v_{is}, w_j) \in E\},$$
$$p_{is}^{min} = min\{p_{ij}|(v_{is}, w_j) \in E\}.$$

A non-negative weight function $z : E \to [0, 1]$ is a *fractional matching* if for each node $u \in V \cup W$ (of the bipartite graph) the sum $\sum_{v|(u,v)\in E} z(u, v) \leq 1$. A node is *exactly matched* if the sum is exactly 1. We have an *integral matching* if the weights $z(u, v) \in \{0, 1\}$. The weight function x' constructed for the optimal solution $\bar{x}$ is a fractional matching in $B(\bar{x})$ of cost at most C. In this fractional matching, each node $w_j \in W$ and each node v_{is} for $i = 1, \ldots, m$ and $s < k_i$ is exactly matched. Since the jobs are sorted according to the processing times on machine i, we have $p_{is}^{min} \geq p_{is+1}^{max}$ for each $s = 1, \ldots, k_i - 1$.

The algorithm to construct a feasible schedule works as follows:

Algorithm:
Step 1: Compute an optimum solution $\bar{x}$ of the linear program.
Step 2: Build the bipartite graph $B(\bar{x})$ with weight function x'.
Step 3: Compute a minimum cost (integer) matching M that matches exacly all job nodes in $B(\bar{x})$.
Step 4: For each edge $(v_{is}, w_j) \in M$ schedule job j on machine i.

Theorem 1. *The schedule generated by the algorithm above has makespan at most 2T and total cost at most C.*

Proof. We know already that x' is a fractional matching in $B(\bar{x})$ of cost at most C. Then, there exists an integral matching M in $B(\bar{x})$ of cost at most C (see [2]). This implies that the constructed schedule has cost at most C. We prove now that the matching M generates a schedule in Step 4 with makespan at most $2T$. To show this consider machine i and the k_i nodes corresponding to machine i in $B(\bar{x})$. Since for each machine node there is most one incident edge in M, the total processing time on machine i can be bounded by $\sum_{s=1}^{k_i} p_{is}^{max}$.

Using the inequality $p_{is}^{min} \geq p_{is+1}^{max}$ for $s = 1, \ldots, k_i - 1$ and $p_{i1}^{max} \leq T$ we obtain:

$$\sum_{s=1}^{k_i} p_{is}^{max} = p_{i1}^{max} + \sum_{s=2}^{k_i} p_{is}^{max} \leq p_{i1}^{max} + \sum_{s=1}^{k_i-1} p_{is}^{min}$$
$$\leq p_{i1}^{max} + \sum_{s=1}^{k_i-1} \sum_{j|(v_{is},w_j)\in E} p_{ij} x'(v_{is}, w_j)$$
$$\leq T + \sum_{j=1}^{n} p_{ij}\bar{x}_{ij} \leq 2T.$$

$\square$

We suppose that $n \geq m$. The linear program in our example can be described as a *fractional packing problem* of the form described in [20, 10]:

$$\sum_{j=1}^{n} p_{ij} x_{ij} \leq T \quad i = 1, \ldots, m$$
$$\sum_{i,j} c_{ij} x_{ij} \leq C$$
$$\sum_{i=1}^{m} x_{ij} = 1 \quad j = 1, \ldots, n$$
$$x_{ij} \geq 0 \qquad \text{if } p_{ij} \leq T$$
$$x_{ij} = 0 \qquad \text{if } p_{ij} > T$$

The m machine constraints and the cost constraint are the packing constraints, and the remaining constraints correspond to a polytope P (the product of n simplices). The techniques in [20, 10] can be used to generate an approximative solution of the packing program where the load and cost constraints are relaxed by a factor of $1 + \epsilon$. The running time of the algorithm in [20] is $O(mn^2 \log m)$, and the running time of the algorithm in [10] is $O(m^2 n \log m)$. Furthermore, the minimum cost matching problem can be solved in $O(n^2 m + n^2 \log n)$ time [2].

For non-negative costs and any fixed $\epsilon > 0$, Shmoys and Tardos [25] have given also a randomized algorithm that generates a schedule of cost at most $(1 + \epsilon)C$ and makespan at most $(2 + \epsilon)T$ and that runs in expected $O(n^2 \log n)$ time. Recently, for constant number of machines m, an approximation algorithm that generates a schedule with cost at most $(1 + \epsilon)C$ and makespan at most $(1 + \epsilon)T$ that runs in $O(n)$ time has been found [14].

3 Semidefinite Programming

In this section we describe an interesting method based on semidefinite programming to get good approximation algorithms. As an example we demonstrate a randomized approximation algorithm for the maximum cut (MAX CUT) problem that generates solutions of expected value of at least .87856 times the optimal value. This algorithm uses an elegant technique that randomly rounds the solution of a nonlinear programming relaxation. This algorithm given by Goemans and Williamson [9] represents the first use of semidefinite programming for approximation algorithms. By using semidefinite programming Karger, Motwani and Sudan [15] have shown how to color a k-colorable graph with $\tilde{O}(n^{1-\frac{3}{k+1}})$ colors in polynomial time. Further approximation results based on semidefinite programming have been obtained in the last years for different combinatorial optimization problems (see e.g. [5, 6, 7, 26, 28]).

A matrix $A \in \mathbb{R}^{n \times n}$ is *positive semidefinite* if $x^T A x \geq 0$ for any vector $x \in \mathbb{R}^n$. For a symmetric matrix A the following statements are equivalent:

(1) A is positive semidefinite.
(2) $A = B^T B$ for some matrix $B \in \mathbb{R}^{m \times n}$.

A *semidefinite program* has the following form:

$$max \ \sum_{i,j} c_{ij} x_{ij}$$
$$\sum_{i,j} a_{ij}^{(k)} x_{ij} = b_k \quad k = 1, \ldots, \ell$$
$$X = (x_{ij}) \qquad \text{symmetric, positive semidefinite}$$

Semidefinite programming is similar to linear programming; e.g. the simplex method can be generalized to semidefinite programs [19]. For any $\epsilon > 0$, a semidefinite program can be solved within an additive error of ϵ in time polynomial in the size of the input and $\log \frac{1}{\epsilon}$ (see e.g. [3, 11, 18, 31]).

In the following we describe the MAX CUT problem. Let $G = (V, E)$ be an undirected graph with non-negative weights $w(i, j)$ on the edges $(i, j) \in E$. For simplicity, we use $w(i, j) = 0$ for $(i, j) \notin E$. The *maximum cut problem* is the problem of finding a partition of V into two sets V_1 and V_2 such that the weight of the edges with one endpoint in V_1 and one endpoint in V_2

$$w(V_1, V_2) = \sum_{v_1 \in V_1, v_2 \in V_2} w(v_1, v_2)$$

is maximized. We call such a partition a *cut*. The MAX CUT problem is NP-complete even for unit weights ($w(i, j) = 1$ for $(i, j) \in E$) and simple graph classes like chordal graphs or complement of bipartite graphs [4]. Furthermore, Håstad [12] has proved that the MAX CUT problem is not approximable with a factor of 0.94127. The best previous algorithm with approximation bound 0.5 was given by Sahni and Gonzales [24] in 1976. We now present a semidefinite program for MAX CUT and, later, the randomized approximation algorithm by Goemans and Williamson.

First, we give a quadratic integer program for MAX CUT. For each vertex $i \in V$, we use a variable x_i to indicate whether $i \in V_1$ or $i \in V_2$:

$$x_i = \begin{cases} -1 & i \in V_1 \\ 1 & i \in V_2 \end{cases}$$

Then, MAX CUT is equivalent to the problem

$$max \ \sum_{i<j} w(i, j) \frac{1 - x_i x_j}{2}$$
$$x_i \in \{-1, +1\} \qquad i = 1, \ldots, n.$$

We note that the partition $V_1 = \{i | x_i = -1\}$, $V_2 = \{i | x_i = 1\}$ corresponds to a cut with weight $w(V_1, V_2) = \sum_{i<j} w(i, j) \frac{1 - x_i x_j}{2}$.

Again, solving an integer program is NP-complete. For the MAX CUT problem we use a nonlinear program instead of a linear program relaxation. The relaxation consists of allowing x_i to be a n - *dimensional unit length vector* $v_i \in S_n$. The product $x_i x_j$ in the objective function is replaced by the dot product $v_i \cdot v_j$ of the corresponding vectors. The set $S_n = \{v \in \mathbb{R}^n | v \cdot v = 1\}$ is called the n - *dimensional unit sphere*. We get the following relaxation (A):

$$max \ \sum_{i<j} w(i, j) \frac{1 - v_i \cdot v_j}{2}$$
$$v_i \in \mathbb{R}^n, v_i \cdot v_i = 1 \qquad i = 1, \ldots, n.$$

Using $y_{ij} = v_i \cdot v_j$ we can rewrite (A) as the following program (B):

$$max \ \textstyle\sum_{i<j} w(i,j) \ \frac{1-y_{ij}}{2}$$
$$Y = (y_{ij}) \qquad \qquad \text{symmetric, positiv semidefinite}$$
$$y_{ii} = 1 \qquad \qquad \qquad i = 1, \ldots, n.$$

We note that (B) is a semidefinite program and that (A) and (B) are equivalent. To see the second statement: A solution of (A) can be directly transformed into a solution of (B). Furthermore, given a solution of (B) a *Cholesky decomposition* can be used to reconstruct the vectors v_i without changing the objective function.

We present now the randomized algorithm for the MAX CUT problem:

Algorithm:
Step 1: Solve the semidefinite program (B).
Step 2: Using a Cholesky decomposition, obtain an optimal set of vectors v_i.
Step 3: Pick a random unit length vector $r \in S^n$.
Step 4: Set $V_1 = \{i | v_i \cdot r \ge 0\}$ and $V_2 = \{i | v_i \cdot r < 0\}$.

In other words, we choose a random hyperplane (with r as its normal) and partition the vertices V into

- vectors in V_1 that lie above the plane and
- vectors in V_2 that lie below the plane.

Next, we analyse the quality of this solution. Let W denote the value of the cut produced by the algorithm, and let $E[W]$ be the expected value of the partition. We denote with $sgn(z)$ the *sign* of a real z; it is $+1$ if z is non-negative and -1 otherwise.

Theorem 2.
$$E[W] \ge 0.878 \sum_{i<j} w(i,j) \ \frac{1 - v_i \cdot v_j}{2}.$$

Let $W(OPT)$ be the value of a optimum cut, and let $W_{SDP}(OPT)$ be the optimum value of the semidefinite relaxation. Since the right hand side of the inequality above is the optimum value $W_{SDP}(OPT)$ of the relaxation (A) multiplied with 0.878 and since $W_{SDP}(OPT)$ is an upper bound of $W(OPT)$, we get a cut whose expected weight is at least 0.878 times $W(OPT)$. To show the Theorem above, we use first the linearity of the expectation and get

$$E[W] = \sum_{i<j} w(i,j) Pr[sgn(v_i \cdot r) \ne sgn(v_j \cdot r)].$$

Then, the Theorem is implied by the following Lemmas:

Lemma 3.
$$Pr[sgn(v_i \cdot r) \ne sgn(v_j \cdot r)] = \frac{1}{\Pi} arccos(v_i \cdot v_j).$$

Proof. The probability that a random hyperplane separates the vectors v_i and v_j is directly proportional to the angle between the vectors, and the angle $\theta = \arccos(v_i \cdot v_j)$. Furthermore,

$$Pr[sgn(v_i \cdot r) \neq sgn(v_j \cdot r)] = 2Pr[v_i \cdot r \geq 0, v_j \cdot r < 0].$$

The set $\{r | v_i \cdot r \geq 0, v_j \cdot r < 0\}$ intersect with the sphere is a spherical digon of angle θ and has a measure equal to $\frac{\theta}{2\Pi}$ times the measure of the full sphere. This implies that $Pr[v_i \cdot r \geq 0, v_j \cdot r < 0] = \frac{\theta}{2\Pi}$, and shows us the Lemma. $\square$

Lemma 4. *Let* $\alpha = min_{0<\theta\leq\Pi} \frac{2}{\Pi} \frac{\theta}{1-\cos\theta}$. *Then,*

$$E[W] \geq \frac{\alpha}{2} \sum_{i<j} w(i,j)(1 - v_i \cdot v_j).$$

Proof. Using the Lemma above, we get

$$E[W] = \frac{1}{\Pi} \sum_{i<j} w(i,j) \arccos(v_i \cdot v_j).$$

Then, using the non-negativity of the weights $w(i,j)$ and the inequality

$$\frac{1}{\Pi} \arccos(y) \geq \alpha \frac{1}{2}(1-y)$$

for $-1 \leq y \leq 1$ applied to $y = v_i \cdot v_j$ we get the statement of the Lemma. The inequality follows directly by changing the variables $y = \cos\theta$. $\square$

Finally, the quality of the approximation algorithm is given by the estimation of α:

Lemma 5.
$$\alpha \geq 0.87856.$$

Proof. Consider the function $\frac{2}{\Pi} \frac{\theta}{1-\cos\theta}$. First, we observe that $\cos\theta \geq 1 - \frac{2}{\Pi}\theta$ for $0 \leq \theta \leq \frac{\Pi}{2}$ and, equivalent, $\frac{2}{\Pi} \frac{\theta}{1-\cos\theta} \geq 1$ for $0 < \theta \leq \frac{\Pi}{2}$. Furthermore, we observe that the function $f(\theta) = 1 - \cos\theta$ is concave in the interval $[\frac{\Pi}{2}, \Pi]$. This implies

$$f(\theta) \leq f(\theta_0) + (\theta - \theta_0)f'(\theta)$$

for any $\theta_0 \in [\frac{\Pi}{2}, \Pi]$. This can be rewritten to

$$1 - \cos\theta \leq 1 - \cos\theta_0 + (\theta - \theta_0)\sin\theta_0$$
$$= \theta \sin\theta_0 + (1 - \cos\theta_0 - \theta_0 \sin\theta_0).$$

For $\theta_0 = 2.331122$ we have $1 - cos\theta_0 - \theta_0 sin\theta_0 < 0$, and obtain as a consequence

$$1 - \cos\theta < \theta \sin\theta_0.$$

This implies that

$$\alpha = min_{0<\theta\leq\Pi} \frac{2}{\Pi} \frac{\theta}{1-\cos\theta} \geq \frac{2}{\Pi} \frac{1}{\sin\theta_0} > 0.87856.$$

$\square$

Finally, the algorithm can be implemented in polynomial time. We suppose that the weights are integral. Using an approximate algorithm for the semidefinite program, for any $\epsilon > 0$, we get a set of vectors v_i in polynomial time with objective value $> W_{SDP}(OPT) - \epsilon$. Using these vectors, the randomized algorithm produces a cut with weight $\geq \alpha(W_{SDP}(OPT) - \epsilon) \geq (\alpha - \epsilon)W(OPT)$.

4 Random Rounding and Conditional Expectation

Random rounding has been introduced by Raghavan and Thompson [23]. The de-randomized rounding using a pessimistic estimator is due to Raghavan [22]. Both results are also presented in Raghavan's PhD Thesis [21].

Random rounding has been used to develop approximation algorithms for the Maximum Satisfiability problem [8] and the Constraint Satisfaction problem [30]. In these algorithms, the probability distribution used to round the variables is not the solution of the relaxation, but rather a convex combination of the solution of the relaxation and of the uniform distribution. The de-randomization of these algorithms is easier since, basically, any 0/1 solution is feasible.

The performance of rounding can be improved in special cases, for example for resource-constrained scheduling problem [29] and for packing and covering integer linear programs [27]. In both cases, the authors de-randomize their rounding schema using new pessimistic estimators. The framework is as follows. Say that we have a probability space $(\mathbf{Pr}, \{0,1\}^n)$ and a set of "good strings" $A \subseteq \{0,1\}^n$ such that $\Pr(A) \geq \epsilon$ for some $\epsilon > 0$; assume also that the algorithm that we want to to de-randomize uses randomness only to find a string $\mathbf{x} \in \{0,1\}^n$.

A deterministic algorithm can construct such a string in the following way. For $i = 0, 1, \ldots, n$ and $(b_1, \ldots, b_i) \in \{0,1\}^i$, let us call $P^i_{b_1,\ldots,b_i} = \Pr[\mathbf{x} \notin A | x_1 = b_1, \ldots, x_i = b_i]$. Of course we have $P^0 = 1 - \Pr[A] < 1$, moreover we have that, for any i and any $(b_1, \ldots, b_i)$, either $P^{i+1}_{b_1,\ldots,b_i,0} \leq P^i_{b_1,\ldots,b_i}$ or $P^{i+1}_{b_1,\ldots,b_i,1} \leq P^i_{b_1,\ldots,b_i}$. Observe that $P^n_{b_1,\ldots,b_n}$ is either equal to 0 or 1, and is equal to 1 if and only if $(b_1, \ldots, b_n) \notin A$.

Algorithm cond-prob   **for** $i = 1$ **to** n **do**
   if $P^i_{b_1,\ldots,b_{i-1},0} \leq P^{i-1}_{b_1,\ldots,b_{i-1}}$ **then**
     $b_i := 0$
   else
     $b_i := 1$;
return $(b_1, \ldots, b_n)$;

The above algorithm maintains the invariant that, at any iteration of the **for** loop, b_i receives a value such that $P^i_{b_1,\ldots,b_i} \leq P^{i-1}_{b_1,\ldots,b_{i-1}}$. By induction, this implies that $P^n_{b_1,\ldots,b_n} \leq P^0 < 1$, and so $P^n_{b_1,\ldots,b_n} = 0$ and $(b_1, \ldots, b_n) \in A$.

This method could, in principle, be applied to almost any randomized algorithm. In practice, however, the computation of the conditional probabilities is an utterly complicated task.

A careful examination of the proof of correctness of the method reveals that it is not really necessary to exactly compute all the conditional probabilities. This is formalized below

Definition 6. A *pessimistic estimator* for set A and probability distribution Pr is a set of values $\{U^i_{b_1,\ldots,b_i}\}^{i=0,\ldots,n}_{(b_1,\ldots,b_i)\in\{0,1\}^i}$ such that the following properties hold.

1. $U^0 < 1$;
2. $\forall i = 0,\ldots,n-1$, for all $(b_1,\ldots,b_i) \in \{0,1\}^i$,
   $U^i_{b_1,\ldots,b_i} \geq \min\{U^{i+1}_{b_1,\ldots,b_i,0}, U^{i+1}_{b_1,\ldots,b_i,1}\}$;
3. $\forall i = 0,\ldots,n$, for all $(b_1,\ldots,b_i) \in \{0,1\}^i$,
   $P^i_{b_1,\ldots,b_i} \geq U^i_{b_1,\ldots,b_i}$.

If we have an algorithm that computes $U^i_{b_1,\ldots,b_i}$ in poly(n) time, then we are done: we can run algorithm cond-prob using $U^i_{b_1,\ldots,b_i}$ in place of $P^i_{b_1,\ldots,b_i}$. The proof of correctness is the same.

The method of conditional probabilities is a standard way to obtain deterministic constructions out of an existence proof that involves the probabilistic method. A clear exposition is in [1]. Pessimistic estimators are defined in [22].

Randomized rounding is an algorithmic technique that is suitable for derandomization using conditional probabilities. The general framework is as follows: we have a problem that can be formulated as an integer linear program (ILP) with 0/1 variables. We relax the ILP to a linear program (LP) and we solve it to optimality. Then, we interpret the fractional solution obtained on this way as a probability distribution over the variables. The constraints of the LP are satisfied with high probability and the expected value of the objective function is close to the value of the relaxation.

Theorem 7. *Let* $\mathbf{x} = (x_1,\ldots,x_n)$ *be a vector satisfying* $\mathbf{a}^T \cdot \mathbf{x} = b$, $0 \leq x_i \leq 1$. *Define the random variables* $y_1,\ldots,y_n$ *such that* y_i *is equal to 1 with probability* x_i *and equal to 0 with probability* $(1 - x_i)$ *then, for any* $f > 0$, *the following holds with probability at least* $(1 - n^{-f})$:

$$b - a_{\max}\sqrt{fn\log n} \leq \mathbf{a}^T \cdot \mathbf{y} \leq b + a_{\max}\sqrt{fn\log n} \tag{1}$$

where $a_{\max} = \max_i |a_i|$.

The Theorem also holds for rounding inequalities. It is also clear that the Theorem can be extended to systems of m equations; in this case the error will be $a_{\max}\sqrt{fn\log mn}$. Let $\mathbf{x}'$ be a fractional solution to the following linear program.

$$\max \quad \mathbf{c}^T \cdot \mathbf{x}$$
$$\text{Subject to}$$
$$A\mathbf{x} \leq \mathbf{b}$$
$$0 \leq \mathbf{x} \leq 1$$

Construct an integer solution $\mathbf{y}$ probabilistically by setting, independently for any j, $y_j = 1$ with probability x'_j and $y_j = 0$ with probability $1 - x'_j$. With high probability, the resulting solution has cost at least $(1 - o(1))\mathbf{c}^T \cdot \mathbf{x}'$ and satisfies

$$Ay \leq b + O(a_{max}\sqrt{n \log mn}) \qquad (2)$$

where a_{max} is the largest entry of A.

The above fundamental results have direct application to randomized approximation algorithms for routing problems and for problems expressible as integer linear programs in packing or covering forms (that generalize, respectively, hypergraph matching and set cover).

De-randomization uses a pessimistic estimator and yield the following result.

Theorem 8. *There exists a polynomial time algorithm that given a vector* $\mathbf{x} = (x_1, \ldots, x_n)$, $0 \leq x_i \leq 1$, *and a* $m \times n$, *matrix* A, *finds a vector* $\mathbf{y} = y_1, \ldots, y_n \in \{0, 1\}^n$ *such that*

$$A\mathbf{x} - O(a_{\max}\sqrt{n \log mn}) \leq A\mathbf{y} \leq A\mathbf{x} + O(a_{\max}\sqrt{n \log mn}) \qquad (3)$$

where $a_{\max} = \max_{i,j} |a_{i,j}|$. *In addition, for the rows of* A *with all non-negative entries, the stronger bound*

$$\sum_i a_{i,j} x_j - O(a_j^{\max} \log n) \leq \sum_j a_{i,j} y_j \leq \sum_i a_{i,j} x_j + O(a_j^{\max} \log n)$$

where $a_j^{\max} = \max_i |a_{i,j}|$.

The very notion of pessimistic estimator has been introduced in order to prove Theorem 8 [22].

References

1. N. Alon and J. Spencer, *The Probabilistic Method*, Wiley Interscience, 1992.
2. R.K. Ahuja, T.L. Magnanti and J.B. Orlin, Network Flows, Prentice Hall, Englewood Cliffs, 1993.
3. F. Alizadeh, Interior point methods in semidefinite programming with applications to combinatorial optimization, *SIAM Journal on Optimization* (1995), 13-51.
4. H.L. Bodlaender and K. Jansen, On the complexity of the maximum cut problem, *Symposium on Theoretical Aspects of Computer Science* STACS 94, LNCS 775, 769-780.
5. B. Chor and M. Sudan, A geometric approach to betweeness, *European Symposium on Algorithms* ESA 95, LNCS 979, 227-237.
6. U. Feige and M.X. Goemans, Approximating the value of two prover proof systems, with applications to MAX 2SAT and MAX DICUT, *Israel Symposium on Theory of Computing and Systems* ISTCS 95, 182-189.
7. A. Frieze and M. Jerrum, Improved approximation algorithms for MAX k-CUT and MAX BISECTION, *Algorithmica* 18 (1997), 67-81.
8. M.X. Goemans and D.P. Williamson, New 3/4-approximation algorithms for the maximum satisfiability problem, *SIAM Journal on Discrete Mathematics* 4 (1994), 656-666.

9. M.X. Goemans and D.P. Williamson, Improved approximation algorithms for maximum cut and satisfiability problems using semidefinite programming, *Journal of the ACM* 42 (1995), 1115-1145.

10. M.D. Grigoriadis and L.G. Khachiyan, Coordination complexity of parallel price-directive decomposition, *Mathematics of Operations Research* 21 (1996), 321-340.

11. M. Grötschel, L. Lovász and A. Schrijver, Geometric Algorithms and Combinatorial Optimization, Springer, Berlin, 1988.

12. J. Håstad, Some optimal in-approximability results, *ACM Symposium on the Theory of Computing* STOC 97, 1-10.

13. D. Hochbaum, Approximation Algorithms for NP-hard Problems, PWS Publishing Company, Boston, 1997.

14. K. Jansen and L. Porkolab, Linear time approximation schemes for scheduling on unrelated machines, in preparation.

15. D. Karger, R. Motwani and M. Sudan, Approximate graph coloring by semidefinite programming, *IEEE Symposium on Foundations of Computer Science* FOCS 94, 2-13.

16. L.G. Khachian, A polynomial time algorithm in linear programming, *Soviet Mathematics Doklady* 20 (1979), 191-194.

17. J.K. Lenstra, D.B. Shmoys and E. Tardos, Approximation algorithms for scheduling unrelated parallel machines, *Mathematical Programming* 46 (1990), 259-271.

18. Y. Nesterov and A. Nemirovskii, Interior Point Polynomial Methods in Convex Programming, Society for Industrial and Applied Mathematics, Philadelphia, 1994.

19. G. Pataki, Cone-LP's and semidefinite programs: Geometry and a Simplex type method, *Integer Programming and Combinatorial Optimization* IPCO 96, LNCS 1084, 162-174.

20. S.A. Plotkin, D. Shmoys and E. Tardos, Fast approximation algorithms for fractional packing and covering problems, *Mathematics of Operations Research* 20 (1995), 257-301.

21. P. Raghavan, *Randomized Rounding and Discrete Ham-Sandwich Theorems: Provably Good Algorithms for Routing and Packing Problems*, PhD thesis, University of California at Berkeley, 1986.

22. P. Raghavan, Probabilistic construction of deterministic algorithms: approximating packing integer programs, *Journal of Computer and System Sciences*, 37 (1988), 130-143.

23. P. Raghavan and C.D. Thompson. Randomized rounding: a technique for provably good algorithms and algorithmic proofs, *Combinatorica*, 7 (1987), 365-374.

24. S. Sahni and T. Gonzales, P-complete approximation problems, *Journal of the ACM* (1976), 555-565.

25. D.B. Shmoys and E. Tardos, An approximation algorithm for the generalized assignment problem, *Mathematical Programming* 62 (1993), 461-474.

26. M. Skutella, Semidefinite relaxations for parallel machine scheduling, *IEEE Symposium on the Foundations of Computer Science* FOCS 98, to appear.

27. A. Srinivasan. Improved approximations of packing and covering problems. *ACM Symposium on Theory of Computing* STOC 95, 268-276.

28. A. Srivastav and K. Wolf, Finding dense subgraphs with semidefinite programming, *Workshop on Approximation Algorithms for Combinatorial Optimization* APPROX 98, LNCS 1444, 181-191.

29. A. Srivastav and P. Stangier, Algorithmic chernoff-hoeffding inequalities in integer programming, *Random Structures and Algorithms*, 8 (1996), 27-58.

30. L. Trevisan. Positive linear programming, parallel approximation, and PCP's, *European Symposium on Algorithms* ESA 96, LNCS 1136, 62-75.

31. P.M. Vaidya, A new algorithm for minimizing convex functions over convex sets, *IEEE Symposium on the Foundations of Computer Science* FOCS 89, 338-343.

Distributed Systems Technology for Electronic Commerce Applications

Winfried Lamersdorf, Michael Merz, Tuan Tu

Distributed Systems Group
Department of Computer Science, Hamburg University, Germany
http://vsys-www informatik.uni-hamburg.de

Abstract. Based on the specific characteristics of electronic commerce (E-Commerce) requirements for an adequate software system support, this contribution gives an overview of the respective distributed systems technology which is (or will be shortly) available for open and heterogeneous electronic commerce applications. Starting from basic communication mechanisms this includes (transactionally secure) remote procedure call and database access mechanisms, service trading and brokerage functions as well as security aspects including such as notary and non-repudiation functions. Further important elements of a system infrastructure for E-Commerce applications are: common middleware infrastructures, componentware techniques, distributed and mobile agent technologies etc. Increasingly new and important topics in this area are currently: workflow management support for compound and distributed E-Commerce services as well as negotiation protocols to support both the settlement and the fulfillment of electronic contracts in E-Commerce applications. In addition to an overview of the state of the art of the respective technology, the paper also presents briefly some aspects of related projects conducted by the authors jointly with international partners (sponsored by EU/ACTS, EU/ESPRIT, DFG) in order to realize some of the important new functions of a systems infrastructure for open distributed E-Commerce applications.

Keywords: Distributed Systems, Electronic Commerce, Electronic Contracting, Middleware, Workflow Management, Service Trading/Brokerage

1 Introduction

Electronic Commerce (E-Commerce) is frequently considered as *the* most important application area of open worldwide computer network infrastructures such as the Internet. Already existing global computer networks provide access to a nearly unbounded number of different functions and services. System support for such a complex distributed application area like E-Commerce comprises both an increasingly

wide variety of functions and techniques already known from traditional communication, information, and cooperation support systems - as well as more specific
functions in order to support, for example, service selection, trading, contract negotiation, security, and payment activities - to name just a few [12, 9]. It has to fulfill
strong flexibility and interoperability requirements on its respective software components – both at the system support as well as at the application level. It also reflects changing requirements and preferences of globally distributed, heterogeneous,
cooperative organization structures.

1.1 Centralized vs. Decentralized Architectures

For example, many computer system customers demand today a re-centralization of
enterprise computing systems in order to reduce roll-out efforts and maintenance
costs. This development can be considered as a sober response to the idea of distrib-
uting any service at any time on any kind of heterogeneous hardware and operating
system environment. Today, certain "low-level" services are accepted as inherently
distributed such as DNS, NFS, HTTP, SMTP, etc. On the other hand, there are many
others that were expected to be distributed applications in the early 90ies and before: distributed databases, shared editing, application-level extensions to the telecommunication infrastructure. However, they did not succeed in day-to-day practice
by now. Why that?

One may argue that the first services are historically better understood since they
have been developed for over 15 years, but there is yet another reason for the lacking success of the latter: the complexity of their respective specifications. In most
cases in which a centralized alternative existed without prohibitive costs this option
would usually be chosen.

Despite that, however, the Internet has in the meantime established a drastically
decentralized communication platform that flattens hierarchies, overcomes organizational borders and liberates small companies and individuals from high invest-
ment costs for communication services. This development also stimulates the cooperation between distributed business partners in many ways.

Finally, it is trivial to state that major organizations today are usually distributed
across cities, regions, and countries. Since they have to coordinate the exchange of
goods, services, and payments across their organizational boundaries and therefore
usually across long distances as well, there is - for such electronic commerce applications - a quite natural need for a corresponding system software support by appropriate distributed systems. In contrast to the above mentioned areas, here the distribution of separate applications and respective software components is not only an
option but rather a necessary precondition for realizing adequate open system support for such electronic commercial market places.

In the following, we first analyze the application fields for electronic commerce
systems a bit more systematically and then provide some examples for components
of an underlying system support technology.

1.2 Modeling Commercial Transactions

In order to provide a systematic classification of electronic commerce technology, two viewpoints could principally be taken: either a distinction can be made between businesseses, consumers, and public authorities, or between respective roles of, e.g., buyers and sellers of goods and services [6]. However, if we consider single persons as legal entities thus representing an equal market participant like a company, the borders between these categories will blur. For this reason we will follow the so called „phase model" for commercial transactions [19]:

- In the first *information phase*, market participants offer product specifications, look for possible transaction partners, compare product specifications and prices, and evaluate offers.
- Then, after an initial contact has been established between some market participants, respective (service) offers and counter-offers are exchanged during the so called contract *negotiation phase*. This negotiation process may either lead to a situation where agreed terms and conditions have been reached or the negotiation is abandoned.
- In case of a contract establishment, first all participants commit their participation in the contract with their respective signatures, then the agreed assets are exchanged during the contract *performance (or: execution) phase*. The time-span of this phase may reach from a few seconds up to several years.

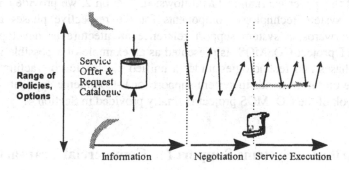

Fig. 1. Phases of Business Transactions

Following these phases, a clear separation of services can be given that are required for an electronic marketplace:

1. *Information phase*: This phase may be supported by (computer) functions like online catalogues, search engines, banner advertising
2. *Negotiation phase*: Here support for telecollaboration, negotiation protocols and strategies may be required.
3. *Execution phase*: During this phase, workflow management, business process integration among market participants, electronic payment systems, EDI-based message exchange functions, etc. may be provided in order to support the automatic execution of E-Commerce applications.

In between these phases, the following additional services may be required:

1. *Brokerage support* in order to select and match respective offers and inquiries, to form a (service providing) consortium or to set-up the negotiation session for all parties of the commercial transaction
2. *Signing support* to enter the execution phase by establishing a contract and ensuring for all parties to sign it. This process may be supported by 'trusted third parties' such as 'certification authorities' or 'electronic notaries'.

In order to keep the model simple, yet without unrealistic abstraction, we consider *any* possible good resp. service as a service; specifically

- also a *payment* is a „service" provided by the customer. The result of the service is the transfer of data which is interpretable as a transfer of a value. This might either be an electronic coin or the settlement authorization between two bank accounts.
- An addition, also a *tangible good* can be represented in the system as a „service": It is selected, ordered and paid electronically and even the physical delivery is accompanied by a range of services and data communications that may be used by the commercial parties (for example: transfers of electronic EDI documents, access to information on the delivery state, etc.).

1.3 Organization of the Rest of the Paper

The rest of this paper is organized as follows: In Section 2, we provide an overview of current system technology components for the respective phases as defined above. Afterwards, a system support reference architecture as developed in the EU/ESPRIT project COSMOS is presented as an example of a possible integration of these phases and technologies under a unified electronic contracting model. A perspective on future trends in system support for E-Commerce applications as well as an outlook of the COSMOS project is finally provided in Section 4.

2   Distributed Systems Support for Commercial Transactions

By following the steps of the phase model, requirements and solutions for distributed systems applications are discussed for the identified electronic commerce areas:

2.1   Catalogue Services

To inform customers about the range of product and their specifications, *catalogue services* are used as a shared information system for both vendors and customers. A catalogue service also establishes a comfortable front-end for the following transaction phases, payment and product delivery. Internally, catalogues are supplied by the vendor's stock management system to keep the information displayed in synch with the physical warehouse.

Today, a catalogue service is deployed by a single vendor who intends to make accessible his range of tangible or intangible ('soft') goods to the customer. For small vendors, a catalogue may be hosted by a third party in the same way as the web server is provided by an Internet Service Provider. In this case, an individual vendor remains responsible for his own 'shop' in terms of presentation and product data. A unified settlement of payments and possibly the delivery of soft goods, however, can be centralized by the shopping mall provider.

As a next step, providers of catalogue services tend to further break down the effort for offering goods in a mall system by allowing vendors to enter single offers into the catalogue: this leads to an offer database, that allows competing market participants to register their offers in a suitable category of the offer database.

This concept has already been addressed several years ago by the ODP trader service [11], that not only suits for storing (*exporting* in ODP lingo) product specifications but also service specifications in a formal sense: services are understood as instances of a *service type* that includes *service attributes* and the *interface type*. A trader additionally provides exporting but also the matching of offers and inquiries. Later-on, this technology has been incorporated into CORBA standardization as the trader Object Service [16].

2.2 Service Brokerage

Usually, a catalogue access ends up in a purchase, which doesn't require any further refinements of a contract or other terms. Usually the good is purchased at the offered price. However, if not only human users are involved, a formalized matchmaking service can be utilized to bring together customers and suppliers or even a group of market participants. In this case a *brokerage service* may be used. To accomplish its task, such a broker requires formal specifications of both the services offered as well as those demanded. Again, the ODP trader suits well for this activity: having already service specifications for different offer categories at hand, an *importing* client then only needs to specify the required service by using an OQL (Object Query Language) statement.

The trader may also be applied to more than two participants in a commercial transaction by specifying a set of required services which are obtained step-by-step from the offer database.

Brokerage services are incorporated into different electronic commerce applications today. To name just a few examples:

- First of all, globally distributed trading/brokerage functions can generally be used for selecting the (according to pre-defined criteria) "best possible" services in an open distributed service environment (such as, e.g., the Internet) [14].
- In the specific context of an open digital library (as an important, dedicated example of an open service market), e.g., the MEDOC project prototype uses a brokerage function for the matching of literature offered and demanded by users of electronic library systems [1].

- Another 'Service Broker' has been developed as a part of the EU/ACTS research project OSM (Open Service Model) [15] in the context of service selection for E-Commerce applications. The respective broker architecture is here based on the OMG CORBA standardization of a Business Object Component Architecture (BOCA) which aims at tying together service offers that have been entered into a common catalogue [17].

2.3 Service Negotiation

Negotiation is the process of reaching an agreement for a service specification. This may take place either out-of-band, by letting market participants negotiate without electronic means, or it may be done on-line. In this case there are several stages of automation possible:

- Use of *collaboration tools*. In this case, human users are involved in the negotiation process. They use, e.g., a shared-editing tool that allows them to concurrently edit a document in a consistent way. The negotiation is free-form, i.e., there are no restrictions for the order of document accesses or the structure of the document.
- Use of *negotiation protocols*. In this case, either human users or software components participate in the negotiation. The negotiation subject is still unstructured, i.e., the participants 'know' how to deal with it. The ordering of document accesses however is formalized and parameterized, .i.e., a negotiation protocol is applied to specify which party delivers which information at which stage to whom. The negotiation can be understood as a workflow process that is driven by a predefined process description.
- Use of *formalized conversations* to further structure the negotiation protocol. Speech act theory (Specifically, the Knowledge Query and Manipulation Language, KQML [2]) provides a linguistic means to define formalized messages that relate - in the case of negotiations - to concepts such as 'offer', 'reject', 'propose', 'accept', etc. This further helps to tailor the involved software systems for the specific application of negotiation support: it may, e.g., react in a different way when it receives an offer instead of a proposal.
- Finally, *the complete negotiation process may be automated* (and therefore delegated to 'autonomous' software components) if the ontology for the negotiation subject has been standardized as well. In this case 'speed' and 'price' are features that a software component is able to reason about. Therefore, AI technologies are applied in this area for knowledge representation and for applying policies that have been defined to control negotiation strategies. Such an intelligent software agent is now capable at least to estimate 'price' and 'speed' and to trade-off their values in a reasonable way [21].

In today's real world, automated negotiation is not used so far for the following reason: Only if the service specification is kept simple (i.e., has only a few 'Quality of Service' attributes), a strategy module can be practically used for negotiating them. The more complex the specification becomes, the more effort needs to be spent for implementing policies and strategies for the agent. If a simple specification is sufficient, the service can be considered as a commodity on the other hand, i.e., a good that is offered by a large number of vendors on the market and for which an individual negotiation would come at prohibitively high costs.

Therefore, the practical integration of negotiation mechanisms won't be feasible unless negotiation support is designed as an integral part of the overall software system.

2.4 Service Configuration

Services offered in an open and heterogeneous environment such as the Internet can only be competitive if they are flexible enough to adapt to a wide variety of user as well as technical requirements. Therefore, appropriate techniques are needed to (re-) *configure* an offered *service dynamically* according to the effective requirements in each case. For example, regarding the involvement of so-called 'third party' services – such as a payment or a notary function – during a business-to-business transaction, as many options as possible should be supported, and moreover, an option common to all transaction parties has to be determined and activated.

A very generic approach to provide system support for such kind of dynamic service configuration consists in using *policy management* mechanisms, in whichso called *policies* provide a formalization of arbitrary requirements which can be evaluated, compared, matched (or unified) and activated in an application independent way [20]. Policies can be added and activated fully automatically at run-time without changing the application code. The configuration effect is achieved by modifying externally accessible properties which are used as system parameters by the applications.

In a broader sense, flexible service configuration also means that arbitrary services should be so configurable that they can be easily plugged together to yield new functionality, i.e. that they can be used as building blocks to assemble new services "on the fly". Providing technical support to fulfill this kind of requirements is precisely the objective of componentware techniques [8] which seem to be the right mean to face the growing challenges in the filed of E-Commerce, especially concerning the requirement of dynamic adaptability. However, there are still a lot of open questions and unsolved problems – for example, the *composition* of an application system out of components has to be distinguished from the *generation* of a new component out of existing ones since they have to fulfill, among other things, very different performance requirements – which are currently being investigated in projects such as DynamiCS [5] in order to make componentware technology applicable in practice.

2.5 Electronic Contract Signing

From the legal perspective, in many cases contracts don't need to be signed explicitly. They often become valid even if they are agreed on orally or by a concluding action. For E-Commerce application, that may mean, for example: whenever a customer hits the 'Buy' button of an electronic shop application, it can be assumed that all the respective consequences are well-known and accepted.

On the other hand, for certain applications there are also several and good reasons that promote the idea of involving an electronic contract into (more secure) explicit online transactions:

- *A written contract cannot be repudiated.* In the case of an electronic contract, this can be signed by the parties as well as by a *trusted third party*. This states who agreed on which terms and at which time. Any arbitration that may be required among these parties can be settled better if there is a version of the contract available that has been archived by a neutral auditor.
- The *legal framework* for online commercial transactions is being established in several countries now. Electronic signatures are at least accepted as an authentication means for the document signed. However, the management of a contract still requires a further harmonization of the national legislation for the participating countries.

  Complex legal situations can be better fixed by using a document as the common form of agreement. It is best practice today that commercial vendors display their terms and conditions as a part of their online presentation. However, it would clarify the legal situation if these documents are not displayed transitionally on the Internet but if they could be escrowed and archived at a third party (e.g. the Chamber of Commerce). This would allow the contracting parties to refer to this document even a long time after it has been replaced by a new one.

  Furthermore, some contracts may be negotiated and closed that require complex specifications such that it is essential to handle them in written form as a shared document. This applies to work plans as well as to complex relationships for obligations and right within consortia.

Finally, in contrast to paper-based contracts, their electronic counterpart are *executable*. Structurally, such contracts incorporate clauses that determine the obligations and rights of each party. From the technical point of view, this can be interpreted for many contracts as an activity or a service that is to be provided at a certain time (payments, delivery of a good or a report, translating a document, or printing, binding and delivering books). Therefore, the *execution phase* of the commercial transaction is not only interpreted in the legal sense as the execution of a contract, but specifically in a technical sense by invoking the corresponding service through remote method invocations.

2.6 Electronic Contract Execution

Considering the final transaction phase, we may view possible levels of electronic support again from several different angles.

- At least, the legal execution can be monitored at the *human level* - as it is the case in 'classical' commerce.
- Since, howvere, deadlines, durations, etc can be represented electronically, this information may also be transferred to a *workflow system* that automatically sends notifications to the parties involved. These notifications refer to the actions the parties agreed upon, e.g., initiating a payment or performing an action. This can then be called a 'supportive' workflow system.
- At the most sophisticated level, these actions may even be triggered by a *workflow engine* that performs method invocations at the different information systems which the parties made available for the others. In this case, a distributed computing infrastructure is assumed that easily enables market participants to be represented not only through Web servers but also through distributed object-oriented software components [13]. Moreover, these components needs to be configurable at run-time in order to integrate them as a part of the commercial transactions

This final situation is, however, only possible if a global network of related objects exists and if these objects can be inspected, refined, combined and integrated as dynamically as a contract is dynamically set-up and executed. A specific requirement is for this reason to transfer the workflow specification that all transaction parties agreed upon into the process definition that is required for a given workflow engine.

Therefore, such an approach can not be successful if the workflow mechanism is isolated from the previously mentioned mechanisms for negotiation and signing. Accordingly, the example E-Commerce infrastructure reference architecture - as developped in the EU/ESPRIT project COSMOS and briefly presented below - has been designed and is currently implemented in such a way.

3   Case Study: The COSMOS Project

As said before, in order to accommodate the different functions mentioned above in a common framework, a *unified* systems architecture is required - at least in terms of an integrated object model and a functional specification of basic software components. Exactly this is the goal of COSMOS (Common Open Service Market fOr SMEs), a European ESPRIT research project that designs and implements important technical software system components for carrying out business transaction across the Internet [4]. In the following, the respective approach is presented in some detail as a case study for demonstrating the use of some typical distributed systems functions and technologies as mentioned above.

Compared with existing electronic commerce architectures such as CommerceNet eCo [3], TINA [22] and the OMG Electronic Commerce Reference Architecture [15], COSMOS is tailored around the concept of a *contract*, which is not only used as a metaphor but as a tangible part of the complete process of a commercial transaction. The COSMOS architecture mainly focuses on software design aspects and less on organizational questions. For the latter we refer to the COSMOS white paper [4].

3.1 COSMOS Contract Model

As the most relevant part of the COSMOS object model, we focus on the modeling of contracts since they serve as the common nexus for most of the transaction phases and building blocks of the implementation.

A COSMOS contract could be considered as structured document composed out of text blocks. In this case, the editing process would be simplified, however, the automated processing of a contract will be very limited. On the other hand, one could attempt to cover the full semantics of a contract by building a 'contracting expert system'. We consider this as a dead end since the expert system overhead is expected as too high – particularly for a Small and Medium Enterprises (SME)/Internet context, characterized by a permanent change of rules, roles, and business subjects.

As a trade-off, the COSMOS contract model aims to identify only those semantically meaningful parts of contract instances which allow for efficient automation and therefore highest increase of the added value. The parts of the contract model can be distinguished by their subject:

- The *'Who'* part: Parties, Persons, and Signatures are related to the participants of the contract. Parties act under a certain role defined by the contract template. They are instantiated as a legal entity which can be in turn a person or an organization. The first may, the latter must be represented by proxies. "Party" only indicates that the legal entity is involved in the contract and abstracts away from the actual tasks which are defined for the corresponding role. Finally each legal entity is associated with a signature when the contract has been closed.

- The *'What'* part is the subject of the contract. It covers all obligation of the involved parties. Each obligation is considered as a transfer of a right which can be either a good, a service, money, or a license. An important feature of the obligation is a list of QoS attributes. It is used for contract templates to specify suitable parties. During contract negotiation, these QoS attributes are subjects of offers and counter-offers. Finally, obligations are to be carried out in the basis of these attributes during contract execution.

- The *'How'* part defines relationships between obligations: when are which services to be delivered? What is the deadline? Which clause will apply when a party falls behind its obligation? The "How" part is used to derive a workflow that defines causal relationships, data transfers, delays and deadlines, and the final termination of the execution phase.

- Finally, some *common clauses* form the fourth part of a contract. These clauses address general terms and conditions at the level of the contract. Also references to applicable external contracts, regulations, and legislation are placed in this part.

Apart from the structural perspective, a contract goes through several steps in line with the transaction phases:

- Initially, a *contract template* is defined, which usually predefines the 'How' and the 'base clauses' parts. Additionally, roles are defined and for each obligation a requested set of conditions. However, the template does not yet identify the contract parties nor the exact obligations: instead of attribute/value pairs (such as 'price per acre = $100' or 'ground's humidity = 20%'), constraint expressions are used as QoS specifications (such as 'price < $150' and 'humidity < 30%').
- *Contract proposal*: By using the broker, the template will be completed if suitable providers can be retrieved from the catalogue. The broker's task is to replace QoS specifications with the corresponding values offered. For each category of obligations a corresponding offer category is required for the catalog. Accordingly, the party objects of a contract template are replaced by the respective participant description taken from the catalog. If the brokerage step leads to a completed contract that can be signed in principle, a *contract proposal* is given.
- During negotiation, contract proposals are exchanged between the parties. Depending on the semantics of such a contract transfer, it may either be considered as a *proposal* (without legal binding) or as an *offer* (with legal binding if the other parties accept). If all parties accept, the contract is in an *agreed* state and ready for signing.
- After all parties (or their proxies) signed the contract, the electronic contracting Service certifies this. Afterwards, the contract is *executable*, i.e. in technical terms, it can be transferred to the workflow system.

3.2 COSMOS Building Blocks

The five functions discussed in Section 2 are covered respectively by five corresponding building blocks in the COSMOS reference architecture underlying the COSMOS prototype implementation (see Fig. 2).

These functions are tightly integrated since they communicate with each other by using contracts as the common representation for the data transferred. All parts of the respective COSMOS prototype may be used optionally by the market participants; It may, for example, happen, that a consortium was already formed before contract negotiations start - such that the catalogue and broker functions are not needed in this case. In other cases, no negotiation is required since the negotiation process itself would be too costly compared with the transaction volume. Finally, one may think of scenarios where no workflow execution is necessary or possible. The configuration of COSMOS components is thus dynamic and depends on the specific business requirements of different kinds of application (i.e. business) transactions.

The COSMOS reference architecture abstracts from implementation technology. This concerns not only its software components but also the contract model. Several current technologies can therefore be used for realizing the respective COSMOS E-Commerce negotiation support prototype implementation, e.g.:

- Current *Web technology* provides the highest performance for online access. This is also the area where new standards emerge at the highest pace.
- *the OMG CORBA standard* promises independence from proprietary hardware and operating systems, here BOCA gains increasing visibility [17]
- Several Frameworks are available for a *'plain Java'* approach, e.g., Voyager [18] for the communication platform or IBM's San Francisco Framework [10] for building component-based applications.
- Finally, also legacy technologies such as EDI has to be supported in the future as an (optionally) integrated part of such an E-Commerce systems infrastructure architecture.

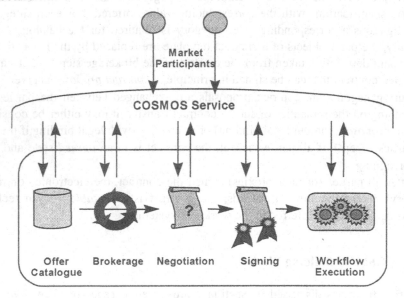

Fig. 2. Building blocks of the COSMOS architecture

4   Conclusions and Further Developments

System support for electronic commerce is a most practically relevant topic for distributed systems research and technology. In order to meet the important inherent openness and flexibility needs of global electronic markets, it requires ad-hoc software integration both at the system as well at the application level. At the same time, these requirements cause several problems for the introduction of electronic commerce applications: On one hand side, they need to be standardized in order to properly cooperate with one another, but they also need to be dynamically deployable, extensible, and integratable on the other. As a result, we face a 'balkanized' separation of electronic commerce tools and technologies today that can only be made interoperable if they adhere to certain standards. However, standardization is a long-term process during which technology development often makes many of the efforts spent there obsolete.

Under this circumstances, the rationale for a generic system infrastructure like the one developed in the COSMOS project is to decompose its functional components into consecutive phases, rather than horizontally into abstraction layers. Then the links between these components can be standardized at the level of the contract model; and, on the other side, any technology decisions for individual component developers are deliberately left open. A most important prerequisite for realizing such a system architecture, however, is a (much more general) *open* and *dynamically* controllable *component based* approach to (also application level) software development.

After having implemented the required functions for the support of commercial transactions, current research developments address additional technological refinements. To give an example, *generic support for auction systems* that is currently being developed at Hamburg University [21] will be integrated to support group negotiation patterns. Another example is the integration of market participants by following the *component-based approach to software integration*. A possible direction has been described in [13].

Finally, *mobile agent technology* is incorporated in the COSMOS project for the transfer of contracts between negotiating parties. Additional rationale for the applicability of this technology is given in [7].

References

1. Adler, W. Lamersdorf, M. Münke, S. Rücker, H. Spahn, U. Berger, A. Brüggemann-Klein, C. Haber "Grey Literature and Multiple Collections in NCSTRL" In: A. Barth, M. Breu, A. Endres, A. de Kemp (Eds.): 'Digital Libraries in Computer Science: The MeDoc Approach', Lecture Notes in Computer Science, vol. 1392, Springer-Verlag, Berlin Heidelberg, New York, 1998, pp. 45-170
2. Chalupsky, T. Finin, R. Fritzson, D. McKay, S. Shapiro, G. Wiederhold: "An overview of KQML: A Knowledge Query and Manipulation Language". Technical Report, April 1992
3. Commerce Net Home Page: http://www.commerce.net
4. COSMOS Project Home Page: http://www.ponton-hamburg.de/cosmos
5. DynamiCS Project Home Page: http://vsys-www.informatik.uni-hamburg.de/projects/dynamics/index.phtml
6. Electronic Commerce Homepage of the European Commission: http://www.ispo.cec.be/ecommerce/
7. Griffel, T. Tu, M. Münke, M. Merz, W. Lamersdorf, M. Mira da Silva "Electronic Contract Negotiation as an Application Niche for Mobile Agents" in: Proc. 1st International Workshop on Enterprise Distributed Object Computing, October 1997
8. Griffel: "Componentware", dpunkt-Verlag, Heidelberg, June 1998
9. Griffel, T. Tu, W. Lamersdorf (Eds.): "Electronic Commerce", dpunkt-Verlag, Heidelberg, June 1998
10. http://www.ibm.com/Java/Sanfrancisco/ technical.html, 1998
11. ISO/IEC IS 13235-1, ITU/T Draft Rec X950 - 1, Part 1; ODP Trader Specification, 1997

12. Lamersdorf, M. Merz (Eds.): "Trends in Distributed Systems for Electronic Commerce", Lecture Notes in Computer Science, vol. 1402, Springer-Verlag, Berlin Heidelberg New York, June 1998
13. Merz, F. Griffel, S. Müller-Wilken, W. Lamersdorf: "Electronic Contracting with COSMOS — How to Establish, Negotiate, and Execute Electronic Contracts on the Internet". In: Proc. 2nd International Workshop on Enterprise Distributed Object Computing, San Diego, Nov. 1998 (to appear)
14. Müller, K. Müller-Jones, W. Lamersdorf, T. Tu: "Global Trader Cooperation in Open Service Markets", in: O. Spaniol, C. Linhoff-Popien, B. Meyer (Hrgs.): Proc. Workshop 'Trends in Distributed Systems: CORBA and Beyond', Lecture Notes in Computer Science, vol. 1161, Springer-Verlag, Heidelberg, Oktober 1996, pp.214-227
15. McConnell, M. Merz, L. Maesano, M. Witthaut: "An Open Architecture for Electronic Commerce". OMG/ECDTF/OSM Response, 1997
16. AT&T, DSTC, DEC, HP, ICL, Nortel, and Novell. Trading Object Service, OMG Document No.: orbos/96-05-06, Version 1.0, 1996
17. Object Management Group: "CORBA BOCA - Business Object Component Architecture", Specification, OMG Document Nr. bom/98-01-07, 1998
18. ObjectSpace. Voyager - Core Technology User Guide, 1997, http://www.objectspace.com/voyager/documentation.html
19. Beat F. Schmid, Markus A. Lindemann (Eds.): Proceedings of the 31st Annual Hawaii International Conference on Systems Science, HICCS'98, Vol. IV, pp. 193-201, Hawaii, January 6-9 1998, 01/1998
20. Tu, F. Griffel, M. Merz, W. Lamersdorf: "Generic Policy Management for Open Service Markets", in: H. Koenig, K. Geihs (Hrsg.): Proc. IFIP International Working Conference on 'Distributed Applications and Interoperable Systemes' (DAIS'97), Chapman & Hall, London/Weinheim/New York, Oktober 1997, pp.211-222
21. Tu, F. Griffel, M. Merz, W. Lamersdorf "A Plug-in Architecture Providing Dynamic Negotiation Capabilities for Mobile Agents" in: K. Rothermel, F. Hohl (Eds.): Proc. 2nd International Workshop on 'Mobile Agents', MA'98, Stuttgart, Lecture Notes in Computer Science, Springer-Verlag, Berlin Heidelberg New York, September 1998
22. Abarca et al.: TINA Service Architecture, Telecommunications Networking Information Architecture Consortium 1997, http://www.tinac.com/u/tinac/97/services/docs/sa/sa5.0/final/

Parallel Interactive Media Server Systems*

Reinhard Lüling, Francisco Cortes Gomez, Norbert Sensen

Department of Mathematics and Computer Science,
University of Paderborn, Germany
{rl,cortes,sensen}@uni-paderborn.de

Abstract. Interactive media server systems play an important role in
the envisioned 'Information society'. Powerful media server systems are
one of the cornerstones of the networked society in which media servers
store news information, product descriptions, customer information, video
clips and many other media elements that are used to inform consumers,
run businesses, or entertain people.
Within this paper we distinguish two types of media objects. Realtime
media on the one hand and non-realtime media objects on the other
hand. Whereas realtime media, e.g. audio and video streams, are mainly
used in information and entertainment applications, non-realtime media
is used in all general purpose applications, e.g. conventional web services.
The paper presents the design of two media server systems, handling
one of the two types of media objects each. The server systems described
in the paper are both based on a distributed memory parallel computer
system. For each of the server systems presented here, a single important
question is studied in detail. This is the data layout question for non-
realtime media servers and the communication scheduling problem for
realtime media servers.

1 Introduction

Digital libraries as they exist today and will be available in the future contain all
kind of media objects. Ranging from simple ASCII text documents, to structured
documents using hyperlinks and integrated animation, sound and video a whole
range of digital libraries exist today or can be envisoned for the near future.

The media components stored by a digital library can be distinguished according to their realtime properties. Media objects as audio and video have
strict realtime requirements for their delivery and presentation from the server
to the client. If a audio/video stream is delivered from the server to a client,
data packets must be send right in time, i.e. not to late to avoid interruption of
the presentation and not to early to avoid buffer overflow on the client. Thus, a
server system delivering continuous media information has to take these realtime
properties into account. As audio and video objects are also usually very large

* This work was partly supported by the MWF Project "Die Virtuelle Wissensfab-
rik", the EU project SICMA, and the DFG Sonderforschungsbereich 1511 "Massive
Parallelität: Algorithmen, Entwurfsmethoden, Anwendungen".

in size and in amount of data that has to be delivered from a server to a client, powerful server systems using a moderate number of processors (SMP systems) or a scaleable number of processors (MPP) are used for the implementation of continuous media servers.

Digital libraries that contain a moderate number of media objects having no realtime characteristic are mostly stored on conventional computer systems (holding at most a moderate number of processors and storage subsystems). If a digital library of this kind is requested by a larger number of clients in parallel (providing short latency times) or the amount of data items stored in the library becomes very large, also here the use of moderate or large parallel systems is favourable.

Within this paper the design of parallel interactive media server systems for the storage and delivery of both kind of media objects is presented, i.e. server systems taking the special characteristics of realtime media into account as well as media servers for the delivery of non-realtime media to a large number of clients are studied. We study the implementation of *Interactive Continuous Media Servers (ICMS)* for the delivery of encoded audio and video streams as well as that of a scaleable web server for the delivery of non-realtime media objects.

The highest level of abstraction considers a parallel interactive media server as a set of storage subsystems, processors, and external communication interfaces (connecting the ICMS to an access and delivery network) which are connected by an internal communication network. Figure 1 presents this abstract model for a parallel media server. We will always consider disks as the storage device, although in real world implementations the storage subsystem itself will consist of a hierarchy of fast memory that can be used for caching, disks and magneto-optic devices for mass storage. A processor can be connected to storage devices, to external communication interfaces, or to both of them.

The internal network is built as a structured graph like the butterfly, the square $n \times n$ grid, or the complete bipartite graph [5]. By using such an internal communication network, the overall communication bandwidth can be considerably increased compared to systems that are based on buses.

The implementation of scaleable servers for the delivery of realtime and non-realtime media objects has gained considerable attention during the last years, as a number of important research questions have to be solved for their optimal implementation.

Within this paper we will focus on two important questions: For the parallel web server system that is studied in section 2 the data layout question is studied, i.e. the question how the media objects should be mapped onto a set of storeage devices is discussed there.

For the parallel ICMS presented in section 3, the question of communication scheduling which becomes very important for distributed memory ICMS is discussed.

Both server systems have been implemented and integrated into various applications which are described shortly in this paper.

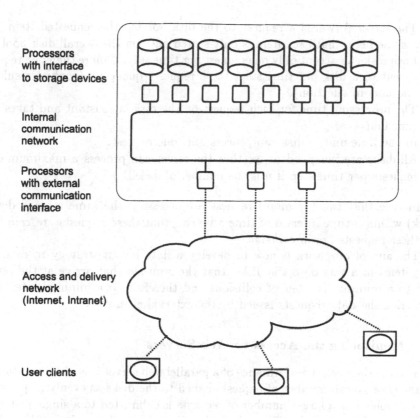

Processors
with interface
to storage devices

Internal
communication
network

Processors
with external
communication
interface

Access and delivery
network
(Internet, Intranet)

User clients

Fig. 1. Abstract model of an ICMS

1.1 Model

To describe the methods used for the determination of a suitable data layout of a parallel web server, the model of the parallel web server used here, is described first. Thus, we concentrate in our model on the aspects that are important for the data layout and model other aspects on a higher level of abstraction.

A parallel web server is build up by the following entities:

- A number of processing modules that are connected by some kind of network or bus architecture.
- A number of communication devices that connect the processing modules to the external clients accessing the server and requesting information.
- A number of storage devices (disks) that are connected to the processing modules.

The parallel web server stores data items (files) on the disks and works as follows:

- The server is able to accept one or more requests arriving via the communication devices from the external clients per time step.

– The server forwards a request to the disk holding the requested item. We assume here, that each item is only stored once on the overall disk pool.

– Each disk can accept only one request per time step. If more than one request is sent to a disk per time step, these requests queue up (conflict resultion via random selection).

– The processing time for each request on the disk is constant and takes one time unit.

– In one time unit, a disk can process only one request.

– All disks are independent, so that the server can process a maximum of n requests per time step if n is the number of disks.

In case that two (or more) request are accessing the same storage device (disk) within a time interval of time δ we say, that these requests are *colliding*, i.e. these requests are in *collision*.

The aim of our work is now to develop a data layout strategy to map the data items in a way onto the disks, that the requests that arrive at the server lead to a minimal number of collisions and therefore to a minimal latency in answering the data requests issued by the external clients.

1.2 Monitoring the Access to Web Servers

To increase the overall performance of a parallel web server it is not important to balance the overall number of requests issued to the disks as evenly as possible, but to avoid that a larger number of requests is submitted to a single disk only while other disks are idle. This means that in each small time interval the load has to be distributed as evenly as possible to all disks, minimizing the latency time for a request this way. Thus, the aim is to minimise the number of collisions on the disks.

To get an impression of the collisions that occur we have taken the log files from the web server of the University of Paderborn (www.uni-paderborn.de) for November and December 1997.

If we study the requests that are issued to all files stored on the web server it is typical for web servers, that some files are accessed very often, while others are requested only seldom. Our observations show, that these frequently requested data items (files) are always the same files. Figure 2 shows the number of requests issued to all files stored on the server on two consecutive days. The x-axis lists all files according to their hit-rate on the first day. The y-axis lists the number of hits for the files. Both axis are drawn with logarithmic scale.

As mentioned above, the overall number of requests that are issued to a single data item on a web server is not as important as the number of collisions of pairs of files. Therefore we build all tuples (i, j) of files i and j stored on the web server in Paderborn and measured the number of collisions, i.e. the number of hits that were made on files i and j within the time interval δ which is choosen to be one second for our experiments.

Figure 3 shows the number of collisions for all pairs of files for two consecutive days sorted by the collisions of the first day. The x-axis lists all tuples (i, j) of

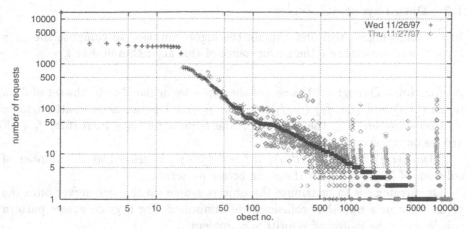

Fig. 2. Distribution of requested data items

files according to the collisions on the first day, and the y-axis lists the number of collisions for each pair of files. Now it is interesting to observe that the collisions are very similar on the two consecutive days, i.e. accesses that collide very often on the first day do this also on the second day.

So if we develop an algorithm, that minimizes the collisions for a typical access pattern of the web server monitored at one day, these collisions will also be reduced on the next day. Thus, we can take the similarity of access patterns into account for the construction of our data layout strategy. This is the basic observation and the foundation of our data layout principle.

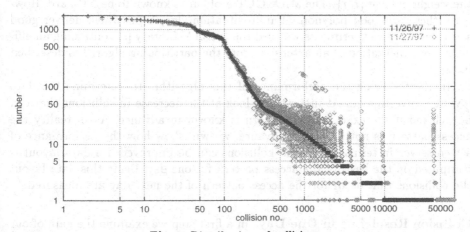

Fig. 3. Distribution of collisions

1.3 Data Layout Strategies

In the following we will first explain the algorithm used to compute the data layout and then evaluate the performance of this algorithm in detail.

Algorithm. Throughout the rest of the paper we define F to be the set of data items (files) and $\{(t_1, f_1), (t_2, f_2), \ldots, (t_m, f_m), \ldots\}$ be an access pattern for a web server where t_i is the time when the request for data item (file) $f_i \in F$ arrives on the server.

Then $c(i, j) = | \{\{(t, i), (t', j)\} \mid |t - t'| \le \delta\} |$ is defined as the number of collisions of files i and j for the given access pattern.

Our strategy is to distribute the objects stored on the web server onto the given disks in a way that collisions are minimised. For a given access pattern this leads to the following algorithmic problem:

given: A set of data items F and a given number of storage devices n.

question: Determine mapping π, $\pi = \min_{l:F \to \{1, \ldots, n\}} \sum_{i,j \in F, l(i) = l(j)} c(i, j)$.

It is easy to map this problem to the MAX-CUT-problem. The MAX-CUT-problem is defined as follows:

given: A graph $G = (V, E)$, weights $w(e) \in I\!N$ for all $e \in E$ and a given number of partitions n.

question: Determine a partition of V into disjoint sets $V_1, \ldots, V_n$, such that the sum of the weights for the edges from E having the endpoints in different V_i is maximal.

The mapping is done in a way that the data items (files) are the nodes of the graph that has to be partitioned and the number of collisions $c(i, j)$ determines the weight of edge $\{i, j\}$. The MAX-CUT problem is known to be NP-hard. However, there are good polynomial approximation algorithms which deliver good solutions. In our experiments we used the PARTY-Library [9] containing an efficient implementation of an extension from the partitioning algorithm described in [3].

In the following the performance of this algorithm to determine the data layout is investigated. At first we will look at the decrease in collisions that can be achived if the exact access pattern is known in advance. As in reality the access pattern is not known in advance, we will show how the performance of a web server in terms of reduced collisions can be improved if a data layout is computed on the basis of the access pattern for one day. Using this data layout the collisions that occur for the access pattern of the next day are measured.

Collision Resolving on One Day. In a first step we examine the gain of our algorithm if the access pattern and therefore the collisions are known in advance.

To do this we took the access statistics of one day and determined the number of collisions of each pair of data items. On the base of these statistics, we built the graph, partitioned the graph, and looked how many collisions had remained and how many had been resolved.

Figure 4 shows in percentage the remaining collisions of a random partition and our partition respectively, based on the access pattern of the server on November 26, 1997. The values are presented in dependence of the number n of storage devices. For a random distribution of the files onto a set of n disks, an edge describing a collision will be cut with probability $\frac{n-1}{n}$. So the expected percentage of remaining collisions is $\frac{1}{n}$.

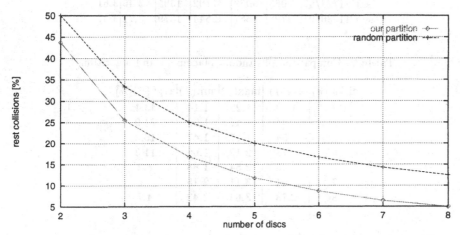

Fig. 4. Percentage of collisions not resolved by random placement and algorithm

The following results can be obtained from Figure 4:

- If there are few discs, only few collisions can be resolved. This can be explained with the existence of larger cliques that cannot be resolved completely when only a few disks are available.
- Our partition resolves clearly more collisions than the random partition.
- The more discs are available the greater is the advantage of our partitioning method in relation to a random mapping.

In the following we compare the results of our algorithm with the random mapping strategy for a number of access patterns. Each access patterns represents exactly all requests that were issued to the server during one day. We compare the number of collisions induced by the access pattern (k_a) with the number of remaining collisions that occur when applying the mapping algorithm described above (k_r). The factor f describes the relation between the number of remaining collisions for the random mapping (which is $\frac{k_a}{n}$) and the mapping that is determined by the algorithm (k_r).

In Table 1 the statistics and results of the partition of one week are shown. The table shows that all collisions up to 4 - 5 percent can be resolved and that the algorithm has about 2 to 3 times the performance of the random mapping.

Table 1. Results for a number of access patterns, each representing one day

day	nodes	edges	k_a	results, $n = 8$		
				k_r	$\frac{k_r}{k_a}[\%]$	f
sun 11/23/97	5533	15148	75334	3152	4.18	2.99
mon 11/24/97	8877	48136	239365	12100	5.06	2.50
tue 11/25/97	7932	43720	228870	11367	4.97	2.52
wed 11/26/97	8206	41172	215825	10800	5.00	2.50
thu 11/27/97	7464	44656	231364	12021	5.20	2.40
fri 11/28/97	6976	30919	174120	8671	4.98	2.51
sat 11/29/97	5065	9059	37702	1305	3.46	3.61
sun 11/30/97	4798	8657	42544	1579	3.71	3.37

Table 2. Comparison of random placement and algorithm

disks (n)	avg(f)	max(f)	min(f)	avg$(\frac{k_r}{k_a})[\%]$
2	1.16	1.22	1.14	43.1
3	1.34	1.47	1.29	24.9
4	1.54	1.77	1.47	16.3
5	1.78	2.12	1.66	11.3
6	2.05	2.54	1.88	8.2
7	2.41	3.11	2.15	6.0
8	2.73	3.64	2.42	4.7

Table 2 shows the influence of the number of disks (n) on the performance of the algorithm. The table presents the results for a number of days where the mapping was determined by the access pattern of day i and this mapping was used to determine the remaining collisions if used for the access pattern of day i. It can be regarded, that the number of resolved solutions is increasing largely when n increases, so that up to 95 percent of all collisions are resolved. It also shows that the performance of the algorithm increases if compared to the random mapping algorithm for larger n.

Optimize the next Day. In the following we examine how much collisions can be resolved if we use the access-statistics of a single day i to determine the data layout and apply this data layout to the access pattern of day $i + 1$ This approach can only be successful if the collisions of successive days have some similarity. We have examined this similarity already above.

Table 3 presents the results for a number of days where the mapping was determined by the access pattern of day i and this mapping was used to for the access pattern of day $i + 1$. The table shows the factor f comparing the performance of the random mapping method with the algorithm presented above in respect to the number of disks n. It also shows the precentage of remaining collisions of day $i + 1$ that could not be resolved. Compared to the number of collisions that can be resolved if the access pattern is known, there is only a very small loss in performance. Also compared to the random mapping method the algorithm still behaves much better.

Table 3. Comparison of random placement and algorithm using access pattern of previous day

disks (n)	avg(f)	max(f)	min(f)	avg$(\frac{k_r}{k_a})$[%]
2	1.11	1.14	1.07	45.2
3	1.22	1.30	1.16	27.4
4	1.34	1.45	1.25	18.7
5	1.47	1.63	1.34	13.7
6	1.61	1.85	1.44	10.5
7	1.76	2.06	1.56	8.2
8	1.87	2.16	1.70	6.7

Table 4 compares the influence on the performance of the data layout method if the exact access pattern is known in advance, or if only the access pattern of the day before is known. Values with the index $_{sd}$ are results from the experiments basing on the statistics of the same day, i.e. the access pattern is known, values with the index $_{db}$ are results that are found if the access pattern of day $i + 1$ is applied to the data layout that is determined using the access pattern of the previous day i.

Table 4. Impact of number of disks on algorithm performance

disks (n)	f_{sd}	f_{db}	$\frac{k_{r,sd}}{k_a}$[%]	$\frac{k_{r,db}}{k_a}$[%]	$\frac{\frac{k_a}{n}-k_{r,db}}{\frac{k_a}{n}-k_{r,sd}}$
2	1.16	1.11	43.1	45.2	0.70
3	1.34	1.22	24.9	27.4	0.70
4	1.54	1.34	16.3	18.7	0.72
5	1.78	1.47	11.3	13.7	0.72
6	2.05	1.61	8.2	10.5	0.73
7	2.41	1.76	6.0	8.2	0.73
8	2.73	1.87	4.7	6.7	0.74

The value of the term $\frac{\frac{k_a}{n}-k_{r,db}}{\frac{k_a}{n}-k_{r,sd}}$ shows the relative performance difference of the random mapping and the data layout determined by the algorithm presented above, for the case that the algorithm knows the exact access pattern or knows only the access pattern of the day before. The values of this term are shown in respect to the parameter n. The results show that the performance of our method decreases by about 30 percent if the data layout is computed on the basis of the access pattern from day $i - 1$ instead of day i if the access pattern of day i is applied. This loss seems to be nearly independent from the number of disks but becomes smaller for larger number of disks.

In general the results show, that the data layout that is based on the access pattern of a previous day leads to a large reduction of the collisions on later days. Thus, if the data layout is determined on the access pattern that is accumulated for one day, it can be expected that this data layout is also very well usable on the next days.

1.4 A high Performance Digital Library System

Based on the data layout strategy described above a parallel distributed memory WWW server has been developed that is the basic element of the 'High Performance Query Server (HPQS)'. This system is developed by our group in co-operation with other groups from the Universities of Bielefeld, Aachen, Dortmund and Hagen. For a full description of the HPQS see [4].

The approach followed by the HPQS system extends and integrates various technologies into one system. The basic features of the HPQS system are:

- Questions can be submitted using a natural language interface making it very convinient to use the system
- The questions is interpreted using a number of problem independent databases and some databases that depend on the application that is targetted, i.e. domain specific knowledge
- A mediator stores metadata information that is extracted from the mass data and uses it for further requests
- A parallel server stores and delivers mass data information and performs search operations on these mass data items.
- High performance specialized processors perform selected search operations on mass data items that demand large computational power.

Figure 5 presents the structure of the HPQS. The system is build up by the following five modules that also represent the operational structure of the HPQS:

NLI: The natural language interface is the user interface of the system. Questions are asked in natural formed sentences. The SZS (semantic inter language) representation is constructed from the questions.

Retrieval-Module: From the SZS representations a FRR (Formal Retrieval Representation) is constructed. It makes use of transformation- and interpretation-knowledge. This FRR is transformed to OQL (Object query language) requests.

Multimedia Mediator: The Multimedia Mediator structures and mediates the available mass data by managing additional meta data. OQL queries are processed by the help of the parallel server.

Parallel Server: The parallel server manages and delivers all available mass data. Additionally, time-consuming methods that work on the mass data informations can be initiated by the Multimedia Mediator and are performed by the parallel server.

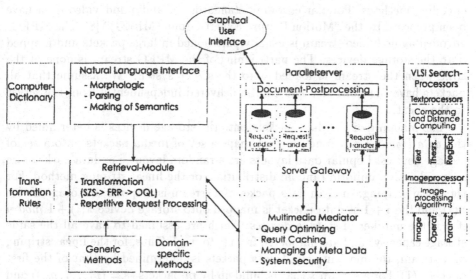

Fig. 5. The High Performance Query Server

Search-Processor: Methods that are frequently used are supported by these specially developed hardware, which is integrated into the parallel server as a co-processor connected via standard PCI interfaces.

An example domain is selected to demonstrate the performance of the HPQS. This special domain can in principal be replaced by every other domain. Within the selected domain of meteorological data, questions on meteorologic data can be submitted to the HPQS. These questions are handled by the different modules of the HPQS and initiate search operations on the mass data stored on the parallel server. Using the results of these search operations, an answer is generated.

In this way, questions can be answered that have a structure like:

- *Where was the most warm place in Germany yesterday ?*
- *How many days were sunny in Berlin in the last month ?*
- *Show me pictures of the formation of clouds over Bavaria in the first week of August !*

1.5 Model

In this section we describe the model of an ICMS that is used in our study. To do this, we mainly study the storage and operational model as the hardware model is similar to that of the parallel web server discussed in the previous section.

Storage Model. The main task of an ICMS is to store and deliver continuous media information. The information has usually large bandwidth (e.g. video encoded with 25 frames per second) and is therefore encoded using sophisticated encoding methods. Popular encoding standards for audio and video data have been proposed by the "Motion Picture Expert Group (MPEG)" [8]. The MPEG-encoded audio/video stream is usually partitioned in large packets and mapped onto the storage devices. The partitioning of the MPEG stream is done at the time when the stream is loaded onto the server system. We assume that all packets have the same size and can be delivered independently from the server to the client.

The mapping of the data packets onto the storage devices is determined by the *data layout*, i.e. a function that maps a set of media packets onto a set of storage devices. Popular data layouts are a random layout, i.e. data packets are mapped with a uniform random distribution, or the linear striping method. For the linear striping, the i-th data packet of a stream is mapped to storage device $\pi(i)$ and the $i + 1$-st data packet is mapped onto storage device $\pi(i) + 1 \ mod \ n$ if n is the number of storage devices (which are assumed to have all the same storage capacity) and are numbered from 0, to $n - 1$. Thus, for the linear striping of a stream, the mapping of all data packets is determined by that of the first packet $\pi(1)$. For a stream s that is build up by m packets $(s = (p_1^s, \ldots, p_m^s))$ and is striped onto n disks, we call $map(s) := \pi(1)$ as the *start disk* of the stream.

Operational Model of an ICMS. From the user's point of view an ICMS behaves like a VCR. If the user logs into the ICMS he selects an audio/video stream and is allowed to play, pause, and stop the stream. Before starting to play a stream, the *admission control algorithm* verifies if the ICMS still provides sufficient resources (disk bandwidth, communication bandwidth, buffer space, processing power) to handle the delivery of the stream. If this procedure is successfully passed and the user is playing a stream, data packets are delivered from the ICMS to the user client according to the defined bitrate of the stream (which is determined when the stream is generated and which is recognized by the ICMS when the stream is loaded onto the ICMS).

The delivery of the data packets from the storage devices to the external communication devices is controlled by a *scheduler* which triggers the delivery of the data packets to the external communication device according to the real time requirements of the stream. A popular scheduling algorithm uses the simple but effective earliest deadline first method, in which a priority queue of events is handled that represent time stamps for the delivery of data packets from the storage devices to the external network interfaces. Whenever the time has expired, the scheduler sends a trigger message to the processor holding the appropriate data packet and informs the processor to deliver it to the appropriate external communication device that connects to the user client. Compared to the communication that takes place from the storage nodes to the nodes holding the external communication devices, the communication that is induced by the trigger message can be neglected.

The main task of the scheduling algorithm is now to assure that the buffer at the user client that holds some data packets to tolerate network latencies, will never become empty. To assure this, we assume that the delay that is induced by the external network connecting the external network interface to the user client is constant. So the task of the scheduling algorithm is to determine the delay that is induced by the internal communication network of the ICMS and by the parallel access of many streams to the same storage device.

1.6 Communication Scheduling in the Beneš and Clos Network

In this section we will investigate how to construct a parallel ICMS that is able to guarantee the communication capability necessary for an ICMS. As a building block for this paralle ICMS we take a Butterfly network $BF(2, n)$, i.e. a Butterfly network of degree 2 and dimension n connecting 2^n storage nodes with 2^n nodes that hold external communication interfaces. A Beneš network (B(2, r) is constructed by two Butterfly networks of the same dimension (BF(2, r)) that are connected back-to-back. For a detailled discussion of both networks see [5]. For the communication scheduling in the Beneš network we use a classical results taken from graph theory:

Theorem 1. *(Permutation Routing in Beneš networks)*

Given any one-to-one mapping π of the 2^{r+1} input links to the 2^{r+1} output links of a Beneš network $B(2, r)$ of dimension r, there is a set of edge-disjoint paths from the inputs to the outputs connecting input i to output $\pi(i)$ for $0 \leq i \leq 2^{r+1} - 1$.

The result of this Theorem enables us to construct an ICMS using a $B(2, r)$ that works as follows:

- Connect a storage device to each of the 2^{r+1} input links and an external communication device to each of the 2^{r+1} outgoing links of the Beneš network.
- Suppose a set of streams $\{s_1, \ldots, s_t\}$ has to be mapped onto the ICMS. All streams are linearly striped onto the storage devices and $map(s_1) = 0$, $map(s_{i+1}) = (map(s_i) + m) \bmod 2^{r+1}$ if m is equal to the number of packets of stream i.
- Operate the ICMS in a synchronized way (rounds) using circuit switching routing, i.e. in each round a storage device can submit a data packet without any congestion to an outgoing link (external communication device).
- In round 1 of the ICMS the idential permutation is routed, i.e. a data packet that is originated at input link j can be submitted to outgoing link j, $0 \leq j \leq 2^{r+1} - 1$.
- In round i of the ICMS a data packet at input link j can be submitted to outgoing link $out(j, i)$ if $(out(j, i) + i) \bmod 2^{r+1} = j$.
- If a user client is connected to the external communication device k and enters the system to retrieve a stream s that starts at storage device j, i.e. the first data packet is stored on storage device j, the set up of the stream is delayed until a round i with $out(j, i) = k$. From this round on, the stream is continuously submitted to the user client.

Figure 6 shows the communication lines that are scheduled in the different rounds. As the theorem states, the communication can be routed without any congestion in each round. Thus, the QoS - requirements of an ICMS can be guaranteed.

Input links from storage devices

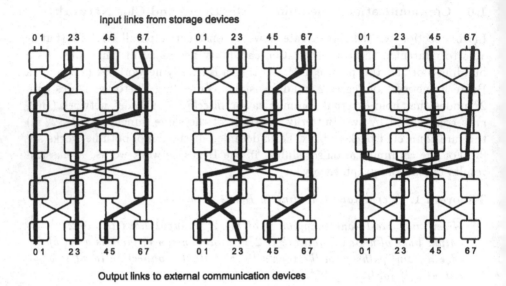

Output links to external communication devices

Fig. 6. Synchronized operation of an ICMS build up by a Beneš network $B(2,3)$

One should notice, that the number of data packets that have to be routed in one round over one path from the input links to the output links of the Beneš network depends directly on the number of users that are located on the respective output link, i.e. if one external network interface connects to two clients, two data packets are routed in one round of the scheduler from the input channel to the output channel. The number of users that are allocated to a single output channel of the Beneš network is determined by the admission control algorithm that will be desrcribed in the next section.

An ICMS that is constructed and operated in the way described above has a number of very important advantages but also some disadvantages.

The most important advantage is, that in each round all communication lines are busy (if all external communication interfaces are used by at least one user), i.e. no hardware in terms of switches and wires is wasted. The routing algorithm is very simple [5] and can be computed online. Thus, the basic principle is ideally suited for the construction of large scale ICMS.

The disadvantages of the network and the operational principle of the ICMS as discussed above are:

- The number of switches that are used for the realization of a Beneš network is very large. In fact the $B(2, r)$ uses $(2r+1)\,2^r$ nodes to connect 2^{r+1} storage nodes and 2^{r+1} external communication devices.
- The network is not scaleable in the way, that the number of storage nodes can be increased without increasing the number of nodes that can hold external communication devices. In fact the outgoing links of the Beneš network can only be used for external communication devices, not to connect additional storage subsystems.
- The overall communication is synchronized, i.e. there might be a decrease in the performance as additional effort (in terms of hardware of control software) is necessary to handle the overall synchronization.

In the following we will stepwise refine the basic ICMS in order to end up with a final version of the structure and operational model that resolves these drawbacks.

Circuit Switching Routing - Store and Forward Routing. The routing model that was described above assumes a circuit switching routing algorithm for the delivery of data packets from the storage devices to the external communication interfaces. As circuit switching models are not very well suited for large scale distributed memory parallel computer systems a store and forward routing scheme would be favorable.

In fact it is also possible to use the same routing method in the store and forward mode. This is because of the leveled structure of the Beneš network. Thus if the complete data packets are send in store and forward modus, the different paths (connecting input and output links of the Beneš network) can be routed in an edge - disjoint way.

Optimization of the Network Structure - Clos Networks. As discussed above, the major disadvantage of the Beneš network if used as the architecture for an ICMS is the fact that the number of input and output edges is similar, what means that one external network interface unit has to be used for one storage device (otherwise the output link is wasted).

A possible solution to overcome this problem is use the so called *folded Beneš network* or *Clos network* [7]. This is constructed by mapping level i and $r - i$ of a network of dimension r on another. In this way, the communication links become bidirectional and the nodes at level 0 provide 2 input and output links each.

The major advantage of this network is, that the number of storage devices and external communication devices can now be scaled to any extend, i.e. network switches are not wasted if only a relative small number of external network devices are used compared to the number of storage devices (as it is usually the case for typical ICMS installations). On the other side, the routing algorithm can be performed in the same way as described for the Beneš network using the bidirectional communication links of the folded network.

1.7   A Parallel ICMS Complying to the RTSP Pprotocol

Based on the data layout and scheduling method that have been presented in
the previous section, a parallel ICMS complying to the RTSP protocol was developed.

RTSP, RTP and RTCP: The 'Real Time Streaming Protocol (RTSP)" is used
to control the delivery of continuous media from an ICMS to the clients. The
associated data delivery protocol RTP (Realtime Transport Protocol) is used
to encapsulate the media elements delivered by the server. Closeley associated
to the RTP protocol is the RTCP (Realtime Transport Control Protocol) that
provides information about packet loss, jitter and other measures to control the
delivery of the data packets via the IP network from the server to the client.

The RTSP protocol was jointly developed by *Progressive Networks, Netscape
Communications*, and *Columbia University* to satisfy the needs for an efficient
delivery of streamed multimedia data over IP networks. Its specification (product of the Multiparty Multimedia Session Control Working Group) has been
approved by the IESG in February 1998. RTSP has its origin in the well known
HTTP protocol. Both protocols can be used homogeneously in a common application and are therefore very well suited to integrate the delivery of both media
types in future client systems.

The idea of using RTSP and RTP is that the control and delivery of continuous media is handled via different channels (IP connections). Whereas the
control messages (issued via RTSP, i.e. STOP, PLAY, PAUSE, ...) are submitted via TCP/IP from the client to the server, the data packets are encapsulated
according to the RTP payload format specification and submitted usually via
UDP/IP from the server to the client.

The parallel RTSP server: The idea of independent channels for control and
delivery of media streams is directly reflected in the design of the software architecture of the RTSP server that is shown in Figure 7. The different modules
shown in this figure (here a configuration with 3 data retriever processes and
2 RTP delivery processes is shown) are mapped onto the processors. The data
retriever processes are performed by those processors that hold a storage device. The RTP data sender modules are mapped onto the processors that hold
an external network interface card. Both types of processes can be scaled. The
scheduler and other control processes are mapped onto one single processor.

The RTSP module accepts incoming requests for a new user session and
forks a new RTSP dealer thread for each session it handles. This dealer thread
performs the RTSP control communication between the client and the server for
the requested session. On start of the session, the admission control algorithm
is invoked in order to decide about the acceptance of the session request, taking
the current resources of the ICMS as well as the necessary resources (bitrate,
memory consumption) of the requested stream into account. If the session is
admitted, one of the RTP data sender modules is identified that provides enough
resources to handle the delivery of the stream and is located on a processor that

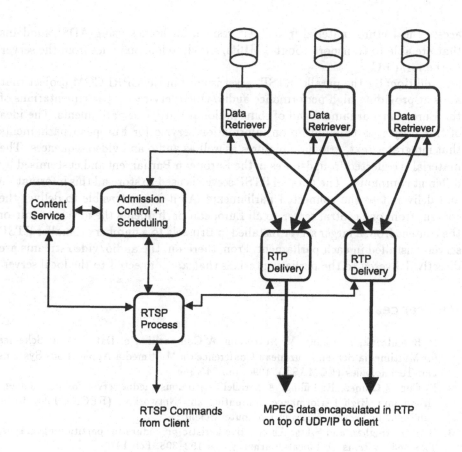

RTSP Commands
from Client

MPEG data encapsulated in RTP
on top of UDP/IP to client

Fig. 7. Software architecture of parallel RTSP server

has an external network interface that is able to access the client. From then on, the scheduler processes takes over the responsibility to trigger the data retriever processes for the delivery of media packets from the disks to the appropriate RTP data sender who encapsulates the data packets for delivery over the network to the client.

For the RTSP server presented here, we used a Clos network as the structure for the internal communication network. In this way it is possible to apply the previous results for the asynchronous scheduling, admission control and data layout to the RTSP server.

Integration of the RTSP server: The RTSP server is used in some European research and development projects. The SICMA project (SICMA = Scaleable Interactive Continuous Media Server - Design and Application) uses the parallel RTSP server for a teleteaching application at the Limburg University in Belgium. Student from different departments can access lectures that contain audio/video material (about 70 GByte of MPEG-1 and MPEG-2 encoded data) from about 45 terminals that are located in the University. At the same time, students can access the lecture material from their residential homes using ADSL modems that are able to transport about 6 MBits/sec via telephone lines from the server to the local PC.

Additionally, the parallel RTSP server is used in the EPRI-COM project that aims at providing high performance audio/video services to parliamentarians of the European Parliament and of some national European parliaments. The idea of this project is to build up an information service for European parliaments that integrates text, graphics, pictures as well as audio and video sequences. The material is collected from debates in the European Parliament and customised by different companies. The parallel RTSP server is used to store all this information and deliver it to the connected parliaments. As it is not feasible to deliver the content from one central server to all European parliaments the idea is to mirror the content from a larger server installed in Brussels to a number of smaller RTSP servers installed in each parliament. From there on, the audio/video streams are directly delivered to the parliamentarians that are connected to the local server.

References

1. P. Berenbrink, R. Lüling, V. Rottmann: A Comparision of Data Layout Schemes for Multimedia Servers, European Conference on Multimedia Applications Systems and Technologies (ECMAST), 1996, pp. 345-366.
2. F. Cortes Gomez, R. Lüling: A parallel continuous media server for Internet environments, High Performance Computing and Networking (HPCN), 1998, to be publisehd in Lecture Notes in Computer Science.
3. B.W. Kernighan and S.Lin. An effective heristic procedure for partitioning graphs, The Bell Systems Technical Journal, pages 192–308, Feb 1970.
4. A. Knoll et.al: HPQS: A High Performance Query Server, European Conference on Research and Advanced Technology for Digital Libraries, September 98
5. F.T. Leighton: Introduction to Parallel Algorithms and Architectures, Arrays, Trees, Hypercubes Morgan Kaufmann Publishers, 1992.
6. F.T. Leighton: Introduction to Parallel Algorithms and Architectures, Arrays, Trees, Hypercubes Section 3.2, The Butterfly, Cube-Connected-Cycles and Benes Network, pp. 439, Morgan Kaufmann Publishers, 1992.
7. B. Monien, R. Lüling, R. Diekmann: The Construction of Large Scale Reconfigurable Parallel Computing Systems – (The Architecture of the SC320), International Journal of Foundations of Computer Science, Vol. 8, No. 3, 1997, pp. 347-361, World Scientific Publishing
8. The Motion Picture Expert Group: WWW Page at http://www.mpeg.org
9. R. Preis and R. Diekmann. The PARTY Partitioning – Library User Guide. Technical Report tr-rsfb-96-024, University of Paderborn.
10. H. Schulzrinne, A. Rao, R. Lanphier: Real Time Streaming Protocol (RTSP), draft-ietf-mmusic-rtsp-09.ps, February, 1998.

On-Line Routing Problems for Broadband Networks

Alberto Marchetti-Spaccamela

Dipartimento di Informatica e Sistemistica,
Università di Roma "La Sapienza", via Salaria 113, 00198 Roma, Italy
alberto@dis.uniroma1.it

Abstract. The area of broadband communication networks gives rise to a large number of on-line problems. One of the most extensively studied problem in this area is the on-line processing of calls; two classes of problems have been considered: call control and load balancing. In the first case a sequence of requests for calls is given on-line to an algorithm which can be either accepted or rejected; the algorithm has to select a virtual circuit between the communicating parties of an accepted call, obeying the network constraints, with the goal of maximizing the total benfit of accepted calls. In load balancing the goal of the algorithm is to find virtual circuits for all calls that minimize the use of network resources.

Algorithms for on-line problems are usually analysed in terms of their competitive ratio, i.e., the worst case, over all input sequences, of the ratio between the values of the solution found by an optimal off-line algorithm (that knows the whole sequence in advance) and by the on-line algorithm.

In this talk we review the main results that have been proposed in the literature by presenting both deterministic and randomized algorithms for various kind of network topologies and discussing lower bounds.

Some Prospects for Efficient Fixed Parameter Algorithms

Rolf Niedermeier*

Wilhelm-Schickard-Institut für Informatik, Universität Tübingen,
Sand 13, D-72076 Tübingen, Fed. Rep. of Germany
`niedermr@informatik.uni-tuebingen.de`

Abstract. Recent time has seen quite some progress in the development of exponential time algorithms for *NP*-hard problems, where the base of the exponential term is fairly small. These developments are also tightly related to the theory of fixed parameter tractability. In this incomplete survey, we explain some basic techniques in the design of *efficient* fixed parameter algorithms, discuss deficiencies of parameterized complexity theory, and try to point out some future research challenges. The focus of this paper is on the design of efficient algorithms and not on a structural theory of parameterized complexity. Moreover, our emphasis will be laid on two exemplifying issues: Vertex Cover and MaxSat problems.

1 Introduction

How to cope with intractability? This is one of the most important problems in the theory and practice of computer science. Several methods to deal with this problem have been developed: approximation, average case analysis, randomization, and heuristics. All of them have their drawbacks as there are hardness of approximability, lack of mathematical tools and results, limited power of the method itself, or the lack of provable performance guarantees at all. Parameterization, whose cantus firmus can be characterized by the words "not all forms of intractability are created equal" [21], is another proposal how to cope with intractability in some cases. This is the basic subject of this paper.

Many hard computational problems have the following general form: given an object x and a natural number k, does x have some property that depends on k? For instance, the *NP*-complete Vertex Cover problem is: given an undirected graph $G = (V, E)$ and a natural number k, does G have a vertex cover of size at most k? Herein, a vertex cover is a subset of vertices $C \subseteq V$ such that each edge in E has at least one of its endpoints in C. In parameterized complexity theory, this natural number k is called the *parameter*. In many applications, the parameter k can be considered to be "very small" in comparison with the size

---

* Supported by a Feodor Lynen fellowship of the Alexander von Humboldt-Stiftung, Bonn, and the Center for Discrete Mathematics, Theoretical Computer Science and Applications (DIMATIA), Prague. Author's address in 1998: DIMATIA MFF UK, Charles University, Malostranské náměstí 25, 118 00 Praha 1, Czech Republic.

$|x|$ of the given object x. Hence, it may be of high interest to ask whether that problems, which usually are *NP*-hard, have deterministic algorithms that *only* are exponential with respect to k, but polynomial with respect to $|x|$.

Parameterized complexity, as mainly developed by Downey and Fellows [1, 17–21], is the perhaps latest approach to attack problems that are (worst case) intractable. The basic observation is that for many hard problems the seemingly inherent "combinatorial explosion" can be restrained to a "small part" of the input, the parameter. So, for instance, the *NP*-complete Vertex Cover problem allows for an algorithm with running time $O(kn + (1.3248)^k k^2)$ [5], where the parameter k is a bound on the maximum size of the vertex cover set we are looking for and n is the number of vertices of the given graph. The fundamental assumption is $k \ll n$. As can easily be seen, this yields an efficient, practical algorithm if only small values of k are involved. In this paper, we focus on issues concerning the development of *efficient* fixed parameter algorithms. However, there are also tight relations to the somewhat more general problem of designing exponential time algorithms with "small" exponential terms.

The writing of this paper was stimulated by the following conception: It is widely agreed that the notion of P versus NP reasonably reflects the difference between tractable and intractable problems. Why? Does an algorithm with running time n^{100}, putting the corresponding problem into P, have practical use? In general, no. The general observation, however, is that most problems in P in fact have $O(n^3)$ algorithms or better [27], which is not that enormous. Of course, from a practical point of view, this may still be unacceptable and usually the ultimate goal are linear or quasilinear time algorithms with small constant factors. For parameterized complexity, expressed conservatively, such an observation is hard to make. Problems are called fixed parameter tractable if they have running time $f(k)n^{O(1)}$ for an arbitrary function f only depending on k. Unfortunately, this $f(k)$ usually cannot be bounded so nicely as in the case of Vertex Cover (where $f(k) = (1.3248)^k$ [5][1]), but grows much faster (e.g., still giving a harmless example, $f(k) = 11^k$ for the Planar Dominating Set problem [20]), making the fixed parameter tractable algorithm already impractical for small values of k. This might be one of the, so far, main deficiencies of parameterized complexity theory. Here, we will survey and explore some results directed to "efficient" fixed parameter tractability as represented by Vertex Cover. In particular, our main focus is on two elementary techniques used in the design of efficient fixed parameter algorithms: kernelization and bounded search trees.

We assume the reader to be familiar with basic notions from algorithms and complexity as, e.g., provided by the text books [13, 27, 41, 44]. We omit material on graph minors, bounded treewidth algorithmics etc., which, on the one hand, play an important role in fixed parameter tractability theory, but, on the other hand, play a minor (sic!) role for the restricted point of view we are taking here—*elementary* methods in designing *efficient* fixed parameter algorithms.

---

[1] Note that, according to the above, we actually have running time $O(kn + (1.3248)^k k^2)$. Assuming, however, $k \ll n$ it is easy to see that this means also a bound of the form $O(f(k)n^{O(1)})$.

Let us mention in passing, however, that for graph problems graph minor theory is one of the main tools for showing fixed parameter tractability [21,48]: If a graph class is minor closed, then this implies fixed parameter tractability of the corresponding problem. For instance, consider the class of graphs having a vertex cover of size at most k, which is closed under taking minors. Consequently, graph minor theory tells us that the problem is fixed parameter tractable. In addition, in the context of bounded treewidth there has been proposed a "design methodology that for many NP-hard problems results in algorithms with time complexity linear in the size of the input graph and only exponential in its treewidth, lowering the exponent of previously known solutions" [50]. Finally, let us mention the existence of a further general FPT method that uses hashing and is called "color-coding," developed by Alon *et al.* [2].

The paper is structured as follows. In the next section, we very briefly provide a general overview on some main topics and ideas of parameterized complexity theory. In Section 3, we take a closer look at the concept of "fixed parameter tractability" and its criticism, thus providing the basic motivation for this paper. Turning to the main approach of theoretical computer science in dealing with intractability, that is, approximation, in Section 4, we sketch some known relations between approximation algorithms and parameterized complexity. In Section 5, based on the Vertex Cover problem, we explain the two basic techniques, kernelization and search trees. We present the basic ideas behind the best known Vertex Cover problem and also discuss related approaches in solving important problems from reconfigurable VLSI. In Section 6, we also discuss efficient fixed parameter algorithms for the maximum satisfiability problem. We end the paper by drawing some general conclusions.

2 A Crash Course in Parameterized Complexity

Given an undirected graph $G = (V, E)$ with vertex set V and edge set E and a natural number k, the NP-complete *Vertex Cover* problem is to determine whether there is a subset of vertices $C \subseteq V$ with k or fewer vertices (where k is a given natural number) such that each edge in E has at least one of its endpoints in C. Vertex Cover is *fixed parameter tractable*: There is an algorithm solving it in time $O(kn + (1.3248)^k k^2)$ [5], making it efficiently solvable for reasonably small values of k. By way of contrast, consider the also NP-complete *Clique* problem: Given an undirected graph $G = (V, E)$, Clique asks whether there is a subset of vertices $C \subseteq V$ with k or fewer vertices (where k is a given natural number) such that C forms a clique by having all possible edges between the vertices in C. Clique appears to be *fixed parameter intractable*: It is *not* known whether it can be solved in time $f(k)n^{O(1)}$, where f might be an arbitrarily fast growing function only depending on k [18]. Moreover, unless $P = NP$, the well-founded conjecture is that no such algorithm exists. Therefore, the best known algorithm solving Clique runs in time $O(n^{ck/3})$ [42], where c is the exponent on the time bound for multiplying two integer $n \times n$ matrices (currently best known, $c = 2.376\ldots$, see [12]). Note that n^k is trivial. The decisive point is that k appears in the exponent of n, and there seems to be no way "to shift the combinatorial explosion only into k", independent from n [21].

The observation that *NP*-complete problems like Vertex Cover and Clique behave completely differently in a "parameterized sense" lies at the very heart of parameterized complexity, which was pioneered by Downey and Fellows and some of their co-authors [18, 20–22, 47]. In this paper, we will focus on the world of fixed parameter tractable problems as, e.g., exhibited by Vertex Cover. Hence, here we only briefly sketch some very basics from the theory of parameterized intractability in order to provide some background on parameterized complexity theory and the ideas behind. For any further details and more discussion, we refer to the extensive literature, e.g., [20–22, 47].

Attempts to prove nontrivial, absolute lower bounds on the computational complexity of problems have made relatively little progress [9]. Hence, it is not surprising that up to now there is no proof that no $f(k)n^{O(1)}$ time algorithm for Clique exists. In a more complexity-theoretic language, where the class of parameterized problems that can be solved in deterministic time $f(k)n^{O(1)}$ is called *FPT*, this can be rephrased by saying that it is unknown whether Clique $\in FPT$. The complexity class *FPT* is called the set of *fixed parameter tractable* problems. Analogously to classical complexity theory, Downey and Fellows developed some way out of this quandary by providing a completeness program. However, the completeness theory of parameterized intractability involves significantly more technical effort. We briefly sketch some integral parts of this theory in the following.

To start with a completeness theory, we first need a reducibility concept: Let $L, L' \subseteq \Sigma^* \times \mathbf{N}$ be two parameterized languages. For example, in the case of Clique the first component is the input graph coded over some alphabet Σ and the second component is the natural number k, that is, the parameter. For complexity theory people, we mention in passing that the parameter k usually is encoded in unary as part of the input. We say that *L reduces to L' by a standard parameterized m-reduction* if there are functions $k \mapsto k'$ and $k \mapsto k''$ from $\mathbf{N}$ to $\mathbf{N}$ and a function $(x, k) \mapsto x'$ from $\Sigma^* \times \mathbf{N}$ to Σ^* such that

1. $(x, k) \mapsto x'$ is computable in time $k''|x|^c$ for some constant c and
2. $(x, k) \in L$ iff $(x', k') \in L'$.

Notably, most reductions from classical complexity turn out *not* to be parameterized [21]. For instance, the reduction from Independent Set to Vertex Cover (see [44]) is not a parameterized one. On the other hand, the reduction from Independent Set to Clique actually turns out to be also a parameterized one.

Now, the "lowest class of parameterized intractability", so-called $W[1]$, can be defined as the class of languages that reduce by a standard parameterized m-reduction to Clique. Hence, Clique is $W[1]$-*complete*. Independent Set is also $W[1]$-complete. A further, interesting $W[1]$-complete problem is *Weighted q-CNF-Sat*: Given a boolean formula F in conjunctive normal form and a positive integer k, does F have a truth assignment of weight k? Herein, the weight of a truth assignment simply is the number t of variables set true. Downey and Fellows provide an extensive list of many more $W[1]$-complete problems [18, 21].

As a matter of fact, a whole hierarchy of parameterized intractability can be defined, $W[1]$ only being the lowest level. In general, the classes $W[t]$ are defined based on "logical depth" (i.e., the number of alternations between unbounded fan-in And- and Or-gates) in boolean circuits. We omit any further details in this direction and just refer to the new monograph [21] or the many papers published on this topic, e.g., [1, 17–20]. There exists a very rich structural theory of parameterized complexity, somewhat similar to classical complexity. Observe, however, that in some respects parameterized complexity appears to be in a sense "orthogonal" to classical complexity: For example, the so-called problem of computing the V-C dimension from learning theory [7, 46], which is not known (and not believed) to be NP-hard, is $W[1]$-complete [16, 20]. Thus, although in the classical sense it appears to be easier than Vertex Cover (which is NP-complete), it appears to be exactly vice versa in the parameterized sense, because Vertex Cover is in FPT.

From a practical point of view, it is probably sufficient to distinguish between $W[1]$-hardness and membership in FPT. So, not being able to show fixed-parameter tractability of a problem, it may be sufficient to give a reduction from Clique or Weighted q-CNF-Sat to the given problem, using a standard parameterized m-reduction. This then gives a concrete indication that, unless $P = NP$, the problem is unlikely to allow for an $f(k)n^{O(1)}$ time algorithm. One circumstantial evidence for this is the result showing that the equality of $W[1]$ and FPT would imply a time $2^{o(n)}$ algorithm for the NP-complete 3-CNF-Sat problem [1, 21], which would mean a breakthrough in computational complexity theory.

In the remainder of this paper, however, we concentrate on the world inside FPT and the potential it carries for improvements and future research. Lots of problems termed fixed parameter tractable by the theory still wait for a proof of real "parameterized efficiency." There seem to be plenty of fields like computational biology or VLSI design, offering natural parameterized problems with efficient fixed parameter algorithms still to be discovered (also see [21, 22, 47]).

3   On the Meaning of Fixed Parameter Tractability

Vertex Cover has an $O(kn + f(k))$ algorithm, where $f(k) = O((1.3248)^k k^2)$ [5]. So, even for values like $k = 70$, this still makes an efficient algorithm, giving this result potential for practical importance. On the other hand, in the definition of FPT, $f(k)$ may take unreasonably large values, e.g.,

$$2^{2^{2^{2^{2^{2^{2^{2^k}}}}}}}$$

Even a less enormous value like $f(k) = 11^k$ for the Planar Dominating Set problem [20] only provides efficient algorithms for quite small values of k. Downey and Fellows [21] introduced so-called klam values to address this. The *klam* value of an algorithm A solving a problem L is defined to be the largest k such that

1. L can be solved by A in time $f(k) + n^{O(1)}$ and

Table 1. Comparing the efficiency of various MaxSat algorithms with respect to the exponential terms involved.

k	2^{2k}	$(1.6181)^k$	$(1.3995)^k$
10	$\approx 10^6$	≈ 124	29
20	$\approx 10^{12}$	≈ 15140	831
30	$\approx 10^{18}$	$\approx 1.9 \cdot 10^6$	≈ 24000
40	$\approx 10^{24}$	$\approx 2.3 \cdot 10^8$	$\approx 6.9 \cdot 10^5$
50	$\approx 10^{30}$	$\approx 2.9 \cdot 10^{10}$	$\approx 2.0 \cdot 10^7$
60	$\approx 10^{36}$	$\approx 3.5 \cdot 10^{12}$	$\approx 5.8 \cdot 10^8$

2. $f(k) \leq U$, where U is some reasonable absolute bound on the maximum number of steps of any computation, e.g., $U = 10^{20}$.

For example, using $U = 10^{20}$, the current klam value for Vertex Cover is approximately 165. Unfortunately, for few parameterized problems klam values of comparable high quality are known. Hence, an important algorithmic challenge concerning *FPT* problems is to provide klam values as large as possible.

To further substantiate the discussion before, let us briefly address another parameterized problem, namely maximum satisfiability for a boolean formula in conjunctive normal form (CNF) with a constant number of literals per clause (also see Section 6 for a more complete treatment). Here, for some time the best known algorithm had running time $O(2^{2k}m)$, where m is the number of clauses [11]. This, assuming a constant number of literals per clause, was first improved to $O(m + k\phi^k) \approx O(m + k(1.6181)^k)$, where ϕ is the golden ratio [40]. and very recently was further improved to $O(m + k(1.3995)^k)$ [43]. Note that for the improvements it is not even necessary to assume a constant number of literals per clause. Then, however, the term m in the time bound has to be replaced by the formula length $|F|$ and the multiplicative factor k has to be replaced by k^2. Let us compare the exponential expressions involved in these three time bounds. Table 3 provides these bounds for some reasonable values of k, implying that the klam value increases significantly and emphasizing the importance of the struggle to make the base of the exponential term as small as possible. So, the klam value for MaxSat corresponding to the three exponential algorithms referred to in Table 3, improves from approximately 35 to 100 to 140.

Finally, to also demonstrate the problematic nature of the comparison "fixed parameter tractable" versus "fixed parameter intractable", let us compare the functions 2^{2^k} and $n^k = 2^{(k \log n)}$. The first refers to fixed parameter tractability, the second to intractability. It is easy to verify that assuming input sizes n in the range from 10^3 up to 10^{15}, the value of k where 2^{2^k} starts to exceed n^k is in the small range $\{6, 7, 8, 9\}$. Hence, this shows how careful one has to be with the term fixed parameter tractable, since, in practice with reasonable input sizes, a fixed parameter intractable problem can easily turn out to have a still more efficient solution than a fixed parameter tractable one. A striking example in this direction is that of computing treewidth. For constant k, there is a famous result giving a linear time algorithm to compute whether a graph has treewidth at most k [8]. However, this algorithm suffers from enormous constant factors (unless $k \leq 3$) and so the $O(n^{k+1})$ algorithm [3] is more practical.

4 Approximation and Parameterization

In this section, we discuss some relations of fixed parameter (in)tractability to approximation. Polynomial time approximation algorithms and schemes are one of the major methods to cope with intractability [27]. Two recent surveys are available [14, 33]. Recently, deep results based on probabilistically checkable proofs have shown that many NP-hard optimization problems are also hard to approximate [4]. This gives rise to the general question of the nature of the relationship between fixed parameter tractability and approximability of problems. In this section, we will sketch some of the known results concerning this relationship and discuss implied consequences.

Results on the relationship between parameterized complexity and approximation come up in at least two ways—a more structural one and a more algorithmic one. We briefly study both of them, but afterwards direct our attention to the more algorithmic nature. Since this short section is anything but complete, for a more comprehensive treatment we refer to the literature [11, 21].

Optimization problems come in two forms: maximization and minimization problems. We concentrate on maximization problems, the minimization case works in analogy. A *maximization problem* is a 3-tuple (I, S, g), where I is the set of input instances, $S(x)$ is the set of feasible solutions for input $x \in I$, and $g(x, y) \in \mathbb{N}$ is the value for each $x \in I$ and $y \in S(x)$. The goal is to maximize $g(x, y)$. The *parameterized version* of a maximization problem is: given $x \in I$ and a positive integer k, is there a $y \in S(x)$ such that $g(x, y) \geq k$.

A maximization problem is *polynomial time approximable to a ratio r* if there is a polynomial time algorithm such that for all input instances $x \in I$ it produces a $y \in S(x)$ such that for the relative error it holds

$$\frac{\max(x)}{g(x, y)} \leq 1 + r,$$

where $\max(x)$ denotes the maximum value of the input instance x. A maximization problem has a *polynomial time approximation scheme (PTAS)* if for all $\epsilon > 0$ there is a polynomial time algorithm that produces a ratio ϵ approximation. Furthermore, it has a *fully polynomial time approximation scheme (FPTAS)* if it has a PTAS where, additionally, the running time of the algorithm is polynomial in the input size *as well as* in $1/\epsilon$.

It is not very difficult to prove the following interesting result [11]: If an NP optimization problem has an FPTAS, then it is in FPT. The basic idea of proof is to make use of the fact that if $\max(x)/g(x, y) \leq 1 + 1/(2k)$, this implies $\max(x) > k$ *iff* $g(x, y) > k$. The contrapositive consequences of this result

appear to be still more important. As a corollary we get that the *NP* optimization problems that are $W[1]$-hard under the standard parameterized m-reduction
have no FPTAS unless $W[1] = FPT$ [11]. Thus, the structural theory concerning
the W-hierarchy surprisingly may give evidence on the non-approximability of
optimization problems. In other words, proving $W[1]$-hardness can be seen as one
way to show non-approximability. Further results of Cai and Chen show that the
parameterized versions of all maximization problems in the class *MaxSNP*, introduced by Papadimitriou and Yannakakis [45], and all minimization problems in
the class $MinF^+ \Pi_1$, introduced by Kolaitis and Thakur [36], are in *FPT*. Hence,
besides the above-mentioned, more structural issues, the subsequent questions
arise:

1. Which problems in *MaxSNP* and $MinF^+ \Pi_1$ admit *efficient* fixed parameter
   algorithms? What are the best time bounds?
2. More generally, can ideas from approximation algorithms be used for the
   design of efficient fixed parameter algorithms and vice versa?
3. For optimization problems a compendium of approximability results exists [14]. Will the future see something analogous for *efficient* fixed parameter
   tractability, giving the best achieved exponential time algorithms?

5   Vertex Cover Problems

The minimization problem Vertex Cover is surely one of the best explored parameterized problems. The problem instance is an undirected graph $G = (V, E)$
and a positive integer k, the question is whether there exists a "vertex cover set"
$C \subseteq V$ with $|C| \leq k$ such that for all edges (u, v) in E, it holds that $u \in C$ or
$v \in C$. Vertex Cover, sometimes called Node Cover, is *NP*-complete. A straightforward greedy algorithm shows that Vertex Cover is approximable to a ratio 1
(cf. [44]), that is, the greedy algorithm always finds a vertex cover of size at most
twice as large as as the optimal one. The simple idea behind the greedy algorithm is to pick any edge from the graph, put both endpoints in the vertex cover,
and delete these endpoints together with their incident edges from the graph.
However, unless $P = NP$, Vertex Cover has no polynomial time approximation
scheme [4] and it is known to be *not* approximable to a ratio 0.1666 [32].

Although Vertex Cover is hard to approximate, it has turned out that it is
"easy to parameterize": Vertex Cover has seen quite some history of progress
with respect to fixed parameter algorithms (see [21] for details). One of the first
results (of mainly theoretical interest) showing its fixed parameter tractability was based on Robertson and Seymour's deep theory of graph minors [25]
leading to an $O(n^3)$ algorithm for constant k. Even a linear time algorithm followed, because graphs with "bounded vertex cover" have bounded treewidth [8].
However, more efficient algorithms based on techniques as *bounded search tree*
[19] and *reduction to problem kernel* [10] have been obtained. Using maximum
matching as a subroutine, Papadimitriou and Yannakakis [46] showed that Vertex Cover admits a polynomial time solution whenever the cover size is $O(\log n)$.
Surprisingly, in essence all this already follows from the elementary search tree

method described in Mehlhorn's text book on graph algorithms [41, page 216], published before all of the above-mentioned papers. Recently, Balasubramanian *et al.* [5] came up with a greatly improved fixed parameter algorithm for Vertex Cover, running in time $O(kn + (1.324718)^k k^2)$. They employ an intricate, improved search tree algorithm. Very recently, this result was slightly improved to $O(kn + (1.31951)^k k^2)$ [22]. Note that according to the authors this "tiny difference amounts to a 21% improvement in the running time for $k = 60$."

In the following subsection, we describe the basic ideas behind the algorithm of Balasubramanian et al. The further improvement was achieved using similar ideas. In particular, studying this concrete problem, the purpose is also to become familiar with the two so far perhaps most successful techniques in designing efficient fixed parameter algorithms—bounded search tree and reduction to problem kernel. Afterwards, in Subsection 5.2, we give one example how to apply this methodology to a problem originating from reconfigurable VLSI—Constraint Bipartite Vertex Cover. This may give sufficient stimulus to pursue further research in this direction.

5.1 General Vertex Cover

Using an intricate, but elementary algorithmic technique, Balasubramanian *et al.* developed a very efficient fixed parameter algorithm to solve Vertex Cover [5]. Let's see how this basically works.

Method 1: reduction to problem kernel. The general idea of this method, which is fairly generally applicable (not only to vertex cover or graph problems), can be expressed as follows.

1. Reduce the given instance to a new instance whose size is *exclusively* bounded by a function of the parameter k.
2. Perform exhaustive search in the new instance, usually employing an exponential time algorithm.

In this way, we get *Buss' algorithm* for Vertex Cover [10, 20, 21], see Fig. 1. Obviously, the new instance has size bounded by $O(k^2)$.

The correctness of Buss' algorithm relies on the idea that "high-degree-vertices", that is, those of degree $> k$, *must* be part of the vertex cover of size $\leq k$ if one exists. It is not difficult to see, using appropriate subalgorithms, that Buss' algorithm has a running time $O(kn + (2k^2)^k k^2)$. Although in the parameterized world, reduction to problem kernel is usually attributed to Buss [20, 21], basically the same technique has been used at least 10 years earlier in VLSI, e.g., by Evans [23]. Reduction to problem kernel is commonly used as some kind of preprocessing to a so-called bounded search tree algorithm, which already can be found in Mehlhorn's textbook [41, page 216].

Input: A graph $G = (V, E)$ and a positive integer k.
Output: A minimum vertex cover of size at most k if one exists.

1. (a) Let H be the set of vertices in V with degree $> k$;
   (b) **if** $|H| > k$ **then** "No size $\leq k$ vertex cover exists"; **exit**;
   (c) Let $G' = (V', E')$ be the graph originating from G by deleting all vertices in H and their incident edges;
   (d) $k' := k - |H|$;
   (e) Delete all isolated vertices in G';
2. **if** $|E'| > kk'$ **then** "No size $\leq k$ vertex cover exists"; **exit**;
3. Perform exhaustive search on G' to find a minimum vertex cover of size k';
4. The minimum vertex cover for G is the minimum vertex cover for G' combined with H.

Fig. 1. Buss' algorithm for Vertex Cover—reduction to problem kernel.

Method 2: bounded search tree. The general idea of this method is to identify a small subset of elements of which at least one must be in *any* feasible solution of the problem. Here comes the application to Vertex Cover based on Mehlhorn's description [41, page 216]. See Fig. 2. It is called *search tree algorithm* and is quite similar in spirit to the greedy approximation algorithm for Vertex Cover, cf. [44]. We use the notion "$G - v$" to express that vertex v and all its incident edges are deleted from G. The time complexity of the algorithm can be easily bounded by $O(2^k n)$.

Using Buss' algorithm as preprocessing phase and directly employing the search tree algorithm, we obtain a vertex cover algorithm running in time $O(kn + 2^k k^2)$. However, combining methods 1 and 2 *and* improving on method 2 leads to the result of Balasubramanian *et al.* [5], which we will focus on next.

An improved search tree algorithm. The key idea of Balasubramanian *et al.* [5] to improve the described search tree method with exponential factor 2^k is to do a careful case distinction by distinguishing between the degree of the vertices of the given graph. Observe that factor 2^k actually is the size of the search tree. So, the goal is to decrease the size of the search tree by using a more sophisticated recursion. Before we describe this in more detail, note that by making use of method 1 as a preprocessing phase, w.l.o.g. we can assume that the subsequent search tree algorithm only has to operate on input graphs of size $O(k^2)$. More precisely, what we do is to run the first two steps of the algorithm in Fig. 1 and to replace the second two steps by an improved version of a bounded search tree (Fig. 2).

The basic structure of the improved search tree algorithm is as follows: We distinguish between five cases in the following order, which is given by the degree of the vertices in the graph: First, we deal with "degree-1-vertices", second, with "degree-2-vertices", third, with "degree-$\geq$ 5-vertices", fourth, with "degree-3-vertices", and, finally, with the remaining graph. Observe that the remaining

Input: A graph $G = (V, E)$ and a positive integer k.
Output: A minimum vertex cover of size at most k if one exists.

1. Construct a complete binary tree of height k;
2. Label the root node $(G, \emptyset)$;
3. Recursively label all tree nodes as follows, where (H, S) shall be an already labeled tree node:
   (a) Pick an arbitrary edge (u, v) in graph H;
   (b) Label left child of (H, S) with $(H - u, S \cup \{u\})$;
   (c) Label right child of (H, S) with $(H - v, S \cup \{v\})$;
4. **if** there is a tree node labeled $(\emptyset, S')$ ($\emptyset$ referring to the "empty graph")
   then "S' is a vertex cover of size $\leq k$"
   else "No size $\leq k$ vertex cover exists".

Fig. 2. Search tree algorithm for Vertex Cover.

graph is 4-regular, that is, each vertex has exactly degree 4. To describe all these cases is out of the scope of this paper. To illustrate the fundamental ideas, however, it is sufficient to describe the first two (and most simple) ones.

The degree-1-vertex case is trivial. If a vertex x has only one neighbor y, then to cover the edge between them, it is always advantageous to pick y for the vertex cover set, because if y has more than one neighbor, we cover more edges this way than by choosing x. By always choosing y, a branching of the recursion in the search tree can be avoided, implying a decrease of its size.

The degree-2-vertex case becomes more involved. We distinguish between three subcases. Assume that the considered degree-2-vertex x has neighbors y and z. If there is an edge between y and z, then we avoid any branching of the recursion by always choosing y and z to be included into the vertex cover set. It is not hard to check that this is always optimal in order to cover the edges (x, y), (x, z), and (y, z) and further possibly incident edges to y and z. Subcase 2 addresses the setting where y and z together have at least two neighbors other than x, say a and b. Then with not too much effort (try!) it can be checked that either $\{y, z\}$ or all neighbors of y and z have to be added to the vertex cover set. Thus we get a branching of our recursion. Denoting by $T(k)$ the size of the recursion tree, this branching leads to the recurrence

$$T(k) = 1 + T(k - 2) + T(k - 3).$$

It is important to emphasize here that this is already one of the worst cases for the improved search tree, that is, the solution of this recurrence already yields the exponential factor $(1.3248)^k$ for the tree size as it is part of the overall result. Finally, subcase 3 ("otherwise") deals with the situation when y and z together have one neighbor other than x, say a. Then again a branching of the recursion can be avoided by the choice $\{a, x\}$ for the vertex cover set. The optimality of this choice is checked easily.

The complete analysis, involving many more and more complicated cases with, however, the same basic flavor, gives an improved search tree of size

$(1.3248)^k$ [5]. All in all, this results in a running time $O(kn + (1.3248)^k k^2)$. What about the potential for improvement of this result (besides the small one to $(1.3195)^k$ already mentioned [22])? It seems to be quite complicated to do this due to the great number of case distinctions involved. In particular, there is more than one worst case and improving some particular cases may not help in bringing down the overall worst case. However, only elementary combinatorial considerations have been used for this result and maybe with the help of machine support one could still find a better recursion.

5.2 Constraint Bipartite Vertex Cover

Kuo and Fuchs studied the *Constraint Bipartite Vertex Cover (CBVC)* problem, deriving from applications in reconfigurable VLSI [38]. The problem is, given a bipartite graph $G = (V_1, V_2, E)$ and two positive integers k_1 and k_2, are there two subsets $C_1 \subseteq V_1$ and $C_2 \subseteq V_2$ such that $|C_1| \leq k_1$ and $|C_2| \leq k_2$ and each edge from E has at least one endpoint in $C_1 \cup C_2$? In addition, motivated by the applications behind, it is interesting to search for *all* solutions to CBVC with minimal values for the vector $(|C_1|, |C_2|)$. CBVC is *NP*-complete in general [38]. Therefore, in practice, heuristic algorithms are used that not always yield optimal solutions. Since the parameter values k_1 and k_2 can be assumed to be quite small for technological reasons (say $k_1 + k_2$ around 50 all in all), algorithms exponential in k_1 and k_2 may be tolerable as long as the running time is linear in the size of the problem instance.

The affinity between CBVC and Vertex Cover is obvious. However, the existence of *two* parameters in combination with the bipartite nature of the graph means a significant hurdle. So, the Vertex Cover algorithm cannot be translated into this new setting. However, the basic techniques as reduction to problem kernel and bounded search tree again apply. Thus, again based on the degree of vertices, the combination of these two techniques yields an $O((k_1 k_2)n + (1.47)^{k_1 + k_2} k_1 k_2)$ algorithm [26]. Here, the case distinction in comparison with the Vertex Cover case gets less complicated and deals as main cases with "vertices of degree at least three" and "vertices of degree at most two". However, note that the seemingly trivial case of vertices with degree at most two requires some care due to the existence of more than one minimal solution (opposite to the general vertex cover case). In particular, this holds true when generalizing CBVC from 2 to even 3 parameters, yielding so-called "3CBVC," which is motivated by applications from reconfigurable programmable logic arrays [31]. The point here is to partition one of the two vertex sets of the given graph into two subsets. Nevertheless, solutions of efficiency comparable to CBVC can be achieved [26]. Besides trying to improve the performance of the proposed (3)CBVC algorithms, there appear to be numerous challenges from VLSI design concerning efficient parameterized algorithms [26], e.g., [30, 31, 35, 37–39, 49, 52].

6 Maximum Satisfiability Problems

Maximum Satisfiability (MaxSat for short) is a problem especially well-known from the field of approximation algorithms [14, 33, 45], having also important practical applications [29]. Hence, many heuristics are in use for MaxSat [6]. The instance is a boolean formula in conjunctive normal form (CNF), the problem is to find a truth assignment that satisfies the most number of clauses. The decision version of MaxSat is NP-complete [27, 44], even if the clauses have at most two literals (so-called Max2Sat). One of the major results in theoretical computer science in recent time shows that if there is a PTAS for MaxSat, then $P = NP$ [4]. On the positive side, it is known that MaxSat is approximable to a ratio 0.3193 [28]. For special cases of MaxSat, better bounds are known: Max$q$Sat is approximable to a ratio $2^{-q}/(1-2^{-q})$ if every clause contains exactly q literals [34], Max3Sat is approximable to a ratio 0.2489 [51], and Max2Sat is approximable to a ratio 0.0741 [24]. On the negative side, Max$q$Sat is not approximable to a ratio $2^{-q}/(1-2^{-q}) - \epsilon$ for any $\epsilon > 0$ and $q \geq 3$ and Max2Sat is not approximable to a ratio 0.0476 [32].

The natural parameterized version of MaxSat requires for an algorithm that determines whether at least k clauses of a CNF formula F can be satisfied. Assume that F contains m clauses and n variables. For each F there always exists a truth assignment satisfying at least $\lceil m/2 \rceil$ clauses: simply pick any assignment— either it does or its bitwise complement does. This can be checked in time $O(|F|)$. This observation was used by Cai and Chen [11] to prove that parameterized Max$q$Sat for some constant q is in FPT, implying that every problem in the optimization class $MaxSNP$ is also in FPT. However, their algorithm relies on the boundedness of clauses, which is not necessary for the algorithms described in the following. Of course, one might argue that the proposed parameterization of MaxSat does not make much sense because for $k \leq \lceil m/2 \rceil$ the problem is trivial and for $k > \lceil m/2 \rceil$ one usually cannot speak any longer of a "small parameter value." This is also why Mahajan and Raman [40] introduced a more meaningful parameterization, asking whether at least $\lceil m/2 \rceil + k$ clauses of a CNF formula F can be satisfied. However, the first parameterization still remains of interest, since from a "non-parameterized point of view," an algorithm with running time exponential in M with a small base for the exponential factor can be of interest. So, we firstly stick to this basic parameterization and afterwards very briefly deal with the "more meaningful" parameterization.

Mahajan and Raman [40] presented an algorithm running in time $O(|F| + k^2 \phi^k) \approx O(|F| + k^2 (1.6181)^k)$ that determines whether at least k clauses of a CNF formula F are satisfiable. This algorithm uses a reduction to problem kernel as well as a bounded search tree.

The *reduction to the problem kernel* relies on the distinction between "large" clauses (i.e., clauses containing at least k literals) and "small" clauses (i.e., clauses containing less than k literals). If F contains at least k large clauses, then it is easy to see that at least k clauses in F can be satisfied. Hence, the subsequent search tree method has only to deal with small clauses. Observe that the size of the remaining "subformula of small clauses" can easily be bounded by $O(k^2)$. This is also owing to the fact that if the number of clauses in F is at least $2k$, then trivially k clauses in F can be satisfied.

Now the *bounded search tree*, here more appropriately called *branching tree*, appears as follows. First, note that we can restrict ourselves to only considering variables that occur both positively and negatively in F, because so-called "pure literals" can always be set true, always increasing the number of satisfied clauses without any disadvantage. The basic technique now is to pick one variable x occurring both positively and negatively in F and then to "branch" into two subformulas $F[x]$ and $F[\bar{x}]$, which arise by setting x to true and false. Clearly, the size of such a branching tree can easily be bounded by 2^k. However, Mahajan and Raman [40] use one further trick, which is basically as follows: Distinguish between two cases. First, if the selected variable occurs exactly twice in F, then one can do a "resolution" avoiding any branching of the recursion:

$$F = (x \vee f_1) \wedge (\bar{x} \vee f_2) \wedge G,$$

where G contains no occurrence of variable x, can be replaced by

$$F' = (f_1 \vee f_2) \wedge G,$$

knowing that one clause in F could be satisfied. Second, if variable x occurs at least three times in F, then we get for the size $T(k)$ of the branching tree the Fibonacci recurrence

$$T(k) \leq 1 + T(k-1) + T(k-2).$$

Altogether, we end up with time complexity $O(|F|+k^2\phi^k)$, where $\phi = (1+\sqrt{5})/2$ is the golden ratio. Independently, in the context of approximation algorithms, basically the same result was also achieved by Dantsin *et al.* [15].

Using many more, carefully designed transformation and splitting rules for propositional formulas, the above result could be improved to time complexity $O(|F|+k^2(1.39995)^k)$ [43]. The fundamental ideas, which all deal with decreasing the size of the branching tree, are as follows. First, there are several "transformation rules", which avoid any branching of the recursion. Besides the described resolution rule, we also have transformation rules called pure literal rule, complementary unit-clause rule, dominating unit-clause rule, small subformula rule, and star rule. Refer to [43] for details. Even more interesting (and more complicated) are the so-called splitting rules, i.e., those rules that lead to a branching of the recursion. The basic idea is to distinguish between the number of occurrences of the variables in formula F. Note that because of some kind of "pre- and postprocessing" done by the transformation rules, we always can restrict attention to variables that occur at least three times in F. Hence, the three main cases now are if a variable x occurs at least 5 times in F, if all variables occur exactly 4 times in F, or if there is some variable that occurs exactly 3 times in F. Obviously, these cover all possibilities. The case of at least 5 variables is quite easy and requires a branching into $F[x]$ and $F[\bar{x}]$. The other two cases, however, are much more complicated and require six, respectively, seven subcases. For the purpose of illustration, we just give one of them, namely, the case that variable x occurs exactly three times in F and F is as follows:

$$F = (\bar{x} \vee \bar{l} \vee \ldots) \wedge (x \vee l \vee \ldots) \wedge (x \vee \ldots) \wedge (l \vee \ldots) \wedge \ldots$$

That is, there is another literal l occurring together with $\bar{x}$ in negated form in one clause, occurring together with x in positive form in a second clause, and occurring in at least one clause not containing variable x. Then the rule "T2" [43] says that we branch (or split) into $F[l]$ and $F[\bar{l}]$. It is not hard to see that in the step from F to $F[l]$ at least two clauses and a further one by applying the resolution rule afterwards are satisfied, and in the step from F to $F[\bar{l}]$ at least one clause and two further clauses by applying the pure literal rule applied to x are satisfied.

All in all, it can be shown that all cases lead to a recursion that yields a branching tree size that can be bounded by $(1.3995)^k$. Interestingly, there is a slightly "better" result if we measure the complexity not in the parameter k of number of clauses to be satisfied, but in the total number m of clauses in F. Then the branching tree size can be bounded by $(1.3803)^m$. Again we refer to [43] for any further details. It is worth noting that in particular the development of the MaxSat algorithm shows how seemingly tight the relation between fixed parameter tractability and the in some sense more general topic of worst case upper bounds for NP-hard problems is. So, both for Vertex Cover and for MaxSat, the best known worst case algorithms also yield the best known parameterized algorithms.

We only mention in passing that the parameterization of MaxSat requiring the satisfiability of at least $\lceil m/2 \rceil + k$ clauses is led back to the case considered above by Mahajan and Raman, thus obtaining a time complexity of $O(|F| + k^2 \phi^{6k}) \approx O(|F| + k^2 (17.9443)^k)$. Plugging in the above described improvements [43], we immediately get $O(|F| + k^2 (1.3995)^{6k}) \approx O(|F| + k^2 (7.5135)^k)$. Furthermore, Mahajan and Raman also study the MaxCut problem [40]. Here, analogous parameterizations as for MaxSat exist. The "conventional" parameterization requiring a cut of size at least k can be led back to a Max2Sat problem [40] and thus can also be improved using the above described results.

7 Conclusion

The purpose of this paper was not to give a complete survey on how to develop algorithms that prove fixed parameter tractability, but, by taking a restricted viewpoint, we concentrated on the techniques of reduction to problem kernel and, even more importantly, bounded search trees. The main intention of this paper was to give an incomplete, but easily understandable review on interesting algorithmic aspects of the field and, in particular, to point out the potential for future algorithmic research topics in this direction. The ultimate goal of this work could be termed as putting the reader into the position to pursue research on efficient parameterized algorithms, maybe even without the need of studying the extensive literature on parameterized complexity.

Also, we concentrated on two core problems: Vertex Cover and MaxSat. Besides the open problems in direct relation with these two, we strongly believe that there is a big potential for research on efficient parameterized algorithms in fields like VLSI design, computational biology, logic, data bases, and several others. Practical algorithms from these fields often use heuristic ideas, and may yield new insight for parameterized algorithm design. It is also promising to test parameterized algorithms in practical applications, e.g., combining or enriching them with some heuristics. Research on efficient parameterized algorithms thus could mean entering a field that offers a link between computer science theory and practice.

Acknowledgment. I'm grateful to Henning Fernau for valuable pointers to the literature. I appreciate having been invited by Jan Kratochvíl and Jarik Nešetřil to give lectures on parameterized complexity at DIMATIA, Prague. In addition, I'm also grateful to Jiří Wiedermann for inviting me to a talk on the presented topic, which together with the lecture notes served as a basis for this paper. Thanks go also to Rod Downey for providing me with a preliminary version of the new monograph [21]. Finally, I'm grateful to Henning Fernau and Ton Kloks for helpful comments on previous drafts of the paper.

References

1. K. A. Abrahamson, R. G. Downey, and M. R. Fellows. Fixed-parameter tractability and completeness IV: On completeness for W[P] and PSPACE analogues. *Annals of Pure and Applied Logic*, 73:235–276, 1995.
2. N. Alon, R. Yuster, and U. Zwick. Color-coding. *J. ACM*, 42(4):844–856, 1995.
3. S. Arnborg, D. G. Corneil, and A. Proskurowski. Complexity of finding embeddings in a k-tree. *SIAM J. Alg. Disc. Meth.*, 8:277–284, 1987.
4. S. Arora, C. Lund, R. Motwani, M. Sudan, and M. Szegedy. Proof verification and hardness of approximation problems. In *Proceedings of the 33d IEEE Conference on Foundations of Computer Science*, pages 14–23, 1992.
5. R. Balasubramanian, M. R. Fellows, and V. Raman. An improved fixed parameter algorithm for vertex cover. *Information Processing Letters*, 65(3):163–168, 1998.
6. R. Battiti and M. Protasi. Reactive Search, a history-base heuristic for MAX-SAT. *ACM Journal of Experimental Algorithmics*, 2:Article 2, 1997.
7. A. Blummer, A. Ehrenfeucht, D. Haussler, and M. K. Warmuth. Learnability and the Vapnik-Chervonenkis dimension. *J. ACM*, 36:929–965, 1989.
8. H. L. Bodlaender. A linear time algorithm for finding tree-decompositions of small treewidth. *SIAM J. Comput.*, 25:1305–1317, 1996.
9. R. B. Boppana and M. Sipser. The complexity of finite functions. In J. van Leeuwen, editor, *Algorithms and Complexity*, volume A of *Handbook of Theoretical Computer Science*, chapter 14, pages 757–804. Elsevier, 1990.
10. J. F. Buss and J. Goldsmith. Nondeterminism within P. *SIAM J. Comput.*, 22(3):560–572, 1993.
11. L. Cai and J. Chen. On fixed-parameter tractability and approximability of NP optimization problems. *J. Comput. Syst. Sci.*, 54:465–474, 1997.
12. D. Coppersmith and S. Winograd. Matrix multiplication via arithmetical progression. *J. Symbolic Computations*, 9:251–280, 1990.

13. T. H. Cormen, C. E. Leiserson, and R. L. Rivest. *Introduction to Algorithms*. The MIT Press, 1990.
14. P. Crescenzi and V. Kann. A compendium of NP optimization problems. Available as http://www.nada.kth.se/theory/problemlist.html, Apr. 1997.
15. E. Dantsin, M. Gavrilovich, E. A. Hirsch, and B. Konev. Approximation algorithms for Max SAT: a better performance ratio at the cost of a longer running time. Technical Report PDMI preprint 14/1998, Steklov Institute of Mathematics at St. Petersburg, 1998.
16. R. G. Downey, P. Evans, and M. R. Fellows. Parameterized learning complexity. In *6th Annual Conference on Learning Theory, COLT'93*, pages 51–57. ACM Press, 1993.
17. R. G. Downey and M. R. Fellows. Fixed parameter tractability and completeness III. In *Complexity Theory: Current Research, Edited by K. Ambos-Spies, S. Homer, and U. Schöning, Cambridge University Press*, pages 191–225. 1993.
18. R. G. Downey and M. R. Fellows. Fixed-parameter tractability and completeness I: Basic results. *SIAM Journal on Computing*, 24(4):873–921, August 1995.
19. R. G. Downey and M. R. Fellows. Fixed-parameter tractability and completeness II: On completeness for W[1]. *Theoretical Computer Science*, 141:109–131, 1995.
20. R. G. Downey and M. R. Fellows. Parameterized computational feasibility. In *P. Clote, J. Remmel (eds.): Feasible Mathematics II*, pages 219–244. Boston: Birkhäuser, 1995.
21. R. G. Downey and M. R. Fellows. *Parameterized Complexity*. Springer-Verlag, 1998.
22. R. G. Downey, M. R. Fellows, and U. Stege. Parameterized complexity: A framework for systematically confronting computational intractability. In F. Roberts, J. Kratochvíl, and J. Nešetřil, editors, *The Future of Discrete Mathematics: Proceedings of the First DIM ATIA Symposium, June 1997*, AMS-DIMACS Proceedings Series. AMS, 1998. To appear. Available through http://www.inf.ethz.ch/personal/stege.
23. R. C. Evans. Testing repairable RAMs and mostly good memories. In *Proceedings of the IEEE Int. Test Conf.*, pages 49–55, 1981.
24. U. Feige and M. X. Goemans. Approximating the value of two prover proof systems, with applications to MAX 2SAT and MAX DICUT. In *3d IEEE Israel Symposium on the Theory of Computing and Systems*, pages 182–189, 1995.
25. M. R. Fellows and M. A. Langston. Nonconstructive advances in polynomial-time complexity. *Information Processing Letters*, 26:157–162, 1987.
26. H. Fernau and R. Niedermeier. Efficient algorithms for constraint bipartite vertex cover problems. Manuscript, July 1998.
27. M. Garey and D. Johnson. *Computers and Intractability: A Guide to the Theory of NP-completeness*. Freeman, San Francisco, 1979.
28. M. X. Goemans and D. P. Williamson. Improved approximation algorithms for maximum cut and satisfiability problems using semidefinite programming. *J. ACM*, 42:1115–1145, 1995.
29. P. Hansen and B. Jaumard. Algorithms for the maximum satisfiability problem. *Computing*, 44:279–303, 1990.
30. N. Hasan and C. L. Liu. Minimum fault coverage in reconfigurable arrays. In *18th Int. Symp. on Fault-Tolerant Computing Systems (FTCS'88)*, pages 348–353. IEEE Computer Society Press, 1988.
31. N. Hasan and C. L. Liu. Fault covers in reconfigurable PLAs. In *20th Int. Symp. on Fault-Tolerant Computing Systems (FTCS'90)*, pages 166–173. IEEE Computer Society Press, 1990.

32. J. Håstad. Some optimal inapproximability results. In *Proceedings of the 29th ACM Symposium on Theory of Computing*, pages 1–10, 1997.

33. D. S. Hochbaum, editor. *Approximation algorithms for NP-hard problems*. Boston, MA: PWS Publishing Company, 1997.

34. D. S. Johnson. Approximation algorithms for combinatorial problems. *J. Comput. Syst. Sci.*, 9:256–278, 1974.

35. J. H. Kim and S. M. Reddy. On the design of fault-tolerant two-dimensional systolic arrays for yield enhancement. *IEEE Transactions on Computers*, 38(4):515–525, Apr. 1989.

36. P. G. Kolaitis and M. N. Thakur. Approximation properties of NP minimization classes. *J. Comput. Syst. Sci.*, 50:391–411, 1995.

37. S.-Y. Kuo and I.-Y. Chen. Efficient reconfiguration algorithms for degradable VLSI/WSI arrays. *IEEE Transactions on Computer-Aided Design*, 11(10):1289–1300, 1992.

38. S.-Y. Kuo and W. Fuchs. Efficient spare allocation for reconfigurable arrays. *IEEE Design and Test*, 4:24–31, Feb. 1987.

39. C. P. Low and H. W. Leong. A new class of efficient algorithms for reconfiguration of memory arrays. *IEEE Transactions on Computers*, 45(5):614–618, 1996.

40. M. Mahajan and V. Raman. Parametrizing above guaranteed values: MaxSat and MaxCut. Technical Report TR97-033, ECCC Trier, 1997. To appear in *Journal of Algorithms*.

41. K. Mehlhorn. *Graph algorithms and NP-completeness*. Heidelberg: Springer, 1984.

42. J. Nešetřil and S. Poljak. On the complexity of the subgraph problem. *Commentationes Mathematicae Universitatis Carolinae*, 26(2):415–419, 1985.

43. R. Niedermeier and P. Rossmanith. New upper bounds for MaxSat. Technical Report KAM-DIMATIA Series 98-401, Faculty of Mathematics and Physics, Charles University, Prague, July 1998. Submitted for publication.

44. C. H. Papadimitriou. *Computational Complexity*. Addison-Wesley, 1994.

45. C. H. Papadimitriou and M. Yannakakis. Optimization, approximation, and complexity classes. *J. Comput. Syst. Sci.*, 43:425–440, 1991.

46. C. H. Papadimitriou and M. Yannakakis. On limited nondeterminism and the complexity of the V-C dimension. *J. Comput. Syst. Sci.*, 53:161–170, 1996.

47. V. Raman. Parameterized complexity. In *Proceedings of the 7th National Seminar on Theoretical Computer Science (Chennai, India)*, pages I-1–I-18, June 1997.

48. N. Robertson and P. D. Seymour. Graph minors—a survey. In I. Anderson, editor, *Surveys in Combinatorics*, pages 153–171. Cambridge University Press, 1985.

49. M. D. Smith and P. Mazumder. Generation of minimal vertex covers for row/column allocation in self-repairable arrays. *IEEE Transactions on Computers*, 45(1):109–115, 1996.

50. J. A. Telle and A. Proskurowski. Algorithms for vertex partitioning problems on partial k-trees. *SIAM Journal on Discrete Mathematics*, 10(4):529–550, 1997.

51. L. Trevisan, G. Sorkin, M. Sudan, and D. P. Williamson. Gadgets, approximation, and linear programming. In *Proceedings of the 37th IEEE Conference on Foundations of Computer Science*, pages 617–626, 1996.

52. L. Youngs and S. Paramanandam. Mapping and repairing embedded-memory defects. *IEEE Design and Test*, 14(1):18–24, 1997.

System Infrastructure for Digital Libraries: A Survey and Outlook

Christos Nikolaou and Manolis Marazakis

Department of Computer Science, University of Crete
and
Institute of Computer Science, FORTH,
PO Box 1385, GR 71110 Heraklion, Greece.
e-mail: {nikolau,maraz}@ics.forth.gr

Abstract. This paper focuses on technical issues regarding the challenge of integrating digital libraries in a work support environment that combines information management with coordination and collaboration. Such broad scope necessitates an extended view of electronic documents to allow for combinations of information content together with executable components. Moreover, as a result of the autonomy of the service and information content providers, this environment takes the form of an *information economy*. This paper provides a brief survey of research results related to architectures, metadata, interoperability and rights management in digital library systems. This survey serves to support a discussion of extending the scope of digital library systems toward integrated work support environments.

1 Introduction

Digital libraries extend and augment their physical counterparts by facilitating access to existing information resources and services, and by providing enhanced support of information-intensive tasks. They offer new levels of access to broader user communities, and create novel opportunities for information exchange understanding, cooperation and problem solving. The vision of a worldwide digital library is actively being pursued by many researchers, developers, and practitioners.

As stated in [15], *interoperability* is the key challenge in realising this vision, requiring *"ways to link the diverse content and perspectives provided by individual digital libraries around the world"* in a loosely coupled federation of autonomous systems, each with its own collection management and access policies, to serve specialized goals and user populations. It is important to note that interoperability needs to be addressed at multiple levels of abstraction, including technical aspects related to system interconnectivity standards and protocols, information-related aspects such as language, metadata, naming, semantics and access interfaces, and interaction-related aspects concerning the rights and obligations of users and organizations. Therefore, digital library systems necessarily address a broad range of technical, informational, and interaction issues.

This paper focuses on technical issues regarding the challenge of integrating digital libraries in a work support environment. We consider a view of digital library systems that goes beyond that of a repository of on-line information, to provide support throughout all phases of work. [10] identifies the integration of information retrieval systems with other information management systems as the most important problem for organizations. [44] makes the point that the activities of users involved in information-intensive tasks can be categorized as discovery, retrieval, interpretation, management, and sharing. Users need to find, analyze and understand information of widely diverse types. Moreover, they need to re-organize the information to use it in multiple contexts, and to manipulate it in collaboration with others. This is a major departure from assuming that the main objective of a digital library system is to locate a particular piece of information. This is further discussed in [33], where, in the context of a critical examination of assumptions that have historically guided the development of networked information systems, it is pointed out that the assumption that *"the correct answer lies in the information"* does not cover the case of *correlations* that require collaborative expertise among individuals interacting with information. Distributed Knowledge Environments are required to provide *"seamless interoperability among searching, authoring, and collaboration facilities"*, advocating a *toolbox metaphor* to support users in their information management and analysis tasks.

[56] argues for a common infrastructure to support both digital libraries and electronic commerce. In our view [35, 41] several important classes of large-scale distributed applications, such as digital library systems, electronic commerce environments and scientific collaborative work environments, share key requirements with emphasis on combining multiple resources made available under restricted terms (and therefore with a limited degree of external control) by independent co-operating partners. We aim for a unified treatment of the problem of supporting such diverse applications via a set of common middleware services. This view fits into the *network centric* application paradigm that is becoming more and more popular in open and dynamic environments, such as the Internet, as a means to utilize widely distributed application components and information resources that are made available by autonomous providers. In such environments, dynamic configuration and composition are key requirements, as the basis for both *coordination*, which entails structured processes involving mainly automated activities, and *collaboration*, which entails mainly unstructured processes with significant human interaction. We are working toward a common infrastructure for large-scale distributed applications that enables on-demand composition and configuration of networks of components made available by autonomous providers, which are coordinated in the context of *work sessions*.

The remainder of this paper is organized as follows. Section 2 briefly surveys recent research results mainly from the areas of interoperability for digital library systems and electronic documents with extended functionality. Section 3 suggests extensions in support of our vision of an integrated work support environment. This section also presents examples of value-added services for digital information objects. Where appropriate, we illustrate the issues presented by referring to our ongoing work toward the development of an infrastructure to support large-scale distributed applications. Finally, Section 4 concludes the paper by summarizing the ideas presented, and outlines our research plan.

2 Current State-of-the-Art

In this section we present a brief survey of research results related mainly to the problem of interoperability in digital library systems. The following subsections provide concise reports on the current state-of-the-art for frameworks and architectures, metadata, interoperability protocols and intellectual property rights. Finally, there is a subsection that surveys work related to extended electronic document models, which we consider essential for extending the functionality of digital library systems. These reports serve to support the discussion in Section 3 of the proposed extension of the scope of digital library systems toward integrated work support environments.

2.1 Frameworks and Architectures

In a seminal paper [23], Kahn and Wilensky proposed a framework for for distributed digital object services, which encompasses digital libraries as well as numerous other services, such as electronic commerce applications. The paper describe the basic entities to be found in such a system, in which information in the form of *digital objects* is stored, accessed, disseminated and managed. A digital object is defined to an instance of an abstract data type with two components, data, in the form of typed digital material, and key-metadata which includes, as a minimum, a *handle* that is globally unique to the digital object. *Repositories* store digital objects and are responsible for securing their resident objects according to their respective *terms and conditions* for access and usage, which are contained in a *properties record* for each digital object. A *dissemination* is the result of an access request on a digital object. It contains the results of the access request (determined by the parameters in the request) and additional components specifying the origin of the dissemination and the specific terms and conditions governing its use. The *repository access protocol* includes services for deposit of digital objects and access to digital objects in repositories.

The Dienst prototype [29] implements part of the framework proposed in [23], focusing mainly on the design of a protocol for accessing digital objects in repositories. [28, 31] present a system design approach to the framework in [23], based on a distributed object model. An important observation in [28] is that a dissemination is not restricted to have the same data as the source digital object. Moreover, a dissemination is not necessarily a subset of the digital object's data. Thus it is possible, for example, for a digital object to be an executable program and disseminations to be produced by running the program using the parameters in the access request as input. This insight is crucial for incorporating computational services in an extended digital library framework.

FEDORA [32] is a digital object and repository architecture designed to provide a reliable and secure means to store and access digital content. Digital objects in FEDORA are *content containers* having a structural kernel which encapsulates content as opaque byte stream packages and a behavior layer that may implement descriptive metadata as well as access functionality for the content packages. Through the structural kernel *disseminators* provide a means to discover and invoke *content-specific* behavior to digital objects. Clients can discover, at run-time, the disseminators associated with a digital object as well as the methods supported by the disseminator. These methods mediate access to information content contained in the digital object. Access control is enforced by *access managers* which are activated when a disseminator is activated. Service requests targeted to a disseminator are intercepted by its associated access manager, which implements rights management policies.

2.2 Metadata

Metadata, in other words machine-understandable structured information objects describing properties of other information objects, are key components of network information services, supporting their interaction with software agents and other services as well as with human users. Metadata support a range of tasks including resource discovery, authentication, rights management, archiving, and system-level interoperability. In this section, we provide a brief survey of metadata development efforts related to digital libraries, with emphasis on interoperability (see also Section 2.3). We also provide a short description of the RDF framework and its potential.

STARTS [21] is a protocol that addresses the main tasks performed by *metasearchers* providing unified query interfaces over multiple sources with varying search interfaces and models. These tasks include selection of the sources to evaluate a query, evaluation of the query at each of the selected sources, and merging the query results. STARTS defines the metadata that each source should export, which include a content summary and a description of available query capabilities.

The Dublin Core [61] is a specification of a set of metadata elements describing essential properties of networked documents, such as title, author and publisher, primarily to support resource discovery. The Warwick framework [30] builds on the Dublin Core to propose a container architecture for aggregating multiple packages of metadata, which are separately accessible and maintainable. [54] combines perspectives from multiple rights-holder communities to present an integrated model for both descriptive and rights metadata. The provision for rights-related metadata provides an important extension to the Dublin Core proposal, explicitly addressing the problem of documenting rights ownership agreements.

An important development currently under way is the Resource Description Framework (RDF) [2], a framework introduced by the W3C Metadata activity, based on the XML metalanguage [8]. RDF is a framework for metadata that aims to provide interoperability between applications that exchange machine-understandable information on the Web. RDF data consists of nodes and attached attribute/value pairs. Nodes represent Web resources, such as servers and pages. Attributes are named properties of the nodes, and their values are either atomic, such as text strings and numbers, or other resources or metadata instances. This mechanism allows the definition of labeled directed graphs that model semantic relationships between nodes. RDF in itself does not contain any predefined vocabularies for authoring metadata. Such vocabularies are expected to emerge as the result of consensus within specific user communities. For example, the Dublin Core vocabulary can be expected to be integrated in the RDF framework to support resource discovery in digital libraries. As another example, the W3C Digital Signature Working Group (DSig) proposes a standard format for making digitally-signed, machine-readable assertions about information resources.

2.3 Interoperability

As a specific example of a full protocol for interoperability among clients and providers, we present an overview of the Z39.50 protocol. [34] provides a concise description of the protocol and a discussion of its deployment. Detailed information about the protocol is available through [1]. The problem of interoperability has been addressed in depth by digital library projects in the context of the NSF Digital Libraries Initiative (DLI) [14, 55]. This section also provides a survey of interoperability-related results from this initiative.

Z39.50 (Information Retrieval (Z39.50); Application Service Definition and Protocol Specification, ANSI/NISO Z39.50-1995) is a protocol which allows a client machine to search databases on a server machine and retrieve the records that are identified as results of such a search. Each server hosts one or more databases containing records. Associated with each database are a set of *access points* (indices) that can be used for searching. The protocol is stateful and connection-oriented. A search produces a set of records, called a "result set", that is maintained on the server; the result of a search is a report of the number of records comprising the result set. Result sets can be combined or further restricted by subsequent searches. Records from the result set can be subsequently retrieved by the client, by issuing requests that contain options for controlling the contents and format of the records to be returned. Z39.50 defines a query language for specifying searches that rely on registered attribute set definitions that specify the names of access points, and various record syntaxes for transferring records from the server to the client, such as the MARC syntax for bibliographic data.

A comprehensive interoperability solution is provided by the InfoBus testbed [46], in the context of the Stanford Integrated Digital Libraries Project, which applies distributed object technology to enable interoperability, by using wrapper objects to present a unified interface of digital library services and a metadata architecture [6, 21] to maintain metadata. The InfoBus set of interoperability protocols have been augmented with support for customized coordination for automating specific types of transactions. An example of such a specific solution is given in [24] which presents event-driven models for different modes of consumer-to-merchant interaction, and an API to facilitate commerce transactions. Shopping models encapsulate the rules for specific types of commerce transactions and instruct the participants what to do next in the way of ordering, payment and delivery. Another example is given in [52] which addresses the issue of rights management and discusses the automation of certain aspects of contract negotiation and enforcement.

In the University of Michigan Digital Library (UMDL) Project [5, 62], interacting software agents cooperate and compete for resources in the context of a virtual information economy to provide library services to users. Each agent performs a highly specialized library task and has a generic communication interface, and represents either a resource or a functional unit of the overall system. In order to service user requests, functional units and resources need to be dynamically combined, by forming teams of agents under the guidance of query planning agents. An essential aspect of this approach is that the capabilities and requirements of any functional unit in the digital library system are explicitly described using a formal language. Using this facility, it is possible for agents to negotiate about provision of complex services as well as resource allocation. A distinguishing aspect of the UMDL testbed is that resource allocation is handled using a market metaphor [39].

An intriguing aspect of interoperability is that, as pointed out in [45], comparing solutions is very difficult since different approaches operate under differing assumptions, and their design goals may be conflicting. Currently there are no quantitative metrics for evaluating interoperability solutions. However, certain criteria provide guidelines for understanding distributed and interoperable digital libraries, by allowing evaluators to articulate the design goals and to understand trade-offs among them [45]. The criteria include the degree of component autonomy, the cost of the infrastructure, scalability in the number of components, the ease and relative cost of contributing and using components, and the breadth of task complexity supported.

2.4 Intellectual Property Rights Management

The protection of intellectual property rights is a fundamental issue for digital library systems, and is closely related to the more general issue of enforcing specific semantics for interactions with information content and services (see Sections 3.2 and 3.4). The notion of *contract* is receiving considerable attention in the context of rights management and access control, which are key issues as the interest in electronic commerce is growing. Contacts provide a powerful framework for expressing and managing complex relationships between transaction participants. The Digital Property Rights Language (DPRL) [60] draws its basic constructs from contract law to provide a framework for specifying specific rights to use and manipulate digital content and actions taken in response to usage of these rights. The Stanford Framework for Interoperable Rights Management (FIRM) [52, 53] defines a programmable rights management service layer to support rights/relationship management. The FIRM Common Rights Language Object Model is an interface specification that describes how generic concepts and principles from contract law are reified digitally. FIRM Object Attribute Models are based on a standard format for defining media-specific or domain-specific rights vocabularies. The RManage relationship manager application is a prototype implementation of the FIRM interface, providing implementations for contracts such as group licenses and subscriptions.

Container technology is the key element in InterTrust Technologies' InterTrust Commerce Platform [9]. The *DigiBox* secure container [59] enables the association (via cryptographic means) of rules and controls with information content, to specify the types of content usage permitted and the consequences of usage (such as payment and report generation). Containers are manipulated using a trusted rights protection application to make the protected content available according to its associated access control rules. Similar functionality is provided by IBM's *Cryptolope* container [19].

2.5   Extendend Document Models

A central argument in this paper is that broadening the scope of electronic documents is essential for extending the functionality of digital library systems. This extension builds upon the capability to encapsulate descriptive metadata within digital objects that allow clients to discover at run-time the functionality supported, as well as the associated terms, conditions and guarantees.

Related work is reported in [11], which describes the *distributed active relationships* model for representing data and metadata in digital library objects, as an extension of the Warwick Container Framework [30] which provides a unifying abstraction for handling metadata that follow diverse standards. This model explicitly expresses the relationships between networked resources and allows these relationships to be dynamically downloadable and executable. Containers are used for aggregating data sets into digital objects, with the ability to support relationships by referencing executable code that may enforce special semantics, as illustrated in a rights management scenario.

[50, 51] describe *ComMentor*, a prototype developed in the context of the Stanford Integrated Digital Libraries Project that enables sharing of structured in-place annotations attached to documents on the WWW. This is presented as a specific instantiation of a general *virtual document* architecture in which viewed documents can incorporate material that is dynamically integrated from distributed sources. The mechanism for shared annotation provides the basis for adding value-added super-structures to WWW documents and supporting online communities by allowing multiple individuals to create lightweight "trails" through the shared document space. Example applications include shared comments, collaborative filtering, seals of approval for content rating, and multiple guided tours through the same content.

The multivalent document model presented in [47] is an attempt to support active and networked documents. A multivalent document is decomposed into *layers* of content, and functionality is provided by *behaviors*, which are dynamically-loaded program objects that manipulate the content. A behavior may communicate with specific layers and other behaviors in order to provide its functionality. Once built, a multivalent document can be extended by adding new layers and behaviors. This model provides a broad framework for documents that incorporate active behavior in response to user interactions, and [47] describes examples of its application, including an example of interaction with a remote service. [48] presents a framework for annotations, which are implemented as special behaviors of multivalent documents.

Developments related to the XML (eXtensible Markup Language) metalanguage [8] make it possible to extend the functionality of electronic documents. XML, which is a subset of SGML [20], provides a standardized text format for describing structured data for use by WWW applications. XML documents are composed of *entities*, which are storage units containing text and/or binary data. Character streams form both a document's data and markup. *Markup*, in the form of tags, describes a document's layout and structure. Thus, XML-encoded data is self-describing. A document may optionally be associated with a *Document Type Definition* (DTD) that defines structuring rules, allowing validation of the data. A *well-formed* XML document is unambiguous, allowing standard browsing and editing tools to read the tags and construct a parse tree representing its hierarchical structure, without requiring the corresponding DTD. Extremely diverse structured data can be encoded using standard tag sets (markup), and exchanged either between applications and clients that need to display and manipulate it, or between application servers for the purposes of automated processing [26, 25, 7]. Examples of data that can be exchanged via XML-encoded documents include purchase orders, invoices, product catalogs, sets of records retrieved from database systems, results from scientific experiments, bibliographic catalogs, and reports with embedded annotations. Since XML is a text-based format, it can be delivered via the HTTP protocol. Furthermore, XML encoding, unlike HTML, separates presentation/rendering issues from actual data content, allowing for example multiple views to be generated from the same data. Finally, the Document Object Model [63] provides a platform- and language-neutral interface allowing programs and scripts to dynamically access and update the content, structure and style of documents.

WIDL [3] is a metadata syntax, implemented in XML, that defines programmatic interfaces to Web content and services, so as to enable automated and structured access by client programs. WIDL definitions include the location (URL) of each service, input parameters to be submitted (via the GET and POST methods of HTTP), and output parameters to be returned by each service (as regions of returned documents). It also possible to specify conditions for successful completion of a service and error indications to be returned to clients. Conditions further enable chaining of services, so that a client can issue requests that incorporate multiple services. A related reference is [16], which presents an approach in which domain-specific markup languages are used to handle interactions in a peer-to-peer system. These languages are understood both by agents and the humans who interact with them. The objective is to dynamically integrate tools into distributed collaborative applications. SGML [20] is used as the metagrammar system for specifying markup languages.

3 Outlook

This section builds on the brief survey of interoperability-related research presented in Section 2 to suggest extensions to support our vision of an integrated work support environment. Broadening the scope of digital library systems to encompass support throughout all aspects of work necessitates an extended view of electronic documents to allow for combinations of information content together with executable components. Section 3.1 makes the point that container technology can provide the necessary framework for building value-added services for digital information objects. Section 3.2 presents specific examples of value-added services for digital information objects that illustrate the issues of integrated work support in an open and dynamic environment. Section 3.3 outlines our view of an integrated work support environment, which is structured as an information economy. Finally, Section 3.4 emphasizes the requirement for mutual respect of terms and conditions by the trading partners of the information economy, and outlines the design of an application model and an infrastructure for interactions in this environment.

3.1 Container Frameworks

A *component* is a software module, encapsulating application code, that can be combined with other components and a *script* to produce a a custom application environment [40]. Components execute within *containers*, which provide the run-time environment for one or more components and a range of standard management and control services for these components. A *component model* defines the guidelines that developers must adhere to, in the form of standard interfaces that enable other active components or applications to invoke its functions and access its data. Moreover, a component model defines the customizable properties exposed by components, allowing a component to be adapted to specific application requirements. Component-based application development involves selecting appropriate components and assembling them into a configuration that supports the functions required for an application.

In the context of digital library systems and electronic documents, it has been demonstrated that container technology enables the encapsulation of information content together with rules and controls specifying the types of content usage permitted, as well as the consequences of usage (such as payment and report generation). There are proposals for using containers as a mechanism for securing intellectual property rights (see Section 2.4). As discussed in more detail in Section 3.2, other applications of container technology are possible as well, including support for compound documents that incorporate active content and automation of processes involving multi-party peer-to-peer interactions for the purposes of collaboration and commerce. Such value-added services are of particular interest in the context of digital libraries aiming to provide functionality extending beyond that of a simple repository of electronic documents. Recent developments in software component frameworks contribute toward such extended functionality. With the emergence of a new generation of component-based software, such as JavaBeans [22], there are now powerful programming environments for building components, basic building-block components for building component ensembles, and component-based applications to address specific business requirements. Components can be combined in a variety of ways, resulting in a high degree of productivity for developers and users. A particularly important aspect is that visual application builders and scripting languages can be used for composition of components. In this setting, extensible containers become essential for managing and deploying components.

Containers in the *Aurora* architecture (see [37] for details) encapsulate software components together with one or more information content modules, and related metadata enabling *introspection*, in other words dynamic discovery and inquiry of the container's capabilities and information content. Containers provide a framework for constructing, managing, and deploying compound documents, with the additional provision of support for active behavior. Such *active compound documents* enable several value-added services for digital objects in a digital library setting. Moreover, they provide the basis for a work session framework, by allowing external entities (such as a session manager) to establish networks of related containers in order to enact desired flows of data and events. This *service flow* paradigm is essential in the unified treatment of diverse applications.

3.2 Value-Added Services for Digital Information Objects

Container technology enables several value-added services for digital information objects. The following examples demonstrate that by taking a broader view of electronic documents it is possible to extend the functionality and scope of digital library systems. This point is elaborated in Section 3.3.

Active Compound Documents A container object can encapsulate multiple modules of information content, together with a software component that mediates access to this content, optionally providing enhanced access services. Thus, a container supports a framework of *active compound documents*. A compound document can incorporate, apart from its main information content, background material to provide additional insight to the document's recipients, as well as capabilities for interaction with data and tools related with the document. Structured documents provide an powerful interaction metaphor, particularly well-suited for collaborative applications.

Electronic Commerce Realising commerce transactions among multiple trading parties involves a complex sequence of interdependent actions, spanning over

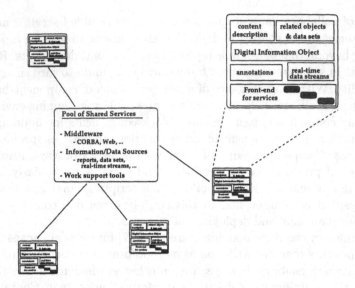

Fig. 1. Active Compound Documents in a Collaborative Work Session.

a long period of time, where each action may involve interactions with information systems as well as humans. Current electronic commerce systems do not support the notion of a complex product/service package consisting of items from multiple providers [17]. They are limited to commerce transactions over items in a single catalog or in an electronic mall that hosts multiple stores. For electronic commerce to reach its full potential, it is necessary to provide an open infrastructure that supports combining functional modules developed and administered by autonomous providers. Scripting can be used to express the required event-driven flow of requests and data among components that implement the required business functions. Support for scripting enables commerce transactions involving product/service packages.

Work Sessions in Scientific Experiments The management of work sessions involving the collection, manipulation, and management of data sets which can be generated from a large number and variety of sources, poses major challenges for current work support technologies, such as information management, computer-supported collaborative work, and workflow automation. The main objective is not necessarily to automate all tasks of the process, but rather to automate the tracking of states of tasks and to allow specification of preconditions to decide when tasks are ready to be executed and of information flow between tasks [38]. This view, together with the requirement for interoperation, motivates the integration of coordination and collaboration technologies with information management (see Section 3.3). Such integration can provide a shared workspace as the basis for collaboration among participants in a work session, allowing participants to invoke services and publish the results they get in response to their requests. Participants can discover at run-time how to invoke a particular service, by looking up the service's registration entry in the directory maintained by the run-time environment. Publish/subscribe communication support [43] allows all "subscribers" to receive the results produced by a invoking a service. Moreover, specialized components may act as large-grain *caches* of data sets. In this case, these components become accessible by registering with the service directory and advertising their capability to provide access to data sets that have been *derived* by a sequence of manipulations on primitive data sets.

Terms, Conditions, and Guarantees Realising an *information economy* requires mechanisms for monitoring and enforcing mutually binding terms and conditions between users and providers of information content and services, and a shift from asset management to relationship management [53]. The encapsulation of metadata within electronic documents is a powerful mechanism for providing documentation of the terms, conditions and guarantees determined by providers of information material and services. This information can be inspected by users at run-time, prior to actual usage of the encapsulated content and services. Moreover, it is possible to design generic enforcement mechanisms. As a specific example, we are developing a service-level management infrastructure in the context of the *Aurora* architecture (see Section 3.4 for details). This functionality is based on the ability to intercept all incoming and outgoing messages targeted at a component that provides access to information content and services. Thus a level of indirection is provided to enable performing authorization checks, logging, and any other pre-processing and post-processing actions required for the enforcement of agreed-upon conditions and guarantees.

3.3 Integrated Work Support

Sharing the views expressed in [57, 58], we believe that information management, as supported by current-generation digital library systems, needs to be augmented with support for coordination and collaboration, as currently supported by workflow [4, 18] and groupware systems [13, 49], in order to provide an integrated work support environment. Such broad scope necessitates an extended view of electronic documents, to evolve from pure containers of information in electronic form toward digital information objects that can be described as *active compound documents*, combining information content together with executable code to introduce active behavior. Moreover, as a result of the autonomy of the service and information content providers, this environment takes the form of an *information economy* where software objects that encapsulate information content and business-oriented services play the role of goods, and objects representing clients and content/service providers play the role of trading partners. A crucial aspect in such an environment, which resembles a marketplace where clients and providers interact by exchanging as well as trading services and information content [12], is the mutual respect of terms and conditions. This requirement, which is also fundamental for the preservation of intellectual property rights in digital library systems, provides us with motivation to develop an infrastructure supporting a form of *electronic contracts* that explicitly declare the terms and conditions under which certain services and information content are to be used, as well as guarantees that providers commit to maintain for their clients.

Along these lines, we are developing *Aurora* [35], an infrastructure for large-scale distributed applications supporting dynamic composition and configuration, as well as contract specification, monitoring and enforcement. *Aurora* supports a *service flow* execution model, where composite services involving multiple resources are realized in the context of *work sessions* as primitive service requests among components that have been configured appropriately to enable interoperation. Components are encapsulated in *containers*, which export uniform interfaces for monitoring and control, as well as management of asynchronous service requests. The developer's task is to identify appropriate components and "plug" them together, via a form of *scripting* as in [40]. Scripts describe the desired configuration of components for realizing a work process; however, this configuration can be inspected and manipulated at run-time. Dynamic configuration [27] is achieved by invoking state inspection and control operations exported by the containers. A federated directory service enables service providers to publish their services and clients to search for offers of interest. This is achieved by having each service provider register entries for the components that it is exporting to provide services to clients. Each such entry includes a list of attribute-value pairs that allow containers, scripts, and development tools to "discover" and utilize a component's capabilities.

3.4   Service-Level Agreements

The concept of *service-level management* [42] comes from enterprise data processing centers, typically based on mainframe computing systems that provide comprehensive monitoring and resource control facilities. The overall goal is to define and maintain required levels of service for the user population of an enterprise. Our ongoing work on the *Aurora* architecture aims to provide this facility in dynamic open systems as well.

A *service-level agreement* (SLA) documents the *expected behavior* of service providers, for a given client or client class. The information contained in the SLA explicitly defines non-functional attributes of the services (such as availability, failure handling, performance, and security) in order to provide guidance to clients. This information, in the form of specifications of the measurements and events that a component exports together with associated control operations, and metadata describing the guarantees and execution policies supported, complements the specification of service functional interfaces. It can be used for selecting among alternative service offers, based on the client's requirements on attributes of the service. *Ongoing proof of conformance* to a SLA requires the ability to produce on-line reports on the delivered service levels, thus achieving *accountability*, which entails that the availability and level of performance of all entities involved in workflow processing be tracked and maintained according to predetermined levels. This aspect is particularly important for work sessions that span organization boundaries. SLA enforcement requires on-line monitoring of the delivered service levels and the actual resource/service demands, and the ability to invoke configuration and control actions to affect the behavior of active sessions. As a specific example, [36] describes the *Aurora* monitoring infrastructure for supporting SLA management.

By allowing clients to obtain up-to-date information on the supported guarantees for reliable execution and expected performance, the SLA specification contributes to making services in a dynamic open environment more predictable, and, in this sense, more manageable. Clients are provided with guidance in planning a strategy for obtaining service despite failures and unpredictable performance, which are inherent characteristics of dynamic open environments such as the Internet. A client can use the information exported by the SLA to set timeouts and to schedule retries and compensating actions in case of failure. Moreover, a client can abort or cancel its requests when the measured service-level parameters (such as transfer rate and response time) become worse than prespecified thresholds. Service providers *explicitly* state, and maintain up-to-date, the guarantees that they can for their service offers under specific run-time conditions and subject to specific terms and conditions of use. In a sense, a *contract* is established between providers and clients, in the context defined by the particular request and current run-time conditions. The *promises* of providers and the corresponding *rights* of clients [52] are documented, and therefore can be continuously monitored.

It is important that the autonomy of service providers is not compromised, as a service provider is the only authority responsible for exporting an interface for use by clients and for establishing and enforcing service attributes such as transactional and performance guarantees. Another important point is that a service provider may combine multiple services, made available by other autonomous providers, in order to provide a *composite service* to a client. A client does not need be aware of this complexity. Moreover, other service providers may not be aware that their services are being used in the context of a composite service request. The SLA exported by a service provider hides such implementation aspects, exporting only aspects related to the service level that a client can expect, together with information about available actions to compensate for actions that were not completed successfully or that the client wishes to revoke.

4 Conclusions

Dynamic composition of services emerges as a key common requirement for several network-centric applications in open environments, such as digital libraries, electronic commerce, and scientific collaborative work [41]. As demonstrated in Section 2.5, container technology is expected to play an increasingly important role as a building block for sophisticated digital library services. We consider a view of digital libraries that goes beyond that of a repository of on-line information, to provide support throughout all phases of work. This vision is incorporated in our ongoing research toward an integrated work support environment that is structured as an *information economy*. A distributed run-time environment based on open protocols serves as the basis of an open and dynamic federation of resources and services owned and managed by autonomous authorities. Towards this end, container technology contributes a framework for encapsulating value-added services in complex-structured documents, including support for active and dynamic content, as well as support for collaborative work and automated interactions with diverse services.

Developments related to the XML and RDF efforts by the W3C Consortium are expected to provide the foundation for machine-understandable self-descriptive information regarding services, information content and other resources. This is essential for supporting automated as well as human-driven processes in the context of an information economy. With the increasing emphasis on open systems comprising widely distributed autonomous providers of services and information content, we consider *service level management* to be an essential requirement, as an integrated approach to handling the issues of terms, conditions and guarantees. Such developments will broaden the scope of digital library system, and contribute towards establishing a comprehensive work support environment, with a profound impact on our lives.

References

1. "The Library of Congress Maintenance Agency Page for International Standard Z39.50". URL: http://lcweb.loc.gov/z3950/agency/.
2. "Resource Description Framework (RDF) Model and Syntax Specification", 1998. Available via URL http://www.w3.org/TR/WD-rdf-syntax/.
3. C. A. Allen. "Automating the Web with WIDL". *World Wide Web Journal*, 2(4), 1997.
4. G. Alonso, D. Agrawal, A.El Abbadi, and C. Mohan. "Functionality and Limitations of Current Workflow Management Systems". *IEEE Expert*, 1(9), 1997. Special Issue on Cooperative Information Systems.
5. D.E. Atkins, W.P. Birmingham, E.H. Durfee, E.J. Glover, T. Mullen, E.A. Rundensteiner, E. Soloway, J.M. Vidal, R. Wallace, and M.P. Wellman. "Toward Inquiry-Based Education Through Interacting Software Agents". *IEEE Computer*, pages 70–76, May 1996.
6. M. Baldonado, C.K. Chang, L. Gravano, and A. Paepcke. "The Stanford Digital Library Metadata Architecture". *Int'l Journal of Digital Libraries*, 1(2), 1997.
7. J. Bosak. "XML, Java, and the Future of the Web". *World Wide Web Journal*, 2(4), 1997.
8. T. Bray, J. Paoli, and C. M. Sperberg-McQueen. "Extensible Markup Language Recommendation (XML) 1.0", 1998. Available via WWW at URL http://www.w3.org/TR/1998/REC-xml.
9. InterTrust Technologies Corp. "Securing the Content, Not the Wire, for Information Commerce", 1996. Available via WWW at URL http://www.intertrust.com.
10. W.B. Croft. "What Do People Want form Information Retrieval?". *D-Lib Magazine*, November 1995. Available via URL http://www.dlib.org.
11. R. Daniel and C. Lagoze. "Distributed Active Relationships in the Warwick Framework". In *Proc. IEEE Metadata Conference*, 1997.

12. M.L. Dertouzos. *"What Will Be : How the New World of Information Will Change Our Lives"*. Harper San Francisco, 1997.
13. C.A. Ellis, S.J. Gibbs, and G.L. Rein (editors). "Groupware: Some Issues and Experiences". *CACM*, 34(1), 1991.
14. E.A. Fox, R. Akscyn, R.Furuta, and J. Legget (editors). "Introduction to Digital Libraries". *CACM*, 38(4), 1995.
15. E.A. Fox and G. Marchionini (editors). "Toward a Worldwide Digital Library". *CACM*, 41(4), 1998.
16. M. Fuchs. "Let's Talk: Extending the Web to Support Collaboration". In *Proc. 5th Workshops on Enabling Technologies: Infrastructure for Collaborative Enterprises*, 1996.
17. H. Garcia-Molina, S.P. Ketchpel, and N. Shivakumar. "Safeguarding and Charging for Information on the Internet". In *Proc. IEEE Int'l Conf. Database Engineering, (ICDE)*, 1998.
18. D. Georgakopoulos, M. Hornik, and A. Sheth. "An Overview of Workflow Management: From Process Modeling to Workflow Automation Infrastructure". *Distributed and Parallel Databases*, 3(2):119–154, April 1995.
19. H.M. Gladney and J.B. Lotspiech. "Safeguarding Digital Library Contents and Users: Assuring Convenient Security and Data Quality ". *D-Lib Magazine*, May 1997. Available via URL http://www.dlib.org.
20. C.F. Goldfarb. *"The SGML Handbook"*. Oxford University Press, 1990.
21. L. Gravano, C.C.K. Chang, H. Garcia-Molina, and A. Paepcke. "STARTS: Stanford Proposal for Internet Meta-Searching". In *Proceedings of the ACM SIGMOD Conference on Management of Data*, 1997.
22. JavaSoft. "JavaBeans API Specification (1.01)", 1997. Available via URL http://java.sun.com:80/beans/docs/spec.html.
23. R. Kahn and R. Wilensky. "A Framework for Distributed Digital Object Services". Technical Report cnri.dlib/tn95-01, Corporation for National Research Initiatives (CNRI), 1995. Available via URL http://www.cnri.reston.va.us/cstr/arch/k-w.html.
24. S.P. Ketchpel, H. Garcia-Molina, and A. Paepcke. "Shopping Models: A Flexible Architecture for Information Commerce". In *Proc. Int'l Conference on Theory and Practice of Digital Libraries*, 1997.
25. R. Khare and A. Rifkin. "Capturing the State of Distributed Systems with XML". *World Wide Web Journal*, 2(4), 1997.
26. R. Khare and A. Rifkin. "XML: A Door to Automated Web Applications". *IEEE Internet Computing*, 1(4), 1997.
27. J. Kramer and J. Magee. "Dynamic Configuration for Distributed Systems". *IEEE Trans. Software Engineering*, 11(4), 1985.
28. C. Lagoze. "A Secure Repository Design for Digital Libraries". *D-Lib Magazine*, December 1995. Available via URL http://www.dlib.org.
29. C. Lagoze and J.R. Davis. "Dienst: an architecture for distributed document libraries". *CACM*, 38(4), 1995.
30. C. Lagoze, C.A. Lynch, and R. Daniel. "The Warwick Framework: A Container Architecture for Aggregating Sets of Metadata". Technical Report TR96-1593, Cornell Computer Science Department, 1996. Available via URL http://cs-tr.cs.cornell.edu:80/Dienst/UI/2.0/Describe/ncstrl.cornell/TR96-1593.
31. C. Lagoze, R. McGrath, E. Overly, and N. Yeager. "A Design for Inter-Operable Secure Object Stores (ISOS)". Technical Report TR95-1558, Cornell Computer Science Department, 1995. Available via URL http://www.ncstrl.org/Dienst/UI/2.0/Describe/ncstrl.cornell

32. C. Lagoze and S. Payette. "An Infrastructure for Open-Architecture Digital Libraries". Technical Report TR98-1690, Cornell Computer Science Department, 1998. Available via URL http://cs-tr.cs.cornell.edu:80/Dienst/UI/1.0/Display/ncstrl.cornell/TR98-1690.
33. R. L. Larsen. "Relaxing Assumptions - Stretching the Vision: A Modest View of Some Technical Issues". *D-Lib Magazine*, April 1997.
34. C.A. Lynch. "The Z39.50 Information Retrieval Standard - Part I: A Strategic View of Its Past, Present and Future". *D-Lib Magazine*, April 1997. Available via URL http://www.dlib.org.
35. M. Marazakis, D. Papadakis, and C. Nikolaou. "The Aurora Architecture for Developing Network-Centric Applications by Dynamic Composition of Services". Technical Report TR 213, FORTH/ICS, 1997.
36. M. Marazakis, D. Papadakis, and C. Nikolaou. "Management of Work Sessions in Dynamic Open Environments". In *Proc. Int'l Workshop on Workflow Management (in conjunction with DEXA'98)*, 1998.
37. M. Marazakis, D. Papadakis, and S.A. Papadakis. "A Framework for the Encapsulation of Value-Added Services in Digital Objects". In *Proc. European Conference on Research and Advanced Technology for Digital Libraries*, 1998.
38. C. Mohan. "Recent Trends in Workflow Management Products, Standards and Research". In *Proc. NATO Advanced Institute (ASI) Workshop on Workflow Management Systems and Interoperability*, 1997. Available via URL http://www.almaden.ibm.com/cs/exotica.
39. T. Mullen and M.P. Wellman. A simple computational market for network information services. In *Proc. 1st International Conference on Multiagent Systems*, June 1995. San Fransisco, CA.
40. O. Nierstrasz, D. Tsichritzis, V. deMey, and M. Stadelmann. "Object + Scripts = Applications". In D. Tsichritzis, editor, *Object Composition*. University of Geneva, 1991.
41. C. Nikolaou, M. Marazakis, D. Papadakis, Y. Yeorgiannakis, and J. Sairamesh. "Towards a Common Infrastructure to Support Large-Scale Distributed Applications". In *Proc. European Conference on Research and Advanced Technology for Digital Libraries*, 1997.
42. J. Noonan. "Automated Service Level Management and its Supporting Technologies". *Mainframe Journal*, October 1989.
43. B. Oki, M. Pfluegl, A. Siegel, and D. Skeen. "The Information Bus - An Architecture for Extensible Distributed Systems". In *Proc. ACM Symposium on Operating System Pronciples*, 1993.
44. A. Paepcke. "Digital Libraries: Searching is not Enough". *D-Lib Magazine*, May 1996. Available via URL http://www.dlib.org.
45. A. Paepcke, C.C.K. Chang, H. Garcia-Molina, and T. Winograd. "Interoperability for Digital Libraries Worldwide". *CACM*, 41(4), 1998.
46. A. Paepcke, S. B. Cousins, H. Garcia-Molina, S. F. Hassan, S. P. Ketchpel, M. Roscheisen, and T. Winograd. "Using Distributed Objects for Digital Library Interoperability". *IEEE Computer*, 29(5), 1996.
47. T.A. Phelps and R. Wilensky. "Toward Active, Extensible, Networked Documents: Multivalent Architecture and Applications". In *Proc. ACM Int'l Conf. on Digital Libraries*, 1996.
48. T.A. Phelps and R. Wilensky. "Multivalent Annotations". In *Proc. European Conference on Research and Advanced Technology for Digital Libraries*, 1997.
49. W. Reinhard, J. Schweitzer, and G. Volksen. "CSCW Tools: Concepts and Architectures". *IEEE Computer*, 27(5), 1994.

50. M. Roscheisen, C. Mogensen, and T. Winograd. "Shared Web Annotations as a Platform for Third-Party Value-Added, Information Providers: Architecture, Protocols, and Usage Examples". Technical Report STAN-CS-TR-97-1582, Stanford Computer Science Department, November 1994. Updated in April 1995.

51. M. Roscheisen, C. Mogensen, and T. Winograd. "Beyond Browsing: Shared Comments, SOAPs, Trails, and On-line Communities". In *Proc. WWW Conference*, 1995.

52. M. Roscheisen and T. Winograd. "The FIRM Framework for Interoperable Rights Management: Defining a Rights Management Service Layer for the Internet". In *Forum on Technology-based Intellectual Property Management*, 1997. Available via URL http://pcd.stanford.edu/rmr/commpacts.html.

53. M. Roscheisen and Terry Winograd. "A Network-Centric Design for Relationship-based Security and Access Control". *Journal of Computer Security*, 1997. Special Issue on Security in the World-Wide Web.

54. G. Rust. "Metadata: The Right Approach - An Integrated Model for Descriptive and Rights Metadata in E-commerce". *D-Lib Magazine*, July/August 1998. Available via URL http://www.dlib.org.

55. B. Schatz and H. Chen (editors). "Building Large-Scale Digital Libraries". *IEEE Computer*, 29(5), 1996.

56. D. Schutzer. "A Need for a Common Infrastructure: Digital Libraries and Electronic Commerce". *D-Lib Magazine*, April 1996. Available via URL http://www.dlib.org.

57. A. Sheth. "From Contemporary Workflow Process Automation to Adaptive and Dynamic Work Activity Coordination and Collaboration". In *Proc. Workshop on Workflow Management in Scientific and Engineering Applications*, 1997.

58. A. Sheth, D. Georgakopoulos, S. Joosten, Rusinkiewicz, W. Scacchi, J. Wilden, and A. Wolf. Report from the NSF Workshop on Workflow and Process Automation in Information Systems. Technical report, University of Georgia, 1996. Available via URL http://LSDIS.cs.uga.edu/publications.

59. O. Sibert, D. Bernstein, and D. Van Wie. "The DigiBox: A Self-Protecting Container for Information Commerce". In *Proc. 1st USENIX workshop on Electronic Commerce*, 1995.

60. M. Stefik and J. Lavendel. "Libraries and Digital Property Rights". In *Proc. European Conference on Advanced Technologies for Digital Libraries*, 1997.

61. S. Weibel, J. Godby, E. Miller, and R. Daniel. "OCLC/NCSA Metadata Workshop Report". 1995. Available via URL http://www.oclc.org:5046/oclc/research/conferences/metadata/.

62. M.P. Wellman, E.H. Durfee, and W.P. Birmingham. "The Digital Library as Community of Information Agents". *IEEE Expert*, 11(3), June 1996.

63. L. Wood, J. Sorensen, S. Byrne, R.S. Sutor, V. Apparao, S. Isaacs, G. Nicol, and M. Champion. "Document Object Model Specification (DOM) 1.0", 1998. W3C Working Draft. Available via WWW at URL http://www.w3.org/TR/WD-DOM.

An Introduction to Cryptology

Bart Preneel*

Katholieke Universiteit Leuven, Dept. Electrical Engineering-ESAT
Kardinaal Mercierlaan 94, B–3001 Heverlee, Belgium
bart.preneel@esat.kuleuven.ac.be

Abstract. This paper provides an overview of the state of the art in the design of cryptographic algorithms. It reviews the different type of algorithms for encryption and authentication and explains the principles of stream ciphers, block ciphers, hash functions, public-key encryption algorithms, and digital signature schemes. Subsequently the design and evaluation procedures for cryptographic algorithms are discussed.

1 Introduction

In our society, digital information and the systems and networks carrying this information are abused under many forms: financial transactions are eavesdropped or modified, sensitive information of individuals and organizations is eavesdropped or stolen, electronic services are used without paying for them, and computer systems and networks are broken into or brought down. The tools to perform this vary from simple bugs, password sniffers, and password crackers, over malicious software such as viruses and malicious applets, to complete hacker workbenches. Traditionally computer networks existed within one organization, and one tried to defend them against an opponent that came from outside the system. Now that we move to open and global networks, and that we are entering an era of electronic commerce, a more complex threat model arises: we cannot even trust the parties we are dealing with, and the system has to be designed to fight fraud within the system. For example, in an electronic transaction system, sellers can deny having sent an order if it turns out badly, and traders can deny having received an order when it turns out profitable (in order to keep the money). The risk for misuse has increased considerably, as potential attackers can operate from all over the globe. Moreover, if someone gains access to an electronic information system, the scale and impact of the abuse can be much larger than in a paper-based system.

These risks create the need for adequate security measures to protect electronic information systems. It is clear that in an electronic world physical security or personnel security by itself cannot be sufficient. An essential component of every secure information system is formed by cryptographic techniques. Other important building blocks are secure operating systems and procedural aspects

---

* F.W.O. postdoctoral researcher, sponsored by the Fund for Scientific Research – Flanders (Belgium).

such as audit tools and management guidelines. Building secure computer systems and networks requires a conservative approach which is not always compatible with the current rapid developments in the industry; moreover, that security has to be kept in mind from the first step of the design.

In this paper we discuss the principles underlying the design of cryptographic algorithms; we distinguish between confidentiality protection (the protection against passive eavesdroppers) and authentication (the protection against active eavesdroppers, who try to modify information). Then we review the different issues that arise when selecting, designing, and evaluating a cryptographic algorithm. Finally we present some concluding remarks.

2 Encryption for Secrecy Protection

The use of cryptography for protection the secrecy of information is as old as writing itself (for an excellent historical overview, see D. Kahn [14]). The basic idea is to apply a 'complicated' transformation to the information to be protected. When the sender (usually called Alice in cryptography) wants to send a message to the recipient (Bob), she will apply to the *plaintext* P the mathematical transformation $E()$. This transformation $E()$ is called the encryption algorithm; the result of this transformation is called the *ciphertext* or $C = E(P)$. Bob will decrypt C by applying the inverse transformation $D = E^{-1}$; this way he recovers P or $P = D(C)$. For a secure algorithm E, the ciphertext C does not make sense to outsiders: Eve, who is tapping the connection, can obtain C, but she cannot obtain (partial information on) the corresponding plaintext P.

This approach only works when Bob can keep the transformation D secret. While this is acceptable for a person-to-person exchange, it is not feasible for large scale use. Bob needs a software or hardware implementation of D: either he has to program it himself, or he has to trust someone to write the program for him. Moreover, he will need a different transformation (and program) for each correspondent, which is not very practical. Bob and Alice always have to face the risk that somehow Eve will obtain D (or E), for example by bribing the author of the software or their system manager, or by breaking into their computer system.

This problem can be solved by introducing into the encryption algorithm $E()$ a secret parameter, the key K. Typically such a key is a binary string of 40 to a few thousand bits. A corresponding key K^* is used for the decryption algorithm D. One has thus $C = E_K(P)$ and $P = D_{K^*}(C)$ (see also Figure 1, which assumes that $K^* = K$). The transformation has to depend strongly (and in a very complicated way) on the keys: if one uses a wrong key $K^{*'} \neq K^*$, one does not obtain the plaintext P but a 'random' plaintext P'. Now it is possible to publish the encryption algorithm $E()$ and the decryption algorithm $D()$; the security of the system relies only on the secrecy of two short keys. This implies that $E()$ and $D()$ can be evaluated publicly and distributed on a commercial basis. One can think of the analogy with a mechanical lock: everyone knows how such a lock works, but in order to open a particular lock, one needs to know the key or the secret combination. The assumption that the algorithm is known to the opponent is known in cryptography as "Kerckhoffs's principle"; Kerckhoffs was a 19th century Dutch cryptographer who was the first to formulate this approach.

A simple example of an encryption algorithm is the so-called 'Caesar cipher,' after the Roman emperor who used it. The plaintext is encrypted letter by letter; the ciphertext is obtained by shifting the letters over a fixed number of positions in the alphabet. The secret key indicates the number of positions. It is claimed that Caesar always used the value of three, such that "AN EXAMPLE" would be encrypted to "DQ HADPSOH". Another example is the name of the computer "HAL" from S. Kubrick's "A Space Odyssey (2001)", which was obtained by replacing the letters of "IBM" by their predecessor in the alphabet. This corresponds to a shift over 25 positions. It is clear that such a system is completely insecure.

A problem which has not yet been addressed is how Alice and Bob exchange the secret key. The easy answer is that cryptography does not solve this problem; cryptography only makes problems easier. In this case the secrecy of a (large) plaintext has been reduced to that of two *short* keys, which can be exchanged on beforehand. The problem of exchanging keys is studied in more detail in an area of cryptography that is called 'key management'. We will not discuss it in further detail here.

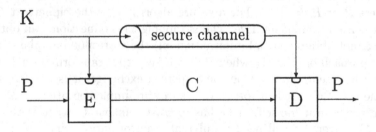

Fig. 1. Model for conventional or symmetric encryption

The branch of science which studies the encryption of information is called *cryptography*. A related branch tries to 'break' encryption algorithms, by recovering the plaintext without knowing the key or by deriving the key from the ciphertext and parts of the plaintext; it is called *cryptanalysis*. The term *cryptology* covers both aspects. For more extensive introductions to cryptography, the reader is referred to [2, 15, 19, 20, 25, 26].

Thus far we have assumed that the key for decryption K^* is equal to the encryption key K, or that it is easy to derive K^* from K. This type of algorithms are called *conventional* or *symmetric* ciphers. In *public-key* or *asymmetric* ciphers, K^* and K are always different; moreover, it should be difficult to compute K^* from K. This has the advantage that one can make K public, which has important implications to the key management problem. The remainder of this section discusses conventional algorithms and public-key algorithms.

2.1 Conventional Encryption

This section introduces the two most common conventional encryption algorithms: additive stream ciphers and block ciphers.

Additive Stream Ciphers. Additive stream ciphers are ciphers for which the encryption consists of a modulo 2 addition (exclusive or, exor) of a key stream to the plaintext (see Figure 2). The plaintext and ciphertext are divided into words of m bits (m is typically 1, 8, or a multiple of 8), and the ith word of the plaintext, ciphertext, and key stream is denoted with p_i, c_i, and k_i, respectively. The encryption operation can then be written as $c_i = p_i \oplus k_i$. Here $\oplus$ denotes addition modulo 2. The decryption operation is identical to the encryption (the cipher is an involution): indeed, $p_i = c_i \oplus k_i = (p_i \oplus k_i) \oplus k_i = p_i \oplus (k_i \oplus k_i) = p_i \oplus 0 = p_i$. It is clear that the m-bit key stream word k_i cannot be a constant (in that case a cryptanalyst can compute the key stream word from a single ciphertext word and the corresponding plaintext word; also repetitions in the plaintext would be visible in the ciphertext). One can show that for a strong cipher the sequence of k_i has to consist of randomly looking strings (see also Sect. 2.2).

In practice one computes the words k_i with a finite state machine. Such a machine stretches a short secret key K into a much longer key stream sequence k_i; this is called a *pseudo-random* string generator. The sequence k_i is eventually periodic. One important (but not sufficient) design criterion for the finite state machine is that the period has to be sufficient long (2^{64} is a typical lower bound). The values k_i should also be uniformly distributed; another condition is that there should be no correlations between (part of) successive words (note that cryptanalytic attacks exist which exploit correlations of less than 1 in 1 million). Formally, the sequence k_i can be parameterized with a security parameter; then on requires that the sequence satisfies every polynomial time statistical test for randomness (here polynomial means polynomial in the security parameter). Another desirable property is that no polynomial time machine can predict the next bit of the sequence (based on the previous outputs) with a probability that is significantly better than 1/2. An important (and perhaps surprising) result in theoretical cryptology by A. Yao shows that these two conditions are in fact equivalent [28].

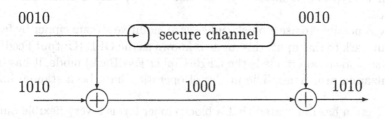

Fig. 2. An additive stream cipher

Block Ciphers. Block ciphers take a different approach to encryption: the plaintext is divided into larger words of n bits, called *blocks*. Every block is enciphered in the same way, using a keyed one-way permutation, i.e., a permutation on the set of n-bit strings that is controlled by a secret key. The simplest way to encrypt a plaintext using a block cipher is as follows: divide the plaintext into n-bit blocks, and encrypt these block by block. The decryption also operates on individual blocks:

$$c_i = E_K(p_i) \qquad \text{and} \qquad p_i = D_K(c_i).$$

This way of using a block cipher is called the ECB (Electronic CodeBook) mode. Note that the encryption operation does *not* depend on the location in the ciphertext as is the case for additive stream ciphers.

Consider the following attack on a block cipher (the so-called tabulation attack): the cryptanalyst collects ciphertext blocks and their corresponding plaintext blocks (this is possible as part of the plaintext is often predictable); this is used to build a large table. With such a table, one can deduce information on other plaintexts encrypted under the same key. In order to preclude this attack, the value of n has to be quite large (e.g., 64 or 128) and the plaintext should not contain any repetitions (or other patterns), as these will be leaked to the ciphertext.

This shows that even if n is large, the ECB mode is not suited to encrypt plaintexts that are not random (such as text, images, etc.). This mode should only be used in very special cases, where the plaintext is already random, such as the encryption of cryptographic keys. There is however an easy way to randomize the plaintext, by using the block cipher in a different mode of operation.

The default mode of operation for a block cipher is the CBC (Cipher Block Chaining) mode. In this mode the different blocks are coupled by adding modulo 2 to a plaintext block the previous ciphertext block:

$$c_i = E_K(p_i \oplus c_{i-1}) \qquad \text{and} \qquad p_i = D_K(c_i) \oplus c_{i-1}.$$

Note that this 'randomizes' the plaintext, and hides patterns. To enable the encryption of the first plaintext block ($i = 1$), one defines c_0 as the initial value IV. By varying this value, one can ensure that the same plaintext is encrypted into a different ciphertext under the same key. The CBC mode allows for random access on decryption: if necessary, one can decrypt only a small part of the ciphertext.

It is also possible to use a block cipher as an additive stream cipher by feeding the output back to the input; this mode is known as the OFB (Output FeedBack) mode. A second stream mode is the CFB (Cipher FeedBack) mode; it has better synchronization properties. The modes of operation have been standardized in [6, 11].

This section has illustrated that a block cipher forms a very flexible building block. The most famous block cipher is the Data Encryption Standard (or DES) [5], which is widely used since 1977. The DES has a block size of 64 bits and a key length of 56 bits; it will be shown in Sect. 4.3 that this is no longer sufficient.

Therefore the US government is planning to replace it by a new block cipher, the AES (Advanced Encryption Standard). Hereto an open call for algorithms has been launched in September '97; 15 candidates have been submitted by the deadline of June '98. Currently the evaluation procedure is under way. The AES will have a block length of 128 bits and a key length between 128 and 256 bits.

2.2 Security of Conventional Algorithms

An essential aspect in the choice of an encryption algorithm is the security level. In 1926 G.S. Vernam has published a simple encryption algorithm for telegraphic messages [27]. The cipher is an additive stream cipher, where the key stream consists of a completely random sequence, generated by a binary symmetric source (all bits are uniformly and identically distributed). In 1949 C. Shannon, the father of information theory, was able to prove mathematically that this scheme offers perfect security, i.e., from observing the ciphertext, the opponent cannot obtain any information on the plaintext, no matter how much computing power he has [24]. The main disadvantage of this scheme is that the secret key is exactly as long as the message (one should never reuse a key stream); C. Shannon also showed that this the best one can do if one wants perfect security. In spite of the long key, the Vernam algorithm is still used by diplomats and spies; it has been used for the 'red telephone' between Washington and Moscow. Spies used to carry key pads with random characters (it is easy to generalize the scheme to arbitrary alphabets). The security of the scheme relies on the fact that every page of the pad is used only once, which explains the name "one-time pad".

In most commercial applications one cannot afford to distribute keys which are as long as the plaintext. Therefore one uses encryption algorithms which do not offer perfect security; this implies that it is *in principle* possible to recover the plaintext and/or the secret key from the ciphertext, in the sense that one has sufficient information to do this. This does not mean that it is also possible *in practice*. For example, additive stream ciphers try to mimic the approach of the Vernam scheme by replacing the random key stream sequence by a pseudo-random sequence generated from a short key.

2.3 Public-Key Encryption

The main problem that is left unsolved by conventional cryptography is the key distribution problem. Especially in a large network it is not feasible to distribute keys between all user pairs (in a network with t users there are $t(t-1)/2$ such pairs). An alternative is to manage all keys in a central location, but this may then become a single point of failure. Public-key cryptography offers a much more elegant solution to this problem.

The concept of public-key cryptography has been invented by in 1976, independently by W. Diffie and M. Hellman [3] and by R. Merkle [18]. The key idea behind public-key cryptography is the concept of *trapdoor one-way functions*. A *one-way function* is a function that is easy to compute, but hard to invert. For example, in a conventional block cipher, the ciphertext has to be a one-way function of the plaintext and the key: it is easy to compute the ciphertext from the plaintext and the key, but given the plaintext and the ciphertext it should be hard to recover the key (otherwise the block cipher would not be secure). Similarly one can show that the existence of additive stream ciphers (pseudo-random string generators) implies the existence of one-way functions. Trapdoor one-way functions are one-way function with an additional property: given some additional information (the trapdoor), it becomes possible to invert the one-way function.

With such functions Bob can send a secret message to Alice without the need for prior arrangement of a secret key. Alice chooses a trapdoor one-way function with public parameter P_A (Alice's public key) and with secret parameter S_A (Alice's secret key). Alice makes her public key widely available (she can put it on her home page, but it can also be included in special directories). Anyone who wants to send some confidential information to Alice, computes the ciphertext as the image of the plaintext under the trapdoor one-way function using the parameter P_A. Upon receipt of this ciphertext, Alice recovers the plaintext by using her trapdoor information S_A (see Figure 3). An attacker, who does not know S_A, sees only the image of the plaintext under a one-way function, and will not be able to recover the plaintext. This assumes that it is infeasible to compute S_A from P_A. Note that if one wants to send a message to Alice, one has to know Alice's public key P_A, and one has to be sure that this key really belongs to Alice (and not to Eve), since it is only the owner of the corresponding secret key who will be able to decrypt the ciphertext. Public keys do not need a secure channel for their distribution, but they do need an authentic channel. As the keys for encryption and decryption are different, and Alice and Bob have different information, public-key algorithms are also known as asymmetric algorithms.

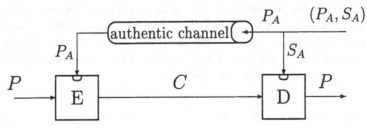

Fig. 3. Model for public-key or asymmetric encryption

The conditions which a public-key encryption algorithm has to satisfy are:
- the generation of a key pair (P_A, S_A) has to be easy;
- encryption and decryption have to be easy operations;
- it should be hard to compute the public key P_A from the corresponding secret key S_A;
- $S_A(P_A(P)) = P$.

Designing a secure public-key encryption algorithm is apparently a very difficult problem. From the large number of proposals, only a few have survived (for example, almost all knapsack-based systems have been broken). The most popular algorithm is the RSA algorithm [22], which was named after its inventors (R.L. Rivest, A. Shamir, and L. Adleman). The security of RSA is based on the fact that it is relatively simple to find two large prime numbers (in 1998 large means 115 decimal digits or more) and to multiply these, while factoring their product (of 230 decimal digits) is not feasible with the current algorithms and computers.

key generation: Find 2 prime numbers p and q with at least 115 digits and compute their product, the modulus $n = p \cdot q$. Compute the Carmichael function $\lambda(n)$, the least common multiple of $p - 1$ and $q - 1$. Choose an encryption exponent e (at least 40 to 64 bits long), which is relatively prime to $\lambda(n)$ and compute the decryption exponent as $d = e^{-1} \bmod \lambda(n)$ (with Euclid's algorithm). The public key consists of the pair (e, n), and the secret key consists of the decryption exponent d or the pair (p, q);

encryption: represent the plaintext as an integer in the interval $[0, n - 1]$ and compute the ciphertext as $C = P^e \bmod n$;

decryption: $P = C^d \bmod n$.

Without explaining the mathematical background of the algorithm, one can observe that decryption requires the extraction of modular eth roots; no algorithm is known for this problem which does not use the prime factors of n; finding the decryption exponent requires knowledge of $\lambda(n)$ and hence of the factors of n. On the other hand, this knowledge is not required for the encryption operation. For the practical use of RSA, one has to take into account many technical details: for example, the plaintext P has to be mapped (with a function that is easy to invert) to a random integer $\in [0, n - 1]$ in order to avoid trivial attacks (e.g., the extraction of natural eth roots when $P^e < n$).

The more complex properties of public-key cryptography seem to require some 'high level' mathematical structure; most public-key algorithms are based on number theoretic problems (such as factoring and discrete logarithm in certain groups). While these number theoretic problems are believed to be difficult, it should be noted that since the invention of public-key cryptography significant progress has been made in factoring: the factorization record in 1975 was 39 decimal digits; in 1985 this was increased to 65 digits, and in 1994 a 130-digit modulus was factored. This evolution is due to a combination of more sophisticated factoring algorithms with progress in hardware and parallel processing. The cryptographer should take this into account by selecting sufficiently large keys for public-key algorithms.

The main advantage of public-key algorithms is the simplified key management. The main disadvantages are the larger keys (typically 64 to 256 bytes) and the slow performance: both in software and hardware public-key encryption algorithms are two to three orders of magnitude slower than conventional algorithms. For example, a 1024-bit exponentiation requires about 0.3 seconds on a 90 MHz Pentium, which corresponds to 3.4 kbit/s. On the same machine, DES runs at 16.9 Mbit/s. Because of the large difference in performance and the larger block length (which influences error propagation), one always employs *hybrid* systems: the public-key encryption scheme is used to distribute a secret key, which is then used in a fast conventional algorithm.

3 Hashing and Signatures for Authentication

Information authentication includes two main aspects:

- *data origin authentication*, or who has originated the information;
- *data integrity*, or has the information been modified.

Other aspects which can be important are the timeliness of the information, the sequence of messages, and the destination of information. These aspects can be accounted for by using sequence numbers and time stamps in the messages and by including addressing information in the data. In data communications, the implicit authentication created by recognition of the handwriting, signature, or voice disappears. The reason is that information becomes much more vulnerable to falsification as the physical coupling between information and its bearer is lost.

Until recently it was widely believed that encryption of information (with a conventional algorithm) was sufficient for protecting its authenticity. The reasoning was that if a certain ciphertext resulted after decryption in a *meaningful* plaintext, it had to be created by someone who knew the key, and therefore it must be authentic. A few counterexamples are sufficient to refute this claim: if a block cipher is used in ECB mode, an attacker can always reorder the blocks. For any additive stream cipher (including the Vernam scheme), an opponent can always modify any plaintext bit (without knowing whether a 0 has been changed to a 1 or vice versa). The concept 'meaningful' information implicitly assumes that the information contains redundancy, which allows to distinguish genuine information from an arbitrary plaintext. However, one can envisage applications where the plaintext contains very little or no redundancy. The separation between secrecy and authentication has also been clarified by public-key cryptography: anyone who knows Alice's public key can send her a confidential message, and therefore Alice has no idea who has actually sent this message.

Two different levels of information authentication can be distinguished. If two parties trust each other and want to protect themselves against malicious outsiders, the term 'conventional message authentication' is used. In this setting, both parties are at equal footing (for example, they share the same secret key). If however a dispute arises between them, a third party (such as a judge) will not be able to resolve it (for example a judge cannot tell whether a message has been created by Alice or by Bob). If protection between two mutually distrustful parties is required (which is often the case in commercial relationships), an electronic equivalent of a manual signature is needed. In cryptographic terms this is called a digital signature.

3.1 Symmetric Authentication

The underlying idea is similar to that for encryption, where the secrecy of a large amount of information is replaced by the secrecy of a short key. In the case of authentication, one replaces the authenticity of the information by the protection of a short string, which is a unique 'fingerprint' of the information. Such a 'fingerprint' is computed as a hash result. This can also be interpreted as adding a special form of redundancy to the information. This process consists of two components. First one compresses the information to a string of fixed length, with a (cryptographic) hash function. Then the resulting string (the hash result) is protected as follows:

- either the hash result is communicated over an authentic channel (e.g., it can be read over the phone). It is then sufficient to use a hash function without a secret parameter, which is called a Manipulation Detection Code or MDC;
- or the hash function uses a secret parameter (the key); it is then called a Message Authentication Code or MAC.

MDCs. If an additional (authentic) channel is available, MDCs can provide authenticity without requiring secret keys. Moreover an MDC is a flexible primitive, which can be used for a variety of other cryptographic applications. An MDC has to satisfy the following conditions:

- it should be hard to find an input with a given hash result (preimage resistance);
- it should be hard to find a second input with the same hash result as a given input (2nd preimage resistance);
- it should be hard to find two different inputs with the same hash result (collision resistance).

An MDC satisfying these three conditions is called a *collision resistant* hash function. For a strong hash function with an n-bit result, solving one of the first two problems requires about 2^n evaluations of the hash function. This implies that $n = 64 \ldots 80$ is sufficient. However, finding collisions is much easier: one will find with high probability a collision in a set of hash results corresponding to $2^{n/2}$ inputs. This implies that collision resistant hash functions need a hash result of 128 to 160 bits. This last property is also known as the birthday paradox based on the following observation: within a group of 24 persons the probability that there are two persons with the same birthday is about 50%. The reason is that a group of this size contains 276 different pairs of persons, which is a large fraction of the 365 days in a year. Note that the birthday paradox plays an essential role in the security of many cryptographic primitives (cf. Sect. 4.3). Examples of MDCs in use today are RIPEMD-160 and SHA-1; both have been standardized in [12]. Not all applications need collision resistant hash functions; sometimes (2nd) preimage resistance is sufficient.

MACs. MACs have been used for more than twenty years in electronic transactions in the banking environment. They require the exchange of a secret key between the communicating parties. The MAC corresponding to a message is a complex function of every bit of the message and every bit of the key; it should be infeasible to derive the key from observing a number of text/MAC pairs, or to compute or predict a MAC without knowing the secret key.

A MAC is used as follows: Alice computes for her message P the value $MAC_K(P)$ and appends this MAC to the message (here MAC denotes both the function and its result). Bob recomputes the value of $MAC_K(P)$ based on the received message P, and verifies whether it matches the received MAC. If the answer is positive, he accepts the message as authentic, i.e., as a genuine message from Alice. Eve, the active eavesdropper, can modify the message P to P', but she is not able to compute the corresponding MAC value $MAC(P')$, as she is not privy to the secret key K. For a secure MAC, the best Eve can do is guessing the MAC. In that case, Bob can detect the modification with high probability: for an n-bit MAC Eve's probability of success is only $1/2^n$. The value of n lies typically between 32 and 64. Note that if encryption and authentication are combined, the key for encryption and authentication need to be different. Moreover, the preferred option is to compute the MAC on the plaintext.

A popular way to compute a MAC is to encrypt the message with a block cipher using the CBC mode (yet another use of a block cipher), and to keep only part of the bits of the last block as the MAC. However, recent research has indicated that this approach is less secure than previously believed [21]; again, the birthday paradox plays a role in this work.

For a MAC, the equivalent of the Vernam scheme exists. This implies that one can design a MAC algorithm which is unconditionally secure, in the sense that the security of the MAC is independent of the computing power of the opponent. The requirement is again that the secret key is used only once. The basic idea of this approach is due to G.J. Simmons and dates back to the seventies (see for example [25]). It turns out that these algorithms can be computationally very efficient, since the properties required from this primitive are combinatorial rather than cryptographic. Recent constructions are therefore one order of magnitude faster than other cryptographic primitives (encryption algorithms, hash functions), and achieve speeds up to 1 Gbit/s on fast processors [9]. A simple example is described here, which is derived from Reed-Solomon codes for error-correction [13]. The key consists of two n-bit words denoted with K_1 and K_2. The plaintext is divided into t n-bit words, denoted with p_1 through p_t. The MAC, which consists of a single n-bit word, is computed based on a simple polynomial evaluation:

$$MAC_{K_1,K_2}(x) = K_1 + \sum_{i=1}^{t} p_i \cdot (K_2)^i,$$

where addition and multiplication are to be computed in the finite field with 2^n elements. It can be proved that the probability of creating another valid message/MAC pair is upper bounded by $t/2^n$. A practical choice is $n = 64$, which results in a 128-bit key. For messages up to 1 Mbyte, the success probability of a forgery is then less than $1/2^{47}$. Note that it turns out to be possible to reuse K_2; however, for every message a new key K_1 is required. This key could be generated from a short initial key using an additive stream cipher, but then the unconditional security is lost. However, one can argue that it is easier to understand the security of this scheme than that of a computationally secure MAC.

3.2 Digital Signatures

A digital signature is the electronic equivalent of a manual signature on a document. It provides a strong binding between the document and a person, and in case of a dispute, a third party can decide whether or not the signature is valid. Of course a digital signature will not bind a person and a document, but will bind a key and a document. Additional measures are then required to bind the person to his or her key. Note that for a MAC, both Alice and Bob can compute the MAC, hence a third party cannot distinguish between them. While block ciphers (and even one-way functions) can be used to construct digital signatures, the most elegant and efficient constructions for digital signature rely on public-key cryptography.

If Alice wants to sign some information P intended for Bob, she adds some redundancy to the information, resulting in $\tilde{P}$, and decrypts the resulting text with her secret key. This operation can only be carried out by Alice. Upon receipt of the signature, Bob encrypts it using Alice's public key, and verifies that the information $\tilde{P}$ has the prescribed redundancy. If so, he accepts the signature on P as valid. Such a digital signature (which is a signature with 'message recovery') imposes an additional condition on the public-key system: $P_A(S_A(P)) = P$. Note that anyone who knows Alice's public key can verify the signature. The RSA public-key encryption scheme is a bijection (a trapdoor one-way permutation), and thus it allows for the construction of digital signatures with message recovery. We leave it as an exercise to the reader to show why the redundancy is essential in this approach.

If Alice wants to sign very long messages (without encrypting them), this approach results in signatures that are as long as the message. Moreover, signing with a public-key system is a relatively slow operation. In order to solve these problems, Alice does not sign the information itself, but the hash result of the information computed with an MDC. The signature now consists of a single block, which is appended to the information (this is called a digital signature 'with appendix'). In order to verify such a signature, Bob recomputes the MDC of the message and encrypts the signature with Alice's public key. If both operations give the same result, Bob accepts the signature as valid. MDCs used in this way need to be collision resistant: otherwise Alice can sign a message P, and later be held accountable for a fraudulent message P' with the same MDC (and thus with the same signature).

Note that there exist other signature schemes with appendix (such as the DSA [7]), which are not derived immediately from a public-key encryption scheme. For these schemes one can define a 'signing operation' (using the secret key) and a 'verification operation' (using the public key), without referring to 'decryption' and 'encryption' operations.

4 Analysis and Design of Conventional Cryptographic Algorithms

In this section we compare three approaches to the design of cryptographic algorithms. Next we describe the typical phases in the life of an algorithm. Then we contrast brute force and shortcut attacks, public and secret algorithms, and weak and strong algorithms.

4.1 Three Approaches in Cryptography

Present day cryptology tries to develop provably secure and efficient cryptographic algorithms. Often such algorithms are not available; therefore cryptographic algorithms are studied following three approaches: the information theoretic approach, the complexity theoretic approach, and the system based approach. These approaches differ in the assumptions about the capabilities of an opponent, in the definition of a cryptanalytic success, and in the notion of security.

The most desirable from the viewpoint of the cryptographer are unconditionally secure algorithms; this design approach is also known as the *information theoretic* approach. However, few such schemes exist: examples are the Vernam scheme (Sect. 2.2), and the MAC based on Reed-Solomon codes (Sect. 3.1). While they are computationally very efficient, the cost in terms of key material may be prohibitively large (certainly for the Vernam scheme). For most applications one has to live with schemes which offer only conditional security.

A second approach is to reduce the security of his scheme to that of other well known difficult problems, or to that of other cryptographic primitives. The *complexity theoretic* approach starts from an abstract model for computation, and assumes that the opponent has limited computing power within this model [8]. This approach has many positive sides:

- It forces the formulation of exact definitions, and to state clearly the security properties and assumptions.
- Once the proofs are written down, anyone can verify them and decide whether or not they are correct.

However, this approach also has some limitations:

- Many cryptographic applications need building blocks, such are one-way functions, one-way permutations, and pseudo-random functions, which cannot be reduced to other primitives. In terms of the existence of such primitives, complexity theory has only very weak results: in non-uniform complexity (Boolean circuits) the best proved thus far is that there exist functions which are twice as hard to invert as to compute, which is far too weak to be of any use in cryptography [10].
- Sometimes the resulting scheme is not very efficient, or the security reduction is quite loose: for example, the correct properties are proved, but the proof is only asymptotic and gives no indication of the exact security level for a concrete instance.

This implies that for many instances, the cryptographer has to rely on the *system-based* or *practical approach*. This approach tries to produce practical solutions; the security estimates are based on the best algorithm known to break the system and on realistic estimates of the necessary computing power or dedicated hardware to carry out the algorithm. By trial and error procedures, several *cryptanalytic principles* have emerged, and it is the goal of the designer to avoid attacks based on these principles. The second aspect is to design *building blocks with provable properties*, and to assemble such basic building blocks to design cryptographic primitives.

4.2 Life Cycle of a Cryptographic Algorithm

A cryptographic algorithm usually starts with a new idea of a cryptographer. A first step should always consist of an evaluation of the resulting algorithm, in which the cryptographer tries to determine whether or not the scheme is secure. If the scheme is unconditionally secure, he has to write the proofs, and to convince himself that the model is correct and matches the application. For computational security, it is again very important to write down security proofs, and to check these for subtle flaws. Moreover, one has to assess whether the assumptions behind the proofs are realistic. For the system-based approach, it is important to prove partial results, and to write down arguments which should convince others of the security of the algorithm. Often such cryptographic algorithms have security parameters (the number of steps, the size of the key, ...); it is then very important to give lower bounds for these parameters, and to indicated the value of the parameters which corresponds to a certain security level.

The next step is the publication of the algorithm at a conference, in a journal, or in an Internet Request for Comment (RFC). This (hopefully) results in an *independent* evaluation of the algorithm. Often more or less subtle flaws are then discovered by other researchers. This can vary from small errors in proofs, to complete security breaks. Depending on the outcome, this can lead to a small fix of the scheme or to abandoning the idea altogether. Sometimes such weaknesses can be found 'in real-time' when the author is presenting his ideas at a conference, but often evaluating a cryptographic algorithm is a very time consuming task; for example, the design effort of the Data Encryption Standard (DES) has been more than 17 man-years, and the open academic evaluation since has taken a multiple of this effort. Cryptanalysis is quite destructive; in this respect it differs from usual scientific activities, even when proponents of competing theories criticize each other.

Few algorithms survive the evaluation stage; ideally, this stage should last for several years. The survivors can be integrated into products and find their way to the market. Sometimes they are standardized by organizations such as NIST (National Institute of Standards and Technology, US), IEEE, IETF, or ISO.

As will be explained below, even if no new security weaknesses are found, the security of a cryptographic algorithm degrades over time; if the algorithm is not modular, the moment will come when it has to be taken out of service.

4.3 Brute Force Attacks Versus Shortcut Attacks

A detailed description of the evaluation procedures for cryptographic algorithms is beyond the scope of this paper. We restrict ourselves to explaining the difference between brute force attacks and shortcut attacks.

Brute Force Attacks. Brute force attacks are attacks which exist against any cryptographic algorithm that is conditionally secure, no matter how it works internally. These attacks only depend on the size of the external parameters of the algorithm, such as the block length of a block cipher, or the key length of any encryption algorithm or MAC. It is the task of the designer to choose the external parameters in such a way that brute force attack are infeasible.

A typical brute force attack against an encryption algorithm or a MAC is an exhaustive key search; it is equivalent to breaking into a safe by trying all the combinations of the lock. The lock should be designed such that this is not feasible in a reasonable amount of time. This attack requires only a few known plaintext/ciphertext (or plaintext/MAC) pairs, which one can always obtain in practice. It can be precluded by increasing the key length: adding one bit to the key doubles the time for exhaustive key search. One should also ensure that the key is selected uniformly at random in the key space.

On a standard PC, trying a single key for a typical algorithm requires a few microseconds. For example, a 40-bit key (which is at present the maximum value allowed by the US government for general purpose export) will be recovered after a few hundred hours. If a LAN with 100 machines can be used, one can find the key in a few hours. For a 56-bit key such as DES (which can be exported from the US under restrictive conditions), a key search requires a few months if several thousand machines are available (as has been demonstrated in the first half of 1997). However, if dedicated hardware is used, a different picture emerges. Recently a 250 000 US$ machine has been built that finds a 56-bit DES key in about 50 hours [4]; the design (that required 50% of the cost) has been made available for free.

One should also take into account "Moore's law" [23], which states that computers double their speed every 18 months (for the same cost). This implies that a 64-bit key, which offers a reasonable security level for the time being, is probably not sufficient for data which needs to be protected for 10 years. Such applications will need keys of at least 80 bits. As the cost of increasing the key size is quite low, it is advisable to design new algorithms with variable key size up to 128...256 bits.

There exist many other brute force attacks. For example, it turns out the security of a block cipher in the CBC mode is decreased by what is called the 'matching ciphertext' attack. As a consequence of the birthday paradox, after $2^{n/2}$ encryptions with a single key, information on the plaintext starts to leak (due to matches in the internal memory, which correspond to matching ciphertexts). This attack can be a problem for present day block ciphers with a 64-bit block length. It can only be prevented by designing new block ciphers with larger block lengths (128 or more), or by changing the key frequently.

Shortcut Attacks. Many algorithms are less secure than suggested by the size of their external parameters. It is often possible to find more effective attacks than trying all keys. Assessing the strength of an algorithm requires cryptanalytic skills and experience, and often hard work. During the last 10 years powerful new tools have been developed: this includes differential cryptanalysis [1], which analyzes the propagation of differences through cryptographic algorithms, linear cryptanalysis [16], which is based on the propagation of bit correlations, and fast correlation attacks on stream ciphers [17].

The design of new algorithms according to the system-based approach is not a memoryless process: when new cryptanalytic techniques are developed, the cryptographers invent new designs which provide complete (or at least improved) resistance against these new attacks. In this way cryptology develops by trial and error procedures.

4.4 Public Versus Secret Algorithms

The open and independent evaluation process described in Sect. 4.2 offers a strong argument for publishing all details of a cryptographic algorithm. Publishing the algorithm opens it up for public scrutiny, and is the best way to guarantee that it is as strong as claimed. (Note that a public algorithm should not be confused with a public-key algorithm.) Published algorithms can be standardized, and will be available from more than one source.

Nevertheless, certain governments and organizations prefer to keep their algorithms secret. They argue (correctly) that obtaining the algorithm raises an additional barrier for the attacker. Moreover, governments want to protect their know-how on the design of cryptographic algorithms. (However, obtaining a description of the algorithm is often not harder than just bribing one person.) This approach is acceptable, provided that sufficient experience and resources are available for *independent* evaluation and re-evaluation of the algorithm.

4.5 Insecure Versus Secure Algorithms

In spite of the fact that secure cryptographic algorithms are available, which offer good performance, in many applications one encounters very insecure cryptographic algorithms. For example, popular software sometimes 'encrypts' data by adding a constant key word to all data words. Several reasons can be indicated for this:

- one excuse is performance: while it is true that adding a constant will always be faster than strong encryption, it should be noted that in software, current encryption algorithms achieve between 20 and 400 Mbit/s; this is sufficient for many applications;
- legal and/or export restrictions: for national security reasons, certain countries (such as the USA) do not allow the export of strong encryption algorithms; some countries (such as France) do not allow for strong encryption within their territory (unless the keys are handed over to the government);

- commercial pressure: companies often rush their security solutions to market, without allowing for sufficient time for the slow evaluation process;
- evolution of computing power: the strength of a cryptographic algorithm erodes over time because of Moore's law; often there exists a large inertia to replace or upgrade an algorithm. A typical example is the DES, that is still widely used in spite of a 56-bit key.
- evolution of cryptanalysis: if designers are not aware of the latest developments in cryptanalysis, it is quite likely that their algorithms will not resist these attacks. For example, the FEAL block cipher with 8 rounds, which was published in 1987, can now be broken with only 10 chosen plaintexts.

5 Concluding Remarks

Securing an application should be based on a careful analysis of the risks and vulnerabilities; this should lead to understanding the security requirements for the data and the communication channels. The next step consists of selecting the right mix of cryptographic algorithms to satisfy these requirements. A very important aspect is the underlying key management infrastructure, which ensures that private and public keys can be established and maintained throughout the system in a secure way. This is where cryptography meets the constraints of the real world.

This paper only scratches the surface of modern cryptology, as the discussion is restricted to a few basic techniques. Other problems solved in cryptography include secure identification, secure sharing of secrets, electronic cash, and copyright protection. Many interesting problems are studied under the umbrella of secure multi-party computation; examples are electronic elections, and the generation and verification of digital signatures in a distributed way.

References

1. E. Biham, A. Shamir, *"Differential Cryptanalysis of the Data Encryption Standard,"* Springer-Verlag, 1993.
2. D.W. Davies, W.L. Price, *"Security for Computer Networks. An Introduction to Data Security in Teleprocessing and Electronic Funds Transfer,"* (2nd Ed.), Wiley, 1989.
3. W. Diffie, M.E. Hellman, "New directions in cryptography," *IEEE Trans. on Information Theory*, Vol. IT–22, No. 6, 1976, pp. 644–654.
4. EFF, *"Cracking DES. Secrets of Encryption Research, Wiretap Politics & Chip Design,"* O'Reilly, May 1998.
5. FIPS 46, *"Data Encryption Standard,"* Federal Information Processing Standard, NBS, U.S. Dept. of Commerce, January 1977 (revised as FIPS 46-2:1993).
6. FIPS 81, *"DES Modes of Operation,"* Federal Information Processing Standard, NBS, US Dept. of Commerce, December 1980.
7. FIPS 186, *"Digital Signature Standard,"* Federal Information Processing Standard, NIST, US Dept. of Commerce, May 1994.

8. M.R. Garey, D.S. Johnson, *"Computers and Intractability: A Guide tot the Theory of NP-Completeness,"* W.H. Freeman and Company, San Francisco, 1979.

9. S. Halevi, H. Krawczyk, "MMH: software message authentication in the Gbit/second rates," *Fast Software Encryption, LNCS 1267*, E. Biham, Ed., Springer-Verlag, 1997, pp. 172–189.

10. A.P.L. Hiltgen, "Construction of feebly-one-way families of permutations," *Proc. Auscrypt'92, LNCS 718*, J. Seberry, Y. Zheng, Eds., Springer-Verlag, 1993, pp. 422–434.

11. ISO/IEC 10116, *"Information technology – Security techniques – Modes of operation of an n-bit block cipher algorithm,"* 1996.

12. ISO/IEC 10118, *"Information technology – Security techniques – Hash-functions, Part 3: Dedicated hash-functions,"* 1998.

13. G.A. Kabatianskii, T. Johansson, B. Smeets, "On the cardinality of systematic A-codes via error correcting codes," *IEEE Trans. on Information Theory*, Vol. IT–42, No. 2, 1996, pp. 566–578.

14. D. Kahn, *"The Codebreakers. The Story of Secret Writing,"* MacMillan, New York, 1967.

15. N. Koblitz, *"A Course in Number Theory and Cryptography,"* Springer-Verlag, 1987.

16. M. Matsui, "The first experimental cryptanalysis of the Data Encryption Standard," *Proc. Crypto'94, LNCS 839*, Y. Desmedt, Ed., Springer-Verlag, 1994, pp. 1–11.

17. W. Meier, O. Staffelbach, "Fast correlation attacks on stream ciphers," *J. of Cryptology*, Vol. 1, 1989, pp. 159–176.

18. R. Merkle, *"Secrecy, Authentication, and Public Key Systems,"* UMI Research Press, 1979.

19. A.J. Menezes, P.C. van Oorschot, S. Vanstone, *"Handbook of Applied Cryptography,"* CRC Press, 1996.

20. *"State of the Art and Evolution of Computer Security and Industrial Cryptography,"* LNCS 741, B. Preneel, R. Govaerts, J. Vandewalle, Eds., Springer-Verlag, 1993.

21. B. Preneel, P.C. van Oorschot, "MDx-MAC and building fast MACs from hash functions," *Proc. Crypto'95, LNCS 963*, D. Coppersmith, Ed., Springer-Verlag, 1995, pp. 1–14.

22. R.L. Rivest, A. Shamir, L. Adleman, "A method for obtaining digital signatures and public-key cryptosystems," *Comm. ACM*, Vol. 21, No. 2, 1978, pp. 120–126.

23. R.R. Schaller, "Moore's law: past, present, and future," *IEEE Spectrum*, Vol. 34, No. 6, June 1997, pp. 53–59.

24. C.E. Shannon, "Communication theory of secrecy systems," *Bell System Techn. J.*, Vol. 28, No. 4, 1949, pp. 656–715.

25. *"Contemporary Cryptology: The Science of Information Integrity,"* G.J. Simmons, Ed., IEEE Press, 1991.

26. D. Stinson, *"Cryptography. Theory and Practice,"* CRC Press, 1995.

27. G.S. Vernam, "Cipher printing telegraph system for secret wire and radio telegraph communications," *J. Am. Inst. Electrical Engineers*, Vol. XLV, 1926, pp. 109–115.

28. A.C. Yao, "Theory and applications of trapdoor functions," *Proc. 23rd IEEE Symposium on Foundations of Computer Science*, IEEE, 1982, pp. 80–91.

Authoring Structured Multimedia Documents

Cécile Roisin

Unité de recherche INRIA Rhône-Alpes
ZIRST - 655 avenue de l'Europe
38330 Montbonnot, France
E-mail: {Cecile.Roisin}@inrialpes.fr

Abstract. This document aims at describing main issues in the area of structured multimedia documents. Documents can be modelled through four main dimensions (logical, hypermedia, spatial and temporal) and will be illustrated by the main corresponding standards (SGML/XML, HTML, CSS, DSSSL/XSL, SMIL). Building authoring tools that are capable to deal with these dimensions (and specially the temporal one) is still a great challenge. We describe some authoring applications and develop temporal aspects of documents through the analysis of new specification and authoring needs required for handling multimedia documents.

Keywords: structured document, style sheet, hypermedia, multimedia document, authoring tool, XML, CSS, HyTime, SMIL

1 Introduction

Electronic documents have been the scope of numerous research activities for years. These works have lead to the identification of the main characteristics attached to documents and to their modeling through several dimensions such as the logical, physical, navigational and temporal ones [2]. One of the major results of that is the emergence of standards such as XML [25] (eXtended Markup Language), HTML [28], HyTime [10], DSSSL [9], SMIL [30], etc. These standards aim at making easier the processing, the exchange and the sharing of documents through different computers, systems, software and networks.

New technologies of data representation and processing allow the use of image, video and sound information in computer applications. Depending on the targeted application, these new media types can be more or less integrated into the whole information system. For example, a video/audio channel of a teleconferencing application is completely independent from other information sources. In this paper, we are interested in applications where combining pieces of information from various media types into a unique entity, called a *multimedia document*, is of high priority. Typical examples are multimedia titles on cdroms or web documents including synchronized video or audio.

This paper provides an overview of major concepts and techniques on which electronic documents technology is based. The first part is devoted to the description of general concepts of documents through the identification of four main dimensions: logical, physical, navigational and temporal. The next one will focus on the management of structured documents; that area will be illustrated by the description of some authoring applications and some transformation techniques. Finally, in the last section we more deeply develop temporal aspects of documents and present new specification and authoring needs required for handling multimedia documents.

2 Models for Electronic Documents

2.1 Electronic Documents

With the advent of hypertext, on-the-fly document generation and multimedia technologies, it becomes more ad more difficult to provide a clear definition of the notion of document. For the purpose of this talk, we will consider a document as a set of basic information entities semantically linked together in order to constitute a message. We will not discuss further where the semantic limit has to be put, but we will focus on the way to express the organization of basic information entities.

The elementary entities that compose documents have either a static or a dynamic nature: static objects include strings, graphics, images or mathematical symbols and dynamic objects include those having a duration such as animations, audios or videos. The duration of a dynamic object may be intrinsic to the object as for audio or cannot be determined before the presentation stage: a typical example is an interaction button whose duration is given at presentation stage by a reader action (a mouse click).

2.2 The Four Dimensions of Documents

Roughly speaking, a document can be considered as a set of basic components organized according to four ways of structuration. These structuration levels can be considered as four independent dimensions:

- The logical dimension (chapters, sections, paragraphs, etc.).
- The navigational dimension (hypertext links, actions).
- The spatial dimension (page layout, presentation, style sheets).
- The temporal dimension (multimédia synchronization, scenario description).

This way of modeling documents provides an homogeneous framework for representing most categories of documents: from conventional documents such as technical reports, letters, scientific articles to graphics or hypermedia structures.

The core of that document model is the expression of object composition in each dimension, as for example:

- Logical composition: "A book is composed of a title, an author and a set of chapters, each of them being a list of paragraphs".
- Spatial composition: "A footnote must be set on the foot of the page in which appears its first reference".
- Navigational composition: "A link is created between each bibliographic entry and all its references", "The architecture of a web site is defined by the HTML links between its pages".
- Temporal composition: "When a company presentation starts, its logo is displayed during 5 seconds, then the manager's picture is shown during his speech; the end of the presentation is composed of a 3 minutes video of the products of the company together with a music".

We can notice that the composition may depend on the nature of the objects that are composed (for instance, a sound has no spatial position).

Numerous models and languages have been proposed for the specification of these different kinds of document composition. Before going further, let's notice that document portability and exchangeability can only be given by composition formats that are independent from any production system. Moreover reusability can be obtained thanks to the definition of generic models.

In the next subsections, we describe models and representative languages for the composition of these dimensions. The temporal dimension will be deeply presented in the last section of this document.

2.3 Models and Languages for Representing Logical Structures of Documents

Models for representing logical structures of documents are based on:

- Basic objects (that cannot be decomposed).
- Composite objects obtained by composition of basic or composite objects.
- Attributes associated with objects (to add semantics).

With such a model, a document is organized as a tree structure (such as the tree representation of a book in Fig. 1) in which the leaves are the basic elements representing the "content" of the document. Basic and composite objects are typed.

We can notice that in traditional word processors, document structures are linear (basically, lists of titles and paragraphs). By opposition, documents represented in a hierarchical and typed way are called *structured documents*.

Main Principles of Generic Logical Structures Languages for defining documents with such typing principles are called *markup languages* because the format intertwines type information (marks or tags) inside document content (basically, the text). For instance, the previous document is defined by: "<book> <title> Mme Bovary </title> <author> Stendhal </author> <chapterList> <chapter1> ....".

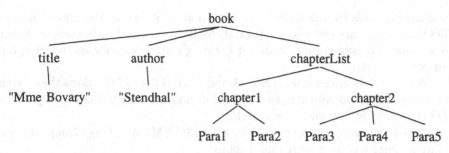

Fig. 1. Logical structure of a book

Due to the great variety of documents (novels, articles, letters, etc.), it was not possible to define an universal markup language including all types of documents authors may create. Instead, languages, called *generic markup languages*, have been defined to specify classes of documents. These languages define grammars to which documents conform.

These principles are nowadays widely applied thanks to the SGML, ODA and XML standards.

SGML/XML SGML [8], Standard Generalized Markup Language, is an ISO standard (ISO 8879:1986) that aims at providing a formal notation for grammar definition of classes of documents called "*DTD: Document Type Definition*".

This standard not only has permitted the emergence of specific DTD adapted for different applications domains (CALS, TEI, HTML), but it has also been used for the definition of new standards:

- HyTime [10] (for hypermédia documents).
- SDML & SSML (for sounds).
- XML [25] ((eXtensible Markup Language) that can be considered as an improvement of SGML.

SGML/XML principles SGML provides a descriptive markup instead of a procedural one. This allows the separation of the "structure+content" part from any information associated with specific processing (formatting, information retrieving, etc.)

As such a marking is a way to type parts of documents through grammar rules (as given by the DTD), typing techniques can be applied for documents: syntactical controls, homogeneous processing.

The standard allows independency from character formats thanks to a string substitution mechanism ("SGML entities").

XML situation XML [25] is a recommendation proposed by the W3 consortium for a new markup language that aims at taking into account new needs for document exchange on the web (more structured documents, carrying more semantics). This specification is an evolution of SGML in the sense that some SGML features are not allowed (mainly omitted tags and inclusions/exclusions) and some extensions are introduced (naming conventions for modularity, links, empty elements).

A major difference between SGML and XML is that XML allows the existence of two kinds of documents: *well-formed documents* which don't always have a DTD, and *valid documents*, which do.

Among the subjects addressed by the W3C XML Working Group, the modeling activity has been split into 4 items:

- Data model, the core for modeling the information contained in an XML document.
- Namespaces for relating names in XML documents with Uniform Resource Identifiers (URIs), in order to associate the local names with global identifiers.
- XLink (XML Linking Language) and XPointer (addressing language for pointing into documents), for specifying constructs to describe simple or complex links between objects (this is an activity of XLL Working Group).
- Structural Schemas, for associating constraints to documents.

The XML syntax plays a central role in the activity of W3C for defining new recommendations in different domains of the web. For instance, the XML syntax is used in:

- Resource Description Format (RDF), the language for representing metadata.
- Synchronized Multimedia Integration Language - (SMIL) [30], for multimedia documents.
- Document Object Model (DOM), for the definition of an applications programming interface that allows active manipulation of the structure, presentation and content of XML and HTML documents

Specific Structures Each DTD defines a specific class of documents. For example, a DTD for describing simple books as the document of Fig. 1, could be defined as follows:

```
<!ELEMENT book (title, author, chapterList)    >
<!ELEMENT chapterList    (chapter)+            >
<!ELEMENT chapter  (para)+                     >
<!ELEMENT (title | author | para) (#PCDATA)    >
```

Fig. 2. A simple DTD for books

Numerous application domains have developed DTD. As an illustration, we list some representative SGML or XML DTD:

- CALS: (Computer-aided Acquisition and Logistic Support), defined by the American DoD for technical documentation.
- TEI: Text Encoding Initiative [22], for encoding a wide variety of commonly encountered textual features in literary and linguistic documents.
- HTML: HyperText Markup Language, which has evolved from basic text and hyperlinks features for the web to the HTML 4.0 Specification [28] for supporting more multimedia options, scripting languages, style sheets, better printing facilities,.
- ISO 12083, for scientific documents defined by the American Association of Publishers and the European Physical Society.
- MathML: this W3C Recommendation [27] is a XML low-level format for describing mathematics as a basis for machine to machine communication. It can be used to encode both mathematical notation, for high-quality visual display, and mathematical content, for more semantic applications

2.4 Models and Languages for Representing Physical Structures of Documents

Principles Among the typographical properties (or presentation properties) that characterize the graphical aspect of documents, we can identify two subsets:

1. Properties depending on the content to be laid out, like fonts, color or typefaces. We call these properties the *style.*
2. Properties depending on the output medium, such as the size of pages, columns, margins and gutters; we call these properties *physical structure* properties.

The expression of presentation properties has evolved in many directions, from low-level commands interspersed within the text (troff, Latex) to style sheets associated to documents in interactive editors (Word, Author/Editor), proprietary stylesheets languages (Panorama and Thot P language [17]) and standard languages (CSS [29], DSSSL [9] and XSL [24]). This evolution follows the evolution of document models, from weakly structured document models to structured document models that contain no presentation information.

With structured documents, the formatting process produces a representation of the document ready to be output (displayed or printed) from the internal representation of that document (its content and logical structure) and the associated presentation properties. One key point of structured document models is their ability to associate presentation properties with document element types, allowing inheritance of properties based on the structural hierarchy [7]. It is worth noting that style properties can be easily related to the logical structure, unlike physical structure properties. In fact, the physical structure of a document can be seen as a hierarchical organization of boxes (see Fig. 3) as defined by Knuth box model; therefore formatting structured documents implies merging two hierarchical structures: the logical one and the physical one [19].

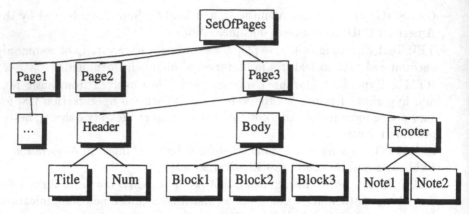

Fig. 3. Hierarchical physical structure of document

Cascading Style Sheets Language In this part, we describe the CSS1/CSS2 suite [29] *Cascading Style Sheets*, the W3C style sheet languages that have been defined for HTML documents. CSS2 Recommendation follows and completes CSS1 Recommendation mainly for supporting media-specific style sheets (browsers, aural devices, printers, etc.), and other high level formatting features such as content positioning, table layout and automatic counters and numbering.

Basic concepts CSS is a simple declarative style sheet language for HTML documents that allows to associate style properties not only with instances but also with element types so that properties can be applied to all elements of the same type. Moreover, CSS syntax allows to have a clear separation between content and presentation.

Properties A property (color, margin, font, etc.) is assigned to a selector in order to manipulate its style. Example: *color: red;*

Selectors Selectors can be defined by one of these three possibilities:

- HTML element: *p { text-indent: 3em }*
- Class selectors: *code.new{ color: green}* with *class* attribute:
  <code class=new> ... </code>
- ID selectors (with *ID* attribute): *#nb554 { font-weight: bold }*

Inheritance The inner selector inherits the surrounding selector's values unless otherwise modified. But there are some exceptions. As an example, the margin-top property is not inherited.

Stylesheet access Styles rules applying for the elements of a document can be put either directly in the head part (with a *style* element) or in a separate file (with extension .css) that is referred with a *link* element as:

```
<link rel=stylesheet href="name.css" type="text/css">
```

The css file contains css rules, as for instance:

```
<style type="text/css">
<!--   h4 \{font: 14pt "Times"; font-weight: bold; color: green\}
       h2 \{font: 16pt "Times"; font-weight: bold; color: blue\}
       p  \{font: 12pt "Times"; color: black\}
-->
</style>
```

Cascading stylesheets With such as way to access to style rules, it is possible that several rules set a value for the same property of the same element. The question is then: which stylesheet definition takes precedence?

The basic rule is the following: the most specific rule wins. However, it is possible to specify rules with an "! important" statement that will override normal rules.

XSL The above example of CSS demonstrates that the principles of section 2.4 can be applied to a single tag set (HTML) for which limited display functions are required. DSSSL [9] and XSL [24] aim at providing a way to describe how to display a document marked up with arbitrary elements as defined with SGML or XML. Their main concepts are:

- Declarative approach: declarative specification allows to describe character-istics and constraints to be used by the formatter. On the contrary, a pro-cedural approach implements the formatting process itself.
- Basic formatting structures called *flow objects* (character, paragraph, se-quence, page, group, link, etc.) having an associated set of formatting char-acteristics that are applied to those objects.
- Tree transformation mechanism, for the transformation of documents from one application to another. For XSL, the target application basically is the formatting process of XML documents: the transformation specifies how each element of a tree source (a XML document) is associated with flow objects that compose the target tree.
- Complete style language for expressing formatting and other document pro-cessing specifications. Typographic requirements range from reordering or duplicating elements to complex page layouts.

XSL is based on DSSSL for its basic principles as described above, but it uses XML syntax. It includes CSS-like style rules and an escape into a scripting language to accommodate more sophisticated formatting.

The association of elements in the source tree to flow objects is through *construction rules* composed of a *pattern* and an *action* to specify a resulting sub-tree of flow objects. Patterns propose a complete selector mechanism in order to identify applicable elements by their context within the source, such as:

element ancestry or descendants, attributes on an element, position of an element relative to its siblings. The action part of the rule describes the structure and the style properties of flow objects that must be created.

2.5 Models and Languages for Representing Hypermedia Structures of Documents

Principles Links aim at representing semantics that cannot be expressed by structural relationships. Typical examples are notes and references in documents. Links can be defined inside a document (internal links) or between documents (external links) providing an hypertext organization of the information that can be used by navigation applications. The most widespread application of this nature is the web itself.

The underlying model for hypertext structures is basically a graph where nodes represent document elements and arcs represent the links between them. This structure is orthogonal to the logical structure of document.

As an illustration of these principles, we briefly describe hyperlinkings aspects of HyTime and XLink, the W3C proposal for hyperlinks.

HyTime and XLink The HyTime standard [10] is an SGML application (it uses SGML syntax) that can be used for hypertext and temporal specifications. Only hyperlinking facilities are described here, see section 4.2 for the temporal aspects of HyTime.

The web Consortium works on the definition of the XML Linking Language (XLink) [26] for the specification of links structures inside XML resources. HTML, HyTime and TEI P3 are the three standards that provide the ground material of XLL working group. More precisely, it uses the same basic concepts than HyTime for link specification. We have chosen the XLink vocabulary for presenting these concepts.

XLink allows the specification of both simple unidirectional links (similar to HTML links) and complex multidirectional, typed links.

Basically, a link is an explicit relationship between two or more local or remote *resources* that are reachable by the use of a *locator*. When a link is traversed (by a user action or by a program), a resource of the link is accessed.

Links are defined by *linking elements* that can be recognized by the applications thanks to a specific attribute named *xml:link* that can take one of the two values: *simple* or *extended*. Other attributes can be defined to associate information with a linking element: role, locators of remote resource and semantics for local and remote resources (specific role, title and behavior when traversed).

A locator is specified by a Uniform Resource Identifiers URI to identify the document together with a XPointer to point to a fragment into the document.

3 Structured Documents Centered Applications

In order to illustrate how the models and languages presented above are used in applications, we describe in the sequel one class of applications, namely editing applications. We then point out new problems raised by structured documents and DTD management when DTD change and we show how transformation techniques can bring solutions to them.

3.1 Editing Tools

Editors based on structured models maintain in memory a logical representation of the document which is used for editing operations. Thanks to this information, the editor guides and controls the user according to the generic structure of the document being edited. In particular, the editor prevents the user from producing a document whose specific structure would not be consistent with the generic structure.

With a structured model of documents, the formatting process produces a representation of the document ready to be output (displayed or printed) from the internal representation of that document (its logical structure) and the style and physical structure properties.

However, an important reason that limits the use of structured document models in document production is the difficulty of developing an editing tool with both logical and physical document representations. Some tools provide structured editing functionalities with poor formatting capabilities while others provide more sophisticated formatting operations but no interactive manipulation (e. g. LaTex). Mixing complex formatting functionalities together with structured document models into an interactive authoring environment is still an open problem [19].

Thot Editor Thot [16], [17] is an experimental authoring system developed by Opera project in order to validate the concepts of structured document into an interactive environment.

Thot is a system designed to produce structured documents. It allows the user to create, to modify and to consult interactively documents that comply with models. These models permit the production of homogeneous documents. Formatting and typography are handled by the system: the user can then focus on the organization and on the contents of documents. Thot performs other operations for the user such as numbering, updating cross references, building index tables, etc.

Thot is an integrated and extensible system. It allows to process with the same tool and within the same document not only structured text but also graphics, complex tables, mathematical formulae, etc.

Thot is also an open system. It is able to exchange documents with other systems through a flexible exporting tool, for example, to convert documents into Latex and HTML. It can also be included in other applications through its programming interface.

Amaya Editor Amaya [18] is the W3C test-bed browser/authoring tool that is used to demonstrate and test many of the new developments in Web protocols and data formats.

It has been developed on top of Thot technology taking advantages of its features such as structure management, multiviews display, multiple presentation handling (for screen and paper). But Amaya is much more than a simple editing tool, it is a complete web browsing and authoring environment for web documents. For instance, a transformation service is included in the tool, allowing the author to change the structure of some parts (lists into tables) or to easily edit mathematical expressions by successive structure changes.

Amaya demonstrates recent web standards such as: (1) a support for CSS [29] which allows Amaya to display documents with style sheets and to create or edit style sheets; and (2) a prototype implementation of MathML [27] which allows users to browse and edit web pages containing mathematical expressions.

3.2 Transformation of Structured Documents

A major drawback of structured documents comes from the basic principle: each document must have a specific logical structure which is consistent with the corresponding generic structure. This implies that: (1) any change in a DTD can have heavy consequences on existing document bases and (2) any change in a document can be done only if the generic structure allows it. In both situations, transformations have to be performed.

DTD Management The logical structure of a document type can evolve. For various reasons it may be necessary to declare new elements, to remove elements that have become useless in some type of document, or to arrange existing elements in a different order. These changes lead to new versions of generic structures and the user has to specify into which new type each old type has to be transformed.

The problem is then to recover documents built with old versions of a generic structure that has evolved. As a number of such documents may exist, it is necessary to transform them automatically, for making them consistent with the new generic structure. This kind of operation is called a *static* transformation because it is usually performed outside an editing session. Filters are typical tools that are used in such situations but they:

- need a specific development for each DTD transformation,
- require an exhaustive description of the translation of each type,
- and imply either simple expressions which only allow limited transformations (such as Balise [3] and Cost [6] tools) or complex expressions [9] which lead to powerful transformation.

Another approach to the transformation of DTD is the automatic one. This approach is based on the comparison between the document to be transformed (source) and the target DTD, using a matching algorithm to find a relation between the structures [20]. However, pure automatic techniques are unable to provide the right results in some situations. Therefore, we study an approach, called *semi-automatic transformation*, which tries to get the advantages of both filters and automatic transformation.

Editing Structured Documents One limitation of current structured editing systems comes from the structural constraints on documents that can be considered too rigid by users. For example, the familiar cut-and-paste command that allows the user to copy or cut a part of a document (the source) and to insert (or paste) it into another part (the target) of a document cannot be easily implemented in an interactive structured editing system. Moreover, the system must allow these types to be defined in different document models, when source and target elements are in different documents.

To allow a cut-and-paste operation when types are different, the structure of source element must be transformed to become consistent with the target generic structure. Usually, the user wants this transformation to be automatic when editing a document, as when he uses an unstructured editing tool. However, he may want to indicate his preferences when several transformations are possible. This kind of transformation performed by an interactive editor is called a *dynamic* transformation. This problem is similar to type conversions as considered in programming languages or object-oriented databases.

The main constraints that have to be taken into account when implementing a dynamic transformation tool are the following:

1. The cut-and-paste operation must not lose any information while keeping as far as possible structural information.
2. The types involved in the operation can be any types known in the system, so no pre-processing can be performed as in static transformations (see above).
3. Performances are critical as the operation is interactive.

Few studies have been made on the specific problem of document types transformations in interactive environments. The second constraint stated above has lead us to explore an automatic transformation technique [20]. The automatic approach is based on the comparison between the document to be transformed (source) and the target DTD, using a matching algorithm to find a relation between the structures.

4 Multimedia Documents: from Temporal Specification to Authoring Environments

A multimedia document is defined as a set of (basic) objects spatially and temporally organized and on which a navigational structure can be set. Multimedia documents combine in time and space different types of elements like video, audio, still-picture, text, synthesized image, ... Compared to classical documents, multimedia documents are characterized by their inherent temporal dimension. Basic media objects, like video, have intrinsic duration. Furthermore, media objects can be temporally organized by the author which adds to the document a temporal structure called *the temporal scenario*. Such an entity can be rendered thanks to a presentation engine by means of the output channels of the computer (screen and speaker).

Today, authors of multimedia documents have often to be programmers because it is the only way for them to specify the complex synchronization of their documents (Lingo scripts in Director [14] documents for example). But it is clear that in order to increase the popularity of such multimedia applications, computer-illiterate people must have direct access to multimedia document creation. That will also drastically reduce production cost of multimedia titles.

Within the past decade, numerous research works (Cmifed [23], Firefly [4], HTSPN [21], Isis [13], Madeus [12]), have presented various ways of specifying temporal scenarios, focusing on a particular understanding of temporal synchronization. Some standards have also been defined for covering temporal specification needs: HyTime [10], MHEG [15] and SMIL [30] are the most representative examples. Before describing them, we analyze what are the main features that are required for multimedia documents environments.

4.1 Multimedia Authoring Requirements

The variety of multimedia approaches reflects the large number of requirements that have to be covered by a multimedia authoring system. But these needs are only partially fulfilled by existing applications. In order to give a structured and readable analysis, we only focus on authoring requirements. We group them in two main classes: expressive power and authoring capabilities.

Expressive power The expressive power of an authoring system is somehow related to the ability of the system to cover a broad range of temporal scenarios required by the author. This criterion is hard to measure since defining an acceptable level of expressive power is strongly dependent on author practice and experience. Authoring requirements can be classified into three sets: (a) the needs arising from the intrinsic nature of the objects composing multimedia documents, (b) those arising from their composition and finally (c) those related to hypermedia navigation.

(a) A multimedia system must be able to handle a wide variety of basic objects (text, sounds, images, videos, etc.) on which the author can set interactivity capabilities and temporal style definitions.

(b) As far as expressive power is concerned, temporal composition aims at expressing any arbitrary ordering between temporal intervals corresponding to the different objects [1].

(c) Hypermedia navigation (see 2.5) is performed through document interactions that can either be global interactions (like usual hyperlinks) or local interactions (the effect applies on a sub-part of the objects).

Authoring capabilities At this point, the relevant question is how long does it take for an author to design a scenario? Authoring capabilities enclose the following criteria:

- Adaptability to computer illiterate people;

- Straightforward design of temporal composition, for example by allowing the user to specify in any order the temporal relations;
- Adaptability to the incremental nature of the editing process, i.e. local modifications must have local consequences;
- Abstraction and multimedia document models capabilities to help the author in the organization of his document (structuration) and to allow reuse parts of documents or templates;
- Multigrids reading support for the access of the same document by different categories of readers (having different native languages or comprehension levels).

One important research activity is the definition of good user interfaces for providing real end-user authoring tools. A good authoring environment will certainly not result by simply packaging an existing programming language: not only the author has to deal with too much low level specifications, but also such authoring tools still provide slow development cycles thanks to the composition-test process (as with MhegDitor which is based on a converter tool [5]). To break down this batch approach, the experiences gained with authoring static documents (see section 3.1) can be considered: the Wysiwyg paradigm has been proven to be the right basis on which editing interfaces have been built. However, such a paradigm cannot be directly apply inside multimedia authoring applications due to the temporal dimension of multimedia documents.

In order to provide the author with good multimedia authoring tools, i. e. close to the Wysiwyg paradigm, it is necessary to allow some way of direct manipulation of the document in the presentation view (the display area where the document is played). However, such a direct edition has to be completed by other features acting on the presentation process (stop/resume) or given through new visual perception mechanisms in order to provide the author with some global perception of the document. Moreover, the author needs more flexible ways to navigate in the document, such as: going faster until some important parts of the document, jumping from a relevant point to another one, etc. Such features must be provided by high level temporal access functionalities such as: direct time point access and different scales of fast forwarding and rewinding.

4.2 Multimedia Languages

Multimedia languages can be classified in two main categories, operational and constraint-based ones, that reflect on how close the document description is to the presentation level:

1. Operational approaches are based on the direct specification of the temporal scenario of the document. The author specifies how a scenario must be executed: based on either a script language or an operational structure (tree or Petri-nets are good examples). Therefore the presentation phase directly implements the operational semantics provided by the used structure. All existing standards belong to this class of languages.

2. Constraint-based approaches set the specification outside this operational scheme. They are based on constraint programming and are characterized by a formatting phase that computes starting times and durations, as required by the scenario. This formatting phase can be seen as a compilation of a declarative specification into an operational structure, which can be interpreted by the presentation phase. Thus, the author specifies what scenario he needs without involvement of how to get the result in terms of operational actions, in a declarative way.

In a previous paper [11], we have shown that constraint-based approaches seem to be more adapted for building powerful authoring tools and they can offer equivalent or higher expressive power capabilities than operational techniques: the author has not to give the duration of all the objects involved in his document. The durations are computed by a temporal formatter, removing the burden of this task from the author and allowing him to obtain reusable scenarios. However, this formatting has to be time-efficient and must provide the solutions desired by the author.

HyTime With HyTime, temporal specification is expressed by placing temporal events (begin and end instants of elements) on an absolute temporal axis. Such an approach is relevant only if objects have a deterministic temporal behavior otherwise it is not possible to define their temporal events in such an absolute way.

The temporal specification of any basic object (text, video or audio) is considered as one dimension of its Finite Coordinate Space (other dimensions can specify spatial positions). Time measurement can differ from one FCS to the other.

HyTime is interesting by its integrated approach of temporal, spatial and hypermedia dimensions of documents. But its intrinsic complexity and its weak temporal composition capabilities prevent the development of tools and applications based on it. TIt is however worth noting that the best successful concepts of HyTime, namely hypertext specifications, have been reused in other standards such as XLink (see 2.5).

SMIL SMIL (Synchronized Multimedia Integration Language) [30] defines a general document format integrating different types of independent media objects. It illustrates operational approaches based on a tree structure. The organization of media objects in the document is given in terms of temporal composition: both sequential and parallel operators are available together with synchronized attributes that be used to specify fine synchronization between objects.

SMIL format is defined as an XML DTD and hyperlinking follows XLink specifications. A SMIL document is composed of two parts: the *Head* part that contains information at document level (basically the spatial organization in terms of *Regions*) and the *Body* part that contains the document scenario. A scenario is a hierarchical structure of parallel or sequential schedules.

The sequential operator expresses the sequential play of the set of children objects. The attribute *Loop* can be used to specify a given number of iterations of sequential structure.

The parallel operator expresses the is simultaneous play of its operands without any constraint on the operand termination: by default, the end time of the construct is defined by the maximum duration of the enclosed elements. This semantics can be changed with the use of the temporal attribute *Endsync*. For instance, if *Endsync=first*, the duration is defined by the minimum duration of the children (the others will be interrupted).

The following example illustrates basic concepts of SMIL and main syntactic features:

```
<smil>
<head>
  <layout type="text/smil-basic">
    <region id="title" left= ... />
    <region id="image"        ... />
  </layout>
</head>
<body>
  <seq>
    <par id="A" endsync="last">
      <audio id="P" dur="20.0 s"
              src="http://www.inria.fr/music.au"/>
      <text id="Name" region="title" dur="5.0 s"
              src="http://www.inria.fr/text.html"/>
      <img id="Hello" region="image"
              src="http://www.inria.fr/hello.gif" dur="10.0 s"/>
      <a id = "H1" href="#Next" show="replace">
          <img id="Button" region="xx"
              src="http://www.inria.fr/button.gif" /> </a>
    </par>
    <video id="V" region="yy" src="http://www.inria.fr/v.mpg"/>
  </seq>
  <par id="Next"> <!-- Next part of the scenario -->
  .....
```

Since its public availability, SMIL is been implemented by numerous vendors: new SMIL players are announced (such as RealNetworks and CWI) and first authoring tools begin to appear (such as VEON authoring tool).

5 Conclusion

The multimedia authoring domain is still in its infancy but lets bet that it will expand considerably very soon. New standards such as SMIL should give a new boost to this domain. Taking into account the distribution of multimedia objects will become a great challenge in the years to come.

Another challenge is the emergence of solutions for providing authoring environments that allow the specification of the different dimensions of documents. The experiences gained with structured editing tools and multimedia environments have to be merged for providing new solutions characterized by:

- the tight-coupling of authoring and presentation functions allowing some forms of direct edition;
- a way to allow the author to access and define each dimension of the documents through several views. Views synchronization can be very helpful to provide accurate perception services on documents;
- and the ability the let the author adapt navigation scales in the time space.

Acknowledgements

I am grateful to all the members of the Opera project at Inria Rhône-Alpes. This paper reflects past and recent research activities of our project: Vincent Quint and Irène Vatton are the main designers and developers of works on structured documents (Thot and Amaya editors); Stéphane Bonhomme works on document transformation based on an approach combining explicit and automatic techniques; the multimedia team (Muriel Jourdan, Nabil Layaïda, Loay Sabry and Laurent Tardif) contributes to the multimedia authoring and presentation area by providing pertinent solutions based on constraint techniques.

References

1. Allen (J. F.), "Maintaining Knowledge about Temporal intervals", *CACM*, vol. 26, num. 11, pp. 832-843, 1983.
2. Andre (J.), Furura (R.), Quint (V.), *Structured documents*, Cambridge University Press, Cambridge, 1989.
3. *Balise 3 Reference Manual*, AIS S.A., 1996.
4. Buchanam (C.), Zellweger (P.T.), "Specifying Temporal Behavior in Hypermedia Documents ", *Proc. of the ACM Conf. on Hypertext*, pp. 262-271, décembre 1992.
5. CCETT, *MhegDitor*, http://www.ccett.fr/mheg/converter.htm, 1998.
6. J. English, "Cost 2 Reference Manual", http://www.art.com/cost/manual.html.
7. R. Furuta, V. Quint, J. André, "Interactively Editing Structured Documents", *Electronic Publishing*, vol. 1, num. 1, pp. 19-44, April 1988.
8. International Standard ISO 8879, *Information Processing - Text and Office Systems - Standard Generalized Markup Language (SGML)*, International Standard Organization, 1986
   [see also]: http://www.sil.org/sgml/sgml.html.
9. ISO, *ISO/IEC DIS 10179.2:1994. Information Technology - Text and Office Systems - Document Style Semantics and Specification Language (DSSSL)*, International Organization for Standardization, Geneva, 1994.

10. ISO/IEC JTC1/SC18/WG8 N1920, *Information Technology: Hypermedia/ Time-based Structuring Language (HyTime), Second edition,* ISO/IEC, août 1997. [see also]: http://www.ornl.gov/sgml/wg8/docs/n1920/html/n1920.html.
11. Jourdan M., Layaïda N., Roisin C., *A survey on authoring techniques for temporal scenarios of multimedia documents,* vol. to be published in Handbook of Multimedia, , CRC Press, April 1998.
12. Jourdan (M.), Layaïda (N.), Roisin (C.), Sabry-Ismaïl (L.), Tardif (L.), "Madeus, an Authoring Environment for Interactive Multimedia Documents", *6th ACM Multimedia'98,* Bristol, 12-16 septembre 1998.
13. Kim (M. Y.), Song (J.), "Multimedia Documents with Elastic Time", *Proc. of the 3rd ACM Conf. on Multimedia,* pp. 143-154, San Francisco, novembre 1995.
14. Macromedia, *Flash and Director,* {En ligne : http://www.macromedia.com, 1998.
15. Meyer-Boudnik (T.) et Eeffelsberg (W.), "MHEG Explained", *IEEE Multimedia Magazine,* vol. 2, num. 1, pp. 26-38, 1995.
16. Opéra, *THOT, A structured document editor,* Inria, 1997. http://www.inrialpes.fr/opera/Thot.en.html.
17. V. Quint, translated by E. Munson, *The languages of Thot,* INRIA , 655 av. de l'Europe, 38330 Montbonnot - France, 1994. [On line]: http://www.inrialpes.fr/opera/thot/doc/languages.toc.html.
18. V. Quint, I. Vatton, "An Introduction to Amaya.", *World Wide Web Journal,* vol. 2, num. 2, pp. 39-46, Spring 1997.
19. C. Roisin, I. Vatton, "Merging Logical and Physical Structures in Documents", *Electronic Publishing – Origination, Dissemination and Design, special issue Proceedings of the Fifth International Conference on Electronic Publishing, Document Manipulation and Typography, EP94,* vol. 6, num. 4, pp. 327-337, April 1994.
20. C. Roisin, P. Claves, E. Akpotsui, "Implementing the Cut-and-Paste Operation in a Structured Editing System", *Mathematical and Computer Modelling,* vol. vol. 26, num. 1, pp. 85-96, 1997.
21. Sénac (P.), Diaz (M.), Léger (A.), De Saqui-Sannes (P.), "Modeling Logical and Temporal Synchronization in Hypermedia Systems", *IEEE Journal of Selected Areas on Communications,* vol. 14, num. 1, pp. 84-103, 1996.
22. TEI, *Text Encoding Initiative,* University of Illinois at Chicago, 1940 W. Taylor St., Room 124 Chicago, IL 60612-7352, USA, 1998. http://www.uic.edu/orgs/tei/index.html.
23. Van Rossum (G.), Jansen (J.) , Mullender (K.) and Bulterman (D.), "CMIFed : a presentation Environment for Portable Hypermedia Documents", *Proc. of the ACM Multimedia Conf.,* California, 1993.
24. W3C Note, *Extensible Specifiaction Language (XSL),* http://www.w3.org/TR/NOTE-XSL.html, 27 August 1997.
25. W3C Recommendation, *Extensible Markup Language (XML) 1.0,* http://www.w3.org/TR/1998/REC-xml-19980210, 10-February 1998.
26. W3C Working Draft, *XML Linking Language (XLink),* http://www.w3.org/TR/WD-xlink, 3-March 1998.
27. W3C Recommendation, *Mathematical Markup Language (MathML) 1.0 Specification,* http://www.w3.org/TR/REC-MathML/, 07-April 1998.
28. W3C Recommendation, *HTML 4.0 Specification,* http://www.w3.org/TR/REC-html40/, 24-April 1998.
29. W3C Recommendation, *Cascading Style Sheets, level 2, CSS2 Specification,* http://www.w3.org/TR/REC-CSS2/, 12-May 1998.
30. W3C Recommendation, *Synchronized Multimedia Integration Language (SMIL) 1.0 Specification,* http://www.w3.org/TR/REC-smil, 15-June 1998.

Engineering Software & Software Engineering

Dieter Rombach

Department of Computer Science, University of Kaiserslautern, Postfach 3049
D-67653 Kaiserslautern, Germany
rombach@informatik.uni-kl.de
http://wwwagse.informatik.uni-kl.de
&
Fraunhofer Institute for Experimental Software Engineering (IESE), Sauerwiesen 6,
D-67661 Kaiserslautern, Germany
rombach@iese.fhg.de
http://www.iese.fhg.de

(Extended Abstract)

1 Introduction

Software has become an indispensable part of most products and services. As a result the need to "engineer software" professionally with high quality at low cost has become important to all branches of industry. The supporting scientific discipline called "software engineering", on the other hand, has matured very slowly, and has only just now arrived at the verge of making a real contribution to truly professionalizing the "engineering of software". This presentation reviews the historic evolution of both the profession of "engineering software" as well as the scientific discipline of "software engineering", points out their symbiotic relationship, and closes with an outlook into a visionary future full of challenges for practitioners, researchers and teachers.

2 The Profession of Software Engineering

Today, most products and services of our daily lives depend highly on complex software. That means that product or service quality is impossible without software quality. This situation has led to increasing pressure on the profession of "engineering software" to transform quickly from a toy discipline (i.e., one hacked software for one's own use) to a development discipline (i.e., one makes money by selling high-demand software without being held responsible for low quality), all the way to an engineering discipline (i.e., quality of software is treated like quality of any regular engineering product).

In consequence this means that a sound scientific basis is needed for describing software products (i.e., software programming languages), for developing software (i.e., software development methods), for coordinating and managing software development (i.e., software development processes), and for assuring the desired qualities of software and improving over time (i.e., quality assurance and management approaches).

Key ideas used in the professional software engineering environment were (in historical order)

- Software (or programming) languages (since 50's): low-level to high-level languages, implementation to design and specification languages, unstructured to structured languages, general to application-specific languages, etc.
- Software development methods (since late 60's): informal to formal/systematic methods, homolythic to scaleable methods both wrt. complexity and formality, etc.
- Software development processes (since late 70's): life-cycle project models to technical process models, isolated (individual) to integrated (team) process models, static to dynamic process models, etc.
- Quality assurance and management approaches (since late 80's): qualitative to quantitative quality assurance, subjective to objective management, improvement by chance to TQM for software, etc.

In the presentation a more detailed review of the professionally used key ideas and technologies will be given.

The main problem still today is that the useful integration of all these ideas and technologies into a competence that contributes to solving the engineering problem of a specific company is not well understood. There exist numerous success and failure stories. However, there is little (re)usable knowledge why a specific language or method worked better or worth in different environments. We - as a community -are over and over surprised if methods proven to work in one environment do fail in a different environment. The main reason for this surprise is indeed a fundamental misunderstanding of the task of "engineering software". Professional software development environments reacted intuitively appropriate by not introducing many of the existing - theoretically promising - research languages and methods into practice - without however understanding its deeper reason.

3 Characteristics of the Software Domain

What is software engineering like? What can we learn from physics, manufacturing or social sciences? In truth, software engineering combines characteristics of all of the above. It is by nature an engineering discipline; however is different from manufacturing in that it is a "design" rather than a "production" task, and is mainly involving human-based processes. There exist many natural science "laws" about the relationship between process and product; however, most of them need to be empirically validated. Finally, like in social sciences, many of the relationships cannot be explained without modeling the human problem solving process. All this explains why one-dimensional approaches like "mathematical transformation ideas" or "management-based approaches" in isolation had to lead to disappointing results. In the presentation a characterization of the software domain will be given and contrasted with other traditional disciplines.

4 The Scientific Discipline of Software Engineering

How has the software engineering discipline (established 1979) responded to these industrial experiences and problems? For a very long time, the discipline evolved in rather independent parallel threads:

- formal methods community: formal specification techniques, formal languages, formal verification, formal transformation, etc.
- system modeling community: architectures, product line approaches, object-orientation, reuse frameworks, etc.
- process community: methods, process models, process standards, life-cycle models, process-sensitive development environments, etc.

As shown by their practical usage in industry, neither one of these communities was able to elevate the engineering of software to a satisfactory "engineering level". When the characteristic of software development - as characterized above - was slowly understood, qualitative changes started to happen. The understanding growing out of the realization that engineering of software is a human-based design process made it obvious, that the creation of software with high quality under changing environmental characteristics required the choice of different languages, methods and or processes. This in turn required an understanding of which language, method or process promises what result under what environmental characteristics. Now many people realized that we had all engaged in producing new languages, methods and processes without understanding their effects.

As a result the importance of empirical studies as an important sub-discipline of software engineering emerged. This has not only led to an addition to the already existing three sub-disciplines, but also to a synergistic whole. Today, more and more people, consider the software engineering discipline as fundamentally "experimental" and composed of

- formal methods community (see above)
- system modeling community (see above)
- process community (see above)
- empirical studies community: experimental designs, quantitative methods, quantitative and qualitative modeling, etc.

The experimental characteristic of our discipline requires the use of empirical studies to identify strengths and weaknesses of existing approaches in objective terms, derive potential for improvement, and evaluate the potential of new languages, methods and processes against such improvement goals. In the presentation, an overview of existing research results the thin traditional three sub-communities will be given, and the need for changing the research paradigm will be motivated.

5 The Experimental Software Engineering Paradigm

The empirical studies community has produced principles, methods and tools for planning and conducting empirical studies in software engineering. Fundamental contributions include methods for defining study goals, designing the appropriate experiments, quantifying observations and modeling phenomena based on measurement data. In addition, languages, methods and tools have been developed for representing software engineering knowledge for reuse. In the presentation a short summary of the existing empirical studies methodologies will be provided.

In order to illustrate the possible improvements to be gained by living the experimental software engineering paradigm in both research and practice realistic examples will be provided. The research example comprises the grown understanding regarding software inspections; the practice example comprises the improvements which have been gained within the NASA SEL development environment.

6 Outlook

Finally, a vision of "software engineering" both as a profession and as a scientific discipline will be painted. Within this vision, the challenges for practitioners, researchers and teachers/trainers will be pointed out.

Efficient Communication Schemes *

Peter Ružička

Institute of Informatics
Faculty of Mathematics and Physics
Comenius University, Bratislava
Slovak Republic
E-mail: ruzicka@dcs.fmph.uniba.sk

Abstract. We give a survey of recent theoretical results for communication problems in *point to point* networks. This survey is based on the previous surveys in [57, 25].
Communication problems are studied as routing path systems satisfying given communication patterns in a network. Efficiency parameters of path systems such as congestion, dilation, stretch factor, compactness and buffer size are considered. We focus on the current research directions and the various techniques that are used. Open problems related to this line of research and an overview of several related research directions are given.

1 Introduction

Communication among the processors in a computer network is a fundamental task in distributed computing. Networks such as wide-area networks are typically sparse point-to-point networks, consisting of a large number of processors, where each processor can directly communicate with only a few neighbors. Telecommunication networks, computer networks or the Internet are examples of networks that perform many communication requests simultaneously (such as e-mails, account transactions or telephone calls.) So the efficiency of communication operations has crucial impact on the effective performance of the whole distributed network.

It is not surprising that great emphasis is devoted to the study of basic communication problems. Among the fundamental problems are efficient routing, broadcasting and gossipping in point-to-point networks. All these problems are currently being studied actively.

In this survey we study communication problems in point-to-point networks. Communication problems are investigated as routing path systems satisfying given communication patterns in a network. This enables us to express broadcasting, accumulation, gossipping and permutation routing by one-to-all, all-to-one, all-to-all and 1-relation patterns, respectively.

The quality of path systems is evaluated according to certain efficiency measures. We focus primarily on efficiency parameters such as congestion, dilation,

* This research has been partially supported by VEGA 1/4315/97.

stretch factor and buffer size. They are independent from any concrete implementation of path systems in the network. We exploit the relationship among
these parameters for various path systems satisfying several significant communication patterns, both on general networks and on some special interconnection
networks, including tori, hypercubes, cube connected cycles, butterflies and star
networks. This approach leads to a variety of interesting combinatorial problems
on path systems and their properties.

Another important issue is related to the space efficient implementation of
the path systems satisfying certain communication patterns on networks. We
consider two compact schemes: interval routing schemes (IRS) [46, 56] and multi-
dimensional interval routing schemes (MIRS) [19]. To measure space complexity
of these compact schemes, we use the compactness measure. We relate the compactness to dilation, congestion and buffer size for IRS and MIRS on general
networks and on certain well-known interconnection networks. We present some
classical efficiency results (also summarized in [57, 25]) and the most recent complexity results in the field of space-efficient communication schemes. The main
focus is on the current research directions and the various techniques that are
used. Open problems related to this line of research are given as well as several
related research directions.

2 Communication Problems

Networks. An *interconnection network* is modeled by an undirected graph
$G = (V, E)$, where V is a set of nodes and E is a set of edges of the network.
Assume $|V| = n$. Each node has a finite set of buffers used for temporarily storing
messages.

Communication Patterns. A *communication request* is an ordered pair of
nodes $(u, v) \in V \times V, u \neq v$. A *communication pattern* $\mathcal{P}$ is a set of communication
requests, i.e. $\mathcal{P} = \{(u, v) \mid u, v \in V, u \neq v\}$. A *set of communication patterns* is
$\{\mathcal{P}^{(i)}\}_{i \in I}$, where each $\mathcal{P}^{(i)}$ is a communication pattern.

We shall consider several significant communication patterns in G.

- A *one-to-all* communication pattern $\mathcal{P} = \{(v, w) \mid w \in V, w \neq v\}$ for a given
  source node v.
- An *all-to-all* communication pattern $\mathcal{P}_A = \{(v, w) \mid v, w \in V, w \neq v\}$.
- A *k-relation* communication pattern $\mathcal{P}_k$ in which each node is the source and
  the destination of at most k requests. A *permutation pattern* is a 1-relation
  $\mathcal{P}_1$.

In static setting we consider static one-to-all and k-relation communication pattern $\{\mathcal{P}\}$, where $\mathcal{P}$ is a one-to-all or k-relation communication pattern, respectively. Similarly, in dynamic setting we have

- *dynamic one-to-all* communication patterns $\{\mathcal{P}^{(v)}\}_{v \in V}$, where
  $\mathcal{P}^{(v)} = \{(v, w) \mid w \in V, w \neq v\}$ for some (not fixed) source node v.
- *dynamic k-relation* communication patterns $\{\mathcal{P}_k^{(i)}\}_{i \in I}$.

Path Systems. Let $p(u,v)$ denote a directed path in G from the node u to v, which consists of consecutive edges beginning at u and ending at v. A *path system* of G is a set of directed paths between nodes in G. A path system $\mathcal{R}$ *satisfies* the communication pattern $\mathcal{P}$ if there is at least one routing path in $\mathcal{R}$ beginning in u and ending in v for each communication request $(u,v) \in \mathcal{P}$.

We distinguish between single and multipath systems. A path system $\mathcal{R}$ satisfying a given communication pattern $\mathcal{P}$ is *single path (deterministic)*, if there is exactly one path $p(u,v)$ in $\mathcal{R}$ for each $(u,v) \in \mathcal{P}$. It is *multipath*, if there can be many paths from u to v in $\mathcal{R}$ for each $(u,v) \in \mathcal{P}$. A path system is *simple (cycle-free)* if no routing path contains the same node more than once, and it is a *shortest (optimal) path* system if for each request $(u,v) \in \mathcal{P}$ only shortest paths from u to v in G are considered. A path system $\mathcal{R}$ satisfying $\mathcal{P}$ is *all shortest (all optimal) path*, if it contains all shortest paths between u and v for each $(u,v) \in \mathcal{P}$.

A cycle-free multipath system $\mathcal{R}$ is *oblivious*, if for each $p(u,v), p(w,v) \in \mathcal{R}$, $u \neq w$, where $p(u,v) = p(u,x)p_1(x,v)$ and $p(w,v) = p(w,x)p_2(x,v)$, also $p(u,x)p_2(x,v) \in \mathcal{R}$ and $p(w,x)p_1(x,v) \in \mathcal{R}$.

Communication Problem. Let G be a network and $\mathcal{P}$ a communication pattern in G. The *communication problem* is specified by $G, \mathcal{P}$. A scheme for the communication problem given by $G, \mathcal{P}$ is an implementation of a path system satisfying the pattern $\mathcal{P}$ in G. In this overview we shall consider only two kinds of compact schemes: interval routing schemes and multidimensional interval routing schemes.

3 Efficiency Parameters

Let G be a network, $\mathcal{P}$ a pattern, and $\mathcal{R}$ a path system satisfying $\mathcal{P}$ in G. In this section we study path systems satisfying the given patterns with respect to dilation, congestion and deadlock-free.

3.1 Dilation, Stretch Factor

The efficiency of a path system is usually measured in terms of its dilation or stretch factor. The *(worst case) dilation* of $\mathcal{R}$, denoted as $dilation(\mathcal{R})$, is the length of the longest routing path in $\mathcal{R}$. The *(worst case) stretch factor* of $\mathcal{R}$, denoted by $stretch(\mathcal{R})$, is the maximum ratio between the length of the routing path in $\mathcal{R}$ and that of the distance between their endpoints.

Now consider single path systems satisfying the all-to-all communication pattern.

The *average dilation* of $\mathcal{R}$ is

$$\frac{1}{n(n-1)} \sum_{u \neq v} |p(u,v)|$$

for $p(u, v) \in \mathcal{R}$, where $|p(u, v)|$ is the length of the path $p(u, v)$.
The *average stretch factor* of $\mathcal{R}$ is

$$\frac{1}{n(n-1)} \sum_{u \neq v} \frac{|p(u, v)|}{distance(u, v)}$$

for $p(u, v) \in \mathcal{R}$, where $distance(u, v)$ is the distance between u and v in G.

3.2 Congestion

For an edge $e \in E$, the edge–congestion $\pi(G, \mathcal{P}, \mathcal{R}, e)$ is the number of paths in $\mathcal{R}$ containing e. The maximum congestion of any edge of G in the path system $\mathcal{R}$ is called the *edge–congestion* of G in the path system $\mathcal{R}$ satisfying the pattern $\mathcal{P}$, i.e. $\pi(G, \mathcal{P}, \mathcal{R}) = max_{e \in E} \pi(G, \mathcal{P}, \mathcal{R}, e)$. $\pi(G, \mathcal{P})$ denotes the minimum congestion of G in any path system $\mathcal{R}$ satisfying the pattern $\mathcal{P}$.

Lemma 1.

- *There exists an n-node network G and a pattern $\mathcal{P}$ such that for each oblivious single path system satisfying $\mathcal{P}$ the following holds:*

$$\pi(G, \mathcal{P}, \mathcal{R}) \geq \frac{n}{2} \pi(G, \mathcal{P}).$$

- *There exists an n-node graph G and a pattern $\mathcal{P}$ such that for each shortest path system $\mathcal{R}$ satisfying $\mathcal{P}$ the following holds:*

$$\pi(G, \mathcal{P}, \mathcal{R}) \geq \frac{n}{2} \pi(G, \mathcal{P}).$$

Competitive Ratio. A general framework was introduced in [8] to deal with congestion issues in dynamic setting. Given a set $\{\mathcal{P}_i\}_{i \in I}$ of communication patterns, a path system $\mathcal{R}$ and a set of path systems $\mathcal{S}$ (all satisfying $\mathcal{P}_i$ for all i), $\mathcal{R}$ is said to be *c-competitive* with respect to $\mathcal{S}$ if

$$max_{i \in I} \left\{ \frac{\pi(G, \mathcal{R}, \mathcal{P}_i)}{\pi(G, \mathcal{R}', \mathcal{P}_i)} \mid \mathcal{R}' \text{ is a path system in } \mathcal{S} \right\} \leq c$$

The competitive ratio relates the behaviour of $\mathcal{R}$ with respect to any other path system from $\mathcal{S}$ on all communication patterns in $\{\mathcal{P}_i\}_{i \in I}$.

The natural question is how much one loses using oblivious or shortest path systems with respect to unrestricted paths systems. Due to the previous lemma we see that there exists an n-node graph G and a set of communication patterns such that any oblivious single path system is at least $n/2$-competitive with respect to unrestricted path systems.

3.2.1 Edge and Vertex Forwarding Indices. The congestion of the path systems has been extensively investigated in the literature. In case of all-to-all patterns, it corresponds to the notion of *edge forwarding index* introduced in [32]. Formally, for the all–to–all pattern $\mathcal{P}_A$, $\pi(G, \mathcal{P}_A)$ is called the *edge–forwarding index* of G. A similar *vertex forwarding index* takes into account the load of nodes in a network [7]. Various results on the minimization of the forwarding indices for various interconnection networks have been obtained in [6, 32, 33, 45, 47, 49].

The following theorem gives edge-forwarding indices for cycles C_n, complete bipartite graphs $K_{n,m}$, hypercubes Q_d, cube connected cycles CCC_d, butterflies BF_d, De Bruijn graphs DB_d and d-dimensional tori $T_{n_1,...,n_d}$.

Theorem 1. [49] *The edge-forwarding index of*

- C_n *is* $\frac{n^2}{4}$ *for n even and* $\frac{n^2-1}{4}$ *for n odd,*
- $K_{n,m}$, $n \geq m$, *is* $\frac{2(n^2+m^2+nm-n-m)}{nm}$,
- Q_d *is* 2^d,
- CCC_d *is* $\frac{5}{4}d^2 2^d (1 - o(1))$,
- BF_d *is* $\frac{5}{4}d^2 2^{d-1} (1 + o(1))$,
- DB_d *is* $d2^{d-1}(1 - o(1))$,
- $T_{n_1,...,n_d}$ *is*

$$(\Pi_{i=1}^d n_i) \ max_{1 \leq i \leq d} \frac{\pi(C_{n_i})}{n_i}$$

where $\pi(C_{n_i})$ is the edge-forwarding index of a cycle C_{n_i}.

We say that $\mathcal{R}$ is of *optimal edge–congestion*, if $\pi(G, \mathcal{P}_A, \mathcal{R}) = \pi(G, \mathcal{P}_A)$, i.e. edge–congestion of $\mathcal{R}$ is equal to the edge–forwarding index of G. The importance of determining the exact values of forwarding indices is that they form lower bounds on the congestion for restricted path systems (e.g. path systems induced by IRS or MIRS schemes in Section 4).

3.3 Deadlock–Free

Given a source, a destination and a current buffer of a message, a *buffer reservation controller* specifies a set of buffers to which the message may move in the next step. The message can move to any of the specified buffers, provided that they are available. (It is assumed that each buffer is large enough to hold exactly one message.) A *deadlock* is a situation in which a set of messages can never reach the destination, because specified buffers of each message are occupied by other messages from the set. A buffer reservation controller is *deadlock-free* if it does not allow the occurrence of a deadlock.

An *orientation DG* of G is a directed graph obtained from G by replacing each undirected edge in G by an arc (i.e. an edge $\{u, v\}$ is replaced by either (u, v) or (v, u)). An orientation is *acyclic* if it does not contain a cycle. An *(alternating) orientation cover* of a path system $\mathcal{R}$ is a sequence of (alternating dual) orientations $DG_1, ..., DG_s$ such that every path $p \in \mathcal{R}$ can be expressed as a concatenation of s paths $p_1, ..., p_s$, where p_i is a path in DG_i for all i. An acyclic orientation cover is an orientation cover consisting of only acyclic orientations.

Given a network G, let $\mathcal{R}$ be an all–to–all shortest path system of G. If there is an acyclic orientation cover for $\mathcal{R}$ of size s, then there exists a shortest path deadlock–free routing algorithm using only s buffers per vertex [50]. A routing algorithm using this strategy is said to be based on acyclic orientations. If there are no restrictions on the strategy used by the routing algorithm then it is said to be based on general strategy.

3.3.1 Buffers.

The following theorems provide necessary and sufficient conditions for the creation of deadlock-free packet routing algorithms, which are oblivious (i.e. every message is forced to take a single, fixed path based on its source and destination nodes).

Theorem 2. [31] *Given any oblivious packet routing algorithm, if there exists a total ordering of the buffers such that every message is always allowed to move to a higher ordered buffer, then the algorithm is deadlock-free.*

Theorem 3. [52] *Given any deadlock-free oblivious packet routing algorithm, there exists a total ordering of the buffers such that every message is always allowed to move to a higher buffer.*

A great deal of research has been devoted to creating efficient deadlock-free routing algorithms [1, 3, 10–14, 30, 38, 42, 51–53, 58, 59].

General Networks. The size of deadlock-free controllers for the optimal (shortest path) packet routing on arbitrary networks strongly depends on the structure of communication patterns. The following fact for all-to-all communication patterns can be found e.g. in [50] and is a consequence of a proposition proven in [52].

Theorem 4. *For any n-node network G and a set of $n(n-1)$ shortest paths connecting every pair of nodes in G, there is a deadlock-free controller of size $D + 1$, where D is the diameter of G.*

The best lower bound on the size of general deadlock-free controllers is $\Omega(\log \log n)$ [9]. However, this lower bound is proved on a rather artificially constructed network. The best lower bound on the size of deadlock-free controllers for well-known interconnection networks is only 3 [10]. It would be interesting to find better upper and lower bounds on the number of buffers required for shortest path deadlock-free routing on general networks. Another interesting issue is to investigate the structure of networks having large size deadlock-free controllers for shortest path deadlock-free packet routing.

Considering all-to-all communication patterns on arbitrary networks, an interesting problem is to determine non-constant lower bound on the size of a deadlock-free controller (based on acyclic orientation covering concept) necessary for the optimal packet routing on well-known interconnection networks.

However, if we assume static one-to-all communication patterns, the requirements for the size of deadlock-free controllers are much lower. Namely, for any network G and a set of $n-1$ shortest paths connecting a source with all other nodes in G, there is trivially a deadlock-free controller (based on acyclic orientation covering) of size 1.

For other types of communication patterns the problems are again unsolved. What is the number of buffers sufficient to realize k-relation (permutation) communication patterns ? Can we do better than $D+1$ buffers per node ?

Specific Networks. We shall now concentrate on specific networks. All-to-all shortest path deadlock-free routing algorithms with constant number of buffers per node are known for many important networks including meshes [42], tori [10], trees [39], hypercubes [42], de Bruijn [9] and shuffle-exchange [9] networks.

Now consider the d-dimensional hypercube. Each node consists of a binary string of length d with two nodes being connected if and only if they differ in exactly one bit. Thus every path in the hypercube corresponds to a sequence of changes of some bits. If the bits are changed in order from left to right, then the path is called *monotone*.

Theorem 5. [9] *Any deadlock-free "dimension-order" routing algorithm on an d-dimensional hypercube Q_d uses at least $\frac{d}{2}+1$ buffers.*

We concentrate on comparing general deadlock-free controllers versus deadlock-free controllers based on acyclic orientation coverings with respect to size.

Theorem 6. [48] *Let $\mathcal{R}$ be an all-to-all shortest path system of a d-dimensional hypercube Q_d with only monotone paths. Every orientation cover of $\mathcal{R}$ has size $\Omega(d/\log d)$.*

This recent result is an improvement over [35], where weaker lower bound in the form $\Omega(\sqrt{d})$ on the size of acyclic orientation covering was proved on the same path system as in Theorem 6. An important consequence of this result is:

Corollary 1. *Every shortest path deadlock-free packet routing algorithm on CCC_d based on acyclic orientations requires $\Omega(d/\log d)$ buffers.*

It is interesting to observe that there exists a shortest path deadlock-free routing algorithm for $\mathcal{R}$ (from Theorem 6) using only 8 buffers per node (which, of course, is not based on acyclic orientations !). In fact, in [48] a graph of size n was presented, which has shortest path deadlock-free packet routing algorithm using only $O(1)$ buffers per node, but every shortest path deadlock-free routing algorithm based on acyclic orientations requires $\Omega(\log n/\log\log n)$ buffers per node. Hence, the technique based on acyclic orientations sometimes does not lead to size optimal deadlock-free packet routing algorithms. It would be interesting to know how large the gap between routing algorithms based on acyclic orientations and general deadlock-free routing algorithms can be.

Covering Problem. The following *covering problem* on the path systems is important for specifying deadlock-free controllers based on acyclic orientations. Given a network G, determine the size (denoted as *rank* in [4]) of alternating acyclic orientation covering for the system of all shortest paths between all pairs of nodes in G.

This covering problem has been studied in [4], where it was shown that to determine the rank is NP-complete in general. Furthermore, in [4] some known upper and lower bounds on the rank were improved for particular topologies, such as grids $G_{p,q}$, tori $T_{p,q}$ and hypercubes Q_d.

Theorem 7. [4]

- $\lceil (2 - \sqrt{2})q \rceil - 1 \leq rank(G_{p,q}) \leq \frac{3}{5}q + o(q)$ *for* $p \geq q$
- $\lfloor \frac{q}{2} \rfloor + 2 \leq rank(T_{p,q}) \leq \lceil \frac{q}{2} \rceil + 4$ *for* $p \geq q$
- $\lceil \frac{d+1}{2} \rceil \leq rank(Q_d) \leq d + 1$

We also present upper and lower bounds on the rank for cube connected cycles CCC_d and butterflies BF_d.

Theorem 8. [35, 48]

- $\Omega(d/\log d) \leq rank(CCC_d) \leq 2d + 6$
- $3 \leq rank(BF_d) \leq 4$

It would be worthwhile to establish the exact values for $q \times q$ grids (the conjecture is $(2 - \sqrt{2})q$ [4]), d-dimensional hypercubes (the conjecture is d [4]) and d-dimensional cube connected cycles (the conjecture is $2d + O(1)$). The main unresolved problem is to determine rank values for other well-known interconnection networks and also for more general classes of networks.

Greedy Controllers. Now consider *greedy* deadlock free controllers. To introduce greedy controllers, we need to recall the definition of path covering. We say that an acyclic orientation sequence $\mathcal{G} = \langle DG_1, ..., DG_s \rangle$ covers a simple path $p(v_1, v_r) = v_1, ..., v_r$ if there exists a sequence of positive integers $j_1, ..., j_{r-1}$ such that $1 \leq j_1 \leq ... \leq j_{r-1} \leq s$ and for every i, $1 \leq i \leq r - 1$, (v_i, v_{i+1}) belongs to DG_{j_i}. We see that a path p need not be covered by $\mathcal{G}$ in a unique way. There could be different sequences $k_1, ..., k_{r-1}$ such that (v_i, v_{i+1}) belongs to DG_{k_i}. We assume that the greedy deadlock-free controller based on $\mathcal{G}$ works with minimal $(r - 1)$-tuples $(k_1, ..., k_{r-1})$ (minimal w.r.t. the lexicographical ordering).

Theorem 9. [35] *There exists a deadlock–free greedy controller of size 2 for the optimal packet routing on a d-dimensional hypercube and of size 4 for the optimal packet routing on a d-dimensional torus.*

Due to Theorem 8 the size of deadlock-free greedy controller for the optimal packet routing on BF_d is at most 4. An interesting question is to determine the size of greedy controllers for other interconnection networks.

4 Communication Schemes

In this section we present communication schemes for efficient implementation of communication problems. The main emphasis is on the implementation of path systems satisfying given communication patterns, which is efficient w.r.t. the space, dilation and buffer size.

4.1 Interval Routing Schemes

An *Interval Labeling Scheme* (ILS) is a scheme of labeling each node in a graph G by a unique integer from the set $\{1, 2, ..., n\}$ and each arc by an interval $[a, b]$, where $a, b \in \{1, 2, ..., n\}$. We allow cyclic intervals $[a, b]$ so that $[a, b] = \{a, a+1, ..., n, 1, ..., b\}$ for $a > b$. The set of all intervals associated with the arcs incident to a node must form a partition of the set $\{1, 2, ..., n\}$. Messages to a destination node having a label l are routed via the arc labeled by the interval $[a, b]$ such that $l \in [a, b]$. An ILS is valid if the path system specified by this ILS satisfies the all-to-all communication pattern. (Thus, if, for all nodes u and v in G, messages sent from u to v reach v correctly, not necessarily via shortest paths.) A valid ILS is also called an *Interval Routing Scheme* (IRS). An IRS thus specifies for each pair of distinct nodes u and v in G a (unique) path from u to v.

In a k-ILS each arc is labeled with up to k intervals, always under the assumption that at every node, all intervals associated with arcs going out from the node form a partition of $\{1, ..., n\}$. At any given node a message with destination node labeled l is routed via the arc labeled by the interval containing l. If k-ILS does not use cyclic intervals, the k-ILS is called *linear* or simply k-LILS. Valid k-ILS and k-LILS are called k-IRS and k-LIRS respectively. A k-IRS (k-LIRS) is said to be *optimal* if it represents a shortest path system containing exactly one shortest path between any pair of nodes.

4.1.1 Compactness. To measure the space efficiency of a given IRS, we use the compactness measure, defined as follows. The *compactness* of a graph G, denoted as *compactness*(G), is the smallest integer k such that G supports a k-IRS of all-to-all single shortest paths, that is, a k-IRS that provides only one shortest path between any pair of nodes.

4.1.1.1 All-to-all Single Shortest Paths Schemes. Matching upper and lower bounds on the compactness of general graphs have been presented in [28].

Theorem 10. [28]

– *Every n–node graph G, $n \geq 1$, satisfies*

$$compactness(G) < \frac{n}{4} + 0.25\sqrt{2n\ln(3n^2)}$$

– *For every sufficiently large integer n, there exists an n–node graph G such that*

$$compactness(G) > \frac{n}{4} - 1.72(n^2 ln\ n)^{1/3}$$

A powerful technique for obtaining lower bounds on the compactness of shortest path interval routing on arbitrary graphs has been introduced in [22] and also used in [23, 29, 36].

The compactness of many graph classes has been studied. Its value is 1 for trees [46], outerplanar graphs [24], hypercubes and meshes [2, 56], 8-directional meshes [34], r-partite graphs [37], interval graphs [40], and unit-circular graphs [23]. It is 2 for tori [56], at most 3 for 2-trees [40], and at most $2\sqrt{n}$ for n-node chordal rings [41]. More results on the compactness of concrete graphs can be found in [5, 25, 41, 57].

It has been proved that compactness $\Theta(n)$ might be required on n-node random graphs [22]. However, there are also certain well-known interconnection networks with large compactness, including shuffle exchange SE_d, cube connected cycles CCC_d, butterflies BF_d and star graphs S_d.

Theorem 11. [36]

– $compactness(SE_d) = \Omega(n^{1/2-\epsilon})$, *for every* $\epsilon > 0$
– $compactness(CCC_d) = \Omega(\sqrt{n/\log n})$
– $compactness(BF_d) = \Omega(\sqrt{n/\log n})$
– $compactness(S_d) = \Omega(n(\log \log n/\log n)^5)$

Following techniques from [36], we can prove the lower bound on the compactness also for De Bruijn graphs DB_d.

Theorem 12. $compactness(DB_d) = \Omega(\sqrt{n/\log n})$

The question is whether above stated lower bounds on the compactness for special interconnection networks can be improved.

4.1.2 Compactness versus Dilation. We now consider the compactness for *dilation bounded IRS*.

Special Networks. Asymptotically optimal trade–offs between the dilation and the compactness have been obtained for some special classes of graphs. The compactness threshold $\Theta(\sqrt{n})$ for the dilation $1.25D - 1$ has been proved on multiglobe graphs and the same threshold $\Theta(\sqrt{n})$ for the dilation D on planar multiglobe graphs (called globe graphs). Moreover, for globe graphs nearly–optimal routing (in the sense of $(1+\epsilon)D$–bounded routing for any given constant $\epsilon > 0$) is achievable with only constant compactness.

The *multiglobe graph* (denoted as $M(s, t, r)$) is obtained from the complete bipartite graph $K_{s,t}$ by replacing all edges by unique path of the length r. Hence, $K_{s,t} = M(t, s, 1)$. Its diameter is $2r$, it has $(r-1)st + s + t$ vertices and rst edges.

Theorem 13. [36]

- There is a multiglobe graph $M(s,t,r)$ such that each k–IRS of M with the dilation bounded by $1.25D - 1$ needs $k = \Omega(\sqrt{n})$.
- There is a $1.25D$–bounded 2–IRS of the multiglobe graph $M(s,t,r)$.
- For any $\epsilon > 0$ there exists a k–IRS of the $M(s,t,r)$ with the dilation bounded by $(1+\epsilon)D$ and $k = \lceil \frac{1}{2}\epsilon \rceil \cdot min(s,t)$.

The *globe graph* (denoted as $G(r,s)$, r odd) is a planar multiglobe graph $M(s,2,\lceil \frac{r}{2} \rceil)$.

Theorem 14. [36]

- Every optimal IRS of the globe graph $G(s,s+1)$ needs compactness $s/4$.
- There is an optimal IRS of $G(r,s)$ with compactness $min(s,r)$.
- There is a $1.5D$–bounded 1–IRS of $G(r,s)$.
- For arbitrary $\epsilon > 0$ there is a $(1+\epsilon)D$–bounded IRS of $G(r,s)$ with constant compactness.

It would be interesting to achieve asymptotically optimal compactness-dilation trade-offs for other classes of interconnection networks (having large compactness requirements).

Two interesting open problems related to the generalization of Theorem 14 towards planar graphs are mentioned. The question [36] is whether for any $\epsilon > 0$ there is a constant k such that every planar graph G of diameter D satisfies

$$k - dilation(G) \leq (1+\epsilon)D.$$

C. Gavoille [25] posed the conjecture that every n-node planar graph has compactness $O(\sqrt{n})$.

General Networks. Note that for every network there is an interval routing scheme with compactness 1 and of dilation $2D$, where D is the diameter of the underlying network [46]. For the dilation bounded interval routing on general graphs, the following nontrivial upper bound result has been obtained with nonconstructive proof.

Theorem 15. [36] *There is an interval routing scheme with the dilation $\lceil 1.5D \rceil$ and the compactness $O(\sqrt{n \log n})$ on n-node networks with the diameter D.*

A technique for lower bounds on the compactness of dilation bounded interval routing has been introduced in [43] and improved in [21, 26, 36, 54, 55]. For linear IRS see [16].

We summarize the best known lower bounds. For the compactness 1, the lower bound on the dilation in the form $2D - 3$ was proved in [55]. They proved the optimality of 1-IRS of dilation $2D$ from [46]. For the compactness k, $2 \leq k \leq \Theta(\sqrt{n})$, the lower bound on the dilation in the form $3D/2 - 3$ appeared in [36]. For the compactness k, $2 \leq k \leq \Omega(n/\log n)$, the following lower bound on the dilation was proved in [21, 26].

Theorem 16. [21, 26]

- For every $D \geq 2$, there exists an n-node graph G such that

$$k - dilation(G) \geq \frac{3}{2}D - 2$$

for every $k \leq O(n/(D \log(n/D)))$.
- For every $D \geq 4 \log n$ there is a bounded degree n-node graph G of diameter D such that

$$k - dilation(G) \geq \frac{3}{2}D - 2 \log \frac{n}{D}$$

for every $k \leq 0.05 \frac{n}{D \log(n/D)}$.

The question remains to determine a tight trade-off between the compactness and the (worst case) dilation for general networks [36]. Another interesting issue is to exploit the relationship between the compactness and the average dilation (average stretch factor) for arbitrary networks [25].

4.1.3 Compactness versus Stretch Factor. The following routing algorithm, constructed in polynomial time, has been presented in [15].

Theorem 17. [15] *For every n-node graph G, with the diameter D, there exists an interval routing scheme on G such that*

- *the compactness is at most $3\sqrt{n(1 + ln\ n)}$,*
- *the worst case stretch factor is at most 5,*
- *the average stretch factor is at most 3.*

4.1.4 Compactness versus Congestion. The competitiveness factor expresses how well the k-IRS behaves with respect to any other scheme on all input communication patterns.

The natural question to ask is how much one loses using k-IRS with respect to unrestricted routing paths systems. There exists an n-node graph G and a set of communication patterns such that any shortest path k-IRS for G is at least $n/2$-competitive.

Moreover, there also exists an n-node graph and a communication pattern such that any optimal k-IRS, $k = O(1)$, is $\Omega(n)$-competitive with respect to non-optimal k-IRS. And finally, there exists an n-node graph and a communication pattern such that any optimal $\sqrt{n}$-IRS is $\Omega(\sqrt{n})$-competitive with respect to non-optimal $O(1)$-IRS.

The main question remains whether there is an n-node graph and functions $f_1(n) << f_2(n)$, $g_1(n) >> g_2(n)$ such that any $f_1(n)$-IRS is at least $g_1(n)/g_2(n)$-competitive with respect to $f_2(n)$-IRS. As a partial solution of this problem, for each fixed $k = O(\sqrt{n})$, there exists an n-node graph and a communication pattern such that the congestion of each path system induced by k-IRS is greater than the congestion of the best path system induced by $(k+1)$-IRS, both satisfying a given communication pattern.

For specific topologies, the next two propositions give basic results on competitiveness for one-to-all and all-to-all communication patterns. We see that matching or nearly matching upper and lower bounds on the competitive ratio hold for many interconnection networks.

Theorem 18. [8]

- *There exists a 1-competitive 1-IRS on chains and trees for arbitrary communication patterns and on rings for dynamic one-to-all patterns.*
- *There exists a 1-competitive 1-IRS on 2-dimensional grids and tori for static one-to-all patterns.*
- *There exists a $(1+\frac{1}{n-1})$-competitive 1-IRS on 2-dimensional tori for dynamic one-to-all patterns.*

Theorem 19. [8]

- *There exists a 1-competitive 1-IRS on any ring for all-to-all patterns.*
- *There exists a $(1+o(1))$-competitive 1-IRS on any d-dimensional grid and a $(1+o(1))$-competitive 2-IRS on any d-dimensional torus for all-to-all patterns.*
- *There exists a $(1.2+o(1))$-competitive 1-IRS on any 2-dimensional tori for all-to-all patterns.*

The following result on tori relates congestion to stretch factor, and is tight as the lower bound on arc-congestion for $T_{n,n}$ is $0.125n^3$.

Theorem 20. [8] *The arc-congestion of any all-to-all path system induced by 1-IRS on 2-dimensional tori $T_{n,n}$ is at most $0.15n^3 + o(n^3)$, with stretch factor at most 2.2.*

4.1.5 Compactness versus Buffers. A (k,s)-DFIRS (deadlock-free IRS) for a graph G is a k-IRS for G together with a deadlock-free controller of size s for G which covers the all-to-all single shortest path system induced by the k-IRS. As all controllers in DFIRS are based on the concept of acyclic orientation covering, the orientations of edges can be saved at nodes of degree δ with additional $O(\delta)$ bits.

We give upper bounds on the trade-offs between the compactness and the size of deadlock-free controllers for certain well-known interconnection networks. The next results for hypercubes and tori are from [18].

Theorem 21. [18]

- *For every i $(1 \le i \le d)$ there exists a $(2^{i-1}, \lceil d/i \rceil + 1)$-DFLIRS for a d-dimensional hypercube.*
- *For every n and i $(1 < i < d)$ there exists a $(\lceil n^i/2 \rceil, 2 \cdot \lceil d/i \rceil + 1)$-DFLIRS on a d-dimensional torus.*

Note that when we consider linear interval routing schemes on d-dimensional hypercubes, the size $d + 1$ can be obtained with compactness 1, and the reduction to size 2 can be achieved with the compactness 2^{d-1}. G. Tel [50] posed the question whether it is possible to obtain the shortest path system induced by a (linear) interval routing scheme, which uses only two buffers per node for deadlock-free packet routing. We argue that there is no deadlock-free linear interval routing scheme (based on acyclic orientations) on a d-dimensional hypercube of the compactness 1 and size 2.

When we consider linear interval routing schemes on d-dimensional tori, the size $2d+1$ can be obtained with the compactness 2, and the restriction to the size 5 can be achieved with the compactness $O(n^{d-1})$. As there exists a deadlock-free controller of size 4 for the optimal packet routing on a d-dimensional tori, it remains an open question the existence of a better deadlock-free IRS.

4.2 Multi–Dimensional Interval Routing Schemes

Multi-dimensional interval routing schemes (MIRS for short) are an extension of interval routing schemes. In (k,d)-MIRS every node is labeled by a unique d-tuple $(l_1, ..., l_d)$, where each l_i is from the set $\{1, ..., n_i\}$ ($1 \leq n_i \leq n$). Each arc is labeled by up to k d-tuples of cyclic intervals $(I_{1,1}, ..., I_{d,1}), ..., (I_{1,k}, ..., I_{d,k})$. In any node a message with destination $(l_1, ..., l_d)$ is routed along any outgoing arc containing a d-tuple of cyclic intervals $(I_1, ..., I_d)$ such that $l_i \in I_i$ for all i. In this case, multiple paths are represented by the scheme, so the intervals on the arcs of a given node may overlap, i.e. they do not form a partition of the nodes in V.

As noted, MIRS can be multipath. A routing based on a multipath routing scheme must choose one arc from the suggested one. If a scheme represents all shortest paths it is called *full-information* shortest path routing scheme.

4.2.1 Compactness.
The upper and lower bounds in Theorem 10 apply also to multi–dimensional interval routing.

4.2.1.1 All-to-all All Shortest Paths Multi-Dimensional Schemes
The first study of space complexity of multi-dimensional schemes appeared in [19].

Theorem 22. [19]

- *For trees, rings and complete graphs there exist full-information shortest path (1, 1)-MIRS.*
- *For complete bipartite graphs there exist full-information shortest path (2, 1)-MIRS.*
- *For every n and i, $1 \leq i \leq d$, there exists a full-information shortest path $(n^{i-1}, \lceil d/i \rceil)$-MIRS on a d-dimensional torus.*
- *For each i, $1 \leq i \leq d$, there exists a full-information shortest path $(\lceil 2^{i-1}/i \rceil, \lceil d/i \rceil)$-MIRS for a d-dimensional hypercube.*

Further study has been presented in [44].

Theorem 23. [44]

- *For a d-dimensional butterfly there exists a full-information shortest path* (2, 3)-*MIRS.*
- *For a d-dimensional CCC there exists a full-information shortest path* $(2d^3, d)$-*MIRS.*

The question remains to determine the parameters of MIRS for star graphs.

DIS and CONS models. A (k, d)-MIRS is denoted in [19] as (k, d)-DIS-MIRS. They also introduced slightly modified CON-MIRS model. In (k, d)-CON-MIRS every node is labeled by a unique d-tuple $(l_1, ..., l_d)$, where each l_i is from the set $\{1, ..., n_i\}$ $(n_i \leq n)$. Each arc is labeled by d-tuple of up to k cyclic intervals

$$(\{I_{1,1}, ..., I_{1,k}\}, ..., \{I_{d,1}, ..., I_{d,k}\}).$$

In any node, a message with destination $(l_1, ..., l_d)$ is routed along any outgoing arc such that for all i the label l_i is contained in the union of intervals in the i-th dimension.

If a graph G has a (k, d)-CON-MIRS, then it has a $(1, k \cdot d)$-MIRS with the same memory requirements per node and the same routing paths. The converse does not hold (as an example we can take full-information shortest path routing on cube connected cycles).

It is known that shortest path routing imposes high memory requirements for any routing scheme. There exist graphs, for which each (k, d)-CON-MIRS and (k, d)-DIS-MIRS requires $k \cdot d = \Omega(n/\log n)$.

In [44] it was shown that the DIS-MIRS model is asymptotically stronger than the CON-MIRS model when considering memory requirements of the full-information shortest path routing schemes of cube connected cycles.

Theorem 24. [44] *For a full-information (k, d)-CON-MIRS of CCC_m graph the following bound holds on k and d:*

$$k \cdot d = \Omega(2^{\sqrt{m/2}})$$

We recall the result of Theorem 23 that for CCC_m, there exists a $(2m^3, m)$-DIS-MIRS with the length of labels $m^2 + m \log m + O(m)$ bits and memory required per node $O(m^5)$ bits.

Even better lower bound has been proved for Cayley graphs.

Theorem 25. [44] *For a full-information (k, d)-CON-MIRS of S_m graph, the following bound holds on k and d:*

$$k \cdot d = \Omega(2^{m/3})$$

The main problem remains to develop effective lower bound technique on $k \cdot d$ also for DIS-MIRS model.

4.2.2 Compactness versus Congestion. There are just few results about multipath MIRS with (asymptotically) optimal congestion on special networks.

Theorem 26. [44] *There exists a multipath* $(2, d + 2)$-*MIRS on* CCC_d *with asymptotically optimal congestion* $(1 + O(\frac{\log d}{d})) \cdot \pi$, *where* π *is the forwarding index of* CCC_d.

We give a trade-off between the congestion and the compactness of multipath MIRS for general graphs.

Theorem 27. [44] *For any graph* G *of maximum degree bounded by* Δ *with forwarding index* π *and a given* s, $1 \leq s \leq n$, *there exists a multipath* $(2 + \lceil n/2s \rceil, 1)$-*MIRS with congestion* $\pi + n\Delta s$.

As a consequence, for any planar graph of constant bounded degree there exists a multipath $(O(\sqrt{n}), 1)$-MIRS with asymptotically optimal congestion.

The previous result is based on the fact that the schemes are multipaths. A natural question arises whether a similar result is possible for deterministic routing schemes too. A positive answer to this question is given below, using the probabilistic method.

Theorem 28. [44] *Let* G *be any connected graph of maximum degree* Δ *with forwarding index* π. *For any* s *such that* $1 \leq s \leq n$, *there exists a* $(2 + n/2s)$-*IRS with congestion* $\alpha \cdot \pi + n\Delta s$, *where* α *satisfies*

$$\left(\frac{e^{\alpha - 1}}{\alpha^\alpha} \right)^{\frac{\pi}{n\Delta s}} < \frac{1}{2n}$$

This theorem has an interesting consequence for planar graphs of bounded degree. For any planar graph, with degree bounded by a constant and with forwarding index π, there exists a $O(\sqrt{n} \log n)$-IRS with asymptotically optimal congestion $O(\pi)$.

4.2.4 Compactness versus Buffers. Efficient deadlock-free MIRS (DFMIRS for short) with respect to the compactness and the size (of buffers) on hypercubes, tori, butterflies and cube connected cycles have been presented in [35].

Theorem 29. [35]

- *For every* i $(1 \leq i \leq d)$ *there exists a* $((2^{i-1}, \lceil d/i \rceil), 2)$-*DFMIRS for a d-dimensional hypercube. (For* $i = 1$, *we obtain a* $((1, d), 2)$-*DFMIRS.)*
- *For every* n *and* i $(1 \leq i \leq d)$ *there exists a* $((n^{i-1}, \lceil d/i \rceil), 4)$-*DFMIRS on a d-dimensional tori. (For* $i = 1$, *we obtain* $((1, d), 4)$-*DFMIRS.)*
- *There is a* $((2, 3), 4)$-*DFMIRS on a d-dimensional butterfly.*
- *There is a* $((2d^3, d), 2d + 6)$-*DFMIRS on a d-dimensional cube connected cycles.*

The above results can be transformed also to an analogous wormhole routing model (as presented in [18]). These results give an evidence that for some well-known interconnection networks there are efficient deadlock-free multidimensional interval routing schemes despite of provable nonexistence of efficient deterministic (i.e. all-to-all single shortest-path) IRS (see lower bounds in Theorem 11). The main question remains whether there are efficient deadlock-free MIRS also for wider classes of graphs, e.g. vertex symmetric graphs, planar graphs, etc.

5 Conclusions

We have presented a survey of recent developments in the complexity of oblivious compact communication schemes in point-to-point networks. Further study of combinatorial properties of path systems can be helpful in the design of efficient communication schemes w.r.t. various efficiency parameters.

Unfortunately, we had to leave out several important lines of research in this area. One of these is the area of universal communication schemes and adaptive communication schemes in point- to-point networks.

Acknowledgements. I would like to thank Richard B. Tan and Daniel Štefankovič for many valuable comments on the manuscript.

References

1. B. Awerbuch, S. Kutten, D. Peleg: *Efficient Deadlock-Free Routing.* In Proceedings of ACM Symposium on Principles of Distributed Computing (PODC'91), 1991, pp. 177–188.
2. E. Bakker, J. van Leeuwen, R.B. Tan: *Linear interval routing schemes.* Algorithms Review 2, 1991, pp. 45–61.
3. P.E. Berman, L. Gravano, G.D. Pifarré, J.L.C. Sanz: *Adaptive Deadlock- and Livelock-Free Routing with All Minimal Paths in Torus Networks.* In Proceedings of the ACM Symposium on Parallel Algorithms and Architectures, 1992, pp. 3–12.
4. J.-C. Bermond, M. Di Ianni, M. Flammini, S. Pérennes: *Acyclic Orientations for Deadlock Prevention in Interconnection Networks.* In 23rd International Workshop on Graph-Theoretic Concepts in Computer Science (WG'97), Lecture Notes in Computer Science, Springer-Verlag, 1997.
5. H.L. Bodlaender, J. van Leeuwen, R.B. Tan, D. Thilikos: *On interval routing schemes and treewidth.* In 21st International Workshop on Graph-Theoretic Concepts in Computer Science (WG'95), Lecture Notes in Computer Science, Springer-Verlag, 1995.
6. A. Bouabdallah, D. Sotteau: *On the Edge Forwarding Index Problem for Small Graphs.* Networks 23, 1993, pp. 249–255.
7. F.R.K. Chung, E.G. Coffman, M.J. Reimann, B.E. Simon: *The forwarding index of communication networks.* IEEE Transactions on Information Theory 33, 1987, pp. 224–232.

8. S. Cicerone, G. Di Stefano, M. Flammini: *Static and Dynamic Low-Congested Interval Routing Schemes.* In 25th International Colloquium ICALP'98, Lecture Notes in Computer Science 1443, Springer-Verlag, 1998, pp. 592–603.

9. R. Cypher: *Minimal, Deadlock-Free Routing in Hypercubic and Arbitrary Networks.* Proceedings of the 7th IEEE Symposium on Parallel and Distributed Processing, 1995.

10. R. Cypher, L. Gravano: *Requirements for Deadlock-Free, Adaptive Packet Routing.* SIAM Journal of Computing 23 (6), 1994, pp. 1266–1274.

11. R. Cypher, L. Gravano: *Storage-Efficient, Deadlock-Free Packet Routing Algorithms for Torus Networks.* IEEE Transactions on Computers 43 (12), 1994, pp. 1376–1385.

12. R. Cypher, F. Meyer auf der Heide, C. Scheideler, B. Vöcking: *Universal algorithms for store-and-forward and wormhole routing.* In Proceedings of the 28th Annual ACM Symposium on Theory of Computing, 1996, pp. 356–365.

13. W.J. Dally, C.L. Seitz: *Deadlock-free message routing in multiprocessor interconnection networks.* IEEE Transactions on Computers, C-36, 1987, pp. 547–553.

14. J. Duato: *Deadlock-Free Adaptive Routing Algorithms for Multicomputers: Evaluation of a New Algorithm.* In 3rd IEEE Symposium on Parallel and Distributed Processing, 1991.

15. T. Eilam, C. Gavoille, D. Peleg: *Compact Routing Schemes with Low Stretch Factor.* LaBRI, Université Bordeaux I, 33405 Talence CEDEX, France, 1998. Submitted for publication.

16. T. Eilam, S. Moran, S. Zaks: *A lower bound for linear interval routing.* In 10th International Workshop on Distributed Algorithms (WDAG'96), Lecture Notes in Computer Science 1151, Springer-Verlag, 1996.

17. T. Eilam, S. Moran, S. Zaks: *The complexity of the characterization of networks supporting shortest-path interval routing.* In 4th International Colloquium on Structural Information and Communication Complexity (SIROCCO'97), 1997.

18. M. Flammini: *Deadlock-Free Interval Routing Schemes.* In 14th Annual Symposium on Theoretical Aspects of Computer Science (STACS), Lecture Notes in Computer Science 1200, Springer-Verlag, 1997, pp. 351–362.

19. M. Flammini, G. Gambosi, U. Nanni, R.B. Tan: *Multi-Dimensional Interval Routing Schemes.* In 9th International Workshop on Distributed Algorithms (WDAG), Lecture Notes in Computer Science, Springer-Verlag, 1995. To appear in Theoretical Computer Science.

20. M. Flammini, G. Gambosi, U. Nanni, R.B. Tan: *Characterization results of all shortest paths interval routing schemes.* In 5th International Colloquium on Structural Information and Communication Complexity (SIROCCO'98), Carleton Press, 1998.

21. M. Flammini, E. Nardelli: *On the path length in interval routing schemes.* Submitted for publication.

22. M. Flammini, J. van Leeuwen, A. Marchetti-Spaccamela: *The complexity of interval routing on random graphs.* In 20th International Symposium on Mathematical Foundations of Computer Science (MFCS'95), Lecture Notes in Computer Science 969, Springer-Verlag, 1995, pp. 37–49.

23. P. Fragniaud, C. Gavoille: *Interval Routing Schemes.* Research Report 94-04, LIP, Ecole Normale Superieure de Lyon, 69364 Lyon Cedex 07, France, 1994. To appear in Algorithmica.

24. G. N. Frederickson, R. Janardan: *Designing networks with compact routing tables.* Algorithmica 3, 1988, pp. 171–190.

25. C. Gavoille: *A Survey on Interval Routing Schemes.* Research Report RR-1182-97, LaBRI, Université Bordeaux I, October 1997. Submitted for publication.
26. C. Gavoille: *On the Dilation of Interval Routing.* In 22nd International Symposium on Mathematical Foundations of Computer Science (MFCS'97), Lecture Notes in Computer Science 1295, Springer-Verlag, 1997, pp. 259–268.
27. C. Gavoille, E. Guévremont: *Worst case bounds for shortest path interval routing.* Journal of Algorithms 27, 1998, pp. 1–23.
28. C. Gavoille, D. Peleg: *The Compactness of Interval Routing.* LaBRI, Université Bordeaux I, 33405 Talence CEDEX, France, 1997. Submitted for publication.
29. C. Gavoille, S. Pérennes: *Lower Bounds for Interval Routing on 3-Regular Networks.* In 3rd International Colloquium on Structural Information and Communication Complexity (SIROCCO'96), Carleton Press, 1996, pp. 88–103.
30. I.S. Gopal: *Prevention of Store-and-Forward Deadlock in Computer Networks.* IEEE Transactions on Communications 33 (12), 1985, pp. 1258–1264.
31. K.D. Günther: *Prevention of Deadlocks in Packet-Switched Data Transport Systems.* IEEE Transactions on Communications 29 (4), 1981.
32. M.C. Heydemann, J.C. Meyer, D. Sotteau: *On Forwarding Indices of Networks.* Discrete Applied Mathematics 23, 1989, pp. 103–123.
33. M.C. Heydemann, J.C. Meyer, D. Sotteau, J. Opatrny: *Forwarding Indices of Consistent Routings and Their Complexity.* Networks 24, 1994, pp. 75–82.
34. R. Královič: *Optimal 1-IRS on 8-directional meshes.* Unpublished manuscript, 1995.
35. R. Královič, B. Rovan, P. Ružička, D. Štefankovič: *Efficient Deadlock-free Multidimensional Interval Routing in Interconnection Networks.* In Distributed Computing (DISC'98), Lecture Notes in Computer Science, Springer-Verlag, 1998.
36. R. Královič, P. Ružička, D. Štefankovič: *The Complexity of Shortest Path and Dilation Bounded Interval Routing.* In 3rd International Euro-Par Conference, Lecture Notes in Computer Science 1300, Springer-Verlag, August 1997, pp. 258–265. Full version will appear in Theoretical Computer Science.
37. E. Kranakis, D. Krizanc, S.S. Ravi: *On multi-label linear interval routing schemes.* In 19th International Workshop on Graph-Theoretic Concepts in Computer Science (WG'93), Lecture Notes in Computer Science 790, Springer-Verlag, 1993, pp. 338–349.
38. T. Leighton: *Introduction to Parallel Algorithms and Architectures: Arrays, Trees, Hypercubes.* Morgan Kaufmann, San Mateo, CA, 1992.
39. P.M. Merlin, P.J. Schweitzer: *Deadlock avoidance in store-and-forward networks.* IEEE Transactions of Communications, COM-27, 1980, pp. 345–360.
40. L. Narayanan, S. Shende: *Characterization of networks supporting shortest-path interval labeling schemes.* In 3rd International Colloquium on Structural Information and Communication Complexity (SIROCCO'96), Carleton University Press, 1996, pp. 73–87.
41. L. Narayanan, J. Opatrny: *Compact routing on chordal rings.* In 4th International Colloquium on Structural Information and Communication (SIROCCO'97), Carleton University Press, 1997.
42. G.D. Pifarré, L. Gravano, S.A. Felperin, J.L.C. Sanz: *Fully-Adaptive Minimal Deadlock-Free Packet Routing in Hypercubes, Meshes and Other Networks.* In Proceedings of the ACM Symposium on Parallel Algorithms and Architectures. 1991, pp. 278–290.
43. P. Ružička: *On efficiency of interval routing algorithms.* In 13th International Symposium on Mathematical Foundations of Computer Science (MFCS'88), Lecture Notes in Computer Science 324, Springer-Verlag, 1988, pp. 492–500.

44. P. Ružička, D. Štefankovič: *On the Complexity of Multi-Dimensional Interval Routing Schemes*. Submitted for publication.

45. R. Saad: *Complexity of the forwarding index problem*. SIAM Journal of Discrete Mathematics 1995.

46. N. Santoro, R. Khatib: *Labelling and implicit routing in networks*. The Computer Journal 28, 1985, pp. 5–8.

47. P. Solé: *Expanding and Forwarding*. Discrete Applied Mathematics 58, 1995, pp. 67–78.

48. D. Štefankovič: *Acyclic Orientations do not Lead to Optimal Deadlock-free Packet Routing Algorithms*. Submitted for publication.

49. F. Shahrokhi, L. Szekely: *An algebraic approach to the uniform concurrent multicommodity flow problem: theory and applications*. Research report CRPDC-91-4, University of North Texas, 1991.

50. G. Tel: *Introduction to Distributed Algorithms. (Chapter 5: Deadlock-free Packet Routing)*. Cambridge University Press, Cambridge, U.K., 1994.

51. S. Toueg: *Deadlock-free and livelock-free packet switching networks*. In Proceedings of Symposium on Theory of Computing (STOCS), 1980, pp. 94–99.

52. S. Toueg, K. Steiglitz: *Some Complexity Results in the Design of Deadlock-Free Packet Switching Networks*. SIAM Journal of Computing 10 (4), 1981, pp. 702–712.

53. S. Toueg, J. Ullman: *Deadlock-free packet switching networks*. SIAM Journal of Computing 10, 1981, pp. 594–611.

54. S.S.H. Tse, F.C.M. Lau: *Lower bounds for multi-label interval routing*. In 2nd International Colloquium on Structural Information and Communication Complexity (SIROCCO'95), Carleton University Press, 1995, pp. 123–134.

55. S.S.H Tse, F.C.M. Lau: *An Optimal Lower Bound for Interval Routing in General Networks*. In 4th International Colloquium on Structural Information and Communication Complexity (SIROCCO'97), Carleton University Press, 1997.

56. J. van Leeuwen, R.B. Tan: *Interval Routing*. The Computer Journal 30, 1987, pp. 298–307.

57. J. van Leeuwen, R.B. Tan: *Compact routing methods: A survey*. In 1st International Colloquium on Structural Information and Communication Complexity (SIROCCO), Carleton Press, 1994, pp. 99–110.

58. J. Vounckx, G. Deconinck, R. Lauwereins, J.A. Peperstraete: *Deadlock-free Fault Tolerant Wormhole Routing in Mesh-Based Massively Parallel Systems*. In Technical Committee on Computer Architecture (TCCA) Newsletter, IEEE Computer Society, Summer-Fall issue, 1994, pp. 49–54.

59. J. Vounckx, G. Deconinck, R. Cuyvers, R. Lauwereins: *Minimal Deadlock-free Compact Routing in Wormhole-Switching based Injured Meshes*. In Proceedings of the 2nd Reconfigurable Architectures Workshop, Santa Barbara, Ca, 1995.

Audit of Information Systems:
The Need for Cooperation

Leon Strous[1]

De Nederlandsche Bank NV, Internal Auditing Department,
Westeinde 1, 1017 ZN, Amsterdam, The Netherlands
strous@iaehv.nl

Abstract. The purpose of auditing an information system is to assess, among others for the organisations' management, that the system functions in the way it was intended. Because of the speed of developments in technology and the increasing complexity of infrastructures and information systems, auditing information systems is becoming more and more difficult. Knowledge of many aspects of information technology is required in order to give an opinion on the quality of information systems. Since it is nearly impossible to combine all this expertise in one person, co-operation between several disciplines is necessary. This paper will give an introduction to the different aspects of it-auditing in general and will demonstrate the difficulties that it-auditors face when, for example, auditing an electronic commerce system. It will indicate the need for co-operation and it will be concluded by suggesting solutions for the auditors' problems.

1 Introduction

1.1 IT-Auditing

IT-auditing (also referred to as ict-auditing, edp-auditing or information systems auditing) is a relatively new profession. That is one of the reasons why many definitions for IT-auditing exist, which is not uncommon also in other areas of information technology. One of these definitions is:

"An IT-audit is an independent and impartial assessment of the reliability, security (including privacy), effectiveness and efficiency of automated information systems, the organisation of the automation department and the technical and organisational infrastructure of the automated information processing. This activity applies to both operational systems and systems under development."

---

[1] This paper is written on a personal basis and in no way represents the opinion of De Nederlandsche Bank NV.

There are three sets of keywords in this definition:
- *Independent and impartial.* This means that the person(s) performing the audit must not have a hierarchical relationship with the auditees or in any other way depend on them (e.g. financially).
- *Reliability, security, effectiveness and efficiency.* These are the so-called quality aspects. In the audit and security literature many different sets of terms can be found. Usually they all cover the same aspects only in a different decomposition.
- *Information systems, automation department and infrastructure.* These are the three possible objects of audits. The infrastructure is the technical as well as the organisational infrastructure.

1.2 Quality Aspects

As said in the previous paragraph, many sets of terms exist for the quality aspects of information technology. For example, according to the Dutch Association of Registered EDP-Auditors (NOREA) an IT-auditor assesses and advises on the following aspects of information technology: effectiveness; efficiency; exclusiveness; integrity; auditability; continuity; controllability.

A more wellknown set of terms is CIA (confidentiality, integrity and availability), often completed with auditibality. It is important that an organisation defines its' set of terms to make sure that everybody has a good understanding of what is covered by each term. In the aim and scope of each audit has to be described what quality aspects will be taken into consideration in that particular audit, e.g. only efficiency or a subset of the security terms.

1.3 Objects of Audit / Types of Audit

The three objects of audit (information systems, automation department and infrastructure) can be refined. Depending on the object of the audit a different type of audit will be performed with different skills / expertise required from the auditor. The following types of audit can be distinguished:
- Computer centre (or data processing centre) audit, performed by the computer centre auditor;
- Technical (hardware, systemsoftware, middleware, datacommunication components) audit, performed by the technical auditor;
- System development audit and audit of selection of software packages, performed by the information system auditor;
- Pre- and post-implementation application system audits also performed by the information system auditor.

1.4 Information Processing Environment

The relationship between the audit objects can be illustrated by a figure [10] that has been derived from a figure used in a publication by the Royal Dutch Institute of Chartered Accountants [6]. The figure originates from a centralised (mainframe) information processing environment, but by referring to functions rather than to departments, the figure is also applicable to decentralised or distributed information processing environments.

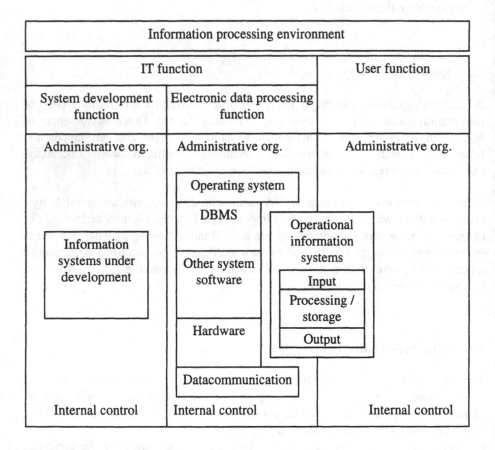

Fig. 1. Information processing environment

1.5 Types of Controls

Generally, the measures to meet the security requirements that are set by an organisation, are divided in three types:
- general controls;
- application controls;
- user controls.

General controls are measures that work for all (or at least for most) applications and they can be found in the automation department (both the development function and the data processing centre) and in the infrastructure. These are organisational controls as well as technical controls in hardware and system software (including middleware, tools and datacommunication components).

Application controls are specific programmed controls in one application system. Usually they are specific for the business processes that are supported by the application.

User controls normally also are specific for one application (or a set of applications that support one business process). These are controls in the administrative organisation and the internal control structure of the user department.

2. Difficulties for IT-Auditors

2.1 Professional Requirements

An IT-auditor is an independent expert in the field of information technology and control theory. In order to meet standards set by professional audit organisations[2], he must have knowledge of:
- Internal control theories and concepts;
- Security principles and measures;
- Information technology (hardware, software, infrastructure);
- Financial/economical aspects of the control processes within an organisation (especially planning, budgeting, decisiontaking, etc.);
- Management and organisation theories;
- Administrative organisation and its models and systems;
- Methods and techniques that are available for performing effective it-audits;
- Generally accepted auditing standards and controlmethods and techniques;
- Knowledge of business processes.

---

[2] e.g. the Dutch Association of Registered EDP-Auditors [7]

Because developments in all these areas go very fast, it is difficult for an auditor to keep up in his own areas of expertise and it is practically impossible to keep pace with the developments in all areas.

2.2 Trends in Information Technology and Control Theories

Two of the most important areas of knowledge of an IT-auditor have shown major developments during recent years. These developments / trends require new knowledge, new approaches and new ways of thinking of an auditor. Everybody knows and can follow in many media the developments in information technology: internet, www, electronic commerce, java, SET, client/server applications, object oriented programming, data mining, integrated system management tools, datacommunication, new chiptechnologies, etc.

The second area where major changes can be seen is in control theories and auditing. International developments concerning internal control and corporate governance indicate that management has to become more aware and has to take more responsibility for the control of an organisation and the reporting on the internal control system. The trend is towards controlling processes rather than controlling products / components.

2.3 Need for Co-operation (1)

Looking at the enumerations in paragraph 2.1 and 2.2 it is obvious that, even within one organisation, too many aspects have to be dealt with in order for one IT-auditor to have all the necessary knowledge. Therefore, depending on the object of the audit, co-operation is necessary with:
- other IT-auditors;
- financial auditors (chartered accountants);
- IT-specialists;
- security specialists;
- software developers / engineers;
- etc.

3   Example: Electronic Commerce

As an example to illustrate the difficulties for an it-auditor, the following figure shows the many parties and components that can be involved in a cross-border electronic commerce trade transaction. This concerns a real business to business transaction and not e.g. the purchase of a book at Amazone by an individual. The transaction starts in Organisation X with an electronic order that is initiated in one of the business applications. This order is then translated into an electronic order message that is sent to the trading partner via the internal and external network. The trading partner delivers the goods and sends an electronic invoice to the organisation X. Organisation X pays the invoice by means of electronic banking. To keep this example simple, we will not take into consideration the possible involvement of a trusted third party / certification authority or a third party service provider.

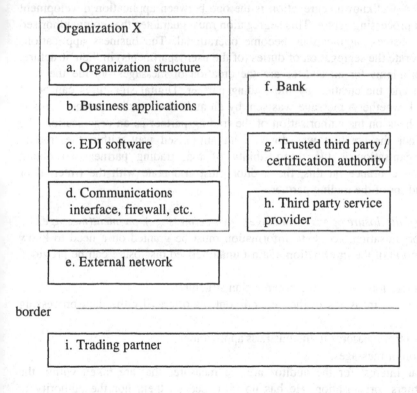

Fig. 2. Parties and components involved in an electronic commerce trade transaction

We are going to look at this transaction from the viewpoint of the internal IT-auditor of Organisation X. What are the consequences for the auditor when management asks the simple question: Is the trade transaction and the processing of it reliable?

The auditor will have to decompose the term reliable in other quality aspects, e.g. authorised, correct and timely. This makes it easier to relate the quality aspects to threats and in that way to necessary measures. In the whole process of the trade transaction a number of threats exist that can occur in various parties or components. In the following list of threats, for each threat a reflection will be given on possible causes and on consequences for the auditor. These reflections do not pretend to be exhaustive and are only intended to illustrate the many different aspects an auditor encounters.

Unauthorised creation or change of an order(message), invoice(message), payment(message)

If the organisation structure does not have an adequate segregation of duties (formalised and approved), the unauthorised creation or change of an order is a real risk. This does not only effect the user departments but also the automation department. A wellknown segregation is the one between application development and the data processing centre. This segregation must guarantee that no unauthorised changes in business applications become operational. The business applications must incorporate the segregation of duties (of the userdepartments) in their structure. Particular problems for an auditor are the creation of messages outside the own organisation and the creation by the trading partner. Digital signatures can be of help to check whether a message was sent by an authorised trading partner. This is however a check on the authorisation of the trading partner as an organisation, the check whether the creation was done in an authorised way within the trading partners' organisation is the responsibility of that trading partner. To obtain information / assurance on this, the auditor must cooperate with the (internal or external) auditor of the trading partner.

Unauthorised disclosure of order(message), invoice(message), payment(message)

Within an organisation, access to information must be granted on a need to know basis. Protection of the information against unauthorised disclosure can be provided by:

- the authorizationmatrix in the organisation structure;
- access control measures in the general controls offered by the data processing centre;
- access control measures in the business applications;
- encryption of messages.

Of particular interest for the auditor are the measures that are taken within the trading partners' organisation. He has no influence on them nor the authority to assess their quality himself. Therefore he has to cooperate with the internal or external auditor of the trading partner.

Unauthorised deletion of order(message), invoice(message), payment(message)

On several occasions when records and messages are stored (e.g. after processing by a business application or after message translation), there is a risk of unauthorised deletion, either intentionally (e.g. to conceal fraudulent transactions) or accidentally (e.g. because of wrong parameter settings concerning retention periods).

The auditor has to be sure that not only appropriate measures exist to prevent the unauthorised deletion, but also measures to detect and restore such a deletion.

Unauthorised processing of a message
The receipt of authorised messages, meaning that they are sent by legitimate, acknowledged trading partners, does not mean that such a message can be processed without further controls. The message must not have been received before, all necessary data elements must be correct, etc. This is the area of edi software (message translation) and application controls in the business applications. The auditor has to check that the necessary controls are built in and that they function correctly.

Denial of sending a message
Both Organisation X and the trading partner must have means to proof that the other party did send a message. If for example the trading partner claims to have received an ordermessage and Organisation X denies to have sent it, technical measures must provide proof. Procedural measures, settled in a trade agreement, must exist for settling a dispute. Also retention periods play a role.

Denial of receiving a message
Denial of receiving a message can be caused by the wish to delay a process (like having to pay the invoice later) or by technical reasons (the message was really not received because it was sent to the wrong address). The auditor has to pay attention to the existence of an acknowledgement mechanism and to the correct address translation.

Claim of receiving a message that was not sent
The trading partner for instance can claim he has received an ordermessage that Organisation X says not to have sent. By means of digital signatures can be shown who is right. The auditor must assess the correct set-up and functioning of the digital signature scheme.

Delay in delivery of messages / Denial of service (availability network, other components)
Malfunctioning of hardware or software components can cause delay in delivery or denial of service. The auditor has to assure himself that for all components, if necessary, back up and fallback measures exist.

Non-compliance with legal/fiscal requirements
In a situation (country) where electronic trade documents have a legal status and original paper documents are no longer required, the auditor must check whether the business applications meet legal and/or fiscal requirements (for example concerning record retention periods or accessibility of records).

In summary, before he can give an answer to the management's' question and thus giving an opinion on the reliability, the auditor has to assess (or rely upon):

- the user controls in the organisation structure;
- the general controls of the automation department;
- the application controls in the business application;
- the user controls around the business application;
- the general controls in the datacommunication infrastructure (including the electronic commerce software, interfaces, firewalls, etc.);
- the general controls concerning the external network;
- controls concerning the trading partner.

3.2 Additional Requirements for the Auditor

Besides the knowledge mentioned in paragraph 2.1 in this example the auditor also must have knowledge of:

- (inter)national legislation on e.g. legal status of electronic trade documents, record retention, data interchange agreements, etc.;
- (inter)national legislation on cryptography, digital signatures, etc.;
- specific IT / technical aspects:
  - strength of cryptographic algorithms used;
  - firewalls;
  - edi software / edi standards;
- evaluation / certification schemes in the country of the trading partner;
- trusted third parties / certification authorities.

3.3 Need for Co-operation (2)

In addition to paragraph 2.3, there is also a need for co-operation with:

- legal specialists
- cryptographers
- auditors of trading partner
- standards bodies
- edi organisations.

4 Possible Solutions

If an IT-auditor would have to seek co-operation with all the parties mentioned in paragraph 2.3 and 3.3 for each audit assignment, audits would take too long and become too expensive. In order to decrease the need for co-operation, a number of activities are possible. These activities have to be undertaken by both individuals and (professional) organisations.

It is emphasised that the need for co-operation is not only a necessity from the viewpoint of the auditor, but just as well it is a necessity for hardware/software developers/engineers to understand audit and control concepts and requirements.

Activities:
- Stimulate the setting up of and participating in working groups, task forces, etc. These working groups will have to study and report on specific issues or subjects. The results of such studies must be made available to all professionals. This must be done both on a national and an international level. Parties that have to play a role in this respect are professional organisations of engineers, auditors, etc. and computer societies.[3]
- Make research results (both universities and industry) broader and easier accessible, make them comprehensible for auditors.
- Make control and audit theories and techniques better-known to researchers and engineers. For example by including this subject in regular education and training programmes.
- Stimulate the use of independent security evaluations. It would be helpful if more technical components, products and systems would be available that are evaluated against generally accepted evaluation criteria (like the harmonised Common Criteria). An auditor would know what to expect from such a product and can make use of that knowledge for his overall judgement without having to perform the evaluation (audit) again.
- Stimulate and participate in the development of standards, both technical as well as procedural (guidelines). Stimulate the use of standards.
- Stimulate the development and use of benchmarks.

References

Following is a list of literature used as general background for this paper and literature used for specific parts. This is only a small selection from the many books and articles that have been written on audit and security of edi, electronic commerce, electronic money and internet.

1. Fred van Blommenstein, *Electronic Commerce, Internet en EDI*, Informatie, January 1998, pp. 14-25, (Dutch language)
2. several articles on Electronic Commerce / Internet Inroads, Communications of the ACM, Volume 39, nr. 6, June 1996.
3. *EDI Control Guide*, EDI Council of Australia / EDP Auditors Association, 1990, 46 pp.

---

[3] For example Working Group 11.5 of Technical Committee 11 of IFIP (the International Federation for Information Processing) organises an annual working conference aiming at having an ongoing dialogue between IT security specialists, internal control specialists (auditors), software/hardware developers and researchers at universities and industry laboratories on the subject of integrity and internal control in information Systems.

4. Linda Garceau / Victor Matos / Santosh K. Misra, *The use of Electronic Money in Electronic Commerce Systems*, IS Audit and Control Journal, Volume III, 1998, Information Systems Audit and Control Association (ISACA), pp. 14-24.

5. Belden Menkus, *Understanding security and audit issues in electronic document interchange*, EDPACS, July 1998, pp. 6-19.

6. Automatisering en Controle deel IV: Mededelingen door de Accountant met betrekking tot de betrouwbaarheid en continu•teit van geautomatiseerde gegevensverwerking. NIVRA Geschrift 26, Amsterdam, The Netherlands, 1982, (Dutch language).

7. Jaarboek 1997/98, Delwel, The Hague, The Netherlands, ISBN 90-6155-847-6, 1997, (Dutch language).

8. Pauline Ratnasingham, *EDI Security: the influences of trust on EDI security*, Computers & Security, volume 17 (1998), number 4, pp. 313-324.

9. William A. Stone, *Electronic Commerce: can internal auditors help to mitigate the risks?*, Internal Auditor, December 1997, pp. 28-34.

10. Leon Strous, *Integrity: definition, subdivision, challenge*, in: Integrity and Internal Control in Information Systems, Volume 1: Increasing the confidence in information systems, Sushil Jajodia et al. (eds.), IFIP / Chapman & Hall, ISBN 0-412-82600-3, 1997, pp. 187-194.

Towards the Use of Dynamic Documents in Business Processes

Christine Vanoirbeek

Swiss Federal Institute of Technolog
Computer Science Department
IN Ecublens
CH-1015 Lausanne, Switzerland
vanoirbeek@epfl.ch

Abstract. Traditional business processes are strongly impacted by the use of emerging information technology that provides new perspectives for strategy and relationship management between the main actors of electronic commerce. The fast-evolving World Wide Web plaftorm emphasizes the need for new paradigms to deal with complex information systems that meet the requirements of innovative economic models.
Integrated secure access to heterogenous information, knowledge publishing, and personnalized content delivery are important issues to be addressed. The paper concentrates on the advantages and limits brought by a document technology approach to deal with new levels of interaction and control in business information and communication systems.

1 Introduction

The rapid growth of the global information infrastructure, essentially organized around the fast evolving Internet and Word Wide Web environments, clearly alters the traditional social, political and economical aspects of the society. Conductlng business over the Internet is inconstestably a domain going through major developments, drastically changing relations between the various actors of electronic commerce. In order to cope with new strategic objectives allowing small and medium enterprises as well as larger organisations to compete in a global market, they need to rely on innovative business models deeply affecting their existing traditional organizational structures and processes.

A major aspect to be addressed is the design and implementation of effective communication and information systems answering the needs of new business processes[12]. The user-friendly and platform independant access to information, through World Wide Web browsers, emphasizes the necessity to provide mechanisms that allow integrated access and manipulation of heterogenous data shared between complex pieces of distributed software. During the last decade, developping applications over the Internet, that address those interoperability issues, has become of major concern for many communities of researchers such as those involved in design of open hypertexts [8], development of CORBA technology and integrated access to distributed databases, development of agent based systems and, definition and use of markup languages (SGML[1], HTML[16], XML[15]) to represent and exchange structured information.

The paper will focuse on the potential benefits to be brougth by the use of a so-called *structured document approach*, based on tagged representation of information, to address the interoperability issues in the framework of electronic commerce applications. The first part presents and summarizes relevant problems to be dealt with in the specific context of business processes, the second one is dedicated to the description of the underlying concepts and evolution of the document technology and, the third one discusses important key issues currently under investigation or to be addressed in future research works.

2 Information Systems in Business Processes

The current evolution of electronic commerce is indubitably promoting the development of an information-based economy emphasizing complex relations between business partners, consumers and administrations. In order to face increasing global competition and customer expectations, the companies are confronted with the redesign of business processes overcrossing their own organization and often jointly owned by the company and its customers or suppliers. The redefinition of such new processes rely on the access and processing of distributed interrelated piece of information where the use of document technology may bring some contributions.

Extensive use of documents - First, the wide variety of activities involved in electronic commerce already makes extensive use of numerous electronic documents: products and services description, project description, spreadsheet documents, mailing, contracts, financial, administrative or technical documents. Unfortunately, most of the documents rely on proprietary formats and exchange of information between different document processing systems remains a difficult problem. Standardization efforts (such as XML) opens attractive perpectives to deal with this problem.

Agent based market systems - In order to face the lack of information and communication structure of web-based electronic commerce applications, many works have been undertaken to develop open agent-based market systems. The paradigm of interacting agents relies on the use of sometimes complex messages to exchange knowledge between agents.

Development of complex Web based workflow - Workflow management systems provide an automated framework for handling complex business processes inside enterprises as well as interactions with economical partners. Many workflow management systems currently provide Web interfaces, unfortunately often limited to different proprietary workflow engines[5]. A combined use of XML and Java technologies could facilitate the implementation of transportable agent to enhance both platform independance and reusability beween processing applications.

Electronic data interchange - Exchange of electronic information in business to business activities has been of great importance for a long time. The EDI (Electronic Data Interchange) standard has been elaborated to answer those needs. The possibility of extending traditional EDI capabilities by the integrated use of XML to define self-describing messages is currently under investigation to facilitate the implementation of a wide range of processing operations such as, validate user input or routing document for workflow applications.

Internationalization - Another important issue relates to the multilingual feature of data, an aspect of the problem brought to light by a global access to information provided by the World Wide Web environment. In this respect, document technology may also bring a valuable contribution. An appropriate representation of the linguistic structure may considerably facilitate the consistency checking of multilingual versions of a document [4] [3].

3 Structuring Electronic Eocuments: an Evolving Technology

3.1 Representing Structured Documents

Designing electronic document models for the production of high quality typographical material has been the original aim of computer scientists involved in the structured document research area. Inspired by the traditional editorial and publishing processes, such models are based on a dual view of the document: *the logical structure* reflecting the author intentions, and the *physical structure*, close to the typographist perception of the document, allowing to specify the use of appropriate typographic resources for emphasizing the author's intentions.

In order to allow the generation of consistent documents and, thus, allowing enhanced processing operations, the concept of *document classes* has been introduced in order to adequately represent various types of documents.

Standardization efforts have been undertaken to facilitate the representation and exchange of such structured documents between various processing applications. SGML (Standard Generalized Markup Language), relying on an attribute grammar formalism to define document classes (DTD - Document Type Definition) and tagged data to represent documents instances, has been and is still used by publishing organisms which have to deal with complex and highly structured documents.

Customized SGML DTDs have been elaborated in order to agree on shared generic document models between specific communities of users or applications.

- The international standard ISO 12083 has been elaborated by the American Association of Publishers and the European Physical Society to provide standard methods for marking up scientific documents.
- CALS (Computer-aided Acquisition and Logistic Support) has been specified for the representation of technical documentation by the American Department of Defense.

- TEI (Text Encoding Initiative) is the result of a collaboration between several research international organisations in order to provide formal guidelines for the representation of textual linguistics documents [19].
- HTML (Hypertext Markup Language) is a well know application of SGML for the representation of documents on the World Wide Web.

The Text Encoding Initiative - The Text Encoding Initiative distinguishes from other DTDs design efforts on the measure that, it was the initial work aiming at providing guidelines for the modular conception of customized DTDs on the basis of an existing sets of logical components. The approach is based on the object oriented paragdigm and implemented by use of the SGML entities mechanism proposed in the SGML standard.

The definition of pre-existing elements are organized in terms of classes; each new element possibly inheriting from a content model and associated attributes.

3.2 Representing Hyperdocuments

The concept of electronic structured documents, initially considered as an abstract representation of their paper counterform, has evolved towards a more complex way of representing semantically rich interrelated pieces of information, so-called hypertext documents[11] [13]. Morevover, the nature of information contained in documents, especially the multimedia components such as sound and video, add a new temporal dimension to be dealt with in various applications.

The ISO standard HyTime (Hypermedia Time/Based Structuring Language) has been elaborated to encompass those important features of electronic documents[10]. HyTime is based on SGML; an SGML document may be considered as a HyTime document by use of the so-called Architectural Form, a mechanism inspired from the object oriented paradigm. HyTime introduces new concepts in order to extend the document model.

Roughly speaking, SGML provides a powerful mean of describing documents as a hierarchy of embedded logical components including cross-references in terms of uni-directional pointers. Additional logical non structural information may be defined by use of an attributes mechanism.

In essence, the HyTime philosophy is comparable to SGML; it provides a way to describe the logical content of documents without providing mechanisms to specify the nature of the processing itself. Those aspects are dealt with in another standard, DSSSL - Document Style Semantics Specification Language[9]. The main contributions of HyTime in comparison with SGML are the following:

- a better link model that allows to represent complex hyperdocuments
- a way of representing multimedia data
- a querying language (HyQ) to retrieve pieces of information into structured documents

The locator concept - In order to refer specific data objects in documents, Hy-Time provides the concept of a *locator* which allows to locate data according to three mechanisms: by *naming* (for example, an SGML identifier), by *counting* (for example, the ninth element of a list) and by *querying* (for example, the element whose attribute value is x). The following examples illustrate potential uses of such locators.

Linking parts of documents - HyTime defines two kinds of links: the contextual links (similar to the references mechanism proposed by SGML) and independant links to be used in numerous purposes such as annotating documents, linking multilingual versions of documents (see figure 1), representing complex hyper-links such as illustrated in figure 2.

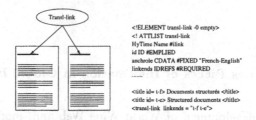

Fig. 1. Use of independant links to represent multilingual documents

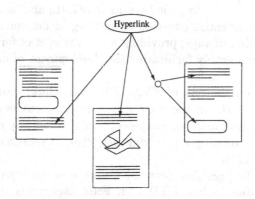

Fig. 2. Representation of complex hyperlinks

Representing a video sequence - To deal with multimedia components, HyTime proposes a model for space and time based on finite axes that each define an addressable range of quanta. Each quantum represents a discrete position along the axis and has a coordinate which must be a positive number. The figure 3 illustrates the definition of a multidimensional space allowing to address clipped regions of video sequences during a given period of time.

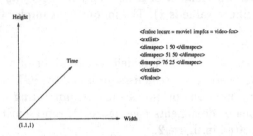

Fig. 3. HyTime multidimensional space representation

3.3 Documents as Pieces of Information in Global Information Systems

The considerable development of World Wide Web and, more specifically, the HTML application of SGML to represent hyperdocuments over the Internet clearly promoted the use of document technology to handle structured data flow of information whitin distributed environments. In this sense, the emergence of XML (Extended Markup Language), a W3c recommendation opens attractive perspectives for many reasons.

First, XML proposes a simplified syntax of SGML, abolishing particular features (such as the potential omission of end tag in documents instances, the potential abbreviation of tags, providing a specific syntax for empty elements, etc.) and, thus considerably facilitating the development of document oriented applications.

Secondly, the combination of XML, XSL and Xlink, integrates the major results of research works in the area of structured documents and hypertext: allowing the separation between document content and any related processing operation as well as offering a powerful formalism to represent complex multimedia hyperdocuments.

Finally, XML distinguishes between *well-formed documents* which are not necessarily associated with a DTD and, *valid documents* that conform to a generic model. This is an important aspect to address the interoperability issues between applications, promoting the independance in regard with proprietary exchange formats of documents.

As application of the emergent XML W3C recommendation, we may cite:

– MathML (Mathematical Markup Language), a W3C Recommendation for describing mathematical notation, aiming at capturing both its structure and contents[17].

– SMIL (Synchronized Multimedia Integration Language) has been designed
to specify hypermedia presentations taking into consideration spatial layout
and timing relations between multimedia components as well as hyperlinking
for time-based media[18].

The specification and evolution of markup languages (SGML, HyTime and
XML) progressively integrated state of the art of research in document and
hypertext representations. Figure 4 gives a synthetic presentation of the relations
between those standards and their application.

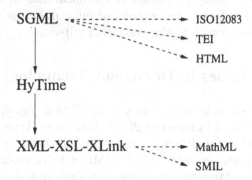

Fig. 4. Relations betweeen markup languages

Representing a video sequence - To summarize the considerations about the evolution of document technology; it appears that the role of electronic documents
in distributed information systems is gaining in importance. They have become
active pieces of information whose content is not only provided by the user but
altered by modifications of the environment (such as an update in a database);
they act as user interfaces (such as WWW forms); they also may be considered
as structured dataflow between various applications [14].

As a consequence, the abstract model of a document is no longer limited
to the editorial logical structure appropriate to print or for visualizing logical
components, but has to rely on an adequate representation to be dealt with by
several applications and users for multiple purposes.

Let us illustrate this idea in the specific business processes domain. An important aspect of electronic commerce is related to the notion of electronic market
mechanisms. As an example in this context, the traditional handling of requests
for proposals may be improved by the use of a flexible structured representation
of the information that takes into consideration the role to be played by various
actors in the decision process.

First, even if the specification of a request for proposal content depends on
the domain it relates to, a generic framework for the specification may be helpful

in many respects. Relying on an agreed established structure provides a powerful means to check the request validity: for example, in the computer science domain, checking consistency between administrative, technical and implementation requirements may be of crucial interest. It helps the clients in formulating their expectations accordingly to a schema that facilitates acurate answers from the suppliers. It finally gives the possibility to automatize, to a certain extent, the process of going through the analysis of answers.

Providing multiple customized partial views on the information is another important issue. An appropriate document model will allow the various actors in the clients organization to access relevant detailed or synthetized parts of the information; annotating his version of the documents or enhancing it with computed information from other sources of information, protecting access to confidential information such as the evaluation criteria.

4 Some Key Issues in Document Technology

Needs for modular representation of documents - The design of formal document descriptions, for instance in terms of SGML Document Type Definitions, often resulted in monolithic definitions of customized document classes, sometimes built in a modular way by use of the SGML entities mechanism. The Text Encoding Initiative addressed the problem of designing document models by taking the benefits of existing predefined document components and proposing explicit guidelines inspired by the object oriented paradigm.

The problem of reusing logical document components is obviously a major issue to be addressed for facing the the problem of interoperability. It is similar to the problem encountered in software engineering and an object oriented design may be considered as a promising approach to deal with those aspects.

In order to enhance the processing capabilities on documents, taking into consideration the structured description of micro structures is another important aspect. Identifying and representing acurately the structure of micro elements, such as dates, URLs or ISBN numbers is part of the problem. HyTime, for instance, introduces the concepts of lexical types to deal with this specific components[6].

Applying multiple structures to documents - The logical organisation of documents highly depends on the processing operations to be applied on them. The so called *logical editorial structure* aimed at describing an abstract representation of the document for multiple rendering purposes, is still the predominant structure in most of the document processing systems. Sharing documents between numerous different applications emphasizes the need of applying several logical structures on a same data content.

For instance, checking consistency between multilingual versions of documents requires a knowledge of the linguistic structure of the information. There is no isomorphism between the editorial subdivision of sentences into paragraphs and the linguistic structure of a document. The SGML standard specifies the possibility of applying concurrent structures on the documents by tagging documents instances accordingly to several DTDs; this feature has been eliminated in the XML specification.

Enhancing logical description of documents with attributes - The abstract structure of documents is not only based on structural properties; the use of attributes to provide additional logical information is another critical issue. The use of meta information, qualifying the documents content, is already used in multiple purposes. In a text processing system, specifying the language of documents components allows to apply appropriate language- dependant spelling ckeckers. In business applications, specifying appropriate rights access to portions of documents appears to be an important aspect of workflow management. Adding meta information in order to improve querying methods is another important use of attributes[7].

Integrating databases and documents - In business applications, highly structured informations have been for a while confined in databases. Promoted by the World Wide Web technology, the use of structured data flow of information is considerably gaining in importance. The problem of storing, accessing and updating them in an efficient and reliable way becomes an important aspect to be dealt with.

In this respect, databases technology offers mechanisms to provide secure and efficient access to information. Providing an appropriate representation of structured files into databases allowing functionalities such as concurrency control, querying and versioning is of major concern and needs to be investigated[2].

References

1. International Standard ISO 8879. *Information Processing - Text and Office Systems - Standard Generalized Markup Language (SGML)*. International Standard Organization, 1986.
2. S. Abiteboul, S. Cluet, and T. Milo. A logical view of structured files. Technical report, INRIA - Verso Project, Technical Report 143, 1997.
3. A. Ballim, G. Coray, A. Linden, and C. Vanoirbeek. The use of automatic alignment on structured multilingual documents. In *Electronic Publishing, Artistics Imaging and Digital Typography, St. Malo, France*, Lecture Notes in Computer Science. Springer, March/April 1998.
4. M. Bryan. Linking html translations. In *WWW Conference, Internationalization Workshop, Paris*, May 1996.
5. T. Cai, P. Gloor, and S. Nog. Dart flow: A workflow management system on the web using tranportable agents. Technical report, Technical Report, Dartmouth College, 1997.
6. S. J. DeRose and D. G. Durand. *Making Hypermedia Work*. Kluwer Academic Publisher, 1994.
7. F. Fourel, P. Mulhem, and M.-F. Bruandet. Dynamic properties of attributes for structured document access. In *International Symposium on Digital Media Information Base (DMIB'97), Nara, Japan*, 1997.

8. K. Gronbaek and R. H. Trigg. Toward a dexter-based model for open hypermedia: Unifying embedded references and link objects. In *Proceedings of the 7th Conference on Hypertext*, March 16-20 1996.

9. ISO. *ISO/IEC DIS 10179.2:1994 Information Technology - Text and Office Systems - Document Style Semantics and Specification Language (DSSSL)*. International Standard Organization, 1994.

10. ISO/IEC JTC1/SC18/WG8 N1920. *Information Technology: Hypermedia/ Time-based Structuring Language (HyTime), second edition*. ISO/IEC, 1997.

11. M. Nanard and J. Nanard. Using structured types to incorporate knowledge in hypertext. In *Proceeding of the ACM Conference on Hypertext*, pages 329–343, December 1991.

12. Y. Pigneur. A framework for designing new information systems. In *The future of information systems: challenges and pitfalls*. University of Namur, Belgium, October 25-26 1996.

13. V. Quint and I. Vatton. Combining hypertext and structured documents in grif. In *Proceedings of the ACM European Conference on Hypertext (ECHT'92*, pages 23–32, Milano, Italy, November 1992.

14. V. Quint and I. Vatton. Making structured documents active. *Electronic Publishing - Origination, Dissemination and Design*, 7(2):55–74, June 1994.

15. W3C Recommendation. *Extensible Markup Language (XML) 1.0*. http://w3.org/TR/1998/REC-xml-19980210, 1998.

16. W3C Recommendation. *HTML 4.0 Specification*. http://www.w3.org/TR/REC-html40/, 1998.

17. W3C Recommendation. *Mathematical Markup Language (MathML) 1.0 Specification*. http://www.w3g.org/TR/REC-MathML, 1998.

18. W3C Recommendation. *Synchronized multimedia Integration Language (SMIL) 1.0 Specification*. http:// wwww.w3.org/TR/REC-smil, 1998.

19. TEI. *Text Encoding Initiative*. University of Illinois at Chicago, USA, 1998.

Computational Power of BSP Computers*

Martin Beran

Faculty of Mathematics and Physics
Malostranské nám. 25, 118 00 Praha 1, the Czech Republic
beran@ss1000.ms.mff.cuni.cz

Abstract. We show how the speed of a BSP (Bulk Synchronous Parallel) computer depends on the parameters p, g, and l of the model. According to the values of parameters, BSP belongs among the first (sequential) or the second (parallel) class models or neither of these classes. The relation between BSP and the class of weak parallel machines is also examined. It turns out that BSP does not fit to the concept of weak (or pipelined) parallelism. Consequences of membership in different machine classes to the physical feasibility of BSP computers are discussed. The main conclusion is that BSP with parameters properly chosen qualifies itself as a practical model, but it is unable to exploit all the parallelism allowed by laws of physics.

1   Introduction

One of the main aims of the research in the area of parallel computing is searching for a good model of parallel computers. Such a model is necessary for design and complexity analysis of parallel algorithms [6]. There is also need for a model which would allow development of a parallel complexity theory better connected to practical parallel computers then the classical theory based on the PRAM model [5, 7]. In past, two main branches of models emerged. Massively parallel algorithms are usually designed for a simple but unrealistic PRAM model. This model is also often used in the complexity theory of parallel algorithms. On the other hand, when developing parallel programs on really existing parallel computers, programmers use models specific for a concrete architecture. Such programs are efficient but they cannot be easily ported to another type of computer. Researchers recognized the need of a *bridging model* of parallel computation. Such a model should serve as a common standard in the same way as von Neumann's machine is used in the sequential computing. Valiant [9] introduced the *bulk-synchronous parallel (BSP)* computer as a candidate for being a bridging model. In BSP, computation runs in *supersteps* on p processors. There are only two other parameters l (communication latency and barrier synchronization time) and g (network bandwidth). The BSP model has been accepted by scientists and programmers, many papers on BSP algorithms were

* This research was partly supported by the grant of the GA CR No. 201/98/0717, by the EU grant INCO-COOP 96-0195 'ALTEC-KIT', and by the grant of the Ministry of Education of CR No. OK-304.

published, research groups were formed [4, 8] and the model was implemented on a broad range of parallel computers. McColl [6] argues that BSP is a good model for general purpose parallel computing because it achieves scalable parallel performance and provides a platform for architecture-independent parallel software.

Van Emde Boas [10] defined the first and the second machine classes. The first class contains the deterministic Turing machine and all the other models which are polynomially time-equivalent and linearly space-equivalent to the Turing Machine. This class is often understood as the class of sequential computers. Machines belonging to the first class are physically feasible, i.e. they can be realized efficiently even when physical limitations (like the speed of light) are taken into account. On the other hand, machines for which time is polynomially equivalent to space of the Turing Machine form the second class. Its members are various kinds of massively parallel machines (PRAM) or they are not deterministic (alternating Turing machine). The disadvantage of the second class machines is their physical infeasibility. Wiedermann [11] introduced the class of weak parallel machines represented by the pipelined parallel Turing machine. Weak parallel machines are physically feasible, slower than members of the second class, but faster than the computers from the first class. Their period (time between starting processing two inputs in a sequence of inputs) is polynomially equivalent to space used on a Turing Machine.

In this paper, we study how the BSP model relates to the above mentioned three machine classes. We show that its computational power depends on values of the BSP parameters p, g, and l. When adding more processors, communication and synchronization become more complicated. So we assume g and l to be functions of the number of processors p. Section 2 gives definitions of BSP and the machine classes and some technical lemmas. Membership of BSP in the first and the second machine class is analyzed in Sect. 3. A BSP computer belongs to the first class for $g(p), l(p) = \Omega(p^a)$ and to the second class for $g(p), l(p) = O(\log^b p)$, where a and b are arbitrary positive constants. With an additional assumption about the relations between complexity classes we can set the parameters so that the resulting computer belongs neither to the first nor to the second class, as is proved in Sect. 4. It does not even belong to the class of weak parallel machines. Section 5 shows that BSP is either too slow (member of the first class) or unrealistically fast (member of the second class) to exploit the potential of physically feasible parallelism represented by the class of weak parallel machines. The concluding Sect. 6 discusses implications for practical usability of the BSP model.

2 Preliminaries

At first we define the BSP computer. Then we present definitions of the first, the second, and the weak parallel machine classes. At the end of this section we give, without proofs, some basic technical lemmas.

Definition 1. The Bulk Synchronous Parallel (BSP) computer *[6, 9] consists of p processors with local memories. Every processor is a RAM with the logarithmic cost. The computation runs in* supersteps. *In the beginning, at most* $\min\{p, O(n)\}$ *processors are active, n denotes the problem size. The input is spread across the local memories of initially active processors. Additional processors can be activated by sending messages to processors which are inactive till this time. During a superstep, processors do computation with locally held data and perform an h-relation, i.e. they send point-to-point messages to other processors so that no processor sends nor receives more than h bits. Supersteps are separated by a barrier synchronization. All messages sent during a superstep are available in their destinations in the beginning of the next superstep.*

The time complexity *of the i-th superstep is* $T_i = w_i + h_i g + l$, *where* w_i *is the maximum amount of computational operations in a processor,* h_i *is the maximum number of bits sent or received by any processor, g is the time spent by sending or receiving a message, and l is the time of the barrier synchronization. The* time complexity of the whole computation *of S superstep is* $T = \sum_{i=1}^{S} T_i$. *We define the* space complexity *of a BSP computer as the sum of space consumed by all the processors.*

We will usually assume that p is potentially unlimited, i.e. that we have exactly as many processors as we need for a particular computation, although only some of them may be active in the beginning of the computation. In such a case p is a function of the problem size n. Performing communication and synchronization is more difficult for larger number of processors. So g and l are not generally constants, but non-decreasing functions of p. In further text, we will denote a BSP computer with particular values of p, g, and l as $\mathrm{BSP}(p, g, l)$. The linear upper limit for the number of initially active processors allows the input to be read in parallel.

Definition 2. The first machine class C_1 *[10] contains the deterministic Turing Machine (DTM) and all the machines which are polynomially time-equivalent and linearly space-equivalent to DTM. Time and space bounds need not be reached by the same simulation.*

Definition 3. The second machine class C_2 *[10] is the class of computational devices with the time complexity polynomially equivalent to the space complexity of DTM.*

Definition 4. The class of weak parallel machines C_{weak} *[11] contains machines with* period *(time between beginnings of processing of two subsequent inputs) polynomially equivalent to the space complexity of DTM.*

Examples of members of C_1 are (multihead and multitape) deterministic Turing Machines and the RAM with the logarithmic cost. The second class contains e.g. the alternating Turing Machine [2] and SIMDAG (also called PRAM) [3, 6]. A representative of the C_{weak} machines is the pipelined parallel Turing Machine [11]. The power of weak parallel computers is in fast processing of (long) sequences of inputs.

Lemma 1. *Following conditions hold for membership in machine classes:*

1. *A machine $\mathcal{M}$ is in $\mathcal{C}_1$ iff there is a machine $\hat{\mathcal{M}} \in \mathcal{C}_1$ such that $\mathcal{M}$ and $\hat{\mathcal{M}}$ are polynomially time-equivalent and linearly space-equivalent.*
2. *A machine $\mathcal{M}$ is in $\mathcal{C}_2$ iff there is a machine $\hat{\mathcal{M}} \in \mathcal{C}_2$ such that $\mathcal{M}$ and $\hat{\mathcal{M}}$ are polynomially time-equivalent.*

Lemma 2. *Let there be p active processors in the beginning of a BSP computation. Then the number of processors that can be activated in $T(n)$ computation steps is bounded by $2^{O(T(n)+\log p)}$.*

Lemma 3. *Let a machine $\mathcal{M}$ simulate a BSP computation having S supersteps. Assume for individual supersteps $\exists c, k > 0 \; \forall i \in \{1, \ldots, S\} : T_i^{\mathcal{M}} \leq c \left(T_i^{\text{BSP}}\right)^k$. Then the whole simulation takes time $T^{\mathcal{M}} = O\left(\left(T^{\text{BSP}}\right)^k\right)$.*

3 Membership in $\mathcal{C}_1$ and $\mathcal{C}_2$

In this section we prove membership of BSP in the first and the second machine classes by mutual simulations of BSP, RAM, Turing Machine, and PRAM. After several auxiliary lemmas, Theorems 1, 2, 3, and 4 establish respective intervals of parameter values. Note that polynomial time and space overheads required for membership in $\mathcal{C}_1$ may be achieved by different simulations.

Lemma 4. *A BSP computer can simulate any deterministic Turing Machine with a polynomial time overhead.*

Proof (sketch). The simulating BSP runs the algorithm for simulation of DTM on RAM. Only one processor is used. □

Lemma 5. *BSP and DTM can be mutually simulated with a linear space overhead.*

Proof (sketch). A BSP computer with only one processor is a RAM which can simulate a Turing Machine in linear space.

DTM writes contents of memories of all the BSP processors to its tape. When simulating a step, Turing Machine sequentially performs one step of every processor. □

Lemma 6. *For any p, g, l, $BSP(p, g, l)$ can be simulated by a Common-CRCW-PRAM with $O(p^4)$ processors with a polynomial slowdown.*

Proof. PRAM uses p processors to simulate p processors of the BSP. Simulation of a superstep runs as follows:

1. local computation – a PRAM processor directly simulates the corresponding BSP processor.

2. communication – for any pair of processors (i, j), an area is reserved in the shared memory for messages from i to j. Then it is necessary to obtain a list of nonempty areas for every destination processor. There is a simple algorithm running in $O(\log p)$ time with p^3 processors. As there are p BSP processor, we need p^4 additional processors.

3. synchronization – one shared memory cell is reserved for synchronization. Each step is augmented by a constant time check of the end of superstep.

We need the common write during the simulation to perform fast communication and synchronization. □

Lemma 7. *For a potentially unlimited number of processors and $g(p) = O(1)$, $l(p) = O(1)$, $BSP(p, g(p), l(p)) \in C_2$.*

Proof. A BSP computation is simulated on a Common-CRCW-PRAM according to the previous lemma.

An EREW-PRAM can be straightforwardly simulated on a BSP by adding a processor for every memory cell of the PRAM. If the PRAM has p processors and uses s memory cells, then BSP has $p + s$ processors. p processors simulate the computation of p PRAM processors. Remaining s processors only handle memory requests. EREW property ensures that all communication requests are 1-relations. □

Theorem 1. *Let p be an arbitrary constant (independent on the input size) and $g(p)$, $l(p)$ any functions. Then $BSP(p, g(p), l(p)) \in C_1$.*

Proof. A BSP with a fixed number of processors can be directly simulated on a RAM. Simulation runs in rounds. In each round, RAM simulates one superstep on all p BSP processors sequentially. This slows down the execution only by a constant factor p. □

Theorem 2. *Let $l(p) = \Omega(p^b)$, for some constant $b > 0$. Then for any p and $g(p)$, $BSP(p, g(p), l(p)) \in C_1$.*

Proof. We simulate a BSP computation on a RAM. In every superstep, the RAM simulates sequentially all the processors of BSP. A superstep takes time $T^{BSP} = w + h + \Omega(p^b)$ on BSP and $T^{RAM} = pw + ph$ on RAM. We analyze three cases:

1. $w \geq p \ \& \ w \geq h \Rightarrow T^{RAM} \leq 2w^2 \leq 2\left(T^{BSP}\right)^2$,
2. $p \geq w \ \& \ p \geq h \Rightarrow T^{RAM} \leq 2p^2 \leq \left(\Omega(p^b)\right)^{2/b} \leq \left(T^{BSP}\right)^{2/b}$,
3. $h \geq w \ \& \ h \geq p \Rightarrow T^{RAM} \leq 2h^2 \leq 2\left(T^{BSP}\right)^2$.

We have got $T^{RAM} = O\left(\left(T^{BSP}\right)^{\max\{2, 2/b\}}\right)$ for each superstep. A polynomial time overhead for the whole computation is obtained by application of Lemma 3. Lemma 5 gives the linear space overhead simulation. A reverse simulation of RAM on BSP with polynomial time overhead follows from Lemma 4. □

Theorem 3. *Let $g(p) = \Omega(p^a)$ for some constant $a > 0$ and $l(p) = \Omega(1)$. Further let us assume that at least one message is sent in each superstep of every BSP computation. Then $BSP(p, g(p), l(p)) \in C_1$.*

Proof. The only nontrivial part of the proof is the simulation of the BSP on a RAM. On BSP, one superstep takes time $T^{\mathrm{BSP}} = w + gh + l = w + h\Omega(p^a) + \Omega(1)$, where $h \geq 1$. The RAM sequentially simulates the BSP processors. It takes time $T^{\mathrm{RAM}} \leq pw + ph$. Further we analyze several cases:

1. $w \leq p \Rightarrow T^{\mathrm{RAM}} \leq p^2 + ph = O\left(hp^2\right)$
   (a) $a \geq 2 \Rightarrow T^{\mathrm{BSP}} \geq \Omega\left(hp^2\right) \geq T^{\mathrm{RAM}}$
   (b) $a \leq 2 \Rightarrow \left(T^{\mathrm{BSP}}\right)^{2/a} \geq \Omega\left(h^{2/a}p^2\right) \geq \Omega\left(hp^2\right) \geq T^{\mathrm{RAM}}$
2. $w \geq p \Rightarrow T^{\mathrm{RAM}} \leq p(w + h)$ & $T^{\mathrm{RAM}} \leq w^2 + ph$
   $\left(T^{\mathrm{BSP}}\right)^2 \geq w^2 + h^2\Omega\left(p^{2a}\right)$
   (a) $a < 1/2$
       i. $h \leq w \Rightarrow T^{\mathrm{RAM}} \leq w^2 + pw \leq 2w^2 \leq 2\left(T^{\mathrm{BSP}}\right)^2$
       ii. $h > w \Rightarrow T^{\mathrm{RAM}} \leq 2ph \leq h\left(\Omega(p^a)\right)^{1/a} \leq \left(h\Omega(p^a)\right)^{1/a} \leq \left(T^{\mathrm{BSP}}\right)^{1/a}$
   (b) $a \geq 1/2 \Rightarrow \left(T^{\mathrm{BSP}}\right)^2 \geq w^2 + h^2\Omega(p) \geq w^2 + h\Omega(p) \geq T^{\mathrm{RAM}}$

We have got a simulation of one BSP superstep on a RAM with a polynomial overhead: $T^{\mathrm{RAM}} = O\left(\left(T^{\mathrm{BSP}}\right)^{\max\{2,2/a\}}\right)$. Consequently, the whole computation is slowed down at most polynomially, according to Lemma 3. □

Theorem 4. *Let us assume a $BSP(p, g(p), l(p))$ of time complexity $T(n) = \Omega(\log(n))$ with $g(p) = O(\log^a p)$, $l(p) = O(\log^b p)$ for some constants $a, b > 0$ and potentially unlimited number of processors. Then $BSP(p, g(p), l(p)) \in C_2$.*

Proof. We simulate $\mathcal{M} = BSP(p, 1, 1)$ – which is in C_2 according to Lemma 7 – running in time $T^{\mathcal{M}}$. Assume also that $\mathcal{M}$ runs in S supersteps. We show that the simulating algorithm runs on the $BSP(p, g(p), l(p))$ in time $T^{\mathrm{BSP}} = O\left(\left(T^{\mathcal{M}}\right)^k\right)$ for a constant $k > 0$. The following inequality holds:

$$T^{\mathrm{BSP}} = \sum_{i=1}^{S} w(i) + g(p)\sum_{i=1}^{S} h(i) + Sl(p) \leq g(p)T^{\mathcal{M}}(n) + S(n)l(p) \ .$$

Clearly $T^{\mathcal{M}}(n) \geq S(n)$ and according to Lemma 2 the number of processors is bounded by $p \leq 2^{O(T^{\mathcal{M}}(n) + \log n)}$. Let us define $c = \max\{a, b\}$.

$$T^{\mathrm{BSP}} \leq T^{\mathcal{M}}(n)(\log^a p + \log^b p) \leq O\left(T^{\mathcal{M}}(n)\left(T^{\mathcal{M}}(n) + \log n\right)^c\right) \ .$$

The assumption $T^{\mathcal{M}}(n) = \Omega(\log n)$ yields $T^{\mathrm{BSP}} \leq O\left(\left(T^{\mathcal{M}}(n)\right)^{c+1}\right)$. We get the desired constant $k = c + 1$.

The reversed simulation of $BSP(p, g, l)$ on $\mathcal{M} = BSP(p, 1, 1)$ runs clearly in time $T^{\mathcal{M}} \leq T^{\mathrm{BSP}}$. □

4 BSP Outside the First and the Second Class

The interval of values of parameters between $\log^k p$ and p^a has remained unexamined from the previous section. The membership of BSP with such parameters in the classes C_1 and C_2 relies on the unproved relation between the complexity classes P and PSPACE, resp. LINSPACE[1]. We show that, under the assumption that there are problems with exponential time lower bound in LINSPACE, BSP with g, l from the above interval does not belong to either of C_1, C_2. On the other hand, if P=PSPACE, then BSP $\in C_1 = C_2$ would hold trivially .

Theorem 5. *Let us suppose that there is a problem $P \in LINSPACE$ with an exponential time lower bound.*
Let [2] *$\forall a > 0 \forall k > 0 : \omega(\log^k p) \le g(p) \le o(p^a)$ & $\omega(\log^k p) \le l(p) \le o(p^a)$.*
Then $BSP(p, g(p), l(p)) \notin C_1$ & $BSP(p, g(p), l(p)) \notin C_2$.

Proof. Assume that P can be solved on the Turing Machine in time TIME$(n) = \Omega(c^n)$ and space SPACE$(n) = O(n)$, where $c > 1$ is some constant. P can be solved in parallel on an EREW-PRAM – and hence on BSP$(p, 1, 1)$, see the proof of Lemma 7 – in time //-TIME$(n) = O(n^l)$ with $p =$ //-PROC$(n) = O(c^{3n})$ processors ($l \ge 1$ is a constant) using the standard transitive closure algorithm [10]. To achieve parallel time //-TIME$(n) = O(n^l)$ the number of processors must be //-PROC$(n) = \Omega(c^n)$, because it is necessary to perform at least the same number of operations as in the sequential computation.

In the worst case, time needed for simulation of BSP$(p, 1, 1)$-computation on BSP$(p, g(p), l(p))$ is BSP-TIME$(n) = o(n^l p^a) = o(n^l c^{3an}) \le o(c^{4an})$. This inequality holds $\forall a > 0$, therefore the speedup is larger than polynomial and hence BSP$(p, g(p), l(p)) \notin C_1$.

Moreover, any BSP$(p, g(p), l(p))$ algorithm – even just one superstep with any h-relation ($h \ge 1$) – slows down the computation more than polynomially: $\forall k \ge 0 :$ BSP-TIME$(n) = \omega(\log^k p) = \omega(\log^k c^n) = \omega(n^k \log^k c) \ge \omega(n^k)$. This means that any BSP with enough processors has too slow communication to meet the polynomial time bound, hence BSP$(p, g(p), l(p)) \notin C_2$. $\square$

5 Relation to the Weak Parallel Machines

The class C_{weak} lies between C_1 and C_2. So a question naturally arises, whether BSP with g and l larger than $\log^k p$ and smaller than p^a could fit into C_{weak}. The following theorem gives a negative answer.

Theorem 6. *Let the assumptions of Theorem 5 hold. Additionally, let every period contain at least one superstep. Then $BSP(p, g(p), l(p)) \notin C_{\text{weak}}$.*

---

[1] class of problems solvable sequentially in linear space

[2] $f(n) = o(g(n)) \overset{\text{def}}{\Longleftrightarrow} \lim_{n \to \infty} f(n)/g(n) = 0$
$f(n) = \omega(g(n)) \overset{\text{def}}{\Longleftrightarrow} \lim_{n \to \infty} g(n)/f(n) = 0$

Proof. Let us take a sequence of N inputs, each having length n. The sequence is processed sequentially in exponential time $N.\text{TIME}(n)$ and linear space $\text{SPACE}(n)$. Execution time of a pipelined parallel computation is $\text{P-TIME}(n) + (N-1)\text{PERIOD}(n)$ where $\text{P-TIME}(n)$ is (exponential) pipeline time complexity and $\text{PERIOD}(n)$ is (polynomial) period. The parallel computation has to perform at least the same number of operations as the sequential computation, therefore the number of processors is $p \geq N.\text{TIME}(n)/(\text{P-TIME}(n) + (N-1)\text{PERIOD}(n))$. From the pipelined computation thesis we get the equality $\text{PERIOD}(n) = O(\text{SPACE}^k(n))$ for some $k > 1$. The limit $\lim_{N \to \infty} p \geq \text{TIME}(n)/\text{SPACE}^k(n)$ gives an exponential number of processors. It can be shown (in the same way as $\text{BSP} \notin C_2$ in the proof of Theorem 5) that the period grows more than polynomially when the pipelined computation is simulated on a $\text{BSP}(p, g(p), l(p))$ computer and consequently $\text{BSP}(p, g(p), l(p)) \notin C_{\text{weak}}$. $\quad\square$

6 Conclusion

The BSP model has been recognized as a practically usable model for general purpose parallel computing [6]. It allows development of efficient, but portable and machine independent parallel programs. In this paper, we have shown the asymptotic power and limitations of the BSP. The computation power of the BSP computers can be tuned in a wide range by setting the parameters. If we allow for enough (exponentially many) processors and very fast communication and synchronization mechanisms, we get a machine from the second class, comparable to PRAM, see Theorem 4. The problem is that such a computer violates basic laws of physics such as the limited speed of light and a lower bound on the processor size. Using arguments from [1], it can be easily proved that in a realistic BSP with a large number of processors, g and l have to be $\Omega(\sqrt[3]{p})$. As we proved in Theorems 2 and 3, such a BSP belongs to the first class. It can still exploit some parallelism, but with much less speedup than the machines from C_2.

The members of C_{weak} are also physically feasible and allow fast processing of sequences of inputs [11]. Unfortunately, the BSP model does not belong to the weak parallel class, as has been shown in Theorem 6. Intuitively, in general BSP, this is caused by the lack of locality of communication. There is an equal distance between any pair of processors. This distance corresponds to the size of the computer and grows with the number of processors. On the other hand, machines in C_{weak} utilize the possibility of fast communication between near processors. Distant processors still communicate slowly, but direct neighbors can communicate in constant time. We may conclude that an efficient realistic model of a parallel computer should include some notion of distance among its processors. One example is the variable-delay-PRAM [7]. Other possibilities would be to allow fast communication and synchronization of BSP submachines of limited size or to define a neighborhood relation on BSP processors and to augment the standard BSP by a fast neighbor-to-neighbor communication mechanism.

References

1. Gianfranco Bilardi and Franco P. Preparata. *Horizons of Parallel Computation*. Technical Report CS-93-20, Department of Computer Science, Universita di Padova, 1993.
2. A. K. Chandra, D. C. Kozen, and L.J. Stockmayer. *Alternation*. Journal of the ACM, 28:114–133, 1981.
3. L. M. Goldschager. *A Universal Interconnection Pattern for Parallel Computers*. Journal of the ACM, 29:1073–1086, 1982.
4. *Harvard BSP group*.
   http://www.deas.harvard.edu/csecse/research/bsp.html
5. Klaus-Jörn Lange. *On the Distributed Realization of Parallel Algorithms*. In Proc. of SOFSEM '97, volume 1338 of Lecture Notes in Computer Science, pages 37–52. Springer-Verlag, 1997.
6. W. F. McColl. *General Purpose Parallel Computing*. In A. M. Gibbons and P. Spirakis, editors, Lectures on parallel Coputation. Proc. 1991 ALCOM Spring School on Parallel Computation, pages 337–391. Cambridge University Press, 1993.
7. Rolf Niedermeier. *Towards Realistic and Simple Models of Parallel Computation*. PhD thesis, Fakultät für Informatik, Eberhard-Karls=Universität Tübingen, Tübingen, 1996.
   http://www-fs.informatik.uni-tuebingen.de/
   ~niedermr/publications/di2.ps.Z
8. *Oxford BSP research group*.
   http://www.comlab.ox.ac.uk/oucl/groups/bsp/
9. Leslie G. Valiant. *A Bridging Model for Parallel Computation*. Communications of the ACM, 33(8):103–111, 1990.
10. P. van Emde Boas. *Machine Models and Simulations*. Handbook of Theoretical Computer Science, A:1–66, 1990.
11. Jiří Wiedermann. *Weak Parallel Machines: A New Class of Physically Feasible Parallel Machine Models*. In I. M. Havel and V. Koubek, editors, Mathematical Foundations of Computer Science 1992, 17th Int. Symposium (MFCS'92), volume 629 of Lecture Notes in Computer Science, pages 95–111, Berlin, 1992. Springer-Verlag.

Modeling of Hypermedia Applications

Radovan Červenka

Dept. of Computer Science, Faculty of Mathematics and Physics
Comenius University, Bratislava
cervenka@fmph.uniba.sk

Abstract. This paper introduces the *Hypermedia Modeling Language - HML*, which constitutes a formal basis for modeling navigation/manipulation, synchronization and media channels handling functionality of applications having some hypermedia features.
We present a logical application architecture framework[1] which forms a principal basis for the HML language. It defines individual hypermedia aspects and determines their position within the application architecture.
Using this framework in the application development process improves transparency of the application architecture and leads to a higher degree of reuse and portability as well as to the ease of maintenance of the application.
For each layer of the framework, we discuss basic principles of its modeling in the HML.

1 Introduction

A number of modern software applications is characterized by some hypermedia features (e.g. navigation or multimedia handling) supported by some technology (e.g. DB, OS, programming languages or GUI). However, they have no clear support in either the application architecture or in the "classical" software engineering application development process. Implementation of these hypermedia features is often mixed with the responsibilities of the business logic and the user interface objects (widgets).

On the other hand, the theory of hypermedia (including hypertext and multimedia) is well developed and offers models of particular hypermedia features, systems and applications, e.g. Nested Context Model [3], Dexter Hypertext Reference Model [5], Trellis hypertext model [4] or Amsterdam Hypermedia Model [6]. The design of hypermedia application can be also supported by some of the existing methodologies, e.g. RMM [8,9], SHDT [1] or OOHDM [11,10]. However, the hypermedia deal mainly with the aspects of external design of applications and do not deal with the business logic or the domain modeling.

This paper identifies and specifies particular aspects of "hypermediality" and determines their responsibilities and locations in the application architecture.

---

[1] "Logical" means that it deals with the logical aspects covered by an application, not with the physical deployment of the system described, for example, by the client-server architecture.

This principle is also reflected by our proposal of the logical application architecture framework. Applying this framework allows us not to differentiate between "pure" hypermedia and non-hypermedia applications from the architecture point of view. We refer to both kinds simply *applications*.

For navigation/manipulation, synchronization and media channels layers of the architecture we define their metamodels and implementation-independent visual modeling language *Hypermedia Modeling Language - HML*.

The HML is designed as an *UML Variant* [12] - a language with well-defined semantics that is built on top of the UML metamodel [14]. In this way the HML inherits all facilities of the UML and extends its complex application modeling by the hypermedia dimension.

In the next section we shall outline our proposal of the logical application architecture framework supporting hypermedia. Sections 3, 4, 5, 6 and 7 describe the domain and application, navigation/manipulation, synchronization, media channels models and presentation modeling principles. Finally, in the section 8, we shall discuss the implementation of the HML in the CASE tool.

2 Logical Application Architecture Framework

From the logical point of view, we can identify different aspects of an application: domain, application logic, navigation/maniputation, media channels, presentation and synchronization. These aspects can be arranged into layers constituting the framework for an application architecture, see Fig. 1.

The *domain layer* implements the information structure and mechanisms of the problem domain independently of the application's intention.

The *application layer* implements a solution of a specific problem - business logic, functionality and overall control of the application. It is intermediate between the domain layer and the user interface layer.

The *navigation/manipulution layer* defines the structure of the information presented to an actor and controls the manipulation of domain and application objects.

The *media channels layer* defines properties and structure of I/O devices used. It also defines the mapping of navigation objects onto these devices.

The *synchronization layer* deals with temporal synchronization of navigation objects.

The *presentation layer* controls presentation of navigation objects and media channels to an actor.

The *actor* is an entity residing outside the application and communicating with the application. Usually it is a user or another cooperating application.

The *system* represents an operating system, a database, a programming language or a hypermedia system, upon which the application is built.

The implementation of an application does not need to support all layers. For example if application does not use multimedia data then the media channel or synchronization are not needed.

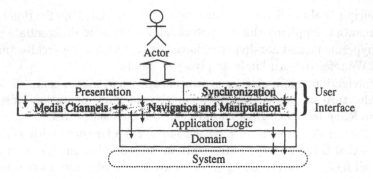

Fig. 1. The generic application architecture. Arrows represent relationship "uses".

Furthermore, this framework also clarifies the application development process by enabling to build each layer separately and using mainly the facilities offered by the underlying layers. The directions of the "uses" relationships among particular layers are depicted on Fig. 1 by arrows.

Each layer is represented by its own model. In the following sections, we shall describe each of them in more detail.

3 Domain and Application Model

Software engineering provides a number of techniques for modeling the domain and the application layers. We shall therefore not discuss this topic here. It suffices to mention that within the context of the HML we shall use for this purpose the modeling techniques of the UML. The domain model is expressed mainly by static structure diagrams and by statechart diagrams. The application layer is modeled by use case diagrams and by realization of uses cases expressed by collaboration or sequence diagrams [13].

To demonstrate the modeling principles described in this paper, we shall use a toy example of the Library Information System (LIS). It is a hypertext information system used for administration of the library archive, readers, book reservations and book borrowings.

Fig. 2 shows its domain model. This model is considerably simplified; for instance class operations or constraints are not specified. This model constitutes just a part of the *conceptual model*. Still it suffices for our purpose.

The LIS application aims to register readers (**Reader** class), books (**Book** class), current book reservations (**Reservation** class) and current book borrowings (**Borrowing** class). Books are partitioned according to the area of interest (**Area** class). Areas themselves are organized into a heterarchy (directed-acyclic graph) based on the subarea-superarea relationship. **Reader**s are special case of **Person**s, used also for keeping the information about book authors.

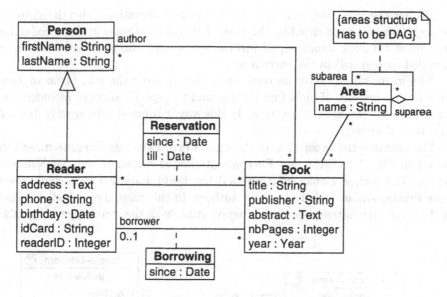

Fig. 2. Simplified domain model of the LIS application

4 Navigation and Manipulation Model

Information and functionality contained within the domain and the application layers would be useless if not accessible by the actors of the application. Customizing the access and structuring of this information according to the needs of a particular actor type is the responsibility of the navigation/manipulation layer.

The navigation/manipulation layer consists of navigation objects, which are called *views* and *hyperlinks* in the HML. Modeling of these navigation elements as well as modeling of navigation contexts , accessing structures and manipulation is outlined in the following subsections.

4.1 Views

The *view* is an object belonging to the navigation layer with the responsibility to structure information and access the behavior offered by domain or application objects. In addition, it can implement the user interface behaviour; e.g. it can dynamically compute the navigation, record and show the navigation history or check the entry values in input forms and dialogues.

The *view class* (*v-class*) generically describes the structure and behaviour of all views of the same kind. The HML denotes the v-class by the stereotype ≪view≫ of a class, or by the icon (as in Fig. 3 and Fig. 4). The view is an instance of a v-class.

Each view has its *owner*, the domain or application object, the properties of which it is viewing. An owner can have many views, depending on the number of ways it needs to be viewed. We can perceive it as a *viewing polymorphism*.

V-class specifies, besides its own attributes and operations, also the structure of the information presented by the view. This information contains a collection, or a more complex structure, of *inclusions* - specifications of views which are included (presented) in the current view.

The inclusion can have its own name, determining the role of an included view in the instance of including v-class, and the specification of included view which can be computed at run time. In this way it is possible to specify dynamic structure of views.

For example the **main** view of the class **Person** (v-class **Person~main**), depicted in Fig. 3, collects two **Person**'s attributes firstName and lastName together. The v-class **Book~bibItem** includes, besides another inclusions, the v-class **Person~main** - a list of book's authors. In this case, the inclusion is specified by the alternative way - as an aggregation with the stereotype ≪hyper≫.

(a)

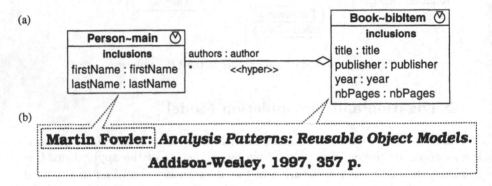

(b)

Fig. 3. (a) Reuse of the v-class **Person~main** in defining the v-class **Book~bibItem** **(b)** Instance of **Book~bibItem**

Employing the inclusion mechanism combined with the template class of UML we can define composite v-classes representing reusable components of the navigation model with a possibility of parametrization.

Taking into account the fact that v-classes are also ordinary classes, we can define very complex structure of the navigation model by inheritance and composition relationships.

4.2 Hyperlinks

In the context of the HML a *hyperlink* constitutes a connection among views in the navigation layer. At the modeling level, a set of hyperlinks of the same kind is specified by a *hyperlink association* (*h-association*). The h-association is modeled by a navigable association with the stereotype ≪hyper≫. The hyperlink is an instance of an h-association.

Each h-association defines a set of *source specifiers* and a set of *destination specifiers*. They are resolved into concrete views at run-time.

Additionally, an *anchor* is specified for each destination. It is a view, which is included into the source view at the place of an activation of the hyperlink. In most cases this is another, simpler view of a destination view's owner.

The HML model supports *in-line* (WWW-like) and *out-of-line* (DHM-like [5]) links (for a more detailed description see [19]). In addition, there is a possibility to model by the HML n-ary hyperlinks [5], dynamically (at run-time) computed hyperlinks and link contexts [7], which are not described in this paper at all.

Fig. 4 illustrates, apart from another things, also defining the set of unary in-line hyperlinks leading from instances of the **Area~bookList** v-class into the views of type **Book~main** having the anchor **Book~simpleBibItem**.

In this example we illustrate both the graphical and the textual forms of specifying the hyperlinks which are semantically equivalent.

4.3 Navigation Contexts and Accessing Structures

The HML also provides for modeling of complex navigation contexts [10] and access structures [8]. To illustrate these possibilities of the HML on the LIS application, we show an example of modeling of the hierarchical index, depicted in Fig. 4.

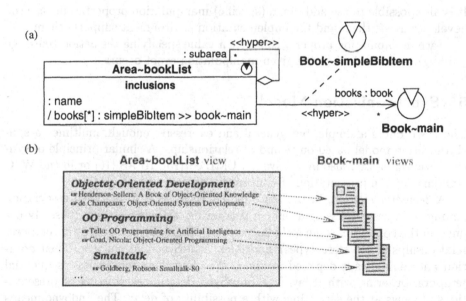

Fig. 4. (a) A hierarchical book index of an area - **Area~bookList** (b) An example of an **Area~bookList** instance

The v-class **Area~bookList** represents an index of all books belonging to the current area of interest. All its subareas and all their books also belong into this area. This recursivity is realized by the inclusion of the v-class **Area~bookList** into itself. The termination of the recurrence is guaranteed by the constraint specified in the domain model (**Area**s structure has to be a directed-acyclic graph).

4.4 Manipulation

The manipulation facility of the navigation/manipulation layer is a possibility to change the domain layer by operations performed on views by an actor.

This is specified by *manipulation properties* attached to the whole v-class (valid for all its inclusions) or particularly its inclusions. The manipulation property specifies the operation, which can be performed with the inclusion. The following manipulation properties are predefined:

in   an inclusion is only input (allows to input some values)
out   an inclusion is only output (shows some values); the default behaviour
inout   an inclusion is input and output
copy   an inclusion can be copied
paste   copied view can be pasted at the inclusion's position
drag   an inclusion can be dragged
drop   dragged view can be dropped at the inclusion's position

It is also possible to use additional (specific) manipulation properties in case the developer needs them and the implementation environment supports them.

Each manipulation property can have a value specifying the action (message sending) performed when the given manipulation event occurs.

5   Synchronization Model

The HML offers a simple, but general and expressive enough, multimedia synchronization model based on temporal relationships. A similar principle of synchronization is used also in the system CMIFed [15], HPAS [16] or in the W3C standard for the presentation of multimedia objects - SMIL [18].

A *temporal relation*, in the sense of the HML, is a stereotyped association among v-classes expressing a temporal ordering of their instances, possibly defined in the context of some including v-class. There are three kinds of temporal relationships (UML stereotypes): SerialLink, StartSync and EndSync. Their notation and semantics is depicted in Fig. 5. The SerialLink represents a sequential temporal ordering with delay. The StartSync determines starting of presentations of views at the same time with a possibility of delay. The EndSync means terminating the presentations of views at the same time with a possibility of delay.

6   Media Channels Model

The application contains data of different media type. Each data has to be presented (played) on some output device. The *media channel* (simply channel)

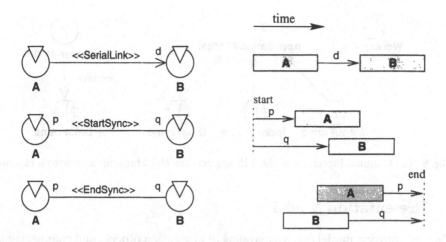

Fig. 5. Temporal relationships; d, p and q are delay parameters

is an abstract input/output device for playing events. This may be, for example, a window or a frame on the screen, an audio or a video output. When the application is running, the channels are mapped onto physical input/output devices.

The *channel type* represents all channels having the same properties, responsibilities and behaviour. It is modeled by a class defining properties of a channel, which are accessible to the application. These properties are expressed by attributes representing the relevant properties of physical devices (size and position of a window; volume, quality, balance, of an audio channel, etc.) and operations intended to exploit the functionality of the instantiated channels (open, play, close, stop the channel, etc.).

The HML denotes the channel type by the stereotype ≪channel≫ of a class, or by the icon (as in Fig. 6). The channel type may be a composition of others (e.g. a view consists of many frames) or it can share properties of the more general channel types by the generalization relationship.

Fig. 6 (a) shows an example of a structure of channel types for the LIS application. The **ApplicationWindow** represents the main application window divided into three frames: the **MenuFrame** containing the menu, the **IndexFrame** (dis)playing the presentation of indices of different kinds (e.g. the book index, the author index, the reader index, etc.) and the **DataFrame** displaying the **main** views of a given domain object selected in the **IndexFrame**. The **Workspace** channel is instrumental in displaying all dialogue types placed on the screen.

The static mapping of views onto a channel is specified by the dependency with the stereotype ≪play≫, leading from the v-class to the channel class. Another kind of mapping a view to channel can be represented by the presentation property (e.g., of the name channel, play or target) whose value specifies the desired channel (it can be computed at run-time).

An example of a channel mapping is depicted in Fig. 6 (b). The **main** view of the **Reader** will be played on the **DataFrame** channel.

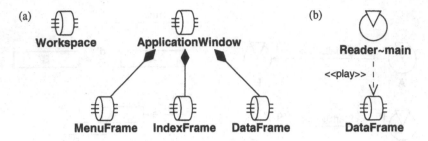

Fig. 6. (a) Channel hierarchy of the LIS application **(b)** Mapping a view to a channel

7 Presentation Model

The presentation model defines mapping of navigation objects and channels onto user interface objects (widgets) and their properties. The presentation is defined by attaching the *presentation specification*, represented by a set of property specifications (in the sense of the UML), to the whole view, to a particular inclusion of a view, to link anchors and targets or to a channel.

The presentation specification depends on the target implementation environment to a large extent, therefore the set of predefined presentation properties and the specification of the syntax and the semantics of their values are out of scope of the HML.

8 HML Implementation

The fact the HML is an UML variant and many modeling constructors use the UML extension mechanisms implies, that an implementation of the software support for HML modeling process can be realized by modifying some existing CASE tool supporting UML and its extension mechanisms. We have chosen Rational Rose 98 [17], which would best fit our requirements.

We have already implemented the core of the navigation, the synchronization and the media channels modeling. Now (August 1998), we are working on implementation of the model management functionality (e.g. browsing of HML elements or finding model inconsistencies) and implementation of the code generator into HTML language supported by JavaScript.

9 Conclusions

We have presented a brief introduction to the Hypermedia Modeling Language - HML. The HML language concerns modeling of the navigation/manipulation, the synchronization and the media channels handling functionality of applications with such hypermedia features.

Detailed description of the syntax, the semantics and the notation can not be presented within the size of this paper. More detailed description of the HML language will appear in the following forthcoming documents: the *HML Summary* introducing the background of the language, the *HML Semantics* defining the semantics and abstract syntax by the HML Metamodel and the *HML Notation* describing the concrete graphical syntax of HML.

Our future work will concern refining the definition of the *navigation* and *interface design patterns* [2] using the HML. We have already defined some navigation patterns of simple access structures (such as index, guided tour or indexed-guided tour). Therefore the HML language also appears to be of significant help in the area of hypermedia pattern languages.

References

1. Bichler, M., Nusser, S. SHDT - The Structured Way of Developing WWW-Sites. *Proceedings of the EICS'96.*
2. Carvalho, S., Rossi, G., and Garrido, A. Design Patterns in an Object-Oriented Framework for Hypermedia. *Patterns Languages of Programs 2*, Vlissides, Coplien and Kerth *eds.*, Addison Wesley, 1996.
3. Casanova, M.A., Tucherman, L. The Nested Context Model for Hyperdocuments. *Proceedings of Hypertext '91*, Dec. 1991.
4. Furuta, R., and Scotts, P.D. The Trellis Hypertext Reference Model. *Proceedings of the NIST Hypertext Standardization Workshop*, January 16-18, 1990.
5. Halasz, F., Schwartz, M. The Dexter Hypertext Reference Model. *Proceedings of the NIST Hypertext Standardization Workshop*, January 16-18, 1990.
6. Hardman, L., Bulterman, D.C.A., and van Rossum, G. The Amsterdam Hypermedia Model: extending hypertext to support real multimedia. Technical Report CS-R9306, Centrum voor Wiskunde en Informatica, The Netherlands, 1993.
7. Hardman, L., Bulterman, D.C.A., and van Rossum, G. Links in Hypermedia: the Requirement for Context. *Proceedings of Hypertext '93.*
8. Isakowitz, T., Stohr, E.A., and Balasubramanian P. RMM: A Methodology for Structured Hypermedia Design. *Commun. ACM 38, 8* (Aug. 1995).
9. Isakowitz, T., Kamis, A., and Koufaris, M. Extending the capabilities of RMM: Russian Dolls and Hypertext. *Proceedings of HICSS-30*, 1997.
10. Schwabe, D., and Barbosa, S.D.J. Navigation Modelling in Hypermedia Applications. Technical report, Departmento de Informatica, PUC RIO, Brasil.
11. Schwabe, D., Rossi, G., Barbosa, S.D.J. Systematic Hypermedia Application Design with OOHDM. *Proceedings of HYPERTEXT '96*, 1996.
12. UML Summary, version 1.1, 1 September 1997. Rational Software Corporation.
13. UML Notation Guide, version 1.1, 1 September 1997. Rational Software Corp.
14. UML Semantics, version 1.1, 1 September 1997. Rational Software Corporation.
15. van Rossum, G., Jansen, J., van Liere, K.S., and Bulterman, D.C.A. CMIFed: a Presentation Environment for Portable Hypermedia Documents. *Proceedings of the First International Conference on Multimedia*, Anaheim, California (Aug. 1993).
16. Yu, J. A Simple, Intuitive Hypermedia Synchronization Model and its Realization in the Browser/Java Environment. *SRC Technical Note 1997-027a* (Apr. 1998), Digital Systems Research Center.

17. Rational SW Corp.: Rational Rose 98. http://www.rational.com/products/rose/.
18. W3C SYMM WG: Synchronized Multimedia Integration Language (SMIL). http://www.w3.org/TR/1998/REC-smil-19980615.
19. W3C XML WG: XML Linking Language (XLink). Working Draft 3-March-1998. http://www.w3.org/TR/1998/WD-xlink-19980303.

On the Klee's Measure Problem
in Small Dimensions

Bogdan S. Chlebus*

Instytut Informatyki, Uniwersytet Warszawski, Banacha 2, 02-097 Warszawa, Poland.
chlebus@mimuw.edu.pl.

Abstract. The Klee's measure problem is to compute the volume of the union of a given set of n isothetic boxes in a d-dimensional space. The fastest currently known algorithm for this problem, developed by Overmars and Yap [6], runs in time $\mathcal{O}(n^{d/2} \log n)$. We present an alternative simple approach with the same asymptotic performance. The exposition is restricted to dimensions three and four.

1 Introduction

The *measure problem* for a d-dimensional Euclidean space, as proposed by Klee in [5], is defined as follows: there is given a collection of n isothetic boxes (their edges are parallel to the coordinate axes) and the task is to compute the measure of their union. Klee [5] gave an $\mathcal{O}(n \log n)$-time algorithm for the case $d = 1$, and later Fredman and Weide [3] proved that this time bound is optimal in the algebraic computation tree model. For $d = 2$ an $\mathcal{O}(n \log n)$-time algorithm was given by Bentley [1]. A straightforward extension of his approach leads to an algorithm that for arbitrary $d \geq 3$ achieves time performance $\mathcal{O}(n^{d-1} \log n)$. Van Leeuwen and Wood [9] showed how to decrease it to $\mathcal{O}(n^{d-1})$. Subsequently this was significantly improved by Overmars and Yap [6] to the time bound $\mathcal{O}(n^{d/2} \log n)$, the fastest algorithm known so far for $d \geq 3$. The question of optimality of computing the volume of a set of isothetic boxes in the Euclidean space of dimension $d > 2$ still remains an open problem.

We present another approach to the measure problem, which is conceptually simpler. Only the special cases of dimension three and four are described, for which algorithms are developed operating in time $\mathcal{O}(n^{3/2} \log n)$ and $\mathcal{O}(n^2 \log n)$, respectively. Generalizing for higher dimensions d, one can obtain algorithms operating in time $\mathcal{O}(n^{d/2} \cdot \log n)$, thus matching the performance of the algorithm of Overmars and Yap [6]. This will be presented in the final version of this paper.

A natural approach to the measure problem is to use the *plane-sweep* technique (cf. [7]), as follows. First select one of the d coordinates, say x. Consider the

---

* This work was supported by the contract KBN 8 T11C 036 14.

set X of all x-coordinates of the corners of all boxes. Sort X in the non-decreasing order, thus creating the *event-point schedule*. Next, view the algorithm as moving a $(d-1)$-dimensional hyperplane perpendicular to the x-axis through all the consecutive points in X, maintaining the *sweep-plane status*, in our case the measure of the intersection K_x of the boxes with the hyperplane. We will refer to K_x as a *cut*. Notice that between two consecutive events $x_1, x_2 \in X$, that is, for $x \in (x_1, x_2)$, the measure of the cut K_x is constant. Therefore the interval (x_1, x_2) contributes $(x_2 - x_1) \cdot Measure(K_x)$ to the total volume, where x is an arbitrary point from (x_1, x_2). Adding these terms together we obtain the total measure of the union of the boxes.

Each event $x \in X$ is a coordinate of a side of some box, which means that, during the hyperplane sweep, when it passes x, we need to either add a $(d-1)$-dimensional box to the cut K_x or remove such a box from K_x. We have $2n$ such events, so the total time complexity will be bounded by $\mathcal{O}(n \cdot t)$, where t is a bound on the time needed to update the measure of K_x. In this way the d-dimensional measure problem reduces to the problem of maintaining the total measure of a varying set of boxes in $(d-1)$-dimensional space. More specifically, we need to design a data structure that implements the following operations on $(d-1)$-dimensional boxes:

Insert: Add a box to K_x ;
Delete: Remove a box from K_x ;
Measure: What is the current $(d-1)$-dimensional measure of K_x?

Our algorithm follows this approach, the novelty being in the way the sweep-plane status is maintained: to this end we use a variant of a quadtree. A quadtree is a data structure used extensively in computational geometry and graphics, it was introduced by Finkel and Bentley [2] for solving range searching problems. More information and references on this and other multidimensional data structures can be found in [4, 8]. A *d-dimensional quadtree* is a composite data structure consisting of the following components: First, there is a *skeleton tree*, second, there are d-dimensional boxes C_v assigned to each node v, called *cells*, and third, there are some additional data structures assigned to each node. Usually all the boxes assigned to the nodes on the same level are a partition of the box assigned to the root.

2 Dimension three

The solution of Overmars and Yap [6] of the measure problem, specialized to dimension three, yields a version of 2-D trees to maintain the area of rectangles. These trees have $\mathcal{O}(\sqrt{n})$ insertion and deletion time. Below we describe another version of the quadtree, that we call *trellis quadtree*, which also has $\mathcal{O}(\sqrt{n})$ time bound for insertions and deletions. Trellis quadtree is conceptually simpler than the original construction of Overmars and Yap for handling rectangles.

Suppose $4n$ points in the plane are given, the vertices of a set of n input rectangles. The following process defines the skeleton tree and the rectangles assigned to each node. Take a rectangle including all the points and divide it into quadrants by drawing horizontal and vertical lines through the median x- and y-coordinates. Repeat this for each quadrant recursively, but taking medians of the *internal points only*. The empty rectangles obtained eventually become assigned to the leaves.

The data structures assigned to a node depend on its kind. For each inner node there is just a counter assigned to it which stores the number of input rectangles completely covering the assigned rectangle. Note that there is no rectangle vertex in a cell assigned to a leaf but there may be horizontal and vertical strips intersecting it. To handle their area we maintain two segment trees (cf. [7]) at each leaf, as follows. Consider a cell C_v assigned to a leaf. Let V be the set of vertical strips crossing C_v and obtained as intersections of the input rectangles with C_v. Consider the set of intervals which are projections of these strips onto the x-axis. The area of the union of the elements of V can be computed from the measure of the union of their projections as

$$Area(\bigcup V) = length(proj_x(\bigcup V)) \cdot length(proj_y(C_v)).$$

The intervals can be stored in a segment tree so that this parameter can be maintained with $\mathcal{O}(\log n)$-time insertions and deletions. A similar situation holds for the set H of horizontal strips. The area of the intersection $Area(\bigcup H \cap \bigcup V)$ is given by

$$Area(\bigcup H \cap \bigcup V) = length(proj_x(\bigcup V)) \cdot length(proj_y(\bigcup H)).$$

Now $Area(\bigcup H \cup \bigcup V)$ can be calculated from the inclusion-exclusion principle formula:

$$Area(\bigcup H \cup \bigcup V) = Area(\bigcup H) + Area(\bigcup V) - Area(\bigcup H \cap \bigcup V).$$

We say that a line *intersects a node* (or intersects the rectangle associated with a node) if it intersects the *interior* of the rectangle associated with the node.

Lemma 1. *A horizontal or vertical line intersects at most* $\sqrt{2}(1 + \sqrt{2}) \cdot \sqrt{n}$ *leaves of the trellis quadtree built for n rectangles.*

Proof. Consider some k points in the plane. Build the skeleton tree and assign rectangles to the nodes, following the principle of construction of the trellis quadtree. Let $T(k)$ denote the maximum number of leaves intersected by a vertical line L, taken over all configurations of k points. Let S be the cell of the root. It is crossed by a vertical line M_v passing through the point with the median x-coordinate, and by a horizontal line M_h passing through the point with the median y-coordinate. The lines M_h and M_v together partition S into four rectangles, of which at most two are intersected by L. If the rectangles intersected by L contain k_1 and k_2 points respectively, where $k_1 + k_2 \leq \frac{k-1}{2}$, then L intersects at most $T(k_1) + T(k_2)$ leaves. Hence the function $T(k)$ is determined by the following recurrence equation:

$$T(k) = \begin{cases} 1 & \text{if } k = 0 \text{ ;} \\ \max_{0 \leq i \leq \lfloor \frac{k-1}{2} \rfloor} \left(T(i) + T\left(\lfloor \frac{k-1}{2} \rfloor - i \right) \right) & \text{if } k > 0 \text{ .} \end{cases}$$

We prove by induction that the inequality

$$T(k) \leq (1 + \sqrt{2}) \cdot \sqrt{k} \tag{1}$$

holds for $k > 0$.

The base of induction: Let $k = 1$, then $T(1) = 2 \cdot T(0) = 2 \leq 1 + \sqrt{2}$.

The inductive step: Suppose first that $\lfloor k/2 \rfloor > i > 0$. Then

$$T(i) + T\left(\lfloor \frac{k-1}{2} \rfloor - i \right) \leq (1 + \sqrt{2})\left(\sqrt{i} + \sqrt{\frac{k}{2} - i} \right)$$
$$\leq (1 + \sqrt{2}) \cdot \sqrt{k} \ .$$

The remaining case is when $i = 0$. Then

$$T(0) + T\left(\lfloor \frac{k-1}{2} \rfloor \right) \leq 1 + (1 + \sqrt{2})\sqrt{\frac{k}{2}}$$
$$\leq (1 + \sqrt{2})\sqrt{k} \ ,$$

for $k \geq 1$ (it is here that the specific value $1 + \sqrt{2}$ is used). To complete the proof, take $k = 2n$ and substitute in inequality 1. $\qquad \square$

The overall time to find the measure of n boxes in 3-dimensional space using trellis quadtrees is as stated in Theorem 1, and is the same as that of algorithm of Overmars and Yap [6].

Theorem 1. *The measure of a union of n 3-dimensional boxes is computed in time $\mathcal{O}(n^{3/2} \log n)$ by the plane-sweep algorithm, if the trellis quadtree is used to maintain the area of intersection of the sweeping plane with the input boxes.*

Proof. First we construct the trellis quadtree. Two copies of each vertex are created, one in an array A_y sorted on the y-coordinates and another in an array A_z sorted on the z-coordinates. The median of the y-coordinates is the y-coordinate of the point stored in the middle of A_y, similarly the median of z-coordinates is the z-coordinate of the point in the middle of A_z. Partition the points into four groups corresponding to four quadrants, in each group storing two copies of a point: one in an array sorted on the y- and in the other on the z-coordinates. The minimum and maximum coordinates of the points in a group are the coordinates of the rectangular region associated with the node. Proceed each node recursively, partitioning the points into four groups and assigning rectangular regions to each node. A node becomes a leaf if no vertex of an input rectangle is located in the interior of the region assigned to the node. This completes the construction of the skeleton tree. Its depth is $\mathcal{O}(\log n)$ and processing a level takes time $\mathcal{O}(n)$, so the time to build the skeleton tree is $\mathcal{O}(n \log n)$. For each input rectangle scan the leaves that it intersects: the intersection is a strip across the cell associated with the leaf, insert the interval being a projection of the strip along its length into the segment tree corresponding to the coordinate of projection. Every rectangle intersects $\mathcal{O}(\sqrt{n})$ leaves by Lemma 1, and each leaf is located and its segment tree updated in time $\mathcal{O}(\log n)$. The total time to construct the tree is thus $\mathcal{O}(n^{3/2} \log n)$.

Next perform the required sequence of insertions and deletions. Each rectangle intersects $\mathcal{O}(\sqrt{n})$ leaves by Lemma 1, and each leaf is located and its parameters updated in time $\mathcal{O}(\log n)$. Therefore the time to process all the boxes is $\mathcal{O}(n^{3/2} \log n)$. □

The bound of Theorem 1 is best possible: it is attained for a set of rectangles with the vertices sufficiently evenly distributed over the input region. The trellis quadtree occupies space $\Theta(n^{3/2})$, however the algorithm can be modified to operate in space $\mathcal{O}(n)$ and within the same time bounds as follows (Overmars and Yap [6] also showed how to implement their algorithm so that it runs in the same time and simultaneously in linear space). The idea is not to first build the tree and then process all the input boxes, but rather construct the leaves one by one and compute the total volume contributed by each leaf, discarding each processed leaf. This corresponds to visiting the nodes of the trellis quadtree depth-first like rather than breadth-first like: when the tree is built as in the proof of Theorem 1 then this is done level by level, that is breadth-first like, alternately, we could store a path to the processed leaf on a stack, that is, scan the nodes depth-first like.

3 Dimension four

The trellis quadtrees generalize to higher dimensions, and in this way we obtain another deterministic solution of the general Klee's measure problem. In this section we consider the case of dimension four. In our framework, the goal is to maintain the volume of the union of 3-D parallelepipeds, again we call them boxes for brevity.

Suppose $6n$ points in the 3-dimensional space are given, determined by the vertices of a set of n input boxes. The following process defines the skeleton tree and the boxes assigned to each node. Take a box B including all the points in its interior, this is to be the region assigned to the root. The points are in three copies each, stored in arrays sorted on the x-, y-, and z-coordinates, respectively. Partition B into eight parts by the planes parallel to pairs of coordinate axes and passing through the median x-, y- and z-coordinates of the points in B. Next assign the points to the obtained parts of B. Suppose a part of B is the following: $P = [x_1, x_2] \times [y_1, y_2] \times [z_1, z_2]$. A point $\langle x, y, z \rangle$ is assigned to the node of P if and only if more than one among the inequalities $x_1 < x < x_2$ and $y_1 < y < y_2$ and $z_1 < z < z_2$ holds. Notice that a point can be assigned to four parts of B during this process. This creates the second level of nodes of the tree. The process is repeated recursively for each node, a node is partitioned into eight parts by the planes passing through the medians of some of the coordinates of the points assigned to the node; say in the case of coordinate x, when $[a, b]$ is the x-edge of the region assigned to the node, then we take the median among all the points with the x coordinates satisfying $a < x < b$, counting multiplicities. A node becomes a leaf if no point is assigned to it. The rule of assigning points to nodes makes it possible to apply the inclusion-exclusion formula in order to compute the volume of the sum of the boxes intersecting the region assigned to a leaf. This is because the intersection of a box with the region assigned to a leaf is a slice of the region bordered by two planes. To be able to use this formula, we need to store the intervals being the projections of the slices on the coordinate axe perpendicular to the slice, to this end we use again interval trees, one for each of the coordinates x, y, and z. The remaining details of the trellis trees handling insertions and deletions of 3-dimensional boxes are similar as in the case of 2-dimensional rectangles.

The performance of the tree can be estimated by bounding the number of leaf cells intersected by a plane parallel to a pair of coordinate axes, analogously to Lemma 1. Consider n points inside or on the sides of a 3-D box. Let n_i, for $1 \leq i \leq 3$, be the number of projections of points on the interior of the i-th side (as depicted on Figure 1). The box is cut by planes parallel to pairs of coordinate axes, and the sides are partitioned into quadrants. The projections on the sides are partitioned accordingly. The number of (projections of) points in the quadrants of the sides are denoted by letters a, b and c with indices, see Figure 1. Consider a plane parallel to two coordinate axes and crossing the box. We are interested in the number of leaf cells intersected by the plane. To be specific, let the plane intersect the sides of the box marked with a_1, a_2, c_1, c_2, its intersection with the box on Figure 1 is shown with dashed lines.

Consider the numbers a_i. They satisfy the following dependencies:

$$a_1 + a_2 = a_3 + a_4 = a_1 + a_3 = a_2 + a_4 = \frac{n_1 - 1}{2},$$

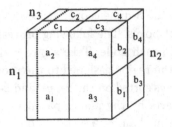

Fig. 1. A 3-D box crossed by a plane

where we assume that n_1 is odd, to avoid the floor notation; later we assume the same about n_2 and n_3. Let $a_1 = a$, then $a_4 = a$ and $a_2 = a_3 = \frac{n_1-1}{2} - a$. If the numbers b_1 and c_1 are denoted as b and c, respectively, then similar dependencies between b_i and c_i hold, and we obtain $b_4 = b$, $b_2 = b_3 = \frac{n_2-1}{2} - b$, $c_4 = c$, $c_2 = c_3 = \frac{n_3-1}{2} - c$. Let $T(n_1, n_2, n_3)$ denote the maximum number of leaf cells intersected by a plane crossing a box, where n_i are the numbers of projections of points on the interiors of three mutually orthogonal sides. We prove by induction that the inequality

$$T(n_1, n_2, n_3) \le 6(n_1 + n_2 + n_3)$$

holds, for $n_1 + n_2 + n_3 > 0$. Indeed, with the notation as in Figure 1, we obtain

$$T(n_1, n_2, n_3) \le T(a_1, b_1, c_1) + T(a_1, b_3, c_2) + T(a_2, b_2, c_1) + T(a_2, b_4, c_2)$$
$$\le T(a, b, c) + T\left(a, \frac{n_2}{2} - b, \frac{n_3}{2} - c\right)$$
$$+ T\left(\frac{n_1}{2} - a, \frac{n_2}{2} - b, c\right) + T\left(\frac{n_1}{2} - a, b, \frac{n_3}{2} - c\right)$$
$$\le 6\Big(a + b + c + a + \frac{n_2}{2} - b + \frac{n_3}{2} - c$$
$$+ \frac{n_1}{2} - a + \frac{n_2}{2} - b + c + \frac{n_1}{2} - a + b + \frac{n_3}{2} - c\Big)$$
$$= 6(n_1 + n_2 + n_3) .$$

The last inequality is correct provided no triple of the arguments of T consists of three zeros, because $T(0, 0, 0) = 1 > 0 + 0 + 0$. If this happens then the worst case is when some three occurrences of $T(\dots)$ are of the form $T(0, 0, 0)$. Then we can estimate:

$$T(n_1, n_2, n_3) \le 3 + T\left(\frac{n_1}{2}, \frac{n_2}{2}, \frac{n_3}{2}\right)$$
$$\le 3 + 6 \cdot \frac{n_1 + n_2 + n_3}{2}$$
$$\le 6(n_1 + n_2 + n_3) .$$

This is for the case as in Figure 1, the other cases are similar. We obtain, as a corollary, that if there are n points inside the box then the number of leaf cells intersected by a plane is at most $18 \cdot n$.

Theorem 2. *The measure of a union of n 4-dimensional boxes is computed in time $\mathcal{O}(n^2 \log n)$ by the plane-sweep algorithm, if the 3-dimensional trellis quadtree is used to maintain the volume of the intersection of the sweeping hyperplane with the input boxes.*

Proof. The situation is similar as in the proof of Theorem 1. Since a plane may intersect up to $\mathcal{O}(n)$ leaves, as proved above, the size of the tree is $\mathcal{O}(n^2)$. It can be built in time $\mathcal{O}(n^2 \log n)$. The sweeping hyperplane status is maintained by inserting and deleting 3-dimensional boxes and computing the volume of their union. A single insertion or deletion is done by processing $\mathcal{O}(n)$ leaves, each in time $\mathcal{O}(\log n)$. The number of these operations is $\mathcal{O}(n)$, hence the total time is $\mathcal{O}(n^2 \cdot \log n)$. $\qquad\qquad\square$

The bound of Theorem 2 is the best possible, and the algorithm can be implemented to run in linear space and within the same time bound.

Acknowledgement. Thanks are due to Marek Chrobak and Larry Larmore for encouraging the author to write this report, and for their criticism of the preliminary versions.

References

1. J.L. Bentley, Algorithms for Klee's rectangle problem, Unpublished notes, Dept. of Computer Science, CMU, 1977.
2. R.A. Finkel and J.L. Bentley, Quad-trees; a data structure for retrieval on composite keys, *Acta Informatica* 4 (1974) 1-9.
3. M.L. Fredman and B. Weide, The complexity of computing the measure of $\bigcup[a_i, b_i]$, *Comm. ACM* 21 (1978) 540-544.
4. S. S. Iyengar, N. S. V. Rao, R. L. Kashyap, and V. K. Vaishnavi, Multidimensional data structures: Review and outlook, *Advances in Computers* 27 (1988) 69-119.
5. V. Klee, Can the measure of $\bigcup[a_i, b_i]$ be computed in less than $\mathcal{O}(n \log n)$ steps?, *Amer. Math. Monthly* 84 (1977) 284-285.
6. M.H. Overmars and C.K. Yap, New upper bounds in Klee's measure problem, *SIAM J. Comput.* 20 (1991) 1034-1045; a preliminary version: New upper bounds in Klee's measure problem, *Proceedings, 29th Ann. Symposium on Foundations of Computer Science*, 1988, pp. 550-556.
7. F.P. Preparata and M.I. Shamos, *Computational Geometry*, Springer-Verlag, 1985.
8. H. Samet, *The Design and Analysis of Spatial Data Structures*, Addison-Wesley, 1990.
9. J. van Leeuwen and D. Wood, The measure problem for rectangular ranges in d-space, *J. Algorithms* 2 (1981) 282-300.

Yet Another Modular Technique for Efficient Leader Election *

Stefan Dobrev and Peter Ružička

Institute of Informatics
Comenius University
Bratislava
Slovakia
E-mail:{dobrev,ruzicka}@dcs.fmph.uniba.sk

Abstract. In this paper we present a general and still flexible modular technique for the design of efficient leader election algorithms in N–node networks. Our approach can be viewed as a generalization of the previous method introduced by Korach, Kutten and Moran [7]. We show how well-known $O(N)$ message leader election algorithms in oriented hypercubes and tori [12, 11, 15, 16] can be derived by our technique. This is in contrast with $\Omega(N \log N)$ message lower bound for the approach in [7].
Moreover, our technique can be used to design new linear leader election algorithms for unoriented butterflies and cube connected cycles, thus demonstrating its usefulness. This is an improvement over the $O(N \log N)$ solutions obtained from the general leader election algorithm [5]. These results are of interest, since tori and corresponding chordal rings were the only known symmetric topologies for which linear leader election algorithms in unoriented case were known [11, 15].

1 Introduction

One of the fundamental problems in distributed systems is the problem of *Leader Election*; that is, the problem of transforming the system from an initial configuration where the processors are in the same initial state, to a final configuration where exactly one processor is in the state *leader* and all other processors are in the state *defeated*. The leader election is widely used in distributed computing, mainly in situations where one processor is required to act as a central coordinator, e.g. as a part of a reinitialization or recovery procedure.

There is a number of leader election algorithms, working on arbitrary networks [5] as well as on special topologies: rings [13, 6], complete graphs [8, 10], chordal rings [2], tori [12] and hypercubes [16, 4, 3]. Much attention has been devoted to different variants of the computational model, depending on the structural information about the underlying network topology available at the processors. It has been shown that more efficient solutions exist for special topologies

---

* The research was partially supported by EU Grant No. INCO-COP 96-0195 "ALTEC-KIT" and by the Slovak VEGA project 1/4315/97.

rather than for arbitrary ones (with or without additional structural information, e.g. sense of orientation).

A general modular technique has been presented in [7], using a traversal algorithm as a building block for leader election. This technique can be applied to arbitrary networks and for some special topologies (e.g. complete graphs) it yields better results than the general leader election algorithm [5]. However, for sparse N-node networks (with $O(N \log N)$ edges) it is not better than the general algorithm.

We propose a modular technique, which overcomes this weakness. Our approach can be seen as a generalization of the previous results from [7, 1], exploiting the ideas from [12, 15]. Designing efficient leader election algorithms for specific topologies can be pretty hard task, thus general and still flexible techniques can be helpful.

We document the last point by using our approach in the case of unoriented butterflies and cube connected cycles. Applications of the general techniques from [5, 7, 1] lead to non-satisfactory $O(N \log N)$ solutions. No better results have been known for these topologies (even in the oriented case). We use our technique to design $O(N)$ leader election algorithms on these topologies, showing that topological awareness alone is sufficient to decrease the communication complexity to $O(N)$ messages.

The paper is organized as follows. In Section 2, we introduce necessary preliminaries. In Section 3, we present our modular technique and in Section 4 we apply it to wrapped butterflies and cube connected cycles.

2 Preliminaries

The computational model is a standard model of asynchronous distributed computing [14]. Every message will be delivered in a finite but unbounded time. FIFO requirements on links are not necessary. All processors are identical and run the same algorithm.

The underlying communication topology is represented by undirected graph $G = (V, E)$, where vertices represent processors and edges represent bidirectional communication channels between them. We will use N for $|V|$.

We consider non-anonymous networks. That means that each processor has unique identification number (id) from some totally ordered set ID. These identities are without topological significance. Moreover, each processor knows only its own identity.

Solving the problem of *Leader Election* means that starting from an initial configuration where all processors are in the same state (the only difference being different *ids*), the system should reach a configuration where exactly one processor is in the state *leader* and all other processors are in the state *defeated*. The computation starts spontaneously in some non-empty subset of processors, the remaining processors join the computation after receiving the first message.

We are interested in *communication complexity*, expressed by the maximum number of messages (usually of size $O(\log N)$ or $O(\log i)$, where i is the maximal *id* used) sent by the algorithm over all possible executions. There are many possible executions, due to the communication asynchronicity or the unknown subset of starting processors. We will use the notion *circumstances* $\mathcal{O}$ for a given fixed pattern of message delays and starting set of processors. If the algorithm is deterministic, for given $\mathcal{O}$ it has only one execution.

Wrapped butterflies and cube connected cycles. The n-dimensional wrapped butterfly can be represented as a graph $BF_n = (V, E)$, where $V = \{(i, c)|0 \le i < 2^n, 0 \le c < n\}$ and $(i, c), (j, c')$ are connected iff $c' = c \pm 1 \bmod n$ and $i = j$ or i and j differ in bit position $\min(c, c')$. By c-column we mean the set $\{(i, c)|0 \le i < 2^n\}$.

The n-dimensional cube connected cycles is a graph $CCC_n = (V, E)$, where V is as before and (i, c) and (j, c') are connected iff $c' = c \pm 1 \bmod n$ and $i = j$ (cycle edges) or $c = c'$ and i and j differ in bit position c (hypercube edge). Columns of the butterfly correspond to cycles created of cycle edges only.

3 The Synchronization Technique

The main idea of our technique comes from the observation that efficiency of leader election algorithms on oriented hypercubes and tori [16, 12] is due to the fact that on these topologies an active processor can claim large territory by marking significantly smaller amount of vertices. Algorithms of Tel and Peterson work in stages and use ad-hoc technique to synchronize the computation. We propose a general synchronization technique which uses arbitrary marking algorithm $\mathcal{A}$ as a building block.

Let $\mathcal{A}$ be a deterministic distributed algorithm initiated at a single vertex, with an integer parameter (later interpreted as the stage number), and with an explicit termination.

Definition 1.

- $\mathcal{A}_{v,i}^{\mathcal{O}}$ denotes $\mathcal{A}$ *invoked at vertex v with a parameter i, running under circumstances $\mathcal{O}$.*
- $\mathcal{R}_{\mathcal{A}_{v,i}^{\mathcal{O}}} = \{u|u$ *is reached by* $\mathcal{A}_{v,i}^{\mathcal{O}}\}$
- **(Collision Set)** $\mathcal{CS}_{\mathcal{A}_{v,i}^{\mathcal{O}}} = \{u|\mathcal{R}_{\mathcal{A}_{v,i}^{\mathcal{O}}} \cap \mathcal{R}_{\mathcal{A}_{u,i}^{\mathcal{O}}} \ne \emptyset\}$
- **(Size of Collision Set)** $\mathcal{CS}_{\mathcal{A}_i} = \min_{v,\mathcal{O}} |\mathcal{CS}_{\mathcal{A}_{v,i}^{\mathcal{O}}}|$
- $f_{\mathcal{A}_i} = \max_{v,\mathcal{O}} (\#$ *of messages used by* $\mathcal{A}_{v,i}^{\mathcal{O}})$

When $\mathcal{A}$ is clear from the context, we will omit it and use shorter terms $\mathcal{R}_{v,i}^{\mathcal{O}}$, $\mathcal{CS}_{v,i}^{\mathcal{O}}$, $\mathcal{CS}_i$ and f_i, respectively.

In the following description of the algorithm we will omit $\mathcal{O}$ indices. All references will be assumed under the circumstances under which this particular execution of the algorithm runs.

The election algorithm $\mathcal{E}$ works in stages. During each stage, actions are initiated by processors active in this stage, resulting in the extinction of some active processors. At the beginning, spontaneously awaked processors are the only active ones. If a processor is awaken by some incoming message, it will become passive for the rest of the computation. Stages are repeated until either only one processor – the leader – remains active or stages cannot be performed efficiently any more. In the second case, another algorithm is launched afterwards to choose the leader from the remaining active processors.

Let v be an active processor in a stage i. Activity launched by v at stage i consists of three phases:

1. **(forward phase)** $\mathcal{A}_{v,i}$ is launched, with suffix $(v, i, \text{forward})$ added to each of its messages. (This suffix is ignored by $\mathcal{A}$). During this phase, the spanning tree $\mathcal{T}_{v,i}$ of $\mathcal{R}_{v,i}$ rooted at v is built.
2. **(backward phase)** Reversed computation proceeds from the leaves of $\mathcal{T}_{v,i}$ backward to v. It is clear when to start, because $\mathcal{A}$ terminates explicitly. During the backward phase collisions are tested. When it is finished, v can tell whether it survives stage i. The processor v survives only if no collision with stronger processor occured (here the suffixes added in the forward phase are used). A processor is stronger if it is in higher stage or it is in the same stage, but with higher id.
3. **(acknowledgement phase)** $\mathcal{T}_{v,i}$ is used to broadcast on $\mathcal{R}_{v,i}$ whether v survived the stage i. $((v, i, \text{ack}, 1), (v, i, \text{ack}, 0)$ are used to signal survived, killed, respectively)

The acknowledgement phase is needed to allow deadlock-free implementation of the backward phase.

If $\mathcal{A}_{v,i}^{\mathcal{O}}$ uses less than $2|\mathcal{R}_{v,i}^{\mathcal{O}}|$ messages and $\mathcal{R}_{v,i}^{\mathcal{O}}$ does not depend on $\mathcal{O}$, it is more efficient to use $\mathcal{A}_{v,i}$ in backward and acknowledgement phase, thus saving the construction of the spanning tree of $\mathcal{R}_{v,i}^{\mathcal{O}}$.

There are some technical difficulties in the backward phase due to the asynchronicity, so we will discuss this phase in more detail.

Backward phase at a leaf u of $\mathcal{T}_{v,i}$:

Test(v,i);

Backward phase at a non-leaf vertex u of $\mathcal{T}_{v,i}$:

<u>Wait</u> for messages $(v, i, \text{backward}, x)$ from all your sons in $\mathcal{T}_{v,i}$;
Compute y as <u>and</u> of all x's fields of these messages;
<u>if</u> $y = 0$ <u>then</u> <u>Send</u>$(v, i, \text{backward}, 0)$ to your father
<u>else if</u> $u \neq v$ <u>then</u> Test(v, i)
    <u>else</u> broadcast (v, i, ack, y) on $\mathcal{T}_{v,i}$;

Procedure Test(v,i) at a vertex u:

Let (w, j) be the maximal pair that u has seen, not taking into account (v, i). If $(w, j, \text{ack}, 1)$ has been received, then take $(w, j + 1)$ instead of (w, j). Let (w^*, j^*) be the maximal pair such that no ack message for it has been received.

<u>if</u> $(w, j) > (v, i)$ <u>then</u> <u>Send</u>$(v, i, \text{backward}, 0)$ to your father
<u>else</u> <u>if</u> $(w^*, j^* + 1) < (v, i)$ <u>then</u> <u>Send</u>$(v, i, \text{backward}, 1)$ to your father
   <u>else</u> <u>Wait</u> for receiving (w', j', ack, x) for all (w', j') such that
        $(w', j' + 1) > (v, i)$ and no ack message has been received for (w', j').
    Compute y as <u>and</u> of all $\neg x$'s fields of these ack messages.
    <u>Send</u>$(v, i, \text{backward}, y)$ to your father;

Lemma 1. *The algorithm $\mathcal{E}$ is deadlock-free.*

Proof. The waiting for actions of some other active processor occurs only in the procedure Test(). Here (v, i) waits for (w', j') only if $(w', j') < (v, i)$ (and $(w', j' + 1) > (v, i)$). (If $(w', j') > (v, i)$ then also $(w, j) > (v, i)$ and no waiting is induced.) That means that in the oriented dependency graph of the waiting relation each edge leads to the weaker vertex, thus no cycle can occur.

Lemma 2. *There always remains at least one active processor.*

Proof. The strongest processor (with the highest (w, j)) can be beaten only by a (slightly weaker) surviving processor.

Lemma 3. *Let u and v be two processors active at stage i (in the execution of $\mathcal{E}$ under circumstances $\mathcal{O}$). If $u \in CS_{v,i}^{\mathcal{O}}$ then at most one of them is active at stage $i + 1$.*

Proof. W.l.o.g. assume $u < v$. (As $u \in CS_{v,i}^{\mathcal{O}}$ implies $v \in CS_{u,i}^{\mathcal{O}}$). If $\exists w \in \mathcal{R}_{v,i}^{\mathcal{O}} \cap \mathcal{R}_{u,i}^{\mathcal{O}}$ such that it received a message $(v, i, \text{forward})$ before receiving $(u, i, \text{forward})$, then u will not survive because of the first test in the procedure Test(u, i) at the vertex w. If there is no such vertex and u survived the stage i, then v will not survive, because it will wait for ack messages for (u, i) in some vertices of $\mathcal{R}_{v,i}^{\mathcal{O}} \cap \mathcal{R}_{u,i}^{\mathcal{O}}$. These ack messages will eventually arrive (because u survives) and kill v.

Corollary 1. *For $i \geq 1$, there are at most $\lfloor N/CS_{i-1} \rfloor$ processors active during the stage i, where $CS_0 = 1$.*

Proposition 1. *Let the algorithm $\mathcal{E}$ run up to k stages, then*

1. *there are at most $\lfloor N/CS_k \rfloor$ active processors,*
2. *$O(N \sum_{i=1}^{k} f_i/CS_{i-1})$ messages are used.*

Proof. Straightforward consequence of the Corollary 1 and the definitions of f_i and CS_i.

Our construction shows how to reduce the problem of designing a leader election algorithm to the problem of choosing a suitable marking algorithm $\mathcal{A}$ such that $\mathcal{A}$ is efficient ($f_i^{\mathcal{A}}$ is preferably low), but it can claim a large territory ($CS_i^{\mathcal{A}}$ is high).

4 Relationship to Known Results

In this section we show how some well-known algorithms for leader election can be viewed as optimized instances of our technique. The algorithm $\mathcal{E}$ is rather clumsy in comparison with these approaches, because it does not exploit properties of the underlying marking algorithm $\mathcal{A}$ (e.g. $\mathcal{A}$ being traversal or the fact that $\mathcal{R}_{v,i}$ and $\mathcal{R}_{u,i}$ may greatly overlap). However, such optimizations improve only the constant factor, but they do not influence the asymptotical behaviour.

Modular technique by Korach, Kutten and Moran [7]. Our technique works different than the construction from [7], but reaches the same complexity:

Take $\mathcal{A}_{v,i}$ to be a traversal algorithm that reaches 2^i vertices. Trivially $\mathcal{CS}_{v,i}^{O} \supset \mathcal{R}_{v,i}^{O}$, so $\mathcal{CS}_i \geq 2^i$. Following arguments from [7] we get the leader election algorithm with the same asymptotical bound on the communication.

Leader election on oriented hypercubes [16]. Choose $\mathcal{A}_{v,i}$ to be two broadcasts: **(a)** on the sub-hypercube spanning the first $\lfloor i/2 \rfloor$ dimensions from v and **(b)** on the sub-hypercube spanning dimensions $\lfloor i/2 \rfloor + 1, \ldots, i$ from v. We get $f_i = O(2^{i/2})$, $\mathcal{CS}_i = O(2^i)$ (the sub-hypercube spanning the first i dimensions from v) and the number of stages $k = \log N$, resulting in the overall communication $O(N \sum_{i=1}^{\log N} 1/2^{i/2}) = O(N)$.

Leader election on (unoriented) tori [12, 15, 11]. Let $\mathcal{A}_{v,i}$ be an algorithm that marks the boundary of a square of side α^i for some $\alpha > 1$ (v is a corner of this square). This can be done using $O(\alpha^i)$ messages even on unoriented tori (see [15, 11]), thus $f_i = O(\alpha^i)$. $\mathcal{CS}_i = \alpha^{2i}$, since there is no vertex inside the marked square that can mark boundary of its square of the same size without crossing the boundary of the surrounding square. k is set to $\log_{\alpha}(\min(n_1, n_2))$, where n_1 and n_2 are sizes of the torus. Following Proposition 1 we get $O(N)$ messages for $\log(n_1/n_2) \in O(1)$. In case of less balanced tori, special termination phase is needed to choose a leader from the remaining active processors (the same as in the original algorithm [12]).

5 New Results

We combine proposed technique with computing preorientation [15,11] and matching technique for hypercubes [16], to achieve linear leader election algorithms for unoriened wrapped butterflies and cube connected cycles. No previous results for these topologies were known and by application of general techniques from [5,7] we get $O(N \log N)$ solutions.

5.1 Leader Election on Unoriented Wrapped Butterflies

Computing preorientation In the butterfly there are just two cycles of length 4 passing through a given vertex, and vertices of each of these cycles lie in the same direction (see Figure 1). This means that after a local precomputation up

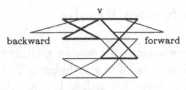

Figure 1.

to distance 2, each vertex can divide its 4 links into two groups - the *forward* and the *backward* links.

There is no global knowledge of what is forward and what is backward direction, however our algorithm does not need it. Note that computing preorientations can be done in $O(N)$ messages, since the degree of the butterfly is constant and we need to look up to constant distance only.

The marking algorithm $\mathcal{A}_i$ (Closely resembles $\mathcal{A}_i$ for oriented hypercubes.)

> Fill(i, forward);
> FarFill(i, forward);
> Fill(i, backward);   *{needed, because there is no global consistency}*
> FarFill(i, backward);   *{of what is forward and what backward}*

Procedure Fill(i, direction)

> At initiator:
>   <u>Send</u>(fill, i) to both neighbours in the desired direction;
> Upon receiving (fill, i):
>   <u>if</u> $i > 1$ <u>then</u> <u>Send</u>(fill, $i-1$) on both links in the opposite direction;

Procedure FarFill(i, direction)

> At initiator:
>   Choose one neighbour in the desired direction and send him
>   (farfill, i, $2i$) message;
> Upon receiving (farfill, i, j):
>   <u>if</u> $j = 1$ <u>then</u> launch Fill(i) in the direction from which you received
>   this message.
>   <u>else</u> <u>Send</u>(farfill, i, $j-1$) to one of the neighbours in the opposite
>   direction.

Note that $\mathcal{A}_i$ is independent of circumstances, so we can omit the index $\mathcal{O}$.

Lemma 4.

1. $f_i \in O(2^i)$
2. $CS_i \geq 2^{2i}$ for $0 \leq i < n/2$
3. $CS_i \geq (2i - n)2^n$ for $n/2 \leq i \leq n$

Proof. 1. The complexity of $\mathcal{A}_i$ is $2 \cdot \text{Fill} + 2 \cdot \text{FarFill} = 4i + 4 \cdot \text{Fill} = $
$= 4i + 4(2^{i+1} - 1) \in O(2^i)$.

2. We will prove the following statement. Let $u = (x, c)$, $v = (y, c)$. If x and y differ only in the substring of $2i$ consecutive bits starting from the position $c + 1$, then $\mathcal{R}_{v,i} \cap \mathcal{R}_{u,i} \neq \emptyset$ ($u \in \mathcal{CS}_{v,i}$). This proves (2), since for each u there are 2^{2i} such v.

Consider a vertex v' from which the procedure Fill$(i, \_)$ was launched from FarFill(). (There are two such v' for each v – take one of them.) v' may differ from u only in $2i$ bits starting from the position $c + 1$. All possibilities of the first i bits are tried in the last layer marked by Fill$(i, \_)$ launched from u to the direction v' lies in. All possibilities of the last i bits (of these $2i$ bits they may differ) are tried at the layer of vertices marked by Fill$(i, \_)$ launched from v'. So, there must be a vertex at the column $(c + i) \bmod n$ which lies in $\mathcal{R}_{v,i} \cap \mathcal{R}_{u,i}$.

3. We will prove the following statement. Let $u = (x, c')$, $v = (y, c)$. If u lies in some of the $2i - n$ columns starting from c, then $u \in \mathcal{CS}_{v,i}$. Since there are 2^n vertices at each column, this shows that $\mathcal{CS}_{v,i} \geq (2i - n)2^n$ for each v.

The proof follows as in the previous case. Let v' be as before. u and v' may now differ in all n bits. All vertices that differ from u only in bits $c' + 1, \ldots, c' + i$ are marked by an invocation of Fill$(i, \_)$ from u. Vertices that differ from v' only in bits $c + i, \ldots, c + 2i$ are marked by the invocation of Fill$(i, \_)$ from v'. Since $2i > N$ and c' is between c and $2i + c$, there is $w \in \mathcal{R}_{v,i} \cap \mathcal{R}_{u,i}$ in each of the columns $c + i, \ldots, c' + i$.

To complete the description of the algorithm, we must ensure that further stages are not needed. This can be done in the following way. If a vertex v is reached by a *fill* message (messages from Fill() launched from FarFill() are not counted) that was initiated by it, then v knows that it is the only surviving processor and broadcasts its identity.

The overall complexity can be computed following Proposition 1 and Lemma 4:

$$N \left(\sum_{i=1}^{\lfloor n/2 \rfloor} \frac{2^i}{2^{2i}} + \sum_{i=\lfloor n/2 \rfloor + 1}^{n} \frac{2^i}{(2i - n)2^n} \right) = O(N)$$

Since the final broadcasting is trivially $O(N)$, we have

Proposition 2. *The leader election algorithm $\mathcal{E}$ on unoriented N–node butterflies uses $O(N)$ messages.*

5.2 Leader Election on Unoriented Cube Connected Cycles

The algorithm for CCC simulates the algorithm for the wrapped butterfly. Since the wrapped butterfly can be embedded in CCC with dilation 2 [9], the complexity of the resulting algorithm is again $O(N)$.

All what is needed to show is how to simulate a preoriented butterfly on an unoriented cube connected cycles of the same dimension. First, we preorient

CCC_n. This can be done in a similar way as in the preorientation of the n–dimensional butterfly. We use the fact that for $n > 8$ there are exactly two circles of length 8 passing through a given vertex. The edge which lies in both circles is the hypercube edge, the remaining two are the cycle edges. The ability to distinguish forward and backward edges on the butterfly corresponds on the CCC to the ability to distinguish consistently left/right when crossing the hypercube edge from one cycle (of length n) to another. This can be done by adding *id* of the left neighbour to the messages. The receiver can distinguish *left* by inspecting which circle (of length 8) contains this left neighbour.

6 Conclusions

We have presented general, but still flexible modular method for the design of efficient (linear) leader election algorithms and shown its suitability for specific topologies (oriented tori and hypercubes, unoriented butterflies and cube connected cycles) over the existing approaches [1, 7].

The linear algorithms for unoriented wrapped butterflies, CCC and tori suggest that on regular graphs of constant degree the global orientation is not necessary for optimal leader election. On the other hand, the $\Omega(N \log N)$ lower bound on unoriented complete graphs [8] shows that the lack of global orientation induces additional $\log N$ factor in this case. $O(N \log \log N)$ algorithm is known for unoriented hypercubes [3], indicating that the additional factor is in this case at most $O(\log \log N)$. These results suggest the following problem:

Prove or disprove $O(N \log d)$ lower bound for leader election on unoriented vertex symmetric graphs of degree d. The stronger version is perhaps even more interesting: *prove/disprove this lower bound for the weaker problem of reducing the number of active vertices to $N/(d+1)$.* (The warrior technique from [3] gives $O(N \log d)$ upper bound for the last problem.)

References

1. Attiya, H.: *Constructing efficient election algorithms from efficient traversal algorithms.* In Proc. 2nd Int. Workshop on Distributed Algorithms, LNCS 312, Springer-Verlag, 1987, pp. 337–344.
2. Attiya, H. – van Leeuwen, J. – Santoro, N. – Zaks, S.: *Efficient elections in chordal ring networks.* Algorithmica 4 (1989), pp. 437–466.
3. Dobrev, S. – Ružička, P.: *Linear broadcasting and $N \log \log N$ election in unoriented hypercubes.* Proc. of the 4th International Colloquium on Structural Information and Communication Complexity (SIROCCO'97), Carleton Press, 1997, pp. 52–68.
4. Flocchini, P. – Mans, B.: *Optimal elections in labeled hypercubes.* Journal of Parallel and Distributed Computing 33 (1), 1996, pp. 76–83.
5. Gallager, R. G. – Humblet, P. A. – Spira, P. M.: *A distributed algorithm for minimum–weight spanning trees.* ACM Trans. Programming Languages and Systems 5 (1983), pp. 66–77.

6. Higham, L. – Przytycka, T.: *A simple, efficient algorithm for maximum finding on rings.* In Proc. 7th Int. Workshop on Distributed Algorithms, LNCS 725, Springer-Verlag, 1993, pp. 249–263.

7. Korach, E. – Kutten, S. – Moran, S.: *A modular technique for the design of efficient leader finding algorithms.* ACM Transactions on Programming Languages and Systems 12 (1990), pp. 84–101.

8. Korach, E. – Moran, S. – Zaks, S.: *Tight upper and lower bounds for some distributed algorithms for a complete network of processors.* Symp. on Principles of Distributed Computing, 1984, pp. 199–207.

9. Leighton, F.T.: *Introduction to Parallel Algorithms and Architectures: Arrays, Trees, Hypercubes.* Morgan Kaufmann Publishers, 1992.

10. Loui, M.C. – Matsushita, T.A. – West, D.B.: *Election in complete networks with a sense of direction.* Information Processing Letters 22 (1986), pp. 185–187. Addendum: Inf. Proc. Lett. 28 (1988), p. 327.

11. Mans, B.: *Optimal Distributed Algorithms in Unlabelled Tori and Chordal Rings.* Journal of Parallel and Distributed Computing 46 (1), 1997, pp. 80–90.

12. Peterson, G. L.: *Efficient algorithms for elections in meshes and complete networks.* Technical Report TR140, Dept. of Computer Science, Univ. of Rochester, Rochester, NY 14627, 1985.

13. van Leeuwen, J. – Tan, R.B.: *An improved upperbound for distributed election in bidirectional rings of processors.* Technical Report RUU-CS-85-23, Dept. of Computer Science, University of Utrecht, August 1985.

14. Tel, G.: *Introduction to Distributed Algorithms.* Cambridge University Press, Cambridge, 1994.

15. Tel, G.: *Sense of Direction in Processor Networks.* In: SOFSEM'95, Theory and Practise of Informatics, LNCS 1012, Springer–Verlag, 1995, pp. 50–82.

16. Tel, G.: *Linear election in oriented hypercubes.* Parallel Processing Letters 5 (1995), pp. 357–366.

Regulated Grammars with Leftmost Derivation

Henning Fernau*

Wilhelm-Schickard-Institut für Informatik, Universität Tübingen
Sand 13, D-72076 Tübingen, Germany
email: fernau@informatik.uni-tuebingen.de

Abstract. In this paper, we investigate various concepts of leftmost derivation in grammars controlled by bicoloured digraphs, especially regarding their descriptive capacity. This approach allows us to unify the presentation of known results regarding especially programmed grammars and matrix grammars, and to obtain new results concerning grammars with regular control, and periodically time-variant grammars. Moreover, we get new results on leftmost derivations in conditional grammars.

1 Introduction

Although leftmost derivations (mostly leftmost derivations of type 3 explained below) played a vital rôle when several rewriting mechanisms have been defined at around 1970, there has been no *systematic* research in that direction. This is surprising: a leftmost restriction may be a means to get rid of the seemingly inherent nondeterminism feature in grammars, see [2], which renders these mechanisms hard to apply. We study leftmost derivations in regulated rewriting systematically by using the framework of graph-controlled grammars, which are an intuitively appealing unifying framework for many seemingly different ways of regulation (see [7, 9, 10]). Hence, we obtain simplified versions of known and many new results on leftmost derivation in regulated rewriting (compare the Section 1.4 in [5]). Moreover, such systematic study is useful to detect unexplored sub-areas, for example concerning leftmost derivation in time-variant grammars. This paper continues our previous works on leftmost derivation, see [4, 11].

The need for such a systematic exposition is underlined by [17] and [6], where ideas from regulated rewriting are applied to parsing theory and database theory, respectively, although the papers indicate that the knowledge of basic facts in regulated rewriting is not too widespread. Note that in [17] programmed grammars with left-1 derivations are used without naming them such.

Conventions: $\subseteq$ denotes inclusion, $\subset$ denotes strict inclusion. $\emptyset$ denotes the empty set. The empty word is denoted by λ. The length of a word x is denoted by $|x|$. We consider two languages L_1, L_2 to be equal iff $L_1 \setminus \{\lambda\} = L_2 \setminus \{\lambda\}$.

Some knowledge about formal languages is assumed on side of the reader, see [5, 16], especially regarding the Chomsky hierarchy $\mathcal{L}(\text{REG}) \subset \mathcal{L}(\text{CF}) \subset \mathcal{L}(\text{CS}) \subset \mathcal{L}(\text{RE})$. Sometimes, we use the following fact:

---

* Supported by Deutsche Forschungsgemeinschaft grant DFG La 618/3-2.

Lemma 1. *Let $\mathcal{L}$ be a trio and let $\mathcal{L}'$ be closed under union and contain all finite languages. If for all $L \in \mathcal{L}$, where $L \subseteq V^*$, and for all $a \in V$ we know that $L\{a\}$ lies in $\mathcal{L}'$ (or, for all $a \in V$ we know that $\{a\}L$ lies in $\mathcal{L}'$), then $\mathcal{L} \subseteq \mathcal{L}'$.*

2 Definitions and known properties

First, we introduce the concept of graph-controlled rewriting, introduced by Wood in [21]. This allows us to present programmed, matrix (set) and time-variant grammars as well as grammars with regular (set) control as special cases, leading to a unified and lucid framework of definitions and arguments as it has been done in [7, 9, 10]. For historic references, we refer to our quoted papers.

A *grammar controlled by a bicoloured digraph* or *G grammar* is an 8-tuple $G = (V_N, V_T, P, S, \Gamma, \Sigma, \Phi, h)$ where

- V_N, V_T, P, S define, as in a phrase structure grammar, the set of nonterminals, terminals, context-free core rules, and the start symbol, respectively;
- Γ is a bicoloured digraph, i.e., $\Gamma = (U, E)$, where U is a finite set of nodes and $E \subseteq U \times \{g, r\} \times U$ is a finite set of directed edges (arcs) coloured by g or r ("green" or "red");
- $\Sigma \subseteq U$ are the initial nodes;
- $\Phi \subseteq U$ are the final nodes;
- $h : U \to (2^P \setminus \{\emptyset\})$ relates nodes with rule sets.

There are two different definitions of the appearance checking (ac) mode in the literature: We say that $(x, u) \Rightarrow (y, v)$ $((x, u) \Rightarrow_c (y, v)$, respectively) holds in G with $(x, u), (y, v) \in (V_N \cup V_T)^* \times U$, if either $x = x_1 \alpha x_2$, $y = x_1 \beta x_2$, $\alpha \to \beta \in h(u)$, $(u, g, v) \in E$ or every (one, respectively) rule of $h(u)$ is not applicable to x, $y = x$, $(u, r, v) \in E$. The reflexive transitive closure of $\Rightarrow$ ($\Rightarrow_c$, respectively) is denoted by $\overset{*}{\Rightarrow}$ ($\overset{*}{\Rightarrow}_c$, respectively). For $m \in \{c, \lambda\}$, the languages generated by G are defined by $L_m(G) = \{x \in V_T^* \mid \exists u \in \Sigma \exists v \in \Phi(S, u) \overset{*}{\Rightarrow}_m (x, v)\}$.

(i) G is said to be with *unconditional transfer* iff $\forall u, v \in U((u, g, v) \in E \iff (u, r, v) \in E)$.

(ii) If $E \cap U \times \{r\} \times U = \emptyset$, G is *without appearance checking*.

Depending on the chosen derivation mode $m \in \{c, \lambda\}$, the language families are denoted by $\mathcal{L}(G_m, \mathrm{CF}, \mathrm{ac})$ (with appearance checking), $\mathcal{L}(G_m, \mathrm{CF}, \mathrm{ut})$ (with unconditional transfer), and $\mathcal{L}(G_m, \mathrm{CF})$ (without appearance checking). "CF" indicates that we allow context-free rules only. Here and in the following, we write $\mathrm{CF} - \lambda$ instead of CF if we do not allow erasing core rules of the form $A \to \lambda$. By definition, we have for $X \in \{\mathrm{CF}, \mathrm{CF} - \lambda\}$, $m \in \{c, \lambda\}$:

$$\mathcal{L}(G_c, X) = \mathcal{L}(G, X) \subseteq \mathcal{L}(G_m, X, \mathrm{ac}), \text{ and } \mathcal{L}(G_m, X, \mathrm{ut}) \subseteq \mathcal{L}(G_m, X, \mathrm{ac}).$$

We consider six special cases of G grammars in the following:

- A *programmed grammar* or *P grammar* has the following features:

- o Every node contains exactly one rule. (Therefore, both modes of ac coincide.)
- o All nodes are both initial and final.
- A *grammar with regular set control* or *rSC grammar* is a G grammar obeying:
  - o If there is a red arc from node u to node v, then there is also a green arc from node u to node v.
- A *grammar with regular control* or *rC grammar* is an rSC grammar such that
  - o every node contains exactly one rule. (Therefore, both modes of ac coincide.)
- A *matrix set grammar* or *MS grammar* is an rSC grammar when:
  - o Only the initial nodes (not necessarily containing rules with left-hand side S) are allowed to have more than one in-going green arc, while only the final nodes are allowed to have more than one out-going green arc. Between every final node and every initial node, there is a green arc.
- A *matrix grammar* or *M grammar* is both an MS and an rC grammar.
- A *(periodically) time-variant grammar* or *TV grammar* has the following features:
  - o If there is a red arc from node u to node v, then there is also a green arc from node u to node v. Every node has exactly one in-going green arc and one out-going green arc. In other words, the graph of green arcs has a simple ring structure.
  - o There is one designated initial node, and every node can be a final node.

Here and in the following, we leave out unnessary components when defining special cases of G grammars, e.g., initial and final nodes need not be specified for P grammars. As language families, we obtain $\mathcal{L}(X, Y, Z)$, where $X \in \{P, rSC_m, rC, MS_m, M, TV_m\}$, $Y \in \{CF, CF - \lambda\}$, $Z \in \{ac, ut, \lambda\}$, $m \in \{c, \lambda\}$.

Obviously, every M[S] grammar is also an r[S]C grammar, and it is not hard to see that every TV grammar is also an rSC grammar. Besides these trivial relations, the following results are known in the area of free derivations [5, 10]:

Theorem 2. *Let* $X \in \{P, M, rC\}$, $Y \in \{CF, CF - \lambda\}$, $Z \in \{ac, ut, \lambda\}$, $Z' \in \{ac, \lambda\}$. *Then, one finds*

1. $\mathcal{L}(X, Y, Z) = \mathcal{L}(G_c, Y, Z) = \mathcal{L}(TV_c, Y, Z) = \mathcal{L}(rSC_c, Y, Z) = \mathcal{L}(MS_c, Y, Z)$;
2. $\mathcal{L}(X, Y, Z') = \mathcal{L}(G, Y, Z') = \mathcal{L}(TV, Y, Z') = \mathcal{L}(rSC, Y, Z') = \mathcal{L}(MS, Y, Z')$;
3. $\mathcal{L}(G, Y, ut) = \mathcal{L}(TV, Y, ut) = \mathcal{L}(rSC, Y, ut) = \mathcal{L}(MS, Y, ut) = \mathcal{L}(M, Y, ac)$.

3 Two Further Derivation Modes

Motivated by the left-2 derivation (as defined in the literature, see discussion in Section 4), it is possible to define a third and fourth derivation mode besides $\Rightarrow$ and $\Rightarrow_c$ for graph-controlled grammars. Let us call these modes the *set modes*, abbreviated as $\Rightarrow_{s_1}$ and $\Rightarrow_{s_2}$. They are defined as follows. Let $G = (V_N, V_T, P, S, \Gamma, \Sigma, \Phi, h)$ with $\Gamma = (U, E)$ be a G grammar. Let $(x, V), (x', V') \in$

$(V_N \cup V_T)^* \times 2^U$. We say that $(x, V) \Rightarrow_{s_1} (x', V')$ $((x, V) \Rightarrow_{s_2} (x', V'))$, respectively) holds in G, if either $x = x_1 \alpha x_2$, $x' = x_1 \beta x_2$, $\alpha \to \beta \in h(v)$, for some $v \in V$, where $V' = \{v' \mid (v, g, v') \in E\}$, or no rule of $\bigcup_{v \in V} h(v)$ is applicable to x, $x' = x$, $V' = \{v' \mid (v, r, v') \in E\}$ for some $v \in V$ in case of $\Rightarrow_{s_1}$ and $V' = \{v' \mid \exists v \in V (v, r, v') \in E\}$ in case of $\Rightarrow_{s_2}$. The reflexive transitive closure of $\Rightarrow_{s_1}$ ($\Rightarrow_{s_2}$, respectively) is denoted by $\overset{*}{\Rightarrow}_{s_1}$ ($\overset{*}{\Rightarrow}_{s_2}$, respectively). The corresponding languages generated by G are defined by $L_s(G) = \{x \in V_T^* \mid \exists V \in 2^U, V \cap \Phi \neq \emptyset$ and $(S, \Sigma) \overset{*}{\Rightarrow}_s (x, V)\}$ for $s \in \{s_1, s_2\}$. As with the $\Rightarrow_c$ mode, we indicate the use of one of the set modes by subscripting.

Remark 3. 1. $L_m(G) = L(G)$ for every $m \in \{c, s_1, s_2\}$ and every G grammar G without ac, since it does not matter whether we choose first the node and then the rule to be applied or whether we choose a rule from the whole set.

2. $L_m(G) = L(G)$ for every $m \in \{s_1, s_2\}$ and every TV grammar G, since there is always only at most one possible continuation node.

3. $L_m(G) = L(G)$ for every $m \in \{c, s_1, s_2\}$ and every RC grammar G by combining the arguments of the first two points: inside the matrices of the MS grammar, there is (at most) one possible continuation (ii), and between (different) matrices, there are only green arcs (i).

Lemma 4. For $Y \in \{CF, CF - \lambda\}$, $Z \in \{ac, ut\}$, $s \in \{s_1, s_2\}$, we can show: $\mathcal{L}(G, Y, Z) \subseteq \mathcal{L}(G_s, Y, Z)$.

For reasons of space, we omit the nearly purely structural construction of the proof of the lemma; similar ideas also work for P, M[S], and r[S]C grammars.

Lemma 5. For $Y \in \{CF, CF - \lambda\}$, $s \in \{s_1, s_2\}$, $\mathcal{L}(G_s, Y, ac) \subseteq \mathcal{L}(G, Y, ac)$.

Proof. Let $G = (V_N, V_T, P, S, \Gamma, \Sigma, \Phi, h)$ with $\Gamma = (U, E)$ be a G grammar with ac. We construct, for $s \in \{s_1, s_2\}$, a G grammar $G_s = (V_N \cup \{F\}, V_T, P \cup \{A \to F \mid A \in V_N\}, S, \Gamma', \{(u, \Sigma) \mid u \in \Sigma\}, \{(u, \Phi) \mid u \in \Phi\}, h')$ with ac; let $h'((u, V)) = h(u) \cup \{A \to F \mid \exists A \to w \in \bigcup_{u' \in V} h(u')\}$, and $\Gamma_s = (U_s, E_s)$ such that $U_s = U \times 2^U$, where E_s is given by

- $((u, V), g, (u', V')) \in E_s$ iff $(u, g, u') \in E$ and $V' = \{\bar{u} \mid (u, g, \bar{u}) \in E\}$;
- $((u, V), r, (u', V')) \in E_{s_1}$ iff $(u, r, u') \in E$ and $V' = \{\bar{u} \mid (u, r, \bar{u}) \in E\}$;
- $((u, V), r, (u', V')) \in E_{s_2}$ iff $(\tilde{u}, r, u') \in E$ for some $\tilde{u} \in V$ and $V' = \{\bar{u} \mid (\tilde{u}, r, \bar{u}) \in E, \tilde{u} \in V\}$. $\quad\square$

It is clear that the previous construction can be changed by serialization of the test rules $A \to F$ in order to work for programmed grammars as well. For matrix (set) grammars, one has to do a similar trick only at the "merging points" between the matrices. Observe that the construction above does not work in case of unconditional transfer. This is no coincidence, as the following lemma tells us.

Lemma 6. For $Y \in \{CF, CF - \lambda\}$, $s \in \{s_1, s_2\}$, $\mathcal{L}(M_s, Y, ut) = \mathcal{L}(M, Y, ac)$.

Proof. The previous lemma and the subsequent remarks show the direction $\subseteq$. For the other direction, consider a P grammar $G = (V_N, V_T, P, S, \Gamma = (U, E), h)$, $V_N = \{A_1, \ldots, A_n\}, U = \{u_1, \ldots, u_k\}$, with ac. We have the following matrices in a simulating M grammar $G' = (V_N', V_T, P', S', \Gamma', h')$ with $V_N' = V_N \cup U \cup \{S', F\}$ (disjoint union!):

- start matrices $(S' \rightarrow uS)$ for all $u \in U$;
- termination matrices $(u \rightarrow \lambda, A_1 \rightarrow F, \ldots, A_n \rightarrow F)$ for every $u \in U$.
- For every $u, u' \in U$ with $(u_i, g, u') \in E$ we take matrix $(A \rightarrow w, u_1 \rightarrow F, \ldots, u_{i-1} \rightarrow F, u_{i+1} \rightarrow F, \ldots u_k \rightarrow F, u_i \rightarrow u')$ for $h(u_i) = \{A \rightarrow w\}$.
- For every $u, u' \in U$ with $(u, r, u') \in E$ we define a matrix $(u \rightarrow u', A \rightarrow F)$ for $h(u) = \{A \rightarrow w\}$.

So, Γ', P' and h' are implicitly defined. Observe that to a sentential form containing at least one nonterminal, one of the (termination or start) matrices is always applicable, so that the first component of each matrix is never applied in ac manner. In the non-erasing case, one can apply lemma 1. ∎

We defer a summary of the obtained results to Section 4.3, since all our reasonings transfer to that case, too.

4 Leftmost Derivations

First, let us discuss what we could mean with the term "leftmost derivation" in the context of graph-controlled grammars and their specializations. Observe that all these definitions coincide in the case of unregulated context-free grammars.

4.1 Leftmost Derivations of Type 1

This mechanism is the strongest form of leftmost interpretation [5, p. 54]: *At each step of a derivation, the leftmost occurrence of a nonterminal is rewritten.*

Observe how the notion of applicability of a rule is affected by this definition: A rule is not applicable if its left-hand side does not equal the leftmost nonterminal symbol in the current sentential form. If a (set of) rule(s) is not applicable, the derivation proceeds according to one of the four modes introduced above. (This has been left a bit unclear in earlier works [5, 14] in our opinion.)

Theorem 7. *Let $X \in \{G, TV, P, M[S], r[S]C\}$, $m \in \{\lambda, c, s_1, s_2\}$, $Y \in \{CF, CF\text{-}\lambda\}$, $Z \in \{ac, ut, \lambda\}$. Then, $\mathcal{L}(X_m, Y, Z, left\text{-}1) = \mathcal{L}(CF)$.*

Proof. It is clear that each context-free language can be be obtained by any of the regulation mechanisms previously introduced when working under leftmost derivations of type 1. So, we only have to show that graph-controlled grammars working under leftmost derivations of type 1 are not more powerful than context-free grammars. We give a direct proof in the following.[1]

---

[1] Observe that the corresponding textbook proofs [5, Lemmas 1.4.1&2] are indirect since they rely on non-trivial properties of type-0 grammars under leftmost derivation, an area which has been investigated by several authors around 1970, see the discussion following [1, Corollary 7].

Let $G = (V_N, V_T, P, S, \Gamma, \Sigma, \Phi, h)$ with $\Gamma = (U, E)$ be a G grammar. We construct a context-free grammar $G'_m = (V'_N, V_T, P'_m, S_0)$ (in a triple-construction manner) with $V'_N = U \times V_N \times U \cup \{S_0\}$, and P'_m consists of the following rules (only in one place we have to distinguish the possible derivation modes $\Rightarrow_m$ with $m \in \{\lambda, c\}$ of G):

1. $S_0 \to (u, S, u')$, if $u \in \Sigma, u' \in \Phi$.

Now, let $A \to w \in h(u)$.

2. Let $(u, r, u'') \in E$ and assume, in case of the $\Rightarrow$-mode, that A is not left-hand side of any rule in u; then take $(u, A, u') \to (u'', A, u')$ into P'; or assume, in case of the $\Rightarrow_c$-mode, that A is not left-hand side of one rule in u; then take $(u, A, u') \to (u'', A, u')$ into P'_c.
3. If $w \in V_T^*$, then put $(u, A, u) \to w$ into P'_m.
4. Assume further that $w = x_0 B_1 x_1 B_2 \cdots x_{r-1} B_r x_r$ with $x_i \in V_T^*$ and $B_i \in V_N$. Put $(u_0, A, u_r) \to x_0(u_0, B_1, u_1)x_1(u_1, B_2, u_2) \cdots x_{r-1}(u_{r-1}, B_r, u_r)x_r$ into P'_m, where all $u_i \in U$ and $(u_0, g, u_r) \in E$.

It is easy to see that the language L generated by G working under leftmost derivations of type 1 in modes $\Rightarrow$ or $\Rightarrow_c$, respectively, equals the language obtained via G' or G'_c, respectively.

For the set modes, we can apply the construction given in lemma 5. $\quad$ ❏

In the literature, the only cases of the preceding theorem that have been treated are M and P grammars with the $\Rightarrow$ derivation mode.

4.2 Leftmost Derivations of Type 2

Again, we quote the general definition from [5]: *At each step of a derivation, the leftmost occurrence of a nonterminal which can be rewritten (note that in regulated grammars only certain nonterminal occurrences can be rewritten in a given stage of derivation) is rewritten.* Grammar derivations falling into this category have been investigated in [3, 5, 18].

This general definition leaves lots of room for interpretation.

Our general idea of leftmost derivations of type 2 will be to define the set of "nonterminals which can be rewritten" according to our four derivation modes separately. This will also allow us to treat ac according to the definitions given above, an issue which has not been tackled in this setting before.

The derivation mode $\Rightarrow_c$: The current state is a pair (x, u), where u is some node and x a sentential form. Then, we choose a rule $A \to w \in h(u)$. So, there is just one "nonterminal which can be rewritten", namely A. (Therefore, we leave the discussion of this mode to Section 4.3.) If A is contained in x, we replace A's leftmost occurrence by w and proceed via one of the green arcs leaving node u. Otherwise, we can apply $A \to w$ in ac mode, so that we leave node u by one of its outgoing red arcs.

The derivation mode $\Rightarrow$: Consider again a current state (x, u). Now, the set N of "nonterminals which can be rewritten" is the set of left-hand sides of rules in $h(u)$. If some symbol from N occurs in x, we look for the leftmost symbol $A \in N$ occurring in the form x. We apply some rule $A \to w \in h(u)$ to this leftmost occurrence of A. Then, we proceed via one of the green arcs leaving node u. If no symbol from N is contained in x, leave node u by one of its outgoing red arcs.

The derivation modes $\Rightarrow_{s_1}$ and $\Rightarrow_{s_2}$: Now, the current state is a pair (x, V), where V is some node set and x a sentential form, and the set N of "nonterminals which can be rewritten" is the set of left-hand sides of rules in $\bigcup_{u \in V} h(u)$. If some symbol from N occurs in x, we look for the leftmost symbol $A \in N$ occurring in the form x. We apply some rule $A \to w \in h(u)$ (for some $u \in V$) to this leftmost occurrence of A. Then, we proceed via one of the green arcs leaving node u. If no symbol from N is contained in x, the set of next nodes is defined via the outgoing red arcs of one (all, respectively) nodes in V.

In case of programmed grammars without ac, this coincides with the usual meaning of "leftmost derivation of type 2". This motivated the introduction of the set derivation modes. The following is known from the literature [5, Theorem 1.4.3] and [11, Theorem 7] regarding programmed grammars:

Theorem 8. Let $s \in \{s_1, s_2\}$, and let $Z \in \{ut, ac, \lambda\}$. Then, we know:
(1) $\mathcal{L}(P_s, CF - \lambda, Z, left\text{-}2) = \mathcal{L}(CS)$; (2) $\mathcal{L}(P_s, CF, Z, left\text{-}2) = \mathcal{L}(RE)$.

Lemma 9. Let $m \in \{\lambda, c, s_1, s_2\}$, and $Z \in \{ut, ac, \lambda\}$. Then, we obviously have:
(1) $\mathcal{L}(G_m, CF - \lambda, Z, left\text{-}2) \subseteq \mathcal{L}(CS)$; (2) $\mathcal{L}(G_m, CF, Z, left\text{-}2) \subseteq \mathcal{L}(RE)$.

Observe that this definition of left-2 derivations in matrix grammars (in any derivation mode) deviates from the classical one given in [5] inspired by Salomaa [18]. The "set modes" correspond to the wl-mode introduced in [4]. Since matrix grammars are matrix set as well as regularly controlled (set) grammars, we get results analogous to the previous theorem for those language classes as well. For the proof in case of unconditional transfer, ideas from the proofs of [11, Theorem 7] and [10, Lemma 4.3] can be adapted. So, we are left with TV grammars and with the $\Rightarrow$-mode of derivation in order to complete the picture.

Theorem 10. Let $Z \in \{ut, ac, \lambda\}$, $m \in \{\lambda, s_1, s_2\}$. We can prove:
(1) $\mathcal{L}(TV_m, CF - \lambda, Z, left\text{-}2) = \mathcal{L}(CS)$; (2) $\mathcal{L}(TV_m, CF, Z, left\text{-}2) = \mathcal{L}(RE)$.

Proof. By the previous lemma, we need to worry about the inclusions $\supseteq$. Further observe that s_1 and s_2 mode coincide for TV grammars. When ac is not involved, we show how to simulate a programmed grammar by a time variant one in the following.[2] Let $G = (V_N, V_T, P, S, \Gamma, h)$ with $\Gamma = (U, E)$ be a P_{s_1} grammar without ac. We construct a TV grammar $G' = (V'_N, V_T, P', S', \Gamma', \Sigma, h')$ without ac simulating the left-2 derivation within G. (First, we give a construction admitting erasing rules.) Let $\Gamma' = (U' = \{v_1, \ldots, v_{2r+2}\}, E')$ possess a ring structure, i.e., $(v_i, g, v_j) \in E'$ iff $j = i \bmod(2r + 2) + 1$. Let $\Sigma = \{v_{2r+2}\}$, $V'_N = V_N \cup V_N \times U \cup \{[u, j] \mid u \in U, 1 \leq j \leq 2\} \cup \{S'\}$. The rules of G' are:

---

[2] The construction of [5, Lemma 2.1.1] is not applicable here.

- $h'(v_i) = \{[u,1] \to [u,1] \mid u \neq u_i\} \cup \{A \to (A,u) \mid (u_i,g,u) \in E\}$ for $1 \leq i \leq r$;
- $h'(v_{r+1}) = \{[u,1] \to [u',2] \mid (u,g,u') \in E\}$;
- $h'(v_{r+1+i}) = \{[u,2] \to [u,2] \mid u \neq u_i\} \cup \{(A,u_i) \to w \mid h(u_i) = \{A \to w\}\}$ for $1 \leq i \leq r$;
- $h'(v_{2r+2}) = \{[u,2] \to [u,1], [u,2] \to \lambda \mid u \in U\} \cup$
  $\{S' \to [u,1]w \mid h(u) = \{S \to w\}\}$.

In the non-erasing case, observe that the corresponding P grammars character-ize the context-sensitive languages which are a trio. Moreover, the time-variant grammars obviously generate a language class which is closed under union. So, we can apply lemma 1, changing the newly introduced erasing rules into $[u,2] \to a$ for some terminal a. Details of the case of unconditional transfer are omitted. ∎

The picture of the leftmost-2 world is completed in the next theorem.

Theorem 11. *Let* $X \in \{G, TV, MS, rSC\}$, $X' \in \{P, M, rC\}$, $m \in \{\lambda, s_1, s_2\}$, $s \in \{s_1, s_2\}$, $Y \in \{CF, CF\text{-}\lambda\}$, $Z \in \{ac, ut, \lambda\}$. *Then,*

1. $\mathcal{L}(X_m, CF - \lambda, Z, \text{left-2}) = \mathcal{L}(X'_s, CF - \lambda, Z, \text{left-2}) = \mathcal{L}(CS)$;
2. $\mathcal{L}(X_m, CF, Z, \text{left-2}) = \mathcal{L}(X'_s, CF, Z, \text{left-2}) = \mathcal{L}(RE)$.

Proof idea. By what we have shown up to this point, we have to treat the MS case in combination with the $\Rightarrow$-mode. It is not too difficult to show the inclusion $\mathcal{L}(P_s, Y, \text{left-2}) \subseteq \mathcal{L}(MS, Y, \text{left-2})$ for $Y \in \{CF, CF\text{-}\lambda\}$. ∎

4.3 Leftmost Derivations of Type 3

Again, we start with the definition from [5]: *to use each rule in a leftmost manner, i.e., the leftmost appearance of its left-hand member is rewritten.* First, we link left-3 derivations with the left-2 derivation cases which are not classified yet.

Lemma 12. *Let* $X \in \{G, TV, MS, rSC, P, M, rC\}$, $Y \in \{CF, CF\text{-}\lambda\}$, $Z \in \{\lambda, ac, ut\}$. *Then, we have* $\mathcal{L}(X_c, Y, Z, \text{left-2}) = \mathcal{L}(X_c, Y, Z, \text{left-3})$.

The next theorem links the different left-3 classes. Proofs are always the same as in case of free derivations. Especially, we can refer to the fourth and fifth section of [10] regarding modes $\overset{*}{\Rightarrow}$ and $\overset{*}{\Rightarrow}_c$ and the preceding section regarding the set modes. Many open questions in this respect are contained in [11].

Theorem 13. *Let* $Y \in \{CF, CF - \lambda\}$, $Z \in \{\lambda, ac\}$, *and* $m \in \{\lambda, c, s_1, s_2\}$. *Then:*

1. $\mathcal{L}(P, Y, Z, \text{left-3}) = \mathcal{L}(X_m, Y, ac, \text{left-3})$ *for* $X \in \{G, M, MS, rC, rSC, TV, P\}$.
2. $\mathcal{L}(P, Y, ac, \text{left-3}) = \mathcal{L}(X_m, Y, ut, \text{left-3}) = \mathcal{L}(X'_s, Y, ut, \text{left-3})$ *for* $m \neq c$, $s \in \{s_1, s_2\}$, $X \in \{G, MS, rSC, TV\}$, $X' \in \{rC, M, P\}$.
3. $\mathcal{L}(P, Y, ut, \text{left-3}) = \mathcal{L}(X_c, Y, ut, \text{left-3}) = \mathcal{L}(X'_m, Y, ut, \text{left-3})$ *for* $m \in \{\lambda, c\}$, $X \in \{G, MS, rSC, TV\}$, $X' \in \{rC, M, P\}$. ∎

Finally, observe the following relations we have shown in [4], solving some open problems contained in [5].[3]

Theorem 14. $\mathcal{L}(P, CF[-\lambda]) \subset \mathcal{L}(P, CF[-\lambda], left\text{-}3) \subset \mathcal{L}(P, CF[-\lambda], ac, left\text{-}3).$ ❏

5 Beyond the Framework: Conditional Grammars

For conditional grammars (K grammars) we refer to [5]. We restrict ourselves mainly to regular conditions. Leftmost derivations have not been considered for these grammars in the literature. It is clear what a K grammar with leftmost derivations of type 1 and 3 should be. As regards left-2 derivations, note that those rules $(\alpha \to \beta, Q)$ with $u \in Q$ are applicable to $u \in (V_N \cup V_T)^*$.

Lemma 15. If $Y \in \{CF - \lambda, CF\}$, $x \in \{2, 3\}$, then $\mathcal{L}(K, Y) \subseteq \mathcal{L}(K, Y, left\text{-}x)$.

Proof idea. In principle, a variant the well-known "colouring trick" will work for the simulation of free derivations by leftmost derivations. ❏

Theorem 16. Let $Y \in \{CF - \lambda, CF\}$. Then, we find $\mathcal{L}(Y) = \mathcal{L}(K, Y, left\text{-}1)$.

For reasons of space, we omit the rather tricky construction of this proof. We found a direct simulation as in Theorem 7. In conclusion, also K grammars are a means for describing levels of the Chomsky hierarchy in a context-free style.

Corollary 17. Let $x \in \{2, 3\}$. We can show the following: $\mathcal{L}(K, CF[-\lambda], left\text{-}1) = \mathcal{L}(CF) \subset \mathcal{L}(K, CF - \lambda[, left\text{-}x]) = \mathcal{L}(CS) \subset \mathcal{L}(K, CF[, left\text{-}x]) = \mathcal{L}(RE).$ ❏

Are there any context-free style derivation mechanisms whose left-1 interpretation yields non-context-free languages? We consider conditional grammars with non-regular context conditions: For example, $\{a^m b^m a^m \mid m \geq 1\}$ is generated by $G = (\{S, T, T'\}, \{a, b\}, P, S)$ with rules

$(S \to aS, \{a, b\}^*S)$, $(S \to bS, \{a, b\}^*S)$, $(S \to T, \{a, b\}^*S)$,
$(T \to T', \{a^m b^m \mid m \geq 1\}a^*)$, $(T' \to \lambda, a^*\{b^m a^m \mid m \geq 1\})$.

Păun and Urbanek [13, 19] proved that the family of languages generable by K grammars with regular core rules and context-free rule conditions strictly contains the intersection closure of the context-free languages. Clearly, that family is contained in the family of languages generable by K grammars with linear core rules and context-free rule conditions, which is included in the family of languages generable by K grammars with context-free core rules and context-free rule conditions working under left-1 interpretation. Is any of those inclusions is strict or not?

---

[3] When admitting erasing rules, those results can be alternatively derived combining results from [5, 8, 12, 20]. More precisely, Virkkunen showed in [20, Lemma 5] how to characterize scattered context languages as morphic images of intersection of unordered scattered context languages with left-3 derivations and regular sets.

References

1. B. S. Baker. Non-context-free grammars generating context-free languages. *Inf. & Contr.*, 24:231–246, 1974.
2. H. Bordihn. A grammatical approach to the LBA problem. In Gh. Păun, A. Salomaa, eds., *New Trends in Formal Languages*, volume 1218 of *LNCS*, pp. 1–9, 1997.
3. A. Cremers, H. A. Maurer, and O. Mayer. A note on leftmost restricted random context grammars. *Inf. Proc. Let.*, 2:31–33, 1973.
4. J. Dassow, H. Fernau, and Gh. Păun. On the leftmost derivation in matrix grammars. Work in progress, 1998.
5. J. Dassow and Gh. Păun. *Regulated Rewriting in Formal Language Theory.* Springer, 1989.
6. G. Dong. Grammar tools and characterizations. In *Proc. 11th ACM SIGACT-SIGMOD-SIGART Symposium on Principles of Database Systems (PODS'92)*, pp. 81–90, 1992.
7. H. Fernau. On unconditional transfer. In W. Penczek and A. Szałas, eds., *MFCS'96*, volume 1113 of *LNCS*, pp. 348–359, 1996.
8. H. Fernau. On grammar and language families. *Fund. Inform.*, 25:17–34, 1996.
9. H. Fernau. Graph-controlled grammars as language acceptors. *J. Aut., Lang. and Comb.*, 2(2):79–91, 1997.
10. H. Fernau. Unconditional transfer in regulated rewriting. *Acta Inform.*, 34:837–857, 1997.
11. H. Fernau and F. Stephan. How powerful is unconditional transfer? —When UT meets AC.—. Technical Report WSI-97-7, Universität Tübingen (Germany), Wilhelm-Schickard-Institut für Informatik, 1997. Short version published in: S. Bozapalidis (ed.) *Proc. of the 3rd Int. Conf. Developments in Language Theory DLT'97*, pp. 249–260.
12. F. Hinz and J. Dassow. An undecidability result for regular languages and its application to regulated rewriting. *EATCS Bull.*, 38:168–173, 1989.
13. Gh. Păun. On the generative capacity of conditional grammars. *Inform. & Contr.*, 43:178–186, 1979.
14. Gh. Păun. On leftmost derivation restriction in regulated rewriting. *Rev. Roumaine Math. Pures Appl.*, 30:751–758, 1985.
15. D. J. Rosenkrantz. Programmed grammars and classes of formal languages. *J. ACM*, 16(1):107–131, 1969.
16. G. Rozenberg and A. Salomaa, eds. *Handbook of Formal Languages (3 volumes)*. Springer, 1997.
17. A. Rußmann. Dynamic LL(k) parsing. *Acta Inform.*, 34(4):267–289, 1997.
18. A. Salomaa. Matrix grammars with a leftmost restriction. *Inf. & Contr.*, 20:143–149, 1972.
19. F. J. Urbanek. A note on conditional grammars. *Rev. Roumaine Math. Pures Appl.*, 28:341–342, 1983.
20. V. Virkkunen. On scattered context grammars. *Acta Universitatis Ouluensis, Series A*, 20, No. 6, 1973.
21. D. Wood. Bicolored digraph grammar systems. *RAIRO Inform. théor. Appl.*, 1:45–50, 1973.

Some Results on the Modelling of Spatial Data

Luca Forlizzi[1] and Enrico Nardelli[1,2]

[1] Dipartimento di Matematica Pura ed Applicata, Univ. of L'Aquila, Via Vetoio,
Coppito, I-67010 L'Aquila, Italia. E-mail: {forlizzi,nardelli}@univaq.it
[2] Istituto di Analisi dei Sistemi ed Informatica, Consiglio Nazionale delle Ricerche,
Viale Manzoni 30, I-00185 Roma, Italia.

Abstract. Formal methods based on the mathematical theory of partially ordered sets (i.e., posets) have been used in the database field for the modelling of spatial data since many years. In particular, the use of the lattice completion (or normal completion) of a poset has been shown by Kainz, Egenhofer and Greasley [13] to be a fundamental technique to build meaningful representations of spatial subdivisions. In fact, they proved that the new elements introduced by the normal completion process can (and have to) be interpreted as being the intersection of poset elements. This is fundamental, from a mathematical point of view, since it means that the lattice resulting from the normal completion is the closure of the given poset with respect to the intersection operation. In this paper we precisely clarify the limitations for the use of lattices as models for spatial subdivisions, by proving sufficient and necessary conditions. Our result gives therefore a sound theoretical basis for the use of lattices built on simplicial complexes as a data model for spatial databases.

1 Introduction

A class of sets together with a set-containment relation among them models many common situations in spatial databases. For example it may represent a containment relation between geographical objects of the plane or a hierarchical relation between administrative units. The set-containment relation is a partial order relation. Formal methods based on the mathematical theory of partially ordered sets (i.e. posets) have been used for the description of spatial relations since many years [13,8,19].

In particular, the use of the lattice completion (or normal completion) of a poset has been shown by Kainz, Egenhofer and Greasley [13] to be a fundamental technique to build meaningful representation of spatial subdivisions. They proposed to represent by means of the elements introduced by the normal completion operator, the set-intersection between sets of the class. Consider for example the class of sets S containing the four sets A, B, C, and D shown in Fig. 1.

Each set is represented with an elliptic shape filled with a different pattern. Zones filled with more than one pattern belong to more than one set.

We can represent the class S with the poset P shown in Fig. 2 left.

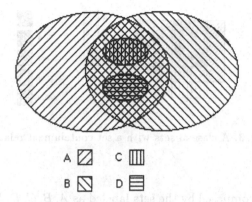

Fig. 1. A class of sets with a set containment relation

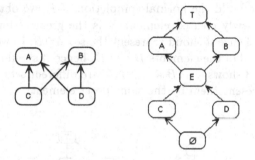

Fig. 2. (left) A poset representation of the class of sets of Fig. 1. (right) The normal completion of the poset in Fig. 2 (left)

Now suppose we want a representation of the closure S' of the class S with respect to the set intersection operator (i.e. the class obtained intersecting each possible pair of sets taken from S). Such a closure is composed by the sets contained in S plus the set $A \cap B$ and the empty set. The set $A \cap B$ is contained in the sets A and B and it contains the sets C and D. The normal completion of poset P is the lattice L, shown in Fig. 2 right. The lattice L is composed by the elements of P plus a top and bottom element, and a new element labeled E, which is smaller than the elements (representing the sets) A and B and greater than those (representing the sets) C and D. Therefore, since the relation of set with respect to other sets of S is analogous to that of the element E with respect to other elements of L, the lattice L can represent the class of sets S', provided that the element E represents the set $A \cap B$.

In the general case, however, using the normal completion operator to represent the set-intersection operator, may lead to incorrect results, as the following example shows. In Fig. 3 a class S of sets with a set containment relation and its closure S' with respect to the set intersection operator are represented.

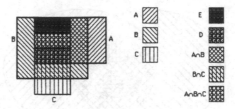

Fig. 3. A class of sets with a set containment relation

The class S is composed by the sets labeled as A, B, C, D, E, D and T, where $T \equiv \bigcup_{x \in S} x$ is the greatest set of the class and it is not represented in Fig. 3. As Fig. 3 shows, the class S' is composed by the sets contained in S plus the sets $A \cap B$, $B \cap C$ and $A \cap C \equiv A \cap B \cap C$. A poset P representing the class S in shown in Fig. 4 left. If we build the normal completion of P, we obtain the lattice in Fig. 4 right. The newly created element X is the greatest lower bound of the elements A and B, hence it shoud represent the set $A \cap B$. However X is also the greatest lower bound of the elements B and C, hence it should represent the set $B \cap C$, but as Fig. 3 shows, $A \cap B$ and $B \cap C$ are different sets and consequently is incorrect to represent them by the same poset element.

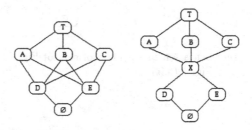

Fig. 4. (left) A poset representation of the class of sets of Fig. 3. (right) The normal completion of the poset in Fig. 4 (left)

In Fig. 5 we see a correct representation of S'. We have built poset in Fig. 5 starting from Fig. 3 (that shows the class S) and not from Fig. 4 left (the poset representation of S). In fact the poset in Fig. 4 left does not provide enough information: for example inspecting Fig. 3 we see that the sets $A \cap C$ and $A \cap B \cap C$ are the same set, but poset in Fig. 4 left cannot carry this information. If $A \cap B \cap C$ was strictly contained in $A \cap C$, see example in Fig. 6, then the poset in Fig. 4 left would still be, without any modification, a representation of this different class.

This fact shows that to represent set intersection operator by means of poset operator we have to provide more information to our representation. A way to do

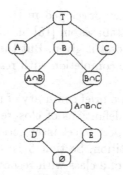

Fig. 5. A representation of the closure with respect to set intersection operator of the class of sets in Fig. 3

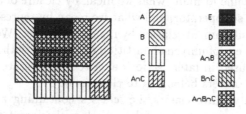

Fig. 6. A class of sets with a set containment relation

this is to include in the class S a spatial subdivision of the whole domain on which S is defined. In a poset that represents such a class there is an element for each of the atomic units of the spatial subdivision of S. We show that when a class S includes a spatial subdivision, the normal completion of its poset representation is a correct representation of S'. This was the case discussed by Kainz, Egenhofer and Greasley [13] since they modeled spatial regions by means of simplicial complexes, that include naturally a spatial subdivision.

We highlight in this paper the fundamental role played by the presence of a spatial subdivision for a correct use of the normal completion operator. We give necessary and sufficient conditions for a correct use of lattices as models for spatial relations.

The use of posets as a modelling structure for realities in spatial databases is largely widespread [2, 13, 8, 15, 19, 11]. Also, a discrete basis for the sets of the class, which is analogous to the universal partition we introduce in Sect. 2, is commonly used in the modelling of geometrical entities [6, 10]. Such a discrete basis is indeed the starting point for many efficient data structure based on a space-partitioning criteria, e.g. quadtree [16], grid-file [14], k-d tree [3], cell-tree [9]. Normal completion plays a central role in posets operations [4, 5]. Various studies has been conducted to develop efficient algorithms for its construction. The most interesting, in our opinion, are [12, 15, 17]. Efficient representation techniques for posets have been developed in [1, 18]. With reference to the use of posets to model spatial databases, in [15] an incremental algorithm to build the normal completion of a poset is given. But the issue of how to interpret the new elements inserted for the completion with respect to the reality of interest is left open.

We close this section with a brief summary of the rest of this paper. In Sect. 2 we introduce formally the definitions of closure of a class of sets with a set-containment relation with respect to set-intersection, of representation of a class of sets and of universal partition. Section 3 is dedicated to the study of the representation of the closure of a class with respect to set-intersection.

2 Representations and Closures

In this section we define formally what we mean by closure of a class of sets with respect to a certain set operator, and what we mean by representation of a class of sets with a set-containment relation by means of a poset. We also introduce in this section the concept of universal partition of a class S with a set-containment relation. It will be used in later sections as a tool to operate efficiently on sets belonging to S and on sets belonging to closures of S.

We consider only finite classes, i.e. classes containing a finite number of sets. For technical reasons it is useful to work with classes of sets with a set-containment relation that contain a greatest set (namely a set that contains every other set of the class) and a least set (namely a set that is contained in every other set of the class). This is not a restriction since if a finite class of sets has not a greatest or a least set, we can always extend it adding respectively the set union of all the sets of the class or the empty set, and then work with the extended class. From now on, when we speak of a class of sets with a set-containment relation, we always refer to the extended class. All results proved in this section are almost straightforward, hence proofs are omitted.

Definition 1. *Let S be a class of sets with a set-containment relation. We define $S^\cap$, the closure of S with respect to set-intersection operator, by the following rules:*

1. *if $s \in S$ then $s \in S^\cap$;*
2. *$\forall s_1, s_2 \in S^\cap$, $s_1 \cap s_2 \in S^\cap$.*

To build correctly the closure of S we need to perform aggregations and subdivisions of sets. For this aim we make use of a universal partition, a subclass of S containing sets that act as building blocks for every other set of S (i.e. every set of S can be obtained applying the set-union operator to a suitable collection of sets of the universal partition).

Definition 2. *Let S be a class of sets with a set-containment relation, and let $U_S \subseteq S$. We say that U_S is a universal partition of S if $\forall r_1, r_2 \in U_S$, we have $r_1 \cap r_2 \equiv \emptyset$, and $\forall s \in S$ there exist $r_1, r_2 \ldots r_n \in U_S$ such that $s \equiv \bigcup_i r_i$.*

To associate to each set of the class its building blocks (i.e. the collection of sets of the universal partition that compose the set) we define a mapping.

Definition 3. *Let S be a class of sets with a set-containment relation and a universal partition U_S. We define the mapping $S_{\text{Base}} : S \mapsto 2^{U_S}$ as*

$$S_{\text{Base}}(s) = \{r \in U_S | r \subseteq s\} .$$

The following proposition shows that for each set s of a class of sets with a set-containment relation, there exists a unique collection of sets of the universal partition whose set-union is equal to s, and that this collection is exactly $S_{\text{Base}}(s)$.

Proposition 1. *If S is a class of sets with a set-containment relation and a universal partition U_S, there exists a unique set $\{r_1, r_2 \ldots r_n\} \in 2^{U_S}$ such that $s \equiv \bigcup_i r_i$. Also $\forall s \in S, s \equiv \bigcup_{r \in S_{\text{Base}}(s)} r$.*

The universal partition U_S of a class S of sets with a set-containment relation is also a universal partition of $S^\cap$.

Corollary 1. *Let S be a class of sets with a set-containment relation and a universal partition U_S. Then U_S is a universal partition of $S^\cap$.*

Thanks to the corollary above, we can apply Definition 3 also to $S^\cap$.

Now we define formally what is a representation by means of a poset of a class of sets with a set-containment relation.

Definition 4. *Let S be a class of sets with a set-containment relation and let $< P, \leq >$ be a poset. We say that P is a representation of S if there exists an isomorphism between S and P.*

In the rest of this paper, every time we deal with a representation P of a class S of sets with a set-containment relation, we refer the isomorphism between S and P as $Rep : S \mapsto P$. Of course there exists $Rep^{-1} : P \mapsto S$. Note that since the classes of sets with a set-containment relation we consider have a greatest and a least set, their representations have a greatest and a least element.

In a representation of a class of sets with a set-containment relation and a universal partition, we need to identify the representants of the sets of the universal partition.

Definition 5. *Let S be a class of sets with a set-containment relation and a universal partition U_S, and let P be a representation of S. We define universal partition on P the set $U_P = \{x \in P | x = Rep(r) \text{ and } r \in U_S\}$.*

Also in the representation we need to refer to representants of the sets of the universal partition whose set-union is a given set. Therefore we introduce the mapping $P_{\text{Base}}(.)$ from elements in P to subsets of the universal partition defined on P.

Definition 6. *Let S be a class of sets with a set-containment relation and a universal partition U_S, and let P be a representation of S. For each $p \in P$, we define the mapping $P_{Base} : P \mapsto 2^{U_P}$ as*

$$P_{Base}(p) = \{x \in P | x = Rep(r) \text{ and } r \in S_{Base}(Rep^{-1}(p))\} .$$

In a class of sets with a set-containment relation and a universal partition, a set is 'composed' by sets of the universal partition by means of the set-union operator. In the representation of the class an analogous 'composition' is obtained by means of the $lub(.)$ operator that assign to each subset of a poset its least upper bound, as the following theorem shows.

Theorem 1. *Let S be a class of sets with a set-containment relation and a universal partition. If P is a representation of S then for each $s \in S$ we have:*

$$Rep(s) = lub(\{y | y = Rep(r) \text{ and } r \in S_{Base}(s)\}) .$$

If one thinks to $P_{Base}(.)$ as a mapping between the posets $< P, \leq >$ and $< 2^{U_P}, \subseteq >$, previous proposition translates into the following corollary:

Corollary 2. *The mapping $P_{Base}(.)$ is an order embedding from the poset $< P, \leq >$ to the poset $< 2^{U_P}, \subseteq >$.*

3 Representation of Set-Intersection Closure

3.1 Introduction

In this section, given a class S of sets with a set-containment relation and its representation P, we study how to derive from P a representation of $S^{\cap}$, the closure of S with respect to the set-intersection operator. Before we proceed with formal investigations on this subject, let us see how the existence of a universal partition modifies the example presented in Fig. 2. In Fig. 7 we show a class S of sets containing five sets A, B, C, D, E which have exactly the same containment relations as the regions in Fig. 2. But the class also contains a universal partition, whose elements coincide with the unit squares of the grid. Sets A, B, C, D, E are shown as aggregations of unit squares identified by different patterns.

A poset representation P for this class of sets is shown in Fig. 8 (the top and the bottom of the poset have been omitted for clarity). We want to construct a representation of $S^{\cap}$, namely a representation which contains also elements that represent sets $A \cap B$, $B \cap C$ and $A \cap B \cap C$.

Comparing P with the poset in Fig. 4 left we can see that the universal partition provides informations on the class S that were missing in the poset in Fig. 4 left. For example elements $1d$, $2d$ and $3d$ represent regions contained in both sets A and B but not in set C. This fact means that $A \cap B$ and $A \cap B \cap C$ are different sets. Figure 9 shows the normal completion $M(P)$ of poset P (in Fig. 9 also, the top and the bottom of the lattice have been omitted for clarity). Inspecting Fig. 9 (and recalling Fig. 5) we can see that $M(P)$ is a correct representation of class $S^{\cap}$, since elements labeled X, Y and Z represent respectively sets $A \cap B$, $B \cap C$ and $A \cap B \cap C$. This is a general fact, as we show formally in the following subsection.

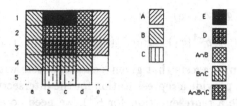

Fig. 7. A class of sets with a set containment relation

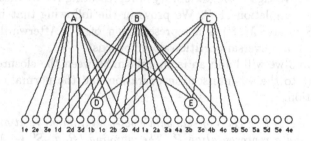

Fig. 8. A poset representation of the class of sets of Fig. 7

3.2 Sufficient Conditions for Representation of Set-Intersection Closure

Proofs of results in this section have been omitted since they are either almost straightforward or rather technical. They can be found in the extended version [7]. The following theorem tells us that given a representation with a universal partition, the greatest lower bound of the representants of two sets represents, if exists, the intersection between the two sets.

Theorem 2. *Let S be a class of sets with a set-containment relation and let P be its representation. Assume P has a universal partition U_P. For every $x_1, x_2 \in P$,*

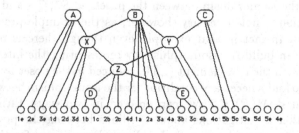

Fig. 9. The normal completion of the poset in Fig. 8

if there exists $x_o = glb(x_1, x_2)$, *then*

$$Rep^{-1}(x_1) \cap Rep^{-1}(x_2) = Rep^{-1}(x_o) \ .$$

Previous theorem suggests that given a class S of sets with a set-containment relation, in order to provide a representation for the intersection of every subclass of S (i.e. to provide a representation for $S^\cap$), we need to extend the representation of S to a poset that has a glb for every subset of its elements, namely a lattice. Since the MacNeille completion of a poset to a lattice is the most common way to realize such an extension (and indeed the resulting lattice has interesting properties) we investigate the possibility of representing $S^\cap$ by means of $M(P)$, the MacNeille completion of P. We prove in the following that if a universal partition of S exists, $M(P)$ is a representation of $S^\cap$. Afterwards we discuss what happens if a universal partition does not exist.

In Theorem 3 we will build an isomorphism between the closure of the class S with respect to the set-intersection operation and the normal completion of its representation.

Theorem 3. *Let S be a class of sets with a set-containment relation, a universal partition U_S, and a representation P. The mapping $IRep : S^\cap \mapsto M(P)$ defined as*

$$IRep(s) = (\{g \in P | g = Rep(r), r \in S_{\text{Base}}\}^*)_*$$

is an isomorphism. Hence $M(P)$ is a representation of $S^\cap$.

The result of Theorem 3, in the restricted formulation for simplicial complexes, where a universal partition always exists, was proved by Kainz, Egenhofer and Greasley [13]. An obvious consequence of Theorem 3 is that $\forall s_1, s_2 \in S, IRep(s_1 \cap s_2) = glb(IRep(s_1), IRep(s_2))$, namely the representant of the intersection of two sets is the glb of the representants of the sets, as we conjectured in Sect. 1.

3.3 Necessary Conditions for Representation of Set-Intersection Closure

Theorem 3 tells us that given a class S of sets with a set-containment relation and its representation P, the existence of a universal partition is a sufficient condition for the isomorphism between the posets $< S^\cap, \subseteq >$ and $< M(P), \leq >$. Such a condition is not necessary, however, as the example presented in Figs. 2 and 3 shows. In fact in that example, even though there is not a universal partition, we can build the isomorphism by representing the intersection of the sets A and B with the new element (E) introduced in the poset by the MacNeille completion. To find a necessary condition for the isomorphism between the posets $< S^\cap, \subseteq >$ and $< M(P), \leq >$, we can proceed in two ways. Either we have to carry out further investigations about the links between the posets $< S^\cap, \subseteq >$ and $< M(P), \leq >$ or we have to find additional conditions for the class S. We now investigate both alternatives. The following definition introduce a mapping $Z : M(P) \mapsto S^\cap$ which we use to show further results for the first alternative.

Definition 7. *Let S be a class of sets with a set-containment relation and let P be a representation of S. We define the mapping* $Z : M(P) \mapsto S^\cap$ *as*

$$Z(x) = \bigcap_{y \in (\uparrow x)\varphi(P)} Rep^{-1}(\varphi^{-1}(y)) \ .$$

The following lemma shows that the mapping $Z(.)$ is an order embedding.

Lemma 1. *The mapping* $Z : M(P) \mapsto S^\cap$ *is an order embedding between the posets* $< S^\cap, \subseteq >$ *and* $< M(P), \leq >$.

From previous lemma an important result follows immediately.

Lemma 2. *Let S be a class of sets with a set-containment relation and a representation P. We have* $|M(P)| \leq |S^\cap|$, *where* $M(P)$ *is the MacNeille Completion of P.*

Given the above lemma, a way to find a necessary condition for the existence of an isomorphism between the posets $< S^\cap, \subseteq >$ and $< M(P), \leq >$ is to find a necessary condition for the sets $S^\cap$ and $M(P)$ to have the same cardinality. We achieve this result by means of the mapping $Z(.)$. The following theorem states a necessary condition for the isomorphism between the posets $< S^\cap, \subseteq >$ and $< M(P), \leq >$.

Theorem 4. *Let S be a class of sets with a set-containment relation and a representation P. If* $S^\cap$ *is isomorphic to* $M(P)$, *then* $\forall s_o, s_1, s_2 \in S$, *if* $Rep(s_o) = glb_P(Rep(s_1), Rep(s_2))$ *then* $s_1 \cap s_2 = s_o$.

Theorem 4 gives a necessary condition for the isomorphism between the posets $< S^\cap, \subseteq >$ and $< M(P), \leq >$, namely the fact that $\forall s_o, s_1, s_2 \in S$, if $Rep(s_o) = glb_P(Rep(s_1), Rep(s_2))$ then $s_1 \cap s_2 = s_o$. Note that this condition is not sufficent, as the example of Fig. 3 discussed in Sect. 1 shows. Inspecting Figs. 3 and 4 left we see that $\forall s_o, s_1, s_2 \in S$, if $Rep(s_o) = glb_P(Rep(s_1), Rep(s_2))$ then $s_1 \cap s_2 = s_o$. However posets $< S^\cap, \subseteq >$ and $< M(P), \leq >$ are not isomorphic since sets $S^\cap$ and $M(P)$ have different cardinalities.

From Theorem 4 the following corollaries follows.

Corollary 3. *Let S be a class of sets with a set-containment relation and a representation P. If* $S^\cap$ *is isomorphic to the Normal Completion of P, then for each* $s_1 \in S_o$ *and for each* $s \in S$ *it is* $s_1 \cap s = s_1$ *or* $s_1 \cap s = \emptyset$, *where* $S_o = \{s \in S | \forall x \in S, \ if \ x \subset s \ then \ x = \emptyset\}$.

Corollary 4. *Let S be a class of sets with a set-containment relation and a representation P. If* $S^\cap$ *is isomorphic to the Normal Completion of P, then for every* $s_1, s_2 \in S_o$, $s_1 \cap s_2 = \emptyset$, *where* $S_o = \{s \in S | \forall x \in S, \ if \ x \subset s \ then \ x = \emptyset\}$.

As discussed earlier, the existence of a universal partition is a sufficient, but not necessary condition for the isomorphism between the closure of a class S of sets with respect to the set-intersection operator and the MacNeille completion of a representation P of S. This means that the converse of Theorem 4 is not true, namely if there exists an isomorphism between $S^\cap$ and $M(P)$ not necessarily a universal partition of S exists (see again the example in Figs. 1 and 2). However, thanks to Corollaries 3 and 4, we can effectively pursue the other alternative towards defining necessary conditions for the isomorphism, namely imposing additional constraints to class S. For this aim we introduce the following definition.

Definition 8. *Let S be a class of sets with a set-containment relation, and let s_T be its greatest set. We say that S is* consistent *with respect to the set-containment relation if* $\bigcup_{x \in S_o} x \equiv s_T$, *where* $S_o = \{s \in S | \forall x \in S, \ if \ x \subset s \ then \ x = \emptyset\}$.

The assumption of a class of sets to be consistent, is reasonable in many cases, since it means that if a set contains strictly another set, then the difference between the two sets is an 'entity' which has to be represented in the class S. For example in a spatial database where a land is represented together with a city contained in it, it seems reasonable that the part of the land outside the city is also identified as an entity.

We can show that for a consistent class S the isomorphism between $S^\cap$ and $M(P)$, implies the existence of a universal partition of S.

Theorem 5. *Let S be a class of sets with a set-containment relation and a representation P. If $S^\cap$ is isomorphic to the Normal Completion of P and S is consistent, then there exists a universal partition on S.*

Putting together Theorem 5 and Theorem 3, we obtain the following corollary that shows how strictly the existence of an isomorphism between $S^\cap$ and $M(P)$ is connected with that of a universal partition on S.

Corollary 5. *Let S be a class of sets with a set-containment relation and a representation P. Let S be consistent. Then $S^\cap$ is isomorphic to the Normal Completion of P iff there exists a universal partition on S.*

This result means that in a spatial database that works with poset representations of consistent classes of sets, the only way to perform spatial intersections among sets by means of the normal completion operator, is to provide the database with a universal partition.

4 Conclusions and Future Works

Partially ordered sets (posets) are widely used to represent classes of sets with a set containment relation. In this paper we have addressed the problem of how to perform natural set manipulations on a class by means of a poset representation of the class. Concerning set intersection we have stated suffcient and necessary conditions for the correct use of the normal completion operator as a representant of set intersection operator. Moreover, for classes of sets satisfying a little more restrictive condition, we found a condition that is both necessary and sufficient.

Our results give further motivations to the use of posets to represent classes of sets with a set containment relation, that was first advocated by Kainz, Egenhofer and Greasley in [13], where proved the importance of normal completion as a formal tool in modelling data for spatial databases. Future work will concentrate on characterizing also the set-union operator.

References

1. H. Aït-Kaci, "A lattice-theoretic approach to computation based on a calculus of partially ordered types", Ph. D. Dissertation, University of Pennsylvania, 1984.
2. E.Apolloni, F.Arcieri, S.Ercoli, E.Nardelli, M.Talamo: "Un modello di riferimento per l'interazione con sistemi per la gestione di dati geografici", (in italian), Convegno Nazionale Sistemi Evoluti per Basi di Dati, Gizzeria Lido, Giugno 1993.
3. J.L.Bentley, "Multidimensional binary search trees used for associate searching", Communications of ACM, 18, 509-517, 1975.
4. G. Birkhoff, "Lattice Theory", American Mathematical Society Colloquium Publications Vol. 25, (Providence, RI: American Mathematical Society), 1967.
5. B.A. Davey, H.A. Priestley, "Introduction to Lattices and Order", Cambridge University Press, 1991.
6. M. Erwing, M. Schneider, "Partition and Conquer", in Spatial Information Theory: A Theoretical Basis for GIS, Vol. 1329 of LNCS, Springer Verlag 1997.
7. L.Forlizzi, E.Nardelli, "On the use of posets as a formal model for spatial data", Technical Report 1/98, Dip. di Matematica, Univ. di L'Aquila, JAN 1998.
8. I. Greasley, "Partially Ordered Sets and Lattices: Correct Metods of Spatial Relations for Land Information Systems", Master's Thesis, University of Maine, Department of Surveying Engineering, Orono, ME, 1990.
9. O.Günther, J.Bilmes, "Tree-based access methods for spatial databases: implementation and performance evaluation", IEEE TKDE, 3(3):342-356, 1991.
10. R.H. Güting, M. Schneider, "Realm-based spatial data types: the ROSE algebra", Fernuniversitat Hagen, Report 141, 1993, VLDB Journal, 4(2), 213-289, April 1995.
11. S.C.Hirtle, "Representational Structures for Cognitive Space: Trees, Ordered Trees and Semi-Lattices", in Spatial Information Theory: A Theoretical Basis for GIS, Vol. 988 of Lecture Notes in Computer Science, Springer Verlag 1995.
12. C. Jard, G.V. Jourdan, J.X. Rampon, "Some online computation of the ideal lattice of posets", IRISA Research Report n.773, 1993.
13. W. Kaintz, M. Egenhofer, I. Greasley, "Modelling spatial relations and operations with partially ordered sets", Int. J. of GIS, vol. 7, no. 3, 215-229., 1993.
14. J. Nievergelt, H.Hinterger, K.C.Sevcik, "The grid file: an adaptable symmetric multikey file structure", ACM TODS, 9(1):38-71, March 1984.
15. L.M. Perry, "Extending (Finite) Partially Ordered Sets to Lattices: An Incremental Approach", Master's Thesis, Univ. of Maine, Dep. of Surv. Eng., Orono, ME, 1990.
16. H. Samet, "The design and analysis of spatial data structures", Addison-Wesley Reading, MA, 1990
17. G. Steiner "An algorithm to generate the ideals of a partial order", Operation Research Letters volume 5 number 6, 1986.
18. M.Talamo, P.Vocca, "An optimal time*space data structure for lattices representation", to be published on SIAM Journal on Computing.
19. M. F. Worboys, "A generic model for planar geographical objects", INT. J. Geographical Information Systems, Vol 6, NO 5, 353-372, 1992.

Randomized Meldable Priority Queues

Anna Gambin and Adam Malinowski

Instytut Informatyki, Uniwersytet Warszawski,
Banacha 2, Warszawa 02-097, Poland,
{aniag,amal}@mimuw.edu.pl

Abstract. We present a practical meldable priority queue implementation. All priority queue operations are very simple and their logarithmic time bound holds with high probability, which makes this data structure more suitable for real-time applications than those with only amortized performance guarantees. Our solution is also space-efficient, since it does not require storing any auxiliary information within the queue nodes.

1 Introduction

In this paper we present a randomized approach to the problem of efficient meldable priority queue implementation. The operations supported by this data structure are the following [10]:

MAKEQUEUE returns an empty priority queue.

FINDMIN(Q) returns the minimum item from priority queue Q.

DELETEMIN(Q) deletes and returns the minimum item from priority queue Q.

INSERT(Q, e) inserts item e into priority queue Q.

MELD(Q_1, Q_2) returns the priority queue formed by combining disjoint priority queues Q_1 and Q_2.

DECREASEKEY(Q, e, e') replaces item e by e' in priority queue Q provided $e' \leq e$ and the location of e in Q is known.

DELETE(Q, e) deletes item e from priority queue Q provided the location of e in Q is known.

(The last two operations are sometimes considered optional.)

In existing priority queue implementations the approach is two-fold. Most data structures require storing additional balance information associated with queue nodes in order to guarantee the worst-case efficiency of individual operations (e.g. leftist trees [8], relaxed heaps [5], Brodal queues [3, 4]). Others achieve good amortized performance by adjusting the structure during some operations rather than struggling to maintain balance constantly (skew heaps [12, 13], pairing heaps [6]). Experiments indicate that the latter approach is more promising in practice [1, 7, 9]. This is due to the fact that the worst-case efficient structures tend to be complex and hard to implement therefore big constant factors hidden in their complexity estimates prevail their theoretically superior performance.

On the other hand, the main disadvantage of the amortized approach is that it cannot be applied in real-time programs, where the worst-case bound on the running time of each individual operation is crucial.

Our solution, both simple and worst-case efficient (in the probabilistic sense), avoids these drawbacks by adopting the randomized approach, earlier applied to construct abstract data structures mainly in the context of dictionaries (e.g. [2, 11]). The idea is loosely based on leftist trees and skew heaps. All other operations are defined in terms of MELD which in both structures is performed along right paths in melded trees. The subtrees of a node on the right path are exchanged in order to keep the path short: in leftist trees – sometimes (depending on their ranks); in skew heaps – always. In our data structure MELD operation is performed along *random* paths in melded trees. This approach has the following advantages:

Simplicity. All operations are easy to implement and the constant factors in their complexity bounds are small, thus, given a fast random number generator, the heaps should perform well in practice.

Space economy. Since we do not need to preserve any balance conditions, no satellite information within nodes is necessary.

Applicability to parallel computations. A single-pass top-down scheme of each operation allows to perform a sequence of operations in a pipelined fashion. Moreover, the loose structure of a heap allows to process disjoint sets of nodes independently.

Worst-case efficiency. The execution time of each individual operation is at most logarithmic with high probability. The expected time behaviour depends on the random choices made by the algorithm rather than the distribution of an input sequence, which allows using this data structure in real-time applications.

The rest of this paper is organized as follows. In Section 2 we describe the data structure and the implementation of meldable priority queue operations. Section 3 is devoted to the efficiency analysis of these algorithms. Section 4 presents some experimental results. Finally, Section 5 contains discussion of some extensions of the data structure and the conclusions.

2 The Randomized Heap

The underlying data structure of the *randomized heap* is a binary tree with one item per node, satisfying *heap property*: if x and y are nodes and x is the parent of y then $item(x) \leq item(y)$. The heap is accessed by the root of the tree.

Let us now describe the implementation of meldable priority queue operations for randomized heap. MAKEQUEUE returns an empty tree and FINDMIN returns an item held in the root. In order to MELD two nonempty trees with roots Q_1 and Q_2, respectively, we compare the items held in the roots. The root with the smaller key, say Q_1, becomes the root of the resulting tree and Q_2, the remaining one, is recursively melded with either left or right child of Q_1, depending on the outcome of a coin toss. More formal definition is given by the following pseudocode:

heap function MELD(**heap** Q_1, Q_2)
    if Q_1 = NULL $\Rightarrow$ **return** Q_2
    if Q_2 = NULL $\Rightarrow$ **return** Q_1
    if $item(Q_1) > item(Q_2) \Rightarrow Q_1 \leftrightarrow Q_2$
    if $toss\_coin$ = HEADS $\Rightarrow left(Q_1) := $ MELD$(left(Q_1), Q_2)$
    else $right(Q_1) := $ MELD$(right(Q_1), Q_2)$
    return Q_1

(The results of Section 3 imply that the recursion depth is at most logarithmic with high probability. Moreover, this tail-recursion is easily removable and serves the purpose of increasing readability only.)

The simplest way to describe all remaining priority queue operations is to define them in terms of MELD. In order to INSERT item e into heap Q we create a single node containing item e and meld it with Q. DELETEMIN melds the left and right subtrees of the root and returns the item held in the (old) root.

For DECREASEKEY and DELETE we need the parent pointer in each node. In order to decrease the value of node x in heap Q we detach the tree rooted at x from Q, adjust the item at x accordingly and then meld Q with the heap rooted at x. Operation DELETE also detaches the tree rooted at x from heap Q, and then performs DELETEMIN on heap rooted at x and finally MELD the resulting heap and Q.

3 The Efficiency Analysis

Since all non-constant-time operations are defined in terms of MELD, it is enough to analyze the complexity of melding two randomized heaps.

Let us fix an arbitrary binary tree Q with n *interior* nodes containing keys and $n + 1$ *exterior* null nodes – the leaves of the tree. Define a random variable h_Q to be the length (the number of edges) of a random path from the root down to an exterior node (the child following each interior node on a path is chosen randomly and independently). In other words, the probability space is the set of all exterior nodes in Q with probability of a node at depth t equal to 2^{-t}, and h_Q is the depth of an exterior node chosen randomly with respect to this distribution.

Lemma 1. *Melding two randomized heaps Q_1 and Q_2 requires time $O(h_{Q_1} + h_{Q_2})$.*

Proof. The melding procedure traverses a random path in each tree until an exterior node in one of them is reached. $\square$

It follows from Lemma 1 that in order to bound the complexity of melding randomized heaps it is enough to estimate h_Q for an arbitrary binary tree Q.

Theorem 1. *Let Q be an arbitrary binary tree with n interior nodes.*

(a) *The expected value $Eh_Q \leq \log(n + 1)$.*
(b) *$Pr[h_Q > (c + 1) \log n] < \frac{1}{n^c}$, for any constant $c > 0$.*

Proof. (a) The proof follows by induction on n. Assume $n > 0$ and let n_L and n_R be the number of interior nodes in the left (Q_L) and right (Q_R) subtree of Q, respectively (thus $n = n_L + n_R + 1$). We have

$$Eh_Q = \frac{1}{2}((1 + Eh_{Q_L}) + (1 + Eh_{Q_R})) \leq 1 + \frac{1}{2}(\log(n_L + 1) + \log(n_R + 1))$$

$$= \log 2\sqrt{(n_L + 1)(n_R + 1)} \leq \log 2 \frac{(n_L + 1) + (n_R + 1)}{2}$$

$$= \log(n_L + n_R + 2) = \log(n + 1)$$

(b) Note that for any fixed path γ from the root to an exterior node the probability that γ is the outcome of a random walk down the tree equals $2^{-|\gamma|}$, where $|\gamma|$ is the length of γ.

Let Γ be the set of all paths from the root to an exterior node in Q with length exceeding $(c + 1) \log n$. We have

$$Pr[h_Q > (c + 1) \log n] = \sum_{\gamma \in \Gamma} 2^{-|\gamma|} < \sum_{\gamma \in \Gamma} 2^{-(c+1)\log n} = |\Gamma| n^{-(c+1)} \leq n^{-c}$$

$\square$

Corollary 1. *The expected time of any meldable priority queue operation on a n-node randomized heap is $O(\log n)$. Moreover, for each constant $\epsilon > 0$ there exists a constant $c > 0$ such that the probability that the time of each operation is at most $c \log n$ exceeds $1 - n^{-\epsilon}$.*

Proof. Immediate by Lemma 1 and Theorem 1. $\square$

4 Experiments

We have carried out some tests to measure the behaviour of the randomized heap in practice. It is not hard to see that the value h_Q is bigger for more balanced trees and smaller for "thinner" ones. When we create a tree by inserting the keys $1, \ldots, n$ in the order of some permutation π then the tree is more balanced if π is closer to the sorted sequence $< 1, \ldots, n >$, and "thinner" if π is closer to the inverted sequence $< n, \ldots, 1 >$. Thus our methodology was the following: for a fixed n subsequently we created a tree

- from an almost sorted permutation ($\frac{n}{2}$ transpositions away from $< 1, \ldots, n >$),
- from a random permutation,

- from an almost inversely sorted permutation ($\frac{n}{2}$ transpositions away from $< n, \ldots, 1 >$),

then we computed the value of h and the total length of paths traversed while melding two such trees (both consisting of keys $1, \ldots, n$). Since we can get different trees even from a fixed permutation, the outcomes were averaged over 100 tests for each value of n.

The results are summarized in the following table (each displayed value is the factor c in expression $c \log(n+1)$):

	Almost sorted permutation		Random permutation		Almost inverted permutation	
n	h	meld	h	meld	h	meld
50	0.85	1.34	0.79	1.28	0.63	0.79
500	0.80	1.39	0.76	1.31	0.50	0.65
5000	0.78	1.41	0.74	1.32	0.40	0.49
15000	0.77	1.42	0.73	1.32	0.36	0.41

It turns out that in case of a tree obtained from a random permutation the value of h is just $\frac{3}{4}$ of the value for the full tree. Moreover, the total length of paths traversed while melding two such trees is about 15% smaller than doubled value of h, as used for an estimation in Lemma 1. (This is not surprising because only one of two random paths is traversed to the very end while melding.)

5 Conclusions

Before the concluding remarks let us note that the flexibility of the randomized heap can be increased by *scaling* it in the manner similar to well known d-ary heaps. Let us fix an integer $d \geq 2$ and make the underlying structure of the heap be a tree with at most d children in each node (kept in an array of size d). The only change to operation MELD is that instead of tossing a symmetric coin we choose value t from $\{1, \ldots, d\}$ at random and recursively meld the tree with the bigger key at the root with t-th subtree of the other tree. An easy adaptation of the proofs from Section 3 gives the following estimates for the complexity of operations on a randomized d-heap with at most n nodes:

- MAKEQUEUE, FINDMIN — $O(1)$
- MELD, DECREASEKEY — $O(\log_d n)$
- INSERT — $O(d + \log_d n)$ (we have to initialize d pointers in the new node to NULL)
- DELETEMIN, DELETE — $O(d \log_d n)$ (we have to meld $O(d)$ heaps)

We have presented a very simple randomized data structure capable to support all meldable priority queue operations in logarithmic time with high probability. The experiments show that the constant factors in the complexity of the operations are in fact even smaller than those derived from the theoretical analysis. Simplicity, flexibility and small memory overhead make the randomized heap seem to be a practical choice for a meldable priority queue with worst-case performance guarantees.

The following question looks as a good starting point for further research: does the randomized approach allow us to lower the asymptotic complexity of some meldable priority queue operations while keeping the data structure simple?

References

1. T. Altman, B. Chlebus, A. Malinowski, M. Ślusarek, manuscript.
2. C. R. Aragon, R. G. Seidel, Randomized search trees. *Algorithmica* 16(1996), 464-497.
3. G. S. Brodal, Fast meldable priority queues, *Proc. 4th Workshop on Algorithms and Data Structures*, vol. 955 of *Lecture Notes in Computer Science*, 282-290, Springer-Verlag, Berlin, 1995.
4. G. S. Brodal, Worst-case efficient Priority Queues, *Proc. 17th ACM-SIAM Symposium on Discrete Algorithms*, 1996, 52-58.
5. J. R. Driscoll, H. N. Gabow, R. Shrairman, R. E. Tarjan, Relaxed heaps: An alternative to Fibonacci heaps with applications to parallel computation. *Comm. ACM* 31(1988), 1343-1354.
6. M. L. Fredman, R. Sedgewick, D. D. Sleator, R. E. Tarjan, The pairing heap: A new form of self-adjusting heap. *Algorithmica* 1(1986), 111-129.
7. D. W. Jones, An empirical comparison of priority queue and event set implementations, *Comm. ACM* 29(1986), 300-311.
8. D. E. Knuth, *The Art of Computer Programming, Volume 3: Sorting and Searching*, Addison-Wesley, Reading, MA, 1973.
9. A. M. Liao, Three priority queue applications revisited. *Algorithmica* 7(1992), 415-427.
10. K. Mehlhorn, A. K. Tsakalidis, Data Structures, In J. van Leeuwen, editor, *Handbook of Theoretical Computer Science, Volume A: Algorithms and Complexity*, MIT Press/Elsevier, 1990.
11. W. Pugh, Skip Lists: A probabilistic alternative to balanced trees, *Comm. ACM*, 33(1990), 668-676.
12. D. D. Sleator, R. E. Tarjan, Self-adjusting binary trees, *Proc. 15th ACM Symp. on Theory of Computing*, 1983, 235-246.
13. D. D. Sleator, R. E. Tarjan, Self-adjusting heaps, *SIAM J. Comput.* 15(1986), 52-69.

The Reconstruction of Convex Polyominoes from Horizontal and Vertical Projections

Maciej Gębala

Institute of Computer Science, University of Wrocław,
ul. Przesmyckiego 20, 51–151 Wrocław, Poland
mgc@tcs.uni.wroc.pl

Abstract. The problem of reconstructing a discrete set from its horizontal and vertical projections (RSP) is of primary importance in many different problems for example pattern recognition, image processing and data compression.

We give a new algorithm which provides a reconstruction of convex polyominoes from horizontal and vertical projections. It costs atmost $O(\min(m,n)^2 \cdot mn \log mn)$ for a matrix that has $m \times n$ cells. In this paper we provide just a sketch of the algorithm.

1 Introduction

1.1 Definition of the Problem

Let R be a matrix which has $m \times n$ cells containing "0"s and "1"s. Let S be a set of cells containing "1"s. Given S we put $h_i(S)$ which is the number of cells containing "1" in the ith row of S and we put $v_j(S)$ which is the number of cells containing "1" in the jth column of S. We call $h_i(S)$ the *ith row projection* of S and $v_j(S)$ the *jth column projection* of S.

We consider the different properties of a set S. We say that a set S of cells satisfies the properties **p**, **v** and **h** if

p: S is a polyomino i.e. S is a connected finite set.

v: every column of S is a connected set i.e. a column in R containing "0" between two different "1"s does not exist.

h: every row of S is a connected set i.e. a row in R containing "0" between two different "1"s does not exist.

The set S belongs to class $(\mathbf{x})$ $(S \in (\mathbf{x}))$ iff it satisfies the properties $\mathbf{x}$.

We can now define the problem of reconstructing a set S from its projections: Given two assigned vectors $H = (h_1, h_2, \ldots, h_m) \in \{1, \ldots, n\}^m$ and $V = (v_1, v_2, \ldots, v_n) \in \{1, \ldots, m\}^n$ we examine whether the pair (H, V) is satisfiable in class $(\mathbf{x})$. It is satisfiable if there is at least one set $S \in (\mathbf{x})$ such that $h_i(S) = h_i$, for $i = 1, \ldots, m$, and $v_j(S) = v_j$, for $j = 1, \ldots, n$. We also say that S satisfies (H, V) in $(\mathbf{x})$.

We define a set S as a convex polyomino if $S \in (\mathbf{p}, \mathbf{v}, \mathbf{h})$.

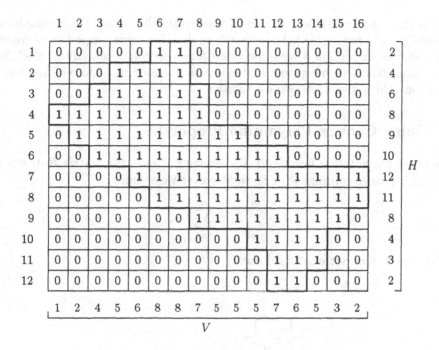

Fig. 1. A convex polyomino that satisfies (H, V)

1.2 Previous Work

First Ryser [4], and subsequently Chang [3] and Wang [5] studied existence of S satisfying (H, V) in the class of sets without any conditions $(\emptyset)$. They showed that the decision problem can be solved in $O(mn)$ time. These authors also developed some algorithms that reconstruct S starting from (II, V).

Woeginger [6] proved that the reconstruction problem in the classes of horizontally and vertically convex sets (**h,v**) and polyominoes (**p**) is an NP-complete problem.

In [1] Barcucci, Del Lungo, Nivat, Pinzani showed that the reconstruction problem is NP-complete in the class of column-convex polyominoes (**p,v**) (row-convex polyominoes (**p,h**)) and in the class of sets having connected columns (**v**) (rows (**h**)). Therefore, the problem can be solved in polynomial time only if all three properties (**p,h,v**) are verified by the cell set.

An algorithm that establishes the existence of a convex polyomino (**p, v, h**) satisfying a pair of assigned vectors (H, V) in polynomial time was described in [1]. The main idea of this algorithm is to construct a certain initial positions of some "0"s and "1"s and to perform a procedure called *filling operation* for each such position. We call them the feet's positions. The number of possible feet's positions in the algorithm is $O(m^2 n^2)$. The *filling operation* procedure costs $O(m^2 n^2)$. Hence, all the algorithm has a complexity $O(m^4 n^4)$.

In this paper we show a variant of above algorithm which has a complexity $O(\min(m,n)^2 \cdot mn \log mn)$. In section 2 we describe some properties of convex polyominoes. In section 3 we show a new *filling operation* procedure which has only complexity $O(mn \log mn)$. And in section 4 we describe a idea of new initial positions which give a correctness solution.

2 Some Convex Polyomino Properties

We follow the notation from [1, 2]. We assume $n \le m$ in the matrix R. If $n > m$ we can exchange columns with rows. Moreover we assume

$$\sum_{j=1}^{m} h_j = \sum_{i=1}^{n} v_i,$$

otherwise it does not exist a solution.

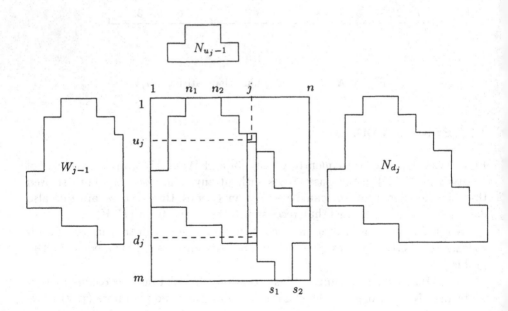

Fig. 2. Some properties of convex polyomino: $N_{u_j-1} \subset W_{j-1} \subset N_{d_j}$

Let $\langle n_1, n_2 \rangle$ be positions of "1"s in upper row, i.e. first row contains "1"s in cells from n_1 to n_2. And let $\langle s_1, s_2 \rangle$ be positions of "1"s in lower (m-th) row. These cells we are called *feet's positions*. Let us introduce the following notations:

$$H_k = \sum_{j=1}^{k} h_j, \qquad V_k = \sum_{i=1}^{k} v_i,$$

$$A = \sum_{j=1}^{m} h_j = \sum_{i=1}^{n} v_i.$$

We assume that $n_2 < s_1$ (the case $s_2 < n_1$ is similar and other cases we do not consider). Let W_j be the set of "1"s in first j columns, and let N_i be a set of "1"s in first i rows (see Fig. 2). Let $R(u_j, j)$ and $R(d_j, j)$ be the upmost and the lowest cells of j-th column containing "1".

Proposition 1. [2] *For all $j \in [n_2 + 1..s_1 - 1]$ we have*

$$N_{u_j-1} \subset W_{j-1} \quad and \quad W_{j-1} \subset N_{d_j}.$$

From above proposition and its variants we get:

Corollary 1. *If $n_2 < s_1$ then for all $j \in [n_2 + 1..s_1 - 1]$ we have*

$$H_{u_j-1} < V_{j-1} \quad and \quad H_{d_j} > V_j,$$
$$A - H_{d_j} < A - V_j \quad and \quad A - H_{u_j-1} > A - V_{j-1}.$$

If $s_2 < n_1$ then for all $j \in [s_2 + 1..n_1 - 1]$ we have

$$H_{u_j-1} < A - V_j \quad and \quad H_{d_j} > A - V_{j-1},$$
$$A - H_{d_j} < V_{j-1} \quad and \quad A - H_{u_j-1} > V_j.$$

We use above properties in section 4 for finding positions of some initial "1"s.

3 Filling Operation

We use the balanced binary trees (like e.g. AVL) in our procedure with the following operations:

empty(*tree*) — a function returning *true* when a *tree* is empty or *false* otherwise. It always costs $O(1)$.

delete(k, *tree*) — a procedure deleting an element k from a *tree*. The complexity of the function is less than $O(\log |tree|)$, where $|tree|$ means size of a *tree* (a number of elements in a *tree*).

insert(k, *tree*) — a procedure putting k in a *tree* where $k \notin tree$ or doing nothing otherwise. The complexity of this function is less than $O(\log |tree|)$.

min(*tree*) — a function returning a minimal element of a *tree*. It costs less than $O(\log |tree|)$.

max(*tree*) — a function returning a maximal element of a *tree*. It costs less than $O(\log |tree|)$.

We have two global variables tree_{col} and tree_{row} which are balanced binary trees. In these trees we will store the numbers of columns and rows, respectively, which we will review in a next step of the main loop in our procedure.

For each row i, where $i \in [1, \ldots, m]$, we define the following auxiliary variables: l^i, r^i, p^i, q^i, $\tilde{l}^i$, $\tilde{r}^i$, $\tilde{p}^i$, $\tilde{q}^i$, free0^i (for each column j, where $j \in [1, \ldots, n]$, we define l_j, r_j, p_j, q_j, $\tilde{l}_j$, $\tilde{r}_j$, $\tilde{p}_j$, $\tilde{q}_j$, free0$_j$, respectively). The variable l is a minimal position containing "1", r is a maximal position containing "1", p is a minimal position without "0" and q is a maximal position without "0", respectively, for all rows and columns. The variables $\tilde{l}$, $\tilde{r}$, $\tilde{p}$, $\tilde{q}$ are temporary values of l, r, p, q, respectively. The variable free0 is the balanced binary tree containing "0" positions which are between $\tilde{p}$ and $\tilde{q}$.

We initialize these variables in a row as follows $l = \tilde{l} = n + 1$, $r = \tilde{r} = 0$, $p = \tilde{p} = 1$, $q = \tilde{q} = n$, free0 = nil (in column $l = \tilde{l} = m+1$, $r = \tilde{r} = 0$, $p = \tilde{p} = 1$, $q = \tilde{q} = m$, free0 = nil, respectively), where nil means the empty tree.

We introduce two auxiliary operations:

put "0" in the ith row in the jth position:

```
if R[i, j] = 1 then exit( fail )      {we break the procedure in this case}
if R[i, j] ≠ 0 then      {it is a new "0"}
    R[i, j] ← 0
    insert( j, tree_col )
    if i < p̃_j + v_j and i ≥ p̃_j then
        p̃_j ← i + 1
        while not empty( free0_j ) and (k ←min( free0_j ))< p̃_j + v_j do
            delete( k, free0_j )
            p̃_j ← k + 1
    if i > q̃_j − v_j and i ≤ q̃_j then
        q̃_j ← i − 1
        while not empty( free0_j ) and (k ←max( free0_j ))> q̃_j − v_j do
            delete( k, free0_j )
            q̃_j ← k − 1
    if p̃_j + v_j ≤ i ≤ q̃_j − v_j then insert( i, free0_j )
```

put "1" in the ith row in the jth position:

```
if R[i, j] = 0 then exit( fail )      {we break the procedure in this case}
if R[i, j] ≠ 1 then      {it is a new "1"}
    R[i, j] ← 1
    insert( j, tree_col )
    if r_j < l_j then      {column j hasn't "1"s}
        l_j ← r_j ← l̃_j ← r̃_j ← i
        if p̃_j < i − v_j + 1 then p̃_j ← i − v_j + 1
        if q̃_j < i + v_j − 1 then q̃_j ← i + v_j − 1
        while not empty( free0_j ) do
            k ←min( free0_j )
            delete( k, free0_j )
            if k < i and k + 1 > p̃_j then p̃_j ← k + 1
            if k > i and k − 1 < q̃_j then q̃_j ← k − 1
    else {column j has "1"s}
        if i < l̃_j then l̃_j ← i
        if i > r̃_j then r̃_j ← i
```

The operations described above retain in memory the number of a column that is modifying when we put new symbol in a row. We analogously define these operations in columns.

Now we define $\oplus, \ominus, \otimes, \odot$ operations described in [1]. They are of the following form:

operation $\oplus$ in the ith row:

if $\tilde{l}^i < l^i$ **then**
  for $j \leftarrow \tilde{l}^i$ **to** $l^i - 1$ **do put** "1" in the ith row in the jth position
  $l^i \leftarrow \tilde{l}^i$
if $\tilde{r}^i > r^i$ **then**
  for $j \leftarrow r^i + 1$ **to** $\tilde{r}^i$ **do put** "1" in the ith row in the jth position
  $r^i \leftarrow \tilde{r}^i$

operation $\ominus$ in the ith row:

if $p^i < \tilde{p}^i$ **then**
  for $j \leftarrow p^i$ **to** $\tilde{p}^i - 1$ **do put** "0" in the ith row i in the jth position
  $p^i \leftarrow \tilde{p}^i$
if $q^i > \tilde{q}^i$ **then**
  for $j \leftarrow \tilde{q}^i + 1$ **to** q^i **do put** "0" in the ith row in the jth position
  $q^i \leftarrow \tilde{q}^i$

operation $\otimes$ in the ith row:

if $l^i > r^i$ and $p^i + h_i - 1 \geq q^i - h_i + 1$ **then**
  $l^i \leftarrow \tilde{l}^i \leftarrow q^i - h_i + 1$
  $r^i \leftarrow \tilde{r}^i \leftarrow p^i + h_i - 1$
  for $j \leftarrow l^i$ **to** r^i **do put** "1" in the ith row in the jth position
if $l^i \leq r^i$ and $q^i - h_i + 1 < l^i$ **then**
  for $j \leftarrow q^i - h_i + 1$ **to** $l^i - 1$ **do**
    put "1" in the ith row in the jth position
  $l^i \leftarrow \tilde{l}^i \leftarrow q^i - h_i + 1$
if $l^i \leq r^i$ and $p^i + h_i - 1 > r^i$ **then**
  for $j \leftarrow r^i + 1$ **to** $p^i + h_i - 1$ **do**
    put "1" in the ith row in the jth position
  $r^i \leftarrow \tilde{r}^i \leftarrow p^i + h_i - 1$

operation $\odot$ in the ith row:

if $l^i \leq r^i$ and $p^i \leq r^i - h_i$ **then**
  for $j \leftarrow p^i$ **to** $r^i - h_i$ **do put** "0" in the ith row in the jth position
  $p^i \leftarrow \tilde{p}^i \leftarrow r^i - h_i + 1$
if $l^i \leq r^i$ and $q^i \geq l^i + h_i$ **then**
  for $j \leftarrow l^i + h_i$ **to** q^i **do put** "0" in the ith row in the jth position
  $q^i \leftarrow \tilde{q}^i \leftarrow l^i + h_i - 1$

The operations $\oplus, \otimes$ put new "1"s in matrix R and the operations $\ominus, \odot$ put new "0"s. We analogously define these operations in columns.

The main loop of the procedure *filling operation* has the following form now:

The main loop of the procedure:

```
repeat
    while not empty( tree_row ) do
        k ←min( tree_row )
        delete( k, tree_row )
        perform operations ⊕,⊖,⊗,⊙ in the kth row
    while not empty( tree_col ) do
        k ←min( tree_col )
        delete( k, tree_col )
        perform operations ⊕,⊖,⊗,⊙ in the kth column
until empty( tree_row ) and empty( tree_col )
```

When we do preprocessing (described in section 4) we put neither "0" nor "1". We only modify variables $\tilde{p}$ and $\tilde{q}$ of a particular row or a column when it is necessary. We put the numbers of these rows or columns in $tree_{row}$ or $tree_{col}$, respectively. We will put "0" or "1" while performing *filling operation* procedure described above (see the $\ominus$ operation and the $\otimes$ operation).

If the *filling operation* procedure returns *fail*, we know that a convex polyomino which has projections H and V (and the same initial position) does not exist.

0	0	0	0	0	0	1	1	0	0	0	0	0	0	0	0	0	0	0	0
0	0	0	0	0	c_1	1	1	c_{18}	0	0	0	0	0	0	0	0	0	0	0
0	0	0	c_{13}	c_7	1	1	1	1	c_{12}	c_6	0	0	0	0	0	0	0	0	0
0	a_1	b_1	1	1	1	1	1	1	1	a_6	b_6	0	0	0	0	0	0	0	0
1	1	1	1	1	1	1	1	1	1	1	1	1	0	0	0	0	0	0	0
1	1	1	1	1	1	1	1	1	1	1	1	1	1	0	0	0	0	0	0
0	a_2	b_2	c_{14}	1	1	1	1	1	1	1	1	1	1	a_3	b_3	c_{15}	0	0	0
0	0	0	0	c_8	c_2	1	1	1	1	1	1	1	1	1	1	1	c_9	c_3	0
0	0	0	0	0	0	1	1	1	1	1	1	1	1	1	1	1	1	1	1
0	0	0	0	0	0	0	1	1	1	1	1	1	1	1	1	1	1	1	1
0	0	0	0	0	0	0	0	1	1	1	1	1	1	1	1	1	1	1	1
0	0	0	0	0	0	0	0	c_{17}	c_{11}	c_5	1	1	1	1	1	c_{16}	c_{10}	c_4	0
0	0	0	0	0	0	0	0	0	0	a_5	b_5	1	1	1	a_4	b_4	0	0	0
0	0	0	0	0	0	0	0	0	0	0	0	1	1	1	0	0	0	0	0

Fig. 3. 3 unjoined cycles: $(a_1, \ldots, a_6)$, $(b_1, \ldots, b_6)$, $(c_1, \ldots, c_{18})$

If trees $tree_{row}$ and $tree_{col}$ are empty, we have two different cases:

case 1: Each cell of R contain "0" or "1". We have the solution. The set S is a convex polyomino and satisfies (H, V).

case 2: Each row contains at least one "1" (we assure this in section 4) and we have some cells in R which contain neither "0" nor "1" (see Fig. 3). If we have any row or any column containing these empty cells and at least one "1", then the auxiliary variables in the row or the column will satisfy the properties:

$$l - \tilde{p} = \tilde{q} - r \neq 0.$$

If any column have not "1", the number of empty cells in this column is equal to double number of "1" that we can put in this column. Moreover, if $R[i, j]$ contains neither "0" nor "1", then it exists $R[i', j']$ containing neither "0" nor "1" and satisfying $i = i'$ and $|j - j'| = h_i$ or $j = j'$ and $|i - i'| = v_j$. In addition the number of empty cells in entire R is equal to double number of missing "1"s. Hence, the cells, which contain neither "0" nor "1", form a cycle or a union of disjoint cycles, each of them contains at least 4 cells. The cells of the cycle are labelled alternately "0" and "1". But some cycles are labelled dependent. In order to fill these cells correctly we build suitable 2-SAT problem, that can be solved in linear time (for more details see [1]). Because the number of empty cells is less than mn the additional cost of solution in this case is at most $O(mn)$.

Now we estimate the complexity of the main loop in the *filling operation* procedure. In each position (i, j) we perform operation **put** only twice (one operation in the ith row and one operation in the jth column). Moreover, when we do operations $\oplus, \ominus, \otimes, \odot$ in a row or in a column in our algorithm, we execute at least one **put** operation. Hence, we review only $O(mn)$ columns and rows and the review of one row costs $O(\log n) + $ [cost of the **put** operations] and the review of one column costs $O(\log m) + $ [cost of the **put** operations]. Therefore, the global cost of the main loop of the algorithm is $O(mn(\log m + \log n)) + $ [cost of all **put** operations].

Now we estimate global cost of all **put** operations. In the ith row when we perform **put** operations we execute at most m insert operations in tree$_{col}$. It costs $O(m \log m)$. For all rows the cost is at most $O(mn \log m)$. In all columns the cost of the insert operations in tree$_{row}$ is at most $O(mn \log n)$, analogously.

Since the insert operations in free0^i in the ith row we are doing no more than one time for each position. There are not more than m delete operations, either. We execute functions min and max only during modifying $\tilde{p}^i$ or $\tilde{q}^i$. Hence, the number of these operations is at most m. All operations in tree free0^i cost at most $O(m \log m)$. For all n rows the cost is at most $O(mn \log m)$. In all m columns the cost of the operation in trees is at most $O(mn \log n)$, analogously.

The complexity of all residual operations is at most $O(mn)$. Hence, the cost of the procedure called *filling operation* is at most $O(mn(\log m + \log n))$.

The proof of the correctness of the procedure is a small modification of the proof from [1].

Theorem 1. *The filling operation procedure costs at most $O(mn \log mn)$.*

4 Main Algorithm

The main idea of the algorithm is testing all possible positions of "1"s into first and last rows, i.e. feet's positions. If we fix any initial positions of upper and lower rows, we will use the Corollary 1 for computing positions of some "1"s in columns between feet's positions. We want to have at least one "1" in each row when we start *filling procedure* described in section 3. It assures the correct effect of working this procedure.

If we have feet's positions $\langle n_1, n_2 \rangle$ and $\langle s_1, s_2 \rangle$ and $n_2 < s_1$, we compute for all $j \in [n_2 + 1..s_1 - 1]$:

$$D_j = \min\{i \in [1..m-1] : A - H_i < A - V_j\},$$
$$U_j = \max\{i \in [2..m] : H_{i-1} < V_{j-1}\}.$$

If $n_1 > s_2$ we compute for all $j \in [s_2 + 1..n_1 - 1]$:

$$D_j = \min\{i \in [1..m-1] : A - H_i < V_{j-1}\},$$
$$U_j = \max\{i \in [2..m] : H_{i-1} < A - V_j\}.$$

It is easy to check that always $U_j \leq D_j$ and moreover, in first case $D_j + 1 \geq U_{j+1}$ and in second case $U_j + 1 \geq D_{j+1}$. Hence, in j-th column we can put "1" in all cells between U_j and D_j and we can put "0" in cells upper $D_j - v_j + 1$ and lower $U_j + v_j - 1$. Moreover, we have all "1"s and "0"s in columns which are appointed by feet's positions. Finally, we have at least one "1" in each row.

Otherwise, if both feet's positions have a common column then its must contain only "1"s because we have "1" on the first and on the last position in this column and a area of "1"s is connected. Hence, in this case we also have at last one "1" in each row.

The preprocessing described above costs at most $0(m + n)$.

We assume, there exists convex polyomino S satisfying (H, V). If we guess the right feet's positions of S (because we tested all feet's positions we must guess it correctly in course the time) we will have all "1"s and "0"s in columns $n_1...n_2$ and $s_1...s_2$. Moreover, we have at least one "1" in each column between feet's positions (if there exist such columns). Finally we have at last one "1" in each row and each of them is correct. Hence, the *filling procedure* cannot answer *fail* and must return the correct polyomino.

If for vectors (H, V) do not exist convex polyomino S satisfying (H, V) the *filling procedure* answers *fail*.

The number of all feet's positions tests is at most n^2 and it is equal to $\min(m, n)^2$. The preprocessing and *filling procedure* costs at most $O(mn \log mn)$. Hence, we have

Theorem 2. *The reconstruction of convex polyomino with vertical and horizontal projections costs at most $O(\min(m, n)^2 \cdot mn \log mn)$.*

Acknowledgements

I would like to thank Leszek Pacholski for his valuable discussions and insightful suggestions.

References

1. Barcucci, E., Del Lungo, A., Nivat, M., Pinzani, R.: Reconstructing convex polyominoes from horizontal and vertical projections. Theor. Comp. Sci. **155** (1996) 321–347
2. Barcucci, E., Del Lungo, A., Nivat, M., Pinzani, R.: Reconstructing convex polyominoes from horizontal and vertical projections II. (1996) Preprint
3. Chang, S.K.: The reconstruction of binary patterns from their projections. Comm. ACM **14** (1971) 21–25
4. Ryser, H.: Combinatorial Mathematics. The Carus Mathematical Monographs Vol. 14 (The Mathematical Association of America, Rahway, 1963)
5. Wang, X.G.: Characterisation of binary patterns and their projections. IEEE Trans. Comput. C-24 (1975) 1032–1035
6. Woeginger, G.J.: The reconstruction of polyominoes from their orthogonal projections. (1996) Preprint

Behavioral Safety in a Model
With Multiple Class Objects

Tomáš Hruška[1,*], Petr Kolenčík[1,*], and Michal Máčel[2]

[1] Department of Computer Science and Engineering
Faculty of Electrical Engineering and Computer Science
Technical University of Brno
Božetěchova 2, 612 66 Brno, Czech Republic
{hruska,kolencik}@dcse.fee.vutbr.cz

[2] VEMA Brno-Computers and Projects, Ltd.
Výstavní 17/19, 603 00 Brno, Czech Republic
macel@vema.cz

Abstract. Considering the extension to the object-oriented model introducing multiple type objects, we faced the problem of disambiguating method dispatching. This issue is closely connected with the conflicts in classes defined by the multiple inheritance. We studied the current works from a broader perspective of conceptual modeling considering both theoretical and practical views. As a result, solution based on the *method redefinition constraints* was proposed. For the presentation of the main ideas, we use the formal tools of category theory. It is in accordance with our former attempts to describe object-oriented models in terms of categorical constructions.

Key words: object-oriented database model, modeling roles, method dispatching, category theory.

1 Introduction

Recent research in the information system design and conceptual modeling shows some practical limitations of the object-oriented paradigm. [8] describes difficulties connected with *modeling roles*. It was pointed out that the assumption usual for the object-oriented models that objects acquire only one type for all their life time is often broken in the real-world situations. As a result, a role model was proposed defining two operations that enable to *acquire* and *discard* types. There were proposed also other approaches to this problem in [1] and [7].

Further studies identified potential complications concerning attribute access and method dispatching in an object-oriented model extended by roles. This issue is closely connected to the conflicts accompanying the multiple inheritance. An object can acquire multiple types at runtime which are equivalent to that

---

* Supported by the grant of the Czech Grant Agency No. 102/96/0986 Object-Oriented Database Model.

ones defined by the multiple inheritance. Thus, we give rise to potential conflicts in state and behavior of objects. Such a problem was recognized in [2] proving that the structural conflict in multiple type objects can be solved by static types (or contexts in which an attribute is referred). Nevertheless, it was shown that the context information is not enough to disambiguate the method dispatching. Two approaches were proposed to solve this problem with discussion of their advantages and disadvantages.

In this paper, we present solution based on the *method redefinition constraints*. Our objective is to show that the problem of method dispatching should not be considered separately but in connection with the semantics of the role model itself. Our approach uses the formal tools of category theory in accordance with our former attempts to describe object-oriented models in terms of categorical constructions (see [5] and [6]). Categorical modeling manifesto [4] assumes that the category theory is especially suited to study the properties of object-oriented models.

2 A Model with Multiple Class Objects

The object-oriented paradigm was developed, besides other things, with the aim to support direct representation of real-world entities. However, the usual assumption that an object has a structure determined once for all of its lifetime breaks this principle. Consider an example of persons, students and readers and suppose that the type *SR* constructed by using the multiple inheritance *has not been defined yet*. In such a database, we can model the roles of the persons by using the types *S* and *R*. However, we can not represent a *person* that studies at the university and is stored in the database of the university library as a *reader* at the same time. Such a situation is common because information systems usually consist of several modules that share the data and each module views them from its specific perspective.

In this case, the object-oriented paradigm provides multiple inheritance to model this semantics. We can combine the properties of *student* and *reader* defining a new type *student-reader*. This technique is adequate for the languages that work with transient objects only. The lifetime of such objects is limited by the lifetime of the application process that created them. However, in the database applications objects are persistent and exist independently on the process that created them. Practical experiences often signify that it is difficult to presume beforehand all the possible combinations of types that an entity can have. With the growing complexity of database applications the problem is even worse. It could lead to combinatorial explosion of the types defined by the multiple inheritance.

To avoid this problem we can introduce so called *multiple type objects* together with two operations for *acquiring* and *discarding* types. This concept will prevent us to build all required types defined by the multiple inheritance and enable objects to play different roles as needed in the real-world situations.

Such an extension to the object-oriented model is considered in [6] presenting formal semantics of the operations *acquire* and *discard*.

As was already stated, in [6] we used category theory to deal with the problem of attribute access in the contex of multiple class objects. There the approach using this theory was very useful. In this paper, category theory will help just to discribe the structure of classes defined by multiple inheritance using simple product notation. In the categorical framework, we can describe the semantics of the inheritance using the notion of *product*:

Definition 1 (Product) Having two objects S and T in a category we define **product** as an object $S \times T$ together with projections $\pi_s : S \times T \to S$ and $\pi_t : S \times T \to T$ such that for any object V and arrows $q_s : V \to S$ and $q_t : V \to T$, there is a *unique* arrow $q : V \to S \times T$ making commute the diagram

$$
\begin{array}{ccc}
 & V & \\
q_t \swarrow & \downarrow q & \searrow q_t \\
S \underset{\pi_s}{\leftarrow} & S \times T & \underset{\pi_t}{\rightarrow} T
\end{array}
$$

□

However, to describe the semantics of multiple inheritance some additional commutativity conditions will be needed as explained in [6]. Particularly, the notion of a *pullback* is used to express the semantics of virtual base types. To illustrate, we will show how to define type hierarchy of types *student* S and *reader* R, having the common ancestor *person* P and a type SR inheriting from S and R using multiple inheritance. This simple university database with library module is shown in Fig. 1.

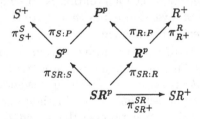

Fig. 1. Inheritance as a *product*

Semantics of the virtual base types can be expressed as a construction of an object SR^P such that the diagram in Fig. 1 commutes and for each possible SR' satisfying this condition there is always unique arrow to SR^P. This construction, described here, is called *pullback* which is a specific case of more general *limit* construction. It can be equivalently stated that SR satisfies the conditions required for $S \times R$ by Definition 1 but the commutativity condition here is extended to the whole diamond diagram of the multiple inheritance.

Thus, the object $SR^p = S^p \times_{P^p} R^p \times SR^+$ is sometimes called *product restricted over* P^p. We use this notation omitting P^p in the superscript of $\times$ to simplify the description of types. Instead of spelling out the detailed *limit* construction we write only the types participating in the *product*. Nevertheless, one can not forget the extended commutativity and uniqueness conditions that must be also satisfied if applicable.

Following this convention, the structure of SR^p can be expressed in various ways as: $SR^p = S^p \times R^p \times SR^+$ (structure of SR in the terms of its most specific classes) $= P^p \times S^p \times R^p \times SR^+$ (structure of SR in the terms of all of its supertypes) $= P^p \times S^+ \times R^+ \times SR^+$ (structure of SR in the terms of its components). Notice, that in the letter case no additional conditions are required to be satisfied. In **Set**, this translates into the following structure:

$$SR^p = \{(p, s, r, sr) \mid p \in P^p, s \in S^+, r \in R^+, sr \in SR^+\}.$$

In a model enabling multiple inheritance together with the notion of *method redefinition*, there can be more than one method with the most specific behavior. The fact that there are no unambiguous implementations of *virtual methods* will be called *behavioral safety*. Condition under which a *virtual method* is *unambiguous* can be expressed as follows:

Definition 2 (Method Unambiguity) The method m is *unambiguous* if and only if for all types $T = T_1 \times T_2 \times \ldots \times T_n$, where $T_1, T_2, \ldots, T_n$ are all the supertypes of T, and for each two $T_i \neq T_j$ that are not in the *subtype relation* and both *implement* m there is always T_k implementing m together with the arrows $\pi_{T_k:T_i} : T_k \to T_i$ and $\pi_{T_k:T_j} : T_k \to T_j$. □

3 Preferred Class and Argument Specificity Approaches

There are two basic solutions to the problem of method dispatching proposed in [2]. One special case is considered separately in the conclusion of that paper. Generally, we have two possibilities how to dispatch the conflicting method m for a SR-object. The first concerns the special situation when m does some initialization. In this case it would be reasonable to call both. Other situations do not enable to invoke both methods and require to choose only one implementation that was most probably meant by the application programmer.

One possibility is to define an order on the types that reimplement the method m separately for each context S and R where m can be invoked. For this reason, this solution is called *preferred class approach*. Notice that this approach supports context dependent behavior since the order is defined for each context in which m can be invoked.

Another way of choosing the right implementation is to compare parameters of the method definitions and choose the one which seems to match the actual parameters better. Even if this *argument specificity approach* is not always able to dispatch a method it ensures a notion of behavior identity. There is also another heuristics that according to the statistics dispatches the method which was invoked more frequently in the past. However, the semantics of the message passing mechanism in such a model would be very indefinite.

4 Constrained Method Redefinition Approach

The solution presented in this paper is inspired by the study of the concept of multiple type objects as related to the real-world situations. We noticed that behavioral conflicts often do not point to a limitation of the model which is seemingly lacking the means to direct the method invocation in the conflicting cases. Rather, they reflect some inconsistency in the database schema itself.

To illustrate, consider a method *get_contact* for *person* redefined in the subtypes *student* and *lecturer*. Suppose that this method returns the name of a *person* (in the case of *lecturer* it adds his degree) and the address for an official correspondence. Let us say that the official contact address for a *person* is his home address, for *student* his university address and for *lecturer* the address of his department. Now we can create an object of the combined type representing, for example, Ph.D. student that works as a *teaching assistant*.

Invoking the method *get_contact* for the objects of type $S^p \times L^p$ in order to write an official letter to a specific person would cause behavioral conflict. Here, some context dependent solution would be preferable. Notice also that it would be possible to return the answer as a set of all the contact addresses and let the user choose what to do with this set. But in a general case the method can change the state of the object thus preventing to get the set of all its possible results without the damaging consequences of its side effects.

This conflicting situation can be solved sensibly also earlier in the process of the database schema design. For the analyst, it is clear from the beginning that *student* and *lecturer* are two roles that the objects in the real world can *acquire* and *discard* independently. The object-oriented database model should enable to express this semantics in the database schema and help to see the possible sources of conflicts thus preventing possible errors in the design process.

Therefore, rather than deciding which method should be dispatched , we disable such a situation at all. The types equivalent to the independent roles will be allowed to redefine its methods only under some strict rules. We call this principle *constrained method redefinition approach*.

5 Refining the Model With Method Redefinition Constraints

Developing the idea to constrain the method redefinition in a way that prohibits behavior conflicts in the multiple type objects, we can find many interesting consequences. First, we will describe the way we recommend to restrict the method redefinition and show how to express the notion in the inheritance hierarchy graph. Second, we will divide subtypes into two disjoint sets. The first will correspond to a set of *exclusive roles* and the other to a set of *independent roles*. Then we will illustrate the close connection between the notions of *method redefinition constraints* and *independent roles*. Finally we will formulate a condition under which objects can *acquire* new types with respect to the *method redefinition constraints*. We will close the presentation by a proof that in a model with the *method redefinition constraints* there are no behavioral conflicts for multiple type objects whose types are changed using the restricted operation *acquire*.

5.1 Constraints as a Property of Direct Method Inheritance

We explain how to constrain the method inheritance first because it is more simple. The motivation that led us to do it this way will be seen later in Section 5.2. The constraints will not be connected with specific methods or types but it will be a property of the inheritance itself. This way the complexity of the model is hold in reasonable limits. Each edge in the inheritance hierarchy will have additional marker that will denote the *constraint*. In the inheritance graph, it will be depicted as a blocked (dashed) edge as shown in Fig. 2. The methods inherited through this edge are blocked and can not be redefined any more at any further subtype down the inheritance hierarchy. It should be emphasized that the block does not concern only the direct subtype but all the subtypes that can be reached through the dashed edge. However, the method can be actually redefined for such a subtype because the graph of the multiple inheritance can provide two paths for method inheritance. This case is allowed but it has direct consequences leading to a greater restriction of the types acquirable by objects. It will be further discussed in Section 5.3.

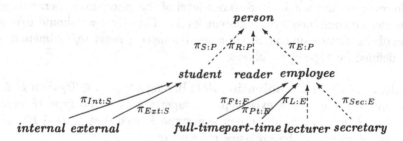

Fig. 2. Graph representation of *method redefinition constraints*

5.2 Constraints and Independent Roles

It is interesting to investigate the connection between the *method redefinition constraints* and *independent roles* played by the objects in the real-world situations. It should be noted that the arrows going to a type define partitioning into two disjoint subsets of the direct subtypes. This can be seen in Fig. 2 where the subtypes of *employee* can be partitioned into two sets {*full-time, part-time*} and {*lecturer, secretary*}. Notice, that all the subtypes of the second set have disabled method redefinition. We will call this set as a set of *independent roles*. This means that such types can be freely combined with each other to form multiple type objects. Thus, the composed objects will not suffer by the behavioral conflicts since there is only one implementation of the most specific method and this is the implementation used for *employees*.

On the other hand, we have the set of *exclusive roles*. Because we enable to redefine the methods for subtypes in this set we must prevent the existence of multiple type objects containing *more than one type* belonging to some *exclusive roles* set excluding all its subtypes as well. This way we ensure that there are no behavioral conflicts in the model. We will define formally which types can be precisely combined in the next section. In the rest of the paper, we will denote the *independent roles* set as T^{ind} and the *exclusive roles* set as T^{ex}.

5.3 Acquirable Types

If the database schema satisfies the *method redefinition constraints* the behavioral conflicts will be prevented provided that an object can acquire only limited set of types.

From the notion of the *independent roles* set one can infer that behavioral safe combinations of the direct subtypes of T are subsets of $T^{ind} \cup \{E\}$ where $E \in T^{ex}$, i.e. arbitrary types from the *independent roles* set and at most one type from the *exclusive roles* set. We will denote the direct safe combination set as T^{dsf}. If there is no unambiguity concerning the methods in T^{dsf} with respect to multiple inheritance there will be no unambiguity in the type combinations based on this set neither.

However, we are not limited to one level of the inheritance hierarchy graph. Types can be combined from different levels. Therefore, we should extend the notion of the direct safe combination set to a more general *safe combination* set A^{safe} defined for type A as follows:

Definition 3 (Safe Combination Set) Having a type $A \in \mathcal{D}_I$ then $B \in A^{safe}$ if and only if there do not exist types G supertype of A and type H supertype of B, $G \neq H$, having distinct direct supertype F such that $G, H \in F^{ex}$ (G and H are not elements of the *exclusive roles* set of F). $\qquad\square$

Notice the symmetry $B \in A^{safe} \Leftrightarrow A \in B^{safe}$ caused by the existence of the same F, G and H in both cases. It seems that in order to combine types A and B it would be enough to require the existence of G and H to be elements of F^{dsf} as opposed to the non-existence condition that G and H are both elements the of *exclusive roles* set. However, the assumption that any method will be redefined only on one path leading through G or H is not true in such a case. The next example in Fig. 3 is used to illustrate that the non-existence requirement is not superfluous.

For the types *pt-student* and *ft-lecturer* there exist two distinct corresponding supertypes *student* and *lecturer* that both seem to prohibit method redefinition

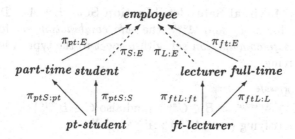

Fig. 3. One special case when *acquire* is restricted

by the dashed edges. However, there is potential conflict in any object derived from *pt-student* and acquiring *ft-lecturer*. This object would have virtual type *assistant* that can have redefined any method inherited from *employee* through the types *part-time* and *full-time* belonging to the *exclusive roles* set of *employee*.

This is easy to check that *ft-lecturer* does not belong to the *safe combination set* of *pt-student* according to our definition since there exist two types *part-time* and *full-time* that break the non-existence condition. We will see the importance of this point later in the next section dealing with the notion of *behavioral safety*.

5.4 Behavioral Safety in the Constrained Model

We conclude the discussion proving that the model with the *constrained method redefinition* and restricted operation *acquire* prevents behavioral conflicts. We can show that there is no behavioral conflict for types in the form $A \times B$, where $B \in A^{safe}$ directly using the Definitions 2 and 3: from the latter we see that any method m can not be implemented in A and B at the same time because there do not exist two paths beginning from F that would enable its redefinition. Thus, if there was no unambiguity for m in A and B itself there can not be found any T_i and T_j according to Definition 2 for the combined type $A \times B$.

Nevertheless, we must consider that the multiple type $A \times B$ can be further extended. Notice, that such a type can not be freely combined with other types from A^{safe}. Rather, the *safe combination set* defines a symmetric but *non transitive* relation over the types that can be combined. We admit reflexivity since it is meaningful with respect to the notion of *method unambiguity*. It is clear that the relation is not transitive looking at the hierarchy in Fig. 2. While *full-time, part-time* $\in student^{safe}$ yet they can not be acquired at the same time. The reason is that the non-existence condition in Definition 3 may not be satisfied because there are no requirements on $B, C \in A^{safe}$ distinct from A.

Thus allowing to combine types $B, C \in A^{safe}$ arbitrarily with the type A does not necessarily mean that we can have an object of the multiple type $B \times C$. All the types that can be combined with the type A are defined using the *maximal safe combination set* A^{msafe}:

Definition 4 (Maximal Safe Combination Set) Let $A \in \mathcal{D}_I$ be a type in the inheritance hierarchy and A^{safe} the *safe combination set* for the type A. Then *maximal safe combination set* with respect to the type A is a set denoted as A^{msafe} satisfying:

(*i*) $A \in A^{msafe}$
(*ii*) $B, C \in A^{msafe} \Rightarrow B \in C^{safe}$ (and also $C \in B^{safe}$)
(*iii*) $\forall X$ satisfying (*i*) and (*ii*) : $A^{msafe} \not\subset X$ □

The first condition states that A is always a part of the A^{msafe}. Second, each pair of A^{msafe} must allow type safe combination. Finally, notice that A^{msafe} is maximal with respect to the types in the inheritance hierarchy, i.e. no other type can be added to A^{msafe} without breaking the condition 2. There can be several *maximal combination sets* for each type A.

Now we can formulate the following proposition for the refined model:

Proposition 1 (Behavioral Safety) Let $\mathcal{D}_I$ be a type hierarchy with *method redefinition constraints* without *behavioral conflicts*. Then for each *maximal safe combination set* with respect to the type $A \in \mathcal{D}_I$: $A^{msafe} = \{A_1, A_2, \ldots, A_n\}$ there is no *behavioral conflict* in the multiple type objects o based on the types from the set A^{msafe}: $o \in \mathbf{MTA} = A_1 \times A_2 \times \ldots \times A_n$.   □

In other words, A^{msafe} defines the types *acquirable* by A-objects at the same time yet ensuring that there is no unambiguity concerning method dispatching. Proposition 1 guarantees *behavioral safety* for all the multiple type objects. Summarize that the restricted product, denoted as $\mathbf{MTA}$, describes the structure of multiple type objects based on the type A extended by all the types from A^{msafe} without the risk of behavioral conflicts.

Proof. We rewrite the multiple type $\mathbf{MTA}$ as $\mathbf{MTA} = T_1 \times T_2 \times \ldots \times T_n$, where $\{T_1, T_2, \ldots, T_n\}$ are all the supertypes $T_i \in \mathcal{D}_I$ of $\mathbf{MTA}$. We also know that T_j does not redefine the methods of T_i if $\pi_{T_j : T_i} : T_j \to T_i$ is constrained. Let us denote by T_i and T_j any two distinct elements of the set $\{T_1, T_2, \ldots, T_n\}$ that are not in the *subtype relation* and suppose that they both implement the method m. Now we have two possibilities.

1. There exists, according to Definition 2, T_k together with the arrows $\pi_{T_k : T_i} : T_k \to T_i$ and $\pi_{T_k : T_j} : T_k \to T_j$. This means that T_k must implement m. Otherwise there would be disambiguity already in the model because $T_k \in \mathcal{D}_I$.

2. T_k, subtype of T_i and T_j, does not exist. In this case, the rest of the proof consist in showing that the method m could be implemented only in one of the types T_i and T_j. Let us suppose that m is reimplemented in both and defined for the first time in F. This means that there must exist at least two different types G and H where G is a supertype of T_i and H supertype of T_j such that H and G are inherited through the non

constrained edges (otherwise the redefinition of m would be restricted and could not be redefined in both T_i and T_j). However, this contradicts the assumption that T_i and T_j belong to the *maximal safe combination* set according to Definitions 3 and 4. Therefore, m can not be implemented in both T_i and T_j and is unambiguous in accordance with Definition 2. $\square$

6 Conclusions

Considering an extension of the object-oriented model by multiple type objects we studied possible solutions to the problem of disambiguating method dispatching. The issue is carefully investigated in [2] providing the proof that structural conflicts cause no problems when the context of attribute access is considered. This led us to propose the semantics of operations *acquire* and *discard* as presented in [6] and study the multiple type objects using the tools of the category theory.

However, the context information is not enough to disambiguate the method dispatching. The two approaches that were proposed to solve this problem in [2] seem to make the database schema design more complicated for practical use.

Thus, while working on an implementation of the object-oriented database model closely following the ODMG-93 standard [3], we proposed another solution enriching the semantics of the method inheritance. *Method redefinition constraints* were introduced, disabling to redefine methods inherited through blocked edges in the rest of the inheritance graph. We could apply this schema for each method separately but it seems that the model would become unnecessarily complex. Therefore, we connect constraints with the inheritance itself. Nevertheless, additional research would be needed to clarify this issue.

We have carefully studied the consequences of such extension providing formal semantics of the concepts. One advantage of the chosen approach is that only meaningful combinations of types are allowed for the multiple type objects. This clarifies the schema design and gives us the possibility to move majority of the runtime checking into the compiletime. Otherwise, it would not be easy to infer whether an *acquired* type is a source of behavioral conflict. Using an algorithm based on Proposition 1 we can generate a table for an effective runtime checking of the operation *acquire*. On the other hand, our approach has the disadvantage of the *argument specificity approach* that disables static typing. Even if methods are always dispatchable, operation *acquire* can cause runtime errors. We have also illustrated how the theoretical results translate into the real-world notions understandable for the database practitioners.

Evaluating the *constrained method redefinition approach*, the problems seem to be clear on the theoretical level. However, there are several possibilities how to restrict the redefinition of methods and, consequently, the corresponding safe combination relation. The effectiveness and usefulness of the *constrained method redefinition approach* must be yet tested in the real environment.

References

1. ALBANO, A., BERGAMINI, R., GHELLI, G., ORSINI, R.: An Object Data Model with Roles. In Proceedings of Nineteenth Int'l Conf. on Very Large Databases, R. Agrawal, S. Baker, and D. Bell, Eds., 1993, pp. 39–51.
2. BERTINO, E., GUERRINI, G.: Objects with Multiple Most Specific Classes. In Proceedings of 9th European Conference ECOOP'95 on Object-Oriented Programming, W. G. Olthoff, Ed., vol. 952 of LNCS, Springer, 1995, pp. 102–126.
3. CATTELL, R.: The Object Database Standard ODMG-93, Release 1.2. Morgan Kaufmann Publishers, 1996.
4. DISKIN, Z., CADISH, B.: Algebraic Graph-Oriented = Category Theory Based. Manifesto of categorizing database theory. Tech. Rep. 9406, Frame Inform Systems, Riga, Latvia, 1994.
5. HRUŠKA, T., KOLENČÍK, P.: Comparison of Categorical Foundations of Object-Oriented Database Model. In Proceedings of 5th International Conference on Deductive and Object-Oriented Databases DOOD'97, F. Bry, R. Ramakrishnan, and K. Ramdmohanarao, Eds., vol. 1341 of LNCS, Springer, 1997, pp. 302–319.
6. HRUŠKA, T., KOLENČÍK, P.: Extending an Object-Oriented Model: Multiple Class Objects. In Proceedings of 16th International Conference ER'97 on Conceptual Modelling, D. W. Embley and R. C. Goldstein, Eds., vol. 1331 of LNCS, Springer, 1997, pp. 229–242.
7. RICHARDSON, J., SCHWARZ, P.: Aspects: Extending Objects to Support Multiple Independent Roles. In Proceedings of the ACM SIGMOD International Conference on Management of Data, J. Clifford and R. King, Eds., 1991, pp. 298–307.
8. VELHO, A. V., CARAPUCA, R.: From Entity-Relationship Models to Role-Attribute Models. In Proceedings of 12th International Conference ER'93 on the Entity-Relationship Approach, R. A. Elmasri, V. Kouramajian, and B. Thalheim, Eds., vol. 823 of LNCS, Springer, 1994, pp. 257–270.

Massively Parallel Suffix Array Construction

Costas S. Iliopoulos[1,2] and Maureen Korda[3]

[1] King's College London, Dept. of Computer Science, London WC2R 2LS, England,
csi@dcs.kcl.ac.uk,
WWW home page: http://www.dcs.kcl.ac.uk/staff/csi
[2] Curtin University of Technology, School of Computing, GPO Box 1987 U, WA,
Australia.
[3] King's College London, Dept. of Computer Science, London WC2R 2LS, England,
mo@dcs.kcl.ac.uk,
WWW home page: http://www.dcs.kcl.ac.uk/pg/mo

Abstract. This paper considers the construction of the suffix array of a
string on the MasPar MP-2 architecture. Suffix arrays are space-efficient
variants of the suffix trees, a fundamental dictionary data structure that
is the backbone of many string algorithms for pattern matching and
textual information retreival. We adapt known PRAM techniques for
implementation on the MasPar: bulletin boards, doubling techniques and
sorting methods. Performance results are presented.

1 Introduction

Given a text $\mathcal{T}$, the retrieval of statistical information about $\mathcal{T}$ can be accomplished using textual search techniques. One such technique is to firstly compute
an index for $\mathcal{T}$ that can subsequently be used to answer a variety of queries. This
index must be efficient in terms of construction time, memory use and storage
space. In the field of string algorithms, the suffix tree data structure ([16], [11])
is an elegant data structure that provides an index and a statistical resource for
a given input text: for a text $\mathcal{T}$ of length n, a suffix tree of $\mathcal{T}$ is a compacted
trie of all the (unique) suffixes of $\mathcal{T}$. It is well known that a suffix tree can be
constructed in linear sequential time and space. However, the constant hidden by
the $O(n)$ space requirement is sufficient to render this data structure impractical in many real applications. Consequently, recent algorithms have been devised
that consider the practical implications of suffix trees where space is traded for
query time ([3],[2]).

An alternative data structure that also provides an index for a given text
is the suffix array [12]. The suffix array of a text $\mathcal{T}$ of length n is an array of
size n such that the i-th entry is the i-th smallest suffix according to the lexicographical ordering of strings. The suffix array therefore represents the leaves of
the *ordered* suffix tree for the text $\mathcal{T}$. Two additional arrays (or a further $2n - 4$
values) associated with longest common prefix information are required to guide
searching in the suffix array. This information represents the inner (branching)
nodes in the equivalent suffix tree. Although the suffix array requires the longer

time of $O(n \log n)$ to construct, it's redeeming feature is that it requires less than half the space of the equivalent suffix tree. The reduction in storage space implies that querying the suffix array is also very efficient since fewer (external) memory references are required.

In parallel computation, a PRAM algorithm was presented in [1] for the construction of a suffix tree requiring $O(n \log n)$ work and $O(\log n)$ time. This algorithm also requires polynomial space; i.e. $n^{1+\epsilon}$ for $0 < \epsilon < 1$. Drawing from the body of fundamental tools developed for parallel string algorithms, we present a practical PRAM algorithm for suffix array construction. By definition, the construction of the suffix array requires sorting techniques. We use the well known bulletin board technique to implement a deterministic naming scheme that also maintains lexicographical order between substrings. The bulletin board is frequently used in parallel string algorithms and our implementation shows how it can be used in practice. Indeed, for realisitic input sizes, the polynomial space requirement of the bulletin board soon exceeds that provided by main computer memory. In this case, we continue the suffix array construction using a parallel radix sort. Our algorithm resembles that of [12] in that it uses the *doubling technique* to derive logarithmic time bounds. However, we feel that a parallel implementation of the Manber and Myers algorithm is not a practical option for the MasPar architecture due to our use of external memory. In the sequel, the description of our algorithm is associated with its practical adaption for the massively parallel MasPar MP-2 2216.

2 Preliminaries and the MasPar

A *string* x is a finite sequence $x[1..n]$ of characters such that each $x[i]$ is drawn from an alphabet Σ. The length of x is n and is denoted $|x|$. A *substring* of x is a string $x[i..j]$ such that $1 \le i \le j \le n$. Furthermore, we say that the substring $x[i..j]$ *occurs* at position i in x. A *prefix* of x is a substring $x[1..j]$ such that $1 \le j \le n$. A *suffix* of x is a substring $x[i..n]$ such that $1 \le i \le n$.

Given an input text $\mathcal{T} = x[1..n]$ and an ordered alphabet Σ, we define the set of suffixes of $\mathcal{T}$ to be $\{s_1, s_2, \ldots s_n\}$ such that $s_i = x[i..n]$. The *suffix array* of $\mathcal{T}$ is a dictionary or indexing data structure consisting of the following components:

(i) An array SA of size n of integers in the range $1..n$ representing the lexico-graphically sorted suffixes of $\mathcal{T}$.

(ii) Two further arrays, LEFT-LCP and RIGHT-LCP, each of size $n - 2$ and containing integers in the range $0..n - 1$. The arrays LEFT-LCP and RIGHT-LCP are used to guide the search during the query procedure.

Each integer value stored in the arrays in (ii) above is the length of the longest common prefix between a pre-determined pair of suffixes of $\mathcal{T}$. These suffix pairs are exactly those equal to all the intervals that arise during a binary search in SA: i.e., let $[j, k], 1 \le j < k \le n$ be any interval that arises during a binary search in SA. Furthermore let $i = \lfloor (j + k)/2 \rfloor$ be the midpoint of this interval. Then the value stored at LEFT-LCP$[i]$ is the longest common prefix between the suffixes associated with SA[i] and SA[j]. Also RIGHT-LCP[i] is the longest common prefix between the suffixes associated with SA[i] and SA[k].

A simple way to determine the supplementary information needed in (ii) above is to firstly compute an array LCP of length $n-1$ that contains the length of the longest common prefix between the suffixes represented by SA[i] and SA[$i+1$] for all $1 \le i < n$. Our implementation uses this approach. Consider the string $\mathcal{T} = abbaabaaababbb$: then the array SA for T

$$\text{SA}[14] = [7, 4, 8, 5, 9, 1, 11, 14, 6, 3, 10, 13, 2, 12]$$

In this example s_7 is the lexicographically smallest suffix and s_{12} is the largest. The accompanying array LCP for SA is:

$$\text{LCP}[13] = [2, 4, 1, 3, 2, 3, 0, 1, 3, 2, 1, 2, 2]$$

An optimal algorithm for computing the minimum value in a given interval can be used to compute LEFT-LCP and RIGHT-LCP from the array LCP.

2.1 The MasPar

The massively parallel idiom is one which gains performance through replication by linking thousands of simple processing elements (PE's) via a suitable interconnection network in a specific topology. In the MasPar MP-2, 16,384 PE's are connected in a 128×128 two-dimensional mesh known as the PE Array. Each PE has 64K of local memory giving an aggregate 1 Gigabyte of distributed memory. In addition, PE's can access a shared memory of size 512K. (See [4] for more details) Communications between PE's are executed in one of two ways. The XNet interconnect furnishes fast local communications such that each PE can communicate with one of its 8 nearest neighbours (i.e., the adjacent horizontal, vertical and diagonal neighbours) in a *register to register* fashion. For more arbitrary communications there is a Global Router that is implemented using a *multi-stage interconnection network*. There is one originating router port and one target port per cluster of 16 PE's. Router communication is constant or independent of the position of the communicating PE's. We implement our algorithms using the MasPar Parallel Application Language, abbreviated to MPL, which allows the programmer specific control over data distribution and inter-processor communications, see [4] for details.

3 Data Structures and Techniques

3.1 Substring Naming

When gathering string statistics for a string x the technique known as *substring naming* is commonly used to group all equal substrings of x together and to associate a unique integer with each group. Substring naming together with recursive doubling (see [7]) are techniques that are widely used in parallel dictionary computations (see [6, 13, 10].) In [1] it was used in the parallel construction of suffix trees.

More formally, let $x[i..j]$ be a substring of an input text $\mathcal{T}$ of length $\ell = j-i+1$ for some $1 \leq i < j \leq n$. A deterministic substring naming function is a function that takes a substring such as $x[i..j]$ as an argument and returns an integer value *name*. We use *ℓ-name* to be the name given to a substring of $\mathcal{T}$ of length ℓ and *ℓ-name(i)* to denote the name of the substring of length ℓ that starts at position i in $\mathcal{T}$. The name for a string of length n can be computed in $\log n$ applications of the following naming function: $f(name1, name2) = newname$, where ($name1$, $name2$) is a tuple of integers, each of which is the name of a substring of length ℓ. Furthermore, *newname* is the *2ℓ-name* of the substring of length 2ℓ that is formed by concatenating the substrings associated with *name1* and *name2*, i.e., the substrings *ℓ-name(i)* and *ℓ-name(i + 2^ℓ)*, $1 \leq i \leq n$.

3.2 Naming using a Bulletin Board

A *bulletin board* BB$[1..n][1..n]$, is a two-dimensional array data structure that is frequently used in CRCW PRAM string algorithms. It enables processors to update the value of a specific parallel variable in constant time as follows: all processors that wish to write to a location BB$[r, c]$ attempt to do so. Depending on which CRCW model is used, a write conflict resolution mechanism is used to determine a winning processor from amongst them that will succeed in writing. For our algorithm, the naming function is computed by associating the rows (r) and columns (c) of BB with the *name1* and *name2* values respectively. We then use BB to convert two values into one as required by the naming function as follows: for all processors associated with positions in $\mathcal{T}$ such that $name1 = r$ and $name2 = c$, the winning processor writes a 1 at location BB$[r, c]$. This location is now said to be *active*. A unique value is then associated with each active location by computing the prefix sums of all active locations. This is the value of the variable *newname*. All processors that attempted to write to BB$[r, c]$ can now read the same value of *newname* from this location. For full details of the above implementation see [8].

The bulletin board is implemented as a set of two dimensional arrays distributed across the memory of the PE array. For a bulletin board of size $n \times n$, and given a total of p processing elements, a simple distribution allocates processor $p_i, i = 0..p-1$ to the bulletin board location [i div $n+1, i$ mod $n+1$]. When $n^2 > p$ this data structure is *virtualised*. Restricting our array bounds to powers of 2 we found that with 1 Gigabyte of PE memory we can implement a bulletin board of size 4096×4096, together with the associated longest common prefix data structures. Therefore each PE is associated with a sub-block consisting of $32 \times 32 = 1024$ BB locations.

Initially, the input alphabet Σ is distributed to all PE's and the size of the first bulletin board required is $|\Sigma|+1$. We now remove all characters from Σ that are not contained in the input text $\mathcal{T}$ and assign *names* to those that remain, since they represent all substrings of length 1 in the text. The input $\mathcal{T}$ is read in consecutive blocks consisting of p contiguous text characters from the external memory assigning one text position to each PE. Initially, it is possible to *stack* the text characters onto the PE's in layers since the bulletin board is very small. All bulletin board updates for each stage of sorting therefore require $O(n/p)$ external memory reads (and writes).

3.3 Longest Common Prefix Computation

Let $\text{lcp}[i,j]_k$ denote the length of the longest common prefix between the substrings of the input text $\mathcal{T}$ starting at positions i and j of length k. For $1 \leq h \leq \log |\mathcal{T}|$ we have

$$\text{lcp}[i,j]_h = \begin{cases} 2^{h-1} + \text{lcp}[i + 2^{h-1}, j + 2^{h-1}]_{h-1}, & \text{if } \text{lcp}[i,j]_{h-1} = 2^{h-1} \\ \text{lcp}[i,j]_{h-1}, & \text{otherwise} \end{cases} \quad (1)$$

The value of the longest common prefix that exists between each suffix and its right neighbour (i.e., the suffix that is currently the next largest one) is updated at each stage of naming using the following arrays:

1. a $q \times q$ array NEW_LCP is used to store the values of the longest common prefix which exist between every pair of *newnames* computed in the *current* stage. (q is the largest name assigned in the current stage.)
2. an $w \times w$ array OLD_LCP is used to store the values of the longest common prefix which exist between every pair of *newnames* computed in the *previous* stage. (w is the largest name assigned in the previous stage.)

These arrays are distributed across PE memory and we exploit the architecture's ability to efficiently broadcast values within the rows and columns of the PE array.

4 Bulletin Board and LCP Table: Performance Results

In Algorithm LCP below we describe how the LCP values are maintained. The algorithm takes as input the array OLD_LCP and it outputs the array NEW_LCP. An "active" processor is one which is associated with a bulletin board location that has been marked 1 (and was therefore written to). Consider the computation to determine the longest common prefix that exists between two ℓ-strings at i and j in $\mathcal{T}$. Let α_1, β_1 denote the values of *name1* and *name2* associated with the substring at position i and α_2, β_2 denote the values of *name1* and *name2* associated with the substring at position j. From (1) we can immediately derive the following lemma that is used to guide the longest common prefix computation:

Lemma 1. Using the α, β representation of substrings, the common prefix between two substrings such that $\alpha_1 \neq \alpha_2$ does not change from the previous iteration of naming.

Algorithm LCP

STEP 1: The first row and first column, r_0 and c_0, of NEW_LCP are initialised as follows: each active processor writes its *name1* value to both α_1 of processor p_δ in row r_0 and to α_2 of processor p_δ in column c_0. The same processor then writes its *name2* value to both β_1 of processor p_δ in row r_0 and to β_2 of processor p_δ in column c_0.

STEP 2: All locations in NEW_LCP are now initialised as follows: processor p_δ of row r_0 broadcasts α_1 and β_1 to all processors in the same column, c_δ. Similarly, each processor p_δ of the column c_0 broadcasts α_2 and β_2 to all the processors in the same row, r_δ.

STEP 3: Each location in NEW_LCP has now received 4 values which are grouped into the two pairs: $\gamma = (\alpha_1, \alpha_2)$ and $\zeta = (\beta_1, \beta_2)$.

STEP 4: All locations in the table NEW_LCP now consider their γ and ζ pairs. If $\alpha_1 \neq \alpha_2$, then by fact (1) and Lemma 1 the longest common prefix value does not change, else the longest common prefix value is equal to $|\alpha_1| +$ OLD_LCP$[\beta_1, \beta_2]$.

Table 1 shows how rapidly the size of the bulletin board grows for increasing lengths of English text and DNA. The results show that the bulletin board size for DNA and English text inputs grows very rapidly and that only 3 and 2 iterations respectively of naming are possible for input sizes larger than 16384: suffixes are sorted according to a uniform prefix of length 8. Indeed, the largest bulletin boards that are made use of are of size 260^2 for DNA and 539^2 for English text.

Table 1. *Iterations* = number of iterations of naming, *Last BB* = largest BB realised, *Next BB* = next BB size required, *Secs* = time in seconds

DNA					English Text				
n	Iterations	Last BB	Next BB	Secs	n	Iterations	Last BB	Next BB	Secs
8k	11	260	6818	88.07	8k	4	4036	4138	31.52
16k	3	260	12002	3.41	16k	2	450	7222	77.34
32k	3	260	21946	4.62	32k	2	487	12389	3.09
64k	3	260	34767	7.83	64k	2	507	15150	4.99
128k	3	260	47664	14.59	128k	2	539	22611	9.09

5   Radix Sort via Merge-Sort

In Section 4 we showed that the bulletin board cannot be used to construct SA for large input sizes due to memory restrictions. When our memory limit is reached say at iteration j of renaming, the input text $\mathcal{T}$ can be represented by an unordered array of integers in the range $1..q$, where q is the largest *newname* computed in the last iteration of the naming stage. By sorting these integers, (each tagged with the index of the suffix it represents), the suffix indices can now be rearranged into their current lexicographic order. In our implementation we do this using parallel merge-sort. In this way, all suffixes that share a common prefix of length at least ℓ are placed into a *partially* completed suffix array in contiguous locations, PART_SA. Furthermore, each suffix can now be encoded by a new, shorter string as follows: let s_i be a suffix of $\mathcal{T}$. We define the q-string of s_i to be $(k_1, k_2, \ldots k_t)$ such that

(i) k_j for some $1 \le j \le t$ is the name of the substring of length ℓ starting at position $i + \ell(j-1)$ in $\mathcal{T}$.
(ii) $0 \le k_j \le q$, for $1 \le j \le t$.

We call each k_j a k-component and use the value 0 to denote a k-component that occurs beyond position n in the input. At this stage the construction of the array SA is completed using a *radix* sort, to base $q + 1$ and each round of this radix sort is a parallel merge-sort.

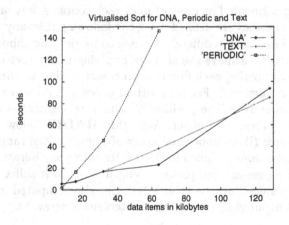

Fig. 1. Merge-Sort applied to DNA, Highly periodic and Text strings

5.1 Parallel Merge-sort

The underlying computational structure of the traditional PRAM algorithm for merge-sort is a complete binary tree. Our merge procedure is an adaption of the $O(\log \log n)$ merging of [9] and [15]. To avoid the communication overheads that are incurred by their $O(1)$ parallel ranking procedure, we implement ranking using a simple binary search. This increases the (theoretical) time complexity for the merging to $O(\log n \log \log n)$. We implement the binary tree computation using a $2 \times n$ array SORT. The merge-sort procedure requires $O(\log^2 n \log \log n)$ time, using n processors. For $p < n$ processors this data structure is virtualised using a cut-and-stack data mapping as in [5]: no two contiguous input elements reside on the same processor. Figure 1 shows the time taken to perform this merge-sort for three different input types.

From Figure 1 we see a sudden jump in the running time for the DNA input of size $32k$. This particular sample contains 29 occurrences of the substring $TTTTTTTT$, the other samples of DNA contain no more than 6 such substrings. In comparison, the input samples of text contain no such repetitive substrings of this length. Substring statistics in relation to suffix trees have been studied extensively by Szpankowski in [14].

5.2 Segmented Merge-sort

Scan primitives can be applied to vectors which are divided into contiguous blocks called *segments*. The segments are defined using *flags* which mark the *end-of-segment* boundaries. If there are m such flags in a given input vector $\mathcal{V}$, the primitive will be executed $m + 1$ times in parallel, once for each segment in $\mathcal{V}$. In our implementation we consider each segment as a bucket, the contents of which are the indices of suffixes of $\mathcal{T}$ that share a common prefix. The buckets are refined using segmented merge-sort until each contains only one suffix index. The segment boundaries are defined using the following rule: any virtual processor that is associated with a different ℓ-*name* to its right neighbour signifies the end of a segment. We achieve the effect of applying merge-sort to all segments in parallel by renumbering each (virtual) processor so that the first processor of each segment has number 0. For each virtual processor, its new processor number *new_iproc* depends on the position at which its segment starts and on its original (virtual) processor number. Algorithm **RADIX** below takes as input the following items: (i) an unordered array of names in the range $1..q$ where q was the largest *newname* assigned in the last iteration, say iteration j, of renaming (each name represents the prefix of length 2^j of each suffix of $\mathcal{T}$); (ii) the associated LCP values; (iii) the table NEW_LCP, also computed in iteration j of renaming. The output is the completely sorted suffix array, SA.

Algorithm RADIX

STEP 1. Each suffix s_i is represented by its q-string $q(i)$. Compute the partial suffix array PART_SA as follows: apply the merge-sort procedure to the first k-component k_1, of each q-string. Each q-string is relocated to its newly sorted position together with the index of the suffix which it represents and the associated LCP value. For $j = 1..\lfloor n/2^\ell \rfloor$ do each of the following substeps:

STEP 2a. Using component k_j as a key, mark all locations t in PART_SA such that the k-component for PART_SA$[t]$ is not equal to the k-component for PART_SA$[t + 1]$. This partitions the array PART_SA into segments such that all locations with the same k-component belong to the same segment or *equivalence class*.

STEP 2b. Compute the *size* of each segment. If all segments are of size 1, then compute the LCP values for the entire input and terminate the computation. Else, for all locations contained in segments of size 1, store the value of k_j in K, $j - 1$ in J and mark the location as "non-active".

STEP 2c. For all "active" segments of size greater than 1, apply the merge-sort procedure using the component k_{j+1} as the sort key. Remove k_j from each $q(i)$ and send the remaining q-string to its new sorted location.

6 Conclusion

We give an algorithm for the parallel construction of the suffix array data structure. Our empirical results show that the PRAM bulletin board technique for naming and sorting substrings requires more main memory than is available on a MasPar MP-2 for practical input sizes. This is partly due to the fact that we also maintain tables for computing longest common prefix information. The theoretical time of $O(\log^2 n)$ "reduces" to $O(kn/p \log n)$ where $k < \log n$ is the number of BB iterations that main memory can accomodate, and p is the number of PE's. However, the bulletin board can be used to reduce the input size and to create a more succinct representation of each suffix, the q-string. Each character in a q-string represents a substring of length 2^ℓ for some $0 \le \ell < \log n$. For DNA and English text the length of q-strings is in the region of $n/4$. A radix sort is then used to complete the suffix array construction. Assuming that the main memory of the PE array holds n integer values, one round of the radix sorting is implemented using a segmented merge-sort and requires $O(n/p \log^2 m \log \log m)$ time, where $m < n$ is the size of the largest segment or bucket to be sorted in the current round. The number of rounds of radix sort required depends on the length of the longest repeated substring in the input: for DNA and English text we found that at most 3 rounds were required to eliminate all but a small fraction of q-strings from the sort.

References

[1] A. Apostolico, C. S. Iliopoulos, G. Landau, B. Schieber, and U. Vishkin. Parallel construction of a suffix tree with applications. *Algorithmica*, 3:347–365, 1988.

[2] A. Andersson, N. J. Larsson, and K. Swanson. Suffix trees on words. In *Proceedings of Combinatorial Pattern Matching*, pages 102–115, 1996.

[3] A. Andersson and S. Nilsson. Efficient implementation of suffix trees. *Software - Practice and Experience*, 25, 2:129–141, 1995.

[4] Digital Equipment Corporation, Maynard, Massachusetts. *DECmpp Programming Language Reference Manual*, 1992.

[5] C. Farrell and D. Kieronska. Implementation of automatic virtualisation into parallel compilers for massively parallel simd architectures. In *SS'93 Conf on High Performance Computing*, pages 55–61, Calgary, Canada, 1993.

[6] Z. Kedem, G. M. Landau, and K. Palem. Optimal parallel suffix-prefix matching algorithm and applications. In *Proc. 1st ACM Symposium on Parallel Algorithms and Architectures*, pages 388–398, 1989.

[7] R. Karp, R. Miller, and A. Rosenberg. Rapid identification of repeated pattrns in strings, trees and arrays. In *Proc. 4th Annual ACM Symposium on Theory of Computing*, pages 125–136, 1972.

[8] M. Korda. *Two dimensional string covering and parallel suffix array construction*. PhD thesis, King's College, University of London, Strand, London, 1998.

[9] C. Kruskal. Searching, merging and sorting in parallel computation. *IEEE Transaction on Computers*, C-32;10:942–946, 1983.

[10] G. M. Landau and U. Vishkin. Pattern matching in a digitized image. *Algorithmica*, 12(4/5):375–408, 1994.

[11] E. M. McCreight. A space-economical suffix tree construction algorithm. *Journal of the ACM*, 23:262–272, 1976.

[12] U. Manber and G. Myers. Suffix arrays: A new method for on-line string searches. In *Proc. 1st ACM-SIAM Symposium on Discrete Algorithms*, pages 319–327, 1990.

[13] S. Muthukrishnan and K. Palem. Highly efficient parallel dictionary matching. In *Proc. 5th ACM Symposium on Parallel Algorithms and Architechtures*, 1993.

[14] W. Szpankowski. Expected behaviour of typical suffix trees. In *Proc. 3rd ACM-SIAM Symposium on Discrete Algorithms*, pages 422–431, 1992.

[15] L. G. Valiant. Parallelism in comparison models. *SIAM Journal on Computing*, 4:348–355, 1975.

[16] P. Weiner. Linear pattern matching algorithm. In *Proc. 14th IEEE Symposium on Switching and Automata Theory*, pages 1–11, 1973.

Weak Bisimilarity and Open Maps

Sławomir Lasota*

Institute of Informatics, Warsaw University,
Banacha 2, 02-097 Warszawa, Poland,
sl@mimuw.edu.pl

Abstract. An alternative proof (to that from [3]) is presented for weak bisimilarity of transition systems to be abstractly definable by open maps [9]. This result arises from an observation that the categories (of transition systems) well suited for studying strong and weak bisimulations are related by an adjunction (for a suitable monad), giving a link between both bisimilarities. We formulate a generalization of this result, hopefully applicable also to other equivalences of processes.

1 Introduction

Recently a categorical generalization of bisimulation was proposed, by means of *open maps* (*open morphisms*) [9, 8], enabling a uniform definition of bisimulation-like equivalences across a range of different models for parallel computations. This setting turned out appropriate for defining, among many others, strong and weak bisimilarity [12], trace equivalence [7], testing equivalence [6] and a bisimilarity of event structures [5]. Open maps can be understood as arrows witnessing a bisimulation, hence two objects A and B in a category are bisimilar if they are related by a span of open maps, representing abstractly a bisimulation.

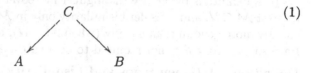

$$(1)$$

In [3] one can find an overview of different equivalence definable by means of open maps. Open maps were also successfully applied to behavioural equivalences [1] of algebras, see [10].

In this paper we focus on weak bisimilarity of transition systems, proved already in [3] to coincide with open-maps bisimilarity in the category of transition systems. The method was similar as in the case of strong bisimilarity, that is open maps were characterized as those satisfying a suitable zig-zag condition, to be mentioned below. The only difference to strong bisimilarity is that category which turned appropriate to work in, was richer in morphisms than the usually considered category of transition systems (which is well suited for strong bisimilarity). We found an abstract categorical characterization of this category as

---

* This work was supported by the KBN grant 8 T11C 046 14.

the Kleisli category for a suitable monad on the category of transition systems. Both categories under consideration are moreover linked by a pair of functors forming an adjunction, which we show to be reflective. These observations lead directly to an alternative prove of coincidence of weak bisimilarity and open-maps bisimilarity, which does not require any explicit characterization of open maps. This is due to properties of open maps, proved recently in [10], which allow to "transport" openness of morphisms (and bisimilarity) via an adjunction.

On a more intuitive level, the adjunction gives an elegant connection between (abstract formulations of) strong and weak bisimilarity. There still rest an interesting question, whether this situation can be shifted to some other equivalences of processes? This is why all the properties of preservation of openness and bisimilarity, formulated in this paper as well as in [10], are intended to be re-usable and as general as possible.

We assume the reader to have some prior knowledge of category theory, in particular to be familiar with adjunctions and monads. As a reference, we propose [11].

2 Bisimulation from Open Maps

Let $\mathcal{U}$ be a category of models of computation, in which we choose a subcategory $\mathcal{P}$ (not necessarily full) of *observation objects*. $\mathcal{P}$ is also called in the sequel a *path subcategory*, as it is intended to contain „paths" for computations to follow. Any morphism $p : O \to A$ from an observation object $O \in |\mathcal{P}|$ is understood as an observable *computation* in A. A morphism $h : A \to B$ between models can be intuitively thought of as a simulation of A in B since h transforms every computation $p : O \to A$ in A to a computation $p; h : O \to B$ in B. Moreover any morphism $m : O \to O'$ in $\mathcal{P}$ making $p = m; p'$ means intuitively that a "larger" computation p' is an extension of p (via m).

In a definition below, we distinguish moreover a subcategory of models of interest $\mathcal{M} \subseteq \mathcal{U}$, and consider bisimilarity only in $\mathcal{M}$. This way we gain a notion slightly more general than usually (when $\mathcal{M} = \mathcal{U}$), following the approach of [3]. Path subcategory $\mathcal{P}$ is not required to be a subcategory of $\mathcal{M}$.

Definition 2.1 (Open maps and bisimilarity). A morphism $h : A \to B$ in $\mathcal{M}$ is $\mathcal{P}$-*open* if for any morphism $m : O \to O'$ in $\mathcal{P}$ and two computations $p : O \to A$ and $p' : O' \to B$ in $\mathcal{U}$, whenever the square

commutes, i.e. $p; h = m; p'$, there exists a diagonal morphism $r : O' \to A$ in $\mathcal{U}$ making two triangles commute, i.e. $p = m; r$ and $p' = r; h$. Two objects A and B are $\mathcal{P}$-*bisimilar*, denoted by $A \sim_{\mathcal{P}} B$, if there exists in $\mathcal{M}$ a span of $\mathcal{P}$-open maps as in (1). We omit prefix $\mathcal{P}$- when obvious from a context. If not stated otherwise, we assume $\mathcal{U} = \mathcal{M}$.

The abstract notion of $\mathcal{P}$-bisimilarity is intended to generalize the strong bisimilarity between transition systems, which will serve as an illustrating example.

2.1 Strong Bisimulation

A *labelled transition system* [13] (over a set L, intended to give labels to transitions) is a triple $T = (S, i, \{ \xrightarrow{a} \}_{a \in L})$ consisting of a set of *states* S with a distinguished initial state $i \in S$ and a family of *transition relations* $_- \xrightarrow{a} _- \subseteq S \times S$. We write $s \xrightarrow{a} s'$ to denote that states s and s' are related by a transition labelled by a.

Morphisms between transition systems are „structure preserving" functions mapping states to states. Formally, a morphism from $T_1 = (S_1, i_1, \{ \xrightarrow{a} \}_{a \in L})$ to $T_2 = (S_2, i_2, \{ \xrightarrow{a} \}_{a \in L})$, is a function $\sigma : S_1 \to S_2$, such that $\sigma(i_1) = i_2$ and $s \xrightarrow{a} s'$ implies $\sigma(s) \xrightarrow{a} \sigma(s')$ (we deliberately overload here symbol $\xrightarrow{a}$, hoping that this causes no troubles). This defines a category TS_L, in which morphisms compose as functions.

Following [14, 12], we say that T_1 and T_2 are *strongly bisimilar* if there exists a strong bisimulation between them; bisimulation is defined as usual, with the only additional requirement to relate initial states. Strong bisimilarity was shown in [9] to coincide with $Bran_L$-bisimilarity in TS_L, where $Bran_L$ is the full subcategory of transition systems consisting of finite sequences of actions:

$$i \xrightarrow{a_1} s_1 \xrightarrow{a_2} \ldots \xrightarrow{a_n} s_n \tag{2}$$

$Bran_L$-open morphisms $\sigma : T_1 \to T_2$, called also *zig-zag*, are those satisfying the following *zig-zag* property: for each reachable $s \in S_1$, whenever $\sigma(s) \xrightarrow{a} s'$, then $s \xrightarrow{a} s''$, for some $s'' \in S_1$ satisfying $\sigma(s'') = s'$.

3 Weak Bisimulation

Consider transition systems over an alphabet L, fixed in the sequel. We assume L to contain a distinguished action τ, being silent or non-observable. *Weak bisimulation*, being less restrictive than strong one, allows an action a to be simulated by a sequence of the form

$$\xrightarrow{\tau} \ldots \xrightarrow{\tau} \xrightarrow{a} \xrightarrow{\tau} \ldots \xrightarrow{\tau} \tag{3}$$

that is by a preceded or followed by an arbitrary number of τ actions. Moreover, τ action need not to be simulated at all. In the formal definition below we use the following notation, proposed in [12]. First, let $s \xRightarrow{a} s'$ denote a sequence of transitions (3), for an arbitrary label a (including τ), that is

$$s \xRightarrow{a} s' \text{ iff } s(\xrightarrow{\tau})^* r \xrightarrow{a} r'(\xrightarrow{\tau})^* s' \text{ for some states r and r',}$$

where $(\xrightarrow{\tau})^*$ stands for the reflexive-transitive closure of $\xrightarrow{\tau}$. Second, treating an action a as a one-element sequence, we define a τ-deleting function $\widehat{\ } : L \to L^*$

by $\widehat{a} =_{def} a$, for $a \neq \tau$, and $\widehat{\tau} =_{def} \epsilon$, the empty sequence. Moreover, we assume $s \xrightarrow{\epsilon} s' \Leftrightarrow s = s'$, implicitly extending the notation $\_ \xrightarrow{a} \_$ to the set L^* of finite sequences of actions.

Definition 3.1. *A weak bisimulation between T_1 and T_2 is any relation $\sim \subseteq S_1 \times S_2$ such that $i_1 \sim i_2$ and whenever $s_1 \sim s_2$ then for every action $a \in L$,*

1. *$s_1 \xrightarrow{a} s_1'$ in T_1 implies $s_2 \xRightarrow{\widehat{a}} s_2'$ in T_2 and $s_1' \sim s_2'$, for some s_2',*
2. *$s_2 \xrightarrow{a} s_2'$ in T_2 implies $s_1 \xRightarrow{\widehat{a}} s_1'$ in T_1 and $s_1' \sim s_2'$, for some s_1'.*

If such $\sim$ exists, we say that T_1 and T_2 are weakly bisimilar.

To deal with weak bisimilarity we choose the appropriate category WTS_L of transition systems whose morphisms $\sigma : T_1 \to T_2$ are functions $\sigma : S_1 \to S_2$, such that $\sigma(i_1) = i_2$ and $s \xrightarrow{a} s'$ implies $\sigma(s) \xRightarrow{\widehat{a}} \sigma(s')$. These morphisms will be called *weak morphisms*; the usual morphisms of transition systems we call *strong* in the sequel. Obviously category TS_L, consisting of strong morphisms, is a subcategory of WTS_L.

As a path subcategory for weak bisimulation we take again the subcategory $Bran_L$ of finite linear transition systems as in (2) together with exclusively strong morphisms between them. Surprisingly, this is the same path subcategory as in the case of strong bisimilarity – this coincidence will be justified and explained below. Obviously $Bran_L$ is not a full subcategory of WTS_L, being full subcategory of TS_L. In [3] it was shown that weak bisimilarity coincides with $Bran_L$-bisimilarity in category of weak morphisms; it was achieved by explicit characterization of $Bran_L$-open maps as those satisfying an appropriate zig-zag property, analogously as in the case of strong bisimilarity.

4 Characterization

Our aim is to show that spans of $Bran_L$-open morphisms in category WTS_L define weak bisimilarity without referring to any explicit formulation of openness. Our considerations will be based on the observation that bisimilarity induced by open morphisms can be transported in some relevant cases via an adjunction. First, open maps are well-behaved with respect to an adjunction:

Lemma 4.1 ([10]). *For arbitrary adjunction $F \dashv G$ between categories $\mathcal{M}$ and $\mathcal{N}$ and for arbitrary subcategory $\mathcal{P}$ of $\mathcal{M}$,*

$$\text{a morphism } h \text{ in } \mathcal{N} \text{ is } F(\mathcal{P})\text{-open} \iff G(h) \text{ is } \mathcal{P}\text{-open in } \mathcal{M}.$$

Second, despite that bisimilarity itself is not transported in a similar way in general, it does when an adjunction is a reflection:

Lemma 4.2. *Assumed that the adjunction from the previous lemma is reflective (i.e. the right adjoint $G : \mathcal{N} \to \mathcal{M}$ is full and faithful), we have*

$$A \sim_{F(\mathcal{P})} B \text{ in category } \mathcal{N} \iff G(A) \sim_{\mathcal{P}} G(B) \text{ in category } G(\mathcal{N})$$

($G(\mathcal{N})$, image of G, is a subcategory of $\mathcal{M}$).

Proof: Assumed that A and B are $F(\mathcal{P})$-bisimilar in $\mathcal{N}$, that is they are related by a span $A \xleftarrow{f} C \xrightarrow{g} B$ of $F(\mathcal{P})$-open maps in $\mathcal{N}$, we can easily construct a span of $\mathcal{P}$-open maps by taking the image of G on C, f and g. By Lemma 4.1, both morphisms forming the span $G(A) \xleftarrow{G(f)} G(C) \xrightarrow{G(g)} G(B)$ are $\mathcal{P}$-open, hence $G(A)$ and $G(B)$ are $\mathcal{P}$-bisimilar.

For the opposite direction, let A and B be arbitrary objects of $\mathcal{N}$ such that $G(A)$ and $G(B)$ are $\mathcal{P}$-bisimilar in $G(\mathcal{N})$. This means that $G(A)$ and $G(B)$ are related by a span $G(A) \xleftarrow{f} C \xrightarrow{g} G(B)$ of $\mathcal{P}$-open maps and moreover there exist some morphisms in $\mathcal{N}$, say f' and g', which are mapped by G to f and g, respectively. Let C' and D' denote domains of f' and g', respectively. Since $G(C') = G(D')$ and G, being full and faithful, reflects isomorphisms, we conclude $C' \simeq D'$ and obtain a span $A \xleftarrow{f'} C' \simeq D' \xrightarrow{g'} B$. Moreover, f' and g' are $F(\mathcal{P})$-open, again by Lemma 4.1, hence $A \sim_{F(\mathcal{P})} B$. $\square$

A careful reader could have noticed that for $\mathcal{P}$-bisimilarity in category $G(\mathcal{N})$, the path subcategory $\mathcal{P}$ is not guaranteed to be a subcategory of $G(\mathcal{N})$. This motivates our general definition of bisimilarity in Section 2.

A fact similar to Lemma 4.1 was proved already in [9], in the situation when the adjunction is a coreflection. For other related results one can consult [4] and [2], where conditions are given for a functor to preserve openness.

We are going now to construct an adjunction between categories TS_L and WTS_L, to which we will apply Lemma 4.2. The adjunction will be obtained automatically by noticing that WTS_L is precisely the Kleisli category for the monad of a suitable endofunctor $W : TS_L \to TS_L$, defined below. Intuitively speaking, for a transition system T, $W(T)$ has the same states but more transitions; these extra ones are all of the form $s \xRightarrow{\hat{a}} s'$. Hence W can be thought of as a closure on all "weak transitions" $s \xRightarrow{\hat{a}} s'$. Formally, for $T = (S, i, \{\xrightarrow{a}\}_{a \in L})$ we take:

$$W(T) = (S, i, \{\xRightarrow{\hat{a}}\}_{a \in L}).$$

For a morphism $f : W(T_1) \to W(T_2)$ we put:

$$W(f) = f : W(T_1) \to W(T_2)$$

i.e. W takes f to the same function. It can be easily checked that functor W equipped with two natural transformations $\eta : Id_{TS_L} \dot{\to} W$ and $\mu : W^2 \dot{\to} W$, consisting of identity functions

$$\eta_T(s) = s, \quad \mu_T(s) = s$$

form a monad, i.e. satisfy the monad laws (cf. [11], page 133). Now consider the Kleisli category for this monad, having the same objects as TS_L and whose morphisms $T_1 \to T_2$ are all morphisms $T_1 \to W(T_2)$ from TS_L. We obtain for free the canonical adjunction between TS_L and the Kleisli category; moreover

Lemma 4.3. *This adjunction is a reflection.*

Proof: We will show that counit ε is a natural isomorphism, that is $T \simeq \mathcal{W}(T)$ in the Kleisli category. To this aim we will show that the following two morphisms

$$l := \eta_T; \eta_{\mathcal{W}(T)} : T \to \mathcal{W}(T) \quad \text{and} \quad r := \varepsilon_T = id_{\mathcal{W}(T)} : \mathcal{W}(T) \to T$$

compose to identities in the Kleisli category. (Codomains of l and r above are in the Kleisli category; note that these morphisms are also morphisms in TS_L, but here they have other codomain objects: $l : T \to \mathcal{W}^2(T)$ and $r : \mathcal{W}(T) \to \mathcal{W}(T)$.) Start by observing that

$$\eta_{\mathcal{W}(T)} = \mathcal{W}(\eta_T). \tag{4}$$

Having this and applying monad laws, it is easy to show that (composing in TS_L)

$$l; \mathcal{W}(r); \mu_T = \eta_T; \eta_{\mathcal{W}(T)}; \mu_T = \eta_T \quad \text{and}$$

$$r; \mathcal{W}(l); \mu_{\mathcal{W}(T)} = id_{\mathcal{W}(T)}; \mathcal{W}(\eta_T); \mathcal{W}(\eta_{\mathcal{W}(T)}); \mu_{\mathcal{W}(T)} = \mathcal{W}(\eta_T) = \eta_{\mathcal{W}(T)}$$

i.e. both l and r compose in both cases to identities in the Kleisli category, which are as usual units of the monad. $\qquad\square$

Finally, one can see that the Kleisli category we are considering is just another formulation of category WTS_L consisting of weak morphisms. Now, applying Lemma 4.2 to the adjunction between TS_L and WTS_L we obtain the following:

Proposition 4.4. *Weak bisimilarity coincides with $Bran_L$-bisimilarity in category WTS_L.*

Proof: Let $F_{\mathcal{W}} \dashv G_{\mathcal{W}}$ denote the functors of the adjunction, with the left adjoint $F_{\mathcal{W}} : TS_L \to WTS_L$. Observe that $F_{\mathcal{W}}(f) = f$, hence $F_{\mathcal{W}}(Bran_L) = Bran_L$. Now, by Lemma 4.2 two transition systems T and U are connected by a span of $Bran_L$-open maps in WTS_L if and only if

$$\mathcal{W}(T) \text{ and } \mathcal{W}(U) \text{ are related by a span of } Bran_L\text{-open maps in } G_{\mathcal{W}}(WTS_L). \tag{5}$$

On the other hand, notice that weak bisimulation could be defined equivalently (cf. [12]) by replacing in Definition 3.1 requirements 1 and 2 by

1. $s_1 \xrightarrow{\hat{a}} s_1'$ in T_1 implies $s_2 \xRightarrow{\hat{a}} s_2'$ in T_2 and $s_1' \sim s_2'$, for some s_2',
2. analogously,

which means that T and U are weakly bisimilar if and only if $\mathcal{W}(T)$ and $\mathcal{W}(U)$ are strongly bisimilar (more precisely, weak bisimulations between T and U are precisely strong bisimulations between $W(T)$ and $W(U)$). Hence T and U are weakly bisimilar if and only if

$$W(T) \text{ and } W(U) \text{ are related by a span of } Bran_L\text{-open maps in } TS_L. \qquad (6)$$

Now we only need to fill the gap between (5) and (6), different only in the category, the spans of open maps are to come from; it suffices to show (6) $\Rightarrow$ (5). Consider any $Bran_L$-open morphism $f : V \to W(T)$ in TS_L. Note that it is necessarily its own adjunct $f^\# = f : V \to T$ in WTS_L. We will show that $G_W(f^\#) = W(f); \mu_T$ is also $Bran_L$-open. First, counit μ_V is open, being an identity function. Moreover, $W(f) : W(V) \to W^2(T)$ is also open (i.e. zig-zag), since zig-zag property from Section 2.1 can be easily proved to hold also for sequences of the form (3). Hence, if $W(T)$ and $W(U)$ are connected by a span of $Bran_L$-open maps from V, then they are also connected by a span of $Bran_L$-open maps from $W(V)$, laying necessarily in $G_W(WTS_L)$. $\qquad\square$

We would like to stress on that in the proof we did not need refer to any explicit characterization of $Bran_L$-open maps in WTS_L, despite that such a characterization exists and is given by a zig-zag condition similar to that in Section 2.1 (cf. [3]): a morphism $\sigma : (S_1, i_1, t_1) \to (S_2, i_2, t_2)$ is $Bran_L$-open in WTS_L iff for each reachable $s \in S_1$, whenever $\sigma(s) \xrightarrow{a} s'$, then $s \xRightarrow{\hat{a}} s''$, for some $s'' \in S_1$ satisfying $\sigma(s'') = s'$. Moreover, it is an interesting observation, that the choice of $Bran_L$ for the path subcategory for weak bisimulation seems to be the only reasonable one. For instance, one can easily check that we obtain a different equivalence when we replace $Bran_L$ by the full subcategory of WTS_L of finite linear transition systems. Surprisingly, bisimilarity induced in such a case would even not relate the following two weakly bisimilar transition systems

$$\bullet \qquad\qquad \bullet \xrightarrow{\ \tau\ } \bullet$$

one of them consisting exclusively of a single initial state.

5 Generalization

Let (W, η, μ) be a monad on some category $\mathcal{M}$. Let $\mathcal{M}_W$ denote its Kleisli category and $F_W \dashv G_W$ denote the usual adjunction between $\mathcal{M}$ and $\mathcal{M}_W$.

Motivated by the example of weak bisimilarity and by its equivalent formulation in points 1 and 2 in the proof of Proposition 4.4, and especially by observation (6), we propose the following general definition:

Definition 5.1. Objects A and B of $\mathcal{M}$ are $\mathcal{P}$-*bisimilar w.r.t.* W, for a subcategory $\mathcal{P}$ of $\mathcal{M}$, if $W(A)$ and $W(B)$ are $\mathcal{P}$-bisimilar (in $\mathcal{M}$).

Before we state a generalization of Proposition 4.4 (Theorem 5.2), let us analyze properties satisfied by W in the previous section. First, the monad is *idempotent* in the sense that μ is a natural isomorphism there. This is sufficient in a general situation for (4), hence implies G_W to be full and faithful. Second, open maps are preserved by W, i.e. whenever f is open, $W(f)$ is open as well. (This fact is implicitly used for proving Proposition 4.4.) Fortunately, these two properties guarantee that $\mathcal{P}$-bisimilarity w.r.t. W is definable by means of open maps:

Theorem 5.2. $\mathcal{P}$-bisimilarity w.r.t. W coincides with $F_W(\mathcal{P})$-bisimilarity in Kleisli category $\mathcal{M}_W$, when monad (W, η, μ) is idempotent and W preserves $\mathcal{P}$-openness.

References

1. Bidoit, M., Tarlecki A. Behavioural satisfaction and equivalence in concrete model categories. *Proc. 20th Coll. on Trees in Algebra and Computing* CAAP'96, Linköping, 241-256, LNCS 1059, 1996.
2. Cattani, G.L., Winskel, G. Presheaf models for concurrency. *Computer Science Logic* CSL'96, LNCS, Springer-Verlag. Preliminary version appeared as BRICS Report RS-96-35.
3. Cheng, A., Nielsen, M. Open maps (at) work. Research series RS-95-23, BRICS, Department of Computer Science, University of Aarhus, 1995.
4. Cheng, A., Nielsen, M. Open Maps, Behavioural Equivalences, and Congruences. Research series RS-96-2, BRICS, Department of Computer Science, University of Aarhus, 1996. A short version of this paper appeared in *Proc. 20th Coll. on Trees in Algebra and Computing* CAAP'96, Linköping, 257-272, LNCS 1059, 1996.
5. Van Glabeek, R.J., Goltz, U. Equivalence notions for concurrent systems and refinement of actions. *Proc. of MFCS*, Springer-Verlag LNCS vol. 379, 1989.
6. Hennesy, M. *Algebraic Theory of Processes*. MIT Press series in the foundations of computing, 1988.
7. Hoare, C.A.R. *Communicating Sequential Processes*. Prentice-Hall, 1985.
8. Joyal, A., Moerdijk, I. A completeness theorem for open maps. *Annals of Pure and Applied Logic* 70(1994), 51-86.
9. Joyal, A., Nielsen, G. Winskel, Bisimulation and open maps. *Proc. 8th Annual Symposium on Logic in Computer Science* LICS'93, 1993, 418-427.
10. Lasota, S. Open Maps as a Bridge between Algebraic Observational Equivalence and Bisimilarity. *Proc. 12th Workshop on Algebraic Developement Techniques, Tarquinia, 1997, LNCS 1376*.
11. Mac Lane, S. *Categories for the Working Mathematician*. Springer, New York, 1971.
12. Milner, R. *Communication and concurrency*. Prentice-Hall International Series in Computer Science, C. A. R. Hoare series editor, 1989.
13. Nielsen, M., Winskel, G. *Models for concurrency*. Chapter 1 of *The Handbook of Logic in Computer Science*, vol. 4, Oxford University Press, eds. S. Abramsky, D. M. Gabbay and T.S. Gabbay, 1995.
14. Park, D.M.R. Concurrency and Automata on Infinite Sequences. *Proc. 5th G.I. Conference*, Lecture Notes in Computer Science 104, Springer-Verlag, 1981.

A Synchronisation Mechanism for Replicated Objects*

Francesc D. Muñoz-Escoí, Pablo Galdámez and José M. Bernabéu-Aubán

Universitat Politècnica de València,
Camí de Vera, s/n,
46071 València, SPAIN
{fmunyoz,pgaldam,josep}@iti.upv.es

Abstract. The HIDRA Concurrency Control (HCC) mechanism provides support for concurrency control in environments where the coordinator-cohort replication model is being used. This replication model allows the arrival of multiple invocations to different object replicas which serve locally those invocations and later make the appropriate checkpoints on the rest of replicas. The HCC uses a service serialiser object (SS) and a set of serialiser agents placed in each replica node. As a result, since the HCC components are replicated, this mechanism is also fault tolerant. Each invocation received by an object replica is processed by the SS which knows the invocations that are currently being processed. So, this agent is able to block or allow the execution of arriving invocations according to their conflicts with the currently active ones and the concurrency specification made when the object interface was declared.

1 Introduction

There are a lot of mechanisms to ensure synchronisation in object-oriented distributed environments. Some of them are based on synchronisation primitives, like distributed locks with two phase locking [5], on mutual exclusion algorithms which use their own protocols [1], or use programming languages with operation-based synchronisation support [12]. However these mechanisms either require a big amount of messages to find out which task may access the object or they do not have good expressive power [3] to allow multiple synchronisation policies. The situation is worst if we consider a replicated resource whose access has to be synchronised. In this case, the typical solution relies either on two phase locking, which is very restrictive because all locks have to be gotten before the first one is released (and this removes the advantages of locks compared to an operation-based granularity mechanism, such as those provided in several programming languages), on dynamic voting [7], which implies a read-write locking mechanism, or on optimistic approaches [6], which may lead to abortion of requests.

The HIDRA [4] Concurrency Control (HCC) mechanism synchronises the accesses to replicated objects using an operation-based granularity. Since HIDRA

---

* This work was partially supported by the CICYT (Comisión Interministerial de Ciencia y Tecnología) under project TIC96-0729.

uses an object request broker (ORB) to manage remote object invocations, HCC is based on extensions to the CORBA [11] interface definition language (IDL). So, it is independent from the programming language, and the programmer has to deal with synchronisation features only when the interface is being defined. When the objects are being implemented no care has to be taken about synchronisation.

HCC has been included in HIDRA because our architecture provides support for object replication. Thus, our concurrency control mechanism uses a special object that serves serialisation requests. These requests are made before the actual replicated object is invoked and their execution thread is associated to that replicated object invocation. The serialiser checks if there are any invocations (either blocked or currently being executed) that have a conflict with the invocation being serialised. In this case, this invocation is blocked; otherwise, it is allowed to go on.

The rest of the paper is organised as follows. Section 2 describes the HCC mechanism. Section 3 shows some synchronisation techniques used in other distributed environments and finally, Sect. 4 gives the conclusion.

2 The HCC Mechanism

The HCC mechanism is needed in HIDRA to serialise all requests that arrive to replicas of an object that uses the coordinator-cohort replication model. In this replication model, an invocation is initially served by only one replica, that processes the request and makes at least one checkpoint to transfer the state updates to the other object replicas. Each object invocation may be served by a different replica. So, multiple invocations may be executed concurrently in all replicas of the object and some distributed concurrency control mechanism is needed.

To decide which operations may proceed simultaneously, an extension of the IDL language is used, providing information about which pairs of operations are mutually conflictive. Basing the concurrency on this property allows the implementation of multiple synchronisation strategies, such as mutual exclusion, readers-writer policy, FCFS policy, etc.

2.1 Objectives

As previously stated, HCC is a concurrency control mechanism that manages replicated object invocations in distributed environments. Its main objectives are:

- The mechanism has to use a pessimistic approach. The object invocation mechanism used in HIDRA assumes that an invocation will be never aborted; this prevents the use of optimistic techniques to manage concurrency.
- The mechanism has to be fault-tolerant; i.e., the failure of part of the components needed by our mechanism has to be tolerated.

```
<op_dcl>    ::= [ <op_scope> ] [ <op_attribute> ] <op_type_spec> <identifier>
              <param_dcls> [ <raises_expr> ] [ <context_expr> ]
              [ <cnc_expr ] [ <cfl_expr> ]

<op_scope> ::= "local"

<cnc_expr> ::= "concurrent" "(" <scoped_name> { "," <scoped_name> }* ")"

<cfl_expr> ::= "conflicts" "(" <scoped_name> { "," <scoped_name> }* ")"
```

Fig. 1. Syntax of the extended operation declaration.

- We have to reduce the possibility of misuse of the mechanism by the programmer. So, the management of the concurrency control tasks has to be as transparent as possible to the programmer.
- Efficiency. The number of messages needed to carry on the concurrency control tasks has to be kept at a minimum.

2.2 Extensions to IDL

The IDL extensions enlarge the optional parts of an operation declaration to include which other operations of each interface instance can be executed concurrently and which operations in different objects cannot proceed simultaneously.

The HCC mechanism assumes initially that all operations of the same object are mutually exclusive. All other operation invocations can proceed concurrently. As a result, all non-extended interfaces are interpreted by the HCC as specifications of objects whose state is protected by exclusive operations.

The new syntax for an operation declaration appears in Fig. 1, where the new local, concurrent and conflicts clauses are shown.

The local keyword means that this operation only has to access one of the object replicas. Thus, other replicas do not have to wait for a checkpoint that notifies the termination of that call.

The concurrent expression gives the list of operations (that by default are in conflict with the operation being declared now) which can proceed simultaneously with this operation. For each pair of concurrent operations, this expression only needs appear in the declaration of one of them.

IDL allows interface inheritance. The HCC considers that all operations of all the interfaces of an object cannot be executed concurrently. So, to build the list of concurrent operations we need scoped names because we have to identify the interface which provides the concurrent operation (it may be any ancestor interface in the hierarchy of interfaces provided by the object).

The conflicts expression gives the list of operations (that by default are allowed to proceed concurrently) which now are in conflict with this operation. In this case, it is assumed that the operations in conflict are provided by two different objects, but these objects share some state and these operations access this shared state. Again, we need scoped names to identify correctly the operations in conflict.

```
struct InvoCtxt {                  interface ServiceSerialiser { // pseudo IDL
    long        Operation,             void Serialise( in RoiID      InvoID,
    CORBA::TypeId Interface,                           in InvoCtxt   Invocation,
    ObjectId    ObjId                                  in TObj       TerminationObject );
};                                 };
```

Fig. 2. Interface of the service serialiser object.

2.3 HCC Components

The HCC mechanism relies on some components that maintain and manage the information needed to allow or suspend invocations on the objects to be controlled. These components are:

– Serialiser object (SS). This object is created when a service (a group of inter-related objects) is registered in the system and it has to decide which invocations on the replicas of the objects that compose that service may proceed.

As the requests arrive to the object replicas, the ORB invokes the serialiser providing information about which object instance is being invoked, which operation and which invocation identifier is being used. The serialiser checks if the incoming invocation conflicts with any one of the active invocations and, if so, blocks the incoming one. As a result, each serialiser has to maintain the identifiers of a collection of active (and still non-terminated) invocations and also, the identifiers and execution threads of all blocked invocations. These are the *blocked* and *active lists*, and they constitute the dynamic state of the serialiser.

– ORB machinery on the server side. Before an invocation reaches the actual object it is calling, the ORB components placed on the server side have to identify and call the appropriate SS. When the call to the serialiser returns, the ORB machinery can invoke the actual object replica.

2.4 Serialisation of Requests

The HCC is managed by the HIDRA's ORB components, becoming a transparent service for the application programmer. Only a requirement is made to the programmer of replicated objects: she or he has to specify in the interface declaration which operations are incompatible, as we have described in Sect. 2.2. Our extended interface compiler generates the CCS object that has to be provided when a replicated service is registered in a running HIDRA system. As a result of this registration, the service serialiser (SS) is created and it receives the CCS object that it uses to make the concurrency control decisions.

The serialisation of a request is made when that invocation arrives to the domain where the replica of the invoked object resides. The ORB components call the `Serialise()` operation of the SS. The declaration of this operation is given in Fig. 2. The arguments needed by this SS operation are the following:

```
interface CCS { // pseudo IDL
    boolean CanBeConcurrent(
        in InvoCtxt        FirstInvocation,
        in InvoCtxt        SecondInvocation
    ) raises (UnknownInterface, BadOperationNumber);
};
```

Fig. 3. Interface of the CCS objects.

- **InvoID.** A reference to a `RoiID` object [10] that identifies the current invocation being serialised. We use the acronym ROI (Reliable Object Invocation) to refer to an invocation on a replicated object.
- **Invocation.** This structure maintains an *invocation context* and is composed by the following objects:
  - **Interface.** This value identifies the interface that is being invoked.
  - **ObjID.** This value is internal to the ORB and identifies the specific instance that is being invoked.
  - **Operation.** The operation number that is being invoked in the interface **Interface**.
- **TerminationObject.** An object needed to detect when this invocation has terminated in all object replicas. See [10] for details on this object.

The information maintained in an *invocation context* is needed to identify the possible conflicts with other previous ROIs.

Once the call to the `Serialise()` operation arrives to the SS, it follows these steps:

1. All invocation contexts in the active and blocked lists are inspected and a call to the `CanBeConcurrent()` operation of the CCS object is made (See Fig. 3) to test if the current invocation and the inspected one can proceed at the same time.
2. In case that the two tested operations could not be concurrent, the identifier of the operation (its `RoiID` reference) in the active or blocked lists is inserted in a set of *precedent operations* associated to the current one.
3. When the two lists have been scanned, if the precedent operations set is empty, this operation is inserted in the list of active operations and its `Serialise()` invocation is replied. However, if the precedent operations set is not empty, the operation is inserted in the list of blocked operations. It will remain there until all the operations in its precedent set have been terminated. When this happens, the invocation context is moved to the active list and the `Serialise()` invocation is also replied.
4. The SS uses the `TerminationObject` associated to each ROI to find out when that invocation has been finished. That happens when this object receives the unreferenced notification, as it is described in [10]. In this case, its `RoiID` is removed from the active list and from all precedent sets where it can be found.

2.5 Expressive Power

In [9], the *expressive power* is defined as the ability of a synchronisation mechanism to implement a range of synchronisation policies. The wider the range of synchronisation policies a mechanism can implement, the greater its expressive power will be.

Bloom [3] gave some criteria to identify the expressive power of a particular synchronisation mechanism. He proposed that six different types of data are necessary to give a good expressive power. These types are: the name of the invoked operation, the relative arrival type of invocations, the invocation parameters, the synchronisation state of the resource, the local state of that resource and history information about ROIs already terminated.

The HCC is able to manage four of these six available types of information. It uses the names (in our case they are given by the TypeId of the interface and the operation number) of the operations being invoked, the relative arrival type of invocations (as they are received, the precedent set is built and thus, the relative arrival time is maintained), the synchronisation state (because the HCC maintains which invocations are active and which others are already serialised but they still have not been started) and it is also able to maintain the history of past invocations on each replicated object.

With all that information, the HCC can implement different synchronisation policies very easily. For instance, two of the most common synchronisation policies are mutual exclusion and readers/writer. To implement mutual exclusion no special action has to be taken in HCC, because it is the default policy. So, for the interface given in Fig. 4.a, all operations are considered mutually exclusive and their invocations are serialised in FCFS order.

```
interface BoundedBuffer {                interface BoundedBuffer {
    void  InsertItem(in Item TheItem);       void  InsertItem(in Item TheItem);
    Item  GetItem();                         Item  GetItem();
    void  PrintBuffer();                     void  PrintBuffer()
                                                   concurrent(BoundedBuffer::PrintBuffer);
    Item  ListItem(in long Position);        Item  ListItem(in long Position)
                                                   concurrent(BoundedBuffer::ListItem,
                                                              BoundedBuffer::PrintBuffer);
    void  PrintItems(in long First,          void  PrintItems(in long First, in long Last)
                     in long Last);                concurrent(BoundedBuffer::PrintBuffer,
};                                                            BoundedBuffer::PrintItems,
                                                              BoundedBuffer::ListItem);
                                         };

              (a)                                          (b)
```

Fig. 4. Example of interface declaration with: (a) mutual exclusion policy, (b) readers-writer policy.

The first two operations modify the state of the buffer, while the other three only read this state. So, we can modify the previous declaration to enforce a readers/writer policy. The resulting declaration is shown in Fig 4.b. In this case, the operations InsertItem() and GetItem() cannot be executed concurrently with any other operation of the same interface because they modify the state of the bounded buffer. On the other hand, `PrintBuffer()`, `ListItem()` and `PrintItem()` only read the state of the object and can be executed concurrently.

2.6 Fault Tolerance

To achieve fault tolerance, a representative of the SS is added in each replica node. This SS agent (or SSA, for short) maintains part of the dynamic state of the SS, enabling its reconstruction in case of failure. When SSAs are considered, the synchronisation tasks are modified in the following way:

- All serialisation requests are initially managed by the SSA placed in the node of the coordinator replica. These SSA objects forward the serialisation request to the unique SS object, except for the case of an invocation to a `local` operation (See Sect. 2.2). The SS does not suspend the execution thread in case of conflicts. It only takes account of this situation and replies immediately, returning the list of precedent invocation contexts.
- The SS maintains in its blocked and active lists, information about all the non-`local` invocations. The SSA maintains in these lists only the information regarding the ROIs with their coordinator in its local node. It also blocks the execution threads associated to the ROIs placed in its blocked list.
- The SSA extends its pseudo-interface to provide locally invocable operations to get and manage references to the TObj objects associated to the ROIs which have a cohort in its node.
  These operations are needed by the SSA to know when a given invocation has finished. When that event happens, the ROI is removed from the precedent sets associated to blocked ROIs and it is also removed from the active list.

In case of failure of the service serialiser or several of its agents, some special actions are needed to reconfigure the state of the HCC components. According to the failure type, two cases are distinguished.

Failure of a SSA. When a SSA crashes, the whole node where it resides has crashed, because our ORB support is in the kernel domain. So, all coordinator replicas for the ROIs controlled by this SSA have also crashed.

We need to replace the faulty SSA because it controls the activation of the blocked ROIs when its precedent operations set becomes empty. To this end, we have to describe how a ROI is restarted when its coordinator replica has crashed.

If the ROI still remained blocked, no special action has to be taken. If the client that initiated the ROI is alive, it will reinitiate the invocation on another replica. Since the RoiID is maintained by the client, the new attempt is identified as a replay by the SS and an updated precedent operations set is returned to the new chosen coordinator's SSA.

If the ROI was already active, our ORB support will choose another coordinator replica and no serialisation request is initiated to do so. When the client reinitiates the invocation on another coordinator replica to pick the results of the previous attempt, its serialisation request will be replied immediately by the SS as in the case described in the previous paragraph.

Failure of the SS and some SSAs. As previously shown, when this failure happens no special action has to be taken to rebuild the state of the crashed SSAs because the ROI mechanism chooses another coordinator replica for all ROIs involved in the crash.

However, the dynamic state of the SS has to be rebuilt. This state consists of the active and blocked lists of ROIs. Both lists have to be rebuilt using the information maintained by the surviving SSAs. In these SSAs, we can find:

- All the information about the blocked ROIs whose coordinator replica is placed on the same node. This includes the RoiID and InvoCtxts of all the precedent operations in each precedent set and the RoiID, InvoCtxt and TObj of the blocked ROI.
- The RoiID and TObj references for the currently active ROIs that have made at least one checkpoint and still have not made the last checkpoint.

Thus, when the SS has crashed, one of the remaining SSAs is promoted to the SS class. To rebuild its active list, the following steps are taken in the reconfiguration phase of the cluster:

1. All surviving SSAs are queried and each of them returns a list with all RoiIDs that have an associated TObj reference. For each one of these ROIs the SSAs return its RoiID, its TObj reference and (if it can be locally found) its InvoCtxt.
2. All the RoiIDs returned in the previous step are inserted in the active list and a TObj object replica is regenerated from its reference and it is associated to its RoiID and InvoCtxt.

To rebuild the blocked list, this sequence of steps is needed:

1. All surviving SSAs are queried and each of them returns all their blocked ROIs and the precedent set for each of these ROIs.
2. All these blocked lists are merged to build the blocked list of the new SS. Thus, the precedent sets for a given ROI are compared and the resulting precedent set only has the ROIs that could be found in all the merged precedent sets (we assume that if in any precedent set a given ROI is missing, then this ROI was detected as terminated by that SSA, which removed it from that precedent set).
3. Finally, all precedent sets are checked to find out if they have some ROI that does not appear in the active nor in the blocked list. If that happens, that ROI is removed from the precedent sets because it corresponds to a ROI that was active but still did not make any checkpoint and whose coordinator replica crashed. A ROI of this class has to be reinitiated and serialised again. When some ROI of this kind is found, the new SS also has to invoke the Terminated() method of all the SSAs using its associated RoiID as input argument. This call removes the ROI from the active lists of all SSAs.

Once these two protocols have been executed, the new SS has a dynamic state that allows the service of new serialisation requests of the HCC.

3 Related Work

HIDRA needs a pessimistic concurrency control mechanism to synchronise the access to replicated objects that follow the coordinator-cohort replication model. The HCC provides such a mechanism with operation granularity.

Other concurrency control mechanisms for replicated objects exist, but the greater part of them are used in databases and are based on *quorum consensus* [8]. These replication models assign a vote to each replica and divide the operations in only two categories (read and write). Each time a read (write) operation must be made, the operation has to access a *read (resp. write) quorum* number of replicas. The property that has to be accomplished by these algorithms is that the sum of the two quorums must exceed the total sum of votes and that the write quorum must be greater than half the sum of all votes. The operations are allowed to proceed if they have collected the required vote quorum.

More advanced techniques are discussed in [6] where two approaches are described: *conflict-based* and *state-based* validation. In the first case, operations are allowed to proceed concurrently if they commute; i.e., if they do not conflict. This is an approach equivalent to ours. The state-based validation needs know which parts of the state are affected by each invocation. In this case, the concurrency control mechanism needs the value of the arguments of each invocation and the current state of each object being invoked. Although this technique allows even greater concurrency than the conflict-based one, the amount of information that needs to be managed and the access to the object state make it infeasible in our environment.

Finally, the replication model also affects the concurrency control mechanism. In the passive and active replication models only a local concurrency control mechanism is needed. However, the coordinator-cohort replication model is not so easy. A concurrency control mechanism for this replication model was already given in [2]. It is based on controlling the *data dependencies* and *precedence dependencies* between the operations being requested. A data dependency exists between two operations when one of them requires the result of the other before it can be started. Precedence dependencies exist between two operations if they conflict. Although precedence dependencies are already controlled by HCC, data dependencies need some control on the arguments of the operations. This enlarges the amount of data that must be managed by the concurrency control mechanism and does not improve so much the concurrency.

4 Conclusions

The HCC mechanism provides an easy-to-use concurrency control support for the programmer of replicated objects. The programmer only has to worry about concurrency when the interface of the replicated objects is being declared; all other support is transparently provided by HCC.

The concurrency control is given at an operation granularity and it allows the implementation of multiple concurrency control policies. Additionally, the objects involved in the HCC support are fault-tolerant, giving as result an appropriate concurrency control mechanism for the coordinator-cohort replication model of HIDRA.

Although other concurrency control mechanisms may be found for replicated object management, HCC is either more comfortable for the programmer or requires less message interchange among the agents involved in that concurrency control or provides support for a greater number of synchronisation policies.

References

1. J. M. Bernabéu-Aubán and M. Ahamad. Applying a path-compression technique to obtain an efficient distributed mutual exclusion algorithm. In J. C. Bermond and M. Raynal, editors, *3rd International Workshop on Distributed Algorithms, Nice, France*, LNCS, pages 33–44. Springer-Verlag, sep 1989.
2. K. P. Birman, T. Joseph, and T. Raeuchle. Concurrency control in resilient objects. Technical report, TR 84-622, Dept. of Computer Science, Cornell Univ., Ithaca, NY, July 1984.
3. Toby Bloom. Evaluating synchronisation mechanisms. In *7th International ACM Symposium on Operating System Principles*, pages 24–32, 1979.
4. P. Galdámez, F. D. Muñoz-Escoí, and J. M. Bernabéu-Aubán. High availability support in CORBA environments. In F. Plášil and K. G. Jeffery, editors, *24th Seminar on Current Trends in Theory and Practice of Informatics, Milovy, Czech Republic*, volume 1338 of *LNCS*, pages 407–414. Springer Verlag, November 1997.
5. Jim Gray. Notes on database operating systems. In R. Bayer, R. Graham, and G. Seegmuller, editors, *Operating Systems: An Advanced Course*. Springer-Verlag, 1979.
6. M. Herlihy. Apologizing versus asking permission: Optimistic concurrency control for abstract data types. *ACM Trans. on Database Sys.*, 15(1):96–124, March 1990.
7. S. Jajodia and D. Mutchler. Dynamic voting algorithms for maintaining the consistency of a replicated database. *ACM Trans. on Database Sys.*, 15(2):230–280, June 1990.
8. A. Kumar and A. Segev. Cost and availability tradeoffs in replicated data concurrency control. *ACM Trans. on Database Sys.*, 18(1):102–131, March 1993.
9. Ciaran McHale. *Synchronisation in Concurrent, Object-oriented Languages: Expressive Power, Genericity and Inheritance*. PhD thesis, Department of Computer Science, Trinity College, Dublin, Ireland, October 1994.
10. F. D. Muñoz-Escoí, P. Galdámez, and J. M. Bernabéu-Aubán. ROI: An invocation mechanism for replicated objects. In *Proc. of the 17th IEEE Symposium on Reliable Distributed Systems, West Lafayette, IN, USA*, October 1998.
11. OMG. *The Common Object Request Broker: Architecture and Specification*. Object Management Group, February 1998. Revision 2.2.
12. U. S. Dept. of Defense. Reference manual of the Ada programming language. Technical report, ANSI/MIL-STD-1815A, DoD, Washington, D.C., 1983.

Data Mining Extension
for Object-Oriented Query Language

Mgr. Vladimir Novacek*

Department of Computer Science, TU Brno
Bozetechova 2, 612 66 Brno
Czech Republic
novacekv@dcse.fee.vutbr.cz

Abstract. Knowledge discovery in databases (KDD) and data mining became very important in data processing and analysing. The combination of powerful KDD and data mining techniques and sophisticated resources of object-oriented database systems brings even more considerable results. But these emerging tools and techniques require a powerful data mining query language which would serve as an interface between applications and data mining tools. This motivates us to propose general conditions and instruments for extending object-oriented query language (OOQL) with the ability of data mining. These instruments will be introduced in two examples of an object-oriented data mining query language, ODAMIL, an extension of Object Comprehensions language, and DMOQL, an extension of OQL language proposed by the ODMG.

1 Introduction

Knowledge Discovery in Databases (KDD, [1]) is general process of discovery of useful knowledge from data. This process involves data pre-processing, data mining itself and interpretation of mined patterns. Patterns interpretation is necessary for distinguishing what patterns constitute knowledge and what don't. Data mining is only one part of the KDD process. It analyses pre-processed data and produces information patterns which are then interpreted.

Development of modern database systems, e.g. object-oriented databases (OODB), has advanced considerably. It is natural then to investigate knowledge discovery in OODB ([2]). The OODB offers richer structure and semantics which can be employed in the KDD process.

In the present time there is a lot of practical applications employing or based on the KDD technology. Just the amount of various applications with various requests for the KDD system requires the introduction of certain standard which could be called Data Mining Query Language (DMQL). The DMQL would offer standard interface

* Supported by grant of the Czech Grant Agency Object-oriented Database Model No. 102/96/0986 and grant of the Advancement fund of MSMT Data Mining in Object-Oriented Database No. 243.

between application and the KDD system. Design of such language for data mining in relational databases is described in [3].

The joining of modern object-oriented database technology and data mining in conjunction with the need to create query language for data mining motivates us to propose general conditions and instruments for extending object-oriented query language (OOQL) with the ability of data mining. This would serve for development of OOQL for data mining which enables an application to obtain knowledge from OODB in certain standard simple way similar to receiving stored data from OODB using OOQL.

These instruments will be described and then introduced in two examples: object-oriented data mining query languages ODAMIL and DMOQL. The language ODAMIL (Object-oriented DAta MIning query Language) is an extension of OOQL Object Comprehensions ([4]). DMOQL (Data Mining OQL) is an extension of OQL language ([5, 6]) proposed by the ODMG group.

The second chapter deals with data mining extension emphasising three basic parts. The first one is data mining input, i.e. OODB being used. The second one describes the data mining output, i.e. particular types of mined rules. And the third one necessary extensions added to the OOQL. The third and fourth chapter introduces two examples of extending OOQL with data mining capabilities: languages DMOQL and ODAMIL. And finally the fifth chapter introduces some examples of the DMOQL and ODAMIL languages usage.

2 Data Mining Extension

Looking at data processing we can see that it is an process taking a database as both input and output, i.e. consuming and producing data. An application puts a query written in OOQL and it causes a database engine to pick some data from a database and give it to the application.

Data mining can also be viewed as an process. But this time it takes a database as an input and produces mined knowledge as an output. Using some data mining query language an application would put a query written in this language and the query would cause some data mining program to pick data from a database, analyse it and give mined knowledge to the application as a result of the query.

The data mining query language would enable an application to get knowledge from OODB in certain standard way similar to receiving stored data from OODB using OOQL. This is the reason for extending OOQL with data mining ability. This extension is possible under satisfying several conditions which will be described in following chapters.

2.1 Database

An object-oriented database ([7, 8]) will be input for data mining process. There are no additional adaptations of the database required for data mining purposes, no completion or adding of attributes, methods or objects. There are no required changes of already existing data or metadata. There is only one exception and it is completion of output definitions, i.e. definitions of mined knowledge and rules, which will be described in the following chapter.

Data mining program takes the OODB as it is. It doesn't worry about a database structure, type or origin of stored data, etc. It retrieves data from OODB using OOQL in the same way as any other database application. So from the data mining point of view no other change concerning the OODB is required.

Solely it is necessary to give the data mining program access to metadata. Data mining program needs the description of analysed data, i.e. objects it is working with. It needs to know description and structure of classes to which analysed objects belong. This information about object attributes and their types, about methods and their parameters are important for proper choice of data mining techniques and algorithms, for proper treatment of analysed data.

Knowing the analysed objects metadata the data mining program can choose optimal data mining strategy and mine interesting knowledge effectively.

2.2 Mined Rules

Data mining output is represented by newly obtained knowledge in the form of mined rules. Formally, the rule is expression E in language L describing the facts in certain subset of data from database ([1]).

For example, the expression „If a customer buys bread, he will also buy milk with probability of p percent" can be a rule for appropriate choice of threshold p.

Rules are characterised by two parameters. The *rule support* generally expresses the rule strength. Thus the higher the rule support, the lower the probability of accidental deducing of the rule only from a few transactions. The *rule confidence* generally expresses the measure of correlation in the database among items of the left and right side of the rule. Higher confidence means again higher rule quality.

There are various rule types ([1]) focusing on particular aspects of relations among data, data structure and content. It is not necessary to involve all these rule types into data mining extension of OOQL. We can constrain ourselves only to limited subset of these rules. In the case of ODAMIL or DMOQL languages mining of only limited number of rule types is supposed. Association, sequential and classification rules are to be mined.

The concept of knowledge and rule specified in this formal way must be expressed and defined by means of OODB, i.e. described in the data definition language (DDL). It is necessary to know the result type already in the moment of putting a query. In the case of OOQL the output is a collection of objects of some already defined class. In the case of data mining the output is a set or collection of rules. These rules must be first defined and their definitions, in other words rule metadata, added to the OODB metadata. Mined rules are formally treated as objects of some class returned as a query result. That's why it is necessary to know rule metadata in advance.

2.3 Query Language Extension

The OOQL serves for data retrieval. But knowledge is nothing else then another sort of data. Mined knowledge is described by metadata stored in the OODB and hence knowledge can be treated in the same way as 'normal' data. From this point of view there is no difficulty with incorporating knowledge discovery into data retrieval, i.e. extending OOQL with data mining ability.

There are some common features required for such extension. Adding rule metadata definitions into OODB is the first one mentioned before. The OOQL extending itself consists in enriching the OOQL with some new construct performing data mining. This new construct, let's say MINE command, would be similar to the SELECT statement from the SQL language or its equivalent from particular OOQL retrieving data from a database.

There are three possible issues with this addition. The first one is not a problem actually. Both OOQL constructs and MINE command retrieve data from OODB, i.e. behave in the same way. The only difference is that OOQL puts data immediately into output while MINE command analyses if first, extract rules from it and then put them into output. So from the point of view of OODB and treating it there's no problem.

The second one is the output problem. OOQL produces data while the MINE command produces knowledge. But knowledge is formally similar to data as mentioned before because both data and knowledge are defined by metadata and are formally treated as objects of some classes. Thus the difference between data and knowledge is wiped away. And the data mining process inside the MINE command does not bother.

The third and last problem is the possibility of adding some new element into OOQL. But OOQLs have usually some constructs such as user defined functions which can be utilised for the purpose of data mining extension. Now adding the MINE command won't be so demanding and factitious. And in addition the OOQL interpreter would have to be modified or rewritten anyway because, in fact, we define new OOQL requiring new interpreter so incorporating some new construct won't be so burdensome.

Of course, the MINE command must have some parameters determining required rule type, relevant data set and other necessary auxiliary components of data mining algorithms such as various thresholds for instance. But these parameters can be entered as parameters or primitives of the MINE command. According to number and type of mined rules it is possible to add only one MINE command or more separate commands for mining each rule type.

So the adding of MINE command is possible and is not so demanding. There are two another difficult things. The first one is choosing or designing advisable data mining algorithm(s) for performing data mining and producing required knowledge. The second one is presentation and utilisation of mined knowledge. But these tasks are not covered in this paper.

Once the OOQL is extended with the command(s) for data mining application can use this feature and obtain knowledge from OODB in the same simple way as retrieving data.

The principles mentioned above are introduced in following two chapters in two examples of object-oriented data mining query languages: ODAMIL and DMOQL.

Instead of abstract MINE command there is used a function `MineRules` as a representative of the data mining command.

3 The DMOQL Language

The DMOQL language arises from the OQL language and that's why we first introduce briefly this object-oriented query language developed by the ODMG group.

3.1 The OQL Language

The ODMG-93 is a reference standard built upon the existing SQL-92 ([9]), OMG and ANSI programming language standards. It includes also OQL (Object Query Language). OQL is an adaptation of the SQL-92 query language and is extended with all features of the ODMG object model. It includes the ability to include operation invocation in queries, to query over object inheritance hierarchies, to invoke inter-object relationships, and to query over arbitrary collections.

OQL is an SQL-like declarative (nonprocedural) language that provides a rich environment for efficient querying of database objects, including high-level primitives for object sets and structures, while retaining compatibility with the SQL-92 SELECT syntax.

OQL is a language where operators can be freely composed, as long as the operands respect the type system. This is a consequence of the fact that the result of any query has a type which belongs to the ODMG type model, and thus can be queried again.

OQL provides a superset of the SQL-92 SELECT syntax. This means that most SQL SELECT statements which run on relational DBMS tables work with the same syntax and semantics on the ODMG collection classes.

3.2 The DMOQL Language Syntax

The DMOQL language is proposed as an extension of object-oriented query language OQL ([5, 6]). The DMOQL is drafted generally and can be complemented for mining of arbitrary rule type. In this paper there is designed mining of basic rule types, namely association, classification and sequential rules. It is also possible to specify necessary auxiliary components of data mining algorithms, such as various thresholds for instance.

In the DMOQL language design there is employed one feature of the OQL language. The OQL language enables to invoke function inside a query. That's why the DMOQL language defines new function `MineRules`. Similarly to the `select` statement which retrieves data from OODB the `MineRules` function performs data mining and extracts knowledge from OODB. Necessary additional information is passed through parameters of the `MineRules` function.

The `MineRules` function definition is given here using a rather informal BNF notation. { symbol } means a sequence of 0 or n symbol(s). [symbol] means an optional symbol.

```
query        ::= MineRules(RuleType, TargSet
                 [, Thresholds] [, RelatedAttrs])

RuleType     ::= 'association' | 'sequential' |
                 'classification'

TargSet      ::= query

Thresholds   ::= set(ThrDef {, ThrDef})

ThrDef       ::= ThrID float_literal

ThrID        ::= 'minsupp' | 'minconf'

RelatedAttrs ::= set(identifier)
```

The `MineRules` function has four parameters with following description :

- Parameter `RuleType` determines the type of mined rules. Particular values determine type of mined rules according to their names.
- Parameter `TargSet` defines the target data set. It is essentially a subquery in the OQL language. The subquery is evaluated and the resulting collection or set of objects represents the target data set. The target data set contains data which are interesting for data mining at the moment. It contains then relevant data which are analysed and from which rules are mined.
- Optional parameter `Thresholds` contains particular thresholds definitions. If this parameter is empty implicit thresholds are used. Otherwise it contains set of definitions each of which sets one threshold.

    There are two threshold types, namely minimal support (determined by keyword `minsupp`) and minimal confidence (determined by keyword `minconf`). It means that the rules will be put as knowledge into output of the `MineRules` function only if their support and confidence will be greater than given minimal thresholds. Threshold's value itself is entered in percentages but written as a number within 0 to 1 interval.
- Parameter `RelatedAttr` contains list of attributes according to which the classification of target data set will be performed. It is entered only for mining of classification rules. In this case the target data set is processed by classification algorithm ([10, 11]) at first. The algorithm classifies the data set, i.e. divides it, into categories according to entered attributes. After this suitable data mining algorithm is executed which will mine classification rules for each data category.

4 The ODAMIL Language

The ODAMIL language is proposed as an extension of object-oriented query language Object Comprehensions ([4]). The ODAMIL language enables mining of basic rule types, namely association, classification and sequential rules but it is possible to complement it for mining of arbitrary rule type. Next it is possible to specify necessary auxiliary components of data mining algorithms, such as various thresholds for instance, by means of this language.

Queries in the Object Comprehensions language are entered similarly to specifying a set in mathematics. For example the set of squares of all odd numbers from the set S would be entered this way :

$\{ x^2 \mid x \in S, \text{Odd} (x) \}$

This standard mathematical notation was inspiration for the Object Comprehensions language. We introduce here one example of query written in this language :

```
Set[ s ← Student, s.address.city = „Prague" | s]
```

This query returns a collection of all students from the class Student who live in Prague as its result.

The Object Comprehensions language contains a lot of other constructs for entering various types of queries. It enables also to use user defined functions which can be parametrised. These functions work with objects in the OODB and return collections of objects as their results. They behave therefore as subqueries.

This feature of Object Comprehensions language is employed in the ODAMIL language design. The ODAMIL language newly defines function MineRules which performs data mining. Mined rule types, target data set and other information is entered through parameters of this function.

```
MineRules(RuleType: TRuleType; TargSet: Set Of Object;
    Thresholds: Set Of TThreshold;
    RelatedAttr: Set Of String) : Set Of Rule;
```

The MineRules function has four parameters with following description :
- Parameter RuleType determines type of mined rules.. Type TRuleType is defined as enumerated this way :

```
TRuleType = Enum(association, sequential,
    classification);
```

Particular values determine type of mined rules according to their names.
- Parameter TargSet defines target data set. It is essentially a query in the Object Comprehensions language. The query is evaluated and the resulting collection of objects represents the target data set.
- Parameter Thresholds can contain particular thresholds definitions. If this parameter is empty implicit thresholds are used. Otherwise it contains set of records each of which sets one threshold. Parameter Thresholds type is defined as follows :

```
TThreshold = Record

  IDThreshold: Enum(minsupp, minconf);

  Value:        Real;

end;
```

Attribute `IDThreshold` determines threshold type. There are two threshold types, namely minimal support (determined by keyword `minsupp`) and minimal confidence (determined by keyword `minconf`). Attribute `Value` contains threshold's value itself which is entered in percentages but written as a number within 0 to 1 interval.

- Parameter `RelatedAttr` contains list of attributes according to which classification of the target set will be performed. It is meaningful then only for mining of classification rules. In other cases is empty and is not relevant. When classification rules are mined the target data set is processed by classification algorithm ([10, 11]) at first. The algorithm classifies the data set, i.e. divides it, into categories according to entered attributes. After this suitable data mining algorithm is executed which will mine classification rules for each data category.

5 Examples of Mined Rules

Both in the ODAMIL and DMOQL languages the `MineRules` function is used in queries in a normal way as other query functions. Usage of both languages will be demonstrated in the following examples. First query is written in the DMOQL language and the second one in the ODAMIL language.

Example 1

```
MineRules('association', select * from Purchases where
   total ≤ 100)

Set[ r ← MineRules(association, Set[ p ← Purchases,
   p.total ≤ 100 | p], Set[], Set[]) | r]
```

This query returns a collection of association rules mined from data about potty purchases as its result. The target data set will be a collection of transactions, i.e. particular customer purchases, which total does not exceed $100. Implicit thresholds will be used during data mining.

Example 2

```
MineRules('sequential', select * from Purchases where
    (date ≥ 1.1.1997) AND (date ≤ 31.12.1997),
    set(minsupp 0.75, minconf 0.8))
```

```
Set[ r ← MineRules(sequential, Set[ p ← Purchases,
    p.date ≥ 1.1.1997, p.date ≤ 31.12.1997  | p], Set
    [Thr(minsupp, 0.75), Thr(minconf, 0.8)], Set[]) | r]
```

This query will mine sequential patterns from data about transactions performed in 1997. The target data set will be collection of transactions performed in 1997. Thresholds will be set so that minimal support of mined rules will be 75% and minimal confidence will be 80%.

Example 3

```
MineRules('classification', select * from Purchases
    where(date ≥ 1.1.1997) AND (date ≤ 31.12.1997),
    Set['Customer.Spending'])
```

```
Set[ r ← MineRules(classification, Set[ p ← Purchases,
    p.date ≥ 1.1.1997, p.date ≤ 31.12.1997 | p], Set[],
    Set['Customer.Spending']) | r]
```

This query will mine classification rules from data about transactions performed in 1997 using implicit thresholds. The target data set will be divided according to customer's spending and then classification rules for each category will be mined, e.g. what goods is bought by rich and poor customers, information which could be useful for marketing, etc.

6 Conclusions

Data mining and knowledge discovery represent a very important area for further research and development. And not only in the area of relational databases but especially in the environment of new progressive database systems such as OODB or deductive object-oriented databases (DOOD). These database systems are capable to hold large amount of data but also involve its structure and mutual relationships. Just these features can be successfully employed in data mining.

In a time of rapid development within this area there is increasing need for data mining query language which would enable simple and uniform entering of various data mining tasks and which would represent standard interface between application and data mining system.

In this paper we described general conditions and instruments for extending OOQL with data mining abilities and a design of object-oriented data mining query languages ODAMIL and DMOQL. These languages are proposed for effective data mining in the OODB.

Future research will probably continue towards the development of new effective algorithms for data mining in the OODB and towards the employment of the DOOD as a progressive tool for handling data and knowledge. Integration of data mining into the environment of DOOD is very interesting and important area.

References

1. Fayyad, U. M.; Piatetsky-Shapiro, G.; Smyth, P.; and Uthurusamy, R.: *Advances in Knowledge Discovery and Data Mining*. Menlo Park, Calif.: AAAI / MIT Press 1996
2. Han, J.; Nishio, S.; and Kawano, H.: *Knowledge Discovery in Object-Oriented and Active Databases*. In Knowledge Building and Knowledge Sharing, ed. F. Fuchi and T. Yokoi, 221-230. Ohmsha, Ltd. and IOS Press 1994
3. Han, J.; Fu, Y.; Wang, W.; Koperski, K.; and Zaiane, O.: *DMQL: A Data Mining Query Language for Relational Databases*
    Available at ftp://ftp.fas.sfu.ca/pub/cs/han/kdd/dmql96.ps
4. Chan, D. K. C.; and Trinder, P. W.: *Object Comprehensions: A Query Notation for Object-Oriented Databases*. In Directions in Databases, LNCS 826, Springer-Verlag, 1994
5. Cattell, R.G.G. *The Object Database Standard: ODMG-93, v1.2*, Morgan Kaufmann Publishers, San Mateo, California. 1994
6. Cattell, R.G.G.; Barry, D.; Bartels, D.; Berler, M.; Eastman, J.; Gamerman, S.; Jordan, D.; Springer, A.; Strickland, H.; and Wade, D. *The Object Database Standard: ODMG 2.0*. Morgan Kaufmann Publishers, San Mateo, California. 1997
7. Beneš, M.: *Object-Oriented Model of a Programming Language*. In: Proceedings of MOSIS 96 Conference, Krnov 1996 MARQ Ostrava and Department of Computer Science Technical University Ostrava 1996, pp. 33-38
8. Beneš, M.; and Hruška, T.: *Objektově orientované databáze*. In: Sborník celostátní konference EurOpen.CZ '97, Borová Lada na Šumavě 22.-25.6.1997, Česká společnost uživatelů otevřených systémů 1997, pp. 5-18
9. Melton, J.; and Simon, A. R. *Understanding the New SQL: A Complete Guide*. Morgan Kaufmann Publishers, 1993
10. Mehta, M.; Agrawal, R.; and Rissanen, J.: *SLIQ: A fast scallable classifier for data mining*. In Proc. International Conference on Extending Database Technology (EDBT'96), Avignon, France, March 1996
11. Winstone, L.; Wang, W.; and Han, J.: *Multiple-level data classification in large databases*. In submitted for publication, March 1996

Constraints with Variables' Annotations and Constraint Hierarchies

Hana Rudová

Faculty of Informatics Masaryk University
Botanická 68a, 602 00 Brno, Czech Republic
e-mail: hanka@fi.muni.cz

Abstract. Variables' annotations in over-constrained problems enable to express preferences for optimal solution selection using preferences on variables. The basic interpretation of variables' annotations is presented and correspondence with hierarchical CSP is described. New local comparator for constraint hierarchy is proposed and used for solving constraints with variables' annotations. The relationships between standard locally-better comparator and the new one are clarified. The potential application areas of variables' annotations are also mentioned.

1 Introduction

Over-constrained problems are usually solved by giving some preferences or weights to individual constraints and defining the solution as such a valuation which minimizes the violations of constraints. There are, however, over-constrained problems with partially or even completely ordered variables. Assigning preferences to variables could be more natural than defining preferences for constraints artificially. We describe a new constraint solving environment where preferences (or annotations) are assigned to individual variables instead of to the constraints themselves [7, 6]. Moreover, the annotations are local to variable occurrences, i.e., any variable may have different annotations in different constraints (in fact, even different occurrences in the same constraint are allowed).

Variables' annotations could be suitable for application areas as for example planning or scheduling. Using of our annotations is advantageous in applications where variables have their own preferences. These preferences could be applied directly instead of creating unnatural preferences over individual constraints. The classical example of such application is the timetabling problem where variables represent teachers (dean, professors, assistants...), rooms (more and less occupied), and different groups of students. For example, the lecture taught by a professor should be more preferred than another lecture taught by an assistant.

Let us consider the small real example illustrating meaning of variable preferences. There is a lecture L and its practice P. The practice should be preferably taught at least one day after the lecture. We would like to express by the following constraint that the professor's lecture is more preferred than the assistant's practice.

`L@strong + 1 #=< P@medium   % c1`

There are two weaker constraints: the lecture has to be taught on Thursday or Friday and the practice from Monday to Thursday:

`L@weak in 4..5            % c2`
`P@weak in 1..4            % c3`

These constraints form a kind of hierarchy: the constraint c1 with the highest preferences must be satisfied first and then we may try to satisfy constraints c2 and c3. It is possible to satisfy c1 but not c2 and c3 taken together. The constraint c2 influences the variable with higher annotations (look at c1), so this constraint is also satisfied. Then, trying to minimize the overall constraint violation, we get (a kind of) optimal solution L=4, P=5. By classical hierarchy where c1 is annotated by **strong** or **medium**, the solution L=3, P=4 is also obtained. But this solution is not optimal from our point of view. The different requirements towards the lecture and practice must be stated by assigning different preferences to c2 and c3 and so these constraints must be ordered. But this could be wrong with respect to other constraints in a more complex problem. Also, the exact location of the two appropriate constraints need not be easy to find in this context.

2 Constraints with Variables' Annotations

A constraint system with variables' annotations is derived from standard constraint satisfaction [5, 8]. As in other frameworks for solving over-constrained problems, an error function $e(c\theta)$ is applied and indicates how nearly constraint c is satisfied for a valuation θ. This error function can be trivial ($e(c\theta) = 0/1$ means c is satisfied/unsatisfied) or we can define the error function by using the domain's metric.

The constraint system is extended by variables' annotations in constraints [7, 6]. Every variable in every constraint has determined special annotation from annotation set: $a : C \times V \to \mathcal{A}$. There is a function $\circledast$ for computing global annotation:

- global variable annotation $av : V \to \mathcal{A}$, $av(v) = \underset{\{c \in C \mid v \in var(c)\}}{\circledast} a(c, v)$,

- constraint annotation $ac : C \to \mathcal{A}$, $ac(c) = \underset{\{v \in var(c)\}}{\circledast} a(c, v)$,

- global constraint annotation $acv : C \to \mathcal{A}$, $acv(c) = \underset{\{v \in var(c)\}}{\circledast} av(v)$,

where $var(c)$ is a set of variables of constraint c.

3 Hierarchy with Global Comparators

Correspondence between constraints with variables' annotations and constraint hierarchies [4, 9] with global comparators is described in this section. The hierarchy is constructed over constraint annotations ac, with additional order imposed by global constraint annotations acv within each level.

The annotation set $\mathcal{A}$ is an interval $(0, 1)$. The greater values of annotations are more preferred. The value 0 is not a member of $\mathcal{A}$ because a variable with such annotation plays no role in the constraint system.

Function $\circledast$ is the geometric average over real numbers. Constraint hierarchy is constructed using ordering of constraints $\leq_c$ which is defined using constraint annotation:

$$c, d \in C : c \leq_c d \equiv ac(c) \geq ac(d) . \tag{1}$$

The hierarchy of constraints $C = C_0 \cup C_1 \cup \ldots \cup C_n$ is a union of disjoint sets C_i where preferences of constraints decrease with increasing value of i:

$$C_0 = \{c \in C \mid ac(c) = 1\} \ldots \text{ level with required constraints },$$
$$C_i = \{c \in C \mid (\forall d \in C_j, j < i : d <_c c) \wedge (\forall e \in C_k, i < k : c <_c e)\} \quad i > 0 . \tag{2}$$

The valuation θ has an error $E(C\theta) = [E(C_1\theta), \ldots, E(C_n\theta)]$, where $E(C_i\theta) = \sum_{\{c \in C_i\}} acv(c)\, e(c\theta)$ holds. The value $E(C_0\theta)$ is not considered because all constraints at the level C_0 have to be satisfied. The value $acv(c)$ is understood as a weight of constraint c. The optimal solution θ has minimal error $E(C\theta)$ compared by weighted-sum-better comparator as in classical hierarchical CSP.

In a similar way, worst-case-better and least-squares-better comparators can be applied:

$$\text{worst-case-better: } E(C_i\theta) = \max_{\{c \in C_i\}} acv(c)e(c\theta) ,$$
$$\text{least-squares-better: } E(C_i\theta) = \sum_{\{c \in C_i\}} acv(c)\, e(c\theta)^2 .$$

The timetabling example from the Introduction solved by the hierarchy with weighted-sum-metric-better comparator describes [6] in detail.

4 Hierarchy with Local Comparators

The standard local comparator [1] uses no weights. Therefore the decomposition of C using only constraint annotation ac is not suitable — all global information of variables would be omitted. On the other hand, use of only global constraint annotation acv can cause that a constraint with smaller variable's annotations is in the more important level than another constraint with higher variable's annotations because the first constraint has higher value of acv. Therefore a combination of ac and acv have to be used for the construction of a hierarchy. This is done by a redefinition of the ordering $\leq_c$ (global comparators use definition (1)):

$$c, d \in C : c \leq_c d \equiv (ac(c) > ac(d)) \ \vee$$
$$((ac(c) = ac(d)) \wedge (acv(c) \geq acv(d))) .$$

---

[1] We recall the definition of locally-better comparator briefly (in detail [4, 9]): $locally\text{-}better(\theta, \delta, C) \equiv \exists k \in 1 \ldots n$ such that $(\forall l \in 1 \ldots k - 1 : (\forall c \in C_l : e(c\theta) = e(c\delta))) \wedge (\exists c \in C_k : e(c\theta) < e(c\delta)) \wedge (\forall d \in C_k : e(d\theta) \leq e(d\delta))$

The hierarchy is constructed as above (2) and the locally-better [1] comparator can be used for the solution selection. There is no reason for decomposing of C_0 using acv because C_0 is required level where all constraints have to be satisfied.

Another possibility is introduced by the definition of a new local comparator, which uses an ordering of constraints at every level. Levels are defined using (1) and (2), the ordering is then defined through global constraint annotation acv.

Definition 1. *A valuation θ is ordered-better than another valuation δ if, for each of the constraints through some level $k-1$, the error after applying θ is equal to that after applying δ, and at the level k the errors are compared with respect to an ordering $\leq_w$ of a set W given by a function $w : C \to W$ (proposition $w(c) \leq_w w(d)$ means c is preferred constraint over d):*

$$
\begin{aligned}
&ordered\text{-}better(\theta, \delta, C) \equiv \\
&\quad \exists k \in 1 \ldots n \text{ such that} \\
&\qquad \forall l \in 1 \ldots k-1 \, \forall c \in C_l : e(c\theta) = e(c\delta) \\
&\qquad \wedge \, \exists c \in C_k : e(c\theta) < e(c\delta) \\
&\qquad \wedge \, \forall d \in C_k \text{ such that } w(d) \leq_w w(c) : e(d\theta) \leq e(d\delta) \; .
\end{aligned}
$$

The valuation θ is ordered-better *if no valuation ω ordered-better than θ exists.*

All constraints at level C_0 have to be satisfied and therefore we may restrict ourselves to levels $1 \ldots n$ only. We can choose trivial error function e ($e(c\theta) = 0/1$ means c is satisfied/unsatisfied) or metric function (using metric of variables' domain), and then we get ordered-predicate-better or ordered-metric-better comparators, respectively.

Now we can define the mapping of constraints with variables' annotations to constraint hierarchy with ordered-better comparator exactly. The hierarchy is constructed using (1)+(2) and the ordered-better comparator chooses a better solution. The function w, the set W, and the ordering $\leq_w$ correspond to acv, $(0, 1)$, and $\geq$ over real numbers, respectively.

4.1 Ordered-Better and Locally-Better Comparators

In this section, the relations between ordered-better and locally-better comparators are clarified. We will also show that both described mappings with local comparators give the same solutions.

In the following, we suppose that $C = \{c_1, c_2, \ldots, c_m\}$ is constraint hierarchy with levels $C_0, C_1, \ldots, C_n$, an ordering $\leq_w$, and function w.

Lemma 1. *Every ordered-better solution θ of hierarchy C is locally-better.*

Proof. Let us assume that ordered-better valuation θ is not locally-better. Then a valuation ω exists which is locally-better than θ. Next let C_k be the first level, where valuations ω and θ have different values of error function on some constraints. Because the valuation ω is locally-better than valuation θ:

$$\forall d \in C_k : e(d\omega) \leq e(d\theta) \; . \tag{3}$$

The level C_k is the first level where any error functions differ, and so the next proposition follows from ordered-better(θ, w, C) (see Definition 1)

$$\exists d \in C_k : e(d\theta) < e(d\omega) \tag{4}$$

which is contradictory with the proposition (3). So, we obtain that no solution ω locally-better than θ exists and the valuation θ has to be the locally-better solution. □

There are locally-better solutions, which are not ordered-better. For example, let us consider hierarchy $C = C_1 = \{c, d\}$ where $w(c) <_w w(d)$ holds. Let there exist solutions ω and θ such that $e(c\omega) > e(c\theta)$, $e(d\omega) < e(d\theta)$. Both solutions could be locally-better but only θ could be ordered-better because it is ordered-better than ω.

The next part concentrates on exact specification of relation between locally-better and ordered-better comparator.

Definition 2. *Let* $C = \bigcup\limits_{i=0}^{n} C_i$ *be hierarchy and* $w : C \to W$ *weight function. Hierarchy refinement* C/w *is defined by* $\bigcup\limits_{i=0}^{n} C_i/w$, $C_i/w = \bigcup\limits_{j=1}^{n_i} C_{ij}$ *if the proposition* $C_0/w = C_0$ *holds and* C_{ij} *is given for* $\forall i \in 1 \ldots n$, $\forall j \in 1 \ldots n_i$ *by a formula* $(\forall c \in C_i \forall d \in C_i : (c \in C_{ij}, d \in C_{il}, l \in 1 \ldots n_i, j < l) \leftrightarrow (w(c) <_w w(d)))$.

The weights have no meaning in required level and we can suppose same weights for every $c \in C_0$. So $C_0/w = C_0 = C_{01}$ is justified.

Hierarchy refinements is a hierarchy, where the level C_{ij} is more important than C_{kl}, iff $(i < k) \vee ((i = k) \wedge (j < l))$ holds. The level C_0 is required and all constraints have to be satisfied for every solution. So, we may restrict ourselves to levels $1 \ldots n$ in comparing of potential valuations.

Lemma 2. *For a given hierarchy* C, *weight function* w, *and valuations* θ *and* δ *the proposition ordered-better*$(\theta, \delta, C) \leftrightarrow$ *locally-better*$(\theta, \delta, C/w)$ *holds.*

Proof. ($\to$): Let θ and δ be valuations of hierarchy C and let θ be ordered-better valuation than δ. Let k be the first level, where the error function on valuations θ and δ differs, and let $c \in C_k$ be a constraint with minimal weight $w(c)$ such that $e(c\theta) \neq e(c\delta)$ holds. Next let $c \in C_{kl}$ holds for some $l \in 1 \ldots n_k$ in hierarchy C/w. We show that θ is locally-better than δ in C/w.

1. $e(d\theta) = e(d\delta)$ holds for every $d \in C_{ij}, i \in 1 \ldots (k-1), j \in 1 \ldots n_i$ because the same holds for every $d \in C_i, i \in 1 \ldots (k-1)$ (error function on θ and δ differs in the level k for the first time).
2. $e(d\theta) = e(d\delta)$ holds for every $d \in C_{kj}, j \in 1 \ldots (l-1)$. The explanation of this fact follows. Firstly $d \in C_k$ and $w(d) <_w w(c)$ is obtained from Definition 2 and $j < l$. The constraint c has minimal weight in C_k such that error function on θ and δ differs. This entails $e(d\theta) = e(d\delta)$ for $d \in C_{kj}$.

3. $e(c\theta) < e(c\delta)$ holds because c is the first by level and weight with distinct values of error function on θ and δ, and θ is ordered-better than δ.
4. $e(d\theta) \leq e(d\delta)$ holds for every $d \in C_{kl}$ because θ is ordered-better than δ, $d \in C_k$ and $w(d) \leq_w w(c)$.

We have shown that proposition $e(d\theta) = e(d\delta)$ holds for $\forall d \in C_{ij}, (i < k) \vee ((i = k) \wedge (j < l)$, next $e(c\theta) < e(c\delta)$ and $\forall d \in C_{kl} : e(d\theta) \leq e(d\delta)$ hold. This means that θ is locally-better than δ in C/w.

($\leftarrow$): This proof is very similar to opposite direction. Let θ be locally-better than δ in C/w. Let error function differ for $c \in C_{kl}$ firstly. So $e(c\theta) < e(c\delta)$ stands. The statement $\forall i < k \forall d \in C_i : e(d\theta) = e(d\delta)$ is implied from locally-better comparator definition ($\forall i \forall j$ such that $(i < k) \vee ((i = k) \wedge (j < l))$ $\forall d \in C_{ij} : e(d\theta) = e(d\delta)$). For the same reason, $e(d\theta) = e(d\delta)$ holds for $\forall d \in C_k$ such that $w(d) <_w w(c)$. The proposition $e(d\theta) \leq e(d\delta)$ holds for $\forall d \in C_k : w(d) =_w w(c)$ because $d \in C_{kl}$ holds, error functions on θ and δ differ on C_{kl} firstly and θ is locallly-better than δ in C/w. So, all necessary conditions are satisfied and θ is ordered-better than δ in C. $\square$

Theorem 1. *The valuation θ is ordered-better solution of hierarchy C with weight function w, iff θ is locally-better solution of hierarchy refinement C/w.*

Proof. Entailment of Lemma 2. $\square$

Now we can go back to our mappings with local comparators. The ordered-better comparator was applied to hierarchy C constructed using ac and to weight function acv. The hierarchy with locally-better comparator was constructed using ac and then acv. Such hierarchy is the hierarchy refinement C/acv. Applying of Theorem 1 is obtained that both mappings compute the same solutions.

4.2 Algorithm for Solving the Hierarchy

This part gives tools for solving system of constraints with variables' annotations using constraint hierarchies with ordered-better comparator. The basic algorithm with its complexity analysis is described in the end.

Definition 3. *A sequence $SC = \langle c_1, \ldots, c_m \rangle$ is hierarchy-ordering of hierarchy C with m constraints if all constraints of SC are sorted by the level of hierarchy ($c_i \in C_k$, $c_j \in C_l$, $k < l$ implies $i < j$) and by the ordering $\leq_w$ (for $c_i, c_j \in C_k$ such that $w(c_i) <_w w(c_j)$ implies $i < j$). A sequence $\langle c_1, c_2, \ldots, c_i \rangle$ is denoted SC_i for $i \leq m$.*

Definition 4. *Let $SC = \langle c_1, c_2, \ldots, c_m \rangle$ be a hierarchy-ordering of hierarchy C. Recursively defined set $S = S_m$ is denoted ordering-solution-set of hierarchy-ordering SC if*

$$S_0 = \{\theta \,|\, \theta \text{ is a valuation of } SC\},$$
$$S_i = \{\theta \,|\, \theta \in S_{i-1} \wedge e(c_i\theta) = min_{w \in S_{i-1}} e(c_i\omega)\} \quad \text{for } i \in 1 \ldots m$$

holds.

Lemma 3. *Let us consider constraint hierarchy C with weight function w. If $w(d) \neq_w w(f)$ holds for every two constraints $d, f \in C_k$ for all $k \in 1 \ldots n$, then a value of error function $e(c\theta)$ is determined for every constraint $c \in C$ and for every ordered-better solution θ uniquely.*

Proof. Let C and w satisfy mentioned properties. There is only one hierarchy-ordering SC of such hierarchy C. We show that the set S_i from Definition 4 is the set of all ordered-better solutions of SC_i for $\forall i \in 1 \ldots m$. So the value of $e(c_i\theta)$ is uniquely determined for every i.

The proof is by induction on i. The base case $i = 0$ is trivial because SC_0 is empty and S_0 is the set of all hierarchy's valuation.

Suppose that the proposition holds for SC_{i-1} and now consider the solutions of $SC_i = \langle c_1, \ldots c_i \rangle$. Let R denote set of all ordered-better solutions of SC_i. Constraint c_i belongs to a higher level of hierarchy than c_j (for $\forall j < i$) or to the same level and then $w(c_j) <_w w(c_i)$ holds. This entails $R \subseteq S_{i-1}$. Let $\omega \in R$ exist such that value $e(c_i\omega)$ is not minimal. Then $\theta \in S_{i-1}$ exists with minimal $e(c_i\theta)$, which entail $\theta \in S_i$ and $e(c_i\omega) > e(c_i\theta)$. Next $e(c_j\omega) = e(c_j\theta)$ is implied for $\forall j < i$ from $\theta, \omega \in S_{i-1}$. So, valuation θ is ordered-better than ω. The valuation ω can not be the member of set R, which consists from ordered-better solutions only. For all $\delta \in R$ the value $e(c_i\delta)$ have to be minimal and so $R = S_i$ is obtained. $\square$

Theorem 2. *Let SC be a hierarchy-ordering of C and a set S be the ordering-solution-set of SC. Then S is the set of ordered-better solutions.*

Proof. The proof is by induction on the number of constraints m. The base case is for $m = 1$. The hierarchy is $C = \{c_1\}$ and only one $SC = \langle c_1 \rangle$ exists. We obtain $S = S_1 = \{\theta \mid \forall \omega : e(c_1\theta) \leq e(c_1\omega)\}$ and so every valuation $\theta \in S$ is an ordered-better solution.

Suppose that the proposition holds for a hierarchy with m constraints and now describe the case with $m + 1$ constraint. Let us suppose $\theta \in S_{m+1}$ and show for every valuation δ that either θ is ordered-better than δ for SC_{m+1} or δ is not ordered-better than θ for SC_{m+1} (θ and δ are not comparable for SC_{m+1}).

1. $\delta \notin S_{m+1} \wedge \delta \in S_m$: The error function for every c_i ($i \in 1 \ldots m$) is defined uniquely which follows from the assumption $\delta \in S_m$ and the definition of ordering-solution-set. Inequality $e(c_{m+1}\theta) < e(c_{m+1}\delta)$ is implied from the assumptions $\delta \notin S_{m+1}$ and minimal value for c_{m+1}'s error function. Together both these properties induce that θ is ordered-better than δ.

2. $\delta \in S_{m+1}$: The error function for every constraint is the same again, so no constraint c_i ($i \in 1 \ldots m + 1$) exists such that $e(c\theta) > e(c\delta)$ (or $<$) and neither δ nor θ is ordered-better than second valuation for SC_{m+1}.

3. $\delta \notin S_m$: $\theta \in S_m$ and so δ can not be ordered-better than θ for SC_m from induction's assumptions. We show that the adding of c_{m+1} does not change this situation for SC_{m+1}. The value of error function for some $i \in 1 \ldots m$ differs for θ and δ (from $\delta \notin S_m$). Let i be the first of them and suppose $c_i \in C_k$ and $e(c_i\theta) < e(c_i\delta)$ (by analogy for $>$). θ and δ are not comparable

for SC_m. So, some $c_j \in C_k$ such that $w(c_j) \leq_w w(c_i)$ and $e(c_j\theta) > e(c_j\delta)$ hold, has to exist. The proposition $w(c_j) =_w w(c_i)$ holds because i is the smallest index $(j > i)$ and SC_m is hierarchy-ordering. These differences induce incomparability for SC_{m+1} too.

Therefore every $\theta \in S$ is an ordered-better solution. $\qquad\qquad\qquad\square$

There are ordered-better solutions, which can not be obtained using any hierarchy-ordering as its ordering-solution-set. Let us consider the example $C = C_1 = \{c1, c2\}$

```
B >= 10 % c1
B =< 8  % c2
```

where $w(c1) = w(c2)$ holds. The valuation $\{B = 10\}$ is obtained for hierarchy-ordering $\langle c1, c2 \rangle$ and $\{B = 8\}$ for $\langle c2, c1 \rangle$. Both valuations are ordered-better but for example a valuation $\{B = 9\}$ is ordered-better, too.

The algorithm for solving constraints with variables' annotation is based on the Theorem 2 and Indigo algorithm [2, 3] for local propagation by means of interval arithmetic [1]. Indigo algorithm manipulates the acyclic set [2] of inequality constraints with the complexity $O(|C| \times |V|)$. The key idea in Indigo is that lower and upper bounds on variables (i.e. intervals) are propagated, and the constraints are processed from strongest to weakest, tightening the bounds on variables using interval arithmetic step by step.

Our solution is divided into three parts:

1. the splitting set of constraints C with variables' annotations to constraint hierarchy $\{C_0, C_1, \ldots, C_n\}$ using constraint annotation ac and ordering $\leq_c$,
2. sorting constraints in every level C_i of hierarchy using global constraint annotation acv to an output sequence of constraints OC_i,
3. the application of the Indigo algorithm with sorted input constraints by the sequence $\langle OC_0, OC_1, \ldots, OC_n \rangle$.

Theorem 3. *Given an acyclic set of constraints, the algorithm computes ordered-metric-better solution.*

Proof. Input constraints for the Indigo algorithm define hierarchy-ordering SC using $OC_0, OC_1, \ldots, OC_n$. The Indigo algorithm minimizes error function in the order given by hierarchy-ordering SC. Those are requirements of Theorem 2 and so we obtain an ordered-metric-better solution as a result of the algorithm. $\quad\square$

Let us denote $m = |C|, k = |V|$ and consider the complexity of algorithm. In the first step, constraint annotation is computed for every constraint. Because every constraint contains maximally k variables, the complexity of this part is $O(mk)$. The complexity of sorting m constraints is $O(m \log m)$. The second step

---

[2] Bipartite constraint graph is acyclic. Vertices of this graph are variables and constraints. An edge is created between variable and constraint when variable occurs in this constraint.

computes global variable annotations and because every variable is contained in maximally m constraints, the complexity $O(mk)$ is obtained. Complexity of computing global constraint annotation is also $O(mk)$ and sorting particular disjoint sets of altogether m constraint takes $O(m \log m)$ steps. The complexity of the last step is $O(mk)$ [3]. As a result, we get the total complexity $O(m(k + \log m))$.

Described algorithm for solving inequality constraints with variables' annotation mapped to the hierarchy with the ordered-better comparator was implemented in Prolog with attributed variables and mutable terms.

5 Conclusions and Future Work

A new approach for solving over-constrained problems using variables' annotations was described. This approach could be suitable for application areas like planning or scheduling. We defined the complete mapping from variables' annotations to constraint hierarchies. We proposed a new local comparator for solving of problems with variables' annotations. We described relation between standard locally-better comparator and new ordered-better comparator. We have shown that the weights used for the ordered-better solution selection enable more exact specification of preferences than locally-better comparator without redefinition of hierarchy.

The future work will consists of the precise interpretation of constraints with variables' annotations which manipulates these constraints more efficiently. We will consider the properties and scope of such interpretation with respect to real problems. We would like to concentrate on an incremental manipulation with our constraints. The incremental manipulation means that adding of a new constraint does not require a complete recomputation of a previously computed solution. The another interesting point is the so called „computation with annotations": let us imagine constraint system with annotations and simplifying of this constraint system together with suitable transformation of annotations so that solutions of both are the same. An attention will be also devoted to study of suitable algorithms for solving systems of constraints with emphasis to variables' annotations and ordered-better comparator.

Acknowledgements

This work is supported by the Universities Development Fund of the Czech Republic under the contract # 0748. I would like to thank my supervisor, Luděk Matyska for exhaustive discussion on topic and reading drafts of this paper.

References

1. Benhamou, F.: Interval Constraint Logic Programming. In: Podelski, A. (ed.): Constraint Programming: Basics and Trends. Lecture Notes in Computer Science, Vol. 910. Springer-Verlag, Berlin Heidelberg New York (1995) 1–21

2. Borning, A., Anderson, R., Freeman-Benson, B.: Indigo: A Local Propagation Algorithm for Inequality Constraints. Proceedings of the 1996 ACM Symposium on User Interface Software and Technology (1996) 129–136
3. Borning, A., Anderson, R., Freeman-Benson, B.: The Indigo Algorithm. Tech. Rep. TR-96-05-01, Department of Computer Science and Engineering University of Washington (1996)
4. Borning, A., Freeman-Benson, B., Wilson, M.: Constraint Hierarchies. Lisp and Symbolic Computation 5, No. 3 (1992) 223–270
5. Freuder, E.C., Mackworth, A.K. (eds.): Constrained-Based Reasoning. MIT Press, (1994). Reprinted from Artificial Intelligence 58, No. 1–3 (1992)
6. Rudová, H.: Constraints with Variables' Annotations. Tech. Rep. FIMU-RS-98-04, Faculty of Informatics Masaryk University, http://www.fi.muni.cz/informatics/reports (1998)
7. Rudová, H.: Constraints with Variables' Annotations. In: Prade, H.: 13th European Conference on Artificial Intelligence, John Wiley & Sons, Ltd. (1998) 261–262
8. Van Hentenryck, P.: Constraint Satisfaction in Logic Programming. MIT Press (1989)
9. Wilson, M., Borning, A.: Hierarchical Constraint Logic Programming. Journal of Logic Programming 16, No. 3,4 (1993) 227–318

Sample Method for Minimization of OBDDs

Anna Slobodová[12] and Christoph Meinel[34]

[1] Compaq, Shrewsbury, Massachusets, USA.
E-mail:slobodov@cadunx.hlo.dec.com
[2] Comenius University, Bratislava,Slovakia
[3] Institute of Telematics, Bahnhofstr. 30-32, 54292 Trier, Germany.
E-mail: meinel@ti.fhg.de
[4] University of Trier, FB IV - Informatik, 54286 Trier, Germany.
E-mail: meinel@uni-trier.de

Abstract. The exact minimization of the size of Ordered Binary Decision Diagrams (OBDD) is known to be an NP-complete problem. The available heuristical solutions of the problem still do not satisfy requirements of the practical applications. Development of the efficient algorithms that find acceptable variable orders within a short time and with a modest memory overhead is hence higly desired.

In this paper we contribute to the solution of the minimization problem by a new variable reordering heuristic that is based on sampling. A small OBDD sample is chosen from the OBDDs that are considered for minimization. Solving the problem for this small sample, we obtain a variable order that is extrapolated and applied to the entire OBDDs. We present the first experimental results with the Sample Reordering targeted at combinatorial verification. The suggested heuristic is substantially faster than Sifting.

1 Introduction

Ordered Binary Decision Diagram (OBDD) as a scheme for representation of Boolean functions is applicable to all problems over a finite domain. Because of its excellent algorithmical properties, OBDD is the favorit data structure in computer-aided design, verification and testing of digital systems. The powerfull computing machinery spent a huge amount of financial resources to support the research aided to development and application of mathematical methods in their design groups. One of the "hot" topics is the BDD-based technology.

Despite deep theoretical investigation and wide practical exploitation of the OBDD model, there are still many theoretical as well as practical problems that remain unsolved. The problem of highest priority for all practical applications that use OBDDs is their conciseness. Since the size of the OBDD representation for a function may vary exponentially for different orders of variables, the

---

[0] This work was partially supported by the German research society (DFG) via the project Me 1077/12-1, while the first author worked with Institute of Telematics. A preliminary version was presented on International Workshop on Logic Synthesis, Lake Tahoe, California.

problem of finding an optimal variable order that realizes the minimal size is of special interest. This problem is known to be NP-complete [18, 4]. The exact algorithm [7–9, 6] works well for small numbers of variables only, and cannot be used for a general purpose. More relevant to the practice are variable reordering heuristics (e.g., [14, 13, 12]).

The variable reordering problem of OBDDs is a typical combinatorial problem with a huge search space of feasible solutions. In addition, there is no known efficient method for exact evaluation of a variable order with respect to the size of corresponding OBDDs. More precisely, having an OBDD for a function f and a variable order π, we have no efficient procedure to compute the size estimation of $\pi\text{OBDD}(f)$. The only way is to construct the OBDD, which can be performed efficiently merely in the case when the size of the resulting OBDD is polynomially related to the size of the initial OBDD (e.g.,[10]). This makes the problem even more complicated, since heuristics that choose several candidates for *a good* order cannot avoid the construction of the OBDDs for their evaluation. This is the reason why methods like simulated annealing [1] or genetic reordering algorithm [5] take too much time.

When a problem appears unsolvable in its full dimension, a natural approach is to reduce it to problems of lower dimensions. This idea can be found in several reordering heuristics: e.g., Sifting [14] looks for *a good* position for one variable, thus obtaining a feasible solution that improves the size of the OBDD. This step is then repeated for all variables. Another example is Block-restricted Sifting [11] where OBDDs are partitioned horizontally into blocks that are minimized independently.

In this paper, we follow the idea mentioned above combining it with the idea of sampling: A part of the considered OBDDs is taken as a representative sample and the variable order problem is solved for it. This subproblem has a substantially lower dimension and hence, it is possible to find quickly a feasible solution for the initial problem. This solution is used as an approximation of *a good* variable order for the entire OBDDs. The goal is to obtain not the best, but an acceptable order in a short time. The suggested Sampling Reordering method is presented as it was implemented in the advanced Decision Diagram package of Colorado University at Boulder [15]. We report the experimental results on an example of symbolic simulation of the circuits that is the core of combinatorial verification. Our experimental evaluation showed the time advantage of the suggested reordering method. There was no clear advantage of any of both methods regarding the final size of the OBDDs. Encouraged by these results we started to work on some other applications, such that as sequential verification. The main idea is to speed up BDD-based operations by focusing on a subset of considered OBDDs. We believe that Sampling is a good basis for such application driven reordering.

The paper is structured by the following way: The next section provides a reader with all necessary notions and facts regarding OBDDs. Implementation details of the sample reordering are discussed in Section 3. Section 4 contains experiments with the method used dynamically during symbolic simulation of benchmark circuits. Evaluation of the method is performed by comparison with the most stable and widely used Sifting Algorithm as proposed by Rudell [14].

2 Preliminaries

2.1 Definitions

In order to make the paper selfcontained, we give definitions of the notions used in this paper. We start by the definition of an OBDD and its interpretation as representation scheme for Boolean functions.

An *Ordered Binary Decision Diagram (OBDD)* P over a set of Boolean variables X_n is a multi-rooted directed accyclic graph with the following properties:

1. Sink-nodes are labelled by Boolean constants 0 and 1.
2. Each internal node is labelled by a variable from X_n and has two distinguishable successors called *low* and *high* son, respectively.
3. On any path, any variable occurs at most once. The order of occurrence of variables defines an order π over X_n, i.e., if x_i precedes x_j on a path, $x_i <_\pi x_j$.

A πOBDD is an OBDD with the variable order π. *The size* of an OBDD P is measured by the number of its non-sink nodes and is denoted by $|P|$.

For any node u of P, an assignment $\alpha : X_n \mapsto \{0,1\}^n$ naturally defines a computational path with the initial point in u and terminal point in a sink: if the path contains a node v labelled by x_i, and $\alpha(x_i) = 0$ ($\alpha(x_i) = 1$), then the path contains the low (respectively, high) son of v. u represents a Boolean function $f(x_1,\ldots,x_n)$, $f : \{0,1\}^n \mapsto \{0,1\}$, if for each assignment α, the corresponding path terminates in a sink labelled by $f(\alpha^{(n)}(x_1),\ldots,\alpha^{(n)}(x_n))$. P represents multiple Boolean functions represented by its roots.

An OBDD is called *reduced*, if no two nodes represent the same function.

The OBDD nodes that are labelled by the same variable form *a node level*.

2.2 OBDD Properties

Due to Shanon decomposition theorem, any Boolean function over X_n has a πOBDD representation, for any variable order π over X_n.

Fact 1 ([3, 16])

1. *Reduced πOBDD for a function f is unique and minimal (w.r.t. its size) πOBDD representation of f.*
2. *Any OBDD can be reduced in linear time.*

The suitability of an OBDD as a data structure for Boolean manipulation is implied by their excellent algorithmical properties:

Fact 2 ([3]) *There are polynomial time algorithms for the following operations over functions represented by OBDDs:*

1. *Boolean binary operations*
2. *building cofactors (i.e., restriction of a function by fixing a value of a variable)*
3. *evaluation of the represented function with respect to a given assignment*
4. *satisfiability and tautology test, and computing the number of satisfiable assignments*
5. *existential and universal quantification over a constant number of variables*

An equivalent modification of an OBDD by exchange of two neighbouring variables in th order is a local operation called *swap*.

Fact 3 ([14]) *Swap operation between the i-th and $(i+1)$-st node levels can be done in time and space $\mathcal{O}(|L_i| + |L_{i+1}|)$.*

Swap operation is the basic step in the most popular variable reordering algorithm Sifting [14]. Sifting consider the Boolean variables in the OBDD to be reordered in the descending order with respect to the size of the corresponding node levels. A processed variable is moved through the whole order by means of swaps and the size of the OBDD is monitored. Afterwards, the variable is placed on the position where the minimal OBDD size was reached. It is not known how precise is the solution found by Sifting. However, because of its universality and easy implementation, it is the mostly used variable reordering heuristic.
Restructering of an OBDD with respect to a new variable order can be performed efficiently, too.

Fact 4 ([18, 10, 2, 17]) *Given an OBDD P over X_n and a variable order π over X_n, construction of an OBDD Q that is functionally equivalent to P and which variable occurence satisfies π can be constructed in time and space polynomial in $|P| + |Q|$.*

3 Sampling Method in Variable Reordering

In this section, we describe Sample Reordering – the suggested application of sampling technique to variable reordering of OBDDs. The main idea is to find a good variable order for a small sample of given OBDDs and to adapt it to the entire multirooted OBDD. There are three basic questions to be discussed:

How to find the sample?
How to minimize it?
How to adapt the variable order of a minimized sample to the entire OBDDs?

Each of these points may have an essential influence on the final solution. From our experience, simple methods are often more effective in practical applications than more sophisticated and complex ones. Hence, we will start with the simplest variant and then discuss possible improvements.

A more appropriate phrasing of the first question would be: "How to find a *good* sample?", where *good* means that any variable order that is optimal for the sample is efficiently transformable into an order that is optimal for the entire OBDDs. Obviously, because of the NP-hardness of the optimal variable order problem, there is no hope to find an efficient algorithm for finding a small (e.g., less than half the size of the considered OBDDs) sample with the desired property mentioned above. Moreover, the same holds if we look for a small sample whose reduction yields an order that is efficiently transformable at least to a better order for the entire OBDDs. Therefore, a real goal is to look for the answer to the following question: How to find a sample that (at least often) assures an order that is better than the initial order of the OBDDs? In the very first step, we choose a sample in a random manner, as it is usual in sampling strategies.

On one hand, this makes the method independent from an application, which can be seen as a positive property. On the other hand, this approach clearly does not exploit the whole potential of the method that could make use of application specific information. In Section 4, we describe the choice of the sample suitable for an application during symbolic simulation of a circuit. The best results were obtained for the sample of 15%–30%. This value may vary with different implementations, and of course, depends on a set of examples.

Another important question is the choice of the size of the sample. A small sample can be reordered fast, but it gives less information about a good variable order for the entire OBDDs than a bigger one. The overhead for copying and reordering of the sample must be in balance with the quality of the order found, i.e., the smaller the sample, the easier the handling, but there will also be less information about the OBDDs. An appropriate value of the sample size parameter can be derived experimentally.

Besides the size of the sample, it is also important what portion of the variables from the support of the entire OBDDs it contains. We do not explicitly require a fixed portion of variables, but the choice of the sample is aimed to cover most of the variables. A potential extension could be an assignment of weights to variables, e.g., the size of the corresponding node levels, that will have an influence on the choice of the sample.

The second question concerning the minimization of the sample partially depends on the OBDD package used and the optimization technique for the minimization of the sample. Considering the implementation details of the CUDD package that we use for our experiments, we chose the following approach: The sample is copied and reordered by Sifting.

The last, but nonetheless important question to be discussed is how to adapt the variable order achieved by minimization of the sample to entire OBDDs. This question actually consists of two parts: how to derive the new variable order for the entire OBDDs from the obtained variable order in the sample, and how to rebuild the OBDDs with respect to this new order. The trivial solution for the new order is to fix the positions of the variables that do not appear in the sample and reorder the rest of variables according to their positions in the reordered sample. In the very first experiments, we have tried to sift the variables that do not appear in the sample, but only in a restricted manner. Each such variable was sifted between two closest positions occupied by the variables that appeared in the sample. This additional reordering did not yield an essential reduction of the size, and we omitted it from the next experiments.

There may be also some restrictions about the positions of variables that are implied by the meaning of the functions represented by the OBDDs. An example for such restrictions in the case of sequential verification is that the present and next state variables of a finite state machine should stay together. These must be met in the new order, too.

We can also try to estimate the quality of a new order and to avoid rebuilding to poor orders. Our conservative estimation is based on the following assumption: If the reordering of a sample did not bring substantial reduction, we do not expect that the order obtained substantially reduces the entire OBDDs.

For reordering to a new order, we use a shuffling procedure that sifts the variables upwards to their new positions, starting with the variable that is positioned on the topmost level in the new order, and proceeding subsequently to lower positions. We have observed that if the size starts to grow, the target order is usually not good. Hence, the rebuilding process is stopped whenever the OBDD size increases beyond a given factor. The rebuilding approach used has an advantage in that we get information about the OBDD size for some other orders that appear on the way to the target one. If one of these intermediate orders happens to be better than the found one, we sift the corresponding variables back to their best found position. If the first attempt fails, we decide whether we try to reorder again, based on another sample.

4   Experiments

The method described in the previous section has been implemented in the Colorado University Decision Diagrams package (CUDD-2.1.2) and used as dynamic reordering method for symbolic simulation of the LGSynth91 benchmark circuits and some circuits contained in the CUDD package. The parameters in CUDD were left at their default values in all experiments. The results are compared to Sifting Algorithm with respect to final size and time. All experiments ran on Pentium Pro 200's with 64MB memory. In this section, we describe some of the experiments and, based on their evaluation, we propose an appropriate parameter setting. The section is closed by the particular application of the sample reordering method to combinatorial verification.

A chosen sample is copied and then reordered by means of Sifting as implemented in CUDD. The variables in the copy are created in the order of their appearance in the copy process. Since we keep the correspondence of the variables in the sample and in the entire OBDDs, we can easily determine a new variable order for the OBDDs from the order in the sample using the strategy described in the previous section. Afterwards, the copy can be discarded.

In order to see whether the idea of sampling works for reordering of OBDDs, we ran several experiments. The measures of interest are the time and OBDD size. The method is compared to Sifting (as implemented in CUDD-2.1.2) with respect to these values. Time is considered as being more important, as long as the size remains acceptable. After initial experiments with one-time reordering, we continued the experiments with dynamic reordering during combinatorial simulation of the circuits. To give an impression of the usability of the method, we present the results for dynamic reordering applied on a sample of larger circuits. Since the number of reorderings done depends on the quality of the variable order found by the heuristic, this type of experiments gives more information than a single application of the method.

The first series of experiments was aimed to help in the choice of the sample parameters: sample size α, the growth factor that determines the size bound for shuffling to the new order β, and the number of reordering attempts allowed for one dynamic invocation of the reordering γ. We have observed that 10% to 20% size growth during the shuffling to a new variable order, and 2 to 3 attempts per invocation of the reordering are satisfying parameter values. Then we held these two parameters constant and ran the experiments with varying sample size. The method was always used for dynamic reordering and for a final reordering of the OBDDs created by the symbolic simulation of circuits. The variable occurence in circuit description implied the initial order in all experiments. The results clearly showed that while a sample of 10% did not yield enough information, the overhead for a 60% sample was too large. There was a clear time saving for sample size of 15% to 30%. Besides that, smaller final size of OBDDs reordered by Sample Reordering was frequent, too.

Sample Reordering Strategy for Combinatorial Verification

In a particular application of the Sampling, we can use additional information for the choice of a sample. The idea is to prefer some roots as more important for minimization then others. These, for any reasons distinguished, roots will be chosen into the sample with a higher preference. We propose a simple reordering strategy with an appropriate parameter setting, targeted to symbolic simulation of circuits:

A small sample is chosen from the newly created roots and copied to be reordered by Sifting (note that any reordering method can be used at this place). The order obtained is applied to the entire OBDDs as described above. If this first attempt fails to reach an acceptable improvement, the same process is repeated for a new sample.

Let us go into details. The new roots obtained as results from the Boolean operations applied during the symbolic simulation, i.e., OBDDs of some internal gates, are pushed onto a stack. Any garbage collection of the unreferenced nodes is completed by cleaning the stack. The size of the stack is bounded. Its capacity can be set according to the considered application and examples (in the presented experiments, we worked with a stack size of 500). The push operation into a full stack discards the bottom item. When the sample reordering is invoked, the sample is preferably built from the roots in the stack. There are several reasons for this: With proceeding computation, the newly created roots represent more and more difficult functions. Hence, their minimization is of high priority. Secondly, they are assumed to survive longer than those created sooner. And finally, the last reordering had been invoked before these roots were existing. Hence, the current order is with high probability not suitable for them.

If the OBDDs whose roots are in the stack do not suffice to cover the requirements on the size of the sample, we choose additional roots randomly. Then we proceed as described above: The sample is reordered using Sifting and the resulting order is used for reordering of the entire OBDDs. If the gain of this reordering amounts to at least 30% of the initial size, we stop the reordering and continue in the application. Otherwise, i.e., if the reduction does not reach the expected value, we try to choose another sample.

The suggested Sampling strategy is evaluated in three series of experiments. The results are summarized in Table 1. Parameter β is set to 1.2, i.e., the allowed size growth during the shuffling of variables to a new order is 20% like the default size growth during the Sifting. The size of the sample is set to 25% in all experiments. The number of attempts is at most 2. In order to avoid using the same sample repeatedly, which may happen if we work with a constant sample size parameter, half of the sample is chosen at random in the second attempt. The first experiment (the column labelled by $2 \times 25\%$) ran as described above. The second experiment (the column labelled by $25\% + 25\%$) differs from the first in that, in the second attempt, we do a conservative pre-estimation of the reduction reachable by reordering to the new order obtained by the reordering of the sample. If the reduction of the sample does not reach the expected value of 30%, then the entire OBDDs are not reordered to the new order. This decreases the number of shuffle attempts and leads to a further decrease of time. In all but the third experiment, the same method is used for dynamic and final reordering. If the resulting OBDDs are processed further in the next computational steps, e.g., in the case of the sequential circuits, if the application continues by reachability analysis, then it makes sense to spend more time by reordering at the end of symbolic simulation. The third experiment differs from the second in that Sifting is used as the final reordering.

The number of reorderings during the symbolic simulation of a circuit varied from 4 to 22 (10 in average) in our experiments. The values of time and size for the Sample Reordering are the average values from 10 runs.

In comparison with Sifting, we have a remarkable saving of time without incurring a penalty with respect to the total value of the final OBDD size.

5 Conclusion

We propose a Sampling Reordering as an efficient heuristic for minimization of OBDDs. The first experimental results with the random sampling proved a remarkable potential of the method. Our current work is focused on the use of Sample Reordering in particular applications where an additional information about the meaning of the represented functions is exploited for the choice of a sample.

Table 1. Experiments for sample size of 25%

Circuit		Sampling			Sifting
		2×25%	25%+25%	25%+25% final Sifting	
bw11x11	time	721.04	**308.66**	388.81	1033.86
	size	150,842	182,269	**136,543**	285,137
bw8x8	time	5.01	**4.22**	4.64	6.11
	size	9,641	9,719	**8,190**	9,050
C499	time	**12.87**	17.62	25.51	20.14
	size	**32,911**	44,238	41,900	26,624
C880	time	7.01	**4.99**	6.90	11.24
	size	13,495	18,665	**10,920**	10,440
C1355	time	23.76	**21.32**	24.17	76.01
	size	**27,063**	29,681	29,192	29,562
C3540	time	91.82	**41.87**	49.57	46.74
	size	34,286	34,060	**31,858**	23,950
C7552	time	91.31	**47.74**	52.92	30.99
	size	69,452	28,440	**15,683**	8,241
i10	time	26.43	**21.62**	35.39	174.83
	size	33,351	34,154	**32,605**	67,971
mm30a	time	18.02	**16.42**	18.79	137.34
	size	21,548	18,433	**17,659**	100,591
s13207.1	time	19.94	**15.21**	16.52	42.02
	size	5,003	6,514	**3,158**	3,008
s15850.1	time	**67.36**	68.94	77.19	75.66
	size	27,409	32,241	**19,812**	12,539
s35932	time	37.97	**34.27**	42.12	50.84
	size	5,866	5,842	**4,987**	5,010
s38584.1	time	59.38	**54.81**	63.37	121.54
	size	28,344	30,860	**16,680**	15,121
s4863	time	93.54	**83.53**	131.97	254.03
	size	80,691	82,612	**69,476**	64,245
s6669	time	52.31	48.74	**48.46**	111.29
	size	25,626	27,299	**22,351**	22,109
Total	time	1,328	**790**	986	2,193
	size	565,528	585,027	**461,014**	683,598

References

1. B. Bollig, M. Löbbig, and I. Wegener. Simulated Annealing to Improve Variable Orderings for OBDDs. *Proc. IWLS*, 5b:5.1–5.10, 1995.
2. J. Bern, Ch. Meinel, and A. Slobodová. Global Rebuilding of OBDDs – Avoiding Memory Requirement Maxima. *Proc. CAV*, (LNCS 939):299–308, 1995.
3. R.E. Bryant. Graph Based Algorithms for Boolean Function Manipulation. *IEEE Transactions on Computers*, (C-35):677–691, 1986.
4. B. Bollig and I. Wegener. Improving the Variable Ordering of OBDDs is NP–complete. *IEEE Transactions on Computers*, (45(9)):993–1002, 1996.
5. R. Drechsler, B. Becker, and N. Göckel. A Genetic Algorithm for Variable Ordering of OBDDs. *IEEE Proc. Computers and Digital Techniques*, 143(6):364–368, 1996.
6. R. Drechsler, N. Drechsler, and W. Günther. Fast Exact Minimization of BDDs. *IEEE/ACM Proc. Design Automation Conference*, 1998.
7. S.J. Friedman, and K.J. Supowit. Finding the Optimal Variable Ordering for Binary Decision Diagrams *IEEE/ACM Proc. DAC*, 348–356, 1987.
8. S.J. Friedman, and K.J. Supowit. Finding the Optimal Variable Ordering for Binary Decision Diagrams *IEEE Transactions on Computers*, 39(5):710–713, 1990.
9. N. Ishiura, H. Sawada, and S. Yajima. Minimization of Binary Decision Diagrams Based on Exchanges of Variables *IEEE Proc. of ICCAD*, 472–475, 1991.
10. Ch. Meinel and A. Slobodová. On the Complexity of Constructing Optimal Ordered Binary Decision Diagrams. *Proc. MFCS*, (LNCS 841):515–525, 1994.
11. Ch. Meinel and A. Slobodová. Speeding up Variable Reordering of OBDDs. *IEEE Proc. of ICCD*, 338–343, 1997.
12. S. Panda and F. Somenzi. Who are the Variables in Your Neighbourhood. *Proc. ACM/IEEE ICCAD*, 74–77, 1995.
13. S. Panda, F. Somenzi, and B.F. Plessier. Symmetry Detection and Dynamic Variable Ordering of Decision Diagrams. *Proc. ICCAD*, 628–631, 1994.
14. R. Rudell. Dynamic Variable Ordering for Ordered Binary Decision Diagrams. *Proc. ACM/IEEE ICCAD*, 42–47, 1993.
15. F. Somenzi. CUDD: CU Decision Diagram Package. Release 2.1.2. *University of Colorado, Boulder(ftp://vlsi.colorado.edu/pub/)*, 1997.
16. D. Sieling, and I. Wegener. Reduction of BDDs in Linear Time, *Information Processing Letters*, 48(3):139-144, 1993.
17. P. Savický, and I. Wegener. Efficient Algorithms for the Transformation Between Different Types of Binary Decision Diagrams *Acta Informatica*, 34:245-256, 1997.
18. S. Tani, K. Hamaguchi, and S. Yajima. The Complexity of the Optimal Variable Ordering Problem of Shared Binary Decision Diagrams. *Proc. ISAAC*, (LNCS 762):389–398, 1993.

Determining Type of TIL Construction
with Verb Valency Analyser

Pavel Smrž and Aleš Horák

Faculty of Informatics, Masaryk University Brno
Botanická 68a, 602 00 Brno, Czech Republic**
{smrz,hales}@fi.muni.cz

Abstract. In our paper we discuss an approach to semiautomatic corpus
processing aimed at analysing verb valencies in Czech and consecutive
determining the type of TIL (Transparent Intensional Logic) construction that belongs to the verb. Obtaining the type of the construction
is a corner-stone of the logical semantic analysis of sentences. TIL is a
highly suitable tool for representing the semantic structure of utterance
as it is presented later in the paper. Our approach is based on the technique of partial syntactic analysis using a special kind of LALR grammar
processing tool.

1 Introduction

Several approaches to semantic analysis have appeared during last decades. Many
authors in computationally oriented semantics work with the assumption that
knowledge of the meaning of a sentence can be equated with knowledge of its
truth conditions: that is, knowledge of what the world would be like if the sentence were true [1]. Traditionally the first order predicate logic was used for
the semantic description of language. As Montague [2] showed, this logic system
is able to capture an important range of the constructs but the range of valid
constructs in natural language is far wider. Montague and his followers try to
overcome this weakness. However, as Tichy showed in his book [3], the Montague Semantics can run into severe problems when analysing certain kind of
sentences, which are commonly used in natural language. That is why TIL was
designed to represent semantic structure of the language by constructions.

TIL, or Transparent Intensional Logic, similarly as Montague Semantics, follows Frege's principle of compositionality, i.e. "The meaning of a sentence is a
function of the meanings of its constituents" [4]. The basic idea of TIL lies in the
presupposition that every well-defined language has a definite intensional base
which can be explicated by an "epistemic" framework. Tichy uses an unspecified
epistemic framework with objectual base E which is a set of four types that
form the basis of type hierarchy. Every entity that can be discussed in a natural
language has its equivalent of the appropriate type over the base E. The TIL

** The research is sponsored by the Czech Ministry of Education under the grant
   VS97028

object that represents the entity described by the analyzed expression is referenced not by some sort of name but rather as a construction of the object. The construction records relations among elementary parts of the discourse (words or word groups with a special meaning as a whole). That is why constructions can be advantageously used for expressing the semantics of natural language.

The aim of TIL semantic analysis is to find an algorithm for associating language expression with equivalent construction. There is a three-leg way from the language expression to the (real world) object it identifies. The first step from the expression to the construction is a subject of semantic analysis. The connection between a construction and the constructed TIL object (the second part) is always fact-independent and it is directed by the mechanism of typed lambda calculus and thus it is well defined. The last leg of the journey is (mostly) dependent on the knowledge of the facts that hold in (and form) the actual world at the actual time.

In computational linguistics researchers try to device analytical tools that can process large amounts of corpus data without the need of human supervision. Automatic analysis based on TIL needs to find a translation algorithm that takes as its input a natural language sentence and outputs the corresponding TIL construction. The corner-stone of sentence meaning analysis is the semantics of the verb group with its arguments. Analysis of the verb groups are often based on Fillmore's semantic cases [5], verb frames and verb valencies.

Fillmore's semantic cases and verb frames are not suitable enough for Czech language which displays quite complicated case system (7 cases in both numbers). In Czech grammatical tradition, which prefers rather dependency oriented approach to syntax, valencies are widely used. If we decided to use Fillmore's semantic cases, we would have to somehow solve the conflicts between "deep" semantic cases and "real" grammatical cases existing in Czech. Our valency notation makes it possible to work with all 7 cases (nominative, genitive, dative, accusative, vocative, locative and instrumental) directly (to show an example). If there is a further need for semantic specification of the cases, it can be done by means of the appropriate semantic features and selectional restrictions.

2   Verb Valencies

In the following text we use the concepts of *valency expression* and *valency pattern* or valency. Valency expression is a schematic notation of a noun or adverb group or a clause, that expresses the requested obligatory attributes of the group or clause. Valency pattern for a given verb is formed by a set of valency expressions that express a scheme of a semantically correct part of sentence which contains the verb and appropriate noun or adverb groups or clauses. For example, the verb vyvozovat (infer) has two different valency patterns:

```
vyvozovat něco z něčeho      infer something from something
vyvozovat z něčeho , že      infer from something that
```

The format used for valency representation must be designed so that complies with the following requirements:

1. it describes all the syntactic information of the relationship between verbs and its arguments
2. it is easy to parse with computer tools
3. at the same time it must be effectively decodable by a human

The format we present meets the above points. The format describes the valency expression schema using the attribute-value pairs. The basic attributes and their values are enlisted in table 1.

Table 1. The basic attributes of used valency notation

attribute h type (semantic features)	attribute c case (grammatical features)	attribute s clause (syntactic features)	attribute r preposition (syntactic features)
P, person	1, nominative	I, infinitive	*particular*
T, thing	2, genitive	C, conj. až	*preposition*
Q, quality	3, dative	D, conj. že	*in curly*
R, reflexive	4, accusative	F, conj. zda	*braces*
M, amount	5, vocative	P, conj. at'	
L, location	6, locative	R, rel. clause	
A, direction from	7, instrumental	U, conj. aby	
F, direction to		Z, conj. jak	
D, gen. direction			
W, time			

The transcription of valency patterns for the above mentioned verb vyvozo-vat then looks like this:

```
vyvozovat <v>hTc4-hTc2r{z},hTc2r{z}-sD
```

One can make an objection to the readability of the format. Actually linguists working with valencies may use the "verbose" format which corresponds to the linguistic tradition of valency notation in Czech. Of course, both the formats are equivalent to the feature structure representations usually assumed in recent grammatical theories.

3   Building a Valency List

Linguistics has been using the concept of verb valency for a long time, but, without the advantage of computer tools, the work with valencies is a very lengthy and inevitably incomplete process, the results of which are of informative value only. At present new ways of getting and exploiting a valency list of a language seem to appear.

1. The first technique of building a list of verb valencies is the "manual" technique, when a researcher writes down valencies according to his or her linguistic knowledge or intuition. This technique, even if it may look archaic and inefficient way in computer processing, seems to be a needful one. Until complete and errorless tools for automatic processing of valencies are developed, the "manual" technique is convenient for making corrections and additions to the list or for building the core of the list.

2. The next technique, that is good to begin with when creating a valency list, consists in taking up a list of valencies that can be found in the form of a dictionary (see [6], [7]) after converting it into the electronic form. Although this technique is a good starting point, some typical difficulties arise during its realization, like a lack of the electronic version of the printed dictionary or inconsistent and out-of-date contents of such "manually" created list.

3. The third technique is based on exploring a language via its representative — text corpus (see [8, 9]). If the corpus is large enough and satisfactorily exemplifying the language (which are the assumptions of a well built corpus), then this corpus technique is the most accurate one of all the stated techniques of building a valency list. It is highly probable that we can find all (used) variants of a given verb in corpus, and it is certain that all valency patterns which are obtained from corpus, are up-to-date, they are being used. An important feature of this technique is the possibility to obtain complete results, that do not contain processing errors, in a rather short time (when compared to the "manual" techniques). An initial disadvantage of the corpus technique is the need of tools working with raw natural language texts and capable of getting the verb valency patterns out of the text only with knowledge of grammatical attributes of the words that can be found in a tagged corpus. If we do not have tools for syntactic analysis or its output available, then the necessary tools must be relatively sophisticated programs, especially in case of variform Slavonic languages (Czech).

4 The Technique of Partial Syntactic Analysis

The partial syntactic analysis is conducted by the GC system. This system works with an LALR(1) grammar that allows the shift-reduce conflict to appear in any state. Such conflict is solved by successive processing of both branches of analysis.

The input to GC is essentially context-free grammar in machine-readable Backus-Naur Form (BNF) [10]. The description of contextual actions connected to each rule of the grammar contains higher grammatical functions that perform additional tests. The grammar is entered in this form:

```
noun-with-proper-names-group  -> NOUN
```

```
              propagate_all($1)
noun-with-proper-names-group  ->  proper-name-group
              propagate_all($1)
noun-with-proper-names-group  ->  NOUN proper-name-group
              agree_case_number_gender_and_propagate($1,$2)
```

The GC system reads an input sequence of tokens (words tagged with a morphological analyser) and processes it according to the grammatical rules. If the input is correct, the system outputs a derivative tree of the given natural language sentence.

As we mentioned above some pre-defined grammatical tests and procedures can be used in the description of context actions associated with each grammatical rule of the system. We use the following tests:

- grammatical case test for particular words and noun groups

```
noun-genitive-group  ->  noun-group noun-group
            test_genitive($2)
            propagate_all($1)
```

- agreement test of case in prepositional construction

```
prepositional-group  ->  PREPOSITION noun-group
            agree_case_and_propagate($1,$2)
            add_prep_ngroup($1)
```

- agreement test of number and gender for relative pronouns

```
noun-group-with-rel-pron  ->  noun-group ',' rel-pron-group
            agree_number_gender_and_propagate($1,$3)
```

- agreement test of case, number and gender for noun groups

```
adj-noun-group  ->  adj-group noun-group
            agree_case_number_gender_and_propagate($1,$2)
```

- test of agreement between subject and predicate
- test of the verb valencies

```
clause  ->  subj-part verb-part
            agree_subj_pred($1,$2)
            test_valency_of($2)
```

The contextual actions propagate_all and *_and_propagate propagate all relevant grammatical information from the nonterminals on the right hand side to the one on the left side of the rule.

During the analysis the GC system builds a list of noun groups and adverbial groups (procedures add_ngroup, add_prep_ngroup and add_adverb_group) and a list of verb forms (add_verb). The relevant grammatical features of noun and adverbial groups are extracted and translated into valency patterns of found verbs. Eventually the valencies may be confronted with valencies from the existing list [11].

5 Assigning TIL Type According to Valencies Found

We use the valency list obtained by means of the GC system when we want to find the logical construction that corresponds to the verb meaning.

Having the valency list we want to find a distribution of all verbs into classes of equivalence. As equivalent we regard those verbs whose valency lists are similar. The algorithm of finding the similar valency lists for verbs first modifies the original valency list. The modifications are as follows:

1. In the valency list the valency expressions that are formed by a noun group with preposition (hPr{} or hTr{}) are (where it is possible) replaced by one of the expression hL (location), hF (direction from), hA (direction to), hD (way description) or hW (time).
   This mechanism is very important since we work with "raw" data from syntactic analysis as described in the previous paragraph. Thus the information about location, direction or time is often expressed in the form of a noun group with preposition which has to be translated into the corresponding valency.
2. The valency expressions of location and time are deleted from the valency patterns. The reason for this is that these expressions often represent adjuncts that display circumstantial meaning.
3. The valency lists for verbs modified in the previous steps are then sorted and duplicate valency expressions are left out. Resulting valency lists are compared eventually.

In such a way it is possible to define a decomposition of the set of verbs into classes of equivalence. The verbs in each class then share the same type of logical construction.

The Transparent Intensional Logic works with a hierarchy of types with the following four basic types: ι (individuals), o (truth values), τ (real numbers or time moments) and ω (possible worlds). Other types are then created as functions from one type to another one or as types of higher rank, that can run over constructions. Some important types are $\iota_{\tau\omega}$ (individual role), $(o\iota)_{\tau\omega}$ (a class of individuals or a property) or $(o\alpha\beta)_{\tau\omega}$ (an intensional relation between objects of types α and β).

If we want to translate a sentence into a construction, we first need to know the type of constructions that correspond to particular words in the sentence. Among them the construction representing a verb usually forms the basic part of the resulting construction and constructions of other words form its arguments. To determine the type of the verb construction seems to be more difficult than it is perhaps with a noun.

The classification of verbs described above divides verbs into groups with the same type of construction. Moreover, it is possible to formulate rules for deducing the type directly from the valency list for a verb. We derive the type from the valency list of a verb class in the following way — first we construct a set of all valency expressions that appear in the valency list for a verb, so called multi-valency. The multi-valency is a schema of all possible expressions that can be tied with the verb, the verb "arguments". It also shows the number and kind of each argument. We assume that the verb expresses a relation between (at most) these arguments. In the sentence where some of these expressions are not present, the corresponding arguments are filled with null values. This approach allows to fill in a value of an argument that is missing in the sentence but is known from the preceding text and thus it semantically belongs to the verb.

The expressions are translated to verb arguments in the following ways:

1. hQ (property) is regarded as a property of individuals, $(o\iota)_{\tau\omega}$-objects.
2. hM (amount) expresses a number of some individuals, it is an extensional (not dependent on the actual world or time) relation between a number and an individual or individuals, a $(o\tau\iota)$-object (logical object of type $(o\tau\iota)$).
3. hP (person) and hT (thing) can express an individual role or a class of individuals, thus it has type $\iota_{\tau\omega}$ or $(o\iota)_{\tau\omega}$. Only during the analysis of a particular sentence it can be determined which one of these types should be used and in some cases it cannot be determined at all since the respective expression can be ambiguous.
4. hA (where to), hF (where from), hD (which way) and hR (reflexive pronoun) usually serve as modificators of the verb meaning. Therefore they do not change the type of the verb construction, they are functions that show the logical object expressing the modified meaning of a verb.
5. all sX expressions refer to another construction, thus they are of a higher rank type $*_n$.

For example, if we process the valency list of the verb mít (have) with the algorithm, we obtain a multi-valency hA-hF-hPTc4-hPTc4r{za}-hPTc7r{s}-sI, which yields the following construction[1]:

$$\lambda w/\omega.\lambda t/\tau.\lambda k do/I.\lambda koho\_co/I.\lambda za\_koho\_co/I.\lambda s\_kym\_cim/I.\lambda inf/*_n .$$
$$[^0 kam/((o*_n IIII)(o*_n IIII)_{\tau\omega})_{wt}$$
$$[^0 odkud/((o*_n IIII)(o*_n IIII)_{\tau\omega})_{wt}$$
$$^0 mit/(o*_n IIII_{\tau\omega})_{wt}]],$$

where $I = \iota_{\tau\omega}$ or $(o\iota)_{\tau\omega}$.

The construction can be schematically written as

```
modifier_where_to(modifier_where_from(
   have(
      sb_nomin,sb_st_accus,as sb_st_accus,with sb_st_instr,inf
   )
))
```

The constructions obtained by means of verb valencies represent the way how to extract the attributes of the verb meaning from the syntactic structure of the sentence.

---

[1] The object and variable names in the construction translated to English:
$\lambda w.\lambda t.\lambda sb\_nomin.\lambda sb\_st\_accus.\lambda as\_sb\_st\_accus.\lambda with\_sb\_st\_instr.\lambda inf.$
$[^0 where\_to_{wt} [^0 where\_from_{wt} {}^0 have_{wt}]]$

6 Conclusions

The most important results lie in the implementation of the algorithm of partial syntactic analysis of Czech language that can automatically discover verb valencies in corpus data. We have also introduced an algorithm for determining the type of TIL construction associated with the verb meaning according to the list of its valency patterns. This procedure plays a key role in the system of TIL semantic analysis.

References

1. Pulman, S. G.,Language Analysis and Understanding, in *Survey of the State of the Art in Human Language Technology*, R. A. Cole, editor, pp 122–129, URL: http://www.cse.ogi.edu/CSLU/HLTsurvey/
2. Montague, R., The Proper Treatment of Quantification in Ordinary English, in *Approaches to Natural Language*, Hintikka, J., editor, pp 221–242, Reidel, 1973
3. Tichý, P.: *The Foundations of Frege's Logic*, de Gruyter, Berlin, New York, 1988
4. Frege G., Über sinn und bedeutung (On Sense and Reference), in Geach and Black, editors, *Translations from the Philosophical Writings of Gottlob Frege*, Blackwell, Oxford, translation 1960
5. Fillmore, C., "The Case for Case," *Universals in Linguistic Theory*, New York, 1968, pp. 1-88
6. Filipec, J., et al., *Slovník spisovné češtiny* (The Dictionary of Literary Czech), Academia, Prague, 1994
7. *Slovník spisovného jazyka českého* (The Dictionary of Literary Czech Language), Academia, Prague, 1989
8. Pala, K., Rychlý, P., Smrž, P., DESAM — approaches to disambiguation. Technical Report FIMU-RS-97-09, Faculty of Informatics, Masaryk University, Brno, 1997.
9. Pala, K., Rychlý, P., Smrž, P., "DESAM — Annotated Corpus for Czech," *Lecture Notes in Computer Science 1338*, SOFSEM'97, pp. 523–530
10. Aho, A. V., Sethi, R., Ullman, J. D., *Compilers — Principles, Techniques, and Tools*, Addison-Wesley, 1986.
11. Pala, K., Ševeček, P., "Valence českých sloves" (Valencies of Czech Verbs), *Proceedings of Works of Philosophical Faculty at the University of Brno*, Brno, 1997, pp. 41-54

Off-Line Recognition of Cursive Handwritten Czech Text

Pavel Smrž, Štěpán Hrbáček and Michal Martinásek

Faculty of Informatics, Masaryk University Brno
Botanická 68a, 602 00 Brno, Czech Republic
E-mail: {smrz,xhrbacek,xmartin}@fi.muni.cz

Abstract. In this paper a part of the system for recognising off-line cursive Czech text is presented. Recently, various systems for recognition of cursive English text has been developed, however, to our knowledge no method has been presented yet for Czech, a language rich in diacritic marks. This paper deals with preprocessing which is different for Czech and English handwritten texts. For finding the letter boundaries a method based on minimising a heuristic cost function has been used.

1 Introduction

Handwritten form of a language is used in notebooks, personal letters, on envelopes, cheques, etc. Taking into account the possible importance of these documents the benefits of automatic recognition of handwritten texts are obvious.

The problem of handwritten character recognition can be subdivided into two categories: off-line recognition [1–3] and on-line recognition [4, 5]. On-line recognition deals with real-time data processing and has the ability to integrate pen-movement and pressure information. Off-line recognition, however, is based on a static input of the data and relies only on pixel information for the recognition of each word [6].

Off-line cursive script recognition has progressed in the past thirty years from a novelty to a technology that can be implemented into commercial applications. Processing the characters with diacritic marks that are common in Czech, however, still represents a problem and has not been satisfactory solved yet. This paper deals with the preprocessing part of cursive script recognition in which specific features of a language rich in diacritic marks play the key role.

2 Finding Text Line Boundaries

Before starting let us define a useful term we will use in the following text: Smoothed pixel density histogram s is a histogram defined as follows:

$$s(i) = \sum_{j=-2..2} h(i+j),\qquad(1)$$

where $h(i)$ is a pixel density histogram at the point i.

Splitting the page to rows is the first step which needs specific handling in Czech. The typical profile of a horizontal smoothed pixel density histogram for an English text is shown in the Fig. 1a. In the case of a Czech text this typical form is disturbed due to the acute accents and inverted circumflexes that influence especially the characteristic form in the ascender part (see Fig. 1b). Algorithms looking for the boundaries of the text rows could not be therefore based on searching characteristic patterns in the horizontal histogram because the style of the upper part of the histogram differs in Czech texts not only according to the style of writing (the slant of acute accents and position of writing of the inverted circumflexes) but also to the contents of the text (the number of diacritic marks above the characters on the row).

(a)   (b)

Fig. 1. Histograms of handwriting: a) in English, b) in Czech

The second problem we deal with in this part is the position of acute accents and inverted circumflexes above the text. Acute accents and inverted circumflexes may be too high above the text and a simple algorithm for finding the text rows could consider them an independent row. We have solved this problem in this way: We suppose that the rows have approximately the same height on the whole page. After an initial estimation of text lines the algorithm adjoins too low rows to the following row. Based on our experiments it is reasonable to assume that true rows are only those which are higher than a half of an average row.

We have tried to find the borders of a line as precisely as possible. The rows of a written text in Czech usually have not straight line boundaries. The boundaries are often overlapped due to acute accents and inverted circumflexes and due to characters descending beneath the lower boundary. For the first approximation of boundaries we should calculate the horizontal smoothed histogram and estimate the baselines for all rows. Then the contour following algorithm may be used for the parts of characters which overlap the low borderline in order to find precise row boundaries. Possible problems with some thin and slanted strokes can be avoided by using the 3x3 Gaussian mask for the scanned picture of handwriting before the algorithm is applied.

3 Splitting Rows To Words

The first phase of row processing is based on finding the reference lines. The reference lines of a text line are the four horizontal lines that mark the top of the ascenders, the top of the main bodies of letters, the baseline and the bottom of the descenders [7]. This phase should not be biased by Czech diacritic marks. The only exception may be the situation when the acute accents and inverted circumflexes are positioned too low above the text. In this case it may be a problem to find the top reference line.

Let us suppose that the slant of a writing on a particular row is known and we are trying to use it for splitting the row to words which is a logical continuation of the whole process. The problems which arise are similar to that with splitting a page to rows so that we can use an analogous way to solve them. First we calculate the vertical histogram at the same angle as that of the slant of written text and smooth it again. Then the spaces between the words may be estimated using the values of calculated histogram (text density). This approach works well if a good method for the estimation is employed. Corrections of erroneously split rows are possible after the words are recognised by comparing them with a dictionary.

Serious problems could arise by an improper positioning of acute accents and inverted circumflexes at the end of a word. If they are written too far behind the text the algorithm could separate them as an individual word. To avoid this situation a horizontal histogram for every short word is computed. The process reveals whether the word found in this way is located on the baseline of the text. A diacritic mark found in this way is joined to the precedent word.

4 Extracting Style Parameters of Czech Text

In the previous section we supposed that the slant of writing is known. The way to obtain its value along with other important characteristics of writing is described in following text.

Histograms are not sufficient for the phase of splitting the words. The inner structure of particular words is more complex than the structure of the whole page or a row. Therefore, it is necessary to calculate the following parameters that characterise the word to be split:

- dominant slant of writing
- thickness of the pen
- average width of characters
- average height of characters

It is obvious that the result of splitting the words largely depends on the accuracy of determination of particular parameters. To minimise the inaccuracy it is necessary to work not only with average values of these parameters but also with their deviations and to take them into consideration when the word is split.

The basic parameter used in handling with words is the slant of writing. All the methods mentioned in the following text are based on it. Let h be a histogram. Define $d(h)$ as a sum of differences of all pairs of adjacent values in histogram h. To determine the slant of writing the vertical histograms at angles of $-20, -10, 0, 10, 20, 30$ degrees are created and the value of $d(h)$ is calculated for all of them. The angle with a minimum value is to be considered the dominant slant.

The vertical histogram for the dominant slant of writing can be used to find the thickness of the pen. As the average thickness of the pen the average of the set containing the smallest non-zero elements of the histogram in a given range is employed.

To determine the average width of characters we calculate the vertical histogram at the dominant slant angle. Then we search for places where the histogram value approximately equals to the determined width of the pen and the histogram values are rising on the right side. We calculate the average of the distances between these points as well as their deviations. The determination of the average width of characters already in this phase is rather difficult and the result is not fully reliable. Moreover, the characters like **n, u, m, w**, etc. can be misread as pairs or triples of letters. This problem can be eliminated in the phase of recognition and postprocessing only.

In the determination of the average height of characters we can considerably simplify the task by using the height of the highest character as the searched value.

Vertical histograms are influenced by the diacritic marks much more than the horizontal ones. The determination of the slant of writing is influenced by diacritic marks because the slant of the acute accents and the style of writing of inverted circumflexes considerably affect the histogram computed at different angles. The style of writing diacritic marks may differ from writing style of true letters and there is a risk that the slant of writing the marks could override the true slant of writing in case of short rows with a relative large number of letters with diacritic marks. The determination of the average width of characters could be also influenced by an improper position of acute accents. The influence of diacritic marks can be eliminated by a proper heuristics. Therefore, we use the values based on the histogram of the whole rows in which the deviation are eliminated by averaging.

5 Finding Letter Boundaries

The process of splitting words can begin after all style parameters are determined. The influence of diacritic marks is critical in this part of processing. In this stage we work only with particular words. Therefore, the deviations in vertical histograms are not eliminated by averaging so that they can lead to misinterpretation of data. The slant of acute accents manifests itself by strong jumps in the histogram which prevent the algorithm from finding the position of letters. Simply, the algorithm designed for splitting letters in English texts does not work for Czech texts.

The solution of this problem can be temporal elimination of diacritic marks. It is performed by using the algorithm for finding single graphical objects in the upper part of the row. Then the original algorithm for splitting words into particular characters can be applied. However, problems may arise where diacritic marks are adjoined back to the letters because the acute accents and inverted circumflexes are not written at the constant place with respect to the position of the letter they belong to. Therefore, we decided not to attach the diacritics back to the text in this phase but to process it separately. A Czech text in which diacritic marks are absent is processed in the same way as an English text (including the recognition of particular letters). Diacritic marks are then adjoined to the final text. Re-attachement of diacritic marks based on a language model only to the letters where it is possible considerably improves usefulness of the algorithm.

The algorithm for splitting words is described in the following paragraphs [7]:

In the first phase the procedure is similar to the determination of the width of characters. Based on the prevalent slant of writing we choose the set of four angles in its neighbourhood and apply the algorithm for the determination of the width of characters to the histograms at corresponding slants with the following changes: When a proper place for division is found we add its position to the set M which was initialised to be empty. This process is repeated for all chosen angles. The set M can be, therefore, considered the set of candidates for division of a given word and our task is to use the most appropriate one. It is useful to order the set M after all candidates are added.

The first point in the ordered set M is chosen as the initial new point of division. Then we create the set N of points which are from the initial point distant of less than a half of the average width of character. This points we remove from the set M. In the next step we remove the point with the smallest value of the cost function (defined later) from the set N and insert it to the set Q of the final division points. This process is repeated until the set M is empty. Finally we unify the points in the set Q the inter-distance of which is less than a quarter of the width of characters. It is probable that such points correspond to the same boundary of a character.

The detailed algorithm can be described by the following steps:

1. Find the division point p
2. Let the threshold point t be at a distance of a half of the width of character from p.
3. Let the set N be the set of division points between p and t
4. If there are more division points with the same angle in the set N, delete all the points after the second one.
5. Chose the division point q with the smallest value of the cost function from the set N and insert it to the set Q
6. Unify the points in the distance less than one quarter of a character in the set Q

Finally we need to define the above mentioned cost function:

$$cost\,(\alpha, p) = w_1 \left(\frac{p - pp}{ew}\right)^2 - w_2 \left(\frac{p - pp}{ew}\right) + w_3\,(tc) + w_4\,(hc) \qquad (2)$$

The function is defined for the pair (α, p) where α is the angle of the division line and p is the position of the division point on the baseline. pp is the position of the previous division point on the baseline, ew is the average width of characters, tc is the number of pixels intersected by the division line normalised by the average width of the pen, and hc is the height of the highest point intersected by the division line normalised by the height of the row. Experimentally found constants w_1, w_2, w_3, w_4 control the correct division of letter pairs and triplets.

References

1. C. Faure and E. Lecolinet. OCR: Handwriting. In R. A. Cole et al, editor, *Survey of the State of the Art in Human Language Technology*, pages 86–89. Center for Spoken Language Understanding, Oregon Graduate Institute, 1995. http://www.cse.ogi.edu/CSLU/HLTsurvey/ch2node6.html.
2. P. Smrž. Handwritten characters recognition, 1995. (in Czech).
3. A. W. Senior. Off-line handwriting recognition: A review and experiments. Technical Report CUED/F-INFENG/TR 105, Cambridge University Engineering Department, December 1992.
4. C. Higgins and P. Bramall. An on-line cursive script recognition system. In M. L. Simner, C. G. Leedham, and A. J. W. M. Thomassen, editors, *Handwriting and Drawing Research — Basic and Applied Issues*, pages 285–298. IOS Press, 1996.
5. R. K. Powalka, N. Sherkat, L. J. Evett, and R. J.Whitrow. Dynamic cursive script recognition: A hybrid approach. In *Advances in Handwriting and Drawing: A multidisciplinary approach*, 1994.
6. S. Wesolkowski. Cursive script recognition: A survey. In M. L. Simner, C. G. Leedham, and A. J. W. M. Thomassen, editors, *Handwriting and Drawing Research — Basic and Applied Issues*, pages 267–284. IOS Press, 1996.
7. B. A. Yanikoglu and P. A. Sandon. Off-line cursive handwriting recognition using style parameters. Technical Report PCS-TR93-192, Department of Mathematics and Computer Science, Dartmouth College, Hanover, NH, June 1993.

Automated Theorem Proving in a Combination of Theories with Disjoint Signatures

Pavel Vanousek

Dpt. of theoretical Computer Science, MFF, Charles University,
Malostranské nám. 25, 118 00 Prague 1, Czech Republic
vanousek@kti.ms.mff.cuni.cz

Abstract. We present a method for automated theorem proving in a combination of theories with disjoint signatures. The Nelson-Oppen combination technique for decision procedures is used to combine separate theorem provers in different theories. The provers being combined are based on the Prolog Technology Theorem Proving method and they use the SLD resolution (alternatively Model Elimination) as an inference system. Our approach enables to tune up the provers for different theories separately and increases the efficiency of automated theorem proving in a combination of theories.

1 Introduction

The specifications of hardware and software systems often involve huge sets of axioms and that is the reason, why such systems are often described in a modular fashion - using structured specifications [10, 24]. The theorem proving is needed to support the process of the development of such systems from their formal specifications. The modularity of the structured specifications may be used in the process of theorem proving, as it enables to prove something in a context of a given subspecification without considering the whole structured specification. Although such a process typically requires user interaction, some parts of it can be automated.

Since first order automated theorem proving can be used to support this process of systems development [11, 15, 16], it is desirable to study the techniques of automated theorem proving in structured specifications, so that the automated theorem prover can benefit from the modularity of the theory.

This paper deals with the automation of the process of proving in a combination of theories, keeping the proving activities in the combined theories separated. We show that this approach can improve the efficiency of automated theorem proving in the combination of theories in comparison with the method of *flattening* of the theory, when the axioms of the combined theories are treated in one set.

The paper is organized as follows: Section 2 describes the Nelson-Oppen combination technique for decision procedures. In section 3, we present an algorithm that combines this technique with the SLD resolution. The extension of the algorithm for Non-Horn theories is shortly discussed in section 4. In section 5 we present some experimental results and the last section concludes.

2 The Nelson-Oppen combination technique

In this section, we will describe the Nelson-Oppen combination technique for decision procedures [5, 12, 20]. The method integrates decision procedures for quantifier free decidable theories (denoted T_i) with disjoint signatures ($sig(T_i) \cap sig(T_j)$ is empty for $i \neq j$) into a decision procedure for their union.

We say that t is an *i-term* if it is a variable or it has a form $f(s)$ and $f \in sig(T_i)$. A subterm s of t is an *alien subterm* if t is an i-term and s is maximal subterm of t, such that s is a j-term for $j \neq i$. If the *i-term* t contains only symbols from $sig(T_i)$ and variables, we call it a *pure* (i-)term. These definitions can be straightforwardly extended to atomic formulas (we can separate them into theories using the predicate symbol instead of the top function symbol of a term). We will refer to the theories T_i as *basic theories*.

To decide a formula F in a combination of theories $T = \bigcup_i T_i$ with the above stated properties:

1. Convert the formula $\neg F$ into a disjunctive normal form. It is sufficient to show that any conjunction is unsatisfiable to determine the validity of F

2. In the conjunction Φ, *homogenize* each literal (based on its predicate / top term for equality) so that alien subterms are replaced by variables and appropriate equality is added to this conjunct. Exactly, for a literal L with predicate belonging to the theory T_i (or a top term function symbol belonging to T_i in case the literal is an equality) find in each argument the (largest) subterm t with the top function symbol f such that f does not belong to signature of T_i. This subterm t is replaced by a new variable x (we will call these newly introduced variables shared variables) and an equality $x = t$ is added to the conjunction. This process is applied recursively and to all the literals, so that after the homogenization each literal contains just predicate and function symbols from one theory (we will say that the literal belongs to T_i). (See example on Fig.1)

3. Split the resulting conjunction to conjunctions Φ_i such that just all the literals from Φ_i belong to T_i .

4. If Φ_i is unsatisfiable in T_i for some i, then Φ is unsatisfiable in T

5. If a disjunction of equalities for shared variables $x_1 = y_1 \vee \ldots \vee x_k = y_k$ can be deduced from Φ_i in T_i (This can be decided using decision procedure for $\Phi_i \wedge x_1 \neq y_1 \wedge \ldots \wedge x_k \neq y_k$. Further, there are finitely many shared variables and therefore finitely many possible disjunction of equalities, i.e. the problem of finding all the disjunctions is decidable) propagate the equalities into other theories. Exactly, for any disjunct of equalities $x_j = y_j$ add $x_j = y_j$ to Φ_k for any k and apply recursively this procedure (from point 4). If for all disjuncts the result is unsatisfiable, then Φ is unsatisfiable in T. If there are no disjunctions that can be deduced from any Φ_i in T_i (and the point 4. did not determine unsatisfiability) or for some deduced equality $x_j = y_j$, $\Phi_k \wedge x_j = y_j$ is satisfiable for all k, then Φ is satisfiable in T.

In the example (Fig.1), we can see the case, when the propagation of a disjunction of equalities between theories is necessary to show unsatisfiability.

$T_1 \equiv \{\forall x, y \, (q(x, y) \wedge (x = y) \Rightarrow p(x))\}$
$T_2 \equiv \{\forall x (f(f(x)) = f(x) \vee f(f(f(x))) = f(x))\}$
$T \equiv T_1 \cup T_2$
We want to decide if : $T \vdash q(f(x), f(f(f(x)))) \wedge q(f(x), f(f(x)))) \Rightarrow p(f(x))$

1. negation: $q(f(x), f(f(f(x)))) \wedge q(f(x), f(f(x)))) \wedge \neg p(f(x))$
2. homogenization: $q(u, v) \wedge u = f(x) \wedge v = f(f(f(x)))$
   $\wedge \, q(u', v') \wedge u' = f(x) \wedge v' = f(f(x))) \wedge \neg p(w) \wedge w = f(x)$
3. $\Phi_1 = q(u, v) \wedge q(u', v') \wedge \neg p(w)$,
   $\Phi_2 = (u = f(x) \wedge v = f(f(f(x)))) \wedge u' = f(x) \wedge v' = f(f(x))) \wedge w = f(x))$
4. $T_2, \Phi_2 \vdash w = u$
5. $T_2, \Phi_2 \vdash w = u'$
6. $T_2, \Phi_2 \vdash u = v \vee u' = v'$
7. $T_1, \Phi_1, w = u, w = u', u = v$ is unsatisfiable
8. $T_1, \Phi_1, w = u, w = u', u' = v'$ is also unsatisfiable and therefore
   $T, q(f(x), f(f(f(x)))) \wedge q(f(x), f(f(x)))) \wedge \neg p(f(x))$ is unsatisfiable i.e.
   $T \vdash q(f(x), f(f(f(x)))) \wedge q(f(x), f(f(x)))) \Rightarrow p(f(x))$

Fig. 1. Example of the use of Nelson-Oppen combination method

The disjunction of equalities causes branching (called split in [12]) in the above described algorithm and therefore has an impact on its efficiency. It is often the case, that just single equalities (and not the disjunctions with two or more members) can be deduced from the theories. These theories are called *convex* theories.

The algorithm given above is complete with further assumptions on the theories [2, 20]: The theories T_i have to be *stably infinite*, which means, that every formula F is satisfiable in T_i iff it is satisfiable in some infinite model of T.

3   Combination of Nelson-Oppen procedure with SLD resolution

The combination techniques for decision procedures over union of theories can be rather straightforwardly extended for theorem proving in a combination of theories. We will require, that the combined theories have disjoint signature (the result is extendable to the case when they can share constant symbols using results from [2]). We have to overcome several difficulties to use theorem proving procedures instead of decision procedures:

1. As the theories considered may be undecidable, one has to cope with the fact, that the theorem proving procedures need not terminate in contrast with the decision procedures.
2. Proofs have to be assembled into a proof of the formula being proved. Another question arises in the context of a concrete deterministic algorithm: How to determine, which equalities among shared variables shall we try to solve (and in what theory) ?

We will concentrate on Horn theories, where SLD resolution (a goal driven strategy used in logic programming, also called backward chaining) is complete [1]. For Horn theories, there can be no splits in Nelson-Oppen algorithm. i.e. Horn theories are convex. The reason is that for a Horn theory, we have the least Herbrand model M_H of T [1] and therefore a proper disjunction of equalities (i.e. such that only one equality is valid in some models and only the second one in other models) cannot be a consequence of T.

Our algorithm uses iterative deepening search, i.e. the depth of a proof is restricted when searching for the proof. In case the proof cannot be found with a given depth bound, the depth bound is increased for the further attempt. That is the method of overcoming the potential undecidability of the theory. The propagation of equalities among underlying provers for different theories is ensured by a pool, where the proven equalities are stored, and which is accessible from all theories. As the underlying prover, we use a procedure realizing SLD resolution with bounded depth of search and with unit-lemma caching [14, 21]. We use some PROLOG notation in the following text, in particular we denote variables by uppercase letters and we speak about facts (unit clauses) and rules (non-unit clauses) of a theory.

Since the theorem prover based on SLD resolution is goal-driven, it is natural to generate equalities between shared variables, that would help to solve the goal and to store them in a second pool, where they can form a goal for proving in another theories. In these pools, the goals are stored along with their proofs. We will call the pools Pool-done (contains proved literals) and Pool-todo (contains equalities inferred by backward chaining as subgoals).

In the process of homogenization, we use terms of a form $v(x)$, $v(y)$ etc., instead of variables (here x and y mean constants). The reason is, we have to distinguish shared variables from the original variables. Our algorithm *solve_NOP* extends the underlying prover for unstructured theories:

The procedure *solve_NOP(Thy, Goal)*:

1. Do with a given depth limit for all proofs:
2. If a (homogenized) literal shall be proved in a combination of basic theories (*Thy*), select the theory where it belongs (using its signature) and try to prove it using the underlying prover (with proper facts and rules). The literals from *Pool-done* are accessible as facts in all basic theories.
3. If the literal of the form (i.e. unifiable with) $eq(v(X), v(Y))$, that means equality between shared variables, is the original goal or it is encountered as a subgoal, then
   (a) If the literal $eq(v(x), v(y))$ is on the *Pool-done*, then the subgoal is solved
   (b) If the literal $eq(v(x), v(y))$ is not on *the Pool-todo*, then insert it on this Pool and call *solve_iter_pool*
   (c) If the literal $eq(v(x), v(y))$ is on the *Pool-todo* and not on the *Pool-done*, then call *solve_iter_pool*
4. If the original literal was not solved (neither step 2 succeeded, nor it is on the *Pool-done*), increase the depth bound (add a positive number to current depth bound) and go to 1.

Procedure *solve_iter_pool* goes over all goals on the *Pool-todo* and over all combined theories and tries to solve the goals with a given depth limit until both *Pool-done* and *Pool-todo* become stable.

The procedure *solve_iter_pool*:

1. repeat
2. for all Goals ∈ *Pool-todo* do
3. for all Theories ∈ Combined Theory do
4. *solve_NOP(Theory, Goal)* but dont call *solve_iter_pool* recursively (!)
5. if Goal was solved then move it from *Pool-todo* to *Pool-done* (along with its proof)
6. od
7. od
8. until there is neither a change on *Pool-todo* nor any new literal on *Pool-done*

The underlying prover with the depth restriction will always terminate and it is correct and complete for Horn theories. The procedure *solve_NOP* without call to *solve_iter_pool* will therefore also halt. Then the *solve_iter_pool* procedure must be terminating as well, as there are just finitely many shared variables and therefore finitely many states of pools. From that we can immediately conclude that *solve_NOP* (including recursive calls to *solve_iter_pool*) is terminating for a given depth limit (i.e. with the depth limit bounded in the step 4, steps 2 and 3 will always terminate). For the proof of completeness, we assume that we combine two theories T_1 and T_2 (the proof for more theories being an obvious generalization). The notation $T_1 \cup T_2 \rhd A$ will in the following mean that the algorithm will find the proof of a positive literal A in a theory which is the combination of basic theories with axioms T_1 and T_2. $T_1 \cup T_2 \vdash A$ means, that A is provable from the union of axioms $T_1 \cup T_2$ using SLD resolution.

Theorem 1. *The above stated algorithm is sound and complete for theorem proving in a union of Horn theories with disjoint signatures i.e. $T_1 \cup T_2 \rhd A$ if and only if $T_1 \cup T_2 \vdash A$ We assume that the two theories T_1 and T_2 fulfill the requirements of the algorithm (solve_NOP) i.e. they have disjoint signatures, they are stably infinite and their union is consistent.*

Informally: We will denote Eq the contents of *Pool-done*. From the completeness of backward chaining and from axioms for equality, when it is possible to prove $T_i \cup Eq \vdash A$, we will get Eq as a subgoal using SLD resolution (as it will be in the body of some clause from T_i or some clause describing equality axioms). The subgoals $Eq_k \in Eq$ will get to the *Pool-todo* and will trigger the *solve_iter_pool* procedure (even in the case, the goal is already on the Pool). The *solve_iter_pool* procedure will solve Eq_k if it is possible in any T_j wrt. a given depth limit. While new equations are encountered as subgoals during *solve_iter_pool*, the procedure is repeated and therefore all possible equations among shared variables, deducible from T_j within the given depth limit that can help to establish $T \vdash A$ (using rules and facts from T_j) are proved and stored on Pool-done after the run of *solve_iter_pool*. As all the equalities stored on *Pool-done* are accessible to the provers in all theories, completeness wrt. a given depth limit follows from completeness of Nelson-Oppen technique and of underlying prover.

Formally: We want to prove: If $T_1 \cup T_2 \vdash A$ then $T_1 \cup T_2 \triangleright A$. As $T_1 \cup T_2 \vdash A$ then from completeness of SLD resolution there exists a SLD-refutation of $\neg A$ from $T_1 \cup T_2$. We will represent this refutation in a form of a proof tree with the root A, in which every branching corresponds to an application of a rule (with proper substitution propagated up through the tree, cf. [13, 21]). We will consider the whole tree with the resulting answer substitution δ applied to its nodes. The leafs of the tree correspond to the successful unifications with the facts (see Fig. 2). We will also assume that we run our algorithm with a depth limit big enough to construct the tree (that will always happen as the depth limit is iteratively increased until the goal is proved).

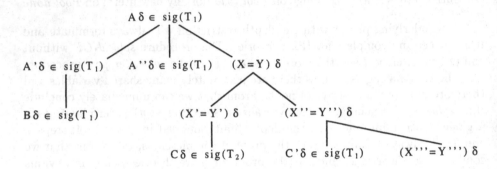

Fig. 2. A proof tree for goal A

Our proof is based on the fact, that the only nodes that can switch between theories are the nodes containing an equality between shared variables. More precisely, if there are two nodes on a path from root that contain literals expressed in different signatures $sig(T_i)$ and $sig(T_j)$ for $i \neq j$, then there has to be a node containing an equality between shared variables between these two nodes. The reason is that the signatures of the theories are disjoint (but for the pred. symbol of equality). We will prove the theorem using induction on the height of highest subtree of the proof tree that contains equality between shared variables in its root.

1. If there is no equality between shared variables in the tree, then all the literals in the tree belong syntactically to the same theory T_i, given by A. Hence $T_i \vdash A$ and $T_i \triangleright A$ i.e. our algorithm proves A (as the SLD resolution in a single theory is built in it - see *solve_NOP*, step 2).

2. If there is an equality between shared variables in the leaf of the tree, this equality has to be a fact in some T_i. In the SLD resolution process, this equality will be established as a subgoal and thus it will get to *Pool-todo* (in step 3 of our algorithm). After the call to *solve_iter_pool* it will get to *Pool-done* and algorithm succeeds for that subgoal (step 4). Hence, if the tree

contains equalities between shared variables just in the leafs, the algorithm will succeed for goal A by the same arguments as in the previous point, augmented by the fact that equalities in the leafs will be proved.

3. If there is a highest subtree of height k with an equality between shared variables $(X = Y)$ in the root of the proof tree, we will prove that the algorithm succeeds by induction on k. We got the result for $k = 1$ in point 2. As we have a complete inference mechanism (underlying prover - SLD resolution) built in our algorithm, we get some instantiation of the root equality literal as a subgoal $(X = Y)\sigma$. This subgoal gets to *Pool-todo* in step 3 of our algorithm and *solve_iter_pool* is called that tries to solve this subgoal in both theories using a recursive call of the algorithm. The algorithm will succeed on the subgoal and an instantiation $(X = Y)\delta$ will get to *Pool-done* by induction assumption (there can be just subtrees with equality in the root of the height less than k in the proof tree of the goal).

When the subgoal $(X = Y)\delta$ gets to the *Pool-done* the algorithm succeeds on A (point 1 of proof). In point 3 of our proof, it is necessary to consider the fact that *solve_iter_pool* is not called recursively, which seems to damage induction assumption. Nevertheless, the recursive call to *solve_iter_pool* is replaced by iteration of *solve_iter_pool* until *Pool-todo* becomes stable. Correctness of the algorithm *solve_NOP* follows directly from the fact that every derivation computed by *solve_NOP* is also a SLD derivation in $T_1 \cup T_2$.

4 Non Horn theories

The algorithm *solve_NOP* can be extended to cope with non-Horn theories. It can be combined with the method of Model Elimination [3, 18, 19] (resp. its variant Restart Model Elimination [3]) in order to become complete for the combination of any first order quantifier free theories with disjoint signatures. The basic idea of this extension is to store equalities on pool along with the set of their ancestors. The context of a goal, formed by its ancestors, can be used to perform reduction steps that extend the SLD inference mechanism to become complete. As we cannot describe this method more thoroughly here, due to the lack of space, we refer to [23] for details.

5 Experimental results

We have undertaken several experiments with our prover, based on the ideas described in previous sections. The prover was implemented in Prolog, based on ideas of Prolog Technology Theorem Prover [14, 18, 19] with caching [14, 21]. We used examples from the domain of formal methods, namely we proved some statements in the specifications of data structures like lists or arrays combined with theories describing linear arithmetics and equality for uninterpreted function and predicate symbols. The tasks 1,2 come from [5], where they are solved using Nelson-Oppen technique and decision procedures, task 3 is based on a structured specification from [6]. For exact axiomatization see [23]. As an example, we present task 2, which was to prove:

$$(x \leq y \wedge y \leq x + Head([0,x]) \wedge P(f(x) - f(y))) \Rightarrow P(0)$$

where P resp. f are uninterpreted function symbols and $Head$ means a head of a list.

We compared our (structured) approach with the case, when the structure was *flattened*, i.e. the axioms of all the theories being combined were grouped together into one resulting theory. The results showed that the theorem proving in structured specifications can benefit from keeping the structure even when the theorem provers for separate theories are not specifically tuned up (using different heuristics and/or term weights etc.).

In the following tables, there are summarized three parameters for each task: The runtime, the number of inferences and the number of database hits. The inference is counted whenever some literal is inferred i.e. when $solve(.., Subgoal, ..)$ returns some instance of *Subgoal*. The number of hits summarizes all accesses to database of input rules and facts and to cache. It is incremented whenever a rule (or a fact) or a subgoal instance is retrieved from the database or cache in an attempt to solve a subgoal.

Table 1. Experimental results

Task no.	solve_NOP			flattened		
	time	*inferences*	*hits*	*time*	*inferences*	*hits*
1	24	1625	7827	20	129	3483
2	314	7343	57064	1200*	4701	63557
3	35	2237	9293	105	1409	14917

* The computation was aborted as the time limit was achieved

The results show (Table 1), that in all cases the number of inferences is less for the flattened form of input. The reason is, that when the Pool is used, the equalities are repeatedly tried to be solved in different theories. On the other hand, in the case of more difficult tasks (2,3) the algorithn *solve_NOP* is better both in time and in the number of hits. The reason for this behavior can be found when one examines the cached solutions. The number of cached solutions is summarized in Table 2.

The number of cached solutions is significantly smaller in the case of *solve_NOP* and this leads to the better results of our algorithm comparing to the underlying prover on the flattened form of input. The reason for the smaller number of cached solutions is the syntactical restriction on terms (and literals) imposed by *solve_NOP*. Mixed terms and literals containing function symbols from different theories may not be formed and this leads to the restriction of the search space and to the restriction of the cache size too.

Table 2. Cache content

Task no.	Cache content	
	solve_NOP	flattened
1	20	24
2	175	444*
3	27	141

* The computation was aborted as the time limit was achieved

As an example, we may consider an equality $f(v(y)) = f(v(y) + 0)$ that is inferred in a flattened form of task 2 and that says that application of any function f on a shared variable $v(y)$ gives the same result as its application on $v(y) + 0$, which is based on the fact that $v(y) = v(y) + 0$. The algorithm will also infer and store in cache many other similar equalities like $f(v(y)) = f(v(y)+0+0)$ etc. On the other hand, none of these equalities can be inferred by the *solve_NOP* algorithm as they use symbols from more theories $(0, +$ from the theory of linear arithmetics and f from the theory of uniterpreted function symbols).

The extra-inferred literals are of proper types and therefore it is not possible to achieve similar effect using type control. Our algorithm *solve_NOP* restricts the connection between these theories to shared variables and in that way it avoids repeatable work, as it enables to infer just "syntactically pure" literals.

6 Conclusion

We presented a method of automated theorem proving in a combination of theories with disjoint signatures that keeps the proving activities in different theories separate. The method is based on a propagation of equalities between shared variables in the spirit of Nelson-Oppen combination technique for decision procedures. Our method is useful from two points of view: It can be used to tune up the provers for different theories separately and even when the provers with the same setup are used in all basic theories, it increases the efficiency of theorem proving.

In future, we would like to extend this technique for the use with many sorted first order logic. Further, our method could provide a basis for integration of theorem proving and decision procedures [4]. We are also interested in automated theorem proving in general structured specifications i.e. including operations like renaming and parameterization [24] that are not used here.

References

1. Apt K.R, Introduction to Logic Programming (Revised and Extended Version), Report CS-R8826, Centre for Math. and Comp. Science, 1986 Amsterdam
2. Baader F., Tinelli C.: A New Approach for Combining Decision Procedures for the Word Problem and Its Connection to the Nelson-Oppen Combination method, pg. 19-33 in proc. CADE-14 , LNAI 1249, ed. W. McCune, Springer 1997

3. Baumgartner P., Furbach U.: Model Elimination Without Contrapositives and its Application to PTTP, in Proc. CADE-14 , LNAI 1249, ed. W. McCune, Springer 1997

4. Bjorner N.S., Stickel M.E., Uribe, T.E.: A Practical Integration of First-Order Reasoning and Decision procedures, pg. 101-115 in proc. CADE-14 , LNAI 1249, ed. W. McCune, Springer 1997

5. Boulton R.J.: Combining Decision Procedures in the HOL system, pg. 75-89 , LNCS 971, Higher Order Logic Theorem Proving and Its Applications, 1995

6. Burstall R.M, Sanella D.T.: Structured theories in LCF, Proceedings of the 8th Colloquium on Trees in Algebra and Programming, L'Aquila, Italy, 1983

7. Busch H.: First-Order Automation for Higher-Order-Logic Theorem Proving, pg. 97-112, LNCS 859, Higher Order Logic Theorem Proving and Its Applications 1994

8. Chang C.L., Lee R.C.: Symbolic Logic and Mechanical Theorem Proving, Academic Press, New York,1973

9. Dahn B.I., Gehne J., Honigmann Th., Wolf A.: Integration of Automated and Interactive Theorem Proving in ILF, pg. 57-60 in proc. CADE-14 , LNAI 1249, ed. W. McCune, Springer 1997

10. Harper R., Sanella D., Tarlecki A.: Structured theory presentations and logic representations, p. 113-160, Annals of pure and Applied Logic, North Holland 1994

11. Harrison J.: First Order Logic in Practice, Proceedings of FTP97 Workshop, 1997, RISC report No 97-50

12. Nelson G., Oppen C.: Simplification by cooperating Decision Procedures, pg. 245-257, ACM Transactions on Programming Languages and Systems, 1/2, 1979

13. Nilsson N.J.: Principles of Artificial Intelligence, Tioga Publishing Co., Palo Alto, California (1980),193-275

14. Plaisted D.A.: Non-Horn Clause Logic Programming Without Contrapositives, pg. 287- 325, Journal of Automated Reasoning 4 (1988)

15. Reif W., Schellhorn G.: Proving properties of Finite Enumerations: A Problem Set for Automated Theorem Provers, Technical Report Nr. 97-12, Department of Computer Science, University of Ulm

16. Reif W., Schellhorn G.: Theorem Proving in Large Theories, Proceedings of FTP97 Workshop, 1997, RISC report No 97-50

17. Shostak, R.E.: Deciding combinations of theories, LNCS 138, 6th Conference on Automated Deduction, (CADE 6), LNCS 138, ed. D.W. Loveland, Springer 1982

18. Stickel M.E.: A Prolog technology theorem prover: a new exposition and implementation in Prolog, pg. 109-128, Theoretical Computer Science 104 (1992)

19. Stickel M.E.: A Prolog Technology Theorem Prover: Implementation by an Extended Prolog Compiler, pg. 353-380, Journal of Automated Reasoning 4 (1988)

20. Tinelli.C., Harandi. M.: A new correctness proof of the Nelson-Oppen combination procedure, proc. of the 1st International Workshop Frontiers of Combining Systems,1996

21. Vanousek P.: Implication based theorem proving (in Czech), Diploma Thesis, MFF Charles University Prague, 1995

22. Vanousek P.: Automated Theorem Proving in Structured Theory Specifications (Choosing implementional environment), Tech rep. 98-03, MFF Charles University Prague, 1998

23. Vanousek P.: Automated Theorem Proving in Structured Theory Specifications, Dissertation Thesis (in progress), MFF Charles University Prague, 1998

24. Wirsing M., Proofs In Structured Specifications, MIP - 9008, 1991 University Passau

Author Index

Lecture Notes in Computer Science

For information about Vols. 1–1439

please contact your bookseller or Springer-Verlag